CompTIA Network+ Study Guide

N10-004 Exam Objectives

OBJECTIVE	CHAPTER

Sybex®
An Imprint of
WILEY

OBJECTIVE	CHAPTER

Exam specifications and content are subject to change at any time without prior notice and at CompTIA's sole discretion. Please visit CompTIA's website (www.comptia.org) for the most current information on their exam content.

Sybex®
An Imprint of
WILEY

OBJECTIVE	CHAPTER

4.0 NETWORK MANAGEMENT

Sybex®
An Imprint of

WILEY

NOTE

Sybex®
An Imprint of
WILEY

CompTIA
Network+®
Study Guide

CompTIA
Network+®
Study Guide

Todd Lammle

WILEY

Wiley Publishing, Inc.

Acquisitions Editor: Jeff Kellum
Development Editor: Susan Herman
Technical Editors: Steven Johnson and Derek Lewis
Production Editor: Christine O'Connor
Copy Editor: Tiffany Taylor
Production Manager: Tim Tate
Vice President and Executive Group Publisher: Richard Swadley
Vice President and Publisher: Neil Edde
Project Manager 1: Laura Moss-Hollister
Associate Producer: Shawn Patrick
Media Quality Assurance: Angie Denny
Book Designer: Judy Fung, Bill Gibson
Compositor: Craig Woods, Happenstance Type-O-Rama
Proofreader: Publication Services, Inc.
Indexer: Jack Lewis
Project Coordinator, Cover: Lynsey Stanford
Cover Designer: Ryan Sneed

Copyright © 2009 by Wiley Publishing, Inc., Indianapolis, Indiana

Published simultaneously in Canada

ISBN: 978-0-470-42747-7

For general information on our other products and services or to obtain technical support, please contact our Customer Care Department within the U.S. at (877) 762-2974, outside the U.S. at (317) 572-3993 or fax (317) 572-4002.

Wiley also publishes its books in a variety of electronic formats. Some content that appears in print may not be available in electronic books.

Library of Congress Cataloging-in-Publication Data.
Lammle, Todd.
  CompTIA Network+ study guide (Exam N10-004) / Todd Lammle. — 1st ed.
      p. cm.
   ISBN 978-0-470-42747-7 (paper/cd-rom) -- ISBN 978-0-470-42748-4 (cloth/cd-rom) 1. Computer networks— Examinations—Study guides. 2. Electronic data processing personnel--Certification. I. Title.
   TK5105.5.L3555 2009
   004.6076—dc22

                                   2009001904

10 9 8

Dear Reader,

Thank you for choosing the *CompTIA Network+ Study Guide* from Sybex, a proud Authorized Gold Partner in the CompTIA Authorized Partner Program (CAPP) for content developers. The learning material in this book, which meets the exacting standards of CompTIA's content assurance program, was written by an outstanding author who combines practical experience with a passion for teaching.

Sybex was founded in 1976, and more than thirty years later we're still committed to producing consistently exceptional books and learning products. With each of our titles, we're working hard to set a new standard for the industry.

I hope you see these efforts reflected in the pages that follow. I'm always interested to hear from customers about how we're doing here at Sybex. Feel free to let me know what you think about this or any other Sybex book by sending me an e-mail at nedde@wiley.com.

If you think you've identified a typo or a technical error, please visit our customer service web site at http://sybex.custhelp.com.

Feedback is critical to our efforts, and yours is always welcome.

Best regards,

Neil Edde
Vice President and Publisher
Sybex, an Imprint of Wiley

Wiley Publishing, Inc.

Acknowledgments

Monica Lammle's writing style, editing ability, encouragement, and dedication to ensuring that my books are concise yet highly readable has been invaluable to the success of this and many other projects.

Susan Herman was the development editor of this, the newest book in the Sybex CompTIA series. Thank you, Susan, for having the patience of Job, and for working so hard on this book with me. I'm so happy (and relieved) that you took on the job and, most of all, that you didn't run screaming from the room the next day!

Jeff Kellum is instrumental to my success in the Cisco world and is my acquisitions editor for this new CompTIA Network+ book. Jeff, thanks for your guidance and continued patience for all our books we've published together!

In addition, Christine O'Connor was an excellent production editor and she worked really hard to get the book done as quickly as possible, without missing the small mistakes that are so easy to over look. I am always very pleased when I hear that she will be working with me on a new project. Tiffany Taylor was latest copy editor, and she was patient, helpful, and detailed, but yet worked extremely hard to get this book out the shelf as fast as possible, and for that I thank her tremendously.

Steven Johnson literally hashed and rehashed each topic in this guide with me at all hours of the day and night, scrutinizing the material until we both agreed it was verifiably solid. Thank you, Steve!

I also want to mention Patrick Conlan, who tech-edited my CCNA book and is writing the Sybex Cisco Network Professional's Advanced Internetworking Guide. Pat was very helpful in throwing ideas at me for this book, and was the photographer for all the pictures I put in this book.

About the Author

Todd Lammle, CompTIA Network+, CCSI, CCNA/CCNP, CCSP/CCVP, MCSE, CEH/CHFI, FCC RF Licensed, is the authority on Network Certification and internetworking. He is a world-renowned author, speaker, trainer, and consultant. Todd has over 25 years of experience working with LANs, WANs, and large licensed and unlicensed wireless networks. He's president and CEO of GlobalNet Training and Consulting, Inc., a network-integration and training firm based in Dallas, Texas. You can reach Todd through his forum at www.lammle.com.

Contents at a Glance

Contents

Introduction

If you're like most of us in the networking community, you probably have one or more network certifications. If that's you, you're very wise in choosing to go for a Network+ certification to proudly add to your repertoire, because that achievement will make you all the more valuable as an employee. And in these challenging economic times, keeping ahead of the competition—even standing out among your present colleagues—could make a big difference in whether you gain a promotion or possibly keep your job instead of being the one who gets laid off! Or maybe this is your first attempt at certification because you've decided to venture into a new career in information technology (IT). You've realized that getting into the IT sector is a good way to go because as the Information Age marches on, the demand for knowledgeable professionals in this dynamic field will only be intensify dramatically.

Either way, certification is one of the best things you can do for your career if you are working in, or want to break into, the networking profession, because it proves that you know what you're talking about regarding the subjects you're certified in. It also powerfully endorses you as a professional in a way that's very similar to a physician being "board certified" in a certain area of expertise.

In this book, you'll find out what the Network+ exam is all about, because each chapter covers a part of the exam. I've included some great review questions at the end of each chapter to help crystallize the information you learned and solidly prepare you to ace the exam.

A really cool thing about working in IT is that it's constantly evolving so there are always new things to learn and fresh challenges to master. Once you obtain your Network+ certification and discover that you're interested in taking it further by getting into more complex networking (and make more money), the Cisco CCNA certification is definitely your next step; you can get the skinny on that and even more in-depth certifications on my blog at www.lammle.com.

What Is the Network+ Certification?

Network+ is a certification developed by the Computing Technology Industry Association (CompTIA) that exists to provide resources and education for the computer and technology community. This is the same body that developed the A+ exam for computer technicians.

Way back in 1995, members of the organization got together to develop a new certification that tests skills for IT. To ensure industry-wide support, it was sponsored by many past and present IT industry leaders like these:

- Compaq Computers
- Digital Equipment Corporation (a part of Compaq)
- IBM
- Lotus

- Microsoft
- Novell
- TSS
- U.S. Robotics
- US West
- Wave Technologies

The Network+ exam was designed to test the skills of network technicians with 18 to 24 months of experience in the field. It tests areas of networking technologies such as the definition of a protocol, the Open Systems Interconnect (OSI) model and its layers, and the concepts of network design and implementation—the minimum knowledge required for working on a network and some integral prerequisites for network design and implementation.

Why Become Network+ Certified?

The Network+ certification is a relatively new certification, and it's the next certification in the lineup of CompTIA certifications beginning with the A+ certification. Because CompTIA is a well-respected developer of vendor-neutral industry certifications, becoming Network+ certified proves you're competent in the specific areas tested by Network+.

Three major benefits are associated with becoming Network+ certified:

- Proof of professional achievement
- Opportunity for advancement
- Fulfillment of training requirements

Proof of Professional Achievement

Networking professionals are pretty competitive when it comes to collecting more certifications than their peers. And because the Network+ certification broadly covers the entire field of networking, technicians want this certification a lot more than having just Microsoft certs—Net+ is a lot more prestigious and valuable. Because it's rare to gain something that's worth a lot with little effort, I'll be honest—preparing for the Network+ exam isn't exactly a lazy day at the beach. (However, beaches do happen to be really high on my personal list of great places to study!) And people in IT know that it isn't all that easy to pass the Net+ exam, so they'll definitely respect you more and know that you've achieved a certain level of expertise about vendor-independent networking-related subjects.

Opportunity for Advancement

We all like to get ahead in our careers—advancement results in more responsibility and prestige, and it usually means a fatter paycheck, greater opportunities, and added options.

In the IT sector, a great way to make sure all that good stuff happens is by earning a lot of technology certifications, including Network+.

Network+, because of its wide-reaching industry support, is recognized as a baseline of networking information. Some companies actually specify the possession of both Network+ and A+ certifications as job requirements before they'll even consider hiring you, or maybe before your next review. And often, gaining a Network+ certification will get you a pay raise at review time.

How to Become Network+ Certified

The simplest way to become Network+ certified is to take the exam. It is administered by Pearson VUE and Thomson Prometric, which you're already familiar with if you've taken other computer certification exams. If you haven't, surprise—the test is administered by a computer.

The test is 90 minutes long, with 100 questions. That is less than one minute per question, but as of the time of this writing, all question are multiple choice, so that makes it somewhat of an easier test then a test with simulations and drag and drop questions. Also to your benefit, you can review your answers before you finish your test, which gives you a review period if you finish before 90 minutes. You need to get a score of 720 out of 1000

To register to take the exam, call Thomson Prometric (not the testing center) at 888-895-6116 or Pearson VUE at 877-551-PLUS. Be prepared to pay for the exam at registration time with a major credit card like Visa or MasterCard. Check CompTIA's website, because prices may vary.

 This book covers everything about CompTIA Network+. For up-to-date information about Todd Lammle CompTIA bootcamps, audio training, and training videos, please see www.lammle.com and/or www.globalnettraining.com.

You can take the CompTIA exam at any of the more than 800 Prometric Authorized Testing Centers around the world (www.2test.com), or call 800-204-EXAM (3926). You can also register and take the exams at a Pearson VUE authorized center (www.vue.com) or call (877) 404-EXAM (3926).

To register for a CompTIA exam, do the following:

1. Determine the number of the exam you want to take—the CompTIA Network+ exam number is N10-004.

2. Register with the nearest Prometric Registration Center or Pearson VUE testing center. Like I said, you have to pay for the exam in advance; at this writing, the exam costs $239 and must be taken within one year of payment. You can schedule an exam up to six weeks in advance or as late as the same day you want to take it. If something comes up and you need to cancel or reschedule your exam appointment, contact Prometric or Pearson VUE at least 24 hours in advance.

3. When you schedule the exam, you'll get instructions regarding all appointment and cancellation procedures, the ID requirements, and information about the testing-center location.

At the end of the exam, your score report will be displayed on the screen and printed out so that you have a hard copy.

Who Should Buy This Book?

You—if want to pass the Network+ exam, and pass it confidently, that is! This book is chock full of the exact information you need that directly maps to Net+ exam objectives; so if you use it to study for the exam, your odds of passing shoot way up.

And in addition to including every bit of knowledge you need to learn to pass the exam, I've also included some really great tips and solid wisdom to equip you even further to successfully work in the real IT world.

What Does This Book Cover?

This book covers everything you need to know in order to pass the CompTIA Network+ (N10-004) exam. But in addition to studying the book, it's a good idea to practice on an actual network if you can.

Here's a list of the 20 chapters in this book. At the end each of them, I've included a written lab and some key review questions to help you hone your skills:

Chapter 1, Introduction to Networks   An introduction to what a network is, and an overview of the most common physical network topologies you'll find in today's networks.

Chapter 2, The Open Systems Interconnection Specifications   This chapter covers the OSI model, what it is, what happens at each of its layers, and how each layer works.

Chapter 3, Networking Topologies, Connectors, and Wiring Standards   This chapter covers the various networking media and topologies, plus the cable types and properties used in today's networks.

Chapter 4, The Current Ethernet Specifications   This chapter covers how a basic Ethernet LAN works, and describes and categorizes the different Ethernet specifications.

Chapter 5, Networking Devices   It's important for you to understand all the various devices used in today's networks, and this chapter will describe how hubs, routers, and switches and some other devices work within a network.

Chapter 6, Introduction to Internet Protocol (IP)   This is your introduction to the all-important IP protocol stack.

Chapter 7, IP Addressing   This chapter will take up from where Chapter 6 left off and move into IP addressing. It also contains information about public versus private addressing and DHCP.

Chapter 8, IP Subnetting, Troubleshooting IP, And Introduction to NAT   Beginning where Chapter 7 ends, we'll be tackling IP subnetting in this one. But no worries here— I've worked hard to make this not-so-popular yet vital topic as painless as possible.

Chapter 9, Introduction to IP Routing   This is an introduction to routing that basically covers what routers do and how they do it. This chapter, along with Chapters 10 and 11, cover routing and switching in much more detail than what is necessary to meet the CompTIA Network+ objectives, because this knowledge is so critical to grasp when working with today's networks.

Chapter 10, Routing Protocols   This chapter goes into detail describing the protocols that run on routers and that update routing tables to create a working map of the network.

Chapter 11, Switching and Virtual LANs (VLANs)   This chapter covers Layer 2 switching, the Spanning Tree Protocol (STP), and Virtual LANs. Just as I went in deeper than needed for the exam with the routing chapters, I'll cover switching and virtual LANs (which are also vital in today's corporate networks) more thoroughly as well.

Chapter 12, Wireless Technologies   Because wireless is so important for both home and business networks today, this chapter is loaded with all the information you need to be successful at wireless networking at home and work.

Chapter 13, Authentication and Access Control   This is the first of three security chapters. There are tons of exam objectives about network security that are so important that I took three chapters to cover all of them. In this chapter, I'll introduce security, security filtering, tunneling, and user authentication.

Chapter 14, Network Threats and Mitigation   This is probably the most fun of the three security chapters because I'll tell you all about security threats and how to stop them. The only way to get good at network security is to implement it, and this chapter shows you how.

Chapter 15, Physical and Hardware Security   This chapter's focus is on explaining basic firewalls, security devices, and device security.

Chapter 16, Wide Area Networks   In this chapter, you get to learn all about things like frame relay, E1/T1, DSL, cable modems, and more. All the CompTIA Network+ WAN objectives are covered in this chapter.

Chapter 17, Command-Line Tools   This is also a fun chapter because again, you can follow along and run all the commands yourself. And I repeat, it's a really good idea to do that!

Chapter 18, Software and Hardware Tools   This chapter introduces you to the network tools you will use to help you run your networks. Both software and hardware tools will be discussed.

Chapter 19, Network Troubleshooting   In almost every chapter, I discuss how to verify and fix problems, but this chapter will get really into the nuts and bolts of detailed network troubleshooting and documentation.

Chapter 20, Management, Monitoring, and Optimization   This last chapter will provide configuration-management documentation and covers wiring, logical diagrams, baselines, policies, and regulations.

How to Use This Book

If you want a solid foundation for the serious effort of preparing for the CompTIA Network+ (N10-004) exam, then look no further, because I've spent countless hours putting together this book with the sole intention of helping you to pass the Network+ exam!

This book is loaded with valuable information, and you will get the most out of your study time if you understand how I put the book together. Here's a list that describes how to approach studying so you get the most out of it:

1. Take the assessment test immediately following this introduction. (The answers are at the end of the test, but no peeking!) It's okay if you don't know any of the answers—that's what this book is for. Carefully read over the explanations for any question you get wrong, and make note of the chapters where that material is covered.

2. Study each chapter carefully, making sure that you fully understand the information and the test objectives listed at the beginning of each one. Again, pay extra-close attention to any chapter that includes material covered in questions you missed on the assessment test.

3. Complete the Written Lab at the end of each chapter. Do *not* skip these written exercises, because they directly map to the CompTIA objectives and what you've got to have nailed down to meet them.

4. Answer all the Review Questions related to each chapter. (The answers appear at the end of the chapters—no cheating!) Specifically note any questions that confuse you, and study those sections of the book again. And don't just skim these questions—make sure you understand each answer completely.

5. Try your hand at the bonus exams included on the companion CD. The questions in these exams appear only on the CD. Check out www.lammle.com for more CompTIA Network+ exam prep questions. The questions found at www.lammle.com will be updated at least monthly, maybe weekly or even daily. Before you take your test, be sure and visit my website for questions, videos, audios, and other useful information.

6. Test yourself using all the flashcards on the CD. These are brand-new and updated flashcard programs to help you prepare for the latest CompTIA Network+ exam, and they're really great study tools.

I tell you no lies—learning every bit of the material in this book is going to require applying yourself with a good measure of discipline. So try to set aside the same time period every day to study, and select a comfortable and quiet place to do so. If you work hard, you will be surprised at how quickly you learn this material.

If you follow the steps listed here, study, and practice the Review Questions, bonus exams, electronic flashcards, and all the written labs, you would almost have to try to fail the CompTIA Network+ exam. However, studying for the Network+ exam is like training for a marathon—if you don't go for a good run every day, you're not likely to finish very well.

What's on the CD?

I worked hard to provide some really great tools to help you with your certification process. All of the following tools should be loaded on your workstation when you're studying for the test.

The Sybex Test Engine

The test-preparation software prepares you to pass the CompTIA Network+ exam. In this test engine, you will find all the review and assessment questions from the book, plus two bonus exams.

 If you purchased the Deluxe Edition of this book, there are four additional bonus exams, for a total of six.

Electronic Flashcards for PC, Pocket PC, and Palm Devices

To prepare for the exam, you can read this book, study the review questions at the end of each chapter, and work through the practice exams included in the book and on the companion CD. But don't neglect the flashcards included on the CD—if you can get through these tough questions and understand the answers, you'll know you're ready for the CompTIA Network+ exam.

The flashcards include 150 questions specifically written to hit you hard and make sure you are ready for the exam. Between the review questions, the bonus exams, and the flashcards on the CD, you'll be more than prepared for the exam.

 If you purchased the Deluxe Edition of this book, there are 150 additional flashcards, for a total of 300.

PDF of Book

Sybex offers the Study Guide in PDF on the CD so you can read the book on your PC or laptop. (Acrobat Reader is also included on the CD.)

CompTIA Network+ Virtual Lab as Part of Deluxe Edition

If you purchased the Deluxe Edition of this book, we include the Network+ Virtual Lab. This is the most powerful practical tool in the market today. It will allow you to create a virtual network and work with simulated devices such as routers, switches, and server and client hardware. Also included are hands-on labs. Complete instructions are included on a PDF version of the Network+ Virtual Lab manual and README file found on the CD-ROM.

System Requirements for the Virtual Lab include Internet Explorer 4.0 or later; Pentium 133 (Pentium II 266 or higher recommended); 32MB of RAM (64MB recommended); Windows NT (SP3 or higher), 2000, or XP, or Vista; 25MB of free hard-disk space, 8x CD-ROM drive, and a mouse or other pointing device.

Exam Objectives

Speaking of objectives, you're probably pretty curious about those, right? CompTIA asked groups of IT professionals to fill out a survey rating the skills they felt were important in their jobs, and the results were grouped into objectives for the exam and divided into six domains.

This table gives you the extent by percentage that each domain is represented on the actual examination.

Domain	% of Examination
1.0 Network Technologies	20%
2.0 Network Media and Topologies	20%
3.0 Network Devices	17%
4.0 Network Management	20%
5.0 Network Tools	12%
6.0 Network Security	11%
Total	100%

Next, I'm going to give you the outline of the Network+ exam objectives.

 The specific objectives and weighting percentages can change at any time, so check CompTIA's website at www.comptia.org for a list of the most current ones.

1.0 Network Technologies (20%)

The objectives for this domain are as follows:

1.1 Explain the function of common networking protocols

- TCP
- FTP
- UDP
- TCP/IP suite
- DHCP
- TFTP
- DNS
- HTTP(S)
- ARP
- SIP (VoIP)
- RTP (VoIP)
- SSH
- POP3
- NTP
- IMAP4
- Telnet
- SMTP
- SNMP2/3
- ICMP
- IGMP
- TLS

1.2 Identify commonly used TCP and UDP default ports

TCP ports:

- FTP – 20, 21
- SSH – 22

- TELNET – 23
- SMTP – 25
- DNS – 53
- HTTP – 80
- POP3 – 110
- NTP – 123
- IMAP4 – 143
- HTTPS – 443
  UDP ports:
- TFTP – 69
- DNS – 53
- BOOTPS/DHCP – 67
- SNMP – 161

1.3 Identify the following address formats

- IPv6
- IPv4
- MAC addressing

1.4 Given a scenario, evaluate the proper use of the following addressing technologies and addressing schemes

  Addressing technologies:

- Subnetting
- Classful vs. classless (e.g. CIDR, Supernetting)
- NAT
- PAT
- SNAT
- Public vs. private
- DHCP (static, dynamic APIPA)
  Addressing schemes:
- Unicast
- Multicast
- Broadcast

1.5 Identify common IPv4 and IPv6 routing protocols

  Link state:

- OSPF
- IS-IS

Distance vector:

- RIP
- RIPv2
- BGP

Hybrid:

- EIGRP

1.6 Explain the purpose and properties of routing

- IGP vs. EGP
- Static vs. dynamic
- Next hop
- Understanding routing tables and how they pertain to path selection
- Explain convergence (steady state)

1.7 Compare the characteristics of wireless communication standards 802.11 a/b/g/n

- Speeds
- Distance
- Channels
- Frequency

Authentication and encryption:

- WPA
- WEP
- RADIUS
- TKIP

2.0 Network Media and Topologies (20%)

The objectives for this domain are as follows:

2.1 Categorize standard cable types and their properties

Types:

- CAT3, CAT5, CAT5e, CAT6
- STP, UTP
- Multimode fiber, single-mode fiber
- Coaxial
  - RG-59
  - RG-6

- Serial
- Plenum vs. Non-plenum

Properties:

- Transmission speeds
- Distance
- Duplex
- Noise immunity (security, EMI)
- Frequency

2.2 Identify common connector types

- RJ-11
- RJ-45
- BNC
- SC
- ST
- LC
- RS-232

2.3 Identify common physical network topologies

- Star
- Mesh
- Bus
- Ring
- Point to point
- Point to multipoint
- Hybrid

2.4 Given a scenario, differentiate and implement appropriate wiring standards

- 568A
- 568B
- Straight vs. cross-over
- Rollover
- Loopback

2.5 Categorize WAN technology types and properties

Types:

- Frame relay
- E1/T1
- ADSL

- SDSL
- VDSL
- Cable modem
- Satellite
- E3/T3
- OC-x
- Wireless
- ATM
- SONET
- MPLS
- ISDN BRI
- ISDN PRI
- POTS
- PSTN

  Properties:
- Circuit switch
- Packet switch
- Speed
- Transmission media
- Distance

2.6 Categorize LAN technology types and properties

  Types:
- Ethernet
- 10BaseT
- 100BaseTX
- 100BaseFX
- 1000BaseT
- 1000BaseX
- 10GBaseSR
- 10GBaseLR
- 10GBaseER
- 10GBaseSW
- 10GBaseLW
- 10GBaseEW
- 10GBaseT

Properties:

- CSMA/CD
- Broadcast
- Collision
- Bonding
- Speed
- Distance

2.7 Explain common logical network topologies and their characteristics

- Peer to peer
- Client/server
- VPN
- VLAN

2.8 Install components of wiring distribution

- Vertical and horizontal cross connects
- Patch panels
- 66 block
- MDFs
- IDFs
- 25 pair
- 100 pair
- 110 block
- Demarc
- Demarc extension
- Smart jack
- Verify wiring installation
- Verify wiring termination

3.0 Network Devices (17%)

The objectives for this domain are as follows:

3.1 Install, configure and differentiate between common network devices

- Hub
- Repeater
- Modem

- NIC
- Media converters
- Basic switch
- Bridge
- Wireless access point
- Basic router
- Basic firewall
- Basic DHCP server

3.2 Identify the functions of specialized network devices

- Multilayer switch
- Content switch
- IDS/IPS
- Load balancer
- Multifunction network devices
- DNS server
- Bandwidth shaper
- Proxy server
- CSU/DSU

3.3 Explain the advanced features of a switch

- PoE
- Spanning tree
- VLAN
- Trunking
- Port mirroring
- Port authentication

3.4 Implement a basic wireless network

- Install client
- Access point placement
- Install access point
    - Configure appropriate encryption
    - Configure channels and frequencies
    - Set ESSID and beacon
- Verify installation

4.0 Network Management (20%)

The objectives for this domain are as follows:

4.1 Explain the function of each layer of the OSI model

- Layer 1 – physical
- Layer 2 – data link
- Layer 3 – network
- Layer 4 – transport
- Layer 5 – session
- Layer 6 – presentation
- Layer 7 – application

4.2 Identify types of configuration management documentation

- Wiring schematics
- Physical and logical network diagrams
- Baselines
- Policies, procedures and configurations
- Regulations

4.3 Given a scenario, evaluate the network based on configuration management documentation

- Compare wiring schematics, physical and logical network diagrams, baselines, policies and procedures and configurations to network devices and infrastructure
- Update wiring schematics, physical and logical network diagrams, configurations and job logs as needed

4.4 Conduct network monitoring to identify performance and connectivity issues using the following:

- Network monitoring utilities (e.g. packet sniffers, connectivity software, load testing, throughput testers)
- System logs, history logs, event logs

4.5 Explain different methods and rationales for network performance optimization
Methods:

- QoS
- Traffic shaping
- Load balancing
- High availability
- Caching engines
- Fault tolerance

Reasons:

- Latency sensitivity
- High bandwidth applications
  - VoIP
  - Video applications
- Uptime

4.6 Given a scenario, implement the following network troubleshooting methodology

- Information gathering – identify symptoms and problems
- Identify the affected areas of the network
- Determine if anything has changed
- Establish the most probable cause
- Determine if escalation is necessary
- Create an action plan and solution identifying potential effects
- Implement and test the solution
- Identify the results and effects of the solution
- Document the solution and the entire process

4.7 Given a scenario, troubleshoot common connectivity issues and select an appropriate solution

Physical issues:

- Cross talk
- Nearing crosstalk
- Near End crosstalk
- Attenuation
- Collisions
- Shorts
- Open impedance mismatch (echo)
- Interference

Logical issues:

- Port speed
- Port duplex mismatch
- Incorrect VLAN
- Incorrect IP address
- Wrong gateway
- Wrong DNS
- Wrong subnet mask

Issues that should be identified but escalated:

- Switching loop
- Routing loop
- Route problems
- Proxy arp
- Broadcast storms

Wireless Issues:

- Interference (bleed, environmental factors)
- Incorrect encryption
- Incorrect channel
- Incorrect frequency
- ESSID mismatch
- Standard mismatch (802.11 a/b/g/n)
- Distance
- Bounce
- Incorrect antenna placement

5.0 Network Tools (12%)

The objectives for this domain are as follows:

5.1 Given a scenario, select the appropriate command line interface tool and interpret the output to verify functionality

- Traceroute
- Ipconfig
- Ifconfig
- Ping
- Arp ping
- Arp
- Nslookup
- Hostname
- Dig
- Mtr
- Route
- Nbtstat
- Netstat

5.2 Explain the purpose of network scanners

- Packet sniffers
- Intrusion detection software
- Intrusion prevention software
- Port scanners

5.3 Given a scenario, utilize the appropriate hardware tools

- Cable testers
- Protocol analyzer
- Certifiers
- TDR
- OTDR
- Multimeter
- Toner probe
- Butt set
- Punch down tool
- Cable stripper
- Snips
- Voltage event recorder
- Temperature monitor

6.0 Network Security (11%)

The objectives for this domain are as follows:

6.1 Explain the function of hardware and software security devices

- Network based firewall
- Host based firewall
- IDS
- IPS
- VPN concentrator

6.2 Explain common features of a firewall

- Application layer vs. network layer
- Stateful vs. stateless
- Scanning services
- Content filtering

- Signature identification
- Zones

6.3 Explain the methods of network access security

Filtering:

- ACL
  - MAC filtering
  - IP filtering
- Tunneling and encryption
  - SSL VPN
  - VPN
  - L2TP
  - PPTP
  - IPSEC
- Remote access
  - RAS
  - RDP
  - PPPoE
  - PPP
  - VNC
  - ICA

6.4 Explain methods of user authentication

- PKI
- Kerberos
- AAA
  - RADIUS
  - TACACS+
- Network access control
  - 802.1x
- CHAP
- MS-CHAP
- EAP

6.5 Explain issues that affect device security

- Physical security
- Restricting local and remote access

- Secure methods vs. unsecure methods
  - SSH, HTTPS, SNMPv3, SFTP, SCP
  - TELNET, HTTP, FTP, RSH, RCP, SNMPv1/2

6.6 Identify common security threats and mitigation techniques

Security threats:

- DoS
- Viruses
- Worms
- Attackers
- Man in the middle
- Smurf
- Rogue access points
- Social engineering (phishing)

Mitigation techniques:

- Policies and procedures
- User training
- Patches and updates

Assessment Test

1. What is the basic purpose of a local area network (LAN)?

    A. To interconnect networks in several different buildings

    B. To connect one or more computers together so they can share resources

    C. To interconnect 2 to 10 routers

    D. To make routers unnecessary

2. Which of the following describes a VLAN?

    A. It is a device that provides IP addresses to hosts.

    B. It uses firewalls.

    C. It virtually separates subnets using switches.

    D. It virtually separates subnets using routers.

3. IP resides at which layer of the OSI model?

    A. Application

    B. Data Link

    C. Network

    D. Physical

4. Layer 2 of the OSI model is named _____.

    A. Application layer

    B. Network layer

    C. Transport layer

    D. Data Link layer

5. Which RG rating of coax is used for cable modems?

    A. RG-59

    B. RG-58

    C. RG-6

    D. RG-8

6. Which UTP wiring uses four twisted wire pairs (eight wires) and is rated for 250MHz?

    A. Category 3 UTP

    B. Category 5 STP

    C. Category 5 UTP

    D. Category 6 UTP

7. If you are running half-duplex Internet, which of the following is true. (Choose all that apply)?

  A. Your digital signal cannot transmit and receive data at the same time.

  B. Hosts use the CSMA/CD protocol to prevent collisions.

  C. The physical connection consists of one wire pair.

  D. All of the above

8. You need to connect a hub to a switch. You don't like this idea because you know that it will create congestion. What type of cable do you need to use to connect the hub to the switch?

  A. EtherIP

  B. Crossover

  C. Straight-through

  D. Cable Sense, Multiple Access

9. Your boss asks you why you just put in a requisition to buy a bunch of switches. He said he just bought you a bunch of hubs five years ago! Why did you buy the switches?

  A. Because each switch port is its own collision domain.

  B. The cable connecting devices to the hub wore out, and switches were cheaper than new cable.

  C. There were too many broadcast domains, and a switch breaks up broadcast domains by default.

  D. The hubs kept repeating signals but quit recognizing frames and data structures.

10. Which device would connect network segments together, creating separate collision domains for each segment but only a single broadcast domain?

  A. Hub

  B. Router

  C. Switch

  D. Modem

11. Most Application-layer protocols only use UDP or TCP at the Transport layer. Which of the following could use both?

  A. TCP

  B. Microsoft Word

  C. Telnet

  D. DNS

12. HTTP, FTP, and Telnet work at which layer of the OSI model?

  A. Application

  B. Presentation

  C. Session

  D. Transport

13. IPv6 uses multiple types of addresses. Which of the following would describe an anycast address used by an IPv6 host?

    A. Communications are routed to the most distant host that shares the same address.

    B. Packets are delivered to all interfaces identified by the address. This is also called one-to-many addressing.

    C. This address identifies multiple interfaces, and the anycast packet is only delivered to one address. This address can also be called one-to-one-of-many.

    D. Anycast is a type of broadcast.

14. Which of the following IP addresses are not allowed on the Internet? (Choose all that apply.)

    A. 11.255.255.1

    B. 10.1.1.1

    C. 172.33.255.0

    D. 192.168.0.1

15. What is the subnetwork address for a host with the IP address 200.10.5.168/28?

    A. 200.10.5.156

    B. 200.10.5.132

    C. 200.10.5.160

    D. 200.10.5.0

    E. 200.10.5.255

16. If you wanted to verify the local IP stack on your computer, what would you do?

    A. ping 127.0.0.0

    B. ping 127.0.0.1

    C. telnet 1.0.0.127

    D. ping 127.0.0.255

    E. telnet 255.255.255.255

17. The OSI model uses an encapsulation method to describe the data as it is encapsulated at each layer of the OSI. What is the encapsulation named at the Data Link layer?

    A. Bits

    B. Packets

    C. Frames

    D. Data

    E. Segments

18. Where does a Data Link layer frame have to carry a Network layer packet if the packet is destined for a remote network?

  A. Router

  B. Physical medium

  C. Switch

  D. Another host

19. Which of the following are not Distance Vector routing protocols? (Choose all that apply.)

  A. OSPF

  B. RIP

  C. RIPv2

  D. IS-IS

20. Which of the following uses both Distance Vector and Link State properties?

  A. IGRP

  B. OSPF

  C. RIPv1

  D. EIGRP

  E. IS-IS

21. You need to break up broadcast domains in a Layer 2 switched network. What strategy will you use?

  A. Implement a loop-avoidance scheme

  B. Create a flatter network structure using switches

  C. Create a VLAN

  D. Disable spanning tree on individual ports

22. Why do most switches run the Spanning Tree Protocol by default?

  A. It monitors how the network is functioning.

  B. It stops data from forwarding until all devices are updated.

  C. It prevents switching loops.

  D. It manages the VLAN database.

23. Which of the following describes MIMO correctly?

  A. A protocol that requires acknowledgment of each and every frame

  B. A data-transmission technique in which several frames are sent by several antennae over several paths and are then recombined by another set of antennae

  C. A modulation technique that allows more than one data rate

  D. A technique that packs smaller packets into a single unit, which improves throughput

24. Which two practices help secure your wireless access points from unauthorized access?

    A. Assigning a private IP address to the AP

    B. Changing the default SSID value

    C. Configuring a new administrator password

    D. Changing the mixed-mode setting to single mode

    E. Configuring traffic filtering

25. IPSec is defined at what layer of the OSI model?

    A. Network

    B. Physical

    C. Layer 4

    D. Layer 7

26. You want your users to log in and authenticate before they can get onto your network. Which of the following services would you use?

    A. RADIUS

    B. TACACS+

    C. Virtual Network Computing

    D. Remote desktop protocol

27. Someone calls you and asks for your bank-account number because the bank is having problem with your account. You give them this information and later find out that you were scammed. What type of attack is this?

    A. Phishing

    B. Calling-scam

    C. Analog-scam

    D. Trust-exploration attack

    E. Man-in-the-middle attack

    F. Rogue access point

28. Which three of the following are types of denial of service attacks?

    A. Ping of Death

    B. Stacheldraht

    C. SYN flood

    D. Virus FloodSyn

29. You want to stop a hacker in their tracks. Which of the following devices are proactive in providing this service?

   A. Access control list (ACL)

   B. Content filtering

   C. Security zones

   D. Intrusion Prevention System (IPS)

   E. Network Address Translation

   F. Virtual LAN's

30. You connected your company to the Internet, and security is a concern. What should you install?

   A. Higher-quality cables

   B. Firewall

   C. DNS

   D. Switches

31. Which of the following are WAN protocols or technologies? (Choose all that apply.)

   A. ATM

   B. ISDN

   C. MPLS

   D. RIP

32. The rate at which the frame-relay switch agrees to transfer data is referred to as _____.

   A. BE

   B. FECN

   C. CIR

   D. BECN

33. Which two arp utility switches perform the same function?

   A. –g

   B. –z

   C. –d

   D. –a

   E. –h

   F. –b

34. You need to purge and reload the remote NetBIOS name table cache. Which `nbtstat` utility switch will you use?

    A. –r

    B. –R

    C. /r

    D. /R

    E. –a

    F. –A

35. Which tool is used to attach ends to network cables?

    A. Punch-down tool

    B. Crimper

    C. VLAN tool

    D. Strippers

    E. ARP tool

36. You are using a TDR. Which three of the following actions can you do with this device?

    A. Estimate cable lengths

    B. Find splice and connector locations and their associated loss amounts

    C. Display unused services

    D. Define cable-impedance characteristics

37. Which of the following are considered cabling issues? (Choose all that apply.)

    A. Crosstalk

    B. Shorts

    C. Open impedance mismatch

    D. DNS configurations

38. A workstation gives an error message to a user. The message states that a duplicate IP address has been detected on the network. After developing a hypothesis, what should the next step be according to the standard troubleshooting model?

    A. Test and observe an action plan.

    B. Determine if anything has changed.

    C. Implement an action plan.

    D. Document the solution and the entire process.

39. Which network-performance-optimization technique can delay packets that meet certain criteria to guarantee usable bandwidth for other applications?

A. Traffic shaping

B. Jitter control

C. Logical network mapping

D. Load balancing

E. Access lists

40. You need to optimize network traffic by spreading it across multiple connections. Which strategy should be used?

A. Load balancing

B. Traffic shaping

C. Add VLAN's

D. A 1Gbps connection

E. Following the regulations

Answers to Assessment Test

1.   B. LANs generally have a geographic scope of a single building or smaller. They can be simple (two hosts) to complex (with thousands of hosts). See Chapter 1 for more information.

2.   C. Virtual LANs (VLANs) separate subnets (Layer 3 networks) using switches instead of routers. See Chapter 1 for more information.

3.   C. IP is a Network-layer protocol. Internet Explorer is an example of an Application layer protocol; Ethernet is an example of a Data Link–layer protocol; and T1 can be considered a Physical-layer protocol. See Chapter 2 for more information.

4.   D. Layer 2 of the OSI model is the Data Link layer, which provides the physical transmission of the data and handles error notification, network topology, and flow control. See Chapter 2 for more information.

5.   C. Cable modems use RG-6 coax cables. See Chapter 3 for more information.

6.   D. To get the high data-transfer speed, like 1Gbps, you need to use a wire standard that is highly rated, such as Category 5e or Category 6. See Chapter 3 for more information.

7.   D. A, B, and C are true. With half-duplex, you are using one wire pair with a digital signal either transmitting or receiving (but not both at once). Carrier Sense Multiple Access with Collision Detection (CSMA/CD) helps packets that are transmitted simultaneously from different hosts share bandwidth evenly. See Chapter 4 for more information.

8.   B. To connect two switches together or a hub to a switch, you need a crossover cable. See Chapter 4 for more information.

9.   A. For the most part, switches are not cheap; however, one of the biggest benefits of using switches instead of hubs in your internetwork is that each switch port is actually its own collision domain. A hub creates one large collision domain. Switches still can't break up broadcast domains (do you remember which devices do?). Hubs do not recognize frames and data structures but switches do. See Chapter 5 for more information.

10. C. A switch creates separate collision domains for each port but does not break up broadcast domains by default. See Chapter 5 for more information.

11. D. DNS uses TCP for zone exchanges between servers and UDP when a client is trying to resolve a hostname to an IP address. See Chapter 6 for more information.

12. A. HTTP, FTP and Telnet use TCP at the Transport layer; however, they are all Application-layer protocols, so the Application layer is the best answer for this question. See Chapter 6 for more information.

13. C. Anycast is a new type of communication that replaces broadcasts in IPv4. Anycast addresses identify multiple interfaces, which is the same as multicast; however, the big difference is that the anycast packet is delivered to only one address: the first one it finds defined in the terms of routing distance. This address can also be called one-to-one-of-many. See Chapter 7 for more information.

14. B, D. The addresses in the range 10.0.0.0 through 10.255.255.255, and 172.16.0.0 through 172.31.255.255, as well as 192.168.0.0 through 192.168.255.255 are all considered private, based on RFC 1918. Use of these addresses on the Internet is prohibited so that they can be used simultaneously in different administrative domains without concern for conflict. See Chapter 7 for more detail on IP addressing and information on private IP addresses.

15. C. This is a pretty simple question. A /28 is 255.255.255.240, which means that our block size is 16 in the fourth octet. 0, 16, 32, 48, 64, 80, 96, 112, 128, 144, 160, 176, and so on. The host is in the 1604 subnet. See Chapter 8 for more information.

16. B. To test the local stack on your host, ping the loopback interface of 127.0.0.1. See Chapter 8 for more information.

17. C. The Data Link layer is responsible for encapsulating IP packets into frames and for providing logical network addresses. See Chapter 9 for more information.

18. A. Packets specifically have to be carried to a router in order to be routed through a network. See Chapter 9 for more information.

19. A, D. RIP and RIPv2 are Distance Vector routing protocols. OSPF and IS-IS are Link State. See Chapter 10 for more information.

20. D. EIGRP is called a hybrid routing protocol because it uses the characteristics of both Distance Vector and Link State routing protocols. However, EIGRP can only be run on Cisco routers and is not vendor-neutral. See Chapter 10 for more information.

21. C. Virtual LANs break up broadcast domains in Layer 2 switched internetworks. See Chapter 11 for more information.

22. C. The Spanning Tree Protocol (STP) was designed to stop Layer 2 loops. All enterprise model switches have STP by default. See Chapter 11 for more information.

23. B. Part of the 802.11n wireless standard, MIMO sends multiple frames by several antennae over several paths; they are then recombined by another set of antennae to optimize throughput and multipath resistance. This is called spatial multiplexing. See Chapter 12 for more information.

24. B, C. At a minimum, you need to change the default SSID value on each AP and configure new usernames and passwords on the AP. See Chapter 12 for more information.

25. A. IPSec works at the Network layer of the OSI model (Layer 3) and secures all applications that operate above it (Layer 4 and above). Additionally, because it was designed by the IETF and designed to work with IPv4 and IPv6, it has broad industry support and is quickly becoming the standard for VPNs on the Internet. See Chapter 13 for more information.

26. A. RADIUS combines user authentication and authorization into one profile. See Chapter 13 for more information.

27. A. Social engineering or phishing refers to the act of attempting to illegally obtain sensitive information by pretending to be a credible source. Phishing usually takes one of two forms: an email or a phone call. See Chapter 14 for more information.

28. A, B, C. A denial of service (DoS) attack prevents users from accessing the system. All of the above are all possible denial of service attacks except Virus FloodSyn. See Chapter 14 for more information.

29. D. Changing network configurations, terminating sessions, and deceiving the attacker are all actions that can be taken by an Intrusion Prevention System (IPS) device. These are all proactive approaches to security. See Chapter 15 for more information.

30. B. Firewalls help provide perimeter network security by allowing or denying connections and types of traffic in or out of the network. See Chapter 15 for more information.

31. A, B, C. Routing Information Protocol (RIP) is not a WAN protocol, but a routing protocol used in local area connections. See Chapter 16 for more information.

32. C. The Committed Information Rate (CIR) is the rate, in bits per second, at which the frame-relay switch agrees to transfer data. See Chapter 16 for more information.

33. A, D. The arp utility's –a and –g switches perform the same function. They both show the current ARP cache. See Chapter 17 for more information.

34. B. To purge and reload the remote NetBIOS name cache, you must use nbtstat –R. Remember that the *R* must be uppercase, and it will not work correctly without the hyphen before it. See Chapter 17 for more information.

35. B. A wire crimper or crimper is used to attach ends onto different types of network cables. See Chapter 18 for more information.

36. A, B, D. Due to sensitivity to any variation and impedance to cabling, answers A, B and D are all reasons you'd use a TDR. See Chapter 18 for more information.

37. A, B, C. Because most of today's networks still consist of large amounts of copper cable, they can continue to suffer from the physical issues (the options are not a complete list) that have plagued all networks since the very beginning of networking. See Chapter 19 for more information.

38. C. Creating an action plan and a solution, and identifying the potential effects, would be the next step according to the standard troubleshooting model. See Chapter 19 for more information.

39. A. Traffic shaping, also known as packet shaping, is another form of bandwidth optimization. See Chapter 20 for more information.

40. A. Load balancing refers to a technique used to spread work out to multiple computers, network links, or other devices. You can load-balance work on servers by clustering servers so that multiple machines all provide the same service. See Chapter 20 for more information.

Chapter

1

Introduction to Networks

THE FOLLOWING COMPTIA NETWORK+ EXAM OBJECTIVES ARE COVERED IN THIS CHAPTER:

✓ **2.3 Identify common physical network topologies**

- Star
- Mesh
- Bus
- Ring
- Point to point
- Point to multipoint
- Hybrid

✓ **2.7 Explain common logical network topologies and their characteristics**

- Peer to peer
- Client/server
- VPN
- VLAN

You'd have to work pretty hard these days to find someone who would argue that our computers have become invaluable to us personally and professionally. Our society has become highly dependent on these resources and on sharing them with each other. The ability to communicate with those we need to—whether they're in the same building or in some far-away land—completely hinges on our capacity to create and maintain solid, dependable networks.

And those vitally important networks come in all shapes and sizes—ranging from small and simple, to humongous and super complicated. But whatever their flavor, they all need to be maintained properly; and in order to do that well, you've got to understand networking basics. The various types of devices and technologies that are used to create networks, as well as how they work together, is what this book is about, and I'll go through this critical information one step at a time with you. Understanding all of this will not only equip you with a rock-solid base to build on as you grow in your IT knowledge and career, but will also arm you with what you'll need to ace the Network+ certification exam!

There are two other topics under Objective 2.7—virtual private networks (VPNs) and virtual local area networks (VLANSs)—that I'll only be introducing to you in this chapter. So make a little note to yourself that I'm going to cover VPNs thoroughly later on in Chapter 13, "Authentication and Access Control," and I'll tell you all about VLANs in Chapter 11, "Switching and Virtual LANs."

To find up-to-the-minute updates for this chapter, please see www.lammle.com or www.sybex.com/go/comptianetwork+studyguide.

First Things First: What's a Network?

The dictionary defines the word *network* as "a group or system of interconnected people or things." Similarly, in the computer world, the term *network* means two or more connected computers that can share resources like data and applications, office machines, an Internet connection, or some combination of these, as shown in Figure 1.1.

Okay—Figure 1.1 shows a really basic network made up of only two host computers connected together; they share resources like files and even a printer hooked up to one of the hosts. These two hosts "talk" to each other using a computer language called *binary code*, which consists of lots of 1s and 0s in a specific order that describes exactly what they want to "say."

FIGURE 1.1   A basic network

Next, I'm going to tell you about local area networks (LANs), how they work, and even how we can connect LANs together. Then, later in this chapter, I'll describe how to connect remote LANs together through something known as a wide area network (WAN).

The Local Area Network (LAN)

Just as the name implies, a *local area network (LAN)* is usually restricted to spanning a particular geographic location like an office building, a single department within a corporate office, or even a home office.

Back in the day, you couldn't put more than 30 workstations on a LAN, and you had to cope with strict limitations on how far those machines could actually be from each other. Because of technological advances, all that's changed now, and we're not nearly as restricted in regard to both a LAN's size and the distance a LAN can span. Even so, it's still best to split a big LAN into smaller logical zones known as *workgroups* to make administration easier.

In a typical business environment, it's a good idea to arrange your LAN's workgroups along department divisions; for instance, you would create a workgroup for Accounting, another one for Sales, and maybe another for Marketing—you get the idea. Figure 1.2, which shows two separate LANS, each as its own workgroup.

FIGURE 1.2   A small LAN Two separate LANs (workgroups)

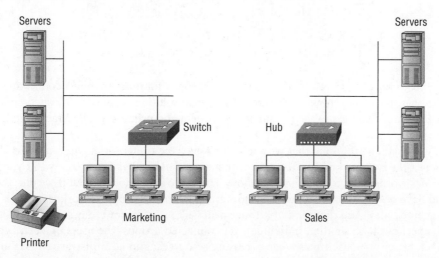

First, don't stress about the devices labeled *hub* and *switch*—these are just connectivity devices that allow hosts to physically connect to resources on a LAN. Trust me; I'll describe them to you in much more detail later in Chapter 5, "Networking Devices."

Anyway, back to the figure… Notice that there's a Marketing workgroup and a Sales workgroup. These are LANs in their most basic form. Any device that connects to the Marketing LAN can access the resources of the Marketing LAN—in this case, the servers and printer. If you want to access resources from the Sales LAN, then you must connect directly to the Sales LAN.

There are two problems with this:

1. You must be physically connected to each LAN to get the resources from that specific workgroup's LAN.

2. You can't get from one LAN to the other LAN and use its server data and printing resources remotely.

This is a typical network issue that's easily resolved by using a cool device called a router to connect the two LANs together, as shown in Figure 1.3.

FIGURE 1.3   A router connects LANs together.

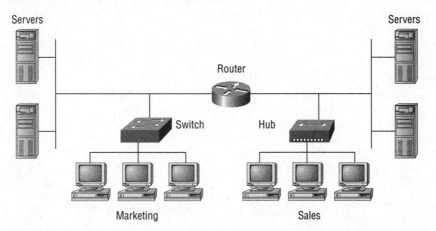

Nice—problem solved! Even though you can use routers for more than just connecting LANs together, the router shown in Figure 1.3 is a great solution because the host computers from the Sales LAN can get to the resources (server data and printers) of the Marketing LAN, and vice versa.

Now, you might be thinking that we really don't need the router—that we could just physically connect the two workgroups together with a type of cable that would allow the Marketing and Sales workgroups to hook up somehow. True—we could do that, but if we did, then we would have only one big, cumbersome workgroup instead of separate workgroups for Marketing and Sales. And that kind of arrangement isn't practical for today's networks.

This is because with smaller, individual, yet connected groups, the users on each LAN enjoy much faster response times when accessing resources; and administrative tasks are a lot easier, too. Larger workgroups run more slowly because in them, a legion of hosts are all trying to get to the same resources simultaneously. So the router shown in Figure 1.3, which separates the workgroups while still allowing access between them, is a really great solution after all.

> Like I said—don't worry about the network connectivity devices I've mentioned so far in this chapter, like hubs, switches, and routers. I promise to cover them all in detail in Chapter 5. At this stage, I really want you to focus on understanding the concepts that I'm presenting. For now, all you need to know is that hubs and switches are devices that connect other devices together, and routers connect networks together.

So now, let me define those other terms I've used so far: workstations, servers, and hosts.

Common Network Components

There are a lot of different machines, devices, and media that make up our networks. Right now, I'm going to tell you about three of the most common:

- Workstations
- Servers
- Hosts

Workstations

Workstations are often seriously powerful computers that run more than one central processing unit (CPU) and whose resources are available to other users on the network to access when needed. Don't confuse workstations with client machines, which can be workstations but aren't always. A *client machine* is any device on the network that can ask for access to resources from a workstation—for instance, a printer.

> The terms *workstation* and *host* are used interchangeably because computers have become more and more powerful and the terms have become somewhat fuzzy. The term *host* is used to describe pretty much anything that takes an IP address.

Servers

Servers are also powerful computers. They get their name because they truly are "at the service" of the network and run specialized software for the network's maintenance and control known as the *network operating system*.

In a good design that optimizes the network's performance, servers are highly specialized and are there to handle one important labor-intensive job. This is not to say that a single server can't do many jobs; but more often than not, you'll get better performance if you dedicate a server to a single task. Here's a list of common dedicated servers:

File server   Stores and dispenses files.

Mail server   The network's post office, which handles email functions.

Print server   Manages all printers on the network.

Web server   Manages web-based activities by running Hypertext Transfer Protocol (HTTP) for storing web content and accessing web pages.

Fax server   The "memo maker" that sends and receives paperless faxes over the network.

Application server   Manages network applications.

Telephony server   Handles the call center and call routing and can be thought of as a sophisticated network answering machine.

Remote-access server   Provides remote users with access to the network through modems, an IP connection, or wirelessly.

Proxy server   Handles tasks in the place of other machines on the network.

    See how the name of each kind of server indicates what it actually does—how it serves the network? This is an excellent way to remember them.

Okay, like I said, servers are usually dedicated to doing one specific important thing within the network. But not always—sometimes they have more than one job. But whether servers are designated for one job or are network multitaskers, they all maintain the network's data integrity by backing up the network's software and hardware. And no matter what, they all serve a number of client machines.

Back in Figure 1.2, I showed you an example of two really simple LAN networks. I want to make sure you know that servers must have considerably superior hard-drive space—a lot more than a simple workstation's capacity—because they serve many client machines and provide any resources they require. Because they're so important, you should always put your servers in a very secure area. My company's servers are in a locked server room because not only are they really pricey workhorses, but they also store huge amounts of important and sensitive company data; so, they need to be kept safe from any unauthorized access.

In Figure 1.4, you can see a network populated with both workstations and servers. You also see that the hosts can access the servers across the network—pretty much the general idea of having a network.

You probably noticed that there are more workstations here than servers, right? Think of why that is... If you answered that it's because one server can provide resources to what can sometimes be a huge number of individual users at the same time, but workstations don't, you've got it!

FIGURE 1.4   A network populated with servers and workstations

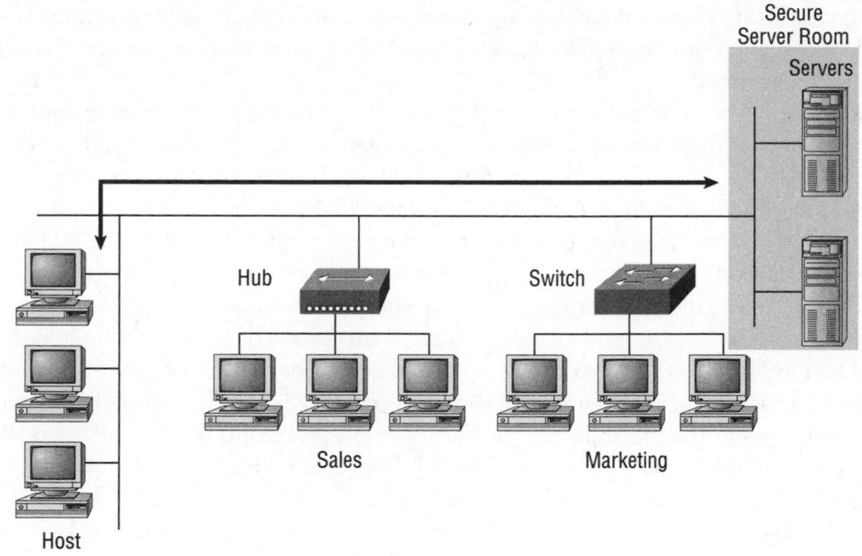

Hosts

It can be kind of confusing because when people refer to hosts, they really can be referring to almost any type of networking devices—including workstations and servers. But
if you dig a bit deeper, you'll find that usually this term comes up when people are talking about resources and jobs that have to do with Transmission Control Protocol/Inter-
net Protocol (TCP/IP). The scope of possible machines and devices is so broad because,
in TCP/IP-speak, a *host* means any network device with an IP address. Yes, you'll hear
IT professionals throw this term around pretty loosely; but for the Network+ exam,
stick to the definition being network devices, including workstations and servers, with
IP addresses.

Here's a bit of background: The name *host* harkens back to the Jurassic period of networking when those dinosaurs known as *mainframes* were the only intelligent devices to roam
the network. These were called *hosts* whether they had TCP/IP functionality or not. In that
bygone age, everything else in the network-scape was referred to as *dumb terminals*, because
only mainframes—hosts—were given IP addresses. Another fossilized term from way back
then is the use of *gateways* when talking about any Layer 3 machines like routers. We still use
these terms today, but they've evolved a bit to refer to the many intelligent devices populating
our present-day networks, each of which has an IP address. This is exactly the reason why
you hear *host* used so broadly.

Now, let's dive a tad deeper into the workgroup subject I started when I described a
basic LAN to you in the beginning of this chapter.

Virtual LANs (VLANs)

It's time to stop using the word *workgroups* when referring to the hosts and resources on a LAN and start using the words *virtual LANs (VLANs),* which are pretty much the same thing with a new name.

A VLAN is really no different than a LAN or LAN workgroup, except that it's not physically built to look anything like the individual LANs shown in Figure 1.2. Instead, it's built *logically.* They both work exactly the same way—the hosts, server, and printers are configured exactly the same—and it's even possible that the router will be configured the same way, too.

So where does the word *virtual* fit in here, and how is this different than the earlier definition of a workgroup? Well, back in Figure 1.2, your network resources were all physically connected together locally. You had to physically walk to the Sales department to get to its resources like servers. The router in Figure 1.3 fixed this problem because it made it so that you could be physically on the Marketing LAN and get to the Sales servers via the router. I've got to tell you—doing this is not a solution I'd recommend. "What!? But Todd, you just said that's why we put the router in Figure 1.3—so one LAN can talk to the other one!"

Yes, true, we want to make our workgroups (VLANs) small, and the router helped us accomplish this. But in today's networks, we don't want to send data through a router unless we absolutely have to. We want resources like servers and printers local to the hosts—meaning right there on the same LAN. This isn't always possible in a network designed as shown in Figures 1.2 and 1.3 because people move around so much in today's possibly worldwide networks. So it's VLANs to the rescue!

Okay, because this can get confusing fast, so let me clarify what I've said so far: In a LAN, your host is connected to a network, which is the workgroup where it resides—for example, in Sales. In a VLAN, your host still resides in a network (or VLAN), but where you're physically connected within your network is no longer relevant. You can be hanging out on the same floor where the Marketing workgroup people work, but you can still access the Sales resources as if you were physically on the Sales LAN without going through a router to get there. This makes network access to the resources you need faster for you; plus, it can provide some nice security benefits because, by default, your host cannot communicate outside the VLAN. So even though you're connected to the Marketing floor, you can still only communicate on the Sales VLAN.

How does this work? It comes down to the particular port you're plugged into (physically connected to). That port is configured for the LAN workgroup you're a member of—if that's the Sales VLAN, you're a Sales local to the Sales servers, even if you're not actually in the Sales department. This type of network is illustrated Figure 1.5, which shows three VLANs.

This type of port configuration is called a *VLAN membership,* and it's got to be configured by an administrator on a network device called a *switch.* VLANs are seriously important in today's networks, and like I said, I'll cover them thoroughly in Chapter 11. For now, remember that VLANs are the new workgroups, and they define the same thing: a group of users sharing network resources. The difference is that VLANs allow you to be anywhere on the physical network and still be local to the specific network resources you need—sweet!

 VLANs help isolate network traffic

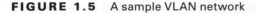

FIGURE 1.5   A sample VLAN network

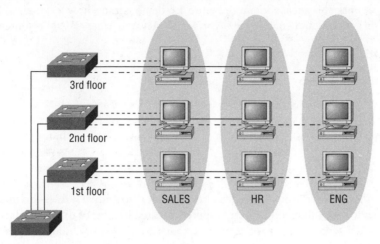

Wide Area Network (WAN)

There are legions of people who, if asked to define a *wide area network (WAN)*, couldn't do it. Yet most of them use the Big Dog of all WANs—the Internet—every day! With that in mind, you can imagine that WAN networks are what we use to span large geographic areas and truly go the distance. Like the Internet, WANs usually employ both routers and public links, so that's generally the criteria used to define them.

> WANs are so important that I have dedicated an entire chapter to them: Chapter 16, "Wide Area Networks."

Here's a list of some of the important ways that WANs are different from LANs:

- They usually need a router port or ports.
- They span larger geographic areas and/or can link disparate locations.
- They're usually slower.
- We can choose when and how long we connect to a WAN. A LAN is all or nothing— our workstation is either connected permanently to it or not at all, although most of us have dedicated WAN links now.
- WANs can utilize either private or public data transport media like phone lines.

We get the word *Internet* from the term *internetwork*. An internetwork is a type of WAN that connects of a bunch of networks, or *intranets*. In an internetwork, hosts still use hardware addresses to communicate between each host on the LAN. However, in an internetwork, hosts use logical addresses (IP addresses) to communicate with hosts on a different LAN (other side of the router).

And *routers* are the devices that make this possible. Each connection into a router is a different logical network (broadcast domain). Figure 1.6 demonstrates how a router is employed to create an internetwork and enable our LANs (or VLANs) to access WAN resources.

FIGURE 1.6   An internetwork

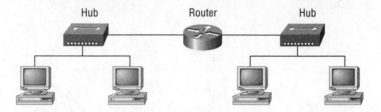

The Internet is a prime example of what's known as a *distributed WAN*—an internetwork that's made up of a lot of interconnected computers located in a lot of different places. There's another kind of WAN, referred to as *centralized*, that's composed of a main, centrally located computer or location that remote computers and devices can connect to. A good example is remote offices that connect to a main corporate office.

Okay, so now we have our LANs from corporate headquarters connecting with a WAN to our remote offices. This is all good, but what if we want the hosts at the remote site to be able to access secure servers at the corporate office? Well, if you like to live dangerously, you could just open your corporate network up to the Internet so the whole world could easily get in there to your secure servers. But because that's a really bad idea, you can use *virtual private networks (VPNs)* instead.

Virtual Private Networks (VPNs)

No worries—VPNs aren't really that hard to understand. A VPN fits somewhere between a LAN and WAN and many times may seem just like a WAN link because your computer, on one LAN, connects to a different, remote LAN, and uses its resources remotely. The key difference with VPNs is a big one—security! So the definition of connecting a LAN (or VLAN) to a WAN may sound the same, but a VPN is much more.

Here's the difference: A typical WAN connects two or more remote LANs together using someone else's network like, say, your Internet service provider (ISP), using a router. Your local host and router see these networks as remote networks and not as local networks or local resources. This would be a WAN in its most general definition. A VPN actually makes your local host part of the remote network by using the WAN link that connects you to the remote LAN. The VPN will make your host appear as though it's actually local on the remote network! This means that we now have access to the remote LANs resources, and that access is very secure.

This may sound a lot like the VLAN definition I just used, and really, the concept is the same: "Take my host and make it appear local to the remote resources." Just remember that for networks that are physically local, using VLANs is a good solution; but for networks that are physically remote—those that span a WAN—we'd opt for using VPNs instead.

For a simple VPN example, let's use my home office in Boulder, Colorado. Here, I have my personal host, but I want it to appear as if it's on a LAN in my corporate office in Dallas, Texas, so I can get to my remote servers. VPN is the solution I use for this because I need the security it provides.

Figure 1.7 shows this example of my host using a VPN connection from Boulder to Dallas, which allows me to access the remote network services and servers as if my host is right there on the same VLAN as my servers.

FIGURE 1.7   Example of using a VPN network

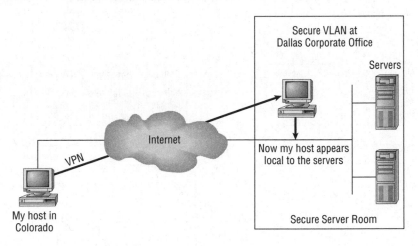

Why is this so important? If you answered, "because my servers in Dallas are secure, and only the hosts on the same VLAN are allowed to connect to them and use the resources of these servers," you nailed it! A VPN allows me to connect to these resources by locally attaching to the VLAN through a VPN across the WAN. The other option is to open up my network and servers to everyone on the Internet or another WAN service, in which case my security goes "poof!" So you can see that it's a very good thing I have a VPN.

Network Architecture: Peer-to-Peer or Client/Server?

So, we've developed networking as a way to share resources and information, and how that's achieved directly maps to the particular architecture of the network operating system software. There are two main network types you need to know about: peer-to-peer and client/server. And by the way, it's really tough to tell the difference just by looking at a diagram or even by checking out live video of the network humming along, but the difference between peer-to-peer and client/server architectures are major. They're not just physical; they're logical differences. You'll see what I mean in a bit.

Peer-to-Peer Networks

Computers connected together in *peer-to-peer networks* do not have any central, or special authority—they're all *peers,* meaning that when it comes to authority, they're all equals. This means it's up to the computer that has the resource being requested to perform a security check for access rights to its resources.

It also means that the computers existing in a peer-to-peer network can be client machines that access resources and server machines that provide them to other computers. This works really well if there's not a huge number of users on the network, each user handles backing things up locally, and your network doesn't require a lot of security.

If your network is running Windows, Mac, or Unix in a local LAN workgroup, you have a peer-to-peer network. Figure 1.8 gives you a snapshot of a typical peer-to-peer network. Peer-to-peer networks present some challenges. For example, backing up company data becomes an iffy proposition.

FIGURE 1.8   A peer-to-peer network

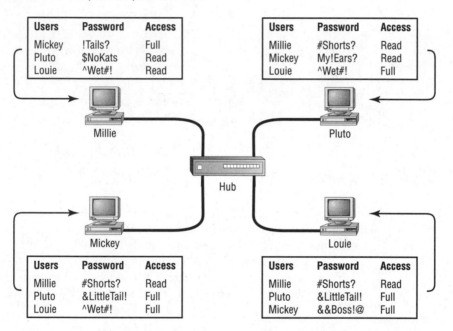

Since it should be clear by now that peer-to-peer networks are all sunshine,—backing up all that super-important data is not only vital, it can be really challenging. What if you forget where you put a badly needed file (haven't we all done that)? And then there's that security issue to tangle with. Because security is not centrally governed, each and every user has to remember and maintain a list of users and passwords on each and every machine. Worse, some of those all-important passwords for the same users change on different machines—even for accessing different resources. Yikes!

Client/Server Networks

Client/server networks are pretty much the polar opposite of peer-to-peer networks because in them, a single server is specified that uses a network operating system for managing the whole network. So a client machine's request for a resource goes to the main server, which responds by handling security and directing the client to the resource it wants, instead of the request going directly to the machine with the desired resource.

This arrangement definitely has its benefits. First, because the network is much better organized and doesn't depend on users remembering where needed resources are, it's a whole lot easier to find the files you need because everything is stored in one spot on that special server. Your security also gets a lot tighter because all usernames and passwords are on that server (which, by the way, isn't ever used as a workstation). You even gain scalability—client/server networks can have legions of workstations on them. And even with all those demands, their performance is actually optimized.

Check out Figure 1.9. Looking at it, you see a client/server network with a server that has a database of access rights, user accounts, and passwords.

FIGURE 1.9   A client/server network

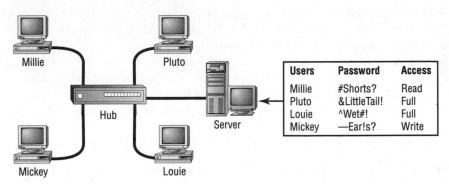

Users	Password	Access
Millie	#Shorts?	Read
Pluto	&LittleTail!	Full
Louie	^Wet#!	Full
Mickey	—Ear!s?	Write

Many of today's networks are a healthy (we hope) combination of the peer-to-peer and client/server architectures with carefully specified servers that permit the simultaneous sharing of resources from devices running workstation operating systems. Even though the supporting machines can't handle as many inbound connections at a time, they still run the server service reasonably well. If this type of mixed environment is designed well, most networks benefit greatly by having the capacity to take advantage of the positive aspects of both worlds.

Physical Network Topologies

Just as a topographical map shows the shape of the terrain, the *physical topology* of a network is also a type of map. It defines the specific characteristics of a network, such as where all the workstations and other devices are located, and the precise arrangement of all the physical media like cables. On the other hand, *logical topologies*, which were covered in the previous section, delineate exactly how data moves through the network. And though these two topologies are usually a lot alike, a particular network can have physical and logical topologies that are very different. But basically, what you want to remember is that a network's physical topology essentially gives you the lay of the land, and the logical topology shows how data navigates through that layout.

Here is a list of the various topologies you're most likely to run in to these days:

- Bus
- Star
- Ring
- Mesh
- Point-to-point
- Point-to-multipoint
- Hybrid

Bus Topology

This type of topology is the most basic one of the bunch, and it really does sort of resemble a bus. (Well, okay—actually, it looks more like a bus that's been in a pretty nasty wreck!) Anyway, the *bus topology* consists of two distinct and terminated ends, with each of its computers connecting to one unbroken cable running its entire length. Back in the day, we used to attach computers to that main cable with wire taps, but this didn't work all that well so we began using drop cables in their place (unless you're dealing with 10Base-2 Ethernet, in which case you would slip a "T" into the main cable anywhere you wanted to connect a device to it, instead of using drop cables).

Figure 1.10 depicts what a typical bus network's physical topology looks like.

FIGURE 1.10   A typical bus network's physical topology

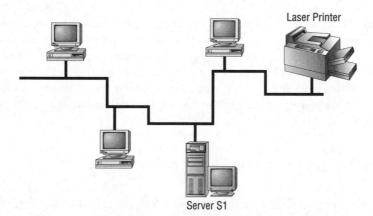

Even though all the computers on this kind of network see all the data flowing through the cable, only the one computer that the data is specifically addressed to actually gets it. Some of the benefits in favor of using a bus topology are that it's easy to install and it's not very expensive, in part because it doesn't require as much cable as the other types of physical topologies. But it also has some drawbacks: For instance, it's hard to troubleshoot, change, or move, and it really doesn't offer much in the way of fault tolerance because everything is connected to that single cable.

> By the way, *fault tolerance* is the capability of a computer or a network system to respond to a condition automatically, often resolving it, which reduces the impact on the system. If fault-tolerance measures have been implemented correctly on a network, it's highly unlikely that any of that network's users will know that a problem even existed.

Star Topology

A *star topology's computers are* connected to a central point with their own individual cables or wireless connections. You'll often find that central spot inhabited by a device like a hub, a switch, or an access point.

Star topology offers a lot of advantages over bus topology, making it more widely used even though it obviously requires more physical media. One of its best features is that because each computer or network segment is connected to the central device individually, if the cable fails, it brings down only that particular machine or network segment. That's truly a great benefit because it makes the network much more fault tolerant as well as a lot easier to troubleshoot. Another great thing about a star topology is that it's a lot more scalable—all you have to do if you want to add to it is run a new cable and connect to the machine at the core of the star. In Figure 1.11, you'll find a great example of a typical star topology.

FIGURE 1.11   Typical star topology with a hub

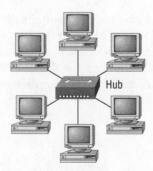

Okay, although it is called *star* topology, it really looks a lot more like the imaginary pictures people draw of the sun. (Yes, the sun is a star—but it definitely doesn't look like how we usually depict it, does it?) You could also get away with saying it looks like a bike wheel with spokes connecting to the hub in the middle of the wheel and extending outward to connect to the rim. And just like that bike wheel, it's the hub device at the center of a star-topology network that can give you the most grief if something goes wrong with it. If that hub in the middle of it all happens to fail, down comes the whole network, so it's a very good thing hubs don't fail often!

Just as it is with pretty much everything, a star topology has its pros and cons. But the good news far outweighs the bad, which is why people are choosing to go with a star topology more and more. Here's a list of benefits gained by opting for a star topology:

- New stations can be added easily and quickly.

- A single cable failure won't bring down the entire network.

- It is relatively easy to troubleshoot.

The disadvantages of a star topology include the following:

- The total installation cost can be higher because of the larger number of cables (but prices are constantly becoming more competitive).

- It has a single point of failure (the hub or other central device).

There are two more sophisticated implementations of star topology. The first is called *point-to-point link*, where you have not only the device in the center of the spoke acting as a hub, but also the one on the other end. This is still a star-wired topology, but as I'm sure you can imagine, it gives you a huge amount of scalability!

Another refined version is the wireless flavor; but to understand this version well, you've really got to have a solid grasp of the capabilities and features of all the devices populating the wireless star topology. No worries, though—I'll be covering wireless access points later on in Chapter 12, "Wireless Networking." For now, it's good enough for you to know that access points are pretty much just wireless hubs or switches that behave like their wired counterparts. Basically, they set up by point-to-point connections to endpoints and other wireless access points.

Ring Topology

In this type of topology, you'll find that each computer is directly connected to other computers within the same network. Looking at Figure 1.12, you can see that the network's data flows from computer to computer back to the source, with the network's primary cable forming a ring. The problem is, the *ring topology* has a lot in common with the bus topology because if you want to add to the network, you have no choice but to break the cable ring—something that is probably going to bring down the entire network.

FIGURE 1.12   A typical ring topology

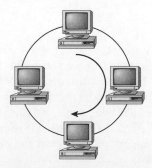

This is one big reason why this topology isn't all that popular—you just won't run into it a lot as I did in the 1980s and early 1990s. A few more reasons include the fact that it's pricey because you need several cables to connect each computer; it's really hard to reconfigure; and as you've probably guessed, it's not fault tolerant.

However, with all that being said, if you work at an ISP, you may find a physical ring topology in use for a technology called SONET or possibly some other WAN technology. You just won't find any LANs in physical rings anymore.

Mesh Topology

In this type of topology, you'll find that there's a path from every machine to every other one in the network. That's a lot of connections—in fact, the *mesh topology* wins the prize for "most physical connections per device"! You won't find it used in LANs very often, if ever, these days, but you will find a modified version of it known as *hybrid mesh* used in a restrained manner on WANs including the Internet.

Often, hybrid mesh topology networks will have quite a few connections between certain places to create redundancy (backup). And other types of topologies can sometimes be found in the mix too, which is also why it's dubbed *hybrid*. At any rate, it isn't a full-on full mesh topology if there isn't a connection between all devices in the network. But it's still respectably complicated—Figure 1.13 shows just how much only four connections can complicate things.

FIGURE 1.13   A typical mesh topology

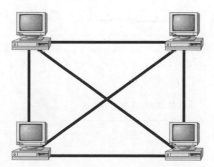

As shown in the figure, things just get more and more complex as both the wiring and the connections multiply. For each *n* locations or hosts, you end up with $n(n-1)/2$ connections. This means that in a network consisting of only four computers, you have $4(4-1)/2$, or 6 connections. And if that little network grows to, say, a population of 10 computers, you'll have a whopping 45 connections to cope with—yikes! That's a huge amount of overhead, so only small networks can really use this topology and manage it well. On the bright side, you get a very respectable level of fault tolerance. But it is nice that we don't use these in corporate LANs any longer, because they were very complicated to manage.

A Full Mesh physical topology has the absolute least likelihood of having a collision.

This is the reason you will usually find the hybrid version in today's WANs. In fact, the mesh topology is actually pretty rare these days. It's mainly used because of the robust fault tolerance it offers—because you've got a multitude of connections, if one goes on the blink, computers and other network devices can simply switch to one of the many redundant connections that are up and running. But as you can imagine, all that cabling in the mesh topology requires makes it really costly. Plus, you can make your network management much less insane by using what's known as a *partial mesh topology* solution instead, so why not go that way? You may lose a little fault tolerance; but if you go the partial-mesh route, you still get to use the same technology between all the network's devices. Just remember that with partial mesh, not all devices will be interconnected, so it's very important to choose wisely the ones that are.

Point-to-Point Topology

As its name implies, in a *point-to-point* topology you have a direct connection between two routers, giving you one communication path. The routers in a point-to-point topology can either be linked by a serial cable, making it a physical network, or be far apart and only connected by a circuit within a frame relay network, making it a logical network.

Figure 1.14 gives you a prime specimen of a T1, or WAN point-to-point connection.

FIGURE 1.14   Three point-to-point connections

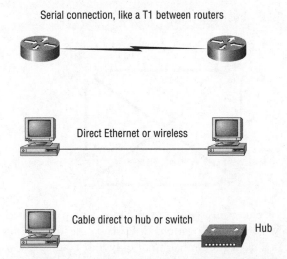

Serial connection, like a T1 between routers

Direct Ethernet or wireless

Cable direct to hub or switch   Hub

What you see here is a lightning bolt and a couple of round things with a bunch of arrows projecting from them, right? Well, the two round things radiating arrows represent our network's two routers, and that lightning bolt represents a WAN link. (These symbols are industry standard and I'll be using them throughout this book, so it would a good idea to get used to them.)

Part two of the diagram shows two computers connected by a cable—a point-to-point link. By the way, this should remind you of something we just went over… remember our talk about peer-to-peer networks? Good! I hope you also happen to remember that a big drawback related to peer-to-peer network sharing is that it is not very scalable. With this in mind, you probably won't be all that surprised that even if both machines have a wireless point-to-point connection, the network won't be very scalable.

You'll usually find point-to-point networks within many of today's WANs; and as you can see in part three of Figure 1.14, a link from a computer to a hub or switch is also a valid point-to-point connection. A common version of this setup consists of a direct wireless link between two wireless bridges that's used to connect computers in two different buildings together.

Point-to-Multipoint Topology

Again as the name suggests, a *point-to-multipoint* topology consists of a succession of connections between an interface on one router to multiple destination routers—one point of connection to multiple points of connection. Each of the routers and every one of their interfaces involved in the point-to-multipoint connection are part of the same network.

Figure 1.15 shows a WAN to best demonstrate a point-to-multipoint network that depicts a single corporate router connecting to multiple branches.

FIGURE 1.15   A point-to-multipoint network, Example 1

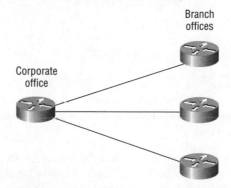

Figure 1.16 shows another prime example of a point-to-multipoint network: a college or corporate campus.

FIGURE 1.16   A point-to-multipoint network, Example 2

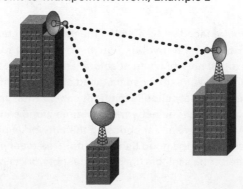

Hybrid Topology

I know I talked about hybrid network topology back in the section about mesh topology, but I didn't give you a picture of it in the form of a figure. I also want to point out that *hybrid topology* means just that—a combination of two or more types of physical or logical network topologies working together within the same network.

Figure 1.17 depicts a simple hybrid network topology. Here you see a LAN switch or hub in a star topology configuration that connects to its hosts via bus topology:

FIGURE 1.17:   A Simple Hybrid Network

Hub

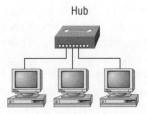

Physical Star, Logical Bus

 Real World Scenario

They're just cables, right?

Wrong! Regardless of the type of network you build, you need to start thinking about quality at the bottom and work up.

Think of it as if you were at an electronics store buying the cables for your sweet new home-theater system. You've already spent a bunch of time and money getting the right components to meet your needs. In fact, you've probably parted with a respectable chunk of change, so why would you stop there and connect all these great devices together with the cable equivalent of twine? No, you're smarter than that. You know that picking out the exact cables that will maximize the sound and picture quality of your specific components can also protect them.

It's the same thing when you're faced with selecting the physical media for a certain network (such as your new client-server network)—you just don't want to cut corners here. Because it's the backbone of the network, you absolutely don't want to be faced with having to dig up everything that's already been installed after the fact. Doing this costs a lot more than taking the time to wisely choose the right cables and spending the money it takes to get them in the first place. The network downtime alone can cost a company a bundle (pun intended). Another reason for choosing the network's physical media correctly is that it's going to be there for a good 5 to 10 years. This means two things: It better be solid quality, and it better be scalable, because that network is going to grow and change over the years.

Topology Selection, Backbones, and Segments

Okay—now that you're familiar with many different types of network topologies, you're ready for some tips on selecting the right one for your particular network. You also need to know about backbones and segments—the very last part of this chapter.

Selecting the Right Topology

As you now know, not only do you have a buffet of network topologies to choose from, but each one also has pros and cons to implementing it. But it really comes down to that well-known adage, "ask the right questions." First, how much cash do you have? And how much fault tolerance do you really need? Also, is this network likely to grow like a weed—is it probably going to need to be quickly and easily reconfigured often? In other words, how scalable does your network need to be?

For instance, if your challenge is to design a nice, cost-effective solution that only involves a few computers in a room, getting a wireless access point and some wireless network cards is definitely your best way to go because you won't need to pony up for a bunch of cabling and it's super simple to set up. Alternately, if you're faced with coming up with a solid design for a growing company's already-large network, you're probably good to go using a wired star topology because it will nicely allow for future changes. Remember, a star topology really shines when it comes to making additions to the network, moving things around, and making any kind of changes happen quickly, efficiently, and cost effectively.

If, say, you're hired to design a network for an ISP that needs to be up and running 99.9% of the time with no more than eight hours a year allowed downtime, well, you need Godzilla-strength fault tolerance. Do you remember which topology gives that up the best? (Hint—Internet.) Your primo solution is to go with either a hybrid or a partial-mesh topology. Remember that partial mesh leaves you with a subset of $n(n-1)/2$ connections to maintain—a number that could very well blow a big hole in your maintenance budget!

Here's a list of things to keep in mind when you're faced with coming up with the right topology for the right network:

- Cost
- Ease of installation
- Ease of maintenance
- Fault-tolerance requirement

The Network Backbone

Today's networks can get pretty complicated, so we've got have a standard way of communicating with each other intelligibly about exactly which part of the network we're referring to. This is the reason we divide networks into different parts called *backbones* and *segments*.

Figure 1.18 illustrates a network and shows which part is the backbone and which parts are segments.

FIGURE 1.18   Backbone and segments on a network

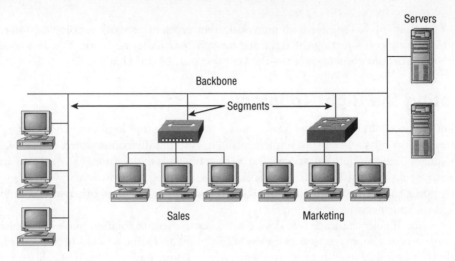

You can see that the network backbone is actually kind of like our own. It's what all the networks segments and servers connect to and what gives the network its structure. As you can imagine, being such an important nerve center, the backbone must use some kind of seriously fast, robust technology—often that's Gigabit Ethernet. And to optimize network performance (that is, speed and efficiency), it follows that you would want to connect all of the network's servers and segments directly to the network's backbone.

Network Segments

When we refer to a segment, we can mean any small section of the network that may be connected to, but isn't actually a piece of, the backbone. The network's workstations connect to its servers, which in turn connect to the network backbone; you can see this by taking another look at Figure 1.18, which displays three segments.

Summary

This chapter created a solid foundation for you to build your networking knowledge on as you go through this book.

In it, you learned what, exactly, a network is, and you got an introduction to some of the components involved in building one: routers, switches, and hubs, as well as the jobs they do in a network.

You also learned that having the components required to build a network isn't all you need—understanding the various types of network connection methods like peer-to-peer and client/server is also vital.

Also covered were key networking technologies like VLANs and VPNs—the latter being the secure way to connect remote networks.

Further, you learned about the various types of logical and physical network topologies and the features and drawbacks of each. We wrapped up the chapter with a short discussion about network backbones and segments, and equipped you with the right questions to ask yourself to ensure that you come up with the right network topology for your networking needs.

Exam Essentials

Know your network topologies.   Know the names and descriptions of the topologies. Be aware of the difference between physical networks—what humans see—and logical networks—what the equipment "sees."

Know the advantages and disadvantages of the topologies.   It is important to know what each topology brings to the table. Knowing the various characteristics of each topology comes in handy during troubleshooting.

Understand the term *virtual private network*.   You need to understand why and how to use a VPN between two sites.

Written Labs

Provide the answers to the following questions:

1. What are the three primary LAN topologies?

2. What common WAN topology often results in multiple connections to a single site, leading to a high degree of fault tolerance?

3. What is the term for a device that shares its resources with other network devices?

4. What network model draws a clear distinction between devices that share their resources and devices that do not?

5. Which network topology or connection type can be implemented with only two endpoints?

6. What device is an example of an Ethernet technology implemented as a star topology?

7. What does VPN stand for?

8. What does VLAN stand for?

9. Will a computer that shares no resources most likely be connected to the backbone or to a segment?

10. Which LAN topology is characterized by all devices being daisy-chained together with the devices at each end being connected to only one other device?

(The answers to the Written Lab can be found following the answers to the Review Questions for this chapter.)

Review Questions

1. You need a network that provides centralized authentication for your users. Which of the following logical topologies should you use?

   A. VLANs

   B. Peer-to-peer

   C. Client/Server

   D. Mesh

2. You need a topology that is scalable to use in your network. Which of the following will you install?

   A. Bus

   B. Ring

   C. Star

   D. Mesh

3. Which of the following physical topologies has the least likelihood of having a collision?

   A. Bus

   B. Star

   C. Ring

   D. Mesh

4. In a physical-star topology, what happens when a workstation loses its physical connection to another device?

   A. The ring is broken, so no devices can communicate.

   B. Only that workstation loses its ability to communicate.

   C. That workstation and the device it's connected to lose communication with the rest of the network.

   D. No devices can communicate because there are now two unterminated network segments.

5. You want to remotely log into an office computer using remote desktop in a secure manner. Which of the following should you use?

   A. VPN

   B. Tagged packets

   C. VLANs

   D. Telnet

   E. SSH

6. What is a logical grouping of network users and resources connected to administratively defined ports on a switch?

   A. Host

   B. Hub

   C. VLAN

   D. VTP

7. Which of the following is a concern when using peer-to-peer networks?

   A. Where to place the server

   B. Whose computer is least busy and can act as the server

   C. The security associated with such a network

   D. Having enough peers to support creating such a network

8. Which of the following is an example of when a point-to-multipoint network is called for?

   A. When a centralized office needs to communicate with many branch offices

   B. When a full mesh of WAN links is in place

   C. When multiple offices are daisy-chained to one another in a line

   D. When there are only two nodes in the network to be connected

9. Which of the following is an example of a LAN?

   A. Ten buildings interconnected by Ethernet connections over fiber-optic cabling

   B. Ten routers interconnected by frame-relay circuits

   C. Two routers interconnected with a T1 circuit

   D. A computer connected to another computer so they can share resources

10. Which of the following is a disadvantage of the star topology?

   A. When a port on the central concentrating device fails, the attached end device loses connectivity to the rest of the network.

   B. When the central concentrating device experiences a complete failure, all attached devices lose connectivity to the rest of the network.

   C. In a star topology, a more expensive type of host must be used when compared to the host used when implementing a physical bus.

   D. It is more difficult to add stations and troubleshoot than with other topologies.

11. What is a difference between a LAN and a WAN?

   A. WANs need a special type of router port.

   B. WANs cover larger geographical areas.

   C. WANs can utilize either private or public data transport.

   D. All of the above.

12. What does the acronym VPN stand for?

   A. Virtual processor network

   B. Virtual passive network

   C. Virtual private network

   D. Variable-length private network

13. In what type of network are all computers considered equals and do they not share any central authority?

   A. Peer-to-peer

   B. Client-server

   C. Physical topology

   D. None of the above

14. What advantage does the client-server architecture have over peer-to-peer?

   A. Easier maintenance

   B. Greater organization

   C. Tighter security

   D. All of the above

15. An example of a hybrid network is which of the following?

   A. Ethernet

   B. Ring topology

   C. Bus topology

   D. Star topology

16. You have a network with multiple devices and need to have a smaller broadcast domain while working with a tight budget. Which of the following is the best solution?

   A. Use static IP addresses

   B. Add more hubs

   C. Implement more switches

   D. Create VLANs

17. Which type of topology has the greatest number of physical connections?

   A. Point-to-multipoint

   B. Star

   C. Point-to-point

   D. Mesh

18. What type of topology gives you a direct connection between two routers so that there is one communication path?

  A. Point-to-point

  B. Star

  C. Bus

  D. Straight

19. Which network topology is a combination of two or more types of physical or two or more types of logical topologies?

  A. Point-to-multipoint

  B. Hybrid

  C. Bus

  D. Star

20. When designing a network and deciding which type of network topology to use, which item(s) should be considered? (Select all that apply.)

  A. Cost

  B. Ease of installation

  C. Ease of maintenance

  D. Fault-tolerance requirements

Answers to Review Questions

1. C. A client/server logical topology allows you to have a centralized database of users so that authentication is provided in one place.

2. C. To install a physical topology that provides ease of scalability use a star network. This is a hub or switch device, and this is the most common LAN networks today.

3. D. Only a Mesh physical topology has point-to-point connections to every device, so it has the least likelihood of ever having a collision.

4. B. In a star topology, each workstation connects to a hub, switch, or similar central device, but not to other workstations. The benefit is when connectivity to the central device is lost, the rest of the network lives on.

5. A. To connect to remote office securely, you need to use a Virtual Private Network (VPN).

6. C. VLANs allow you to be anywhere on the physical network and still be local to the network resources you need.

7. C. Security is easy to relax in a peer-to-peer environment. Because of the trouble it takes to standardize authentication, a piecemeal approach involving users' personal preferences develops. There are no dedicated servers in a peer-to-peer network, and such a network can be created with as few as two computers.

8. A. When a central office, such as a headquarters, needs to communicate directly with its branch offices, but the branches do not require direct communication with one another, the point-to-multipoint model is applicable. The other scenarios tend to indicate the use of a point-to-point link between sites.

9. D. LANs generally have a geographic scope of a single building or smaller. They can range from simple (two hosts) to complex (with thousands of hosts).

10. B. The only disadvantage mentioned is the fact that there is a single point of failure in the network. However, this topology makes troubleshooting easier; if the entire network fails, you know where to look first. The central device also ensures that the loss of a single port and the addition of a new device to an available port do not disrupt the network for other stations attached to such a device.

11. D. A typical WAN connects two or more remote LANs together using someone else's network (your ISP's) using a router. Your local host and router see these networks as remote networks and not as local networks or local resources.

12. C. Virtual private networks (VPNs) allow for the creation of private networks across the Internet. A VPN makes your local host part of the remote network by using the WAN link that connects you to the remote LAN.

13. A. In a peer-to-peer network, all computers are considered equals. It is up to the computer that has the resource being requested to perform a security check for access rights to its resources.

14. D. In client-server networks, requests for resources go to a main server that responds by handling security and directing the client to the resource it wants, instead of the request going directly to the machine with the desired resource (as in peer-to-peer).

15. A. The best answer to this question is Ethernet, which uses a star physical topology with a logical bus technology.

16. D. If you have a switch, you can break up a layer-2 switched networks into smaller broadcast domains by creating VLAN's.

17. D. In the mesh topology, there is a path from every machine to every other one in the network. A mesh topology is used mainly because of the robust fault tolerance it offers—if one connection goes on the blink, computers and other network devices can simply switch to one of the many redundant connections that are up and running.

18. A. As its name implies, in a point-to-point topology you have a direct connection between two routers, giving you one communication path. The routers in a point-to-point topology can either be linked by a serial cable, making it a physical network, or be far away and only connected by a circuit within a frame-relay network, making it a logical network.

19. B. A hybrid topology is a combination of two or more types of physical or logical network topologies working together within the same network.

20. A, B, C, D. Each topology has its own set of pros and cons regarding implementation, so asking the right questions and considering cost, ease of installation, maintenance, and fault tolerance are all important factors to be considered.

Answers to Written Labs

1. Bus, ring, and star

2. Mesh

3. Server

4. Client/server

5. Point-to-point

6. Hub

7. Virtual private network

8. Virtual LAN

9. A segment

10. Bus

Chapter

2

The Open Systems Interconnection Specifications

THE FOLLOWING COMPTIA NETWORK+ EXAM OBJECTIVES ARE COVERED IN THIS CHAPTER:

✓ **4.1 Explain the function of each layer of the OSI model**

- Layer 1 – physical
- Layer 2 – data link
- Layer 3 – network
- Layer 4 – transport
- Layer 5 – session
- Layer 6 – presentation
- Layer 7 – application

In this chapter, I'm going to dissect the Open Systems Interconnection (OSI) model and describe each part to you in detail, because you need a solid foundation on which to build your networking knowledge. The OSI model has seven hierarchical layers that were developed to enable different networks to communicate reliably between disparate systems.

Because this book is centering upon all things Network+, it's crucial for you to understand the OSI model as CompTIA sees it, so I'll present each of its seven layers in that light.

I'll finish this chapter with an introduction to encapsulation. *Encapsulation* is the process of encoding data as it goes down the OSI stack.

To find up-to-the-minute updates for this chapter, please see www.lammle.com or www.sybex.com/go/comptianetwork+studyguide.

Internetworking Models

When networks first came into being, computers could usually communicate only with computers from the same manufacturer. For example, companies ran either a complete DECnet solution or an IBM solution—not both together. In the late 1970s, the *Open Systems Interconnection (OSI) reference model* was created by the International Organization for Standardization (ISO) to break through this barrier.

The OSI model was meant to help vendors create interoperable network devices and software in the form of protocols so that different vendor networks could work with each other. Like world peace, it'll probably never happen completely, but it's still a great goal.

The OSI model is the primary architectural model for networks. It describes how data and network information are communicated from an application on one computer through the network media to an application on another computer. The OSI reference model breaks this approach into layers.

In the following section, I'll explain the layered approach and how you can use this approach to help troubleshoot internetworks.

The Layered Approach

Basically, a *reference model* is a conceptual blueprint of how communications should take place. It addresses all the processes required for effective communication and divides these processes into logical groupings called *layers*. When a communication system is designed in this manner, it's known as *layered architecture*.

Think of it like this: Say you and some friends want to start a company. One of the first things you'll do is sit down and think through what tasks must be done, who will do them, the order in which they will be done, and how they relate to each other. Ultimately, you might group these tasks into departments. Let's say you decide to have an order-taking department, an inventory department, and a shipping department. Each of your departments has its own unique tasks, keeping its staff members busy and requiring them to focus only on their own duties.

In this scenario, I'm using departments as a metaphor for the layers in a communication system. For things to run smoothly, the staff of each department has to trust and rely heavily on the others to do their jobs and competently handle their unique responsibilities. In your planning sessions, you'll probably take notes, recording the entire process to facilitate later discussions about standards of operation that will serve as your business blueprint or reference model.

Once your business is launched, your department heads, each armed with the part of the blueprint relating to their own department, will need to develop practical methods to implement their assigned tasks. These practical methods, or protocols, must be compiled into a standard-operating-procedures manual and followed closely. The procedures in your manual will have been included for different reasons and have varying degrees of importance and implementation. If you form a partnership or acquire another company, it will be imperative that its business protocols—its business blueprint—matches yours (or at least be compatible with it).

Similarly, software developers can use a reference model to understand computer communication processes and see what types of functions need to be accomplished on any one layer. If they're developing a protocol for a certain layer, all they need to concern themselves with is that specific layer's functions, not those of any other layer. Another layer and protocol will handle the other functions. The technical term for this idea is *binding*. The communication processes that are related to each other are bound, or grouped together, at a particular layer.

Advantages of Reference Models

The OSI model is hierarchical, and the same benefits and advantages can apply to any layered model. The primary purpose of all such models, especially the OSI model, is to allow different vendors' networks to interoperate.

Advantages of using the OSI layered model include, but are not limited to, the following:

- It divides the network communication process into smaller and simpler components, thus aiding component development, design, and troubleshooting.

- It allows multiple-vendor development through standardization of network components.

- It encourages industry standardization by defining what functions occur at each layer of the model.

- It allows various types of network hardware and software to communicate.

- It prevents changes in one layer from affecting other layers, so it doesn't hamper development and makes application programming easier.

The OSI Reference Model

One of the greatest functions of the OSI specifications is to assist in data transfer between disparate hosts—meaning, for example, that they enable you to transfer data between a Unix host and a PC or a Mac.

The OSI model isn't a physical model, though. Rather, it's a set of guidelines that application developers can use to create and implement applications that run on a network. It also provides a framework for creating and implementing networking standards, devices, and internetworking schemes. The OSI model has seven layers:

- Application (Layer 7)

- Presentation (Layer 6)

- Session (Layer 5)

- Transport (Layer 4)

- Network (Layer 3)

- Data Link (Layer 2)

- Physical (Layer 1)

Figure 2.1 shows a summary of the functions defined at each layer of the OSI model. With this in hand, you're now ready to explore each layer's function in detail.

FIGURE 2.1 Layer functions

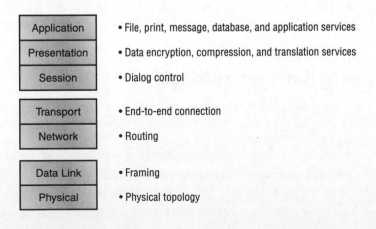

Some people like to use the mnemonic Please Do Not Throw Sausage Pizza Away to remember the seven layers (starting at Layer 1 and moving up to Layer 7).

The seven layers are divided into two groups. The top three layers define how the applications within the end stations will communicate with each other and with users. The bottom four layers define how data is transmitted end to end. Figure 2.2 shows the three upper layers and their functions, and Figure 2.3 shows the four lower layers and their functions.

When you study Figure 2.2, understand that the user interfaces with the computer at the Application layer and also that the upper layers are responsible for applications communicating between hosts. Remember that none of the upper layers knows anything about networking or network addresses. That's the responsibility of the four bottom layers.

FIGURE 2.2 The upper layers

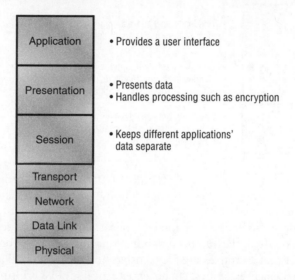

Figure 2.3 illustrates that the four bottom layers define how data is transferred through physical media, switches, and routers. These bottom layers also determine how to rebuild a data stream from a transmitting host to a destination host's application.

Let's start at the Application layer and work our way down the stack.

The Application Layer

The *Application layer* of the OSI model marks the spot where users actually communicate to the computer. This layer comes into play only when it's apparent that access to the network will be needed soon. Take the case of Internet Explorer (IE). You could uninstall every trace of networking components from a system, such as TCP/IP, the NIC card, and so on, and you could still use IE to view a local HTML document—no problem. But things would definitely get messy if you tried to do something like view an HTML document that had to be retrieved using HTTP or nab a file with FTP or TFTP. That's because IE responds to requests such as those by attempting to access the Application layer. And what's happening is that the Application layer acts as an interface between the application program—which isn't part of the layered structure—and the next layer down by providing ways for the application to send information down through the protocol stack. In other words, IE doesn't reside within the Application layer—it interfaces with Application-layer protocols when it needs to deal with remote resources.

FIGURE 2.3   The lower layers

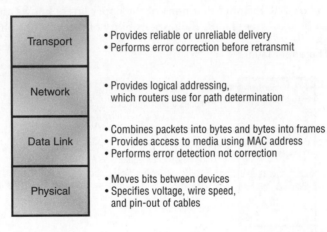

The Application layer is also responsible for identifying and establishing the availability of the intended communication partner and determining whether sufficient resources for the intended communication exist.

These tasks are important because computer applications sometimes require more than just desktop resources. Often, they unite communicating components from more than one network application. Prime examples are file transfers and email, as well as enabling remote access, network-management activities, client/server processes like printing, and information location. Many network applications provide services for communication over enterprise networks; but for present and future internetworking, the need is fast developing to reach beyond the limits of current physical networking.

It's important to remember that the Application layer acts as an interface between application programs. This means that Microsoft Word, for example, doesn't reside at the Application layer but instead interfaces with the Application-layer protocols. Chapter 5 will present some programs that actually reside at the Application layer—for example, FTP and TFTP.

The Presentation Layer

The *Presentation layer* gets its name from its purpose: It presents data to the Application layer and is responsible for data translation and code formatting.

This layer is essentially a translator and provides coding and conversion functions. A successful data-transfer technique is to adapt the data into a standard format before transmission. Computers are configured to receive this generically formatted data and then convert the data back into its native format for reading (for example, EBCDIC to ASCII). By providing translation services, the Presentation layer ensures that data transferred from one system's Application layer can be read by the Application layer of another one.

The OSI has protocol standards that define how standard data should be formatted. Tasks like data compression, decompression, encryption, and decryption are associated with this layer. In addition, some Presentation-layer standards are involved in multimedia operations.

The Session Layer

The *Session layer* is responsible for setting up, managing, and then tearing down sessions between Presentation-layer entities. This layer also provides dialogue control between devices, or nodes. It coordinates communication between systems and serves to organize their communication by offering three different modes: *simplex*, *half duplex*, and *full duplex*. To sum up, the Session layer basically keeps applications' data separate from other applications' data.

The Transport Layer

The *Transport layer* segments and reassembles data into a data stream. Services located in the Transport layer segment and reassemble data from upper-layer applications and unite it onto the same data stream. They provide end-to-end data transport services and can establish a logical connection between the sending host and destination host on an internetwork.

The Transport layer is responsible for providing mechanisms for multiplexing upper-layer applications, establishing sessions, and tearing down virtual circuits. It also hides details of any network-dependent information from the higher layers by providing transparent data transfer.

You may be familiar with TCP and UDP already. (If you're not, no worries—I'll tell you all about them in Chapter 6, "Introducing the Internet Protocol.") If so, you know that both work at the Transport layer and that TCP is a reliable service and UDP is not. This means application developers have more options because they have a choice between the two protocols when working with TCP/IP protocols.

The term *reliable networking* can be used at the Transport layer. It means that acknowledgments, sequencing, and flow control will be used.

The Transport layer can be connectionless or connection-oriented. However, it's important that you understand the connection-oriented portion of the Transport layer. The following sections will provide the skinny on the connection-oriented (reliable) protocol of the Transport layer.

Connection-Oriented Communication

Before a transmitting host starts to send segments down the model, the sender's TCP process contacts the destination's TCP process to establish a connection. What is created is known as a *virtual circuit*. This type of communication is called *connection-oriented*. During this initial *handshake*, the two TCP processes also agree on the amount of information that will be sent in either direction before the respective recipient's TCP sends back an acknowledgment. With everything agreed on in advance, the path is paved for reliable communication to take place.

Figure 2.4 depicts a typical reliable session taking place between sending and receiving systems. Looking at it, you can see that both hosts' application programs begin by notifying their individual operating systems that a connection is about to be initiated. The two operating systems communicate by sending messages over the network confirming that the transfer is approved and that both sides are ready for it to take place. After all of this required synchronization takes place, a connection is fully established and the data transfer begins. This virtual circuit setup is called *overhead*.

FIGURE 2.4   Establishing a connection-oriented session

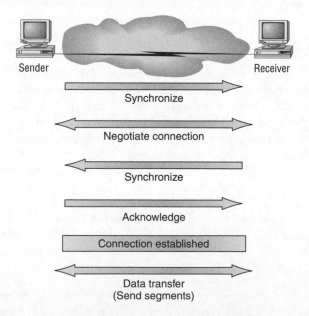

While the information is being transferred between hosts, the two machines periodically check in with each other, communicating through their protocol software to ensure that all is going well and that the data is being received properly.

Let me sum up the steps in the connection-oriented session—the three-way handshake—pictured in Figure 2.4:

- The first "connection agreement" segment is a request for synchronization.

- The second and third segments acknowledge the request and establish connection parameters—the rules—between hosts. These segments request that the receiver's sequencing is synchronized here as well so that a bidirectional connection is formed.

- The final segment is also an acknowledgment. It notifies the destination host that the connection agreement has been accepted and that the connection has been established. Data transfer can now begin.

 Although I broke this connection setup into much detail, it really is just called the "three-way handshake" as I already mentioned, and is known as "SYN, SYN-ACK, SYN", or synchronize, synchronize-acknowledgment, syncronize.

Sounds pretty simple, but things don't always flow so smoothly. Sometimes congestion can occur during a transfer because a high-speed computer is generating data traffic a lot faster than the network can handle transferring it. A bunch of computers simultaneously sending datagrams through a single gateway or destination can also botch things up. In the latter case, a gateway or destination can become congested even though no single source caused the problem. In either case, the problem is basically akin to a freeway bottleneck—too much traffic for too small a capacity. It's not usually one car that's the problem; it's that there are simply too many cars on that particular freeway.

Flow Control

Data integrity is ensured at the Transport layer by maintaining *flow control* and by allowing users to request reliable data transport between systems. Flow control provides a means for the receiver to govern the amount of data sent by the sender. It prevents a sending host on one side of the connection from overflowing the buffers in the receiving host—an event that can result in lost data. Reliable data transport employs a connection-oriented communications session between systems, and the protocols involved ensure that the following will be achieved:

- The segments delivered are acknowledged back to the sender upon their reception.

- Any segments not acknowledged are retransmitted.

- Segments are sequenced back into their proper order upon arrival at their destination.

- A manageable data flow is maintained in order to avoid congestion, overloading, and data loss.

Okay, so what happens when a machine receives a flood of datagrams too quickly for it to process? It stores them in a memory section called a *buffer*. But this buffering action can solve the problem only if the datagrams are part of a small burst. If not, and the datagram deluge continues, a device's memory will eventually be exhausted, its flood capacity will be exceeded, and it will react by discarding any additional datagrams that arrive.

This sounds pretty bad, but there aren't really any huge worries here thanks to the transport function—network flood-control systems actually work quite well. How do they work? Well, instead of just dumping resources and allowing data to be lost, the transport can issue a "not ready" indicator to the sender, or source, of the flood (as shown in Figure 2.5). This mechanism works kind of like a stoplight, signaling the sending device to stop transmitting segment traffic to its overwhelmed peer. After the peer machine's receiver processes the segments abounding in its memory reservoir (its buffer), it sends out a "ready" transport indicator. When the machine waiting to transmit the rest of its datagrams receives this "go" indictor, it resumes its transmission.

During fundamental, reliable, connection-oriented data transfer, datagrams are delivered to the receiving host in exactly the same sequence they're transmitted—and the transmission fails if this order is breached! So if any data segments are lost, duplicated, or damaged along the way, a failure notice is transmitted. This problem is solved by making sure the receiving host acknowledges that it has received each and every data segment in the correct order.

To summarize, a service is considered connection-oriented if it has the following characteristics:

- A virtual circuit is set up (such as a three-way handshake).
- It uses sequencing.
- It uses acknowledgments.
- It uses flow control.

FIGURE 2.5   Transmitting segments with flow control

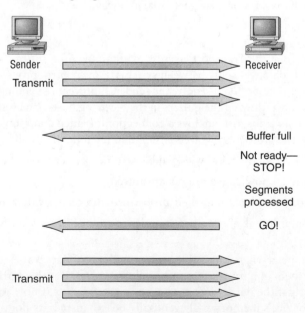

Windowing

Ideally, data throughput happens quickly and efficiently. And as you can imagine, it would be slow if the transmitting machine had to wait for an acknowledgment after sending each segment. But because time is available *after* the sender transmits the data segment and *before* it finishes processing acknowledgments from the receiving machine, the sender uses the break as an opportunity to transmit more data. The quantity of data segments (measured in bytes) that the transmitting machine is allowed to send without receiving an acknowledgment for them is called a *window*.

Windows are used to control the amount of outstanding, unacknowledged data segments.

It's important to understand that the size of the window controls how much information is transferred from one end to the other. Although some protocols quantify information by observing the number of packets, TCP/IP measures it by counting the number of bytes.

Figure 2.6 illustrates two window sizes—one set to 1 and one set to 3. In our simplified example, both the sending and receiving machines are workstations.

When you've configured a window size of 1, the sending machine waits for an acknowledgment for each data segment it transmits before transmitting another. If you've configured a window size of 3, the sending machine is allowed to transmit three data segments before an acknowledgment is received. In reality, this isn't done in simple numbers but in the amount of bytes that can be sent.

FIGURE 2.6 Windowing

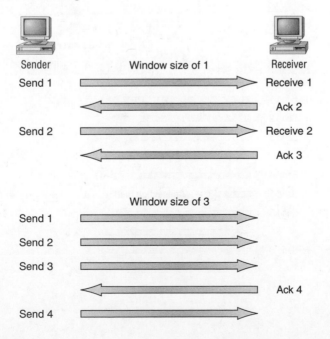

> If a receiving host fails to receive all the segments that it should acknowledge, the host can improve the communication session by decreasing the window size.

Acknowledgments

Reliable data delivery ensures the integrity of a stream of data sent from one machine to the other through a fully functional data link. It guarantees that the data won't be duplicated or lost. This is achieved through something called *positive acknowledgment with retransmission*—a technique that requires a receiving machine to communicate with the transmitting source by sending an acknowledgment message back to the sender when it receives data. The sender documents each segment it sends and waits for this acknowledgment before sending the next segment. When it sends a segment, the transmitting machine starts a timer and retransmits if it expires before an acknowledgment is returned from the receiving end.

In Figure 2.7, the sending machine transmits segments 1, 2, and 3. The receiving node acknowledges it has received them by requesting segment 4. When it receives the acknowledgment, the sender then transmits segments 4, 5, and 6. If segment 5 doesn't make it to the destination, the receiving node acknowledges that event with a request for the segment to be re-sent. The sending machine will then resend the lost segment and wait for an acknowledgment, which it must receive in order to move on to the transmission of segment 7.

FIGURE 2.7   Transport layer reliable delivery

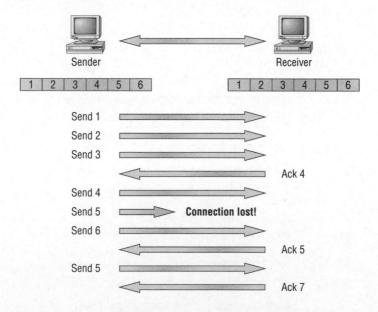

The Transport layer doesn't need to use a connection-oriented service (this is up to the application developer). It's safe to say that if you're connection-oriented, meaning that you've created a virtual circuit, you're using TCP. If you aren't setting up a virtual circuit, then you're using UDP and are considered connection-less.

Transport Control Protocol (TCP) and User Datagram Protocol (UDP) are protocols that work at the Transport layer and are covered in detail in Chapter 6.

Devices Used in an Internetwork

The following network devices operate at all seven layers of the OSI model:

- Network management stations (NMSs)
- Web and application servers
- Gateways (not default gateways)
- Network hosts

Several devices operate primarily at the Physical layer of the OSI model. These devices manipulate mainly the physical aspects of a network data stream (such as the voltages, signal direction, and signal strength). The most popular of these are the following:

- Network Interface Cards (NICs)
- Transceivers
- Repeaters
- Hubs

These devices are discussed in detail in Chapter 5, "Networking Devices."

The Network Layer

The *Network layer* manages device addressing, tracks the location of devices on the network, and determines the best way to move data, which means that the Network layer must transport traffic between devices that aren't locally attached. Routers (Layer 3 devices) are specified at the Network layer and provide the routing services within an internetwork.

It happens like this: First, when a packet is received on a router interface, the destination IP address is checked. If the packet isn't destined for that particular router, the router looks up the destination network address in the routing table. Once the router chooses an exit interface, the packet is sent to that interface to be framed and sent out on the local network. If the router can't find an entry for the packet's destination network in the routing table, the router drops the packet.

Two types of packets are used at the Network layer:

Data packets These are used to transport user data through the internetwork. Protocols used to support data traffic are called *routed protocols*. Two examples of routed protocols are Internet Protocol (IP) and Internet Protocol version 6 (IPv6), which you'll learn about in Chapter 7, "IP Addressing."

Route-update packets These are used to update neighboring routers about the networks connected to all routers within the internetwork. Protocols that send route-update packets are called routing protocols; examples of some common ones are Routing Information Protocol (RIP), RIPv2, Enhanced Interior Gateway Routing Protocol (EIGRP), and Open Shortest Path First (OSPF). Route-update packets are used to help build and maintain routing tables on each router.

Figure 2.8 shows an example of a routing table. The routing table used by a router includes the following information:

Network addresses These are protocol-specific network addresses. A router must maintain a routing table for individual routing protocols because each routing protocol keeps track of a network with a different addressing scheme (IP, and IPv6,for example). Think of it as a street sign in each of the different languages spoken by the residents who live on a particular street. If there were American, Spanish, and French folks on a street named Cat, the sign would read Cat/Gato/Chat.

FIGURE 2.8 Routing table used in a router

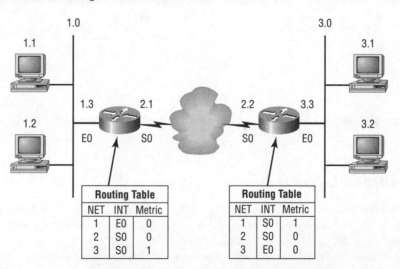

Interface This is the exit interface a packet will take when destined for a specific network.

Metric This value equals the distance to the remote network. Different routing protocols use different ways of computing this distance. I'll cover routing protocols in Chapter 9,

"Introduction to Routing"; for now, just know that some routing protocols (namely RIP) use something called a *hop count*—the number of routers a packet passes through en route to a remote network—whereas others use bandwidth, delay of the line, or something known as a tick count (1/18 of a second).

Routers break up broadcast domains, which means that by default, broadcasts aren't forwarded through a router. Why is this a good thing? Routers also break up collision domains, but this can be accomplished using Layer 2 (Data Link layer) switches as well.

Broadcast and collision domains are covered in detail in Chapter 5. For now, remember that routers break up broadcast domains and switches break up collision domains.

Because each interface in a router represents a separate network, it must be assigned unique network identification numbers, and each host on the network connected to that router must use the same network number. Figure 2.9 demonstrates how a router works within an internetwork.

FIGURE 2.9   A router in an internetwork

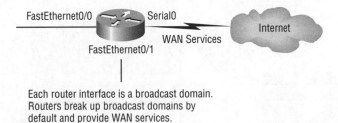

Each router interface is a broadcast domain.
Routers break up broadcast domains by
default and provide WAN services.

Here are some points about routers that you should definitely commit to memory:

- Routers, by default, won't forward any broadcast or multicast packets.
- Routers use the logical address in a Network-layer header to determine the next hop router to forward the packet to.
- Routers can use access lists, created by an administrator, to control security on the types of packets that are allowed to enter or exit an interface.
- Routers can provide Layer 2 bridging functions if needed and can simultaneously route through the same interface.
- Layer 3 devices (routers, in this case) provide connections between virtual LANs (VLANs).
- Routers can provide quality of service (QoS) for specific types of network traffic.

Routers can also be referred to as a Layer-3 switch. These terms are interchangeable.

The Data Link Layer

The *Data Link layer* provides the physical transmission of the data and handles error notification, network topology, and flow control. This means the Data Link layer ensures that messages are delivered to the proper device on a LAN using hardware addresses, and translates messages from the Network layer into bits for the Physical layer to transmit.

The Data Link layer formats the message into pieces, each called a *data frame*, and adds a customized header containing the destination and source hardware address. This added information forms a sort of capsule that surrounds the original message in much the same way that engines, navigational devices, and other tools were attached to the lunar modules of the Apollo project. These various pieces of equipment were useful only during certain stages of flight and were stripped off the module and discarded when their designated stage was complete. This is a great analogy for data traveling through networks because it works very similarly.

Figure 2.10 shows the Data Link layer with the Ethernet and Institute of Electrical and Electronics Engineers (IEEE) specifications. When you check it out, notice that the IEEE 802.2 standard is not only used in conjunction with the other IEEE standards; it also adds functionality to those standards.

FIGURE 2.10   Data Link layer

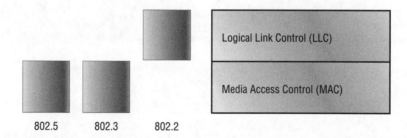

It's important for you to understand that routers, which work at the Network layer, don't care about where a particular host is located. They're only concerned about where networks are located and the best way to reach them—including remote ones. Routers are totally obsessive when it comes to networks. And for once, this obsession is a good thing! The Data Link layer is responsible for the unique identification of each device that resides on a local network.

For a host to send packets to individual hosts on a local network as well as transmit packets between routers, the Data Link layer uses hardware addressing. Each time a packet is sent between routers, it's framed with control information at the Data Link layer; but that information is stripped off at the receiving router, and only the original packet is left completely intact. This framing of the packet continues for each hop until the packet is finally delivered to the correct receiving host. It's important to understand that the packet itself is never altered along the route; it's only encapsulated with the type of control information required for it to be properly passed on to the different media types.

The IEEE Ethernet Data Link layer has two sublayers:

Media Access Control (MAC)   Defines how packets are placed on the media. Contention media access is "first come/first served" access where everyone shares the same bandwidth—hence the name. Physical addressing is defined here, as well as logical topologies. What's a logical topology? It's the signal path through a physical topology. Line discipline, error notification (not correction), ordered delivery of frames, and optional flow control can also be used at this sublayer.

Logical Link Control (LLC)   Responsible for identifying Network-layer protocols and then encapsulating them. An LLC header tells the Data Link layer what to do with a packet once a frame is received. It works like this: A host receives a frame and looks in the LLC header to find out where the packet is destined—say, the IP protocol at the Network layer. The LLC can also provide flow control and sequencing of control bits.

Project 802

One of the major components of the Data Link layer is the result of the IEEE's 802 subcommittees and their work on standards for local area and metropolitan area networks (LANs/MANs). The committee met in February 1980, so they used the "80" from 1980 and the "2" from the second month to create the name Project 802. The designation for an 802 standard always includes a dot (.) followed by either a single or a double digit. These numeric digits specify particular categories within the 802 standard. These standards are listed in Table 2.1.

TABLE 2.1   IEEE 802 Networking Standards

Standard	Topic
802.1	LAN/MAN Management (and Media Access Control Bridges)
802.2	Logical Link Control
802.3	CSMA/CD
802.4	Token Passing Bus
802.5	Token Passing Ring
802.6	Distributed Queue Dual Bus (DQDB) Metropolitan Area Network (MAN)
802.7	Broadband Local Area Networks
802.8	Fiber-Optic LANs and MANs
802.9	Isochronous LANs

TABLE 2.1 IEEE 802 Networking Standards *(continued)*

Standard	Topic
802.10	LAN/MAN Security
802.11	Wireless LAN
802.12	Demand Priority Access Method
802.15	Wireless Personal Area Network
802.16	Wireless Metropolitain Area Network (also called WiMAX)
802.17	Resilient Packet Ring
802.18	LAN/MAN Standards Committee

The Physical Layer

Finally, we're hitting bottom. Well, not in a bad way—we've now arrived at the *Physical layer*, which does two important things: It sends bits and receives bits. Bits come only in values of 1 or 0—a Morse code with numerical values. The Physical layer communicates directly with the various types of actual communication media. Different kinds of media represent these bit values in different ways. Some use audio tones, and others employ *state transitions*—changes in voltage from high to low and low to high. Specific protocols are needed for each type of media to describe the proper bit patterns to be used, how data is encoded into media signals, and the various qualities of the physical media's attachment interface.

The Physical layer specifies the electrical, mechanical, procedural, and functional require-ments for activating, maintaining, and deactivating a physical link between end systems. This layer is also where you identify the interface between the *data terminal equipment (DTE)* and the *data communication equipment (DCE).* (Some older phone-company employees still call DCE data circuit-terminating equipment.) The DCE is usually located at the service provider, whereas the DTE is the attached device. The services available to the DTE are most often accessed via a modem or *channel service unit/data service unit (CSU/DSU).*

The Physical layer's connectors and different physical topologies are defined by the OSI as standards, allowing disparate systems to communicate.

Finally, the Physical layer specifies the layout of the transmission media (its topology, in other words). A physical topology describes the way the cabling is physically laid out (as opposed to a logical topology, discussed earlier in the section "The Data Link Layer"). The physical topologies include Bus, Star, Ring, and Mesh, and were described in Chapter 1, "Introduction to Networks."

Introduction to Encapsulation

When a host transmits data across a network to another device, the data goes through *encapsulation*: It's wrapped with protocol information at each layer of the OSI model. Each layer communicates only with its peer layer on the receiving device.

To communicate and exchange information, each layer uses *Protocol Data Units (PDUs)*. These hold the control information attached to the data at each layer of the model. They're usually attached to the header in front of the data field but can also be in the trailer, or end, of it.

At a transmitting device, the data-encapsulation method works like this:

1. User information is converted to data for transmission on the network.

2. Data is converted to segments, and a reliable connection is set up between the transmitting and receiving hosts.

3. Segments are converted to packets or datagrams, and a logical address is placed in the header so each packet can be routed through an internetwork.

4. Packets or datagrams are converted to frames for transmission on the local network. Hardware (Ethernet) addresses are used to uniquely identify hosts on a local network segment.

5. Frames are converted to bits, and a digital encoding and clocking scheme is used.

Figure 2.11 shows how user data is encapsulated at a transmitting host.

After you learn more foundational material about networking in the next few chapters, I'll come back to the encapsulation method and discuss it in more detail in Chapter 6, as well as in even more detail in Chapter 9.

FIGURE 2.11: Data encapsulation

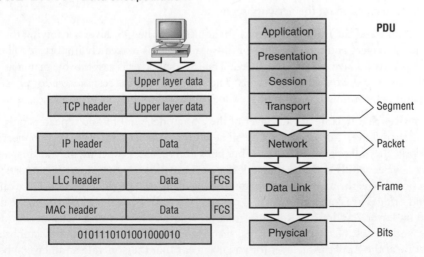

Summary

You're now armed with a ton of fundamental information. You're set to build on it and are well on your way to certification.

Let's take a minute to go over what you've learned in this chapter. We started by discussing internetworking models and the advantages of having them. I then discussed the OSI model—the seven-layer model used to help application developers design applications that can run on any type of system or network. Each layer has its special jobs and select responsibilities within the model to ensure that solid, effective communications do, in fact, occur. I provided you with complete details of each layer and discussed how you need to view the specifications of the OSI model.

This chapter finished with a brief introduction to the encapsulation method used in networking. Encapsulation is a highly important concept to understand, and I'll continue to discuss it throughout this book.

Exam Essentials

Remember the OSI layers.   You absolutely must remember and understand the seven layers of the OSI model as well as what function each layer provides. The Application, Presentation, and Session layers are upper layers and are responsible for communicating from a user interface to an application. The Transport layer provides segmentation, sequencing, and virtual circuits. The Network layer provides logical network addressing and routing through an internetwork. The Data Link layer provides framing and placing of data on the network medium. The Physical layer is responsible for taking 1s and 0s and encoding them into a digital signal for transmission on the network segment.

Know the sublayers of the Data Link layer.   In addition to the OSI layers, knowing the only layer that has sublayers and the functions of those sublayers is extremely important. The Data Link layer has two sublayers: LLC and MAC. The LLC sublayer is responsible primarily for the multiplexing of Network-layer protocols. The MAC sublayer is responsible for physical addressing and determining the appropriate time to place data on the network.

Know the devices that operate at each layer of the OSI model.   Hubs and repeaters only see bits, making them Layer 1 devices. Because all networking devices have physical connectivity to the network, they all operate at Layer 1, but hubs and repeaters operate only at this layer. Nevertheless, we generally consider that a device operates at the highest layer it supports; that layer's functionality is the main reason we implement the device on the network. For example, switches and bridges are considered Layer 2 devices because they understand and make decisions based on Layer 2 addresses. Routers are Layer 3 devices for a similar reason; they deal with Layer 3 addresses. Networking devices, such as workstations, that run applications are said to operate at the Application layer (or you may hear that they operate at all layers) because they must include Application-layer protocols that offer services to networked applications.

Written Lab

1. Which layer chooses and determines the availability of communicating partners along with the resources necessary to make the connection, coordinates partnering applications, and forms a consensus on procedures for controlling data integrity and error recovery?

2. Which layer is responsible for converting data packets from the Data Link layer into electrical signals?

3. At which layer is routing implemented, enabling connections and path selection between two end systems?

4. Which layer defines how data is formatted, presented, encoded, and converted?

5. Which layer is responsible for creating, managing, and terminating sessions between applications?

6. Which layer manages the transmission of data across a physical link and is primarily concerned with physical addressing and the ordered delivery of frames?

7. Which layer is used for reliable communication between end nodes over the network and provides mechanisms for establishing, maintaining, and terminating virtual circuits as well as controlling the flow of information?

8. Which layer provides logical addressing that routers use for path determination?

9. Which layer specifies voltage, wire speed, and connector pinouts and moves bits between devices?

10. Which layer combines bits into bytes and bytes into frames and uses MAC addressing?

(The answers to the Written Lab can be found following the answers to the Review Questions for this chapter.)

Review Questions

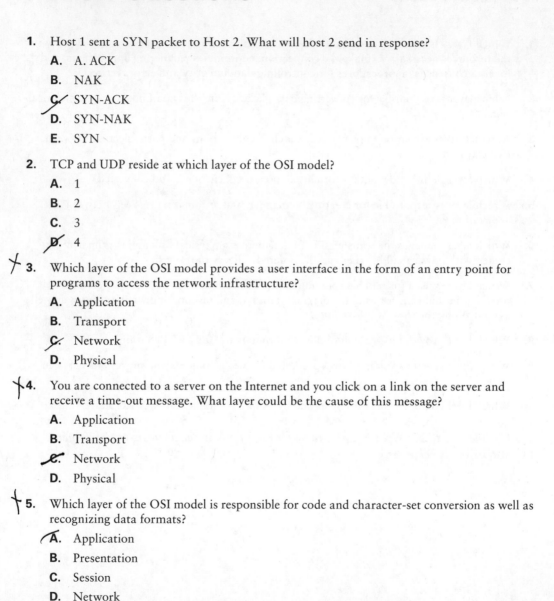

1. Host 1 sent a SYN packet to Host 2. What will host 2 send in response?

   A. A. ACK

   B. NAK

   C. SYN-ACK

   D. SYN-NAK

   E. SYN

2. TCP and UDP reside at which layer of the OSI model?

   A. 1

   B. 2

   C. 3

   D. 4

3. Which layer of the OSI model provides a user interface in the form of an entry point for programs to access the network infrastructure?

   A. Application

   B. Transport

   C. Network

   D. Physical

4. You are connected to a server on the Internet and you click on a link on the server and receive a time-out message. What layer could be the cause of this message?

   A. Application

   B. Transport

   C. Network

   D. Physical

5. Which layer of the OSI model is responsible for code and character-set conversion as well as recognizing data formats?

   A. Application

   B. Presentation

   C. Session

   D. Network

6. At which layers of the OSI model do bridges, hubs, and routers primarily operate, respectively?

   A. Physical, Physical, Data Link

   B. Data Link, Data Link, Network

   C. Data Link, Physical, Network

   D. Physical, Data Link, Network

7. Which layer of the OSI model is responsible for converting data into signals appropriate for the transmission medium?

   A. Application

   B. Network

   C. Data Link

   D. Physical

8. A receiving host has failed to receive all the segments that it should acknowledge. What can the host do to improve the reliability of this communication session?

   A. Send a different source port number.

   B. Restart the virtual circuit.

   C. Decrease the sequence number.

   D. Decrease the window size.

9. Which Layer 1 devices can be used to enlarge the area covered by a single LAN segment? (Choose two.)

   A. Switch

   B. NIC

   C. Hub

   D. Repeater

   E. RJ-45 transceiver

10. Segmentation of a data stream happens at which layer of the OSI model?

    A. Physical

    B. Data Link

    C. Network

    D. Transport

11. When data is encapsulated, which is the correct order?

    A. Data, frame, packet, segment, bits

    B. Segment, data, packet, frame, bits

    C. Data, segment, packet, frame, bits

    D. Data, segment, frame, packet, bits

12. What are two purposes for segmentation with a bridge?

    A. To add more broadcast domains

    B. To create more collision domains

    C. To add more bandwidth for users

    D. To allow more broadcasts for users

13. Acknowledgments, sequencing, and flow control are characteristic of which OSI layer?

    A. Layer 2

    B. Layer 3

    C. Layer 4

    D. Layer 7

14. Which of the following are types of flow control? (Choose all that apply.)

    A. Buffering

    B. Cut-through

    C. Windowing

    D. Congestion avoidance

    E. VLANs

15. What is the purpose of flow control?

    A. To ensure that data is retransmitted if an acknowledgment is not received

    B. To reassemble segments in the correct order at the destination device

    C. To provide a means for the receiver to govern the amount of data sent by the sender

    D. To regulate the size of each segment

16. At which layer of the OSI model would you find IP?

    A. Transport

    B. Network

    C. Data Link

    D. Physical

17. Of the following, which is the highest layer in the OSI model?

    A. Transport

    B. Session

    C. Network

    D. Presentation

18. Routers perform routing at which OSI layer?

   A. Physical

   B. Data Link

   C. Network

   D. Transport

   E. Application

19. Which of the following mnemonic devices can you use to remember the first letter of the name of each layer of the OSI model in the proper order?

   A. All People Seem To Need Processed Data

   B. Always Should People Never Threaten Dog Police

   C. Please Do Not Throw Sausage Pizza Away

   D. All Day People Should Try New Professions

20. Which IEEE standard specifies the protocol for CSMA/CD?

   A. 802.2

   B. 802.3

   C. 802.5

   D. 802.11

Answers to Review Questions

1. C. To set up a connection-oriented session, this is called a three-way handshake and the transmitting host sends a SYK packet, the receiving host sends a SYK-ACK, and the transmitting host replies with the last SYN packet. The session is now set up.

2. D. TCP and UDP are Transport-layer protocols. The Transport layer is Layer 4 of the OSI model.

3. A. The top layer of the OSI model gives applications access to the services that allow network access.

4. A. If the remote server is busy or does not respond to your web browser request, this is an Application layer problem.

5. B. The Presentation layer makes data "presentable" for the Application layer.

6. C. Bridges, like switches, are Data Link-layer devices. Hubs, like repeaters, are Physical-layer devices. Routers are Network-layer devices.

7. D. The Physical layer's job is to convert data into impulses that are designed for the wired or wireless medium being used on the attached segment.

8. D. A receiving host can control the transmitter by using flow control (TCP uses windowing by default). By decreasing the window size, the receiving host can slow down the transmitting host so the receiving host does not overflow its buffers.

9. C, D. Not that you really want to enlarge a single collision domain, but a hub (multiport repeater) will provide this functionality for you.

10. D. The Transport layer receives large data streams from the upper layers and breaks these up into smaller pieces called segments.

11. C. The encapsulation order is data, segment, packet, frame, bits.

12. B, C. Bridges and switches break up collision domains, which allow more bandwidth for users.

13. C. A reliable Transport-layer connection uses acknowledgments to make sure all data is received reliably. A reliable connection is defined by the use of acknowledgments, sequencing, and flow control, which is characteristic of the Transport layer (Layer 4).

14. A, C, D. The common types of flow control are buffering, windowing, and congestion avoidance.

15. C. Flow control allows the receiving device to control the pace of the transmitting device so the receiving device's buffer does not overflow.

16. B. IP is a Network-layer protocol. TCP is an example of a Transport-layer protocol, Ethernet is an example of a Data Link-layer protocol, and T1 can be considered a Physical-layer protocol.

17. D. The Presentation layer is the sixth layer of the model. Only the Application layer is higher, but it is not listed. Session is Layer 5, Transport is Layer 4, and Network is Layer 3.

18. C. A router is specified at the Network layer and a router routes packets. Routers can also be called layer-3 switches.

19. C. The phrase "Please Do Not Throw Sausage Pizza Away" contains the first letters of the layers in order from Layer 1 through Layer 7. "All People Seem To Need Data Processing" works from the top down, but that's not exactly how the option that looks similar reads. The other options have all the right letters, just not completely in the right order.

20. B. The 802.3 standard, commonly associated with Ethernet, specifies the media-access method used by Ethernet, which is known as Carrier Sense Multiple Access with Collision Detection (CSMA/CD).

Answers to Written Lab

1. The Application layer is responsible for finding the network resources broadcast from a server and adding flow control and error control (if the application developer chooses).

2. The Physical layer takes frames from the Data Link layer and encodes the 1s and 0s into a digital signal for transmission on the network medium.

3. The Network layer provides routing through an internetwork and logical addressing.

4. The Presentation layer makes sure that data is in a readable format for the Application layer.

5. The Session layer sets up, maintains, and terminates sessions between applications.

6. PDUs at the Data Link layer are called frames. As soon as you see *frame* in a question, you know the answer.

7. The Transport layer uses virtual circuits to create a reliable connection between two hosts.

8. The Network layer provides logical addressing, typically IP addressing, and routing.

9. The Physical layer is responsible for the electrical and mechanical connections between devices.

10. The Data Link layer is responsible for the framing of data packets.

Chapter

3

Networking Topologies, Connectors, and Wiring Standards

THE FOLLOWING COMPTIA NETWORK+ EXAM OBJECTIVES ARE COVERED IN THIS CHAPTER:

✓ **2.1 Categorize standard cable types and their properties**

- Type:
- CAT3, CAT5, CAT5e, CAT6
- STP, UTP
- Multimode fiber, single-mode fiber
- Coaxial
    - RG-59
    - RG-6
- Serial
- Plenum vs. Non-plenum
- Properties:
- Transmission speeds
- Distance
- Duplex
- Noise immunity (security, EMI)
- Frequency

✓ **2.2 Identify common connector types**

- RJ-11
- RJ-45

- BNC
- SC
- ST
- LC
- RS-232

✓ **2.4 Given a scenario, differentiate and implement appropriate wiring standards**

- 568A
- 568B
- Straight vs. cross-over
- Rollover
- Loopback

✓ **2.8 Install components of wiring distribution**

- Vertical and horizontal cross connects
- Patch panels
- 66 block
- MDFs
- IDFs
- 25 pair
- 100 pair
- 110 block
- Demarc
- Demarc extension
- Smart jack
- Verify wiring installation
- Verify wiring termination

The idea of connecting a bunch of computers together hasn't changed a whole lot since the mid-1980s, but how we go about doing that certainly has. Like everything else, the technologies and devices we create our networks with have evolved dramatically and will continue to do so in order to keep up with the ever-quickening pace of life and the way we do business.

When you connect computers together to form a network, you want error-free, blazingly fast communication, right? Although "error-free" and reality don't exactly walk hand in hand, keeping lapses in communication to a minimum and making that communication happen really fast is definitely possible. But it isn't easy, and understanding the types of media and network topologies used in networking today will go far in equipping you to reach these goals. So will being really knowledgeable about and familiar with the array of components and devices used to control network traffic.

All of these networking ingredients are going to be the focus of this chapter. In it, I'll cover different types of networking media, discuss common topologies and devices, and compare the features that they all bring into designing a solid network that's as problem free and turbo charged as possible.

To find up-to-the-minute updates for this chapter, please see www.lammle.com or www.sybex.com/go/comptianetwork+.

Physical Media

A lot of us rely on wireless networking methods that work using technologies like radio frequency and infrared, but even wireless depends on a physical media backbone in place somewhere. And the majority of installed LANs today communicate via some kind of cabling, so let's take a look at the three types of popular cables used in modern networking designs:

- Coaxial
- Twisted pair
- Fiber optic

Coaxial Cable

Coaxial cable, referred to as *coax*, contains a center conductor made of copper that's surrounded by a plastic jacket, with a braided shield over it. A plastic such as polyvinyl chloride (PVC) or fluoroethylenepropylene (FEP, commonly known as Teflon) covers this metal shield. The Teflon-type covering is frequently referred to as a *plenum-rated coating*, and it's definitely expensive but often mandated by local or municipal fire code when cable is hidden in walls and ceilings. Plenum rating applies to all types of cabling and is an approved replacement for all other compositions of cable sheathing and insulation like PVC-based assemblies.

The difference between plenum and non-plenum cable come down to how each is constructed and where you can use it. Many large multi-story buildings are designed to circulate air through the spaces between the ceiling of one story and the floor of the next; this space between floors is referred to as the *plenum*. And it just happens to be a perfect spot to run all the cables that connect the legions of computers that live in the building. Unless there's a fire—if that happens, the plenum cable becomes a serious hazard because its insulation gives off poisonous smoke that gets circulated throughout the whole building. Plus, plenum cables can actually become "wicks" for the fire, helping it quickly spread from room to room and floor to floor—yikes!

Because it's a great goal to prevent towering infernos, the National Fire Protection Association (NFPA) demands that cables run within the plenum have been tested and guaranteed as safe. They must be fire retardant and create little or no smoke and poisonous gas when burned. This means you absolutely can't use a non-plenum-type cable in the plenum, but it doesn't mean you can't use it in other places where it's safe. And because it's a lot cheaper, you definitely want to use it where you can.

Thin Ethernet, also referred to as *Thinnet* or 10Base-2, is a thin coaxial cable. It is basically the same as thick coaxial cable except it's only about ¼ in diameter. Thin Ethernet coaxial cable is Radio Grade 58 or just RG-58. Figure 3.1 shows an example of Thinnet.

Oh, by the way, if you use Thinnet cable, you've got to use *BNC* connectors to attach stations to the network, as shown in Figure 3.2.

 NOTE   You don't have to know much about most coax cable types in networks anymore, especially the Thinnet and Thicknet types of coaxial cable. Thicknet was known as RG-8 A/U. Nowadays, we use 75ohm coax for cable TV; using coax in the Ethernet world is pretty much a thing of the past. RG-6 or CATV coax is used in our brave new broadband world.

Anyway, you can attach BNC connector with a crimper that looks like a weird pair of pliers and has a die to crimp the connector. A simple squeeze crimps the connector to the cable. You can also use a screw-on connector, but I avoid doing that because it's not very reliable.

Table 3.1 lists some specifications for the different types of coaxial cable, but understand that we only use RG-59 and RG-6 in today's world.

FIGURE 3.1   A stripped-back Thinnet

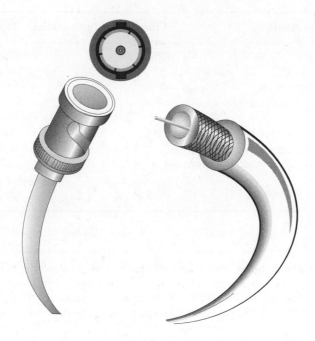

FIGURE 3.2   Male and female BNC connectors

Male

Female

TABLE 3.1   Coaxial Cable Specifications

RG Rating	Popular Name	Ethernet Implementation	Type of Cable
RG-58 U	N/A	None	Solid copper
RG-58 A/U	Thinnet	10Base-2	Stranded copper

TABLE 3.1   Coaxial Cable Specifications *(continued)*

RG Rating	Popular Name	Ethernet Implementation	Type of Cable
RG-8	Thicknet	10Base-5	Solid copper
RG-59	Cable television Low cost, short distance	N/A	Solid copper
RG-6	Cable television, cable modems Longer distances than RG-59; some power implementations	N/A	Solid copper
RG-62	ARCnet (obsolete)	N/A	Solid/stranded

An advantage of using coax cable is the braided shielding that provides resistance to electronic pollution like *electromagnetic interference (EMI)*, *radio frequency interference (RFI)*, and other types of stray electronic signals that can make their way onto a network cable and cause communications problems.

Twisted-Pair Cable

Twisted-pair cable consists of multiple individually insulated wires that are twisted together in pairs. Sometimes a metallic shield is placed around them; hence the name *shielded twisted-pair (STP)*. Cable without outer shielding is called *unshielded twisted-pair (UTP)*, and it's used in twisted-pair Ethernet (10Base-T, 100Base-TX, 1000Base-TX) networks.

Ethernet Cable Descriptions

Ethernet cable types are described using a code that follows this format: *N<Signaling>-X*. The *N* refers to the signaling rate in megabits per second, *<Signaling>* stands for the signaling type—either baseband or broadband—and the *X* is a unique identifier for a specific Ethernet cabling scheme.

Here's a common example: 100Base-X. The 100 tells us that the transmission speed is 100Mb, or 100 megabits. The *X* value can mean several different things, and the *T* is short for *twisted-pair*. This is the standard for running 100-Megabit Ethernet over two pairs (four wires) of Category 5, 5e, or 6 UTP.

So why are the wires in this cable type twisted? Because when electromagnetic signals are conducted on copper wires in close proximity—like inside a cable—it causes interference called *crosstalk*. Twisting two wires together as a pair minimizes interference and even protects against interference from outside sources. This cable type is the most common today for the following reasons:

- It's cheaper than other types of cabling.
- It's easy to work with.
- It allows transmission rates that were impossible 10 years ago.

UTP cable is rated in these categories:

Category 1 Two twisted wire pairs (four wires). It's the oldest type and is only voice grade—it isn't rated for data communication. People refer to it as plain old telephone service (POTS). Before 1983, this was the standard cable used throughout the North American telephone system. POTS cable still exists in parts of the Public Switched Telephone Network (PSTN) and supports signals limited to the 1MHz frequency range.

Category is often shortened to *Cat.* Today, any cable installed should be a minimum of Cat 5e because some cable is now certified to carry bandwidth signals of 350MHz or beyond. This allows unshielded twisted-pair cables to exceed speeds of 1Gbps—fast enough to carry broadcast-quality video over a network.

Category 2 Four twisted wire pairs (eight wires). It handles up to 4Mbps, with a frequency limitation of 10MHz, and is now obsolete.

Category 3 Four twisted wire pairs (eight wires) with three twists per foot. This type can handle transmissions up to 16MHz. It was popular in the mid-1980s for up to 10Mbps Ethernet, but it's now limited to telecommunication equipment and, again, is obsolete for networks.

Category 4 Four twisted wire pairs (eight wires), rated for 20MHz. Also obsolete.

Category 5 Four twisted wire pairs (eight wires), rated for 100MHz. But why use Cat 5 when you can use Cat 5e for the same price? I am not sure you can even buy plain Cat 5 anymore!

Category 5e (enhanced) Four twisted wire pairs (eight wires), rated for 100MHz, but capable of handling the disturbance on each pair that's caused by transmitting on all four pairs at the same time—a feature that's needed for Gigabit Ethernet. Any category below 5e shouldn't be used in today's network environments.

Figure 3.3 shows a basic Cat 5e cable with the four wire pairs twisted to reduce cross-talk.

Category 6 Four twisted wire pairs (eight wires), rated for 250MHz. Cat 6 became a standard back in June 2002. You would usually use it as riser cable to connect floors together. If you're installing a new network in a new building, there's no reason to use anything but Category 6 UTP cabling as well as running fiber runs between floors.

FIGURE 3.3   Cat 5e UTP cable

Connecting UTP

BNC connectors won't fit very well on UTP cable, so you need to use a *Registered Jack (RJ)* connector, which you're familiar with because most telephones connect with them. The connector used with UTP cable is called RJ-11 for phones that use four wires; RJ-45 has four pairs (eight wires), as shown in Figure 3.4.

 Real World Scenario

Category 5e Cabling Tips

If you want data rates faster than 10Mbps over UTP, ensure that all components are rated to deliver this and be really careful when handling all components. If you yank on Cat 5e cable, it will stretch the number of twists inside the jacket, rendering the Cat 5e label on the outside of the cable invalid. Also, be certain to connect and test all four pairs of wire. Although today's wiring usually uses only two pairs (four wires), the standard for Gigabit Ethernet over UTP requires that all four pairs (eight wires) be in good condition.

Also be aware that a true Cat 5e cabling system uses rated components from end to end, patch cables from workstation to wall panel, cable from wall panel to patch panel, and patch cables from patch panel to hub. So if any components are missing, or if the lengths don't match the Category 5e specification, you just don't have a Category 5e cabling installation. And certify that the entire installation is Category 5e compliant. Be warned that doing this requires some pretty pricey test equipment to make the appropriate measurements.

FIGURE 3.4   RJ-11 and RJ-45 connectors

Most of the time, UTP uses RJ connectors; you use a crimper to attach them to a cable, just as you would with BNC connectors. The only difference is that the die that holds the connector is a different shape. Higher-quality crimping tools have interchangeable dies for both types of cables. We do not use RJ-11 for local area networks (LANs), but we do use them for our home Digital Subscriber Link (DSL) connections.

RJ-11 uses two wire pairs, and RJ-45 uses four wire pairs.

Fiber-Optic Cable

Because fiber-optic cable transmits digital signals using light impulses rather than electricity, it's immune to EMI and RFI.

Anyone who's seen a network's UTP cable run down an elevator shaft would definitely appreciate this fiber feature. Fiber cable allows light impulses to be carried on either a glass or a plastic core. Glass can carry the signal a greater distance, but plastic costs less. Whichever the type of core, it's surrounded by a glass or plastic cladding with a different refraction index that reflects the light back into the core. Around this is a layer of flexible plastic buffer that can be wrapped in an armor coating that's usually Kevlar, which is then sheathed in PVC or plenum.

The cable itself comes in either single-mode fiber (SMF) or multimode fiber (MMF); the difference between them is in the number of light rays (the number of signals) they can carry. Multimode fiber is most often used for shorter-distance applications and single-mode fiber for spanning longer distances.

Although fiber-optic cable may sound like the solution to many problems, it has pros and cons just like the other cable types.

Here are the pros:

- Is completely immune to EMI and RFI
- Can transmit up to 40 kilometers (about 25 miles)

And here are the cons:

- Is difficult to install
- Is more expensive than twisted-pair
- Troubleshooting equipment is more expensive than twisted-pair test equipment
- Is harder to troubleshoot

Single-Mode Fiber

Single-mode fiber-optic cable (SMF) is a very high-speed, long-distance media that consists of a single strand—sometimes two strands—of fiber glass that carries the signals. Light-emitting diodes (LEDs) and laser are the light sources used with SMF. The light source is transmitted from end to end and pulsed to create communication. This is the type of fiber cable employed to span really long distances because it can transmit data 50 times further than multimode fiber at a faster rate.

Clearly, because the transmission media is glass, the installation of SMF can be a bit tricky. Yes, there are outer layers protecting the glass core, but the cable still shouldn't be crimped or pinched around any tight corners.

Multimode Fiber

Multimode fiber-optic cable (MMF) also uses light to communicate a signal; but with it, the light is dispersed on numerous paths as it travels through the core and is reflected back. A special material called *cladding* is used to line the core and focus the light back onto it. MMF provides high bandwidth at high speeds over medium distances (up to about 3,000 feet), but beyond that it can be really inconsistent. This is why MMF is most often used within a smaller area of one building; SMF can be used between buildings.

MMF is available in glass or in a plastic version that makes installation a lot easier and increases the installation's flexibility.

Fiber-Optic Connectors

A whole bunch of different types of connectors are available to use with fiber-optic cables, but the two most popular are the *straight tip (ST)* and *subscriber* (or *square*) *connector (SC)*. The ST fiber-optic connector (developed by AT&T) is one of the most widely used fiber-optic connectors; it uses a BNC attachment mechanism similar to Thinnet's that makes connections and disconnections fairly frustration free. In fact, this is the feature that makes this connector so popular. Figure 3.5 shows an example of an ST connector. Notice the BNC attachment mechanism.

The SC connector is another type of fiber-optic connector. As you can see in Figure 3.6, SC connectors are *latched*—a mechanism holds the connector in securely and prevents it from falling out.

SC connectors work with either single-mode or multimode optical fibers and will last for around 1,000 matings. They're being used more now but still aren't nearly as popular as ST connectors for LAN connections.

FIGURE 3.5   An example of an ST connector

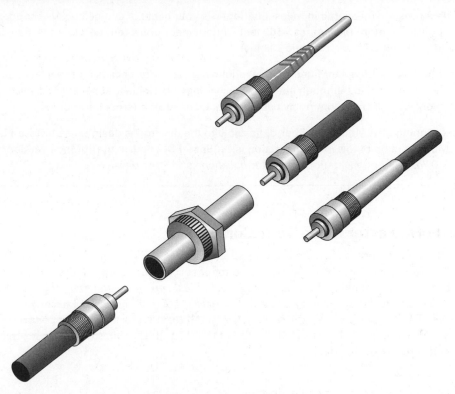

FIGURE 3.6   A sample SC connector

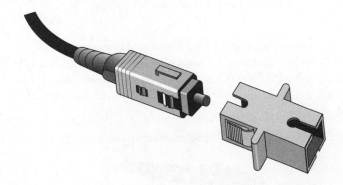

Real World Scenario

Should I Use Copper or Fiber?

If your data runs are measured in miles, fiber optic is your cable of choice because copper just can't give you more than about 1,500 feet without electronics regenerating the signal. The standards limit UTP to a pathetic 328 feet.

Another good reason to opt for fiber is if you require high security, because it doesn't create a readable magnetic field. Although fiber-optic technology was initially super expensive and nasty to work with, it's now commonly used for Gigabit or 10GB Internet backbones.

Ethernet running at 10Mbps over fiber-optic cable to the desktop is designated 10Base-FL; the 100Mbps version of this implementation is 100Base-FX. The *L* in the 10Mbps version stands for *link*. Other designations are *B* for *backbone* and *P* for *passive*.

Small Form Factor Fiber-Optic Connectors

Another cool fiber-optic connector is the *small form factor (SFF)* connector, which allows more fiber-optic terminations in the same amount of space than its standard-sized counterparts. The two most popular versions are the *mechanical transfer registered jack (MT-RJ or MTRJ)*, designed by AMP, and the *Local Connector (LC)*, designed by Lucent.

The MT-RJ fiber-optic connector was the first small form factor fiber-optic connector to be widely used, and it's only one-third the size of the SC and ST connectors it most often replaces. It offers these benefits:

- Small size
- TX and RX strands in one connector
- Keyed for single polarity
- Pre-terminated ends that require no polishing or epoxy
- Easy to use

Figure 3.7 shows an example of an MT-RJ fiber-optic connector.

LC is a newer style of SFF fiber-optic connector that's pulling ahead of the MT-RJ. It is especially popular for use with Fibre-Channel adapters (FCs) and is a standard used for fast storage area networks and Gigabit Ethernet adapters. Figure 3.8 depicts an example of the LC connector.

FIGURE 3.7   A sample MT-RJ fiber-optic connector

FIGURE 3.8   A sample LC fiber-optic connector

It has similar advantages to MT-RJ and other SFF-type connectors but is easier to terminate. It uses a ceramic insert just as standard-sized fiber-optic connectors do.

Serial Cables

Except for multi-mode fiber, all the cable flavors I've talked about so far are considered serial cable types. In network communications, *serial* means that one bit after another is sent out onto the wire or fiber and interpreted by a network card or other type of interface on the other end.

Each 1 or 0 is read separately and then combined with others to form data. This is very different from parallel communication where bits are sent in groups and have to be read together to make sense of the message they represent. A good example of a parallel cable is an old printer cable—which has been replaced by USB, as I'll get to in a minute.

RS-232

Recommended Standard 232 (RS-232) was a cable standard commonly used for serial data signals connecting data-terminal equipment and data-communications equipment, as when you connect a computer's serial port to an external modem.

Figure 3.9 shows an example of one of the many types of RS-232 cables.

Because most laptops don't even come with these types of connectors anymore, they've pretty much been replaced by things like USB and FireWire.

Universal Serial Bus (USB)

Universal Serial Bus (USB) is now the built-in serial bus du jour of most motherboards. You usually get a maximum of 4 external USB interfaces, but add-on adapters can take that up to as many as 16 serial interfaces. USB can actually connect a maximum of 127 external devices, and it's a much more flexible peripheral bus than either serial or parallel.

We use USB to connect printers, scanners, and a host of other input devices like keyboards, joysticks, and mice. When connecting USB peripherals, you've got to connect them either directly to one of the USB ports (as shown in Figure 3.10) on the PC or to a USB hub that is connected to one of those USB ports.

FIGURE 3.9   An RS-232 cable end

FIGURE 3.10   A USB port

Hubs can be chained together to provide multiple USB connections; but even though you can connect up to 127 devices, it's really not practical to go there. Each device has a USB plug, as shown in Figure 3.11.

FIGURE 3.11   A USB plug

Properties of Cables

The reason we use so many different types of cables in a network is that each type has its own set of properties that specifically make it the best to use for a particular area or purpose. Different types vary in transmission speeds, distance, duplex, noise immunity, and frequency, and I'll cover each of these next.

Transmission Speeds

Based on the type of cable or fiber you choose and the network that it's installed in, network administrators can control the speed of a network to meet the network's traffic demands. Admins usually permit, or would like to have, transmission speeds of up to 10Gbps or higher on the core areas of their networks that connect various network segments. In the distribution and access areas, where users connect to switches, it's typically 100Mbps per connection; but transmission speeds are creeping up because the traffic demand is getting higher.

Distance

A deciding factor used in choosing what cable type to use is often the topology of a network and the distance between its components. Some network technologies can run much further than others without communication errors, but all network communications technologies are prone to *attenuation*—the degradation of signal due to the medium itself and the distance signals have to travel. Some cable types suffer from attenuation more than in others. For instance, any network using twisted-pair cable should have a maximum segment length of only 328 feet (100 meters).

Duplex

All communications are either half-duplex or full-duplex. The difference is whether the communicating devices can "talk" and "listen" at the same time.

During half-duplex communication, a device can either send communication or receive communication, but not both at the same time. Think walkie-talkie—when you press the button on the walkie-talkie, it turns the speaker off, and you can't hear anything the other side is saying.

In full-duplex communication, both devices can send and receive communication at the same time. This means that the effective throughput is doubled and communication is much more efficient. Full-duplex is typical in most of today's switched networks. I'll discuss both full and half duplex in more detail in Chapter 4, "The Current Ethernet Specifications."

Noise Immunity (Security, EMI)

Any time electrons are pushed through two wires next to each other, it creates a magnetic current. And we can create a current in the wires. This is good because without *magnetic flux*, we wouldn't be using computers—the power that surges through them is a result of it. The bad news is that it also creates two communications issues.

First, because the wire is creating a current based on the 1s and 0s coursing through it, with the right tools in hand, people can read the message in the wire without cutting it or even removing the insulation. You've heard of this—it's called *tapping* the wire, and it's clearly a valid security concern. In ancient history, high-security installations like the Pentagon actually encased communication wires in lead shielding to prevent them from being tapped. STP wires make tapping a little harder, but not hard enough.

The best way to solve the magnetic-flux problem caused by electricity is to not use these wires at all. As I said, fiber-optic cables carry the signal as light on a glass or really pure plastic strand, and light is not susceptible to magnetic flux, making fiber optics a whole lot harder to tap. It's still not impossible—you can do it at the equipment level, but you have to actually cut and then repair the cable to do that, which isn't likely to go unnoticed.

The second magnetic-flux issue comes from the outside in instead of from the inside out. Because wires can take on additional current if they're near any source of magnetism, you've got to be really careful where you run your cables. You can avoid EMI by keeping copper cables away from all powerful magnetic sources like electric motors, speakers, amplifiers, fluorescent light ballasts, and so on. Just keep them away from anything that can generate a magnetic field!

Frequency

Each cable type has a specified maximum frequency that gives you the transmission bandwidth it can handle. Cat 5e cable is tested to 100MHz maximum frequency and can run 1Gbps signals for relatively short distances. That's maxing it out, but it's still good for connecting desktop hosts at high speeds. On the other hand, Cat 6 is a 250MHz cable that can handle 1Gbps data flow all day long with ease. Cat 6 has a lot more twists and thicker cables, so it is best used when connecting floors of a building.

Although signal is measured as bandwidth, the capacity to carry the signal in a cable is measured as frequency.

Wiring Standards

Ethernet cabling is an important thing to understand, especially if you're planning to work on any type of LAN network. There are different types of wiring standards available:

- Straight-through cable (568A)
- Crossover cable (568B)
- Rolled cable (rollover)
- Hardware loopback

We will look into each one of these, and then I'll end this section with some examples for you.

568A vs. 568B

If you look inside a network cable, you will find four pairs of wires twisted together to prevent crosstalk; they're also twisted like this to help prevent EMI and tapping. The same pins have to be used on the same colors throughout a network to receive and transmit; but how do you decide which color wire goes with which pin? The good news is that you don't have to decide—at least not completely. Two wiring standards have surfaced that have been agreed on by over 60 vendors including AT&T, 3Com, and Cisco (although there isn't 100 percent agreement). In other words, over the years, some network jacks have been pinned with the 568A standard and some have used the 568B standard, which can cause a bit of confusion if you don't know what you're looking at in your network.

If you're thinking, "What's the difference, and why does it matter?" the answer is the position of four wires on one side of the cable—that's it! There are eight wires in each UTP cable; pins 4, 5, 7, and 8 aren't used in either standard.

If you're installing new cabling to each cubicle and/or office, you need to make sure to connect all eight pins—and use Cat 5e or Cat 6. Voice over IP (VoIP) uses all eight pins, and it's really common to have voice and data on the same wire at the same time in today's networks.

This only leaves the wire pairs to connect to pins 1, 2, 3, and 6. If we connect the green-white, green, orange-white, and orange wires to pins 1, 2, 3, and 6, respectively, on both sides of the cable, we're using the 568A standard and creating the kind of straight-through cable that's regularly implemented as a regular *patch cable* for most networks. On the other hand, if we switch from pin 1 to pin 3 and from pin 2 to pin 6 on one side only, we've created a *crossover cable* for most networks.

Straight-Through Cable

The straight-through cable is used to connect a host to a switch or hub, or a router to a switch or hub.

No worries—I'll tell you all about devices like switches, hubs, and routers in detail in Chapter 5, "Networking Devices."

Four wires are used in straight-through cable to connect Ethernet devices. It's really pretty simple to do this; Figure 3.12 depicts the four wires used in a straight-through Ethernet cable.

Notice that only pins 1, 2, 3, and 6 are used. Connect 1 to 1, 2 to 2, 3 to 3, and 6 to 6, and you'll be up and networking in no time. Just remember that this would be a 10/100 Ethernet-only cable, and it wouldn't work with 1000Mbps Ethernet, voice, Token Ring, ISDN, and so on.

FIGURE 3.12   Straight-through Ethernet cable

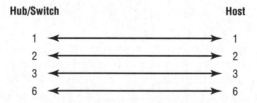

Crossover Cable

The same four wires are used in this cable; and just as with the straight-through cable, you just connect the different pins together. Crossover cables can be used to connect these devices:

- Switch to switch
- Hub to hub
- Host to host

- Hub to switch
- Router direct to host

Check out Figure 3.13, which demonstrates how each of the four wires are used in a crossover Ethernet cable.

FIGURE 3.13   Crossover Ethernet cable

Okay—did you notice that instead of connecting 1 to 1, 2 to 2, and so on, we connected pins 1 to 3, and 2 to 6, on each side of the cable? A crossover cable is typically used to connect two switches together, but it can also be used to test communications between two workstations directly, bypassing the switch.

A crossover cable is used only in Ethernet UTP installations. You can connect two workstation NICs or a workstation and a server NIC directly with it.

You're going to find out a lot more about how important it is to label basically everything. But for now, make sure to label a crossover cable as what it is so that no one tries to use it as a workstation patch cable. If they do that, the workstation won't be able to communicate with the hub and the rest of the network!

It's really cool that you can carry a crossover cable with you in your tool bag along with your laptop—then, if you want to ensure that a server's NIC is functioning correctly, you can just connect your laptop directly to the server's NIC using your handy crossover cable. You should be able to log in to the server if both NICs are configured correctly.

Use a cable tester to make sure that what you're dealing with is in fact a crossover cable. The tester can also tell you if there's a problem with the cable. Figure 3.14 shows an inexpensive cable tester for UTP.

This cost-effective little tool will tell you beyond a shadow of a doubt if you have a straight-through or crossover cable—or even if there's a problem with the cable.

Rollover Cable

Although rollover cable isn't used for hooking Ethernet connections together, you can use it to connect a host to a router console serial communication (com) port.

And if you have a router or switch, you use this cable to connect your PC running Hyper-Terminal or some other terminal-emulation program to the hardware. Eight wires are used in this cable to connect serial devices, although not all eight are used to send information (just as in Ethernet networking). Figure 3.15 shows the eight wires used in a rolled cable.

FIGURE 3.14 An inexpensive cable tester

FIGURE 3.15 Rolled Ethernet cable

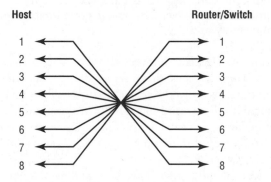

These are probably the easiest cables to make because you just cut the end off on one side of a straight-through cable, turn it over, and put the connector back on—using a new connector, of course.

Hardware Loopback

In any talk about wiring, loopback isn't so much a wiring standard as it is a way to redirect data flow. Sometimes you may need a computer to think it has a live connection to a network when it doesn't, because it's a good testing strategy and because you need a live network to install. In these cases, you will need to trick the PC into seeing its own output as input; and you do this with a loopback plug. It works a lot like a crossover cable except that it connects the transmit pins directly to the receive pins, as shown in Figure 3.16. It's used by the NIC's software diagnostics to test transmission and reception capabilities, and you just can't completely test an NIC without one of these cool devices.

FIGURE 3.16   A hardware loopback and its connections

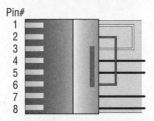

Pin#

In a loopback, pins 1 & 3 and
pins 2 & 6 are connected

Usually, the hardware loopback is no bigger than a single RJ-45 connector with a few small wires on the back. If a NIC has hardware diagnostics that can use the loopback, the hardware loopback plug will be included with the NIC. To use it, simply plug the loopback into the RJ-45 connector on the back of the NIC, and start the diagnostic software. Select the option in your NIC's diagnostic software that requires the loopback, and start your diagnostic routine. These diagnostics will tell you if the NIC can send and receive data.

Test Your Cable Understanding

You've taken a look at the various RJ-45 UTP cables. With that in mind, what cable is used between the switches in the following?

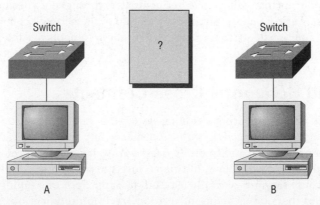

In order for host A to ping host B, you need a crossover cable to connect the two switches together. But what types of cables are used in the network shown in the following?

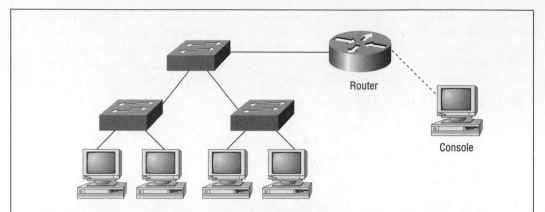

In the second example, there are a variety of cables in use. For the connection between the switches, we'd clearly use a crossover cable like the one you saw in the earlier example. The trouble is, here we have a console connection that uses a rolled cable. Plus, the connection from the router to the switch is a straight-through cable, which is also what's running between the hosts to the switches.

Installing Wiring Distributions

By now, you're probably getting the idea that there are a lot more components in the average computer networks than meets the eye, right? If this isn't exactly a news bulletin to you, then you either already are, or have been, involved in the initial installation of the network. If the latter describes you, you probably will be, or already are, involved in the purchase and installation of the components that will connect the computers throughout your organization's building. And it may also be up to you to verify that all of the network components have been installed properly and tested. So, let's go over each of these components and the process of verifying their proper installation.

Vertical and Horizontal Cross-Connects

A *cross-connect* is a location within a cabling system that facilitates the termination of cable elements, plus the reconnection of those elements with jumpers, termination blocks, and/or cables to a patch panel and so on. In other words, it's where all the wires come together. Cables that run from communications closets to wall outlets are known as *horizontal cables*, because they are generally used on the same floor of a building.

Backbone cables that connect equipment rooms, telecommunications rooms, and other physical termination points are referred to as *vertical cables*, because they often go from floor to floor in a building. All of these cables will eventually connect to each other and finish off the network cabling for the building. The exact pieces involved depend on the size of the installation, the needs of the organization, and the structure in which they're installed.

The maximum length of a Cat-3 horizontal cross-connect (meaning from wall outlet to closet) is 100 meters (328 feet).

Patch Panels

A *patch panel* is usually a rack or wall-mounted structure that houses cable connections. A patch cable generally plugs into the front side, while the back holds the punched-down connection of a longer, more permanent cable. The purpose of the patch panel is to give the administrator a non-grief-ridden way to change the path of a signal quickly when needed. Figure 3.17 depicts a modern patch panel.

FIGURE 3.17   A patch panel

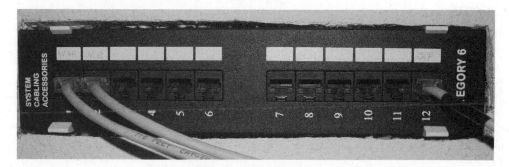

These come in really handy if a cable inside a wall becomes damaged or fails because a network administrator can "patch around" the dead cable by simply changing the connection on two patch panels.

66 Block

In the past, one of the most common types of patch panels was known as a *66 block*. Even though these are now considered legacy equipment, they're still listed as an objective on the exam. Figure 3.18 shows a 66 block.

We don't use them much anymore because they're very large in comparison to newer wire-terminating devices, and they have a relatively small (25-pair) capacity. The final nail in their coffin is that they are unsuited for any network communications faster than 10Mbps. But once in a while, you still see these used in some telephone installations.

FIGURE 3.18   A 66 block

MDF/IDF

The *main distribution frame (MDF)* is a wiring point that's generally used as a reference point for telephone lines. It's installed in the building as part of the pre-wiring, and the internal lines are connected to it. After that, all that's left is to connect the external (telephone company) lines to the other side to complete the circuit. Often, another wire frame called an *intermediate distribution frame (IDF)* is located in an equipment or telecommunications room. It is connected to the MDF and is used to provide greater flexibility for the distribution of all the communications lines to the building. It is typically (and better be) a sturdy metal rack designed to hold the bulk of cables coming from all over the building!

25 Pair

A *25-pair cable* consists of 25 individual pairs of wires all inside one common insulating jacket. It's not generally used for data cabling, just for telephone cabling, and especially for backbone and cross-connect cables because it reduces the cable clutter significantly. This type of cable is often referred to as a *feeder cable* because it supplies signal to many connected pairs. In the picture of the 66 block, Figure 3.18, a 25-pair wire is connected to the 66 block to provide connectivity to the IDF.

100 Pair

100-pair feeder cables can be used for really huge telephone company installations. They combine 100 pairs of wires into one large, insulated cable. These large cables are also used in aerial installations and sometimes in buried and duct-type installations that run up and down a building. To keep the pairs unique, you've got to use colors other than the traditional networking ones.

110 Block

A newer type of wiring distribution point called a *110 block* has replaced most telephone wire installations and is also used for computer networking. On one side, wires are punched down; the other side has RJ-11 (for phone) or RJ-45 (for network) connections.

110 blocks come in sizes from 25 to more than 500 wire pairs, and some are capable of carrying 1Gpbs connections when used with Category 6 cables. The hitch is that using Cat 6 with the 110 block is really difficult because of the size of the Cat 6 wiring.

Demarc/Demarc Extension

The *demarc* (short for demarcation) is the last point of responsibility of the service provider. It's often at the MDF in your building connection (if your building is large), but it's usually just an RJ-45 jack that your channel service unit/data service unit (CSU/DSU) connects into from your router to wide area network (WAN) connections (CSU/DSU's are explained in detail in Chapter 5).

When troubleshooting, network admins often test for connectivity on both sides of the demarc to determine if the problem is internal or external. The length of copper or fiber that begins after the demarc but still doesn't reach all the way up to your office is referred to as a *demarc extension*.

Smart Jack

A *smart jack*, also called a network interface device (NID) or network interface unit, is owned by the PSTN and is a special network interface that's often used between the service provider's network and the internal network. You can't physically test to an actual demarc because it is just an RJ-45 jack, but the service provider may install a NID that has power and can be looped for testing purposes.

The smart-jack device may also provide for code and protocol conversion, making the signal from the service provider usable by the devices on the internal network like the CSU/DSU.

 Real World Scenario

Above and Beyond the Network+!

If you have a Cisco router that is having a problem—such as a serial WAN connection issue—and you're using a serial port on your router to connect to a port on a CSU/DSU, type this at the enabled Cisco router console or telnet port:

```
config t
int s0/0
loopback
```

At this point, your interface will come up and look like it is working. That is, of course, if your connection from the router to the CSU/DSU is working properly. If not, you have a local problem.

Verifying Correct Wiring Installation

Because most of us aren't insecure enough to constantly go around thinking that we've made a whole bunch of mistakes, it's common for installers to assume that they haven't made any at all. Yes, they may test a cable or two for good measure, but they really do leave most cables totally untested and worse—they either keep incomplete, sketchy records or no records at all. A truly professional installer will verify each cable's connectivity and keep detailed records of when it was tested and when it passed the connectivity test.

Oh… and let me count the ways things can go wrong when pulling a network cable. Copper cables can be placed a little too close to a magnetic source and can be affected by EMI. Cable jackets can be ripped off completely when pulling the cable through a tight space or around a corner. Cables can be cut wrong and extended beyond the maximum length for their type. Fiber-optic cables are really fragile and can be easily and expensively damaged if they're handled roughly or poorly installed.

The best cable-installer companies assume that some of these things will go wrong, and therefore they will test, test, and test again. So if you're handling your own installation, you should do the same things. Consider yourself your own customer—you want to keep yourself happy, don't you? Seriously, the old carpenter's rule of "measure twice, cut once" applies to cable installations as well, both literally and figuratively.

The moral of this story is that you should test frequently during installation and again when you're done. And definitely make sure you keep complete and detailed records to refer to, just in case something nasty happens later.

Verifying Proper Wiring Termination

By the way, the number of things that can go wrong when terminating copper wires totally dwarfs the number that can happen when pulling cables. With a minimal amount of training and a little patience, almost anyone can pull a network cable without damaging it—at least, most of the time. Proper termination of copper cables to a punch-down block is much trickier and requires practice to get right, so save yourself that pain by always inspecting the installation and verifying that all wires are terminated properly in the right order.

Fiber-optic termination requires extra-special (read, expensive) equipment and training. Unless your installers spend hours cutting, stripping, polishing, and terminating the fiber-optic cable and look for any mistakes or damage as thoroughly as a CSI looks for clues at a crime scene, they probably won't get it done right the first time. You should always test a new connection with the appropriate tool. We will discuss the tools used to test connections in Chapter 18, "Software and Hardware Tools."

The tools to test the installation and termination of both UTP and fiber are covered in Chapter 18.

Summary

I know getting through this chapter probably wasn't the most fun you've had recently. But understanding all those types of wires and cabling, along with their unique capacities, their associated standards, and the right connectors to use with them plus where to place them is integral to having a solid, foundational understanding of the things that make a great network run quickly and reliably.

It's critical for you to grasp the basics of networking. Having the facts about how a good network is designed and implemented and what goes into that process will make you an effective and efficient technician—and maybe, some day, a highly paid system administrator.

Exam Essentials

Understand the various types of cables used in today's networks.   Coaxial (other than for cable modems) is rarely used, but twisted-pair and fiber optics are very common in today's networks.

Understand the various types of ends that are used on each type of cable.   Coax uses BNC; twisted-pair uses RJ-11 for voice and RJ-45 for data; and fiber uses various ends, depending on its use.

Understand what a 568A cable is.   A 568A cable is also known as an Ethernet straight-through cable and is used to connect hosts to switches, for example.

Understand what a 568B cable is.   A 568B cable is also known as an Ethernet cross-over cable and is used to connect switches to switches, for example.

Written Lab

1.   Which UTP wiring uses four twisted wire pairs (eight wires) and is rated for 250MHz?

2.   The point at which the operational control or ownership changes from your company to a service provider is referred to as_____.

3.   Which type of cable will you use to connect switches?

4.   Which RG rating of coax is used for cable modems?

5.   Which UTP uses four twisted wire pairs (eight wires), is rated for 100MHz, and is capable of handling the disturbance on each pair caused by transmitting on all four pairs at the same time?

6.   You want to connect a host to a switch port. What type of Ethernet cable will you use?

7.   What type of hardware do you need to make a computer think it has a live connection to a network even when it doesn't?

8.   568A uses which pins to make a connection?

9.   568B uses which pins to make a connection?

10. What are two advantages of fiber-optic cabling?

   (The answers to the Written Lab can be found following the answers to the Review Questions for this chapter.)

Review Questions

1. Why would a network administrator use plenum-rated cable during an installation? (Choose 2)

   A. Low combustion temperature

   B. High combustion temperature

   C. Reduces toxic gas released during a fire

   D. Is not susceptible to any interference

2. Which of the following Ethernet unshielded twisted-pair (UTP) cables types is most commonly used?

   A. 10Base-T

   B. 100Base-TX

   C. 1000Base-TX

   D. All of the above

3. UTP cable is rated in the following categories except:

   A. Category 2

   B. Category 3

   C. Category 5e

   D. Category 8

4. What type of connector does UTP cable typically use?

   A. BNC

   B. ST

   C. RJ-45

   D. SC

5. Which of the following provides the longest cable run distance?

   A. Single-mode fiber

   B. multi-mode fiber

   C. category 3 UTP

   D. Coax

6. You need to crimp on a connector using an RJ-45 connector. Which pin-out configuration would you use to connect a host into a switch?

   A. UTP

   B. 568A

   C. 568B

   D. Rolled

7.   Fiber-optic cable is immune to electromagnetic interference (EMI) and radio frequency interference (RFI) because it:

   A.   Transmits analog signals using electricity

   B.   Transmits analog signals using light impulses

   C.   Transmits digital signals using light impulses

   D.   Transmits digital signals using electricity

8.   What type of cable transmits lights from end-to-end?

   A.   Coax

   B.   Fiber-optic

   C.   UTP

   D.   Category 2

9.   What is the main difference between single-mode fiber (SMF) and multimode fiber (MMF)?

   A.   Electrical signals

   B.   Number of light rays

   C.   Number of digital signals

   D.   Signal mode can be run a shorter distance

10.   What type of cable should be used if you need to make a cable run longer than 100 meters?

   A.   Category 5e

   B.   Category 6

   C.   Fiber-optic

   D.   Wireless link

11.   Which of the following are fiber-optic connectors? (Select three.)

   A.   BNC

   B.   ST

   C.   RJ-11

   D.   SC

   E.   LC

   F.   RJ-45

12.   You need to connect two devices on a vertical connect and they need to send voice traffic. Which of the following cable will you use?

   A.   Cat-3

   B.   Cat -5

   C.   Crossover

   D.   Rolled

13. How many hosts on a half-duplex segment can talk at one time?

    A. 0

    B. 1

    C. 2

    D. Unlimited

14. Which type of cable does EMI have the least effect on?

    A. Coax

    B. Fiber-optic

    C. UTP

    D. STP

15. How many devices can be connected to a full-duplex segment?

    A. 0

    B. 1

    C. 2

    D. 4

16. How many wires are used in UTP during transmission?

    A. 2

    B. 4

    C. 6

    D. 8

17. A cross-over cable is used to connect all of the following except:

    A. Switch to switch

    B. Host to host

    C. Hub to switch

    D. Host to switch

18. Which type of cable should be used to connect to the console port on a router?

    A. Console cable

    B. Cross-over cable

    C. Straight-through cable

    D. USB

19. The purpose of the demarcation point is to separate the customer from whom?

  A. The branch office

  B. Headquarters

  C. The data center

  D. The service provider

20. You need to make a 568B cable. How many pairs will you use?

  A. 1

  B. 2

  C. 3

  D. 4

Answers to Review Questions

1. **B, C.** Plenum-rated cable means that the coating doesn't begin burning until a much higher temperature of heat; doesn't release as many toxic fumes as PVC when it does burn; and is rated for use in air plenums that carry breathable air, usually as non-enclosed fresh-air return pathways that share space with cabling.

2. **D.** UTP is commonly used in twisted-pair Ethernet like 10Base-T, 100Base-TX, 1000Base-TX, and so on.

3. **D.** Unshielded twisted-pair has standards from Category 2–6 for use on Ethernet networks. There is no Category 8 defined.

4. **C.** UTP usually connects with RJ-45. You use a crimper to attach an RJ connector to a cable.

5. **A.** Single mode fiber allows for the maximum cable run distances.

6. **B.** You would use a straight-through cable to connect a host to a switch, and that pin-out is called 568A.

7. **C.** Fiber-optic cable transmits digital signals using light impulses rather than electricity; therefore it is immune to EMI and RFI.

8. **B.** Remember that fiber-optic cable transmits a digital signal using light impulses. Light is carried on either a glass or a plastic core.

9. **B.** The difference between single-mode fibers and multimode fibers is in the number of light rays (and thus the number of signals) they can carry. Generally speaking, multimode fiber is used for shorter-distance applications and single-mode fiber for longer distances.

10. **C.** Standards limit UTP to a mere 100 meters. Different fiber-optic types have different maximum lengths, but fiber-optic is the only cable type that can extend well beyond 100 meters.

11. **B, D, E.** There are many different types of fiber-optic connectors. SC, ST, LC, and MT-RJ are some of the more typical connectors in use today.

12. **B.** To connect two devices for voice on a vertical connect, the minimum cable you can use is category 5.

13. **B.** In half-duplex communication, a device can either send communication or receive communication, but it cannot do both at the same time.

14. **B.** Fiber-optic cable only transmits light (not electricity like UTP), so EMI has zero effect on it.

15. **C.** Full-duplex communication requires a point-to-point configuration because the collision-avoidance circuit is disabled.

16. **B.** Both wiring standards for UTP (568A and 568B) utilize only pins 1, 2, 3, and 6.

17. D. All devices that are pinned the same for transmit and receive require a cross-over cable to communicate directly.

18. A. A rolled cable or console cable would be used to connect a host to a router console serial communication (com) port.

19. D. The demarcation point or demarc is the point at which the operational control or ownership changes from your company to a service provider. This is often at the MDF in relation to telephone connections and the CSU/DSU in regard to WAN connections.

20. B. A 568B is a crossover cable and this cable uses two pairs of wires.

Answers to Written Lab

1. Category 6

2. Demarcation point or demarc

3. Crossover or 568B

4. RG-6

5. Category 5e

6. Straight-through or 568A

7. A hardware loopback

8. 1, 2, 3, and 6

9. 1 to 3 and 2 to 6

10. It is completely immune to EMI and RFI and can transmit up to 40 kilometers (about 25 miles).

Chapter
4

The Current Ethernet Specifications

THE FOLLOWING COMPTIA NETWORK+ EXAM OBJECTIVES ARE COVERED IN THIS CHAPTER:

✓ **2.6 Categorize LAN technology types and properties**

- Types:
  - Ethernet
  - 10BaseT
  - 100BaseTX
  - 100BaseFX
  - 1000BaseT
  - 1000BaseX
  - 10GBaseSR
  - 10GBaseLR
  - 10GBaseER
  - 10GBaseSW
  - 10GBaseLW
  - 10GBaseEW
  - 10GBaseT
- Properties
  - CSMA/CD
  - Broadcast
  - Collision
  - Bonding
  - Speed
  - Distance

Before we move on and explore networking devices, the TCP/IP and DoD models, IP addressing, subnetting, and routing in the upcoming chapters, you've got to understand the big picture of LANs and learn the answer to the key questions: "How is Ethernet used in today's networks, and what are Media Access Control (MAC) addresses and how are they used?"

This chapter will answer those questions and more. I'll not only discuss the basics of Ethernet and the way MAC addresses are used on an Ethernet LAN, but I'll also cover the protocols used with Ethernet at the Data Link layer as well. You'll also learn about the various Ethernet specifications.

So now, let's get started with the fundamentals of connecting two hosts together.

For up-to-the-minute updates for this chapter, please see www.lammle.com or www.sybex.com/go/comptianetwork+studyguide.

Network Basics

Networks and networking have grown exponentially over the last 20 years—understandably so. They've had to evolve at light speed just to keep up with huge increases in basic mission-critical user needs ranging from sharing data and printers to more advanced demands like videoconferencing. Unless everyone who needs to share network resources is located in the same office area (an increasingly uncommon situation), the challenge is to connect the sometimes large number of relevant networks together so all users can share the networks' wealth.

As I started to discuss in Chapter 1, "Introduction to Networks," let's take a look at how communication happens on a basic local area network (LAN). Starting with Figure 4.1, you get a picture of a basic LAN network that's connected together using an Ethernet connection to a hub. This network is actually one collision domain and one broadcast domain, but don't stress if you have no idea what this means—I'm going to talk about both collision and broadcast domains in depth in Chapter 5, "Networking Devices."

Okay, about Figure 1.1... How would you say the PC named Bob communicates with the PC named Sally? Well, they're both on the same LAN connected with a multiport repeater (a hub). So does Bob just send out a data message, "Hey Sally, you there?" or does Bob use Sally's IP address and put things more like, "Hey 192.168.0.3, are you there?" I hope you picked the IP address option, but even if you did, the news is still bad—both answers are wrong! Why?

Because Bob is actually going to use Sally's MAC address (known as a *hardware address*), which is burned right into the network card of Sally's PC, to get hold of her.

FIGURE 4.1   The basic network

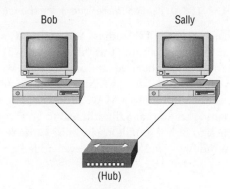

This is all good, but how does Bob get Sally's MAC address when Bob knows only Sally's name and doesn't even have her IP address? Bob is going to start by using name resolution (hostname to IP address resolution), something that's usually accomplished using Domain Name Service (DNS). And note that if these two hosts are on the same LAN, Bob can just broadcast to Sally asking her for the information (no DNS needed)—welcome to Microsoft Windows, Vista included!

Here's the output from a network analyzer depicting a simple name-resolution process from Bob to Sally:

```
Time        Source      Destination   Protocol   Info
53.892794   192.168.0.2  192.168.0.255  NBNS   Name query NB SALLY<00>
```

As I already mentioned, because the two hosts are on a local LAN, Windows (Bob) will broadcast to resolve the name Sally (the destination 192.168.0.255 is a broadcast address). Let's take a look at the rest of the information:

```
EthernetII,Src:192.168.0.2(00:14:22:be:18:3b),Dst:Broadcast(ff:ff:ff:ff:ff:ff)
```

This output shows that Bob knows his own MAC address and source IP address but not Sally's IP address or MAC address; so, Bob sends a broadcast address of all *f*s for the MAC address (a Data Link layer broadcast) and an IP LAN broadcast of 192.168.0.255. Again, no worries—you're going to learn all about broadcasts in Chapter 6, "Introduction to Internet Protocol (IP)."

Before the name is resolved, the first thing Bob has to do is broadcast on the LAN to get Sally's MAC address so he can communicate to her PC and resolve her name to an IP address:

```
Time       Source       Destination Protocol Info
5.153054   192.168.0.2  Broadcast   ARP Who has 192.168.0.3? Tell 192.168.0.2
```

Next, check out Sally's response:

```
Time       Source      Destination   Protocol  Info
5.153403 192.168.0.3 192.168.0.2  ARP  192.168.0.3 is at 00:0b:db:99:d3:5e
5.53.89317  192.168.0.3 192.168.0.2 NBNS Name query response NB 192.168.0.3
```

Okay, sweet—Bob now has both Sally's IP address and her MAC address. These are both listed as the source address at this point because this information was sent from Sally back to Bob. So, *finally*, Bob has all the goods he needs to communicate with Sally. And just so you know, I'm going to tell you all about Address Resolution Protocol (ARP) and show you exactly how Sally's IP address was resolved to a MAC address a little later in Chapter 6.

By the way, I want you to understand that Sally still had to go through the same resolution processes to communicate back to Bob—sounds crazy, huh? Consider this a welcome to IPv4 and basic networking with Windows—and we haven't even added a router yet.

Ethernet Basics

Ethernet is a contention media-access method that allows all hosts on a network to share the same bandwidth of a link. Ethernet is popular because it's readily scalable, meaning that it's comparatively easy to integrate new technologies, such as Fast Ethernet and Gigabit Ethernet, into an existing network infrastructure. It's also relatively simple to implement in the first place, and with it, troubleshooting is reasonably straightforward. Ethernet uses both Data Link and Physical layer specifications, and this section of the chapter will give you both the Data Link layer and Physical layer information you need to effectively implement, troubleshoot, and maintain an Ethernet network.

Collision Domain

The term *collision domain* is an Ethernet term that refers to a particular network scenario wherein one device sends a packet out on a network segment, thereby forcing every other device on that same physical network segment to pay attention to it. This is bad because if two devices on one physical segment transmit at the same time, a *collision event*—a situation where each device's digital signals interfere with another on the wire—occurs and forces the devices to retransmit later. Collisions have a dramatically negative effect on network performance, so they're definitely something we want to avoid!

The situation I just described is typically found in a hub environment where each host segment connects to a hub that represents only one collision domain and one broadcast domain. This begs the question, "What's a broadcast domain?"

Broadcast Domain

Here's that answer... A *broadcast domain* refers to the set of all devices on a network segment that hear all the broadcasts sent on that segment.

Even though a broadcast domain is typically a boundary delimited by physical media like switches and repeaters, it can also reference a logical division of a network segment where all hosts can reach each other via a Data Link layer (hardware address) broadcast.

That's the basic story, but rest assured that I'll be delving deeper into the skinny on collision and broadcast domains a bit later in Chapter 5.

CSMA/CD

Ethernet networking uses *Carrier Sense Multiple Access with Collision Detection (CSMA/CD)*, a protocol that helps devices share the bandwidth evenly without having two devices transmit at the same time on the network medium. CSMA/CD was created to overcome the problem of those collisions that occur when packets are transmitted simultaneously from different hosts. And trust me—good collision management is crucial, because when a host transmits in a CSMA/CD network, all the other hosts on the network receive and examine that transmission. Only bridges and routers can effectively prevent a transmission from propagating throughout the entire network.

So, how does the CSMA/CD protocol work? Let's start by taking a look at Figure 4.2.

FIGURE 4.2   CSMA/CD

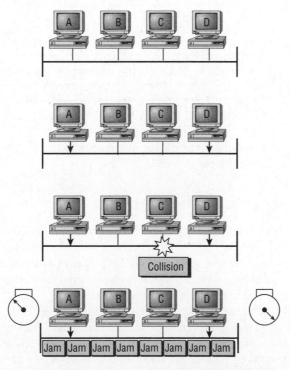

Carrier Sense Multiple Access with Collision Detection (CSMA/CD)

When a host wants to transmit over the network, it first checks for the presence of a digital signal on the wire. If all is clear, meaning that no other host is transmitting, the host will then proceed with its transmission. But it doesn't stop there. The transmitting host constantly monitors the wire to make sure no other hosts begin transmitting. If the host detects another signal on the wire, it sends out an extended jam signal that causes all hosts on the segment to stop sending data (think busy signal). The hosts respond to that jam signal by waiting a while before attempting to transmit again. Backoff algorithms determine when the colliding stations can retransmit. If collisions keep occurring after 15 tries, the hosts attempting to transmit will then time out. Pretty clean!

When a collision occurs on an Ethernet LAN, the following happens:

- A jam signal informs all devices that a collision occurred.

- The collision invokes a random backoff algorithm.

- Each device on the Ethernet segment stops transmitting for a short time until the timers expire.

- All hosts have equal priority to transmit after the timers have expired.

And following are the effects of having a CSMA/CD network sustaining heavy collisions:

- Delay

- Low throughput

- Congestion

Backoff on an 802.3 network is the retransmission delay that's enforced when a collision occurs. When a collision occurs, a host will resume transmission after the forced time delay has expired. After this backoff delay period has expired, all stations have equal priority to transmit data.

In the following sections, I'm going to cover Ethernet in detail at both the Data Link layer (Layer 2) and the Physical layer (Layer 1).

Half- and Full-Duplex Ethernet

Just so you know, half-duplex Ethernet is defined in the original 802.3 Ethernet specification. Basically, when you run half duplex, you're using only one wire pair with a digital signal either transmitting or receiving. This really isn't all that different from full duplex because you can both transmit and receive—you just don't get to do that at the same time running half duplex like you can if you're running full duplex.

Here's how it works: If a host hears a digital signal, it uses the CSMA/CD protocol to help prevent collisions and to permit retransmitting if a collision does occur. Half-duplex Ethernet—typically 10Base-T—is only about 30 to 40 percent efficient because a large 10Base-T network will usually provide only 3 to 4Mbps at most. Although it's true that 100Mbps Ethernet can and sometimes does run half duplex, it's just not very common to find that happening these days.

In contrast, full-duplex Ethernet uses two pairs of wires at the same time instead of one measly wire pair like half duplex employs. Plus, full duplex uses a point-to-point connection between the transmitter of the sending device and the receiver of the receiving device. This means that with full-duplex data transfer, you not only get faster data-transfer speeds, but you also get collision-prevention too—sweet!

You don't need to worry about collisions because now it's like a freeway with multiple lanes instead of the single-lane road provided by half duplex. Full-duplex Ethernet is supposed to offer 100 percent efficiency in both directions—for example, you can get 20Mbps with a 10Mbps Ethernet running full duplex or 200Mbps for Fast Ethernet. But this rate is something known as an *aggregate rate*, which translates as "you're supposed to get" 100 percent efficiency. No guarantees, in networking as in life.

Full-duplex Ethernet can be used in many situations; here are some examples:

- With a connection from a switch to a host
- With a connection from a switch to a switch
- With a connection from a host to a host using a crossover cable

 You can run full duplex with just about any device except a hub.

You may be wondering: If it's capable of all that speed, why wouldn't it deliver? Well, when a full-duplex Ethernet port is powered on, it first connects to the remote end and then negotiates with the other end of the Fast Ethernet link. This is called an *auto-detect mechanism*. This mechanism first decides on the exchange capability, which means it checks to see if it can run at 10, 100, or even 1000Mbps. It then checks to see if it can run full duplex; and if it can't, it will run half duplex instead.

Hosts usually auto-detect both the Mbps and the duplex type available (the default setting), but you can manually set both the speed and duplex type on the network interface card (NIC) card, as shown in the following graphic:

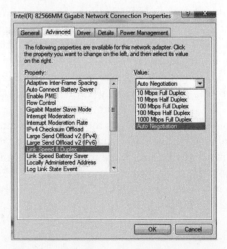

It is pretty rare these days to go into a NIC configuration on a host and change these settings, but this example shows that you can do that if you want.

 Remember that half-duplex Ethernet shares a collision domain and provides a lower effective throughput than full-duplex Ethernet, which typically has a private collision domain and a higher effective throughput.

Last, remember these important points:

- There are no collisions in full-duplex mode.
- A dedicated switch port is required for each full-duplex host.
- The host network card and the switch port must be capable of operating in full-duplex mode.

Now let's take a look at how Ethernet works at the Data Link layer.

Ethernet at the Data Link Layer

Ethernet at the Data Link layer is responsible for Ethernet addressing, commonly referred to as *hardware addressing* or *MAC addressing*. Ethernet is also responsible for framing packets received from the Network layer and preparing them for transmission on the local network through the Ethernet contention media-access method.

Ethernet MAC addresses are made up of hexadecimal addresses. So before I discuss MAC addresses, let's start by talking about binary, decimal, and hexadecimal addresses and how to convert one to another.

Binary to Decimal and Hexadecimal Conversion

Understanding the differences between binary, decimal, and hexadecimal numbers and how to convert one format into the other is very important before we move to discussing the TCP/IP protocol stack and IP addressing in Chapter 6 and Chapter 7, "IP Addressing."

So let's get started with binary numbering. It's pretty simple, really. Each digit used is limited to either a 1 (one) or a 0 (zero), and each digit is called 1 bit (short for *bi*nary digi*t*). Typically, you count either 4 or 8 bits together, with these being referred to as a *nibble* and a *byte*, respectively.

What's interesting about binary numbering is the value represented in a decimal format—the typical decimal format being the base-10 number scheme that we've all used since kindergarten. The binary numbers are placed in a value spot, starting at the right and moving left, with each spot having double the value of the previous spot.

Table 4.1 shows the decimal values of each bit location in a nibble and a byte. Remember, a nibble is 4 bits and a byte is 8 bits.

TABLE 4.1   Binary Values

Nibble Values	Byte Values
8 4 2 1	128 64 32 16 8 4 2 1

What all this means is that if a one digit (1) is placed in a value spot, then the nibble or byte takes on that decimal value and adds it to any other value spots that have a 1. And if a zero (0) is placed in a bit spot, you don't count that value.

Let me clarify things for you—if we have a 1 placed in each spot of our nibble, we then add up 8 + 4 + 2 + 1, to give us a maximum value of 15. Another example for our nibble values is 1010, which means that the 8 bit and the 2 bit are turned on and equal a decimal value of 10. If we have a nibble binary value of 0110, then our decimal value is 6, because the 4 and 2 bits are turned on.

But the byte values can add up to a value that's significantly higher than 15. This is how— if we count every bit as a one (1), then the byte binary value looks like this (remember, 8 bits equal a byte):

11111111

We then count up every bit spot because each is turned on. It looks like this, which demonstrates the maximum value of a byte:

128 + 64 + 32 + 16 + 8 + 4 + 2 + 1 = 255

A binary number can equal plenty of other decimal values. Let's work through a few examples:

10010110

Which bits are on? The 128, 16, 4, and 2 bits are on, so we'll just add them up: 128 + 16 + 4 + 2 = 150.

01101100

Which bits are on? The 64, 32, 8, and 4 bits are on, so we add them up: 64 + 32 + 8 + 4 = 108.

11101000

Which bits are on? The 128, 64, 32, and 8 bits are on, so we add the values: 128 + 64 + 32 + 8 = 232.

You should memorize Table 4.2 before braving the IP sections in Chapters 6 and 7.

TABLE 4.2   Binary-to-Decimal Memorization Chart

Binary Value	Decimal Value
10000000	128
11000000	192
11100000	224

TABLE 4.2   Binary-to-Decimal Memorization Chart *(continued)*

Binary Value	Decimal Value
11110000	240
11111000	248
11111100	252
11111110	254
11111111	255

Hexadecimal addressing is completely different than binary or decimal—it's converted by reading nibbles, not bytes. By using a nibble, we can convert these bits to hex pretty simply. First, understand that the hexadecimal addressing scheme uses only the numbers 0 through 9. And because the numbers 10, 11, 12, and so on can't be used (because they are two-digit numbers), the letters *A*, *B*, *C*, *D*, *E*, and *F* are used to represent 10, 11, 12, 13, 14, and 15, respectively.

Hex is short for *hexadecimal*, which is a numbering system that uses the first six letters of the alphabet (*A* through *F*) to extend beyond the available 10 digits in the decimal system. Hexadecimal has a total of 16 digits.

Table 4.3 shows both the binary value and the decimal value for each hexadecimal digit.

TABLE 4.3   Hex-to-Binary to Decimal Chart

Hexadecimal Value	Binary Value	Decimal Value
0	0000	0
1	0001	1
2	0010	2
3	0011	3
4	0100	4
5	0101	5
6	0110	6

TABLE 4.3 Hex-to-Binary to Decimal Chart *(continued)*

Hexadecimal Value	Binary Value	Decimal Value
7	0111	7
8	1000	8
9	1001	9
A	1010	10
B	1011	11
C	1100	12
D	1101	13
E	1110	14
F	1111	15

Did you notice that the first 10 hexadecimal digits (0–9) are the same values as the decimal values? If not, look again. This handy fact makes those values super easy to convert.

So suppose you have something like this: 0x6A. (Some manufacturers put *0x* in front of characters so you know that they're a hex value, while others just give you an "*h*". It doesn't have any other special meaning.) What are the binary and decimal values? To correctly answer that question, all you have to remember is that each hex character is one nibble and two hex characters together make a byte. To figure out the binary value, first put the hex characters into two nibbles and then put them together into a byte. 6 = 0110 and A (which is 10 in hex) = 1010, so the complete byte is 01101010.

To convert from binary to hex, just take the byte and break it into nibbles. Here's how you do that:

Say you have the binary number 01010101. First, break it into nibbles—0101 and 0101—with the value of each nibble being 5 because the 1 and 4 bits are on. This makes the hex answer 0x55. And in decimal format, the binary number is 01010101, which converts to 64 + 16 + 4 + 1 = 85.

Okay, now try another binary number:

11001100

Our answer is 1100 = 12 and 1100 = 12 (therefore, it's converted to CC in hex). The decimal conversion answer is 128 + 64 + 8 + 4 = 204.

One more example, and then we need to get working on the Physical layer. Suppose we're given the following binary number:

10110101

The hex answer is 0xB5, because 1011 converts to B and 0101 converts to 5 in hex value. The decimal equivalent is 128 + 32 + 16 + 4 + 1 = 181.

 See the Written Lab for more practice with binary/hex/decimal conversion.

Ethernet Addressing

Now that you've got binary to decimal to hexadecimal address conversion down, we can get into how Ethernet addressing works. It uses the *Media Access Control (MAC) address* burned into each and every Ethernet NIC. The MAC, or hardware, address is a 48-bit (6-byte) address written in a hexadecimal format.

Figure 4.3 shows the 48-bit MAC addresses and how the bits are divided.

FIGURE 4.3   Ethernet addressing using MAC addresses

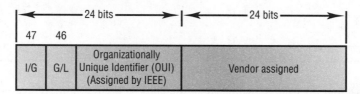

The *organizationally unique identifier (OUI)* is assigned by the Institute of Electrical and Electronics Engineers (IEEE) to an organization. It's composed of 24 bits, or 3 bytes. The organization, in turn, assigns a globally administered address (24 bits, or 3 bytes) that is unique (supposedly—no guarantees) to each and every adapter it manufactures. Look closely at the figure. The high-order bit is the Individual/Group (I/G) bit. When it has a value of 0, we can assume that the address is the MAC address of a device and may well appear in the source portion of the MAC header. When it is a 1, we can assume that the address represents either a broadcast or multicast address in Ethernet or a broadcast.

The next bit is the Global/Local bit (G/L, also known as U/L, where *U* means *universal*). When set to 0, this bit represents a globally administered address (as standardized by the IEEE). When the bit is a 1, it represents a locally governed and administered address. The low-order 24 bits of an Ethernet address represent a locally administered or manufacturer-assigned code. This portion commonly starts with 24 0s for the first card made and continues in order until there are 24 1s for the last (16,777,216th) card made. You'll find that many manufacturers use these same six hex digits as the last six characters of their serial number on the same card.

Ethernet Frames

The Data Link layer is responsible for combining bits into bytes and bytes into frames. Frames are used at the Data Link layer to encapsulate packets handed down from the Network layer for transmission on a type of physical media access.

The function of Ethernet stations is to pass data frames between each other using a group of bits known as a MAC frame format. This provides error detection from a cyclic redundancy check (CRC). But remember—this is error detection, not error correction. The 802.3 frames and Ethernet frame are shown in Figure 4.4.

Encapsulating a frame within a different type of frame is called *tunneling*.

FIGURE 4.4   802.3 and Ethernet frame formats

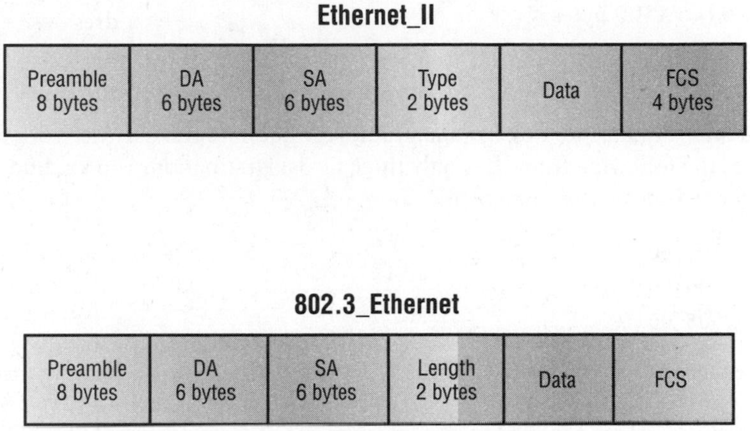

Ethernet_II

Preamble 8 bytes	DA 6 bytes	SA 6 bytes	Type 2 bytes	Data	FCS 4 bytes

802.3_Ethernet

Preamble 8 bytes	DA 6 bytes	SA 6 bytes	Length 2 bytes	Data	FCS

Following are the details of the different fields in the 802.3 and Ethernet frame types:

The following section regarding frame headings and the various types of Ethernet frames are beyond the CompTIA Network+ objectives. Throughout the rest of this book, I will show you screen shots from a network analyzer. It's always good to understand what you are looking at, so I put this section in to help you understand a frame structure.

Preamble   An alternating 1,0 pattern provides a 5MHz clock at the start of each packet, which allows the receiving devices to lock the incoming bit stream.

Start Frame Delimiter (SFD)/Synch   The preamble is seven octets, and the SFD is one octet (synch). The SFD is 10101011, where the last pair of 1s allows the receiver to come into the alternating 1,0 pattern somewhere in the middle and still sync up and detect the beginning of the data (this field is not shown in the figure).

Destination Address (DA)   This transmits a 48-bit value using the least significant bit (LSB) first. The DA is used by receiving stations to determine whether an incoming packet is addressed to a particular host. The DA can be an individual address or a broadcast or multicast MAC address. Remember that a broadcast is all 1s (or *F*s in hex) and is sent to all devices, but a multicast is sent only to a similar subset of hosts on a network.

Source Address (SA)   The SA is a 48-bit MAC address used to identify the transmitting device, and it uses the LSB first. Broadcast and multicast address formats are illegal within the SA field.

Length or Type   802.3 uses a Length field, but the Ethernet frame uses a Type field to identify the Network layer protocol. 802.3 by itself cannot identify the upper-layer routed protocol and must be used with a proprietary LAN—Internetwork Packet Exchange (IPX), for example.

Data   This is a packet sent down to the Data Link layer from the Network layer. The size can vary from 64 to 1500 bytes.

Frame Check Sequence (FCS)   FCS is a field at the end of the frame that's used to store the CRC.

Okay—let's take a minute to look at some frames caught on our trusty network analyzer. You can see that the following frame has only three fields: Destination, Source, and Type (shown as Protocol Type on this analyzer):

```
Destination:    00:60:f5:00:1f:27
Source:         00:60:f5:00:1f:2c
Protocol Type: 08-00 IP
```

This is an Ethernet_II frame. Notice that the type field is IP, or 08-00 (mostly just referred to as 0x800) in hexadecimal.

The next frame has the same fields, so it must be an Ethernet_II frame too:

```
Destination:    ff:ff:ff:ff:ff:ff Ethernet Broadcast
Source:         02:07:01:22:de:a4
Protocol Type: 08-00 IP
```

Did you notice that this frame was a broadcast? You can tell because the destination hardware address is all 1s in binary, or all *F*s in hexadecimal.

Let's take a look at one more Ethernet_II frame. I'll talk about this next example again when we use IPv6 in Chapter 6, but you can see that the Ethernet frame is the same Ethernet_II frame we use with the IPv4 routed protocol. The difference is that the Type field has 0x86dd when we are carrying IPv6 data; and when we have IPv4 data, we use 0x0800 in the Protocol field:

```
Destination: IPv6-Neighbor-Discovery_00:01:00:03 (33:33:00:01:00:03)
Source: Aopen_3e:7f:dd (00:01:80:3e:7f:dd)
Type: IPv6 (0x86dd)
```

This is the beauty of the Ethernet_II frame. Because of the Protocol field, we can run any Network layer routed protocol and it will carry the data because it can identify that particular Network layer protocol.

Channel Bonding

Channel bonding (also known as *Ethernet bonding*) is a computer-networking arrangement where two or more network interfaces on a host are combined for redundancy and/or increased throughput. There are various names for this technology, but Link Aggregation is the most common. Cisco calls this EtherChannel. Figure 4.5 shows some examples of Ethernet channel bonding.

FIGURE 4.5   Ethernet channel bonding example

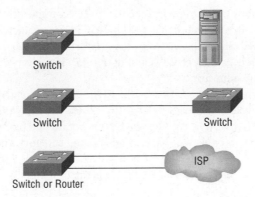

In Figure 4.5, you can see that bonding can be used to attach multiple connections to a server, between switches, and even for connections to the Internet, providing fault tolerance as well as improved throughput.

Ethernet at the Physical Layer

Ethernet was first implemented by a group called DIX (Digital, Intel, and Xerox). They created and implemented the first Ethernet LAN specification, which the IEEE used to create the IEEE 802.3 Committee. This was a 10Mbps network that ran on coax, then on twisted-pair, and finally on fiber physical media.

The IEEE extended the 802.3 Committee to two new committees known as 802.3u (Fast Ethernet) and 802.3ab (Gigabit Ethernet on Category 5+) and then finally 802.3ae (10Gbps over fiber and coax).

Figure 4.6 shows the IEEE 802.3 and original Ethernet Physical layer specifications.

When designing your LAN, it's really important to understand the different types of Ethernet media available to you. Sure, it would be great to run Gigabit Ethernet to each desktop and 10Gbps between switches (and to servers), and although this is just starting to happen, justifying the cost of that network today for most companies would be a pretty hard sell. But if instead, you mix and match the different types of Ethernet media methods currently available, you can come up with a cost-effective network solution that works great.

FIGURE 4.6   Ethernet Physical layer specifications

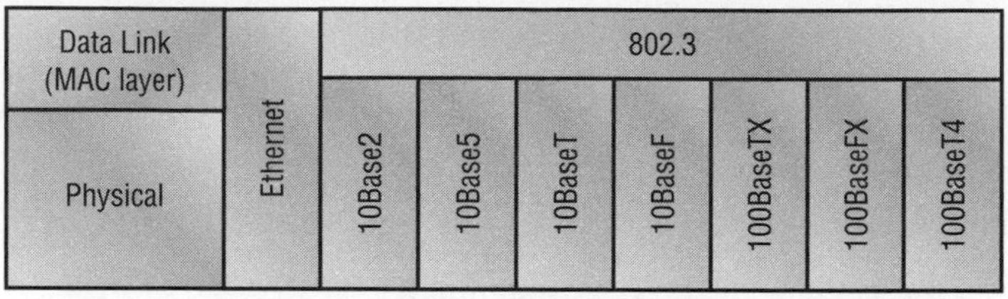

The Electronic Industries Association and the newer Telecommunications Industry Alliance (EIA/TIA) is the standards body that creates the Physical layer specifications for Ethernet. The EIA/TIA specifies that Ethernet use a *Registered Jack (RJ) connector* with a 4 5 wiring sequence on *unshielded twisted pair (UTP)* cabling (RJ-45). However, the industry is calling this just an 8-pin modular connector.

Each Ethernet cable type that is specified by the EIA/TIA has something known as *inherent attenuation*, which is defined as the loss of signal strength as it travels the length of a cable, and is measured in decibels (dB). The cabling used in corporate and home markets is measured in categories. A higher-quality cable will have a higher-rated category and lower attenuation. For example, Category 5 is better than Category 3 because Category 5 cables have more wire twists per foot and therefore less crosstalk. *Crosstalk* is the unwanted signal interference from adjacent pairs in the cable.

Here are the original IEEE 802.3 standards:

10Base-2   10Mbps baseband technology, up to 185 meters in length. Known as *Thinnet* and can support up to 30 workstations on a single segment. Uses a physical and logical bus with Attachment Unit Interface (AUI) connectors. The 10 means 10Mbps, *Base* means baseband technology—a signaling method for communication on the network—and the 2 means almost 200 meters. 10Base-2 Ethernet cards use BNC (British Naval Connector, Bayonet Neill-Concelman, or Bayonet Nut Connector) and T-connectors to connect to a network.

10Base-5   10Mbps baseband technology, up to 500 meters in length. Known as *Thicknet*. Uses a physical and logical bus with AUI connectors. Up to 2,500 meters with repeaters and 1,024 users for all segments.

10Base-T   10Mbps using Category 3 UTP wiring. Unlike on 10Base-2 and 10Base-5 networks, each device must connect into a hub or switch, and you can have only one host per segment or wire. Uses an RJ-45 connector (8-pin modular connector) with a physical star topology and a logical bus.

Each of the 802.3 standards defines an AUI, which allows a one-bit-at-a-time transfer to the Physical layer from the Data Link media-access method. This allows the MAC address to remain constant but means the Physical layer can support both existing and new technologies. The original AUI interface was a 15-pin connector, which allowed a transceiver (transmitter/receiver) that provided a 15-pin-to-twisted-pair conversion.

There's an issue, though—the AUI interface can't support 100Mbps Ethernet because of the high frequencies involved. So basically, 100Base-T needed a new interface, and the 802.3u specifications created one called the Media Independent Interface (MII) that provides 100Mbps throughput. The MII uses a *nibble*, which you of course remember is defined as 4 bits. Gigabit Ethernet uses a Gigabit Media Independent Interface (GMII) and transmits 8 bits at a time.

802.3u (Fast Ethernet) is compatible with 802.3 Ethernet because they share the same physical characteristics. Fast Ethernet and Ethernet use the same maximum transmission unit (MTU) and the same MAC mechanisms, and they both preserve the frame format that is used by 10Base-T Ethernet. Basically, Fast Ethernet is just based on an extension to the IEEE 802.3 specification, and because of that, it offers us a speed increase of 10 times 10Base-T.

Here are the expanded IEEE Ethernet 802.3 standards, starting with Fast Ethernet:

100Base-TX (IEEE 802.3u)   100Base-TX, most commonly known as Fast Ethernet, uses EIA/TIA Category 5, 5E, or 6, UTP two-pair wiring. One user per segment; up to 100 meters long (328 feet). It uses an RJ-45 connector with a physical star topology and a logical bus.

100Base-FX (IEEE 802.3u)   Uses fiber cabling 62.5/125-micron multimode fiber. Point-to-point topology; up to 412 meters long. It uses ST and SC connectors, which are media-interface connectors.

Ethernet's implementation over fiber can sometimes be referred to as 100Base-TF, although this isn't an actual standard. It just means that Ethernet technologies are being run over fiber cable.

1000Base-CX (IEEE 802.3z)   Copper twisted-pair called twinax (a balanced coaxial pair) that can run only up to 25 meters and uses a special 9-pin connector known as the High Speed Serial Data Connector (HSSDC).

1000Base-T (IEEE 802.3ab)   Category 5, four-pair UTP wiring up to 100 meters long (328 feet).

1000Base-SX (IEEE 802.3z)   The implementation of Gigabit Ethernet running over multimode fiber-optic cable (instead of copper twisted-pair cable) and using short wavelength laser. Multimode fiber (MMF) using 62.5- and 50-micron core; uses an 850 nanometer (nm) laser and can go up to 220 meters with 62.5-micron, 550 meters with 50-micron.

1000Base-LX (IEEE 802.3z)   Single-mode fiber that uses a 9-micron core and 1300 nm laser and can go from 3 km up to 10 km.

10GBase-T   10GBase-T is a standard proposed by the IEEE 802.3an committee to provide 10Gbps connections over conventional UTP cables (Category 5e, 6, or 7 cables). 10GBase-T allows the conventional RJ-45 used for Ethernet LANs. It can support signal transmission at the full 100-meter distance specified for LAN wiring.

10GBase-SR   An implementation of 10 Gigabit Ethernet that uses short-wavelength lasers at 850 nm over multimode fiber. It has a maximum transmission distance of between 2 and 300 meters (990 feet), depending on the size and quality of the fiber.

10GBase-LR   An implementation of 10 Gigabit Ethernet that uses long-wavelength lasers at 1,310 nm over single-mode fiber. It also has a maximum transmission distance between 2 meters and 10 km (which is 6 miles!), depending on the size and quality of the fiber.

10GBase-ER   An implementation of 10 Gigabit Ethernet running over single-mode fiber. It uses extra-long-wavelength lasers at 1,550 nm. It has the longest transmission distances possible of the 10-Gigabit technologies: anywhere from 2 meters up to 40 km, depending on the size and quality of the fiber used.

10GBase-SW   10GBase-SW, as defined by IEEE 802.3ae, is a mode of 10GBase-S for MMF with a 850 nm laser transceiver with a bandwidth of 10Gbps. It can support up to 300 meters of cable length. This media type is designed to connect to SONET equipment.

10GBase-LW   10GBase-LW is a mode of 10GBase-L supporting a link length of 10 km on standard single-mode fiber (SMF) (G.652). This media type is designed to connect to SONET equipment.

10GBase-EW   10GBase-EW is a mode of 10GBase-E supporting a link length of up to 40 km on SMF based on G.652 using optical-wavelength 1550 nm. This media type is designed to connect to SONET equipment.

If you want to implement a network medium that is not susceptible to electromagnetic interference (EMI), fiber-optic cable provides a more secure, long-distance cable that is not susceptible to EMI at high speeds like UTP is.

Table 4.4 summarizes the cable types.

TABLE 4.4   Common Ethernet Cable Types

Ethernet Name	Cable Type	Maximum Speed	Maximum Transmission Distance	Notes
10Base-5	Coax	10Mbps	500 meters per segment	Also called Thicknet, this cable type uses vampire taps to connect devices to cable.
10Base-2	Coax	10Mbps	185 meters per segment	Also called Thinnet, a very popular implementation of Ethernet over coax.
10Base-T	UTP	10Mbps	100 meters per segment	One of the most popular network cabling schemes.
100Base-TX	UTP, STP	100Mbps	100 meters per segment	Two pairs of Category 5 UTP.

TABLE 4.4 Common Ethernet Cable Types *(continued)*

Ethernet Name	Cable Type	Maximum Speed	Maximum Transmission Distance	Notes
10Base-FL	Fiber	10Mbps	Varies (ranges from 500 meters to 2,000 meters)	Ethernet over fiber optics to the desktop.
100Base-FX	MMF	100Mbps	2,000 meters	100Mbps Ethernet over fiber optics.
1000Base-T	UTP	1000Mbps	100 meters	Four pairs of Category 5e or higher.
1000Base-SX	MMF	1000Mbps	550 meters	Uses SC fiber connectors. Max length depends on fiber size.
1000Base-CX	Balanced, shielded copper	1000Mbps	25 meters	Uses a special connector, the HSSDC.
1000Base-LX	MMF and SMF	1000Mbps	550 meters multimode/ 2000 meters single mode	Uses longer wavelength laser than 1000Base-SX. Uses SC and LC connectors.
10GBase-T	UTP	10Gbps	100 meters	Connects to the network like a Fast Ethernet link using UTP.
10GBase-SR	MMF	10Gbps	300 meters	850 nm laser. Max length depends on fiber size and quality.
10GBase-LR	SMF	10Gbps	10 kilometers	1310 nm laser. Max length depends on fiber size and quality.
10GBase-ER	SMF	10Gbps	40 kilometers	1550 nm laser. Max length depends on fiber size and quality.
10GBase-SW	MMF	10Gbps	300 meters	850 nm laser transceiver.

TABLE 4.4   Common Ethernet Cable Types *(continued)*

Ethernet Name	Cable Type	Maximum Speed	Maximum Transmission Distance	Notes
10GBase-LW	SMF	10Gbps	10 kilometers	Typically used with SONET.
10GBase-EW	SMF	10Gbps	40 kilometers	1550 nm optical wavelength.

 An advantage of 100Base-FX over 100Base-TX is longer cable runs, however, 100Base-TX is easier to install.

I know there's a lot of information to remember about the various Ethernet and fiber types used in today's networks, but for the CompTIA Network+ exam, you really need to know them. Trust me, I haven't inundated you with unnecessary information!

Armed with the basics covered in the chapter, you're equipped to go to the next level and put Ethernet to work using various network devices. But to ensure you're really ready, read the summary, go over the Exam Essentials and do the Written Lab and Review Questions for this chapter.

Summary

In this chapter, you learned the fundamentals of Ethernet networking, how hosts communicate on a network, as well as how CSMA/CD works in an Ethernet half-duplex network.

I also talked about the differences between half- and full-duplex modes and discussed how Ethernet channel bonding can be used to attach multiple connections between Ethernet devices.

I finished the chapter with a description of the common Ethernet cable types used in today's networks. And by the way, you'd be wise to study that section really well!

Exam Essentials

Understand basic Ethernet communication.   Know how hosts use hardware addresses to communicate on an Ethernet LAN.

Understand Ethernet addressing.   Know the hexadecimal addressing scheme used to create an Ethernet address.

Understand binary, decimal, and hexadecimal addressing.   Know the different addressing types, and also use the Written Lab to practice your conversions.

Understand the basic definition of channel bonding.   Know the various ways you can use channel bonding to make your network more resilient and add bandwidth between devices.

Written Lab

1. Convert from decimal IP address to binary format.

    Complete the following table to express 192.168.10.15 in binary format.

128	64	32	16	8	4	2	1	Binary

    Complete the following table to express 172.16.20.55 in binary format.

128	64	32	16	8	4	2	1	Binary

    Complete the following table to express 10.11.12.99 in binary format.

128	64	32	16	8	4	2	1	Binary

2. Convert the following from binary format to decimal IP address.

Complete the following table to express 11001100.00110011.10101010.01010101 in decimal IP address format.

128	64	32	16	8	4	2	1	Decimal

Complete the following table to express 11000110.11010011.00111001.11010001 in decimal IP address format.

128	64	32	16	8	4	2	1	Decimal

Complete the following table to express 10000100.11010010.10111000.10100110 in decimal IP address format.

128	64	32	16	8	4	2	1	Decimal

3. Convert the following from binary format to hexadecimal.

Complete the following table to express 11011000.00011011.00111101.01110110 in hexadecimal.

128	64	32	16	8	4	2	1	Hexadecimal

Complete the following table to express 11001010.11110101.10000011.11101011 in hexadecimal.

128	64	32	16	8	4	2	1	Hexadecimal

Complete the following table to express 10000100.11010010.01000011.10110011 in hexadecimal.

128	64	32	16	8	4	2	1	Hexadecimal

Review Questions

1. On an Ethernet switched network, what address does one host computer use to communicate with another?
   A. IP address
   B. MAC address
   C. Street address
   D. HUB address

2. Which of the following can run full-duplex and achieve 200Mbps with CAT5e cable?
   A. 100Base-F
   B. 100Base-T
   C. 1000Base-F
   D. 1000Base-T

3. How many devices in a collision domain have to listen when a single host talks?
   A. 2
   B. 3
   C. 1
   D. All

4. If you are using a cable medium called 100Base-TF, what does this mean?
   A. That you are running Ethernet over cable
   B. Ethernet over fiber
   C. Ethernet over ThickNet
   D. That you are bundling multiple connections

5. What protocol helps devices share the bandwidth evenly without having two devices transmit at the same time on the network medium?
   A. TCP/IP
   B. CSMA/CD
   C. HTTPS
   D. TFTP

6. What is the maximum distance of 10GBase-SR?
   A. 100 meters (328 feet)
   B. 302 meters (990 feet)
   C. 305 meters (1000 feet)
   D. 1593 km (6 miles)

7. How many wire pairs are used with half duplex?
    - A. 2
    - B. 1
    - C. 4
    - D. None of the above

8. How many wire pairs are used with 100Base-T full duplex?
    - A. 2
    - B. 1
    - C. 4
    - D. A or C

9. What is the maximum distance of 10GBase-LR?
    - A. 1 mile
    - B. 3 miles
    - C. 6 miles
    - D. 25 miles

10. What is the effective total throughput increase with a full-duplex connection?
    - A. None
    - B. Twice as much
    - C. Four times as much
    - D. Ten times as much

11. What device can you not use full-duplex communication with?
    - A. Host
    - B. Hub
    - C. Switch
    - D. Router

12. What is the decimal equivalent of this binary number:
    11000000.10101000.00110000.11110000?
    - A. 192.168.48.192
    - B. 192.168.48.240
    - C. 192.168.64.224
    - D. 192.168.32.248

13. Which technology increases the bandwidth for network transmission by joining together multiple connections in one logical connection?

A. Bonding

B. VLANs

C. STP

D. Traffic Shaping

14. How is the decimal value 10 represented in binary?

A. 1000

B. 1001

C. 1010

D. 1011

15. What is the decimal value for the binary number 11101000?

A. 128

B. 194

C. 224

D. 232

16. What is the decimal number 10 in hexadecimal?

A. 9

B. A

C. C

D. B

17. How many bits is a MAC address?

A. 16

B. 32

C. 48

D. 64

18. The maximum distance of 1000Base-T is?

A. 100 Meters (328 feet)

B. 128 meters (420 feet)

C. 1000 meters (3280 feet)

D. 1024 meters (3360 feet)

19. What is the purpose of the Frame Check Sequence (FCS) in an Ethernet frame?

   A. Error correction

   B. Error detection

   C. Error recovery

   D. Creating errors

20. What does the Base mean in 100Base-TX?

   A. Broadband

   B. 100Mbps

   C. Baseband

   D. Twisted pair at 100Mbps

Answers to Review Questions

1. B. On an Ethernet Network, the MAC address (hardware address) is used for one host to communicate with another.

2. B. 100Base-T uses CAT5e and can run 200Mbps when using full-duplex. 100Base-TX is only CAT-5, not CAT5e

3. D. When one device sends a packet out on a network segment, all other devices on the same physical network segment must wait and let it be transmitted.

4. B. 100Base-TF means that you have an Ethernet over fiber cable implementation.

5. B. Carrier Sense Multiple Access with Collision Detection (CSMA/CD) helps packets that are transmitted simultaneously from different hosts share bandwidth evenly.

6. B. A 10GBase-SR cable can have a maximum distance of 990 feet (302 meters).

7. B. With half duplex, you are using only one wire pair with a digital signal either transmitting or receiving.

8. A. Full-duplex Ethernet uses two pairs of wires at the same time.

9. C. A 10GBase-LR implementation can go a distance of up to 6 miles

10. B. Double up! You can get 20Mbps with a 10Mbps Ethernet running full duplex or 200Mbps for Fast Ethernet.

11. B. Full-duplex communication cannot be used with a hub, because a hub is a half-duplex single communication device. A host, switch and router have the ability to process traffic (frames), whereas a hub is a multiport repeater.

12. B. 11000000 is 192, 10101000 is 168, 00110000 is 48, and 11110000 is 240.

13. A. Bonding can increase bandwidth and provide redundancy for devices that have multiple links connected together.

14. C. Nibble values are 8 + 4 + 2 + 1, giving us a maximum value of 15. If we have a decimal value of 10, that means the 8 bit and the 2 bit are turned on.

15. D. The 128, 64, 32, and 8 bits are on, so just add the values: 128 + 64 + 32 + 8 = 232.

16. B. The first 10 hexadecimal digits (0–9) are the same values as the decimal values. We already know the binary value for the number 10 is 1010—in hex, the number 10 needs to be displayed as a single character. To display double-digit numbers as a single character, we substitute letters. In our example, 10 is A.

17. C. A MAC, or hardware, address is a 48-bit (6-byte) address written in hexadecimal format.

18. A. 100Base-T and 1000Base-T both have a maximum distance of 100 meters, or 328 feet.

19. B . The FCS can detect frames in the sequence by calculating the cyclic redundancy check (CRC), which verifies that all the bits in the frame are unchanged.

20. C. The 100 means 100Mbps. The Base means baseband, which means baseband technology— a signaling method for communication on the network.

Answers to Written Lab

1. Convert from decimal IP address to binary format.

   Complete the following table to express 192.168.10.15 in binary format.

Decimal	128	64	32	16	8	4	2	1	Binary
192	1	1	0	0	0	0	0	0	11000000
168	1	0	1	0	1	0	0	0	10101000
10	0	0	0	0	1	0	1	0	00001010
15	0	0	0	0	1	1	1	1	00001111

Complete the following table to express 172.16.20.55 in binary format.

Decimal	128	64	32	16	8	4	2	1	Binary
172	1	0	1	0	1	1	0	0	10101100
16	0	0	0	1	0	0	0	0	00010000
20	0	0	0	1	0	1	0	0	00010100
55	0	0	1	1	0	1	1	1	00110111

Complete the following table to express 10.11.12.99 in binary format.

Decimal	128	64	32	16	8	4	2	1	Binary
10	0	0	0	0	1	0	1	0	00001010
11	0	0	0	0	1	0	1	1	00001011
12	0	0	0	0	1	1	0	0	00001100
99	0	1	1	0	0	0	1	1	01100011

2. Convert the following from binary format to decimal IP address.

Complete the following table to express 11001100.00110011.10101010.01010101 in decimal IP address format.

Binary	128	64	32	16	8	4	2	1	Decimal
11001100	1	1	0	0	1	1	0	0	204
00110011	0	0	1	1	0	0	1	1	51
10101010	1	0	1	0	1	0	1	0	170
01010101	0	1	0	1	0	1	0	1	85

Complete the following table to express 11000110.11010011.00111001.11010001 in decimal IP address format.

Binary	128	64	32	16	8	4	2	1	Decimal
11000110	1	1	0	0	0	1	1	0	198
11010011	1	1	0	1	0	0	1	1	211
00111001	0	0	1	1	1	0	0	1	57
11010001	1	1	0	1	0	0	0	1	209

Complete the following table to express 10000100.11010010.10111000.10100110 in decimal IP address format.

Binary	128	64	32	16	8	4	2	1	Decimal
10000100	1	0	0	0	0	1	0	0	132
11010010	1	1	0	1	0	0	1	0	210
10111000	1	0	1	1	1	0	0	0	184
10100110	1	0	1	0	0	1	1	0	166

3. Convert the following from binary format to hexadecimal.

Complete the following table to express 11011000.00011011.00111101.01110110 in hexadecimal.

Binary	128	64	32	16	8	4	2	1	Hexadecimal
11011000	1	1	0	1	1	0	0	0	D8
00011011	0	0	0	1	1	0	1	1	1B
00111101	0	0	1	1	1	1	0	1	3D
01110110	0	1	1	1	0	1	1	0	76

Complete the following table to express 11001010.11110101.10000011.11101011 in hexadecimal.

Binary	128	64	32	16	8	4	2	1	Hexadecimal
11001010	1	1	0	0	1	0	1	0	CA
11110101	1	1	1	1	0	1	0	1	F5
10000011	1	0	0	0	0	0	1	1	83
11101011	1	1	1	0	1	0	1	1	EB

Complete the following table to express 10000100.11010010.01000011.10110011 in hexadecimal.

Binary	128	64	32	16	8	4	2	1	Hexadecimal
10000100	1	0	0	0	0	1	0	0	84
11010010	1	1	0	1	0	0	1	0	D2
01000011	0	1	0	0	0	0	1	1	43
10110011	1	0	1	1	0	0	1	1	B3

Chapter 5

Networking Devices

THE FOLLOWING COMPTIA NETWORK+ EXAM OBJECTIVES ARE COVERED IN THIS CHAPTER:

✓ **3.1 Install, configure and differentiate between common network devices**

- Hub
- Repeater
- Modem
- NIC
- Media converters
- Basic switch
- Bridge
- Wireless access point
- Basic router
- Basic firewall
- Basic DHCP server

✓ **3.2 Identify the functions of specialized network devices**

- Multilayer switch
- Content switch
- IDS/IPS
- Load balancer
- Multifunction network devices
- DNS server
- Bandwidth shaper
- Proxy server
- CSU/DSU

In this chapter, I'll tell you all about the networking devices I've introduced so far. I'll go into much greater detail about each device, and yes—I'm going to present even more of them to you! Because all the components that you'll learn about shortly are typically found in today's networks and internetworks, it's very important that you be familiar with them.

We'll start by covering the more common network devices that you would be most likely to come across, and then move on to discuss some of the more specialized devices that you may or may not always find running in a network.

I'll finish the chapter by using examples to discuss how routers, hubs, and switches work within internetworks today.

For up-to-the-minute updates for this chapter, please see www.lammle.com or www.sybex.com/go/comptianetwork+studyguide.

Common Network Connectivity Devices

Okay—by now, you should be fairly savvy regarding the various types of network media and connections, so it's time to learn about some of the devices they hook up to that are commonly found on today's networks.

First, I'll define the basic terms; then, later in this chapter, I'll show you how these devices actually work within a network. At that time, I'll give you more detailed descriptions of these devices and terms used along with them.

Because these devices connect network entities, they're known as *connectivity devices*. Here's a list of the devices I'll be covering in this chapter:

- Hub
- Repeater
- Modem
- Network Interface Card (NIC)
- Transceiver (media converter)
- Bridge
- Basic switch
- Wireless access point (AP)

- Basic router
- Basic firewall
- Basic Dynamic Host Configuration Protocol (DHCP) server
- Other specialized devices

Hub

As you learned earlier, a *hub* is the device that connects all the segments of the network together in a star topology Ethernet network. Every device in the network connects directly to the hub through a single cable and is used to connect multiple devices without segmenting a network. Any transmission received on one port will be sent out all the other ports in the hub, including the receiving pair for the transmitting device, so that Carrier Sense Multiple Access with Collision Detection (CSMA/CD) on the transmitter can monitor for collisions.

So, basically, this means that if one station sends a broadcast, all the others will receive it; yet based on the addressing found in the frame, only the intended recipient will actually listen to it. This arrangement simulates the physical bus that the CSMA/CD standard was based on, and it's why we call the use of a hub in an Ethernet environment a physical star/logical bus topology.

Figure 5.1 depicts a typical hub as you might find it employed within a home network. Most of the time, hubs really aren't recommended for corporate networks because of their limitations.

FIGURE 5.1 A typical hub

It's important to note that hubs are nothing more than glorified repeaters that are incapable of recognizing frames and data structures—the reason why they act with such a lack of intelligence. A broadcast sent out by any device on the hub will be propagated to all devices connected to it. And just as in a physical bus topology configuration, any two or more of those connected devices have the potential of causing a collision with each other, which means that this hardware device will create a LAN with the most network traffic collisions. Hubs are not suggested in today's corporate network for this reason.

Repeater

Most of the time, repeaters were used in the old Thinnet networks of yesteryear. Today, they're just employed as the multi-port repeaters that we call hubs.

But there's another way we currently use them—Figure 5.2 shows a repeater being used to connect two unshielded twisted-pair (UTP) connectors. This configuration will provide an extension to your Ethernet segment and give you a gain of another 100 meters (328 feet).

FIGURE 5.2   Ethernet repeater

UTP Cable
100 meters

UTP Cable
100 meters

I really don't recommend using a repeater in networks because of the latency involved, but it can be a good thing if you employ one in a very limited role. Even so, I'd personally go with using a wireless network for a solution in a long-distance connection instead of a repeater because it will provide you with good distance without losing bandwidth or adding latency. In other words, just say no—repeaters and hubs shouldn't be used in today's networks because there are better solutions available!

It is important to remember that both hubs and repeaters are layer-1 devices and do not segment a network in any way.

Modem

You're probably (ummm—I hope) familiar with modems, but you may not be aware of their formal description. A *modem* is a device that modulates digital data onto an analog carrier for transmission over an analog medium and then demodulates from the analog carrier to a digital signal again at the receiving end. A mouthful, yes, but the term *modem* is actually an acronym that stands for MOdulator/DEModulator.

When you hear the term *modem*, three different types should come to mind:

- Traditional (plain old telephone service [POTS])
- DSL
- Cable

Traditional (POTS)

Most modems you find in computers today fall into the category of traditional modems. These modems convert the signals from your computer into those that travel over plain old telephone service (POTS) lines. The majority of modems that exist today are POTS modems, mainly because PC manufacturers include one with the computer, built right into the motherboard.

DSL

Digital subscriber line (DSL) has replaced traditional modem access because it offers higher data throughput rates for a reasonable cost. Plus, you get to make regular, land-line phone calls while online. DSL uses higher frequencies (above 3200Hz) than regular voice phone calls use, which provides greater bandwidth than regular POTS modems—up to several megabits per second. And it does so while still allowing standard voice data to travel in its normal frequency range and remain compatible with traditional POTS phones and devices.

DSL "modems" are the devices that allow the network signals to pass over phone lines on these higher frequencies. Check out Figure 5.3.

FIGURE 5.3   A typical DSL modem setup

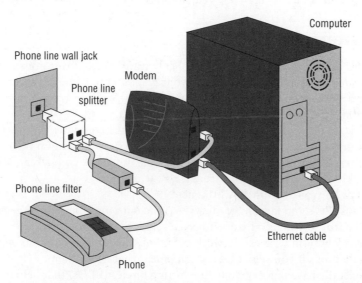

Usually, when you sign up for DSL service, the company you sign up with will send you a DSL modem for free or pretty close to it. This modem is generally an external one (although internal DSL modems are available), and it usually has both a phone line and an Ethernet connection. You have to connect the phone line to a wall jack and the Ethernet connection to your computer (shown in Figure 5.3), so it follows that you need to have an Ethernet NIC in your computer to connect to the DSL modem. Sometimes a router, hub, or switch is connected to the Ethernet port of the DSL modem, increasing the options for your Ethernet network.

If you have DSL service on the same phone line you use to make voice calls, you must install DSL filters on all the phone jacks where you have a phone (again, shown in Figure 5.3). Or, DSL filters may be installed after the DSL modem for all the phones in a building. Unless, of course, you can put up with an overwhelmingly annoying hissing noise (the DSL signals) on your voice calls!

Cable

Another popular high-speed Internet-access technology is cable-modem access. Cable modems connect an individual PC or network to the Internet using your television cable. The cable TV companies use their existing cable infrastructure to deliver data services on unused frequency bands.

The cable modem itself is a fairly simple device. It has a standard coax connector on the back as well as an Ethernet port. You can connect one PC to a cable modem—again, this requires that your computer have an Ethernet NIC installed—or you can connect the modem to multiple PCs on a network using a hub or switch. And you can always use a router to enhance your Ethernet network's capabilities.

Network Interface Card (NIC)

Those of you who aren't familiar with NICs probably want to be, at this point, so here goes: a *Network Interface Card* (NIC) is installed in your computer to connect, or interface, your computer to the network. It provides the physical, electrical, and electronic connections to the network media.

A NIC either is an expansion card or is built right into the computer's motherboard. The NIC usually connects to the computer through *expansion slots* located on the motherboard that allow peripherals to be plugged in directly. In some notebook computers, NIC adapters can be connected to the printer port or through a PC card slot.

Figure 5.4 shows a typical 100Mbps Ethernet NIC.

Nowadays, most PC's and laptops of all types come with an Ethernet connector built into the motherboard, so you usually don't need a separate card. It's also rare to find a laptop today without a built-in wireless network card, but you can buy external wireless cards for desktops and laptops if you've got legacy equipment that needs them.

NIC cards generally have one or two light-emitting diodes (LEDs) that help in diagnosing any functional problems. If there are two separate LEDs on the NIC, one of them is most likely the Link LED, which illuminates when proper connectivity to an active network has been detected. But it's not always that cut and dried—that blinking LED can mean the NIC is receiving a proper signal from the hub or switch, but it can also indicate connectivity to and detection of a carrier on a segment. Another possibility is that it's found connectivity with a router or other end device using a crossover cable.

The other LED is the aptly named Activity LED, which tends to flicker constantly. That activity indicates the intermittent transmission and reception of frames arriving at the network or leaving it.

FIGURE 5.4   Network Interface Card

   The first LED you should verify is the Link LED because if it's not illumi-
nated, the Activity LED simply cannot illuminate.

Transceiver (Media Converter)

Another small device that you might come across on a network is an external transceiver,
otherwise known as a media converter. These simple devices allow a NIC or other networking
device to connect to a different type of media than it was designed to connect to. Many hubs,
switches, and NICs have special connectors that allow for this.

For instance, let's say you've got a 100Base-TX switch, and you want to connect it to
another switch using fiber-optic cabling. To make this happen, you need to connect a fiber
transceiver to each switch's transceiver port and then connect the two transceivers together
with the appropriate fiber-optic cabling. Figure 5.5 shows an Ethernet-to-fiber transceiver.

FIGURE 5.5   A 100Base-TX to 100Base-FX transceiver

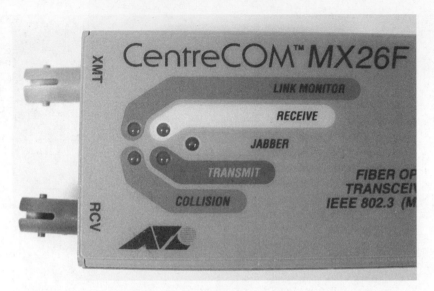

With early Ethernet-style DB-15 female Digital, Intel, and Xerox (DIX) connectors—often referred to as Attachment Unit Interface (AUI) connectors—NIC interfaces are still available as medium-independent connectors on more advanced NICs and other networking devices. But you'll need an external transceiver to convert the electrical signal from the device to one that's compatible with the cabling medium.

Figure 5.6 shows a router with a DIX (AUI) connector.

FIGURE 5.6   Router with a DIX (AUI) connector

All *x*Base-T standards, and all other popular types of Ethernet technology, have a built-in transceiver (which transceives digital data) on the NIC card or device interface. With these technologies, an external transceiver is only required to act as a media converter, as shown in Figure 5.7.

FIGURE 5.7   DIX to RJ-45 transceiver

I'm surprised when I find these in today's networks; but believe it or not, I use them myself at times with some routers. This is the reason that you still need to know about them.

Bridge

A *bridge*—specifically, a transparent bridge—is a network device that connects two similar network segments together. Its primary function is to keep traffic separated on either side of the bridge, breaking up collision domains, as pictured in Figure 5.8.

FIGURE 5.8   Bridges break up collision domains.

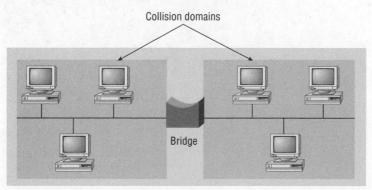

What we can see here is that traffic is allowed to pass through the bridge only if the transmission is intended for a station on the opposite side. The main reasons you would place a bridge in your network would be to connect two segments together or to divide a busy network into two segments.

Bridges are software based; so, interestingly, you can think of a switch as a hardware-based, multiport bridge. In fact, the terms, *bridge* and *switch* are often used interchangeably because the two devices used basically the same bridging technologies. The past tense is there for a reason—you'd be hard-pressed to buy a bridge today.

Switch

Switches connect multiple segments of a network together much like hubs do, but with three significant differences—a switch recognizes frames and pays attention to the source and destination MAC address of the incoming frame as well as the port on which it was received. Hubs don't do those things. They simply send out anything they receive on one port out to all the others.

So, if a switch determines that a frame's final destination happens to be on a segment that's connected via a different port than the one on which the frame was received, the switch will only forward the frame out from the specific port on which its destination is located. If the switch can't figure out the location of the frame's destination, it will flood the frame out every port except the one on which the frame port was received.

Figure 5.9 shows a typical low-cost Ethernet switch. It looks a lot like a hub. However, switches can come in very large, expensive sizes.

FIGURE 5.9   Typical Ethernet switch

That's as far as we're going with switches right now. I'll bring them up later on in this chapter and cover them in much greater detail in Chapter 11, "Switching and Virtual LANs (VLANs)." For now, you can think of a switch as a faster, smarter bridge that has more ports.

Switches are a Layer 2 device, which means they segment the network with MAC addresses. If you see the term "Layer 3 switch", that means you are talking about a router, not a Layer 2 switch. The terms router and Layer 3 switch are interchangeable.

Wireless Access Point (AP)

A *wireless access point (AP)* allows mobile users to connect to a wired network wirelessly via radio frequency technologies. Using wireless technologies, APs also allow wired networks to connect to each other and are basically the wireless equivalent of hubs or switches because they can connect multiple wireless (and often wired) devices together to form a network.

Figure 5.10 shows a typical low-cost access point

FIGURE 5.10   A typical low-cost access point

One of the most popular uses for APs today is to provide Internet access in public areas like libraries, coffee shops, hotels, and airports. You may think WAPs are hard to set up, but they're not—basically, you just need to plug them in to a wired network, power them up, and—voila! Another big plus is that without the clutter and added expense of cables, WAPs make ideal foundations for small business networks.

You'll learn all the critical details a Network+ technician needs to know about APs later, in Chapter 12, "Wireless Technologies."

Router

A *router* is a network device used to connect many, sometimes disparate, network segments together, combining them into what we call an *internetwork*. A well-configured router can make intelligent decisions about the best way to get network data to its destination. It gathers the information it needs to make these decisions based on a network's particular performance data.

Figure 5.11 shows a Small Office, Home Office (SOHO) router that provides wired and wireless access for hosts and connects them to the Internet without any necessary configuration. But know that I certainly don't recommend leaving a router with the default configuration! No worries, though—I'll go over the configuration process with you in Chapter 12.

FIGURE 5.11   Router connected to the Internet, providing access for hosts

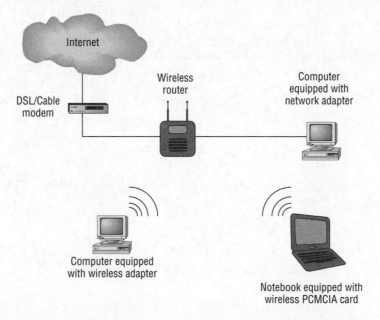

Routers can be multifaceted devices that behave like computers unto themselves with their own complex operating systems—for example, Cisco's IOS. You can even think of them as CPUs that are totally dedicated to the process of routing packets. And due to their complexity and flexibility, you can configure them to actually perform the functions of other types of network devices (like firewalls, for example) by simply implementing a specific feature within the router's software.

 Routers can have many different names: layer-3 switch and multilayer switch are the most common, besides the name router, of course. Remember, if you just hear the word "switch", that means a layer-2 device. Routers, layer-3 switches, and multilayer switches are all layer-3 devices.

Firewall

So what, exactly, is a *firewall*? Basically, firewalls are your network's security guards; and to be real, they're probably the most important thing to implement on your network. That's because today's networks are almost always connected to the Internet—a situation that makes security crucial! A firewall protects your LAN resources from invaders that prowl the Internet for unprotected networks, while simultaneously preventing all or some of your LAN's computers from accessing certain services on the Internet. You can employ them to filter packets based on rules that you or the network administrator create and configure to strictly delimit the type of information allowed to flow in and out of the network's Internet connection.

A firewall can be either a stand-alone "black box" or a software implementation placed on a server or router. Either way, the firewall will have at least two network connections: one to the Internet (known as the *public* side) and one to the network (known as the *private* side). Sometimes, there is a second firewall, as shown in Figure 5.12. This firewall is used to connect servers and equipment that can be considered both public and private (like web and email servers). This intermediary network is known as a *demilitarized zone (DMZ)*.

FIGURE 5.12 Example of firewalls with a DMZ

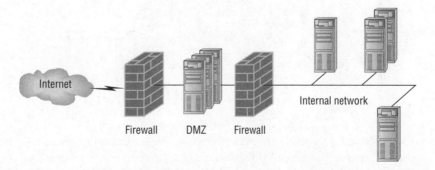

Firewalls are the first line of defense for an Internet-connected network. Without them in place, any network that's connected to the Internet is essentially wide open to anyone with a little technical savvy who seeks to exploit LAN resources and/or access your network's sensitive information.

Dynamic Host Configuration Protocol (DHCP) Server

Even though I'm going to get into the finer points of DHCP soon, in Chapter 6, "Introduction to Internet Protocol (IP)," I want to give you some basic insight into this server service here.

In essence, DHCP servers assign IP addresses to hosts. This protocol gives us a much easier way to administrate—by automatically providing IP information—than the alternative and tedious method known as static IP addressing, where we have to address each host manually. It works well in any network environment, from tiny to huge, and allows all types of hardware to be employed as a DHCP server, including routers.

It works like this: A DHCP server receives request for IP information from a DHCP client using a broadcast (as Chapter 6 will show you in detail). The only hitch is that if the DHCP server isn't on the same segment as the DHCP client, the broadcast won't be received by the server because by default, routers won't forward broadcasts, as shown in Figure 5.13.

FIGURE 5.13   DHCP client sends broadcasts looking for a DHCP server

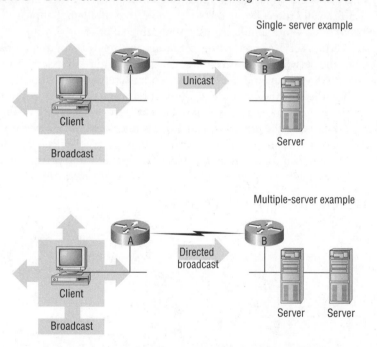

In Figure 5.13, Router A is configured with the IP helper address command on interface E0 of the router. Whenever interface E0 receives a broadcast request, Router A will forward those requests as a unicast (meaning instead of a broadcast, the packet now has the destination IP address of the DHCP server).

So, as shown in the figure, you can configure Router A to forward these requests and even use multiple DHCP servers for redundancy, if needed. This works because the router has been configured to forward the request to a single server using a unicast or by sending the request to multiple servers via a directed broadcast.

Personally, most of the time I use a Windows server to act as the DHCP server for my entire internetwork and have my routers forward client requests. It is possible to have a DHCP server on every network segment, but that is not necessary because of the routers' forwarding ability.

Figure 5.14 shows a picture of a Windows server with something called Scope Options.

FIGURE 5.14   A Windows DHCP server's Scope Options

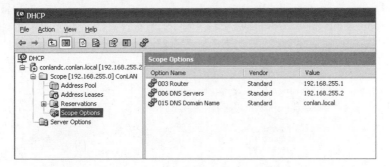

Scope Options provide IP configuration for hosts on a specific subnet. Below the Scope Options, you'll find Server Options, which provide IP information for all scopes configured on the server. If I had just one Domain Name Service (DNS) server for the entire network, I'd configure the Server Options with my DNS server information; that DNS server information would then show up automatically in all scopes configured on my server.

So, what exactly does a DHCP client ask for, and what does a DHCP server provide? Is it just an IP address, a mask, and a default gateway? No, it is much more than that. Let's take a look at a DHCP client request on an analyzer. Figure 5.15 shows the options that the client is requesting from the DHCP server.

FIGURE 5.15   DHCP client request to a DHCP server

```
⊞ Frame 33 (344 bytes on wire, 344 bytes captured)
⊞ Ethernet II, Src: Usi_d0:e9:35 (00:1e:37:d0:e9:35), Dst: Broadcast (ff:ff:ff:ff:ff:ff)
⊞ Internet Protocol, Src: 0.0.0.0 (0.0.0.0), Dst: 255.255.255.255 (255.255.255.255)
⊞ User Datagram Protocol, Src Port: bootpc (68), Dst Port: bootps (67)
⊟ Bootstrap Protocol
    Message type: Boot Request (1)
    Hardware type: Ethernet
    Hardware address length: 6
    Hops: 0
    Transaction ID: 0xb16f1532
    Seconds elapsed: 0
  ⊞ Bootp flags: 0x8000 (Broadcast)
    Client IP address: 0.0.0.0 (0.0.0.0)
    Your (client) IP address: 0.0.0.0 (0.0.0.0)
    Next server IP address: 0.0.0.0 (0.0.0.0)
    Relay agent IP address: 0.0.0.0 (0.0.0.0)
    Client MAC address: Usi_d0:e9:35 (00:1e:37:d0:e9:35)
    Server host name not given
    Boot file name not given
    Magic cookie: (OK)
  ⊞ Option: (t=53,l=1) DHCP Message Type = DHCP Discover
  ⊞ Option: (t=116,l=1) DHCP Auto-Configuration
  ⊞ Option: (t=61,l=7) Client identifier
  ⊞ Option: (t=50,l=4) Requested IP Address = 10.100.36.38
  ⊞ Option: (t=12,l=14) Host Name = "globalnet-todd"
  ⊞ Option: (t=60,l=8) Vendor class identifier = "MSFT 5.0"
  ⊞ Option: (t=55,l=12) Parameter Request List
    End Option
```

First, you can see that the DHCP service runs on top of the bootP protocol (port 68) and that the DHCP client is looking for a bootp server (port 67). The client IP address is 0.0.0.0, and the client doesn't know the DHCP server address either because this is a broadcast to 255.255.255.255 (the Data Link layer broadcast shows ff:ff:ff:ff:ff:ff). Basically, all the DHCP client knows for sure is its own MAC address.

The DHCP client Parameter Request List option shown at the end of Figure 5.15 has been expanded and is shown in Figure 5.16. The client is "requesting" a certain IP address because this is the IP address it received from the server the last time it requested an IP address.

FIGURE 5.16 DHCP client parameter request list

```
⊟ Option: (t=55,l=12) Parameter Request List
     Option: (55) Parameter Request List
     Length: 12
     Value: 010F03062C2E2F1F2179F92B
     1 = Subnet Mask
     15 = Domain Name
     3 = Router
     6 = Domain Name Server
     44 = NetBIOS over TCP/IP Name Server
     46 = NetBIOS over TCP/IP Node Type
     47 = NetBIOS over TCP/IP Scope
     31 = Perform Router Discover
     33 = Static Route
     121 = Classless Static Route
     249 = Classless Static Route (Microsoft)
     43 = Vendor-Specific Information
   End Option
```

That is quite a request list! The DHCP server will respond with the options that it has configured and available to provide to a DHCP client. Let's take a look and see what the server responds with. Figure 5.17 shows the DHCP server response.

FIGURE 5.17 DHCP server response

```
⊞ Frame 34 (359 bytes on wire, 359 bytes captured)
⊞ Ethernet II, Src: Cisco_90:ed:80 (00:0b:5f:90:ed:80), Dst: Broadcast (ff:ff:ff:ff:ff:ff)
⊞ Internet Protocol, Src: 10.100.36.33 (10.100.36.33), Dst: 255.255.255.255 (255.255.255.255)
⊞ User Datagram Protocol, Src Port: bootps (67), Dst Port: bootpc (68)
⊟ Bootstrap Protocol
     Message type: Boot Reply (2)
     Hardware type: Ethernet
     Hardware address length: 6
     Hops: 0
     Transaction ID: 0xb16f1532
     Seconds elapsed: 0
   ⊞ Bootp flags: 0x8000 (Broadcast)
     Client IP address: 0.0.0.0 (0.0.0.0)
     Your (client) IP address: 10.100.36.38 (10.100.36.38)
     Next server IP address: 10.100.36.12 (10.100.36.12)
     Relay agent IP address: 10.100.36.33 (10.100.36.33)
     Client MAC address: Usi_d0:e9:35 (00:1e:37:d0:e9:35)
     Server host name not given
     Boot file name not given
     Magic cookie: (OK)
   ⊞ Option: (t=53,l=1) DHCP Message Type = DHCP Offer
   ⊞ Option: (t=1,l=4) Subnet Mask = 255.255.255.224
   ⊞ Option: (t=58,l=4) Renewal Time Value = 11 hours, 30 minutes
   ⊞ Option: (t=59,l=4) Rebinding Time Value = 20 hours, 7 minutes, 30 seconds
   ⊞ Option: (t=51,l=4) IP Address Lease Time = 23 hours
   ⊞ Option: (t=54,l=4) Server Identifier = 10.100.36.12
   ⊞ Option: (t=15,l=16) Domain Name = "globalnet.local"
   ⊞ Option: (t=3,l=4) Router = 10.100.36.33
   ⊞ Option: (t=6,l=8) Domain Name Server
   ⊞ Option: (t=44,l=4) NetBIOS over TCP/IP Name Server = 10.100.36.13
   ⊞ Option: (t=46,l=1) NetBIOS over TCP/IP Node Type = H-node
     End Option
```

The client is going to get the IP address that it asked for (10.100.36.38), a subnet mask of 255.255.255.224, a lease time of 23 hours (the amount of time before the IP address and other DHCP information expires on the client), the IP address of the DHCP server, the default gateway (router), the DNS server IP address (it gets two), the domain name used by DNS, and some NetBIOS information (used by Windows for name resolution).

The lease time is important and can even be used to tell you if you have a DHCP problem, or more specifically, that the DHCP server is no longer handing out IP addresses to hosts. If hosts start failing to get onto the network one at a time as they try to get a new IP address as their lease time expires, you need to check your server settings.

Here is another example of a possible DHCP problem: you arrive at work after a weekend where some hosts were left on and some were shut down. The hosts that were left running and not shut down are still working, but the hosts that were shut down and were restarted on Monday morning do not get a new IP address. This is a good indication that you need to head over to your DHCP server and take a look at what is going on.

A DHCP server can also be configured with a reservation list so that a host always receives the same IP address. You would use this reservation list for routers or servers if they were not statically assigned. However, you can use reservation lists for any host on your network as well.

Other Specialized Devices

In addition to the network connectivity devices I've discussed with you, there are several devices that, while maybe not directly connected to a network, do actively participate in moving network data. Here's a list of them:

- Multilayer switch
- Content switch
- Intrusion Detection or Prevention System (IDS/IPS)
- Load balancer
- Multifunction network devices
- DNS server
- Bandwidth shaper
- Proxy server
- Channel Service Unit/Data Service Unit (CSU/DSU)

Multilayer Switch

A *multilayer switch* (MLS) is a computer networking device that switches on Open Systems Interconnection (OSI) Layer 2 like an ordinary network switch but provides extra functions on higher OSI layers, like Layer 3, for routing.

The major difference between the packet-switching operation of a router and that of a Layer 3 or multilayer switch lies in the physical implementation. In routers, packet switching takes place using a microprocessor, whereas a Layer 3 switch handles this by using application-specific integrated circuit (ASIC) hardware. I'd show you a picture of a Layer 3 switch, but they look just like regular Layer 2 switches and you already know what those look like. The differences are the hardware inside and the operating system.

Content Switch

Believe it or not, we have switches around today that are capable of utilizing up to OSI Layer 7 information. Here's a list of these cool devices:

- Layer 4–7 switches
- Content switches
- Content services switches
- Web switches
- Application switches

We use the power given us by content switches for something known as *load balancing* within a whole group of servers. It really comes in handy dealing with things like application Transmission Control Protocol/Internet Protocol (TCP/IP) data, HTTP, HTTPS, and/or a virtual private network (VPN) concerning a particular port.

A good point to remember is that load balancing frequently requires Network Address Translation (NAT), which I'll talk about in Chapter 8, "IP Subnetting, Troubleshooting IP, and Introduction to NAT." Client machines connected to load-balanced services are totally in the dark about the specific server that's responding to the client. What's more, some Layer 4–7 switches are so fast they actually execute NAT at wire-speed rates that make it look as though the switch isn't even on the network because the latency, or response time, is so low, it's basically absent.

You can also use content switches for important tasks like encryption and decryption, as well as for streamlining the administration of digital certificates (these are all important terms you'll learn about in Chapters 13, "Authentication and Access Control"; in 14, "Network Threats and Mitigation"; and in 15, "Physical and Hardware Security"). The capabilities of these switches greatly minimize the load on any servers receiving network traffic and really enhance network performance.

Intrusion Detection or Prevention System (IDS/IPS)

Intrusion Detection System (IDS) is exactly what it sounds like—a powerful security tool that detects a plethora of nasty tactics that bad guys use to exploit systems, including unauthorized logins and privilege increases that can give them access to your sensitive data and files. Attacks on network resources, services, and applications—even the vile practice of placing viruses, worms, and trojans—are also detected by IDS. However, IDS only identifies, detects, and reports attempts of unauthorized access to the network as well as any suspicious activity, and is the best software type for identifying an attack. However, if you want to stop the attack in its track you need to add an IPS device.

An *Intrusion Prevention System (IPS)* provides computers with security by vigilantly watching for any suspicious and potentially malicious tactics. It works in real time and, as its name suggests, prevents these evil activities. For instance, network-based IPS monitors the network's traffic, looking for malicious code and other attacks and simply drops any offensive packets while permitting all proper network traffic to flow unimpeded. So, unlike IDS, which can identify an attack and report it, IPS can stop the attack in its tracks by shutting down a port or dropping certain types of packets.

Load Balancer

Your average router just sends incoming packets to their specified, correlative IP address on the network; but a *load balancer* can actually send incoming packets to multiple machines hidden behind one IP address—cool, right?

Today's load-balancing routers follow various rules to determine specifically how they will route network traffic. Depending on your needs, you can set rules based on the least load, fault tolerance, the fastest response times, or just dividing up (balancing) outbound requests for smooth network operations.

In fact, the fault tolerance, or redundancy, as well as the scalability so vital to large networking environments and e-commerce include some of the great benefits we gain using load balancers.

Think about this scenario: Say you have a web site where people are placing orders for the stuff you've got for sale. Obviously, the orders placed vary in size and the rate at which that they come in; and you definitely wouldn't want your servers becoming so overloaded that they hose up and crash your site, causing you to lose lots of money, now would you? That's where balancing the load of traffic between a group of servers comes to the rescue, because even if one of them freezes, your customers will still be able to access your site and place orders.

Multifunction Network Devices

This term applies to any multifunction device that's connected to the network, which provides any combination of printing, copying, faxing, and scanning. Figure 5.18 shows a multifunction network device.

These devices are all-in-one solutions, and you will find them in pretty much every network these days. Why buy a printer, a copier, and a separate fax machine when one machine can do it all for basically the same price?

Domain Name Service (DNS) Server

A *Domain Name Service (DNS) server* is one of the most important servers in your network and on the Internet as well. Why? Because without a DNS server, you would have to type **http://206.123.114.186** instead of simply entering **www.lammle.com**. So it follows that you can pretty much think of a DNS server as the phone book of the Internet.

FIGURE 5.18   A multifunction network device

A host name is typically the name of a device that has a specific IP address; on the Internet, it is part of what is known as a fully qualified domain name (FQDN). An FQDN consists of a host name and a domain name.

The process of finding the IP address for any given host name is known as *name resolution*, and it can be performed in several ways: a HOSTS file (meaning you statically type in all names and IP addresses on each and every host), a request broadcast on the local network (Microsoft's favorite—why ask a server when you can just broadcast, right?), DNS, and Microsoft's Windows Internet Naming Service (WINS). DNS is the most popular today and is the resolution method you really need to know.

On the Internet, domains are arranged in a hierarchical tree structure. The following list includes some of the top-level domains currently in use:

.com   A commercial organization. Most companies end up as part of this domain.

.edu   An educational establishment, such as a university.

.gov   A branch of the U.S. government.

.int   An international organization, such as NATO or the United Nations.

.mil   A branch of the U.S. military.

.net   A network organization.

.org   A nonprofit organization.

Your local ISP is probably a member of the .net domain, and your company is probably part of the .com domain. The .gov and .mil domains are reserved strictly for use by the government and the military within the United States. In other parts of the world, the final part of a domain name represents the country in which the server is located (.ca for Canada, .jp for Japan, .uk for Great Britain, and .ru for Russia, for example). Well over 130 countries are represented on the Internet.

The .com domain is by far the largest, followed by the .edu domain. Some new domain names are becoming popular, however, because of the increasing number of domain-name requests. These include .firm for businesses and companies, .store for businesses selling goods rather than services, .arts for cultural and entertainment organizations, and .info for informational services. The domains .cc, .biz, .travel, and .post are also in use on the Internet.

Let's see how a basic DNS server works in your network. Figure 5.19 shows how, when you type in a human name, the DNS server resolves it, allowing the host to send the HTTP packets to the server.

FIGURE 5.19   DNS resolution example

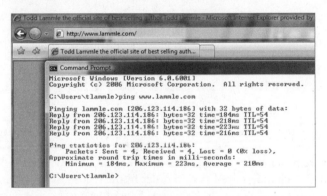

This DOS screen shows how the DNS server can resolve the human name to the IP address of the Lammle.com server when I ping the server by the name instead of the IP address.

It should be easy to imagine how hard life would be without DNS translating human names to IP addresses, routing your packet through the Internet, or internetwork to get to your servers. Figure 5.20 gives you an example of a Windows server configured as a DNS server.

Now the hosts can receive the IP address of this DNS server, and then this server will resolve host names to correct IP address. This is a mission-critical service in today's networks, don't you think? As shown in Figure 5.20, if I ping from a host to conlanpc1, the host will send the name-resolution request to the DNS server and translate this name to IP address 192.168.255.8.

Host (A) is called an A record and is what gives you the IP address of a domain or host. In IPv6, it's called a quad-A or AAAA record. As shown in Figure 5.20, you can see that each name has an A record, which is associated to an IP address. Okay, so "A" record resolve hostnames to IP addresses, but what happens if you know the IP address and want to know the hostname? There is a record for this too! It's called the pointer record (PTR).

FIGURE 5.20 A Windows DNS server

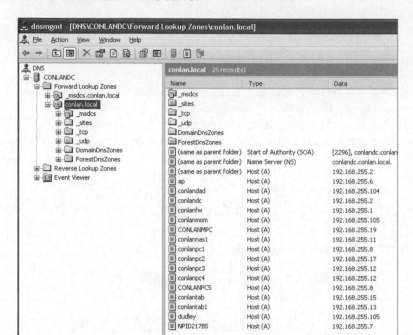

Other typical records found on DNS servers are *mail exchanger (MX) records*, which are used to translate mail records. The MX record points to the mail exchanger for a particular host. DNS is structured so that you can actually specify several mail exchangers for one host. This feature provides a higher probability that email will arrive at its intended destination. The mail exchangers are listed in order in the record, with a priority code that indicates the order in which they should be accessed by other mail-delivery systems.

If the first-priority mail exchanger doesn't respond in a given amount of time, the mail-delivery system tries the second one, and so on. Here are some sample mail-exchange records:

```
hostname.company.com.   IN    MX    10 mail.company.com.
hostname.company.com.   IN    MX    20 mail2.company.com.
hostname.company.com.   IN    MX    30 mail3.company.com.
```

In this example, if the first mail exchanger, `mail.company.com`, does not respond, the second one, `mail2.company.com`, is tried, and so on.

Another important record type on a DNS is the canonical name (*CNAME*) *record*. This is also commonly known as the *alias record* and allows hosts to have more than one name. For example, suppose your web server has the host name www, and you want that machine to also have the name ftp so that users can use FTP to access a different portion of the file system as an FTP root. You can accomplish this with a CNAME record. Given that you already have an address record established for the host name www, a CNAME record that adds ftp as a host name would look something like this:

```
www.company.com.        IN    A       204.176.47.2
ftp.company.com.        IN    CNAME   www.company.com.
```

When you put all these record types together in a zone file, or DNS table, it might look like this:

```
mail.company.com.        IN    A       204.176.47.9
mail2.company.com.       IN    A       204.176.47.21
mail3.company.com.       IN    A       204.176.47.89
yourhost.company.com.    IN    MX      10 mail.company.com.
yourhost.company.com.    IN    MX      20 mail2.company.com.
yourhost.company.com.    IN    MX      30 mail3.company.com.
www.company.com.         IN    A       204.176.47.2
ftp.company.com.         IN    CNAME   www.company.com.
```

Let's take a look a tad deeper for a minute into how resolution takes place between a host and a DNS server. Figure 5.21 shows a DNS query from my host to www.lammle.com from a browser.

FIGURE 5.21   A DNS query to www.lammle.com

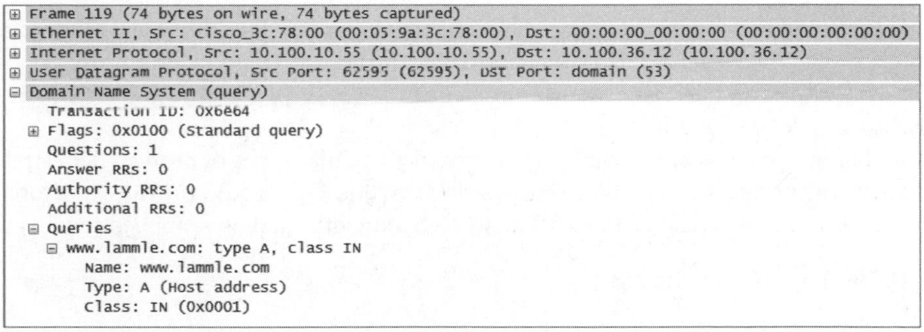

```
⊞ Frame 119 (74 bytes on wire, 74 bytes captured)
⊞ Ethernet II, Src: Cisco_3c:78:00 (00:05:9a:3c:78:00), Dst: 00:00:00_00:00:00 (00:00:00:00:00:00)
⊞ Internet Protocol, Src: 10.100.10.55 (10.100.10.55), Dst: 10.100.36.12 (10.100.36.12)
⊞ User Datagram Protocol, Src Port: 62595 (62595), Dst Port: domain (53)
⊟ Domain Name System (query)
     Transaction ID: 0x6e64
   ⊞ Flags: 0x0100 (standard query)
     Questions: 1
     Answer RRs: 0
     Authority RRs: 0
     Additional RRs: 0
   ⊟ Queries
     ⊟ www.lammle.com: type A, class IN
         Name: www.lammle.com
         Type: A (Host address)
         Class: IN (0x0001)
```

This figure shows that DNS uses User Datagram Protocol (UDP) at the Transport layer (it uses Transport Control Protocol [TCP] if it is updating its phone book pages—we call these *zone updates*), and this query is asking destination port 53 (the DNS service) on host 10.100.36.13 who the heck www.lammle.com is.

Let's take a look at the server's response. Figure 5.22 shows the DNS answer to our query for www.lammle.com.

Port 53 answered from server 10.100.36.13 with the IP address of 206.123.114.186. My host can now go to that server requesting HTTP pages using the IP address.

FIGURE 5.22 The DNS answer to our query

```
⊞ Frame 36 (104 bytes on wire, 104 bytes captured)
⊞ Ethernet II, Src: Cisco_90:ed:80 (00:0b:5f:90:ed:80), Dst: Usi_d0:e9:35 (00:1e:37:d0:e9:35)
⊞ Internet Protocol, Src: 10.100.36.13 (10.100.36.13), Dst: 10.100.36.38 (10.100.36.38)
⊞ User Datagram Protocol, Src Port: domain (53), Dst Port: 59259 (59259)
⊟ Domain Name System (response)
    [Request In: 35]
    [Time: 0.000302000 seconds]
    Transaction ID: 0x070e
  ⊞ Flags: 0x8180 (Standard query response, No error)
    Questions: 1
    Answer RRs: 2
    Authority RRs: 0
    Additional RRs: 0
  ⊟ Queries
    ⊟ www.lammle.com: type A, class IN
        Name: www.lammle.com
        Type: A (Host address)
        Class: IN (0x0001)
  ⊟ Answers
    ▨ www.lammle.com: type CNAME, class IN, cname lammle.com
    ⊟ lammle.com: type A, class IN, addr 206.123.114.186
        Name: lammle.com
        Type: A (Host address)
        Class: IN (0x0001)
        Time to live: 3 hours, 6 minutes, 27 seconds
        Data length: 4
        Addr: 206.123.114.186
```

Bandwidth Shaper

Sometimes referred to as packet shaping or a traffic shaper, a *bandwidth shaper* is essentially another great tool used for optimizing a network's performance. It works by controlling computer network traffic and delaying specified packets to lower response time and maximize the network's available bandwidth.

Traffic shaping really means setting parameters on particular types of profiled data streams that delay the earmarked packets' flow through the network. Figure 5.23 provides a before-and-after snapshot of what data can look like when bandwidth shaping is applied to it.

FIGURE 5.23 Bandwidth shaping

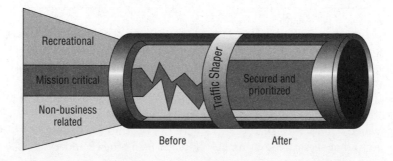

Nice! Why would anyone choose to run a large internetwork without a bandwidth shaper? Because it's expensive, that's why. If you can't shell out the money for your large corporate network to have a bandwidth shaper, just make sure that all the typical porn sites and other popular (nonwork) sites like YouTube, MySpace, Facebook, and so on are blocked from users accessing them inside your network; then, for the most part, you'll be fine.

Proxy Server

A *proxy server* is basically a type of server that handles its client-machine requests by forwarding them on to other servers while allowing granular control over the traffic between the local LAN and the Internet. When it receives a request, the proxy will then connect to the specific server that can fulfill the request for the client that wants it.

Sometimes the proxy modifies the client's request or a server's response to it—or even handles the client's request itself. It will actually cache or "remember" the specific server that would have normally been contacted for the request in case it's needed another time. This behavior really speeds up the network's function, thereby optimizing its performance. However, proxy servers can also limit the availability of the types of sites that users on a LAN have access to, which is a benefit for an administrator of the network if users are constantly connected to nonwork sites and using all the WAN bandwidth.

Figure 5.24 shows where a proxy server would be typically found in a small to medium-size network.

FIGURE 5.24   A proxy server

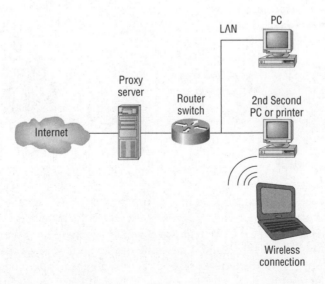

There are two main types of proxy servers you'll typically find working in present-day networks:

Caching proxy server A caching proxy server speeds up the network's service requests by recovering information from a client's or clients' earlier request. Caching proxies keep local copies of the resources requested often, which really helps minimize the upstream use of bandwidth. These servers can greatly enhance network performance.

Web proxy server A web proxy server is usually used to create a web cache. You experience this when you Google a site you've visited before. The web proxy "remembers" you, and the site not only loads faster, but sometimes even recalls your personal information by automatically filling in your username—or even your billing/shipping information when you place another order.

Channel Service Unit/Data Service Unit (CSU/DSU)

The CSU/DSU is a common device found in equipment rooms when the network is connected via a T-series data connection or other digital serial technology like a T1 or Digital Data Server (DDS). It's essentially two devices in one that are used to connect a digital carrier (the T-series or DDS line) to your network equipment—usually to a router. The *Channel Service Unit (CSU)* terminates the line at the customer's premises and also provides diagnostics and remote testing, if necessary. The *Data Service Unit (DSU)* does the actual transmission of the signal through the CSU and can also provide buffering and data-flow control.

Figure 5.25 shows where a typical CSU/DSU would be used for a T1 connection

FIGURE 5.25 Typical placement of a CSU/DSU device

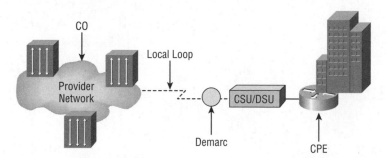

The CSU/DSU connects to your router on one side, and into what is called a demarcation location on the other—which connects your network to the providers WAN.

Both components of a CSU/DSU are required if you are going to connect to a digital transmission medium like a T1 line; and sometimes, one or both of these components may even be built into a router. In the latter case, you can just go ahead and plug the T1 line directly into the router. Otherwise, you'll need some Physical layer specification, like V.35, to cable the interface on the router to the external CSU/DSU.

Okay—with all that in mind, it's time to delve deeper into the particulars of the most common devices found in today's networks: hubs, switches, and routers. The next section will give examples and more detail regarding how these devices are used.

Network Segmentation

It's very likely that at some point you'll have to break up one large network into a bunch of smaller ones because user response will have dwindled to a slow crawl as the network grew and grew. With all that growth, your LAN's traffic congestion will have reached epic proportions. So, now I'm going to show you how to use the segmentation devices I have defined so far in this chapter.

Here's a list of some of the nasty things that commonly cause LAN traffic congestion:

- Too many hosts in a broadcast domain
- Broadcast storms
- Multicasting
- Low bandwidth
- Adding hubs for connectivity to the network

The answer to fixing a huge but slow network is to break it up into a number of smaller networks—something called *network segmentation*. You do this by using devices like routers and switches, which are sometimes still referred to as bridges because switches still use bridging technologies. Figure 5.26 displays a network that's been segmented with a switch so each network segment connected to the switch is now a separate collision domain. But make note of the fact that this network is actually still one *broadcast domain*——the set of all devices on a network segment that hear all the broadcasts sent on that segment.

FIGURE 5.26   A switch can replace the hub, breaking up collision domains.

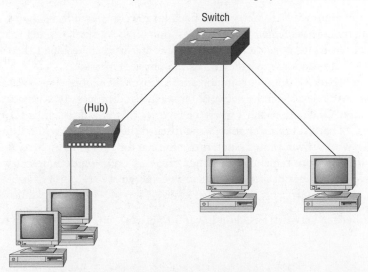

And keep in mind that the hub used in Figure 5.26 just extended the one collision domain from the switch port.

Routers are used to connect networks together and route packets of data from one network to another. (Cisco has become the de facto standard for routers because of its high-quality router products, great selection, and fantastic service.) Routers, by default, break up a broadcast domain. Figure 5.27 shows a router in our little network that creates an internetwork and breaks up broadcast domains.

FIGURE 5.27   Routers create an internetwork.

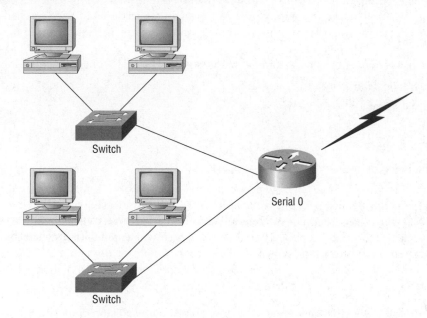

The network in Figure 5.27 is pretty cool. Each host is connected to its own collision domain, and the router has created two broadcast domains. And don't forget that the router provides connections to WAN services as well. The router uses something called a serial interface for WAN connections: specifically, a V.35 physical interface.

Breaking up a broadcast domain is important because when a host or server sends a network broadcast, every device on the network must read and process that broadcast—unless you've got a router. When the router's interface receives this broadcast, it can respond by basically saying, "Thanks, but no thanks," and discard the broadcast without forwarding it on to other networks. Even though routers are known for breaking up broadcast domains by default, it's important to remember that they break up collision domains as well.

There are two advantages of using routers in your network:

- They don't forward broadcasts by default.

- They can filter the network based on Layer 3 (Network layer) information (such as IP address).

Four router functions in your network can be listed as follows:

- Packet switching
- Packet filtering
- Internetwork communication
- Path selection

Remember that routers are really switches; they're actually what we call Layer 3 switches. Unlike Layer 2 switches, which forward or filter frames, routers (Layer 3 switches) use logical addressing and provide what is called *packet switching*. Routers can also provide packet filtering by using access lists; and when routers connect two or more networks together and use logical addressing (IP or IPv6), this is called an *internetwork*. Last, routers use a *routing table* (map of the internetwork) to make path selections and to forward packets to remote networks.

Conversely, switches aren't used to create internetworks (they do not break up broadcast domains by default); they're employed to add functionality to a network LAN. The main purpose of a switch is to make a LAN work better—to optimize its performance—providing more bandwidth for the LAN's users. And switches don't forward packets to other networks as routers do. Instead, they only "switch" frames from one port to another within the switched network. Okay, you may be thinking, "Wait a minute, what are frames and packets?" I'll tell you all about them later in this chapter, I promise.

By default, switches break up collision domains, as mentioned in Chapter 4, "The Current Ethernet Specifications." This is an Ethernet term used to describe a network scenario wherein one particular device sends a packet on a network segment, forcing every other device on that same segment to pay attention to it. At the same time, a different device tries to transmit, leading to a collision, after which both devices must retransmit, one at a time. Not very efficient! This situation is typically found in a hub environment where each host segment connects to a hub that represents only one collision domain and only one broadcast domain. By contrast, each and every port on a switch represents its own collision domain.

Switches create separate collision domains but a single broadcast domain. Routers provide a separate broadcast domain for each interface.

The term *bridging* was introduced before routers and hubs were implemented, so it's pretty common to hear people referring to bridges as switches. That's because bridges and switches basically do the same thing—break up collision domains on a LAN (in reality, you cannot buy a physical bridge these days, only LAN switches; but these switches use bridging technologies, so Cisco still calls them multiport bridges).

So this means a switch is basically just a multiple-port bridge with more brainpower, right? Well, pretty much, but there are differences. Switches do provide this function, but they do so with greatly enhanced management ability and features. Plus, most of the time, bridges only had two or four ports. Yes, you could get your hands on a bridge with up to 16 ports, but that's nothing compared to the hundreds available on some switches.

You would use a bridge in a network to reduce collisions within broadcast domains and to increase the number of collision domains in your network. Doing this provides more bandwidth for users. And keep in mind that using hubs in your network can contribute to congestion on your Ethernet network. As always, plan your network design carefully!

Figure 5.28 shows how a network would look with all these internetwork devices in place. Remember that the router will not only break up broadcast domains for every LAN interface but also break up collision domains.

FIGURE 5.28   Internetworking devices

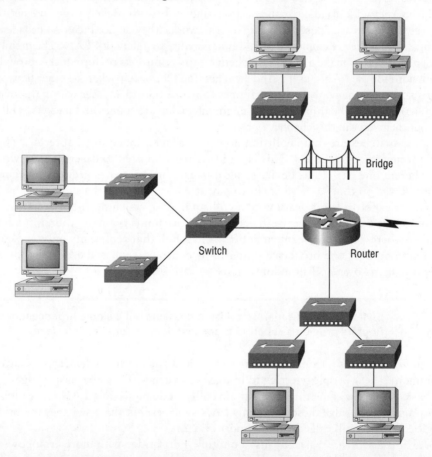

When you looked at Figure 5.28, did you notice that the router is found at center stage and that it connects each physical network together? We have to use this layout because of the older technologies involved—bridges and hubs.

On the top internetwork in Figure 5.28, you'll notice that a bridge is used to connect the hubs to a router. The bridge breaks up collision domains, but all the hosts connected to both hubs are still crammed into the same broadcast domain. Also, the bridge creates only two collision domains, so each device connected to a hub is in the same collision domain as every other device connected to that same hub. This is actually pretty lame, but it's still better than having one collision domain for all hosts.

Notice something else: The three hubs at the bottom that are connected also connect to the router, creating one collision domain and one broadcast domain. This makes the bridged network look much better indeed.

 Although bridges/switches are used to segment networks, they will not isolate broadcast or multicast packets.

The best network connected to the router is the LAN switch network on the left. Why? Because each port on that switch breaks up collision domains. But it's not all good—all devices are still in the same broadcast domain. Do you remember why this can be a really bad thing? Because all devices must listen to all broadcasts transmitted, that's why. And if your broadcast domains are too large, the users have less bandwidth and are required to process more broadcasts, and network response time will slow to a level that could cause office riots.

Once we have only switches in our network, things change a lot. Figure 5.29 shows the network that is typically found today.

FIGURE 5.29   Switched networks creating an internetwork

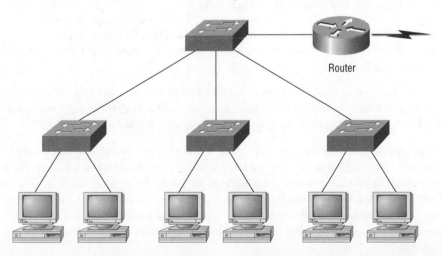

Okay, here I've placed the LAN switches at the center of the network world so the router is connecting only logical networks together. If I implement this kind of setup, I've created virtual LANs (VLANs), something I'm going to tell you about in Chapter 11. So don't stress. But it is really important to understand that even though you have a switched network, you still need a router to provide your inter-VLAN communication, or internetworking. Don't forget that.

Obviously, the best network is one that's correctly configured to meet the business requirements of the company it serves. LAN switches with routers, correctly placed in the network, are the best network design. This book will help you understand the basics of routers and switches so you can make tight, informed decisions on a case-by-case basis.

Let's go back to Figure 5.28 again. Looking at the figure, how many collision domains and broadcast domains are in this internetwork? I hope you answered nine collision domains and three broadcast domains.

The broadcast domains are definitely the easiest to see because only routers break up broadcast domains by default. And because there are three connections, that gives you three broadcast domains. But do you see the nine collision domains? Just in case that's a no, I'll explain. The all-hub network is one collision domain; the bridge network equals three collision domains. Add in the switch network of five collision domains—one for each switch port—and you've got a total of nine.

Now, in Figure 5.29, each port on the switch is a separate collision domain and each VLAN is a separate broadcast domain. But you still need a router for routing between VLANs. How many collision domains do you see here? I'm counting 10—remember that connections between the switches are considered a collision domain.

 Real World Scenario

Should I Replace All My Hubs with Switches?

You're a network administrator at a large company in San Jose. The boss comes to you and says that he got your requisition to buy a switch and is not sure about approving the expense; do you really need it?

Well, if you can, sure—why not? Switches really add a lot of functionality to a network that hubs just don't have. But most of us don't have an unlimited budget. Hubs still can create a nice network—that is, of course, if you design and implement the network correctly.

Let's say that you have 40 users plugged into four hubs, 10 users each. At this point, the hubs are all connected together so that you have one large collision domain and one large broadcast domain. If you can afford to buy just one switch and plug each hub into a switch port, as well as plug the servers into the switch, then you now have four collision domains and one broadcast domain. Not great; but for the price of one switch, your network is a much better thing. So, go ahead! Put that requisition in to buy all new switches. What do you have to lose?

So now that you've gotten an introduction to internetworking and the various devices that live in an internetwork, it's time to head into internetworking models.

As I mentioned earlier, routers break up broadcast domains, which means that by default, broadcasts aren't forwarded through a router. Do you remember why this is a good thing? Routers break up collision domains, but you can also do that using Layer 2 (Data Link layer) switches. Because each interface in a router represents a separate network, it must be assigned unique network identification numbers, and each host on the network connected to that router must use the same network number. Figure 5.30 shows how a router works in an internetwork.

FIGURE 5.30   A router in an internetwork

Here are some points about routers that you should commit to memory:

- Routers, by default, will not forward any broadcast or multicast packets.

- Routers use the logical address in a Network-layer header to determine the next hop router to forward the packet to.

- Routers can use access lists, created by an administrator, to control security on the types of packets that are allowed to enter or exit an interface.

- Routers can provide Layer 2 bridging functions if needed and can simultaneously route through the same interface.

- Layer 3 devices (routers, in this case) provide connections between virtual LANs (VLANs).

- Routers can provide quality of service (QoS) for specific types of network traffic.

Switching and VLANs and are covered in Chapter 11.

Switches and Bridges at the Data Link Layer

Layer 2 switching is considered hardware-based bridging because it uses specialized hardware called an *application-specific integrated circuit (ASIC)*. ASICs can run up to gigabit speeds with very low latency rates.

Latency is the time measured from when a frame enters a port to the time it exits a port.

Bridges and switches read each frame as it passes through the network. The Layer 2 device then puts the source hardware address in a filter table and keeps track of which port the frame was received on. This information (logged in the bridge's or switch's filter table) is what helps the machine determine the location of the specific sending device. Figure 5.31 shows a switch in an internetwork.

FIGURE 5.31   A switch in an internetwork

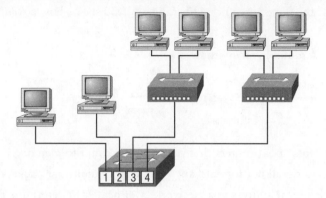

Each segment has its own collision domain.
All segments are in the same broadcast domain.

The real-estate business is all about location, location, location, and it's the same way for both Layer 2 and Layer 3 devices. Although both need to be able to negotiate the network, it's crucial to remember that they're concerned with very different parts of it. Primarily, Layer 3 machines (such as routers) need to locate specific networks, whereas Layer 2 machines (switches and bridges) need to eventually locate specific devices. So, networks are to routers as individual devices are to switches and bridges. And routing tables that "map" the internetwork are for routers as filter tables that "map" individual devices are for switches and bridges.

After a filter table is built on the Layer 2 device, it will forward frames only to the segment where the destination hardware address is located. If the destination device is on the same segment as the frame, the Layer 2 device will block the frame from going to any other segments. If the destination is on a different segment, the frame can be transmitted only to that segment. This is called *transparent bridging*.

When a switch interface receives a frame with a destination hardware address that isn't found in the device's filter table, it will forward the frame to all connected segments. If the unknown device that was sent the "mystery frame" replies to this forwarding action, the switch updates its filter table regarding that device's location. But in the event that the destination address of the transmitting frame is a broadcast address, the switch will forward all broadcasts to every connected segment by default.

All devices that the broadcast is forwarded to are considered to be in the same broadcast domain. This can be a problem; Layer 2 devices propagate Layer 2 broadcast storms that choke performance, and the only way to stop a broadcast storm from propagating through an internetwork is with a Layer 3 device—a router.

The biggest benefit of using switches instead of hubs in your internetwork is that each switch port is actually its own collision domain. (Conversely, a hub creates one large collision domain.) But even armed with a switch, you still can't break up broadcast domains. Neither switches nor bridges will do that. They'll typically simply forward all broadcasts instead.

Another benefit of LAN switching over hub-centered implementations is that each device on every segment plugged into a switch can transmit simultaneously—at least, they can as long as there is only one host on each port and a hub isn't plugged into a switch port. As you might have guessed, hubs allow only one device per network segment to communicate at a time.

Hubs at the Physical Layer

As you know, a hub is really a multiple-port repeater. A repeater receives a digital signal and reamplifies or regenerates that signal and then forwards the digital signal out all active ports without looking at any data. An active hub does the same thing. Any digital signal received from a segment on a hub port is regenerated or reamplified and transmitted out all ports on the hub. This means all devices plugged into a hub are in the same collision domain as well as in the same broadcast domain. Figure 5.32 shows a hub in a network.

FIGURE 5.32   A hub in a network

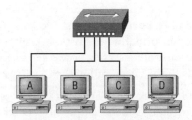

All devices in the same collision domain
All devices in the same broadcast domain
Devices share the same bandwidth.

Hubs, like repeaters, don't examine any of the traffic as it enters and is then transmitted out to the other parts of the physical media. Every device connected to the hub, or hubs, must listen if a device transmits. A physical star network—where the hub is a central device and cables extend in all directions out from it—is the type of topology a hub creates. Visually, the design really does resemble a star, whereas Ethernet networks run a logical bus topology, meaning that the signal has to run through the network from end to end.

Hubs and repeaters can be used to enlarge the area covered by a single LAN segment, although I do not recommend this. LAN switches and/or wireless APs are affordable for almost every situation.

Summary

Whew, this chapter covered quite a bit of information. In this chapter, you learned the difference between a router, a switch (bridge), and a hub and when to use each one. I also covered some devices that you might find in a network today, but not as often, such as a repeater modem and media convertors.

The information I discussed about DNS and DHCP is critical to your success on the Network+ objectives, and I highly suggest that you reread those sections. I covered how both the DNS and DHCP services works on a network.

In addition to the most common devices, I discussed the specialized network devices mentioned in the Network+ objectives. I finished the chapter by discussing collision and broadcast domains in detail as well as how you would use a router, switch, and hub in your networks today.

All of the information in this chapter is fundamental, and you must understand it before moving on to the other chapters in this book.

Exam Essentials

Understand how DHCP works and its purpose.   Dynamic Host Configuration Protocol (DHCP) provides IP configuration information to hosts. It is important to know how a DHCP client requests information from a server, how a server receives this information, and also how the server responds to the client and with what type of information.

Understand how DNS works and its purpose.   Domain Name Service (DNS) is used to resolve human names to binary format. Understanding how DNS resolves these names is critical, as is understanding how a DNS query is sent and how a DNS server responds.

Understand the difference between a hub, a switch (bridge), and a router.   A hub just connects network segments together. A switch/bridge segments the network using MAC addresses, and a router segments the network using logical addressing (IP and IPv6).

Remember the different names for a router   A router is a layer-3 hardware device, but can also be called a layer-3 switch, or a multilayer switch.

Remember the various devices used on networks today and when you would use each one and how.   Understand the differences and how each device works: hubs, repeaters, modems, NICs, media convertors, WAPs, switches, routers, and DHCP.

Understand what IDS and IPS is and what each one does   IDS only identifies, detects, and reports attempts of unauthorized access to the network as well as any suspicious activity, and is the best software type that would be best for identifying an attack. However, if you want to stop the attack in its track you need to add an IPS device. An Intrusion Prevention System (IPS) provides computers with security by vigilantly watching for any suspicious and potentially malicious tactics and prevents these evil activities. Unlike IDS, IPS will identify and possibly shut down a port or drop certain type of packets.

Identify the purpose, benefits, and characteristics of using a proxy service.   A proxy server keeps a LAN somewhat separated from the Internet. Doing so increases security and filtering control and has the tendency to speed up Internet access through caching of recently used web pages.

Written Lab

Complete the table by filling in the appropriate layer of the OSI or hub, switch, or router device.

Description	Device or OSI Layer
This device sends and receives information about the Network layer.	
This layer creates a virtual circuit before transmitting between two end stations.	
A layer-3 switch or multilayer switch	
This device uses hardware addresses to filter a network.	
Ethernet is defined at these layers.	
This layer supports flow control and sequencing.	
This device can measure the distance to a remote network.	
Logical addressing is used at this layer.	
Hardware addresses are defined at this layer.	
This device creates one big collision domain and one large broadcast domain.	
This device creates many smaller collision domains, but the network is still one large broadcast domain.	
This device can never run full duplex.	
This device breaks up collision domains and broadcast domains.	

(The answers to the Written Lab can be found following the answers to the Review Questions for this chapter.)

Review Questions

1. Which is not a common term associated with modems?
    A. POTS
    B. DSL
    C. Cable
    D. NIC

2. What advantage does a switch have over a hub?
    A. It discards frames.
    B. Transmissions received on one port will be sent out all the other ports.
    C. It recognizes frame boundaries and destination MAC addresses of incoming frames.
    D. Any two or more devices the switch connects have the capability of causing a collision with each other.

3. Which device is used to segment a network?
    A. Hub
    B. Switch
    C. Repeater
    D. All of the above

4. What is the primary function of a bridge?
    A. Breaks up collision domains
    B. Allows a NIC or other networking device to connect to a different type of media than it was designed for
    C. Allows mobile users to connect to a wired network wirelessly
    D. None of the above

5. A network device that is used to connect multiple devices together without segmenting a network is a?
    A. Hub
    B. Wireless access point
    C. Switch
    D. Router

6. What is the function of a firewall?
    A. Protects LAN resources from attackers on the Internet
    B. Provides extra bandwidth
    C. Reduces throughput
    D. Allows access to all computers on a LAN

7. Which of the following devices can work at both Layers 2 and 3 of the OSI model?

    A. Hub

    (B) Switch

    C. Repeater

    D. Bridge

8. What is an advantage of using DHCP in a network environment?

    A. More difficult administration of the network

    B. Static IP addressing

    C. Can send an operating system for the PC to boot from

    (D) Assigns IP address to hosts

9. What is a benefit of a multilayer switch (MLS) over a Layer 2 switch?

    A. Less bandwidth

    (B) Routing functions

    C. Fewer features

    D. Fewer ports

10. Which device should be used if you need to send incoming packets to one or more machines that are hidden behind a single IP address?

    A. Switch

    B. Load balancer

    C. Hub

    D. Repeater

11. What role does the "A" record in a Domain Name Service (DNS) server have in your network?

    (A) Translates human name to IP address

    B. Translates IP address to human name

    C. Enables printing, copying, and faxing from one device

    D. Controls network packets to optimize performance

12. Which device does not aid in network segmentation?

    A. Router

    B. Switch

    (C.) Hub

    D. Bridge

13. What is the most common use for a web proxy?

    A. Web cache

    B. Increases throughput

    C. Provides administrative control

    D. Supports user authentication

14. Which is not an advantage of network segmentation?

    A. Reduced congestion

    B. Improved security

    C. Containing network problems

    D. Preventing broadcast storms

15. Users arrive at the office after a weekend and the hosts that were shut down over the weekend are restarted but cannot access the LAN or Internet. Hosts that were not shut down are working fine. Where can the problem be?

    A. The DNS server

    B. The DHCP server

    C. The Proxy server

    D. The Firewall

16. You need a device that detects and reports attempts of unauthorized access to your network, identifies suspicious activity, and is best for identifying an attack. Which device should you install?

    A. Firewall

    B. IDS

    C. IPS

    D. Proxy server

17. Which device creates separate collision domains and a single broadcast domain?

    A. Hub

    B. Router

    C. Switch

    D. Modem

18. Which device by default does not forward any broadcast or multicast packets?

    A. Repeater

    B. Hub

    C. Router

    D. Switch

19. Which type of server in your network uses pointer and A records?

   A. NAT Translation server

   B. IPS/IDS Server

   C. DNS Server

   D. Proxy Server

20. Users on your network are saturating your bandwidth because they are using too many nonwork related sites. What device would limit the availability of the types of sites that users on a LAN have access to while providing granular control over the traffic between the local LAN and the Internet?

   A. Switch

   B. DHCP server

   C. DNS server

   D. Proxy server

Answers to Review Questions

1. D. A modem is a device that modulates digital data onto an analog carrier for transmission over an analog medium and then demodulates from the analog carrier to a digital signal again at the receiving end. Therefore, traditional (POTS), DSL, and cable are all common types of modems. The NIC is the expansion card you install in your computer to connect, or interface, your computer to the network.

2. C. Like a hub, a switch connects multiple segments of a network together, with one important difference. Whereas a hub sends out anything it receives on one port to all the others, a switch recognizes frame boundaries and pays attention to the destination MAC address of the incoming frame as well as the port on which it was received.

3. B. Hubs don't segment a network; they just connect network segments together. Repeaters don't segment the network; they repeat a signal and allow the distance covered to be increased. So the only correct option is B, a switch.

4. A. The primary function of a bridge is to keep traffic separated on both sides of the bridge, breaking up collision domains.

5. A. Hubs create one collision domain and one broadcast domain.

6. A. Firewalls are the first line of defense for an Internet-connected network. If a network was directly connected to the Internet without a firewall, an attacker could theoretically gain direct access to the computers and servers on that network with little effort.

7. B. A switch is typically just a Layer 2 device segmenting the network by using MAC addresses. However, some higher-end switches can provide Layer 3 services.

8. D. Remember that DHCP servers assign IP addresses to hosts. Thus DHCP allows easier administration than providing IP information to each host by hand (called static IP addressing).

9. B. Multilayer switches (also called layer-3 switches) don't have any fewer features, less bandwidth, or fewer ports than a normal switch; they just allow routing functions between subnets.

10. B. A load balancer uses a little trickery and sends incoming packets to one or more machines that are hidden behind a single IP address. Modern load-balancing routers can use different rules to make decisions about where to route traffic, which can be based on least load, fastest response times, or simply balancing requests.

11. A. DNS translates human names to IP addresses for routing your packet through the Internet. Hosts can receive the IP address of this DNS server and then resolve host names to IP addresses.

12. C. Routers, switches, and bridges are all devices that help break up big networks into a number of smaller ones—also known as network segmentation. Hubs don't segment networks—they just connect network segments together.

13. A. Web cache, of course! Most proxy programs provide a means to deny access to certain URLs in a blacklist, thus providing content filtering, usually in corporate environments.

14. D. Options A, B, and C all aid in boosting network performance, so the only option left is broadcast storms. Increased traffic will increase LAN congestion.

15. B. If the DHCP server has stopped functioning, it will not hand out IP addresses to hosts that are restarted. However, the hosts that were not shut down still have an IP addresses because the lease time has not expired.

16. B. An IDS device can detect and report suspicious activity, but unlike an IPS, it does not stop attacks. IDS is best for identifying an attack.

17. C. Switches create separate collision domains but a single broadcast domain. Remember that routers provide a separate broadcast domain for each interface.

18. C. Routers don't forward any broadcast or multicast packets by default, but they do have plenty of other functions like using the logical address, using access lists, and providing Layer 2 bridging functions.

19. C. A DNS server uses many types of records. An "A" record is a hostname to IP address record and a pointer record is an IP address to hostname record.

20. D. A proxy server can provide many functions. A proxy server can use a caching engine so repeated access request for web information would accelerate repeated access for users, and they can also limit the availability of web sites.

Answers to Written Lab

Complete the table by filling in the appropriate layer of the OSI or hub, switch, or router device.

Description	Device or OSI Layer
This device sends and receives information about the Network layer.	Router
This layer creates a virtual circuit before transmitting between two end stations.	Transport
A layer-3 switch, or multilayer switch	Router
This device uses hardware addresses to filter a network.	Bridge or switch
Ethernet is defined at these layers.	Data Link and Physical
This layer supports flow control and sequencing.	Transport
This device can measure the distance to a remote network.	Router
Logical addressing is used at this layer.	Network
Hardware addresses are defined at this layer.	Data Link (MAC sublayer)
This device creates one big collision domain and one large broadcast domain.	Hub
This device creates many smaller collision domains, but the network is still one large broadcast domain.	Switch or bridge
This device can never run full duplex	Hub
This device breaks up collision domains and broadcast domains.	Router

Chapter

6

Introduction to Internet Protocol (IP)

THE FOLLOWING COMPTIA NETWORK+ EXAM OBJECTIVES ARE COVERED IN THIS CHAPTER:

✓ **1.1 Explain the function of common networking protocols**

- TCP
- FTP
- UDP
- TCP/IP suite
- DHCP
- TFTP
- DNS
- HTTP(S)
- ARP
- SIP (VoIP)
- RTP (VoIP)
- SSH
- POP3
- NTP
- IMAP4
- TELNET
- SMTP
- SMNP2/3
- ICMP
- IGMP
- TLS

✓ **1.2 Identify commonly used TCP and UDP default ports**

- TCP ports
    - FTP – 20, 21
    - SSH – 22
    - TELNET – 23
    - SMTP – 25
    - DNS – 53
    - HTTP – 80
    - POP3 – 110
    - NTP – 123
    - IMAP4 – 143
    - HTTPS – 443
- UDP ports
    - TFTP – 69
    - DNS – 53
    - BOOTPS/DHCP – 67
    - SNMP – 161

✓ **1.4 Given a scenario, evaluate the proper use of the following addressing technologies and addressing schemes**

- DHCP (static, dynamic APIPA)

The *Transmission Control Protocol/Internet Protocol (TCP/IP)* suite was created by the Department of Defense (DoD) to ensure and preserve data integrity, as well as to maintain communications in the event of catastrophic war. So it follows that if designed and implemented correctly, a TCP/IP network can truly be a solid, dependable, and resilient network solution. In this chapter, I'll cover the protocols of TCP/IP.

I'll begin by covering the DoD's version of TCP/IP and then compare this version and its protocols with the OSI reference model discussed in Chapter 2, "The Open Systems Interconnection Specifications."

After going over the various protocols found at each layer of the DoD model, I'll finish the chapter by providing a more detailed explanation of data encapsulation that I started in Chapter 2.

For up-to-the-minute updates for this chapter, please see www.lammle.com or www.sybex.com/go/comptianetwork+studyguide.

Introducing TCP/IP

Because TCP/IP is so central to working with the Internet and intranets, it's essential for you to understand it in detail. I'll begin by giving you some background on TCP/IP and how it came about, and then move on to describing the important technical goals defined by the original designers. After that, you'll find out how TCP/IP compares to a theoretical model—the Open Systems Interconnection (OSI) model.

A Brief History of TCP/IP

The very first Request for Comments (RFC) was published in April 1969, which paved the way for today's Internet and its protocols. Each of these protocols is specified in the multitude of RFCs, which are observed, maintained, sanctioned, filed, and stored by the Internet Engineering Task Force (IETF).

TCP/IP first came on the scene in 1973. Later, in 1978, it was divided into two distinct protocols: TCP and IP. Then, back in 1983, TCP/IP replaced the Network Control Protocol

(NCP) and was authorized as the official means of data transport for anything connecting to ARPAnet, the Internet's ancestor that was created by ARPA, the DoD's Advanced Research Projects Agency way back in 1957 in reaction to the Soviet's launching of Sputnik. ARPA was soon re-dubbed DARPA, and it was divided into ARPAnet and MILNET (also in 1983); both were finally dissolved in 1990.

But contrary to what you might think, most of the development work on TCP/IP happened at UC Berkeley in Northern California, where a group of scientists were simultaneously working on the Berkeley version of UNIX, which soon became known as the BSD, or Berkeley Software Distribution series of UNIX versions. Of course, because TCP/IP worked so well, it was packaged into subsequent releases of BSD UNIX and offered to other universities and institutions if they bought the distribution tape. So basically, BSD UNIX bundled with TCP/IP began as shareware in the world of academia, and as a result, became the basis of the huge success and exponential growth of today's Internet as well as smaller, private and corporate intranets.

As usual, what may have started as a small group of TCP/IP aficionados evolved, and as it did, the U.S. government created a program to test any new published standards and make sure they passed certain criteria. This was to protect TCP/IP's integrity and to ensure that no developer changed anything too dramatically or added any proprietary features. It's this very quality—this open-systems approach to the TCP/IP family of protocols—that pretty much sealed its popularity, because it guarantees a solid connection between myriad hardware and software platforms with no strings attached.

TCP/IP and the DoD Model

The DoD model is basically a condensed version of the OSI model—it's composed of four, instead of seven, layers:

- Process/Application layer
- Host-to-Host layer
- Internet layer
- Network Access layer

Figure 6.1 shows a comparison of the DoD model and the OSI reference model. As you can see, the two are similar in concept, but each has a different number of layers with different names.

When the different protocols in the IP stack are discussed, the layers of the OSI and DoD models are interchangeable. In other words, the Internet layer and the Network layer describe the same thing, as do the Host-to-Host layer and the Transport layer. The other two layers of the DoD model are composed of multiple layers of the OSI model.

A vast array of protocols combine at the DoD model's *Process/Application layer* to integrate the various activities and duties spanning the focus of the OSI's corresponding top three layers (Application, Presentation, and Session). We'll be looking closely at those protocols in the next part of this chapter. The Process/Application layer defines protocols for node-to-node application communication and also controls user-interface specifications.

FIGURE 6.1   The DoD and OSI models

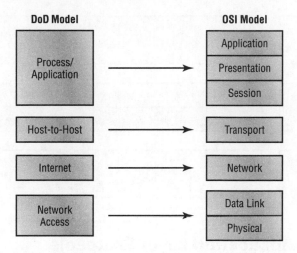

The *Host-to-Host layer* parallels the functions of the OSI's Transport layer, defining protocols for setting up the level of transmission service for applications. It tackles issues such as creating reliable end-to-end communication and ensuring the error-free delivery of data. It handles packet sequencing and maintains data integrity.

The *Internet layer* corresponds to the OSI's Network layer, designating the protocols relating to the logical transmission of packets over the entire network. It takes care of the addressing of hosts by giving them an IP address, and it handles the routing of packets among multiple networks.

At the bottom of the DoD model, the *Network Access layer* monitors the data exchange between the host and the network. The equivalent of the Data Link and Physical layers of the OSI model, the Network Access layer oversees hardware addressing and defines protocols for the physical transmission of data.

The DoD and OSI models are alike in design and concept and have similar functions in similar layers. Figure 6.2 shows the TCP/IP protocol suite and how its protocols relate to the DoD model layers.

In the following sections, we'll look at the different protocols in more detail, starting with the Process/Application layer protocols.

FIGURE 6.2   The TCP/IP protocol suite

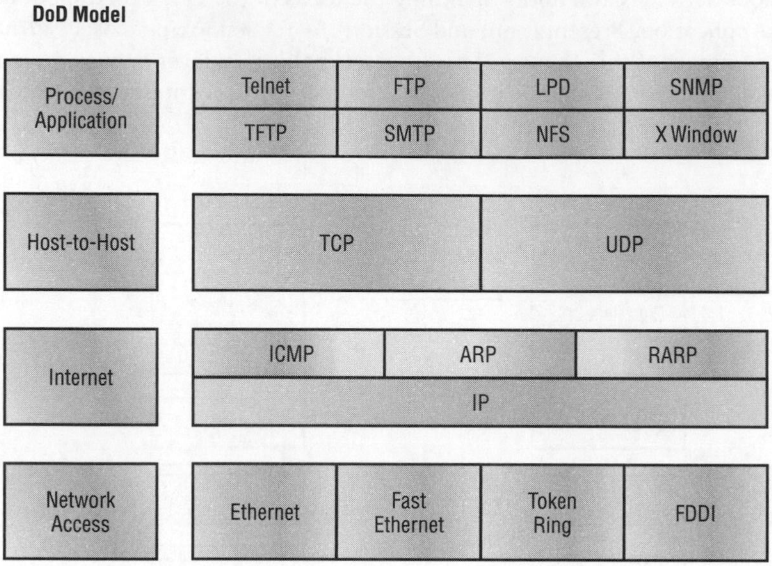

DoD Model

| Process/ Application | Telnet | FTP | LPD | SNMP |
| | TFTP | SMTP | NFS | X Window |

| Host-to-Host | TCP | | UDP | |

| Internet | ICMP | ARP | | RARP |
| | IP | | | |

| Network Access | Ethernet | Fast Ethernet | Token Ring | FDDI |

The Process/Application Layer Protocols

In this section, I'll describe the different applications and services typically used in IP networks.

Telnet

Telnet is the chameleon of protocols—its specialty is terminal emulation. It allows a user on a remote client machine, called the Telnet client, to access the resources of another machine, the Telnet server. Telnet achieves this by pulling a fast one on the Telnet server and making the client machine appear as though it were a terminal directly attached to the local network. This projection is actually a software shell—a virtual terminal that can interact with the chosen remote host.

These emulated terminals are of the text-mode type and can execute refined procedures such as displaying menus that give users the opportunity to choose options and access the applications on the duped server. Users begin a Telnet session by running the Telnet client software and then logging into the Telnet server.

Telnet offers no security or encryption and is being replaced by Secure Shell (SSH) when security across the remote-configuration session is needed or desired.

File Transfer Protocol (FTP)

File Transfer Protocol (FTP) is the protocol that actually lets you transfer files across an IP network, and it can accomplish this between any two machines using it. But FTP isn't just a protocol; it's also a program. Operating as a protocol, FTP is used by applications. As a program, it's employed by users to perform file tasks by hand. FTP also allows for access to both directories and files and can accomplish certain types of directory operations, such as relocating files into different directories. FTP can team up with Telnet to transparently log you into the FTP server and then provides for the transfer of files.

Accessing a host through FTP is only the first step, though. Users must then be subjected to an authentication login that's probably secured with passwords and usernames implemented by system administrators to restrict access. You can get around this somewhat by adopting the username *anonymous*—although what you'll gain access to will be limited.

Even when employed by users manually as a program, FTP's functions are limited to listing and manipulating directories, typing file contents, and copying files between hosts. It can't execute remote files as programs.

Secure File Transfer Protocol (SFTP)

Secure File Transfer Protocol (SFTP) is used when you need to transfer files over an encrypted connection. It uses an SSH session (more on this later), which encrypts the connection. Apart from the secure part, it's used just as FTP is—for transferring files between computers on an IP network, such as the Internet.

Trivial File Transfer Protocol (TFTP)

Trivial File Transfer Protocol (TFTP) is the stripped-down, stock version of FTP, but it's the protocol of choice if you know exactly what you want and where to find it—plus it's easy to use, and it's fast too! It doesn't give you the abundance of functions that FTP does, though. TFTP has no directory-browsing abilities; it can do nothing but send and receive files. This compact little protocol also skimps in the data department, sending much smaller blocks of data than FTP; and there's no authentication as with FTP, so it's insecure. Few sites support it because of the inherent security risks.

 Real World Scenario

When Should You Use FTP?

The folks at your San Francisco office need a 50MB file emailed to them right away. What do you do? Most email servers would reject the email because they have size limits. Even if there's no size limit on the server, it would still take a while to send this big file. FTP to the rescue!

If you need to give someone a large file or you need to get a large file from someone, FTP is a nice choice. Smaller files (less than 5MB) can be sent via email if you have the bandwidth of DSL or a cable modem. However, most ISPs don't allow files larger then 5MB to be emailed; so FTP is an option you should consider if you need to send and receive large files, even if they're compressed. (Who doesn't, these days?) To use FTP, you'll need to set up an FTP server on the Internet so that the files can be shared.

Besides, FTP is faster than email, which is another reason to use FTP for sending or receiving large files. In addition, because it uses TCP and is connection-oriented, if the session dies, FTP can sometimes start up where it left off. Try that with your email client!

Network File System (NFS)

Network File System (NFS) is a jewel of a protocol specializing in file sharing. It allows two different types of file systems to interoperate. It works like this: Suppose the NFS server software is running on an NT server and the NFS client software is running on a UNIX host. NFS allows for a portion of the RAM on the NT server to transparently store UNIX files, which can, in turn, be used by UNIX users. Even though the NT file system and UNIX file system are unalike—they have different case sensitivity, filename lengths, security, and so on—both UNIX users and NT users can access that same file with their normal file systems, in their normal way.

Simple Mail Transfer Protocol (SMTP)

Simple Mail Transfer Protocol (SMTP), answering our ubiquitous call to email, uses a spooled, or queued, method of mail delivery. Once a message has been sent to a destination, the message is spooled to a device—usually a disk. The server software at the destination posts a vigil, regularly checking the queue for messages. When it detects them, it proceeds to deliver them to their destination. SMTP is used to send mail; POP3 is used to receive mail.

Post Office Protocol (POP)

Post Office Protocol (POP) gives us a storage facility for incoming mail, and the latest version is called POP3 (sound familiar?). Basically, how this protocol works is when a client device connects to a POP3 server, messages addressed to that client are released for downloading. It doesn't allow messages to be downloaded selectively; but once they are, the client/server interaction ends and you can delete and tweak your messages locally at will. Lately we're seeing a newer standard, IMAP, being used more and more in place of POP3. Why?

Internet Message Access Protocol, Version 4 (IMAP4)

Because Internet Message Access Protocol (IMAP) makes it so you get control over how you download your mail, with it, you also gain some much-needed security. It lets you peek at the message header or download just a part of a message—you can now just nibble at the bait instead of swallowing it whole and then choking on the hook hidden inside!

With it, you can choose to store messages on the email server hierarchically, and link to documents and user groups too. IMAP even gives you search commands to use to hunt for messages based on their subject, header, or content. As you can imagine, it has some serious authentication features—it actually supports the Kerberos authentication scheme that MIT developed. And yes, IMAP4 is the current version.

Transport Layer Security (TLS)

Both Transport Layer Security (TLS) and its forerunner, Secure Sockets Layer (SSL), are cryptographic protocols that come in really handy for enabling secure online data-transfer activities like browsing the Web, instant messaging, internet faxing, and so on. They're so similar it's not within the scope of this book to detail the differences between them.

SIP (VoIP)

Session Initiation Protocol (SIP) is a hugely popular signaling protocol used to construct and deconstruct multimedia communication sessions for many things like voice and video calls, video conferencing, streaming multimedia distribution, instant messaging, presence information, and online games over the Internet.

RTP (VoIP)

Real-time Transport Protocol (RTP) describes a packet-formatting standard for delivering audio and video over the Internet. Although initially designed as a multicast protocol, it's now used for unicast applications too. It's commonly employed for streaming media, video-conferencing, and push-to-talk systems—all things that make it a de-facto standard in Voice over IP industries.

Line Printer Daemon (LPD)

The Line Printer Daemon (LPD) protocol is designed for printer sharing. The LPD, along with the Line Printer (LPR) program, allows print jobs to be spooled and sent to the network's printers using TCP/IP.

X Window

Designed for client/server operations, *X Window* defines a protocol for writing client/server applications based on a graphical user interface (GUI). The idea is to allow a program, called a client, to run on one computer and have it display things through a window server on another computer.

Simple Network Management Protocol (SNMP)

Simple Network Management Protocol (SNMP) collects and manipulates valuable network information. It gathers data by polling the devices on the network from a management station at fixed or random intervals, requiring them to disclose certain information. When all is well, SNMP receives something called a *baseline*—a report delimiting the operational traits of a healthy network. This protocol can also stand as a watchdog over the network, quickly notifying managers of any sudden turn of events. These network watchdogs are called *agents*, and when aberrations occur, agents send an alert called a *trap* to the management station. In addition, SNMP can help simplify the process of setting up a network as well as the administration of your entire internetwork.

Secure Shell (SSH)

Secure Shell (SSH) protocol sets up a secure Telnet session over a standard TCP/IP connection and is employed for doing things like logging into other systems, running programs on remote systems, and moving files from one system to another. And it does all of this while maintaining a nice, strong, encrypted connection. You can think of it as the new-generation protocol that's now used in place of `rsh` and `rlogin`—even Telnet.

> ### SNMP versions 1, 2, and 3
>
> SNMP versions 1 and 2 are pretty much obsolete. This doesn't mean you won't see them in a network at some time, but v1 is super old and, well, obsolete. SNMPv2 provided improvements, especially in security and performance. But one of the best additions was what was called "GETBULK", which allowed a host to retrieve a large amount of data at once. However, v2 never really caught on in the networking world. SNMPv3 is now the standard and uses both TCP and UDP, unlike v1, which used only UDP. V3 added even more security and message integrity, authentication, and encryption. So, be careful when running SNMPv1 and v2 as they are susceptible to a packet sniffer reading the data.

Hypertext Transfer Protocol (HTTP)

All those snappy websites comprising a mélange of graphics, text, links, and so on—the Hypertext Transfer Protocol (HTTP) is making it all possible. It's used to manage communications between web browsers and web servers and opens the right resource when you click a link, wherever that resource may actually reside.

Hypertext Transfer Protocol Secure (HTTPS)

The Hypertext Transfer Protocol Secure (HTTPS) is also known as Secure Hypertext Transfer Protocol. Sometimes you'll see it referred to as SHTTP or S-HTTP, but no matter—as indicated, it's a secure version of HTTP that arms you with a whole bunch of security tools for keeping transactions between a web browser and a server secure. It's what your browser needs to fill out forms, sign in, authenticate, and encrypt an HTTP message when you make a reservation or buy something online.

 Both SSH (port 22) and HTTPS (port 443) is used to encrypt packets over your intranet and the internet.

Network Time Protocol (NTP)

Kudos to Professor David Mills of the University of Delaware for coming up with this handy protocol that's used to synchronize the clocks on our computers to one standard time source (typically, an atomic clock). Network Time Protocol (NTP) works in conjunction with other synchronization utilities to ensure all computers on a given network agree on the time. This may sound pretty simple, but it's very important because so many of the transactions done today are time- and date-stamped. Think about your precious databases, for one. It can mess up a server pretty badly if it's out of sync with the machines connected to it, even by mere seconds (think crash!). You can't have a transaction entered by a machine at, say, 1:50 a.m., when the server records that transaction as having occurred at 1:45 a.m. So basically, NTP works to prevent "back to the future sans DeLorean" from bringing down the network—very important indeed!

The Requests for Comments (RFCs) form a series of notes, started in 1969, about the Internet (originally the ARPAnet). The notes discuss many aspects of computer communication; they focus on networking protocols, procedures, programs, and concepts but also include meeting notes, opinion, and sometimes humor. You can find the RFCs by visiting www.iana.org.

Network News Transfer Protocol (NNTP)

Network News Transfer Protocol (NNTP) is how you access the Usenet news servers that hold the legion of specific message boards called *newsgroups*. As you likely know, these groups represent pretty much any special interest humans have under the sun. For instance, if you happen to be a classic car buff or a WWII aircraft enthusiast, odds are good there're lots of newsgroups available to join based upon those interests. NNTP is specified in RFC 977. And because it's complicated to configure a news reader program, lots of websites—even search engines—are the entities we usually depend upon to access these many and varied resources.

Secure Copy Protocol (SCP)

FTP is great. It's a super easy, user-friendly way to transfer files—if you don't need to transfer those files securely. That's because when you use FTP for transferring data, usernames and passwords get sent right along with the file request in the clear for all to see with no encryption whatsoever! Kind of like Hail Mary passes, you basically just throw them out there and hope your information doesn't fall into the wrong hands and get intercepted.

That's where Secure Copy Protocol (SCP) comes to your rescue—its whole purpose is to protect your precious files. Through SSH, it first establishes and then sustains a secure, encrypted connection between the sending and receiving hosts until file transfer is complete. When armed with SCP, your Hail Mary pass can be caught only by your intended receiver—snap! In today's networks, however, the more robust SFTP is used more commonly than SCP.

Lightweight Directory Access Protocol (LDAP)

If you're the system administrator of any decent-sized network, odds are you've got a type of directory in place that keeps track of all your network resources, such as devices and users. But how do you access those directories? Through the Lightweight Directory Access Protocol (LDAP), that's how. This protocol standardizes how you access directories, and its first and second inceptions are described in RFCs 1487 and 1777, respectively. There were a few glitches in those two earlier versions, so a third version—the one most commonly used today—was created to address those issues, and is described in RFC 3377.

Internet Group Management Protocol (IGMP)

Internet Group Management Protocol (IGMP) is the TCP/IP protocol used for managing IP multicast sessions. It accomplishes this by sending out unique IGMP messages over the network to reveal the multicast-group landscape and to find out which hosts belong to which multicast group. The host machines in an IP network also use IGMP messages to become members of a group and to quit the group, too. IGMP messages come in seriously handy for tracking group memberships as well as active multicast streams.

Line Printer Remote (LPR)

When printing in an unblended, genuine TCP/IP environment, a combination of Line Printer (LPR) and the Line Printer Daemon (LPD) is typically what's used to get the job done. LPD, installed on all printing devices, handles both printers and print jobs. LPR acts on the client, or sending machine, and is used to send the data from a host machine to the network's print resource so you end up with actual printed output.

Domain Name Service (DNS)

Domain Name Service (DNS) resolves hostnames—specifically, Internet names, such as www.lammle.com, to their corresponding IP addresses.

You don't have to use DNS; you can just type in the IP address of any device you want to communicate with. An IP address identifies hosts on a network and the Internet as well. However, DNS was designed to make our lives easier. Think about this: What would happen if you wanted to move your web page to a different service provider? The IP address would change, and no one would know what the new one was. DNS allows you to use a domain name to specify an IP address. You can change the IP address as often as you want, and no one will know the difference.

DNS is used to resolve a *fully qualified domain name (FQDN)*—for example, www.lammle.com or todd.lammle.com. An FQDN is a hierarchy that can logically locate a system based on its domain identifier.

If you want to resolve the name *todd*, you must either type in the FQDN of todd.lammle.com or have a device, such as a PC or router, add the suffix for you. For example, on a Cisco router, you can use the command `ip domain-name lammle.com` to append each request with the lammle.com domain. If you don't do that, you'll have to type in the FQDN to get DNS to resolve the name.

> An important thing to remember about DNS is that if you can ping a device with an IP address but can't use its FQDN, then you might have some type of DNS configuration failure.

Dynamic Host Configuration Protocol (DHCP)/Bootstrap Protocol (BootP)

Dynamic Host Configuration Protocol (DHCP) assigns IP addresses to hosts with information provided by a server. It allows easier administration and works well in small to even very large network environments. Many types of hardware can be used as a DHCP server, including routers.

DHCP differs from Bootstrap Protocol (BootP) in that BootP assigns an IP address to a host but the host's hardware address must be entered manually in a BootP table. You can think of DHCP as a dynamic BootP. But remember that BootP is also used to send an operating system that a host can boot from. DHCP can't do that.

But there is a lot of information a DHCP server can provide to a host when the host is requesting an IP address from the DHCP server. Here's a partial list of the information a DHCP server can provide:

- IP address
- Subnet mask
- Domain name
- Default gateway (routers)
- DNS
- Windows Internet Naming Service (WINS) information

A DHCP server can give even more information than this, but the items in the list are the most common.

A client that sends out a DHCP DISCOVER message in order to receive an IP address sends out a broadcast at both Layer 2 and Layer 3. The Layer 2 broadcast is all *F*s in hex, which looks like this: FF:FF:FF:FF:FF:FF. The Layer 3 broadcast is 255.255.255.255, which means all networks and all hosts. DHCP is connectionless, which means it uses User Datagram Protocol (UDP) at the Transport layer, also known as the Host-to-Host layer, which we'll talk about next.

In case you don't believe me, here's an example of output from my trusty analyzer:

```
Ethernet II, Src: 192.168.0.3 (00:0b:db:99:d3:5e), Dst: Broadcast➡
  (ff:ff:ff:ff:ff:ff)
Internet Protocol, Src: 0.0.0.0 (0.0.0.0), Dst: 255.255.255.255➡
  (255.255.255.255)
```

The Data Link and Network layers are both sending out "all hands" broadcasts saying, "Help—I don't know my IP address!"

Figure 6.3 shows the process of a client/server relationship using a DHCP connection.

The following is the four-step process a client takes to receive an IP address from a DHCP server:

1. The DHCP client broadcasts a DHCP Discover message looking for a DHCP server (Port 67).
2. The DHCP server that received the DHCP Discover message sends a unicast DHCP Offer message back to the host
3. The client then broadcasts to the server a DHCP Request message asking for the offered IP address and possibly other information.
4. The server finalizes the exchange with a unicast DHCP Acknowledgment message.

What happens if you have a few hosts connected together with a switch or hub and you don't have a DHCP server? You can add IP information by hand (this is called *static IP addressing*; or, Windows provides what is called Automatic Private IP Addressing [APIPA], a feature of later Windows operating systems). With APIPA, clients can automatically self-configure an IP address and subnet mask (basic IP information that hosts use to communicate, which is covered in detail in Chapter 7, "IP Addressing," and Chapter 8, "IP Subnetting,

Troubleshooting IP, and Introduction to NAT") when a DHCP server isn't available. The IP address range for APIPA is 169.254.0.1 through 169.254.255.254. The client also configures itself with a default class B subnet mask of 255.255.0.0. If you have a DHCP server and your host is using this IP address, this means your DHCP client on your host is not working, or the server is down or can't be reached because of a network issue.

Now, let's take a look at the Transport layer, or what the DoD calls the Host-to-Host layer.

FIGURE 6.3 DHCP client four-step process

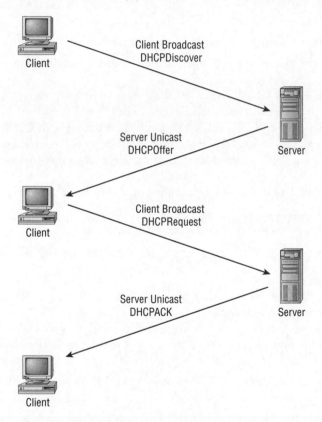

The Host-to-Host Layer Protocols

The main purpose of the Host-to-Host layer is to shield the upper-layer applications from the complexities of the network. This layer says to the upper layer, "Just give me your data stream, with any instructions, and I'll begin the process of getting your information ready to send."

The following sections describe the two protocols at this layer:

- Transmission Control Protocol (TCP)
- User Datagram Protocol (UDP)

In addition, we'll look at some of the key host-to-host protocol concepts, as well as the port numbers.

Transmission Control Protocol (TCP)

Transmission Control Protocol (TCP) takes large blocks of information from an application and breaks them into segments. It numbers and sequences each segment so that the destination's TCP process can put the segments back into the order the application intended. After these segments are sent, TCP (on the transmitting host) waits for an acknowledgment from the receiving end's TCP process, retransmitting those segments that aren't acknowledged.

Remember that in reliable transport operation, a device that wants to transmit sets up a connection-oriented communication with a remote device by creating a session. The transmitting device first establishes a connection-oriented session with its peer system, which is called a *call setup* or a *three-way handshake*. Data is then transferred; and when the transfer is complete, a call termination takes place to tear down the virtual circuit.

TCP is a full-duplex, connection-oriented, reliable, and accurate protocol, but establishing all these terms and conditions, in addition to error checking, is no small task. TCP is very complicated and, not surprisingly, costly in terms of network overhead. And because today's networks are much more reliable than those of yore, this added reliability is often unnecessary.

Because the upper layers just send a data stream to the protocols in the Transport layers, I'll demonstrate how TCP segments a data stream and prepares it for the Internet layer. When the Internet layer receives the data stream, it routes the segments as packets through an internetwork. The segments are handed to the receiving host's Host-to-Host layer protocol, which rebuilds the data stream to hand to the upper-layer protocols.

Figure 6.4 shows the TCP segment format. The figure shows the different fields within the TCP header.

FIGURE 6.4   TCP segment format

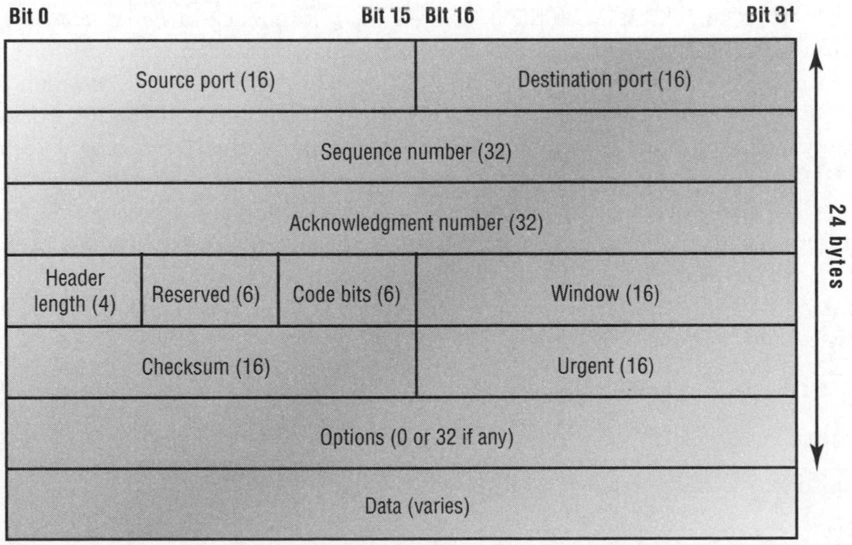

The TCP header is 20 bytes long, or up to 24 bytes with options.

For more detailed information regarding the TCP header, which is beyond the scope of the CompTIA Network+ exam objectives, please see my *CCNA: Cisco Certified Network Associate Study Guide, 6th Edition* (Sybex, 2007).

User Datagram Protocol (UDP)

If you were to compare *User Datagram Protocol (UDP)* with TCP, the former is basically the scaled-down economy model that's sometimes referred to as a *thin protocol*. Like a thin person on a park bench, a thin protocol doesn't take up a lot of room—or in this case, much bandwidth on a network.

UDP doesn't offer all the bells and whistles of TCP either, but it does do a fabulous job of transporting information that doesn't require reliable delivery—and it does so using far fewer network resources.

There are some situations in which it would definitely be wise for developers to opt for UDP rather than TCP. Remember the watchdog SNMP up there at the Process/Application layer? SNMP monitors the network, sending intermittent messages and a fairly steady flow of status updates and alerts, especially when running on a large network. The cost in overhead to establish, maintain, and close a TCP connection for each one of those little messages would reduce what would be an otherwise healthy, efficient network to a dammed-up bog in no time!

Another circumstance calling for UDP over TCP is when reliability is already handled at the Process/Application layer. NFS handles its own reliability issues, making the use of TCP both impractical and redundant. But ultimately, it's up to the application developer to decide whether to use UDP or TCP, not the user who wants to transfer data faster.

UDP does *not* sequence the segments and doesn't care in which order the segments arrive at the destination. But after that, UDP sends the segments off and forgets about them. It doesn't follow through, check up on them, or even allow for an acknowledgment of safe arrival—complete abandonment. Because of this, it's referred to as an *unreliable* protocol. This doesn't mean that UDP is ineffective, only that it doesn't handle issues of reliability. Because UDP assumes that the application will use its own reliability method, it doesn't use any. This gives an application developer a choice when running the IP stack: TCP for reliability or UDP for faster transfers.

Further, UDP doesn't create a virtual circuit, nor does it contact the destination before delivering information to it. Because of this, it's also considered a *connectionless* protocol.

Figure 6.5 clearly illustrates UDP's markedly low overhead as compared to TCP's hungry usage. Look at the figure carefully—can you see that UDP doesn't use windowing or provide for acknowledgments in the UDP header?

FIGURE 6.5   UDP segment

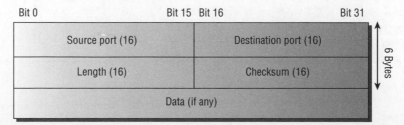

For more detailed information regarding the UDP header, which is beyond the scope of the CompTIA Network+ exam objectives, please see my *CCNA: Cisco Certified Network Associate Study Guide, 6th Edition* (Sybex, 2007).

Key Concepts of Host-to-Host Protocols

Now that you've seen both a connection-oriented (TCP) and connectionless (UDP) protocol in action, it would be good to summarize the two here. Table 2.1 highlights some of the key concepts that you should keep in mind regarding these two protocols. You should memorize this table.

TABLE 6.1   Key Features of TCP and UDP

TCP	UDP
Sequenced	Unsequenced
Reliable	Unreliable
Connection-oriented	Connectionless
Virtual circuit	No virtual circuit
High overhead	Low overhead
Acknowledgments	No acknowledgment
Windowing flow control	No windowing or flow control

A telephone analogy could really help you understand how TCP works. Most of us know that before you speak to someone on a phone, you must first establish a connection with that other person—wherever they are. This is like a virtual circuit with the TCP protocol. If you were giving someone important information during your conversation, you might say, "You know?" or ask, "Did you get that?" Saying something like this is a lot like a TCP acknowledgment—it's designed to get your verification. From time to time (especially on cell phones), people also ask, "Are you still there?" They end their conversations with a "Goodbye" of some kind, putting closure on the phone call. TCP also performs these types of functions.

Alternatively, using UDP is like sending a postcard. To do that, you don't need to contact the other party first. You simply write your message, address the postcard, and mail it. This is analogous to UDP's connectionless orientation. Because the message on the postcard is probably not a matter of life or death, you don't need an acknowledgment of its receipt. Similarly, UDP doesn't involve acknowledgments.

Port Numbers

TCP and UDP must use *port numbers* to communicate with the upper layers because they're what keep track of different simultaneous conversations originated by or accepted by the local host. Originating-source port numbers are dynamically assigned by the source host and will usually have a value of 1024 or higher. Ports 1023 and below are defined in RFC 3232, which discusses what are called *well-known port numbers*.

Virtual circuits that don't use an application with a well-known port number are assigned port numbers randomly from a specific range instead. These port numbers identify the source and destination application or process in the TCP segment.

Figure 6.6 illustrates how both TCP and UDP use port numbers.

FIGURE 6.6   Port numbers for TCP and UDP

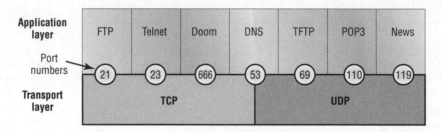

Numbers below 1024 are considered well-known port numbers and are defined in RFC 3232. Numbers 1024 and above are used by the upper layers to set up sessions with other hosts and by TCP to use as source and destination identifiers in the TCP segment.

Table 6.2 gives you a list of the typical applications used in the TCP/IP suite, their well-known port numbers, and the Transport layer protocols used by each application or process. It's important that you study and memorize this table for the CompTIA Network+ objectives.

TABLE 6.2   Key Protocols That Use TCP and UDP

TCP	UDP
Telnet 23	SNMP 161
SMTP 25	TFTP 69
HTTP 80	DNS 53
FTP 20, 21	BOOTPS/DHCP 67
DNS 53	
HTTPS 443	
SSH 22	

TABLE 6.2   Key Protocols That Use TCP and UDP *(continued)*

TCP	UDP
POP3 110	
NTP 123	
IMAP4 143	

Notice that DNS uses both TCP and UDP. Whether it opts for one or the other depends on what it's trying to do. Even though it's not the only application that can use both protocols, it's certainly one that you should remember in your studies.

The Internet Layer Protocols

In the DoD model, there are two main reasons for the Internet layer's existence: routing and providing a single network interface to the upper layers.

None of the other upper- or lower-layer protocols have any functions relating to routing—that complex and important task belongs entirely to the Internet layer. The Internet layer's second duty is to provide a single network interface to the upper-layer protocols. Without this layer, application programmers would need to write what are called *hooks* into every one of their applications for each different Network Access protocol. This would not only be a pain in the neck, but it would also lead to different versions of each application—one for Ethernet, another one for Token Ring, and so on. To prevent this, IP provides one single network interface for the upper-layer protocols. That accomplished, it's then the job of IP and the various Network Access protocols to get along and work together.

All network roads don't lead to Rome—they lead to IP. And all the other protocols at this layer, as well as all those at the upper layers, use it. Never forget that. All paths through the DoD model go through IP. The following sections describe the protocols at the Internet layer:

- Internet Protocol (IP)
- Internet Control Message Protocol (ICMP)
- Address Resolution Protocol (ARP)
- Reverse Address Resolution Protocol (RARP)
- Proxy ARP

Internet Protocol (IP)

Internet Protocol (IP) essentially is the Internet layer. The other protocols found here merely exist to support it. IP holds the big picture and could be said to "see all," in that it's aware of all the interconnected networks. It can do this because all the machines on the network have a software, or logical, address called an IP address, which I'll cover more thoroughly later in this chapter.

IP looks at each packet's destination address. Then, using a routing table, it decides where a packet is to be sent next, choosing the best path. The protocols of the Network Access layer at the bottom of the DoD model don't possess IP's enlightened scope of the entire network; they deal only with physical links (local networks).

Identifying devices on networks requires answering these two questions: Which network is it on? And what is its ID on that network? The first answer is the *software address*, or *logical address* (the correct street). The second answer is the *hardware address* (the correct mailbox). All hosts on a network have a logical ID called an IP address. This is the software, or logical, address and contains valuable encoded information, greatly simplifying the complex task of routing. (IP is discussed in RFC 791.)

IP receives segments from the Host-to-Host layer and fragments them into packets if necessary. IP then reassembles packets back into segments on the receiving side. Each packet is assigned the IP address of the sender and of the recipient. Each router (Layer 3 device) that receives a packet makes routing decisions based on the packet's destination IP address.

Figure 6.7 shows an IP header. This will give you an idea of what the IP protocol has to go through every time user data is sent from the upper layers and is to be sent to a remote network.

FIGURE 6.7 IP header

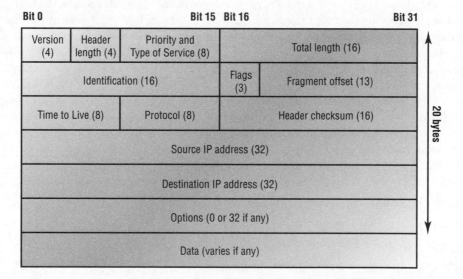

For more detailed information regarding the IP header, which is beyond the CompTIA Network+ exam objectives, please see my *CCNA: Cisco Certified Network Associate Study Guide, 6th Edition* (Sybex, 2007).

Internet Control Message Protocol (ICMP)

Internet Control Message Protocol (ICMP) works at the Network layer and is used by IP for many different services. ICMP is a management protocol and messaging service provider for IP. Its messages are carried as IP packets.

ICMP packets have the following characteristics:

- They can provide hosts with information about network problems.
- They are encapsulated within IP datagrams.

The following are some common events and messages that ICMP relates to:

Destination Unreachable   If a router can't send an IP datagram any further, it uses ICMP to send a message back to the sender, advising it of the situation. For example, take a look at Figure 6.8, which shows that interface E0 of the Lab_B router is down.

FIGURE 6.8   ICMP error message is sent to the sending host from the remote router.

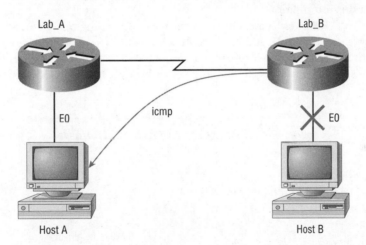

EO on Lab B is down. Host A is trying to communicate to Host B. What happens?

When Host A sends a packet destined for Host B, the Lab_B router will send an ICMP Destination Unreachable message back to the sending device (Host A, in this example).

Buffer Full   If a router's memory buffer for receiving incoming datagrams is full, it will use ICMP to send out this message until the congestion abates.

Hops   Each IP datagram is allotted a certain number of routers, called *hops*, to pass through. If it reaches its limit of hops before arriving at its destination, the last router to receive that datagram deletes it. The executioner router then uses ICMP to send an obituary message, informing the sending machine of the demise of its datagram.

Ping   Ping uses ICMP echo request and reply messages to check the physical and logical connectivity of machines on an internetwork.

Traceroute   Traceroute uses IP packet Time-to-Live time-outs to discover the path a packet takes as it traverses an internetwork.

Both Ping and Traceroute (also just called Trace; Microsoft Windows uses tracert) allow you to verify address configurations in your internetwork.

Address Resolution Protocol (ARP)

Address Resolution Protocol (ARP) finds the hardware address of a host from a known IP address. Here's how it works: When IP has a datagram to send, it must inform a Network Access protocol, such as Ethernet or Token Ring, of the destination's hardware address on the local network. (It has already been informed by upper-layer protocols of the destination's IP address.) If IP doesn't find the destination host's hardware address in the ARP cache, it uses ARP to find this information.

As IP's detective, ARP interrogates the local network by sending out a broadcast asking the machine with the specified IP address to reply with its hardware address. So basically, ARP translates the software (IP) address into a hardware address—for example, the destination machine's Ethernet address. Figure 6.9 shows how an ARP broadcast looks to a local network.

ARP resolves IP addresses to Ethernet (MAC) addresses.

FIGURE 6.9   Local ARP broadcast

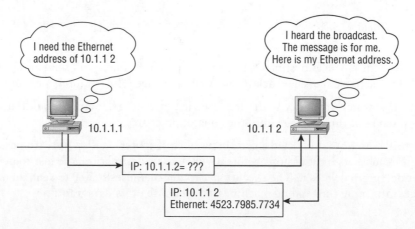

The following trace shows an ARP broadcast—notice that the destination hardware address is unknown and is all 0s in the ARP header. In the Ethernet header, a destination of all *Fs* in hex (all 1s in binary), a hardware-address broadcast, is used to make sure all devices on the local link receive the ARP request.

```
Flags:            0x00
Status:           0x00
Packet Length: 64
Timestamp:        09:17:29.574000 12/06/03
Ethernet Header
Destination:   FF:FF:FF:FF:FF:FF Ethernet Broadcast
Source:           00:A0:24:48:60:A5
Protocol Type: 0x0806 IP ARP
ARP - Address Resolution Protocol
Hardware:                1 Ethernet (10Mb)
Protocol:                0x0800 IP
Hardware Address Length: 6
Protocol Address Length: 4
Operation:               1 ARP Request
Sender Hardware Address: 00:A0:24:48:60:A5
Sender Internet Address: 172.16.10.3
Target Hardware Address: 00:00:00:00:00:00 (ignored)
Target Internet Address: 172.16.10.10
Extra bytes (Padding):
............... 0A 0A 0A 0A 0A 0A 0A 0A 0A 0A 0A 0A 0A
  0A 0A 0A 0A 0A
Frame Check Sequence: 0x00000000
```

Reverse Address Resolution Protocol (RARP)

When an IP machine happens to be a diskless machine, it has no way of initially knowing its IP address. But it does know its MAC address. *Reverse Address Resolution Protocol (RARP)* discovers the identity of the IP address for diskless machines by sending out a packet that includes its MAC address and a request for the IP address assigned to that MAC address. A designated machine, called a *RARP server*, responds with the answer, and the identity crisis is over. RARP uses the information it does know about the machine's MAC address to learn its IP address and complete the machine's ID portrait.

Figure 6.10 shows a diskless workstation asking for its IP address with a RARP broadcast.

FIGURE 6.10   RARP broadcast example

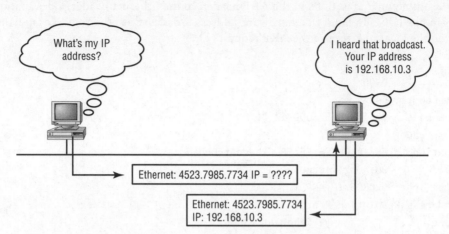

Proxy Address Resolution Protocol (Proxy ARP)

On a network, your hosts can't have more than one default gateway configured. Think about this: What if the default gateway (router) happens to go down? The host won't just start sending to another router automatically—you've got to reconfigure that host. But Proxy ARP can actually help machines on a subnet reach remote subnets without configuring routing or even a default gateway.

One advantage of using Proxy ARP is that it can be added to a single router on a network without disturbing the routing tables of all the other routers that live there too. But there's a serious downside to using Proxy ARP. Using Proxy ARP will definitely increase the amount of traffic on your network segment, and hosts will have a larger ARP table than usual in order to handle all the IP-to-MAC-address mappings. And Proxy ARP is configured on all Cisco routers by default—you should disable it if you don't think you're going to use it.

One last thought on Proxy ARP: Proxy ARP isn't really a separate protocol. It's a service run by routers on behalf of other devices (usually PCs) that are separated from their query to another device by a router, although they think they share the subnet with the remote device.

Data Encapsulation

I started to discuss data encapsulation in Chapter 2, but I could only provide an overview at that point in the book because you needed to have a firm understanding of how ports work in a virtual circuit. With the last five chapters of foundational material under your belt, you're ready to get more into the details of encapsulations.

When a host transmits data across a network to another device, the data goes through *encapsulation*: It's wrapped with protocol information at each layer of the OSI model. Each layer communicates only with its peer layer on the receiving device.

To communicate and exchange information, each layer uses *Protocol Data Units (PDUs)*. These hold the control information attached to the data at each layer of the model. They're usually attached to the header in front of the data field but can also be in the trailer, or end, of it.

Each PDU attaches to the data by encapsulating it at each layer of the OSI model, and each has a specific name depending on the information provided in each header. This PDU information is read only by the peer layer on the receiving device. After it's read, it's stripped off, and the data is then handed to the next layer up.

Figure 6.11 shows the PDUs and how they attach control information to each layer. This figure demonstrates how the upper-layer user data is converted for transmission on the network. The data stream is then handed down to the Transport layer, which sets up a virtual circuit to the receiving device by sending over a synch packet. Next, the data stream is broken up into smaller pieces, and a Transport layer header (a PDU) is created and attached to the header of the data field; now the piece of data is called a *segment*. Each segment is sequenced so the data stream can be put back together on the receiving side exactly as it was transmitted.

Each segment is then handed to the Network layer for network addressing and routing through the internetwork. Logical addressing (for example, IP) is used to get each segment to the correct network. The Network layer protocol adds a control header to the segment handed down from the Transport layer, and what we have now is called a *packet* or *datagram*. Remember that the Transport and Network layers work together to rebuild a data stream on a receiving host, but it's not part of their work to place their PDUs on a local network segment—which is the only way to get the information to a router or host.

FIGURE 6.11   Data encapsulation

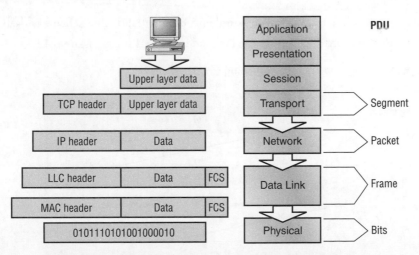

It's the Data Link layer that's responsible for taking packets from the Network layer and placing them on the network medium (cable or wireless). The Data Link layer encapsulates each packet in a *frame*, and the frame's header carries the hardware address of the source and destination hosts. If the destination device is on a remote network, then the frame is sent to a router to be routed through an internetwork. Once it gets to the destination network, a new frame is used to get the packet to the destination host.

To put this frame on the network, it must first be put into a digital signal. Because a frame is really a logical group of 1s and 0s, the Physical layer is responsible for encoding these digits into a digital signal, which is read by devices on the same local network. The receiving devices will synchronize on the digital signal and extract (decode) the 1s and 0s from the digital signal. At this point, the devices build the frames, run a cyclic redundancy check (CRC), and then check their answer against the answer in the frame's Frame Check Sequence (FCS) field. If it matches, the packet is pulled from the frame and what's left of the frame is discarded. This process is called *de-encapsulation*. The packet is handed to the Network layer, where the address is checked. If the address matches, the segment is pulled from the packet and what's left of the packet is discarded. The segment is processed at the Transport layer, which rebuilds the data stream and acknowledges to the transmitting station that it received each piece. It then happily hands the data stream to the upper-layer application.

At a transmitting device, the data-encapsulation method works like this:

1. User information is converted to data for transmission on the network.

2. Data is converted to segments, and a reliable connection is set up between the transmitting and receiving hosts.

3. Segments are converted to packets or datagrams, and a logical address is placed in the header so each packet can be routed through an internetwork.

4. Packets or datagrams are converted to frames for transmission on the local network. Hardware (Ethernet) addresses are used to uniquely identify hosts on a local network segment.

5. Frames are converted to bits, and a digital encoding and clocking scheme is used.

To explain this in more detail using the layer addressing, I'll use Figure 6.12.

FIGURE 6.12 PDU and layer addressing

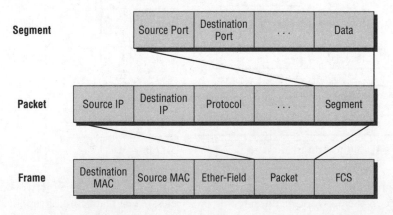

Remember that a data stream is handed down from the upper layer to the Transport layer. As technicians, we really don't care who the data stream comes from because that's a programmer's problem. Our job is to rebuild the data stream reliably and hand it to the upper layers on the receiving device.

Before we go further in our discussion of Figure 6.12, let's review port numbers and make sure you understand them. The Transport layer uses port numbers to define both the virtual circuit and the upper-layer process, as you can see from Figure 6.13.

The Transport layer takes the data stream, makes segments out of it, and establishes a reliable session by creating a virtual circuit. It then sequences (numbers) each segment and uses acknowledgments and flow control. If you're using TCP, the virtual circuit is defined by the source port number. Remember, the host just makes this up starting at port number 1024 (0 through 1023 are reserved for well-known port numbers). The destination port number defines the upper-layer process (application) that the data stream is handed to when the data stream is reliably rebuilt on the receiving host.

Now that you understand port numbers and how they're used at the Transport layer, let's go back to Figure 6.12. Once the Transport layer header information is added to the piece of data, it becomes a segment and is handed down to the Network layer along with the destination IP address. (The destination IP address was handed down from the upper layers to the Transport layer with the data stream, and it was discovered through a name resolution method at the upper layers—probably DNS.)

FIGURE 6.13   Port numbers at the Transport layer

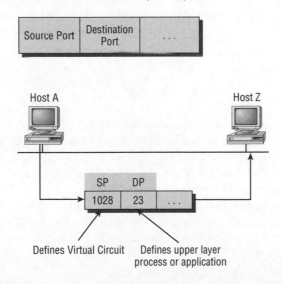

The Network layer adds a header, and adds the logical addressing (IP addresses), to the front of each segment. Once the header is added to the segment, the PDU is called a *packet*. The packet has a protocol field that describes where the segment came from (either UDP or TCP) so it can hand the segment to the correct protocol at the Transport layer when it reaches the receiving host.

The Network layer is responsible for finding the destination hardware address that dictates where the packet should be sent on the local network. It does this by using ARP. IP at the Network layer looks at the destination IP address and compares that address to its own source IP address and subnet mask. If it turns out to be a local network request, the hardware address of the local host is requested via an ARP request. If the packet is destined for a remote host, IP will look for the IP address of the default gateway (router) instead.

The packet, along with the destination hardware address of either the local host or default gateway, is then handed down to the Data Link layer. The Data Link layer will add a header to the front of the packet, and the piece of data then becomes a *frame*. (We call it a frame because both a header and a trailer are added to the packet, which makes the data resemble bookends or a frame, if you will.) This is shown in Figure 6.12. The frame uses an Ether-Type field to describe which protocol the packet came from at the Network layer. Now a CRC is run on the frame, and the answer to the CRC is placed in the FCS field found in the trailer of the frame.

The frame is now ready to be handed down, one bit at a time, to the Physical layer, which will use bit-timing rules to encode the data in a digital signal. Every device on the network segment will synchronize with the clock, extract the 1s and 0s from the digital signal, and build a frame. After the frame is rebuilt, a CRC is run to make sure the frame is okay. If everything turns out to be good, the hosts will check the destination address to see if the frame is for them.

If all this is making your eyes cross and your brain freeze, don't freak—things will become much clearer as we go through the book—really! Soon, I'll be going over exactly how data is encapsulated and routed through an internetwork in even more detail, in an easy to understand, step-by-step manner, in Chapter 9, "Introduction to Routing."

Summary

Protocols, protocols everywhere—so many different reasons for them, and so many jobs they do for us! And sometimes they even work in conjunction with each other. This can seem like way too much information, but no worries—as you become familiar with the various layers and their functions, I promise it will soon become clear that this hierarchical structure is a seriously tight, robust networking foundation.

Similarly, as you understand The TCP/IP big picture, the reason why all those protocols exist and are necessary will also become much easier to understand. They're really like a team that works jointly, from layer to layer, to make our TCP/IP networks the wonderful, great tools they are.

Exam Essentials

Remember the Process/Application layer protocols.   Telnet is a terminal-emulation program that allows you to log into a remote host and run programs. File Transfer Protocol (FTP) is a connection-oriented service that allows you to transfer files. Trivial FTP (TFTP) is a connectionless file transfer program. Simple Mail Transfer Protocol (SMTP) is a send-mail program.

Remember the Host-to-Host layer protocols.   Transmission Control Protocol (TCP) is a connection-oriented protocol that provides reliable network service by using acknowledgments and flow control. User Datagram Protocol (UDP) is a connectionless protocol that provides low overhead and is considered unreliable.

Remember the Internet layer protocols.   Internet Protocol (IP) is a connectionless protocol that provides network address and routing through an internetwork. Address Resolution Protocol (ARP) finds a hardware address from a known IP address. Reverse ARP (RARP) finds an IP address from a known hardware address. Internet Control Message Protocol (ICMP) provides diagnostics and destination-unreachable messages.

Remember the difference between connection-oriented and connectionless network services.   Connection-oriented services use acknowledgments and flow control to create a reliable session. More overhead is used than in a connectionless network service. Connectionless services are used to send data with no acknowledgments or flow control. This is considered unreliable.

Written Lab

1. What might be the problem if a DHCP client suddenly finds itself in a different IP subnet from the one it should be in?

2. Name the protocol that uses both TCP ports 20 and 21.

3. What two well-known port numbers does a DNS server use?

4. Which protocol dynamically reports errors to source hosts by using IP directly to build packets?

5. What could cause a server that you can ping not to provide the particular TCP/IP service, such as FTP, HTTP, and so on, that you expect it to offer?

6. What might cause your email to stop functioning properly when you change Internet service providers?

7. Which UNIX command is used for terminal emulation in the same way Telnet is used?

8. What protocol is at the heart of the `ping` and `tracert` commands in a Windows operating system?

9. Which destination Transport-layer protocol and port number does a TFTP client use to transfer files over the network?

10. What well-known port numbers do SMTP, POP3, and IMAP4 servers use?

(The answers to the Written Lab can be found following the answers to the Review Questions for this chapter.)

Review Questions

1. The OSI has seven layers, which layer does SMTP work at?

    A. Network

    B. Transport

    C. Session

    D. Application

2. You need to have secure communications using HTTPS. What port number is used by default?

    A. 69

    B. 23

    C. 21

    D. 443

3. You want to implement a mechanism that automates the IP configuration, including IP address, subnet mask, default gateway, and DNS information. Which protocol will you use to accomplish this?

    A. SMTP

    B. SNMP

    C. DHCP

    D. ARP

4. What protocol is used to find the hardware address of a local device?

    A. RARP

    B. ARP

    C. IP

    D. ICMP

    E. BootP

5. You need to login to a Unix server across a network that is not secure. Which of the following protocols will allow you to remotely administrator this server securely?

    A. Telnet

    B. SSH

    C. SFTP

    D. HTTP

286
11

6. If you can ping by IP address but not by hostname, or FQDN, which of the following port numbers is related to the server process that is involved?

   A. 21

   B. 23

   C. 53

   D. 69

   E. 80

7. Which of the following describe the DHCP Discover message? (Choose two.)

   A. It uses FF:FF:FF:FF:FF:FF as a Layer 2 broadcast.

   B. It uses UDP as the Transport layer protocol.

   C. It uses TCP as the Transport layer protocol.

   D. It does not use a Layer 2 destination address.

8. What layer 4 protocol is used for a Telnet connection, and what is the default port number?

   A. IP, 6

   B. TCP, 21

   C. UDP, 23

   D. ICMP, 21

   E. TCP, 23

9. Which statements are true regarding ICMP packets? (Choose two.)

   A. They acknowledge receipt of a TCP segment.

   B. They guarantee datagram delivery.

   C. They can provide hosts with information about network problems.

   D. They are encapsulated within IP datagrams.

   E. They are encapsulated within UDP datagrams.

10. Which of the following services use TCP? (Choose three.)

   A. DHCP

   B. SMTP

   C. SNMP

   D. FTP

   E. HTTP

   F. TFTP

11. Which of the following services use UDP? (Choose three.)

    A. DHCP

    B. SMTP

    C. SNMP

    D. FTP

    E. HTTP

    F. TFTP

12. Which of the following are TCP/IP protocols used at the Application layer of the OSI model? (Choose three.)

    A. IP

    B. TCP

    C. Telnet

    D. FTP

    E. TFTP

13. Which of the following protocols is used by e-mail servers to exchange messages with one another?

    A. POP3

    B. IMAP

    C. SMTP

    D. HTTP

14. If you use either Telnet or FTP, which is the highest layer you are using to transmit data?

    A. Application

    B. Presentation

    C. Session

    D. Transport

15. Which of the following protocols can use TCP and UDP, permits authentication and secure polling of network devices, and allows for automated alerts and reports on network devices?

    A. DNS

    B. SNMP

    C. SMTP

    D. TCP

16. You need to transfer files between two hosts. Which two protocol can you use?

    A. SNMP

    B. SCP

    C. RIP

    D. NTP

    E. FTP

17. What layer in the IP stack is equivalent to the Transport layer of the OSI model?

    A. Application

    B. Host-to-Host

    C. Internet

    D. Network Access

18. You need to make sure that your network devices have a consistent time across all devices. What protocol do you need to run on your network?

    A. FTP

    B. SCP

    C. NTP

    E. RTP

19. Which of the following allows a server to distinguish among different simultaneous requests from the same host?

    A. They have different port numbers.

    B. A NAT server changes the IP address for subsequent requests.

    C. A server is unable to accept multiple simultaneous sessions from the same host. One session must end before another can begin.

    D. The MAC address for each one is unique.

20. Which of the following protocols uses both TCP and UDP?

    A. FTP

    B. SMTP

    C. Telnet

    D. DNS

Answers to Review Questions

1. D. SMTP resides at the Application layer of the OSI/DoD model.

2. D. HTTPS, or Secure HTTP uses port 443 by default.

3. C. Dynamic Host Configuration Protocol (DHCP) is used to provide IP information to hosts on your network. DHCP can provide a lot of information, but the most common is IP address, subnet mask, default gateway, and DNS information.

4. B. Address Resolution Protocol (ARP) is used to find the hardware address from a known IP address.

5. B. Secure Shell (SSH) allows you to remotely administer router, switches and even servers securely.

6. C. The problem is with DNS, which uses both TCP and UDP port 53.

7. A, B. A client that sends out a DHCP Discover message in order to receive an IP address sends out a broadcast at both Layer 2 and Layer 3. The Layer 2 broadcast is all *F*s in hex, or FF:FF:FF:FF:FF:FF. The Layer 3 broadcast is 255.255.255.255, which means all networks and all hosts. DHCP is connectionless, which means it uses User Datagram Protocol (UDP) at the Transport layer, also called the Host-to-Host layer.

8. E. Telnet uses TCP at the Transport layer with a default port number of 23.

9. C, D. Internet Control Message Protocol (ICMP) is used to send error messages through the network, but ICMP does not work alone. Every segment or ICMP payload must be encapsulated within an IP datagram (or packet).

10. B, D, E. SMTP, FTP, and HTTP use TCP.

11. A, C, F. DHCP, SNMP, and TFTP use UDP. SMTP, FTP, and HTTP use TCP.

12. C, D, E. Telnet, File Transfer Protocol (FTP), and Trivial FTP (TFTP) are all Application layer protocols. IP is a Network layer protocol. Transmission Control Protocol (TCP) is a Transport layer protocol.

13. C. SMTP is used by a client to send mail to its server and by that server to send mail to another server. POP3 and IMAP are used by clients to retrieve their mail from the server that stores it until it is retrieved. HTTP is only used with web-based mail services.

14. A. Both FTP and Telnet use TCP at the Transport layer; however, they both are Application layer protocols, so the Application layer is the best answer for this question.

15. B. Simple Network Management Protocol, is typically implemented using version 3, which allows for a connection oriented service, authentication and secure polling of network devices, and allows for alerts and reports on network devices.

16. B, E. Secure Copy Protocol (SCP), and File Transfer Protocol (FTP), can be used to transfer files between two systems.

17. B. The four layers of the IP stack (also called the DoD model) are Application/Process, Host-to-Host, Internet, and Network Access. The Host-to-Host layer is equivalent to the Transport layer of the OSI model.

18. C. Network Time Protocol will ensure a consistent time across network devices on the network.

19. A. Through the use of port numbers, TCP and UDP can establish multiple sessions between the same two hosts without creating any confusion. The sessions can be between the same or different applications, such as multiple web-browsing sessions or a web-browsing session and an FTP session.

20. D. DNS uses TCP for zone exchanges between servers and UDP when a client is trying to resolve a hostname to an IP address.

Answers to Written Lab

1. The most likely problem is that a rogue DHCP server has been introduced into the network and is handing this device an incorrect lease.

2. FTP uses both TCP ports 20 and 21 for the data channel and the control channel, respectively.

3. A DNS server uses TCP port 53 for zone transfers and UDP port 53 for name resolutions.

4. ICMP uses IP directly to build error-reporting packets that are transmitted back to the originating source host when issues arise during the delivery of data packets. ICMP is also used during ping and some Traceroute operations.

5. Quite simply, the service might not be running currently on that server. Another possibility might be that a firewall between the client and the server has blocked the protocol in question from passing.

6. Most ISPs have their own mail servers. When you switch service, you might need to point your mail application to the servers provided by the new service provider.

7. The UNIX command `rlogin` functions similarly to Telnet.

8. ICMP is the protocol that the `ping` and `tracert` commands rely on. If you're having trouble getting pings and Traceroutes through a router, you might need to check if ICMP is being allowed thorough.

9. TFTP servers respond to UDP messages sent to port 69.

10. SMTP uses TCP port 25; POP3 uses TCP port 110; IMAP4 uses TCP port 143.

Chapter

7

IP Addressing

THE FOLLOWING COMPTIA NETWORK+ EXAM OBJECTIVES ARE COVERED IN THIS CHAPTER:

✓ **1.3 Identify the following address formats**

- IPv6
- IPv4

✓ **1.4 Given a scenario, evaluate the proper use of the following addressing technologies and addressing schemes**

- Addressing Technologies
  - Public vs. private
  - DHCP (static, dynamic APIPA)
- Addressing schemes
  - Unicast
  - Multicast
  - Broadcast

One of the most important topics in any discussion of TCP/IP is IP addressing. An *IP address* is a numeric identifier assigned to each machine on an IP network. It designates the specific location of a device on the network.

An IP address is a software address, not a hardware address—the latter is hard-coded on a Network Interface Card (NIC) and used for finding hosts on a local network. IP addressing was designed to allow hosts on one network to communicate with a host on a different network regardless of the type of LANs the hosts are participating in.

Before we get into the more complicated aspects of IP addressing, you need to understand some of the basics. First I'm going to explain some of the fundamentals of IP addressing and its terminology. Then you'll learn about the hierarchical IP addressing scheme and private IP addresses.

I'll define unicast, multicast, and broadcast addresses, and then finish the chapter with a discussion on IPv6. And I promise to make it all as painless as possible.

The reason that we would even discuss IPv6 (besides to cover the objectives, of course) is because of the lack of IPv4 addresses available for use in the future networks, which we need to keep our corporate and private networks and even the Internet running. Basically, we're running out of addresses for all our new hosts! IPv6 will fix this for us.

For up-to-the-minute updates for this chapter, please see www.lammle.com or www.sybex.com/go/comptianetwork+studyguide.

IP Terminology

Throughout this chapter, you'll learn several important terms vital to your understanding of the Internet Protocol. Here are a few to get you started:

Bit   A *bit* is one digit, either a 1 or a 0.

Byte   A *byte* is 7 or 8 bits, depending on whether parity is used. For the rest of this chapter, always assume a byte is 8 bits.

Octet   An octet, made up of 8 bits, is just an ordinary 8-bit binary number. In this chapter, the terms *byte* and *octet* are completely interchangeable.

Network address   This is the designation used in routing to send packets to a remote network—for example, 10.0.0.0, 172.16.0.0, and 192.168.10.0.

Broadcast address   The *broadcast address* is used by applications and hosts to send information to all hosts on a network. Examples include 255.255.255.255, which designates all networks and all hosts; 172.16.255.255, which specifies all subnets and hosts on network 172.16.0.0; and 10.255.255.255, which broadcasts to all subnets and hosts on network 10.0.0.0.

> You will find the terms *subnet mask* and *slash notation* (for example, /24) used a few times in this chapter. These terms will be fully defined and used in Chapter 8, "IP Subnetting, Troubleshooting IP, and Introduction to NAT."

The Hierarchical IP Addressing Scheme

An IP address consists of 32 bits of information. These bits are divided into four sections, referred to as *octets* or bytes, and four octets sum up to 32 bits (8×4=32). You can depict an IP address using one of three methods:

- Dotted-decimal, as in 172.16.30.56
- Binary, as in 10101100.00010000.00011110.00111000
- Hexadecimal, as in AC.10.1E.38

Each of these examples validly represents the same IP address. Hexadecimal isn't used as often as dotted-decimal or binary concerning IP addressing, but you still might find an IP address stored in hexadecimal in some programs. The Windows Registry is a good example of a program that stores a machine's IP address in hex.

The 32-bit IP address is known as a structured or hierarchical address, as opposed to a flat, or nonhierarchical address. Although either type of addressing scheme can be used, *hierarchical addressing* has been chosen for a very important reason. The major advantage of this scheme is that it can handle a large number of addresses, namely 4.3 billion (a 32-bit address space with two possible values for each position—either 0 or 1—gives you 2^{32}, or 4,294,967,296). The disadvantage of the flat-addressing scheme, and the reason it's not used for IP addressing, relates to routing. If every address were unique, all routers on the Internet would need to store the address of each and every machine on the Internet. This would make efficient routing impossible, even if only a fraction of all possible addresses were used.

The solution to this problem is to use a two- or three-level hierarchical addressing scheme that is structured by network and host or by network, subnet, and host.

This two- or three-level scheme is comparable to a telephone number. The first section, the area code, designates a very large area. The second section, the prefix, narrows the scope to a local calling area. The final segment, the customer number, zooms in on the specific connection. IP addresses use the same type of layered structure. Rather than all 32 bits being treated as a unique identifier, as in flat addressing, a part of the address is designated as the network address and the other part is designated as either the subnet and host or just the host address.

Next, I'm going to cover IP network addressing and the different classes of address used to address our networks.

Network Addressing

The *network address*—also called the network number—uniquely identifies each network. Every machine on the same network shares that network address as part of its IP address. In the IP address 172.16.30.56, for example, 172.16 is the network address.

The *host address* is assigned to, and uniquely identifies, each machine on a network. This part of the address must be unique because it identifies a particular machine—an individual— as opposed to a network, which is a group. This number can also be referred to as a *host address*. So in the sample IP address 172.16.30.56, the 30.56 is the host address.

The designers of the Internet decided to create classes of networks based on network size. For the small number of networks possessing a very large number of hosts, they created the rank *Class A network*. At the other extreme is the *Class C network*, which is reserved for the numerous networks with a small number of hosts. The class distinction for networks between very large and very small is predictably called the *Class B network*.

Subdividing an IP address into a network and host address is determined by the class designation of your network. Figure 7.1 summarizes the classes of networks—a subject I'll explain in much greater detail throughout this chapter.

FIGURE 7.1   Summary of the three classes of networks

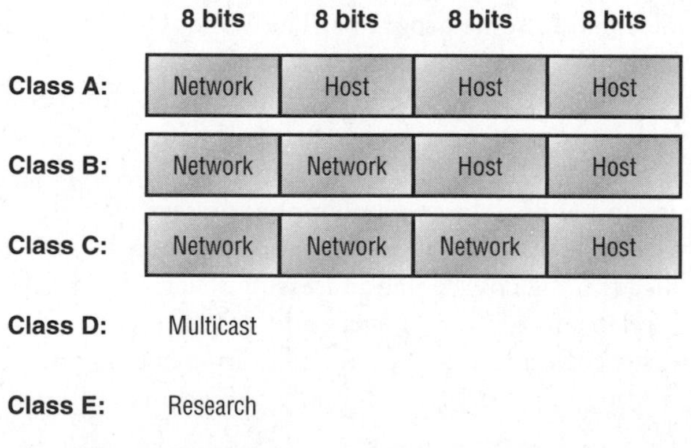

To ensure efficient routing, Internet designers defined a mandate for the leading-bits section of the address for each different network class. For example, since a router knows that a Class A network address always starts with a 0, the router might be able to speed a packet on its way after reading only the first bit of its address. This is where the address schemes define the difference between a Class A, a Class B, and a Class C address. Coming up, I'll discuss the differences between these three classes, followed by a discussion of the Class D and Class E addresses. For now, know that Classes A, B, and C are the only ranges that are used to address hosts in our networks.

Class A Addresses

In a Class A network address, the first byte is assigned to the network address and the three remaining bytes are used for the host addresses. The Class A format is as follows:

network.host.host.host

For example, in the IP address 49.22.102.70, the 49 is the network address and 22.102.70 is the host address. Every machine on this particular network would begin with the distinctive network address of 49.

Class A network addresses are 1 byte long, with the first bit of that byte reserved, and the 7 remaining bits available for manipulation, or addressing. As a result, the maximum number of Class A networks that can be created is 128. Why? Well, each of the 7 bit positions can be either a 0 or a 1, and 2^7 gives you 128.

The designers of the IP address scheme said that the first bit of the first byte in a Class A network address must always be off, or 0. This means a Class A address must be between 0 and 127 in the first byte, inclusive.

Consider the following network address:

0xxxxxxx

If we turn the other 7 bits all off and then turn them all on, we'll find the Class A range of network addresses:

00000000 = 0
01111111 = 127

So, a Class A network is defined in the first octet between 0 and 127, and it can't be less or more.

To complicate matters further, the network address of all 0s (0000 0000) is reserved to designate the default route (see Table 7.1). Additionally, the address 127, which is reserved for diagnostics, can't be used either, which means that you can really only use the numbers 1 to 126 to designate Class A network addresses. This means the actual number of usable Class A network addresses is 128 minus 2, or 126.

Each Class A address has 3 bytes (24-bit positions) for the host address of a machine. This means there are 2^{24}—or 16,777,216—unique combinations and, therefore, precisely that many potential unique host addresses for each Class A network. Because host addresses with the two patterns of all 0s and all 1s are reserved, the actual maximum usable number of hosts for a Class A network is 2^{24} minus 2, which equals 16,777,214. Either way, you can see that's a seriously huge number of hosts to have a network segment!

Here's an example of how to figure out the valid host IDs in a Class A network address:

- All host bits off is the network address: 10.0.0.0.
- All host bits on is the broadcast address: 10.255.255.255.

The valid hosts are the numbers in between the network address and the broadcast address: 10.0.0.1 through 10.255.255.254. Notice that 0s and 255s can be valid host IDs. All you need to remember when trying to find valid host addresses is that the host bits can't ever be all be turned off or all turned on at the same time.

TABLE 7.1   Reserved IP Addresses

Address	Function
Network address of all 0s	Interpreted to mean "this network or segment."
Network address of all 1s	Interpreted to mean "all networks."
Network 127.0.0.1	Reserved for loopback tests. Designates the local host and allows that host to send a test packet to itself without generating network traffic.
Host address of all 0s	Interpreted to mean "network address" or any host on specified network.
Host address of all 1s	Interpreted to mean "all hosts" on the specified network; for example, 128.2.255.255 means "all hosts" on network 128.2 (Class B address).
Entire IP address set to all 0s	Used by Cisco routers to designate the default route. Could also mean "any network."
Entire IP address set to all 1s (same as 255.255.255.255)	Broadcast to all hosts on the current network; sometimes called an "all 1s broadcast" or limited broadcast.

Class B Addresses

In a Class B network address, the first 2 bytes are assigned to the network address and the remaining 2 bytes are used for host addresses. The format is as follows:

network.network.host.host

For example, in the IP address 172.16.30.56, the network address is 172.16 and the host address is 30.56.

With a network address being 2 bytes (8 bits each), we're left with 2^{16} unique combinations. But the Internet designers decided that all Class B network addresses should start with the binary digit 1, then 0. This leaves 14 bit positions available to manipulate, so in reality, we get 16,384 (that is, 2^{14}) unique Class B network addresses.

In a Class B network, the RFCs state that the first bit of the first byte must always be turned on but the second bit must always be turned off. If we turn the other 6 bits all off and then all on, we will find the range for a Class B network:

10000000 = 128
10111111 = 191

As you can see, a Class B network is defined when the first byte is configured from 128 to 191.

A Class B address uses 2 bytes for host addresses. This is 2^{16} minus the two reserved patterns (all 0s and all 1s), for a total of 65,534 possible host addresses for each Class B network.

Here's an example of how to find the valid hosts in a Class B network:

- All host bits turned off is the network address: 172.16.0.0.
- All host bits turned on is the broadcast address: 172.16.255.255.

The valid hosts would be the numbers in between the network address and the broadcast address: 172.16.0.1 through 172.16.255.254.

Class C Addresses

The first 3 bytes of a Class C network address are dedicated to the network portion of the address, with only 1 measly byte remaining for the host address. Here's the format:

network.network.network.host

Using the example IP address 192.168.100.102, the network address is 192.168.100 and the host address is 102.

In a Class C network address, the first three bit positions are always the binary 110. The calculation is as follows: 3 bytes, or 24 bits, minus 3 reserved positions leaves 21 positions. Hence, there are 2^{21}, or 2,097,152, possible Class C networks.

For Class C networks, the RFCs define the first 2 bits of the first octet as always turned on, but the third bit can never be on. Following the same process as the previous classes, convert from binary to decimal to find the range. Here's the range for a Class C network:

```
11000000 = 192
11011111 = 223
```

So, if you see an IP address with a range from 192 up to 223, you'll know it's a Class C IP address.

Each unique Class C network has 1 byte to use for host addresses. This gets us to 2^8 or 256, minus the two reserved patterns of all 0s and all 1s, for a total of 254 available host addresses for each Class C network.

Here's an example of how to find a valid host ID in a Class C network:

- All host bits turned off is the network ID: 192.168.100.0.
- All host bits turned on is the broadcast address: 192.168.100.255.

The valid hosts would be the numbers in between the network address and the broadcast address: 192.168.100.1 through 192.168.100.254.

Class D and E Addresses

The addresses 224 to 255 are reserved for Class D and E networks. Class D (224–239) is used for multicast addresses and Class E (240–255) for scientific purposes. But they're really beyond the scope of this book, so I'm not going to go into detail about them here. But you do need to know that the multicast range is from 224.0.0.0 through 239.255.255.255.

Special Purposes of Network Addresses

Some IP addresses are reserved for special purposes, so network administrators can't ever assign these addresses to hosts. Table 7.1 lists the members of this exclusive little club and the reasons why they're included in it.

Private IP Addresses

The people who created the IP addressing scheme also created what we call *private IP addresses*. These addresses can be used on a private network, but they're not routable through the Internet. This is designed for the purpose of creating a measure of much-needed security, but it also conveniently saves valuable IP address space.

If every host on every network had to have real routable IP addresses, we would have run out of available IP addresses to hand out years ago. But by using private IP addresses, ISPs, corporations, and home users only need a relatively tiny group of bona fide IP addresses to connect their networks to the Internet. This is economical because they can use private IP addresses on their inside networks and get along just fine.

To accomplish this task, the ISP and the corporation—the end users, no matter who they are—need to use something called *Network Address Translation (NAT)*, which basically takes a private IP address and converts it for use on the Internet. Many people can use the same real IP address to transmit out onto the Internet. Doing things this way saves mega-tons of address space—a very good thing for us all!

 Real World Scenario

So, What Private IP Address Should I Use?

That's a really great question: Should you use Class A, Class B, or even Class C private addressing when setting up your network? Let's take Acme Corporation in SF as an example. This company is moving into a new building and needs a whole new network (what a treat this is!). It has 14 departments, with about 70 users in each. You could probably squeeze one or two Class C addresses to use, or maybe you could use a Class B, or even a Class A just for fun.

The rule of thumb in the consulting world is, when you're setting up a corporate network—regardless of how small it is—you should use a Class A network address because it gives you the most flexibility and growth options. For example, if you used the 10.0.0.0 network address with a /24 mask, then you'd have 65,536 networks, each with 254 hosts. Lots of room for growth with that network!

(A /24 tells you that a subnet mask has 24 bits out of 32 bits turned on for network subnet-ing a network. This will be covered in more detail in Chapter 8.)

But if you're setting up a home network, you'd opt for a Class C address because it is the easiest for people to understand and configure. Using the default Class C mask gives you one network with 254 hosts—plenty for a home network.

With the Acme Corporation, a nice 10.1.x.0 with a /24 mask (the x is the subnet for each department) makes this easy to design, install, and troubleshoot.

The reserved private addresses are listed in Table 7.2.

TABLE 7.2   Reserved IP Address Space

Address Class	Reserved Address Space
Class A	10.0.0.0 through 10.255.255.255
Class B	172.16.0.0 through 172.31.255.255
Class C	192.168.0.0 through 192.168.255.255

APIPA

I discussed this in Chapter 6, "Introduction to Internet Protocol (IP)," but it is worth repeating here. What happens if you have a few hosts connected together with a switch or hub and you don't have a DHCP server? You can add static IP information to a host or you can let Win-dows provides what is called Automatic Private IP Addressing (APIPA). I don't recommend this, but APIPA is a "feature" so you do need to remember it, hence mentioning it two chapters in a row!

With APIPA, clients can automatically self-configure an IP address and subnet mask, which is the minimum information needed for hosts to communicate when a DHCP server isn't available.

The IP address range for APIPA is 169.254.0.1 through 169.254.255.254. The client also configures itself with a default class B subnet mask of 255.255.0.0.

Broadcast Addresses

Most people use the term *broadcast* as a generic term, and most of the time, we under-stand what they mean. But not always. For example, you might say, "The host broadcasted through a router to a DHCP server," but, well, it's pretty unlikely that this would ever really happen. What you probably mean—using the correct technical jargon—is, "The host broadcasted for an IP address; a router then forwarded this as a unicast packet to the DHCP server." Oh, and remember that with IPv4, broadcasts are pretty important, but with IPv6, there aren't any broadcasts sent at all—now there's something to look forward to finding out about in the next section on IPv6!

Okay, I've referred to broadcast addresses throughout some of the earlier chapters and even showed you some examples. But I really haven't gone into the different terms and uses associated with them yet. It's about time I did, so here are the four different broadcast (generic term *broadcast)* types that I'd like to define for you:

Layer 2 broadcasts   These are sent to all hosts on a LAN.

Broadcasts (Layer 3)   These are sent to all hosts on the network.

Unicast   These are sent to a single destination host.

Multicast   These are packets sent from a single source and transmitted to many devices on different networks.

First, understand that Layer 2 broadcasts are also known as *hardware broadcasts*—they only go out on a LAN, and they don't go past the LAN boundary (router). The typical hardware address is 6 bytes (48 bits) and looks something like 0c.43.a4.f3.12.c2. The broadcast would be all 1s in binary, which would be all *F*s in hexadecimal, as in FF.FF.FF.FF.FF.FF.

Then there are the plain old broadcast addresses at Layer 3. Broadcast messages are meant to reach all hosts on a broadcast domain. These are the network broadcasts that have all host bits on. Here's an example that you're already familiar with: The network address of 172.16.0.0 255.255.0.0 would have a broadcast address of 172.16.255.255—all host bits on. Broadcasts can also be "all networks and all hosts," as indicated by 255.255.255.255. A good example of a broadcast message is an Address Resolution Protocol (ARP) request. When a host has a packet, it knows the logical address (IP) of the destination. To get the packet to the destination, the host needs to forward the packet to a default gateway if the destination resides on a different IP network. If the destination is on the local network, the source will forward the packet directly to the destination. Because the source doesn't have the MAC address to which it needs to forward the frame, it sends out a broadcast, something that every device in the local broadcast domain will listen to. This broadcast says, in essence, "If you are the owner of IP address 192.168.2.3, please forward your MAC address to me," with the source giving the appropriate information.

A unicast is different because it's a broadcast packet that goes from 255.255.255.255 to an actual destination IP address—in other words, it's directed to a specific host. A DHCP client request is a good example of how a unicast works. Here's an example: Your host on a LAN sends out an FF.FF.FF.FF.FF.FF Layer 2 broadcast and 255.255.255.255 Layer 3 destination broadcast looking for a DHCP server on the LAN. The router will see that this is a broadcast meant for the DHCP server because it has a destination port number of 67 (BootP server) and will forward the request to the IP address of the DHCP server on another LAN. So, basically, if your DHCP server IP address is 172.16.10.1, your host just sends out a 255.255.255.255 DHCP client broadcast request, and the router changes that broadcast to the specific destination address of 172.16.10.1. (In order for the router to provide this service, you need to configure the interfaces with the `ip helper-address` command—this is not a default service.)

Multicast is a different beast entirely. At first glance, it appears to be a hybrid of unicast and broadcast communication, but that isn't quite the case. Multicast does allow point-to-multipoint communication, which is similar to broadcasts, but it happens in a different manner. The crux of multicast is that it enables multiple recipients to receive messages without flooding the messages to all hosts on a broadcast domain.

Multicast works by sending messages or data to IP multicast group addresses. Routers then forward copies (unlike broadcasts, which are not forwarded) of the packet out every interface that has hosts subscribed to that group address. This is where multicast differs from broadcast messages—with multicast communication, copies of packets, in theory, are sent only to subscribed hosts. When I say "in theory," this means that the hosts will receive, for example, a multicast packet destined for 224.0.0.10 (this is a Routing Information Protocol [RIP] packet, and only a router running the RIP protocol will read these). All hosts on the broadcast LAN (Ethernet is a broadcast multi-access LAN technology) will pick up the frame, read the destination address, and immediately discard the frame, unless they are in the multicast group. This saves PC processing, not LAN bandwidth. Multicasting can cause severe LAN congestion, in some instances, if not implemented carefully.

There are several different groups that users or applications can subscribe to. The range of multicast addresses starts with 224.0.0.0 and goes through 239.255.255.255. As you can see, this range of addresses falls within IP Class D address space based on classful IP assignment.

Internet Protocol Version 6 (IPv6)

People refer to IPv6 as "the next-generation Internet protocol," and it was originally created as the answer to IPv4's inevitable, looming address-exhaustion crisis. Though you've probably heard a thing or two about IPv6 already, it has been improved even further in the quest to bring us the flexibility, efficiency, capability, and optimized functionality that can truly meet our ever-increasing needs. The capacity of its predecessor, IPv4, pales in comparison—and that's the reason it will eventually fade into history completely.

The IPv6 header and address structure has been completely overhauled, and many of the features that were basically just afterthoughts and addendums in IPv4 are now included as full-blown standards in IPv6. It's well equipped, poised, and ready to manage the mind-blowing demands of the Internet to come.

Why Do We Need IPv6?

Well, the short answer is, because we need to communicate, and our current system isn't really cutting it anymore—kind of like how the Pony Express can't compete with airmail. Just look at how much time and effort we've invested in coming up with slick new ways to conserve bandwidth and IP addresses. We've even come up with Variable Length Subnet Masks (VLSMs) in our struggle to overcome the worsening address drought.

It's reality, the number of people and devices that connect to networks increases each and every day. That's not a bad thing at all—we're finding new and exciting ways to communicate to more people all the time; something that's become integral to our culture today. In fact, it's now pretty much a basic human need. But the forecast isn't exactly blue skies and sunshine because, as I alluded to in this chapter's introduction, IPv4, upon which our ability to communicate is presently dependent, is going to run out of addresses for us to use. IPv4 has only about 4.3 billion addresses available—in theory—and we know that we don't even get to use all of those. There really are only about 250 million addresses that can be assigned to devices. Sure, the use of Classless Inter-Domain Routing (CIDR) and NAT has helped to extend the inevitable dearth of addresses, but the truth is we will run out of them, and it's going to happen within a few years. China is barely online, and we know a huge population of people and corporations there surely want to be. There are a lot of reports that give us all kinds of numbers, but all you really need to think about to convince yourself that I'm not just being an alarmist is the fact that there are about 6.5 billion people in the world today, and it's estimated that just over 10 percent of that population is connected to the Internet—wow! IPv6 to the rescue!

That statistic is basically screaming at us the ugly truth that, based on IPv4's capacity, every person can't even have a computer with an IP address—let alone all the other devices we use with them. I have more than one computer, and it's pretty likely you do too. And I'm not even including in the mix phones, laptops, game consoles, fax machines, routers, switches, and a mother lode of other devices we use every day! So I think I've made it pretty clear that we've got to do something before we run out of addresses and lose the ability to connect with each other as we know it. And that "something" just happens to be implementing IPv6.

The Benefits of and Uses for IPv6

What's so fabulous about IPv6? Is it really the answer to our coming dilemma? Is it really worth it to upgrade from IPv4? All good questions—you may even think of a few more. Of course, there's going to be that group of people with the time-tested and well-known "resistance to change syndrome," but don't listen to them. If we had done that years ago, we'd still be waiting weeks, even months for our mail to arrive via horseback. Instead, just know that the answer is a resounding YES! Not only does IPv6 give us lots of addresses (3.4×10^{38} = definitely enough), but there are many other features built into this version that make it well worth the cost, time, and effort required to migrate to it.

Today's networks, as well as the Internet, have a ton of unforeseen requirements that simply were not considerations when IPv4 was created. We've tried to compensate with a collection of add-ons that can actually make implementing them more difficult than they would be if they were mandated by a standard. By default, IPv6 has improved upon and included many of those features as standard and mandatory. One of these sweet new standards is IPSec—a feature that provides end-to-end security and that I'll cover in Chapter 16, "Wide Area Networks." Another little beauty is known as *mobility*, and as its name suggests, it allows a device to roam from one network to another without dropping connections.

But it's the efficiency features that are really going to rock the house! For starters, the header in an IPv6 packet has half the fields, and they are aligned to 64 bits, which gives us some seriously souped-up processing speed—compared to IPv4, lookups happen at light speed. Most of the information that used to be bound into the IPv4 header was taken out, and now you can choose to put it, or parts of it, back into the header in the form of optional extension headers that follow the basic header fields.

And of course there's that whole new universe of addresses (3.4×10^{38}) we talked about already. But where did we get them? Did that Chris Angel–Mindfreak dude just show up and, blammo, they all materialized? The obvious answer is no; but that huge proliferation of address had to come from somewhere, right? Well, it just so happens that IPv6 gives us a substantially larger address space, meaning the address is a whole lot bigger—four times bigger, as a matter of fact! An IPv6 address is actually 128 bits in length, and no worries—I'm going to break down the address piece by piece and show you exactly what it looks like coming up in the section "IPv6 Addressing and Expressions." For now, let me just say that all that additional room permits more levels of hierarchy inside the address space and a more flexible address architecture. It also makes routing much more efficient and scalable because the addresses can be aggregated a lot more effectively. And IPv6 also allows multiple addresses for hosts and networks. Plus, the new version of IP now includes an expanded use of multicast communication (one device sending to many hosts or to a select group), which will also join in to boost efficiency on networks because communications will be more specific.

IPv4 uses broadcasts very prolifically, causing a bunch of problems, the worst of which is of course the dreaded broadcast storm—an uncontrolled deluge of forwarded broadcast traffic that can bring an entire network to its knees and devour every last bit of bandwidth. Another nasty thing about broadcast traffic is that it interrupts each and every device on the network. When a broadcast is sent out, every machine has to stop what it's doing and analyze the traffic, whether the broadcast is meant for it or not.

But smile, everyone: There is no such thing as a broadcast in IPv6 because it uses multicast traffic instead. And there are two other types of communication as well: unicast, which is the same as it is in IPv4, and a new type called *anycast*. Anycast communication allows the same address to be placed on more than one device so that when traffic is sent to one device addressed in this way, it is routed to the nearest host that shares the same address. This is just the beginning—we'll get more into the various types of communication in the section "Address Types."

IPv6 Addressing and Expressions

Just as understanding how IP addresses are structured and used is critical with IPv4 addressing, it's also vital when it comes to IPv6. You've already read about the fact that at 128 bits, an IPv6 address is much larger than an IPv4 address. Because of this, as well as the new ways the addresses can be used, you've probably guessed that IPv6 will be more complicated to manage. But no worries! As I said, I'll break down the basics and show you what the address looks like, how you can write it, and what many of its common uses are. It's going to be a little weird at first, but before you know it, you'll have it nailed.

So let's take a look at Figure 7.2, which has a sample IPv6 address broken down into sections.

FIGURE 7.2 IPv6 address example

```
2001:0db8:3c4d:0012:0000:0000:1234:56ab
_____|___|_____
Global prefix   Subnet      Interface ID
```

As you can now see, the address is truly much larger—but what else is different? Well, first, notice that it has eight groups of numbers instead of four and also that those groups are separated by colons instead of periods. And hey, wait a second... there are letters in that address! Yep, the address is expressed in hexadecimal just like a MAC address is, so you could say this address has eight 16-bit hexadecimal colon-delimited blocks. That's already quite a mouthful, and you probably haven't even tried to say the address out loud yet.

One other thing I want to point out is for when you set up your test network to play with IPv6, because I know you're going to want to do that. When you use a web browser to make an HTTP connection to an IPv6 device, you have to type the address into the browser with brackets around the literal address. Why? Well, a colon is already being used by the browser for specifying a port number. So basically, if you don't enclose the address in brackets, the browser will have no way to identify the information.

Here's an example of how this looks:

`http://[2001:0db8:3c4d:0012:0000:0000:1234:56ab]/default.html`

Now obviously, if you could, you would rather use names to specify a destination (like www.lammle.com); but even though it's definitely going to be a pain in the rear, you just have to accept the fact that sometimes you have to bite the bullet and type in the address number. It should be pretty clear that DNS is going to become extremely important when implementing IPv6.

Shortened Expression

The good news is, there are a few tricks to help rescue you when writing these monster addresses. For one thing, you can actually leave out parts of the address to abbreviate it, but to get away with doing that you have to follow a couple of rules. First, you can drop any leading zeros in each of the individual blocks. After you do that, the sample address from earlier would then look like this:

`2001:db8:3c4d:12:0:0:1234:56ab`

Okay, that's a definite improvement—at least you don't have to write all of those extra zeros! But what about whole blocks that don't have anything in them except zeros? Well, you can kind of lose those too—at least some of them. Again referring to our sample address, you can remove the two blocks of zeros by replacing them with double colons, like this:

`2001:db8:3c4d:12::1234:56ab`

Cool—you replaced the blocks of all zeros with double colons. The rule you have to follow to get away with this is that you can only replace one contiguous block of zeros in an address. So if my address has four blocks of zeros and each of them is separated, I don't get to replace them all. Check out this example:

2001:0000:0000:0012:0000:0000:1234:56ab

And just know that you *can't* do this:

2001::12::1234:56ab

Instead, this is the best that you can do:

2001::12:0:0:1234:56ab

The reason why this example is your best shot is that if you remove two sets of zeros, the device looking at the address will have no way of knowing where the zeros go back in. Basically, the router would look at the incorrect address and say, "Well, do I place two blocks into the first set of double colons and two into the second set, or do I place three blocks into the first set and one block into the second set?" And on and on it would go, because the information the router needs just isn't there.

Address Types

We're all familiar with IPv4's unicast, broadcast, and multicast addresses, which basically define who or at least how many other devices we're talking to. But as I mentioned, IPv6 adds to that trio and introduces the anycast. Broadcasts, as we know them, have been eliminated in IPv6 because of their cumbersome inefficiency.

Let's find out what each of these types of IPv6 addressing and communication methods do for us:

Unicast   Packets addressed to a unicast address are delivered to a single interface. For load balancing, multiple interfaces can use the same address. There are a few different types of unicast addresses, but we don't need to get into that here.

Global unicast addresses   These are your typical publicly routable addresses, and they're the same as they are in IPv4.

Link-local addresses   These are like the private addresses in IPv4 in that they're not meant to be routed. Think of them as a handy tool that gives you the ability to throw a temporary LAN together for meetings or for creating a small LAN that's not going to be routed but still needs to share and access files and services locally.

Unique local addresses   These addresses are also intended for non-routing purposes, but they are nearly globally unique, so it's unlikely you'll ever have one of them overlap with any other address. Unique local addresses were designed to replace site-local addresses, so they basically do almost exactly what IPv4 private addresses do—allow communication throughout a site while being routable to multiple local networks.

Multicast   Again, as in IPv4, packets addressed to a multicast address are delivered to all interfaces identified by the multicast address. Sometimes people call them *one-to-many addresses*. It's really easy to spot multicast addresses in IPv6 because they always start with *FF*."

Anycast   Like multicast addresses, an anycast address identifies multiple interfaces, but there's a big difference: the anycast packet is delivered to only one address—actually, to the first IPv6 address it finds defined in terms of routing distance. And again, this address is special because you can apply a single address to more than one interface. You could call them one-to-one-of-many addresses, but just saying "anycast" is a lot easier.

You're probably wondering if there are any special, reserved addresses in IPv6 because you know they're there in IPv4. Well, there are—plenty of them! Let's go over them now.

Special Addresses

I'm going to list some of the addresses and address ranges that you should definitely make a point to remember because you'll eventually use them. They're all special or reserved for specific use; but unlike IPv4, IPv6 gives us a galaxy of addresses, so reserving a few here and there doesn't hurt a thing.

0:0:0:0:0:0:0:0   Equals ::. This is the equivalent of IPv4's 0.0.0.0 and is typically the source address of a host when you're using stateful configuration.

0:0:0:0:0:0:0:1   Equals ::1. The equivalent of 127.0.0.1 in IPv4.

0:0:0:0:0:0:192.168.100.1   This is how an IPv4 address would be written in a mixed IPv6/IPv4 network environment.

2000::/3   The global unicast address range.

FC00::/7   The unique local unicast range.

FE80::/10   The link-local unicast range.

FF00::/8   The multicast range.

3FFF:FFFF::/32   Reserved for examples and documentation.

2001:0DB8::/32   Also reserved for examples and documentation.

2002::/16   Used with 6to4, which is the transition system—the structure that allows IPv6 packets to be transmitted over an IPv4 network without the need to configure explicit tunnels.

Summary

In this chapter, I covered the very basics of both IPv4 and IPv6 and how they work in an internetwork (remember that if the word *IP* is used alone, it is referring to just IPv4). As you now know by reading this chapter, even when discussing and configuring the basics, there is a lot to understand—and we just scratched the surface. But trust me when I say this—you now know more than you'll need to meet the Network+ objectives.

I discussed in detail the difference between each class of address and how to find a network address, broadcast address, and valid host range.

Last, I talked about why we need IPv6 and the benefits associated with it. I followed that up by covering addressing with IPv6 as well as how to use the shortened expressions. And during the talk on addressing with IPv6, I showed you the different address types, plus the special addresses reserved in IPv6.

This next chapter is very important, but it's one that some people find rather challenging; so take a break and get ready for a really fun, but long chapter on IP subnetting. I promise not to torture you too much!

Exam Essentials

Remember the Class A range.   The IP range for a Class A network is 1–126. This provides 8 bits of network addressing and 24 bits of host addressing by default.

Remember the Class B range.   The IP range for a Class B network is 128–191. Class B addressing provides 16 bits of network addressing and 16 bits of host addressing by default.

Remember the Class C range.   The IP range for a Class C network is 192–223. Class C addressing provides 24 bits of network addressing and 8 bits of host addressing by default.

Remember the Private IP ranges.   The Class A private address range is 10.0.0.0 through 10.255.255.255.

The Class B private address range is 172.16.0.0 through 172.31.255.255.

The Class C private address range is 192.168.0.0 through 192.168.255.255.

Understand why we need IPv6.   Without IPv6, the world would soon be depleted of IP addresses.

Understand link-local.   Link-local is like an IPv4 private IP address, but it can't be routed at all, not even in your organization.

Understand unique local.   This, like link-local, is like private IP addresses in IPv4 and cannot be routed to the Internet. However, the difference between link-local and unique local is that unique local can be routed within your organization or company.

Remember IPv6 addressing.   IPv6 addressing is not like IPv4 addressing. IPv6 addressing has much more address space and is 128 bits long, represented in hexadecimal, unlike IPv4, which is only 32 bits long and represented in decimals.

Written Lab

1. What is the valid range of values that may appear in an IPv4 octet? Give your answer in decimal as well as binary.

2. Name some of the benefits of IPv6 over IPv4.

3. What is the term for the auto-configuration technology responsible for addresses that start with 169.254?

4. What does the IP Properties selection Obtain an IP Address Automatically indicate?

5. What effect will an inappropriate DHCP server have on hosts using static IP addresses?

6. What is the name for a 48-bit (6-byte) numerical address physically assigned to a network interface, such as a NIC?

7. What gives IPv6 the ability to reference more addresses than IPv4?

8. What predecessor to DHCP, on which DHCP is based, was used to assign a workstation its IP information and to supply it with a boot image?

9. What is the Class C range of values for the first octet in decimal and in binary?

10. What is the 127.0.0.1 address used for?

(The answers to the Written Lab can be found following the answers to the Review Questions for this chapter.)

Review Questions

1. Which of the following addresses is not allowed on the Internet?
    A. 191.192.168.1
    B. 191.168.169.254
    C. 172.32.255.0
    D. 172.31.12.251

2. A host automatically configured with an address from which of the following ranges indicates an inability to contact a DHCP server?
    A. 169.254.0.X with a mask of 255.255.255.0
    B. 169.254.X.X with a mask of 255.255.0.0
    C. 169.254.X.X with a mask of 255.255.255.0
    D. 169.255.X.X with a mask of 255.255.0.0

3. Which statement regarding private IP addresses is most accurate?
    A. Private addresses cannot be used in intranets that require routing.
    B. Private addresses must be assigned by a registrar or ISP.
    C. A remote host across the Internet cannot ping your host if it has a private address.
    D. Private addresses can only be used by a single administrative domain.

4. Which of the following is a valid Class A address?
    A. 191.10.0.1 255.0.0.0
    B. 127.10.0.1 255.0.0.0
    C. 128.10.0.1 255.0.0.0
    D. 126.10.0.1 255.0.0.0

5. Which of the following is a valid Class B address?
    A. 10.1.1.1 255.255.0.0
    B. 126.1.1.1 255.255.0.0
    C. 129.1.1.1 255.255.0.0
    D. 192.168.1.1 255.255.0.0

6. Which of the following describes a broadcast address?
    A. All network bits are on (1s).
    B. All host bits are on (1s).
    C. All network bits are off (0s).
    D. All host bits are off (0s).

7. Which of the following is a Layer 2 broadcast?

    A. FF:FF:FF:EE:EE:EE

    B. FF:FF:FF:FF:FF:FF

    C. 255.255.255.255

    D. 255.0.0.0

8. In a class C IP address, how long is the network address?

    A. 8 bits

    B. 16 bits

    C. 24 bits

    D. 32 bits

9. Which of the following is true when describing a unicast address?

    A. Packets addressed to a unicast address are delivered to a single interface.

    B. These are your typical publicly routable addresses, just like regular publicly routable addresses in IPv4.

    C. These are like private addresses in IPv4 in that they are not meant to be routed.

    D. These addresses are meant for nonrouting purposes, but they are almost globally unique so it is unlikely they will have an address overlap.

10. A host is rebooted and you view the IP address that it was assigned. The address is 169.123.13.34. Which of the following happened?

    A. The host received an APIPA address

    B. The host received a multicast address

    C. The host received a public address

    D. The host received a private address

11. An IPv4 addresses uses 32 bits. How many bits is an IPv6 address?

    A. 64

    B. 128

    C. 192

    D. 255

12. Which of the following is true when describing a multicast address?

    A. Packets addressed to a unicast address from a multicast address are delivered to a single interface.

    B. Packets are delivered to all interfaces identified by the address. This is also called a one-to-many address.

    C. It identifies multiple interfaces and is delivered to only one address. This address can also be called one-to-one-of-many.

    D. These addresses are meant for nonrouting purposes, but they are almost globally unique so it is unlikely they will have an address overlap.

13. Which of the following is true when describing an anycast address?

    A. Packets addressed to a unicast address from an anycast address are delivered to a single interface.

    B. Packets are delivered to all interfaces identified by the address. This is also called a one-to-many address.

    C. This address identifies multiple interfaces, and the anycast packet is delivered to only one address. This address can also be called one-to-one-of-many.

    D. These addresses are meant for nonrouting purposes, but they are almost globally unique so it is unlikely they will have an address overlap.

14. You want to ping the loopback address of your local host. Which two addresses could you type?

    A. `ping 127.0.0.1`

    B. `ping 0.0.0.0`

    C. `ping ::1`

    D. `trace 0.0.::1`

15. What two statements about IPv6 addresses are true?

    A. Leading zeros are required.

    B. Two colons (::) are used to represent successive hexadecimal fields of zeros.

    C. Two colons (::) are used to separate fields.

    D. A single interface will have multiple IPv6 addresses of different types.

16. What two statements about IPv4 and IPv6 addresses are true?

    A. An IPv6 address is 32 bits long, represented in hexadecimal.

    B. An IPv6 address is 128 bits long, represented in decimal.

    C. An IPv4 address is 32 bits long, represented in decimal.

    D. An IPv6 address is 128 bits long, represented in hexadecimal.

17. Which of the following is a Class C network address?

    A. 10.10.10.0 255.255.255.0

    B. 127.0.0.1 255.255.255.0

    C. 128.0.0.0 255.255.0.0

    D. 192.255.254.0 255.255.255.0

18. Which two of the following are private IP addresses? (Choose two.)

    A. 12.0.0.1

    B. 168.172.19.39

    C. 172.20.14.36

    D. 172.33.194.30

    E. 192.168.24.43

19. Which of the following is a valid IP address that can be used on the Internet (meaning the public addressing scheme)?

   A. 10.10.1.1

   B. 168.16.1.1

   C. 234.1.1.1

   D. 172.30.1.1

20. Which of the following is an invalid IP address for a host?

   A. 10.0.0.1

   B. 128.0.0.1

   C. 224.0.0.1

   D. 172.0.0.1

Answers to Review Questions

1. D. The addresses in the range 172.16.0.0 through 172.31.255.255 are all considered private, based on RFC 1918. Use of these addresses on the Internet is prohibited so that they can be used simultaneously in different administrative domains without concern for conflict. Some experts in the industry believe these addresses are not routable, which is not true.

2. B. APIPA uses the link-local private address range of 169.254.0.0 through 169.254.255.255 and a subnet mask of 255.255.0.0 (see RFC 3330). APIPA addresses are used by DHCP clients that cannot contact a DHCP server and have no static alternate configuration. These addresses are not Internet-routable and cannot, by default, be used across routers on an internetwork.

3. C. Private IP addresses are not routable over the Internet, as either source or destination addresses. Because of that fact, any entity that wishes to use such addresses internally can do so without causing conflicts with other entities and without asking permission of any registrar or service provider. Despite not being allowed on the Internet, private IP addresses are fully routable on private intranets.

4. D. The Class A range is 1–126 in the first octet/byte, so this makes answer B incorrect. Only answer D is a valid Class A address.

5. C. The Class B range is 128–191 in the first octet/byte. Only answer C is a valid Class B address.

6. B. If you turned on all host bits (all of the host bits are 1s), this would be a broadcast address for that network.

7. B. A Layer 2 broadcast is also referred to as a MAC address broadcast, which is in hexadecimal and is FF:FF:FF:FF:FF:FF

8. C. A default class C subnet mask is 255.255.255.0, which means that the first three octets are the network number, or first 24 bits.

9. A. Packets addressed to a unicast address are delivered to a single interface. For load balancing, multiple interfaces can use the same address.

10. C. I wonder how many picked APIPA address as your answer? An APIPA address is 169.254.X.X. The host address in this question is a public address. Somewhat of a tricky question if you did not read carefully.

11. B. An IPv6 address is 128 bits in size.

12. B. Packets addressed to a multicast address are delivered to all interfaces identified by the multicast address, the same as in IPv4. A multicast address is also called a one-to-many address. You can tell multicast addresses in IPv6 because they always start with FF.

13. C. Anycast addresses identify multiple interfaces, which is the same as multicast; however, the big difference is that the anycast packet is delivered to only one address: the first one it finds defined in the terms of routing distance. This address can also be called one-to-one-of-many.

14. A, C. The loopback address with IPv4 is 127.0.0.1. With IPv6, that address is ::1.

15. B, D. In order to shorten the written length of an IPv6 address, successive fields of zeros may be replaced by double colons. In trying to shorten the address further, leading zeros may also be removed. Just as with IPv4, a single device's interface can have more than one address; with IPv6 there are more types of addresses and the same rule applies. There can be link-local, global unicast, and multicast addresses all assigned to the same interface.

16. C, D. IPv4 addresses are 32 bits long and are represented in decimal format. IPv6 addresses are 128 bits long and represented in hexadecimal format.

17. D. Only answer D is in the Class C range of 192–224. It might look wrong because there is a 255 in the address, but this is not wrong—you can have a 255 in a network address.

18. C, E. The Class A private address range is 10.0.0.0 through 10.255.255.255. The Class B private address range is 172.16.0.0 through 172.31.255.255, and the Class C private address range is 192.168.0.0 through 192.168.255.255.

19. B. The private address range is 10.0.0.0 through 10.255.255.255, 172.16.0.0 through 172.31.255.255 and 192.168.0.0 through 192.168.255.255. Also, 224.0.0.0 through 239.255.255.255 is reserved for multicast addressing.

20. C. Answer C is a multicast address and cannot be used to address hosts.

Answers to Written Lab

1. The range of values that an IPv4 octet can take on is 0 through 255 in decimal, which stems from the values 00000000 through 11111111 in binary.

2. IPv6 has the following characteristics, among others, that make it preferable to IPv4: more available addresses, simpler header, options for authentication and other security.

3. Automatic Private IP Addressing (APIPA) is the technology that results in hosts automatically configuring themselves with addresses that begin with 169.254.

4. Filling in the Obtain an IP Address Automatically radio button in IP Properties configures the host as a DHCP client.

5. None; DHCP servers cannot override statically assigned IP information.

6. A MAC address, sometimes called a hardware address or even a burned-in address.

7. The fact that it has 128-bit (16-octet) addresses, compared to IPv4's 32-bit (4-octet) addresses.

8. BootP, the Bootstrap Protocol, used the same port numbers as DHCP but supplied more simplified information to a diskless workstation and allowed the workstation to download a remote boot image.

9. 192–223, 110*xxxxx*.

10. Loopback or diagnostics.

Chapter

8

IP Subnetting, Troubleshooting IP, and Introduction to NAT

THE FOLLOWING COMPTIA NETWORK+ EXAM OBJECTIVES ARE COVERED IN THIS CHAPTER:

✓ **1.4 Given a scenario, evaluate the proper use of the following addressing technologies and addressing schemes**

- Addressing Technologies

    - Subnetting

    - Classful vs. classless (e.g., CIDR, Supernetting)

    - NAT

    - PAT

    - SNAT

    - Public vs. private

This chapter's focus will really zoom in on IP addressing to ensure you have it nailed down tight. This is an integral aspect of networking, and it's important to your success on the exams and as a professional too!

We'll start with subnetting an IP network. You're going to have to really apply yourself, because subnetting takes time and practice in order to do it correctly and quickly. So be patient and do whatever it takes to get this stuff dialed in. This chapter truly is important—possibly the most important chapter in this book for you to understand. Make it part of you!

I'll thoroughly cover IP subnetting from the very beginning. I know this might sound weird to you, but I think you'll be much better off if you can try to forget everything you've learned about subnetting before reading this chapter—especially if you've been to a Microsoft class!

I'll also take you through IP address troubleshooting and walk you through each of the steps recommended when you're faced with troubleshooting an IP network. Finally, I'll finish up with an introduction to Network Address Translation—there are various types of NAT, and you need to know when you would use each one.

So get psyched—you're about to go for quite a ride! This chapter will truly help you understand IP addressing and networking, so don't get discouraged or give up. If you stick with it, I promise that one day you'll look back on this and be really glad you decided to stay the course. It's one of those things that after you understand it, you'll laugh at that time, way back when, when you thought this was hard. So, are you ready now? Let's go!

 For up-to-the-minute updates for this chapter, please see www.lammle.com or www.sybex.com/go/comptianetwork+studyguide.

Subnetting Basics

In Chapter 7, "IP Addressing," you learned how to define and find the valid host ranges used in a Class A, Class B, or Class C network address by turning the host bits all off and then all on. This is very good, but here's the catch: You were defining only one network. What would happen if you wanted to take one network address and create six networks from it? You would have to do something called *subnetting*, because that's what allows you to take one larger network and break it into a bunch of smaller networks.

There are loads of reasons in favor of subnetting, including the following benefits:

- Reduced network traffic

  We all appreciate less traffic of any kind. Networks are no different. Without trusty routers, packet traffic could grind the entire network down to a near standstill. With routers, most traffic will stay on the local network; only packets destined for other networks will pass through the router. Routers create broadcast domains. The more broadcast domains you create, the smaller the broadcast domains and the less network traffic on each network segment.

- Optimized network performance

  This is the very cool reward you get when you reduce network traffic!

- Simplified management

  It's easier to identify and isolate network problems in a group of smaller connected networks than within one gigantic network.

- Facilitated spanning of large geographical distances

  Because WAN links are considerably slower and more expensive than LAN links, a single large network that spans long distances can create problems in every area previously listed. Connecting multiple smaller networks makes the system more efficient.

Next, we're going to move on to subnetting a network address. This is the good part—ready?

How to Create Subnets

To create subnetworks, you take bits from the host portion of the IP address and reserve them to define the subnet address. This means fewer bits for hosts, so the more subnets, the fewer bits left available for defining hosts.

Soon, I'll show you how to create subnets, starting with Class C addresses. But before you actually implement subnetting, you really need to determine your current requirements as well as plan for future conditions.

Follow these steps—they're your recipe for solid design:

1. Determine the number of required network IDs:
   - One for each subnet
   - One for each wide area network connection
2. Determine the number of required host IDs per subnet:
   - One for each TCP/IP host
   - One for each router interface
3. Based on the previous requirements, create the following:
   - One subnet mask for your entire network
   - A unique subnet ID for each physical segment
   - A range of host IDs for each subnet

Understanding the Powers of 2

By the way, powers of 2 are really important to memorize for use with IP subnetting. To review powers of 2, remember that when you see a number with another number to its upper right (an exponent), this means you should multiply the number by itself as many times as the upper number specifies. For example, 2^3 is $2 \times 2 \times 2$, which equals 8. Here's a list of powers of 2 that you should commit to memory:

$2^1 = 2$

$2^2 = 4$

$2^3 = 8$

$2^4 = 16$

$2^5 = 32$

$2^6 = 64$

$2^7 = 128$

$2^8 = 256$

$2^9 = 512$

$2^{10} = 1,024$

$2^{11} = 2,048$

$2^{12} = 4,096$

$2^{13} = 8,192$

$2^{14} = 16,384$

If you hate math, don't get stressed out about knowing all these exponents—it's helpful to know them, but it's not absolutely necessary. Here's a little trick, because you're working with 2s: Each successive power of 2 is double the previous one.

For example, all you have to do to remember the value of 2^9 is to first know that $2^8 = 256$. Why? Because when you double 2 to the eighth power (256), you get 2^9 (or 512). To determine the value of 2^{10}, simply start at $2^8 = 256$, and then double it twice.

You can go the other way as well. If you needed to know what 2^6 is, for example, you just cut 256 in half two times: once to reach 2^7 and then one more time to reach 2^6. Not bad, right?

Subnet Masks

For the subnet address scheme to work, every machine on the network must know which part of the host address will be used as the subnet address. This is accomplished by assigning a *subnet mask* to each machine. A subnet mask is a 32-bit value that allows the recipient of

IP packets to distinguish the network ID portion of the IP address from the host ID portion of the IP address.

The network administrator creates a 32-bit subnet mask composed of 1s and 0s. The 1s in the subnet mask represent the positions that refer to the network or subnet addresses.

Not all networks need subnets, meaning they use the default subnet mask. This is basically the same as saying that a network doesn't have a subnet address. Table 8.1 shows the default subnet masks for Classes A, B, and C. These default masks cannot and do not change. In other words, you can't make a Class B subnet mask read 255.0.0.0. If you try, the host will read that address as invalid and usually won't even let you type it in. For a Class A network, you can't change the first byte in a subnet mask; it must read 255.0.0.0 at a minimum. Similarly, you cannot assign 255.255.255.255, because this is all 1s—a broadcast address. A Class B address must start with 255.255.0.0, and a Class C has to start with 255.255.255.0. Check out Table 8.1.

TABLE 8.1   Default Subnet Mask

Class	Format	Default Subnet Mask
A	*network.host.host.host*	255.0.0.0
B	*network.network.host.host*	255.255.0.0
C	*network.network.network.host*	255.255.255.0

Classless Inter-Domain Routing (CIDR)

Another term you need to know is *Classless Inter-Domain Routing (CIDR)*. It's basically the method that Internet service providers (ISPs) use to allocate an amount of addresses to a company, a home—a customer. They provide addresses in a certain block size; I'll be going into that greater detail later in this chapter.

When you receive a block of addresses from an ISP, what you get will look something like this: 192.168.10.32/28. This is telling you what your subnet mask is. The slash notation (/) means how many bits are turned on (1s). Obviously, the maximum could only be /32 because a byte is 8 bits and there are 4 bytes in an IP address: 4 × 8 = 32. But keep in mind that the largest subnet mask available (regardless of the class of address) can only be a /30 because you've got to keep at least 2 bits for host bits.

Take, for example, a Class A default subnet mask, which is 255.0.0.0. This means that the first byte of the subnet mask is all ones (1s), or 11111111. When referring to a slash notation, you need to count all the 1s bits to figure out your mask. The 255.0.0.0 is considered a /8 because it has 8 bits that are 1s—that is, 8 bits that are turned on.

A Class B default mask would be 255.255.0.0, which is a /16 because 16 bits are ones (1s): 11111111.11111111.00000000.00000000.

Table 8.2 offers a listing of every available subnet mask and its equivalent CIDR slash notation.

TABLE 8.2   CIDR Values

Subnet Mask	CIDR Value
255.0.0.0	/8
255.128.0.0	/9
255.192.0.0	/10
255.224.0.0	/11
255.240.0.0	/12
255.248.0.0	/13
255.252.0.0	/14
255.254.0.0	/15
255.255.0.0	/16
255.255.128.0	/17
255.255.192.0	/18
255.255.224.0	/19
255.255.240.0	/20
255.255.248.0	/21
255.255.252.0	/22
255.255.254.0	/23
255.255.255.0	/24
255.255.255.128	/25
255.255.255.192	/26
255.255.255.224	/27
255.255.255.240	/28
255.255.255.248	/29
255.255.255.252	/30

Make a note to self that the /8 through /15 can only be used with Class A network addresses. /16 through /23 can be used by Class A and B network addresses. /24 through /30 can be used by Class A, B, and C network addresses. This is a big reason why most companies use Class A network addresses. By being allowed the use all subnet masks, they gain the valuable benefit of maximum flexibility for their network design.

Subnetting Class C Addresses

There are many different ways to subnet a network. The right way is the way that works best for you. In a Class C address, only 8 bits are available for defining the hosts. Remember that subnet bits start at the left and go to the right, without skipping bits. This means that the only Class C subnet masks can be the following:

Binary	Decimal	CIDR
00000000	0	/24
10000000	128	/25
11000000	192	/26
11100000	224	/27
11110000	240	/28
11111000	248	/29
11111100	252	/30

We can't use a /31 or /32 because remember, we have to leave at least 2 host bits for assigning IP addresses to hosts.

Okay—get ready for something special... I'm going to teach you an alternate method of subnetting that makes it a whole lot easier to subnet larger numbers in no time. And trust me, you really do need to be able to subnet fast!

Subnetting a Class C Address: The Fast Way!

When you've chosen a possible subnet mask for your network and need to determine the number of subnets, valid hosts, and broadcast addresses of a subnet that the mask provides, all you need to do is answer five simple questions:

- How many subnets does the chosen subnet mask produce?
- How many valid hosts per subnet are available?
- What are the valid subnets?

- What's the broadcast address of each subnet?
- What are the valid hosts in each subnet?

At this point, it's important that you both understand and have memorized your powers of 2. Please refer to the sidebar, "Understanding the Powers of 2," earlier in this chapter if you need some help. Here's how you get the answers to those five big questions:

- *How many subnets?* 2^x = number of subnets. x is the number of masked bits, or the 1s. For example, in 11000000, the number of 1s gives us 2^2 subnets. In this example, there are 4 subnets.

- *How many hosts per subnet?* $2^y - 2$ = number of hosts per subnet. y is the number of unmasked bits, or the 0s. For example, in 11000000, the number of 0s gives us $2^6 - 2$ hosts. In this example, there are 62 hosts per subnet. You need to subtract 2 for the subnet address and the broadcast address, which are not valid hosts.

- *What are the valid subnets?* 256 – *subnet mask* = *block size*, or increment number. An example would be 256 – 192 = 64. The block size of a 192 mask is always 64. Start counting at zero in blocks of 64 until you reach the subnet mask value, and these are your subnets. 0, 64, 128, 192. Easy, huh?

- *What's the broadcast address for each subnet?* Now here's the really easy part. Because we counted our subnets in the last section as 0, 64, 128, and 192, the broadcast address is always the number right before the next subnet. For example, the 0 subnet has a broadcast address of 63 because the next subnet is 64. The 64 subnet has a broadcast address of 127 because the next subnet is 128. And so on. And remember, the broadcast of the last subnet is always 255.

- *What are the valid hosts?* Valid hosts are the numbers between the subnets, omitting all the 0s and all 1s. For example, if 64 is the subnet number and 127 is the broadcast address, then 65–126 is the valid host range—it's *always* the numbers between the subnet address and the broadcast address.

I know this can truly seem confusing. But it really isn't as hard as it seems to be at first—just hang in there! Why not try a few and see for yourself?

Subnetting Practice Examples: Class C Addresses

Here's your opportunity to practice subnetting Class C addresses using the method I just described. Exciting, isn't it? We're going to start with the first Class C subnet mask and work through every subnet that we can using a Class C address. When we're done, I'll show you how easy this is with Class A and B networks too!

Practice Example #1C: 255.255.255.128 (/25)

Because 128 is 10000000 in binary, there is only 1 bit for subnetting, and there are 7 bits for hosts. We're going to subnet the Class C network address 192.168.10.0.

192.168.10.0 = Network address

255.255.255.128 = Subnet mask

Now, let's answer the big five:

- *How many subnets?* Because 128 is 1 bit on (10000000), the answer is $2^1 = 2$.

- *How many hosts per subnet?* We have 7 host bits off (**10000000**), so the equation is $2^7 - 2 = 126$ hosts.

- *What are the valid subnets?* 256 − 128 = 128. Remember, we'll start at zero and count in our block size, so our subnets are 0, 128.

- *What's the broadcast address for each subnet?* The number right before the value of the next subnet is all host bits turned on and equals the broadcast address. For the 0 subnet, the next subnet is 128, so the broadcast of the 0 subnet is 127.

- *What are the valid hosts?* These are the numbers between the subnet and broadcast address. The easiest way to find the hosts is to write out the subnet address and the broadcast address. This way, the valid hosts are obvious. The following table shows the 0 and 128 subnets, the valid host ranges of each, and the broadcast address of both subnets:

Subnet	0	128
First host	1	129
Last host	126	254
Broadcast	127	255

Before moving on to the next example, take a look at Figure 8.1. Okay, looking at a Class C /25, it's pretty clear there are two subnets. But so what—why is this significant? Well actually, it's not, but that's not the right question. What you really want to know is what you would do with this information!

FIGURE 8.1 Implementing a Class C /25 logical network

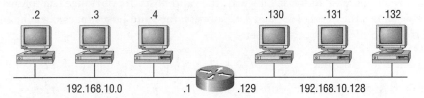

```
Router#show ip route
[output cut]
C 192.168.10.0 is directly connected to Ethernet 0.
C 192.168.10.128 is directly connected to Ethernet 1.
```

The key to understanding subnetting is to understand the very reason you need to do it. And I'm going to demonstrate this by going through the process of building a physical network—and let's add a router. (We now have an internetwork, as I truly hope you already know!) Because we added that router, in order for the hosts on our internetwork to communicate, they must now have a logical network addressing scheme. We could use IPX or IPv6, but IPv4 is still the most popular, and it also just happens to be what we're studying at the moment, so that's what we're going with.

Okay—now take a look back to Figure 8.1. There are two physical networks, so we're going to implement a logical addressing scheme that allows for two logical networks. As always, it's a really good idea to look ahead and consider likely growth scenarios—both short and long term, but for this example, a /25 will do the trick.

Practice Example #2C: 255.255.255.192 (/26)

In this second example, we're going to subnet the network address 192.168.10.0 using the subnet mask 255.255.255.192.

> 192.168.10.0 = Network address

> 255.255.255.192 = Subnet mask

It's time to answer the big five:

- *How many subnets?* Because 192 is 2 bits on (**11**000000), the answer is $2^2 = 4$ subnets.

- *How many hosts per subnet?* We have 6 host bits off (11**000000**), so the equation is $2^6 - 2 = 62$ hosts.

- *What are the valid subnets?* 256 − 192 = 64. Remember, we start at zero and count in our block size, so our subnets are 0, 64, 128, and 192.

- *What's the broadcast address for each subnet?* The number right before the value of the next subnet is all host bits turned on and equals the broadcast address. For the 0 subnet, the next subnet is 64, so the broadcast address for the 0 subnet is 63.

- *What are the valid hosts?* These are the numbers between the subnet and broadcast address. The easiest way to find the hosts is to write out the subnet address and the broadcast address. This way, the valid hosts are obvious. The following table shows the 0, 64, 128, and 192 subnets, the valid host ranges of each, and the broadcast address of each subnet:

The subnets (do this first)	0	64	128	192
Our first host (perform host addressing last)	1	65	129	193
Our last host	62	126	190	254
The broadcast address (do this second)	63	127	191	255

Okay, again, before getting into the next example, you can see that we can now subnet a /26. And what are you going to do with this fascinating information? Implement it! We'll use Figure 8.2 to practice a /26 network implementation.

The /26 mask provides four subnetworks, and we need a subnet for each router interface. With this mask, in this example, we actually have room to add another router interface.

FIGURE 8.2 Implementing a Class C /26 logical network

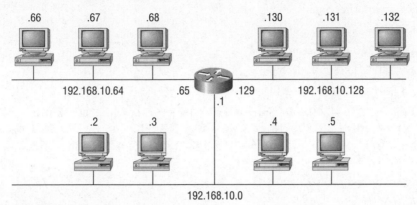

```
Router#show ip route
[output cut]
C 192.168.10.0 is directly connected to Ethernet 0
C 192.168.10.64 is directly connected to Ethernet 1
C 192.168.10.128 is directly connected to Ethernet 2
```

Practice Example #3C: 255.255.255.224 (/27)

This time, we'll subnet the network address 192.168.10.0 and subnet mask 255.255.255.224.

192.168.10.0 = Network address

255.255.255.224 = Subnet mask

- *How many subnets?* 224 is 11100000, so our equation is $2^3 = 8$.

- *How many hosts?* $2^5 - 2 = 30$.

- *What are the valid subnets?* 256 − 224 = 32. We just start at zero and count to the subnet mask value in blocks (increments) of 32: 0, 32, 64, 96, 128, 160, 192, and 224.

- *What's the broadcast address for each subnet (always the number right before the next subnet)?*

- *What are the valid hosts (the numbers between the subnet number and the broadcast address)?*

To answer the last two questions, first just write out the subnets, and then write out the broadcast addresses—the number right before the next subnet. Last, fill in the host addresses. The following table gives you all the subnets for the 255.255.255.224 Class C subnet mask:

The subnet address	0	32	64	96	128	160	192	224
The first valid host	1	33	65	97	129	161	193	225
The last valid host	30	62	94	126	158	190	222	254
The broadcast address	31	63	95	127	159	191	223	255

Practice Example #4C: 255.255.255.240 (/28)

Let's practice on another one:

> 192.168.10.0 = Network address

> 255.255.255.240 = Subnet mask

- *Subnets?* 240 is 11110000 in binary. 2^4 = 16.
- *Hosts?* 4 host bits, or $2^4 - 2$ = 14.
- *Valid subnets?* 256 – 240 = 16. Start at 0: 0 + 16 = 16. 16 + 16 = 32. 32 + 16 = 48. 48 + 16 = 64. 64 + 16 = 80. 80 + 16 = 96. 96 + 16 = 112. 112 + 16 = 128. 128 + 16 = 144. 144 + 16 = 160. 160 + 16 = 176. 176 + 16 = 192. 192 + 16 = 208. 208 + 16 = 224. 224 + 16 = 240.
- *Broadcast address for each subnet?*
- *Valid hosts?*

To answer the last two questions, check out the following table. It gives you the subnets, valid hosts, and broadcast addresses for each subnet. First, find the address of each subnet using the block size (increment). Second, find the broadcast address of each subnet increment (it's always the number right before the next valid subnet); then, just fill in the host addresses. The following table shows the available subnets, hosts, and broadcast addresses provided from a Class C 255.255.255.240 mask:

Subnet	0	16	32	48	64	80	96	112	128	144	160	176	192	208	224	240
First host	1	17	33	49	65	81	97	113	129	145	161	177	193	209	225	241
Last host	14	30	46	62	78	94	110	126	142	158	174	190	206	222	238	254
Broadcast	15	31	47	63	79	95	111	127	143	159	175	191	207	223	239	255

Practice Example #5C: 255.255.255.248 (/29)

Let's keep practicing:

> 192.168.10.0 = Network address

> 255.255.255.248 = Subnet mask

- *Subnets?* 248 in binary = 11111000. 2^5 = 32.
- *Hosts?* $2^3 - 2$ = 6.
- *Valid subnets?* 256 – 248 = 0, 8, 16, 24, 32, 40, 48, 56, 64, 72, 80, 88, 96, 104, 112, 120, 128, 136, 144, 152, 160, 168, 176, 184, 192, 200, 208, 216, 224, 232, 240, and 248.
- *Broadcast address for each subnet?*
- *Valid hosts?*

Take a look at the following table. It shows some of the subnets (first four and last four only), valid hosts, and broadcast addresses for the Class C 255.255.255.248 mask:

Subnet	0	8	16	24	...	224	232	240	248
First host	1	9	17	25	...	225	233	241	249
Last host	6	14	22	30	...	230	238	246	254
Broadcast	7	15	23	31	...	231	239	247	255

Practice Example #6C: 255.255.255.252 (/30)

I know, I know—but just one more:

    192.168.10.0 = Network address
    255.255.255.252 = Subnet mask

- *Subnets?* 64.
- *Hosts?* 2.
- *Valid subnets?*0, 4, 8, 12, and so on, all the way to 252.
- *Broadcast address for each subnet (always the number right before the next subnet)?*
- *Valid hosts (the numbers between the subnet number and the broadcast address)?*

 Real World Scenario

Should We Really Use This Mask That Provides Only Two Hosts?

Imagine you are the network administrator for Acme Corporation in San Francisco, with dozens of WAN links connecting to your corporate office. Right now your network is a classful network, which means that the same subnet mask is on each host and router interface. You've read about classless routing where you can have different size masks, but you don't know what to use on your point-to-point WAN links. Is 255.255.255.252 (/30) a helpful mask in this situation?

Yes, this is a very helpful mask in wide area networks.

If you use the 255.255.255.0 mask, then each network will have 254 hosts, but you only use 2 addresses with a WAN link! That is a waste of 252 hosts per subnet. If you use the 255.255.255.252 mask, then each subnet has only 2 hosts, and you don't waste precious addresses.

The following table shows you the subnet, valid host, and broadcast address of the first four and last four subnets in the 255.255.255.252 Class C subnet:

Subnet	0	4	8	12	...	240	244	248	252
First host	1	5	9	13	...	241	245	249	253
Last host	2	6	10	14	...	242	246	250	254
Broadcast	3	7	11	15	...	243	247	251	255

Subnetting in Your Head: Class C Addresses

It really is possible to subnet in your head. Even if you don't believe me, I'll show you how. And it's not all that hard, either—take the following example:

192.168.10.33 = Host address

255.255.255.224 = Subnet mask

First, determine the subnet and broadcast address of this IP address. You can do this by answering question 3 of the big five questions: 256 – 224 = 32. 0, 32, 64. The address of 33 falls between the two subnets of 32 and 64 and must be part of the 192.168.10.32 subnet. The next subnet is 64, so the broadcast address of the 32 subnet is 63. (Remember that the broadcast address of a subnet is always the number right before the next subnet.) The valid host range is 33–62 (the numbers between the subnet and broadcast address). I told you this is easy!

Okay, let's try another one. We'll subnet another Class C address:

192.168.10.33 = Host address

255.255.255.240 = Subnet mask

What subnet and broadcast address is this IP address a member of? 256 – 240 = 16. 0, 16, 32, 48. Bingo—the host address is between the 32 and 48 subnets. The subnet is 192.168.10.32, and the broadcast address is 47 (the next subnet is 48). The valid host range is 33–46 (the numbers between the subnet number and the broadcast address).

Okay, we need to do more, just to make sure you have this down.

You have a host address of 192.168.10.174 with a mask of 255.255.255.240. What is the valid host range?

The mask is 240, so we'd do a 256 – 240 = 16. This is our block size. Just keep adding 16 until we pass the host address of 174, starting at zero, of course: 0, 16, 32, 48, 64, 80, 96, 112, 128, 144, 160, 176. The host address of 174 is between 160 and 176, so the subnet is 160. The broadcast address is 175; the valid host range is 161–174. That was a tough one.

Okay—one more just for fun. This is the easiest one of all Class C subnetting:

192.168.10.17 = Host address

255.255.255.252 = Subnet mask

What subnet and broadcast address is this IP address a member of? 256 – 252 = 0 (always start at zero unless told otherwise), 4, 8, 12, 16, 20, and so on. You've got it!

The host address is between the 16 and 20 subnets. The subnet is 192.168.10.16, and the broadcast address is 19. The valid host range is 17–18.

Now that you're all over Class C subnetting, let's move on to Class B subnetting. But before we do, let's do a quick review.

So What Do You Know Now?

Here's where you can really apply what you've learned so far and begin committing it all to memory. This is a very cool section that I've been using in my classes for years. It will really help you nail down subnetting!

When you see a subnet mask or slash notation (CIDR), you should know the following:

/25

What do you know about a /25?

- 128 mask
- 1 bits on and 7 bits off (10000000)
- Block size of 128
- 2 subnets, each with 126 hosts

/26

And what do you know about a /26?

- 192 mask
- 2 bits on and 6 bits off (11000000)
- Block size of 64
- 4 subnets, each with 62 hosts

/27

What about a /27?

- 224 mask
- 3 bits on and 5 bits off (11100000)
- Block size of 32
- 8 subnets, each with 30 hosts

/28

And what about a /28?

- 240 mask
- 4 bits on and 4 bits off
- Block size of 16
- 16 subnets, each with 14 hosts

/29

What do you know about a /29?

- 248 mask
- 5 bits on and 3 bits off
- Block size of 8
- 32 subnets, each with 6 hosts

/30

And last, what about a /30?

- 252 mask
- 6 bits on and 2 bits off
- Block size of 4
- 64 subnets, each with 2 hosts

Regardless of whether you have a Class A, Class B, or Class C address, the /30 mask will provide you with only two hosts, ever. This mask is suited almost exclusively for use on point-to-point links.

If you can memorize this "What Do You Know?" section, you'll be much better off in your day-to-day job and in your studies. Try saying it out loud, which helps you memorize things—yes, your significant other and/or coworkers will think you've lost it, but they probably already do if you're in the networking field. And if you're not yet in the networking field but are studying all this to break into it, you might as well have people start thinking you're a little "different" now because they will eventually anyway.

It's also helpful to write these on some type of flashcards and have people test your skill. You'd be amazed at how fast you can get subnetting down if you memorize block sizes as well as this "What Do You Know?" section.

Subnetting Class B Addresses

Before we dive into this, let's look at all the possible Class B subnet masks first. Notice that we have a lot more possible subnet masks than we do with a Class C network address:

255.255.0.0	(/16)
255.255.128.0	(/17)
255.255.192.0	(/18)
255.255.224.0	(/19)
255.255.240.0	(/20)
255.255.248.0	(/21)
255.255.252.0	(/22)

255.255.254.0   (/23)

255.255.255.0   (/24)

255.255.255.128   (/25)

255.255.255.192   (/26)

255.255.255.224   (/27)

255.255.255.240   (/28)

255.255.255.248   (/29)

255.255.255.252   (/30)

We know the Class B network address has 16 bits available for host addressing. This means we can use up to 14 bits for subnetting (because we have to leave at least 2 bits for host addressing). Using a /16 means you are not subnetting with class B, but it is a mask you can use.

> By the way, do you notice anything interesting about that list of subnet values—a pattern, maybe? Ah ha! That's exactly why I had you memorize the binary-to-decimal numbers at the beginning of this section. Because subnet mask bits start on the left and move to the right and bits can't be skipped, the numbers are always the same regardless of the class of address. Memorize this pattern.

The process of subnetting a Class B network is pretty much the same as it is for a Class C, except that you have more host bits and you start in the third octet.

Use the same subnet numbers for the third octet with Class B that you used for the fourth octet with Class C, but add a 0 to the network portion and a 255 to the broadcast section in the fourth octet. The following table shows you an example host range of two subnets used in a Class B 240 (/20) subnet mask:

First subnet	Second Subnet
16.0	32.0
31.255	47.255

Notice that these are the same numbers we used in the fourth octet with a /28 mask, but we moved them to the third octet and added a .0 and .255 at the end. Just add the valid hosts between the numbers, and you're set!

> The preceding example is true only until you get up to /24. After that, it's numerically exactly like Class C.

Subnetting Practice Examples: Class B Addresses

This section will give you an opportunity to practice subnetting Class B addresses. Again, I have to mention that this is the same as subnetting with Class C, except we start in the third octet—with the exact same numbers!

Practice Example #1B: 255.255.128.0 (/17)

172.16.0.0 = Network address

255.255.128.0 = Subnet mask

- *Subnets?* 2^1 = 2 (same as Class C).
- *Hosts?* 2^{15} − 2 = 32,766 (7 bits in the third octet, and 8 in the fourth).
- *Valid subnets?* 256 − 128 = 128. 0, 128. Remember that subnetting is performed in the third octet, so the subnet numbers are really 0.0 and 128.0, as shown in the next table. These are the exact numbers we used with Class C; we use them in the third octet and add a 0 in the fourth octet for the network address.
- *Broadcast address for each subnet?*
- *Valid hosts?*

The following table shows the two subnets available, the valid host range, and the broadcast address of each:

Subnet	0.0	128.0
First host	0.1	128.1
Last host	127.254	255.254
Broadcast	127.255	255.255

Okay, notice that we just added the fourth octet's lowest and highest values and came up with the answers. And again, it's done exactly the same way as for a Class C subnet. We just use the same numbers in the third octet and added 0 and 255 in the fourth octet— pretty simple, huh? I really can't say this enough: It's not hard; the numbers never change; we just use them in different octets!

Practice Example #2B: 255.255.192.0 (/18)

172.16.0.0 = Network address

255.255.192.0 = Subnet mask

- *Subnets?* 2^2 = 4.
- *Hosts?* 2^{14} − 2 = 16,382 (6 bits in the third octet, and 8 in the fourth).
- *Valid subnets?* 256 − 192 = 64. 0, 64, 128, 192. Remember that the subnetting is per-formed in the third octet, so the subnet numbers are really 0.0, 64.0, 128.0, and 192.0, as shown in the next table.

- *Broadcast address for each subnet?*
- *Valid hosts?*

The following table shows the four subnets available, the valid host range, and the broadcast address of each:

Subnet	0.0	64.0	128.0	192.0
First host	0.1	64.1	128.1	192.1
Last host	63.254	127.254	191.254	255.254
Broadcast	63.255	127.255	191.255	255.255

Again, it's pretty much the same as it is for a Class C subnet—we just added 0 and 255 in the fourth octet for each subnet in the third octet.

Practice Example #3B: 255.255.240.0 (/20)

172.16.0.0 = Network address

255.255.240.0 = Subnet mask

- *Subnets?* 2^4 = 16.
- *Hosts?* 2^{12} – 2 = 4094.
- *Valid subnets?* 256 – 240 = 0, 16, 32, 48, and so on, up to 240. Notice that these are the same numbers as a Class C 240 mask—we just put them in the third octet and add a 0 and 255 in the fourth octet.
- *Broadcast address for each subnet?*
- *Valid hosts?*

The following table shows the first four subnets, valid hosts, and broadcast addresses in a Class B 255.255.240.0 mask:

Subnet	0.0	16.0	32.0	48.0
First host	0.1	16.1	32.1	48.1
Last host	15.254	31.254	47.254	63.254
Broadcast	15.255	31.255	47.255	63.255

Practice Example #4B: 255.255.254.0 (/23)

172.16.0.0 = Network address

255.255.254.0 = Subnet mask

- *Subnets?* 2^7 = 128.
- *Hosts?* 2^9 – 2 = 510.

- *Valid subnets?* 256 – 254 = 0, 2, 4, 6, 8, and so on, up to 254.
- *Broadcast address for each subnet?*
- *Valid hosts?*

The following table shows the first five subnets, valid hosts, and broadcast addresses in a Class B 255.255.254.0 mask:

Subnet	0.0	2.0	4.0	6.0	8.0
First host	0.1	2.1	4.1	6.1	8.1
Last host	1.254	3.254	5.254	7.254	9.254
Broadcast	1.255	3.255	5.255	7.255	9.255

Practice Example #5B: 255.255.255.0 (/24)

Contrary to popular belief, 255.255.255.0 used with a Class B network address is not called a Class B network with a Class C subnet mask. It's amazing how many people see this mask used in a Class B network and think it's a Class C subnet mask. This is a Class B subnet mask with 8 bits of subnetting—it's considerably different from a Class C mask. Subnetting this address is fairly simple:

172.16.0.0 = Network address

255.255.255.0 = Subnet mask

- *Subnets?* $2^8 = 256$.
- *Hosts?* $2^8 – 2 = 254$.
- *Valid subnets?* 256 – 255 = 1. 0, 1, 2, 3, and so on, all the way to 255.
- *Broadcast address for each subnet?*
- *Valid hosts?*

The following table shows the first four and last two subnets, the valid hosts, and the broadcast addresses in a Class B 255.255.255.0 mask:

Subnet	0.0	1.0	2.0	3.0	...	254.0	255.0
First host	0.1	1.1	2.1	3.1	...	254.1	255.1
Last host	0.254	1.254	2.254	3.254	...	254.254	255.254
Broadcast	0.255	1.255	2.255	3.255	...	254.255	255.255

Practice Example #6B: 255.255.255.128 (/25)

This is one of the hardest subnet masks you can play with. And worse, it actually is a really good subnet to use in production because it creates over 500 subnets with a whopping 126 hosts for each subnet—a nice mixture. So, don't skip over it!

172.16.0.0 = Network address

255.255.255.128 = Subnet mask

- *Subnets?* $2^9 = 512$.
- *Hosts?* $2^7 - 2 = 126$.
- *Valid subnets?* Okay, now for the tricky part. $256 - 255 = 1$. 0, 1, 2, 3, and so on for the third octet. But you can't forget the one subnet bit used in the fourth octet. Remember when I showed you how to figure one subnet bit with a Class C mask? You figure this out the same way. (Now you know why I showed you the 1-bit subnet mask in the Class C section—to make this part easier.) You actually get two subnets for each third octet value, hence the 512 subnets. For example, if the third octet is showing subnet 3, the two subnets would actually be 3.0 and 3.128.
- *Broadcast address for each subnet?*
- *Valid hosts?*

The following table shows how you can create subnets, valid hosts, and broadcast addresses using the Class B 255.255.255.128 subnet mask (the first eight subnets are shown, and then the last two subnets):

Subnet	0.0	0.128	1.0	1.128	2.0	2.128	3.0	3.128	...	255.0	255.128
First host	0.1	0.129	1.1	1.129	2.1	2.129	3.1	3.129	...	255.1	255.129
Last host	0.126	0.254	1.126	1.254	2.126	2.254	3.126	3.254	...	255.126	255.254
Broadcast	0.127	0.255	1.127	1.255	2.127	2.255	3.127	3.255	...	255.127	255.255

Practice Example #7B: 255.255.255.192 (/26)

Now, this is where Class B subnetting gets easy. Because the third octet has a 255 in the mask section, whatever number is listed in the third octet is a subnet number. However, now that we have a subnet number in the fourth octet, we can subnet this octet just as we did with Class C subnetting. Let's try it out:

172.16.0.0 = Network address

255.255.255.192 = Subnet mask

- *Subnets?* $2^{10} = 1024$.
- *Hosts?* $2^6 - 2 = 62$.
- *Valid subnets?* $256 - 192 = 64$. The subnets are shown in the following table. Do these numbers look familiar?
- *Broadcast address for each subnet?*
- *Valid hosts?*

The following table shows the first eight subnet ranges, valid hosts, and broadcast addresses:

Subnet	0.0	0.64	0.128	0.192	1.0	1.64	1.128	1.192
First host	0.1	0.65	0.129	0.193	1.1	1.65	1.129	1.193
Last host	0.62	0.126	0.190	0.254	1.62	1.126	1.190	1.254
Broadcast	0.63	0.127	0.191	0.255	1.63	1.127	1.191	1.255

Notice that for each subnet value in the third octet, you get subnets 0, 64, 128, and 192 in the fourth octet.

Practice Example #8B: 255.255.255.224 (/27)

This is done the same way as the preceding subnet mask, except that we have more subnets and fewer hosts per subnet available.

172.16.0.0 = Network address

255.255.255.224 = Subnet mask

- *Subnets?* 2^{11} = 2048.
- *Hosts?* $2^5 - 2$ = 30.
- *Valid subnets?* 256 − 224 = 32. 0, 32, 64, 96, 128, 160, 192, 224.
- *Broadcast address for each subnet?*
- *Valid hosts?*

The following table shows the first eight subnets:

Subnet	0.0	0.32	0.64	0.96	0.128	0.160	0.192	0.224
First host	0.1	0.33	0.65	0.97	0.129	0.161	0.193	0.225
Last host	0.30	0.62	0.94	0.126	0.158	0.190	0.222	0.254
Broadcast	0.31	0.63	0.95	0.127	0.159	0.191	0.223	0.255

This next table shows the last eight subnets:

Subnet	255.0	255.32	255.64	255.96	255.128	255.160	255.192	255.224
First host	255.1	255.33	255.65	255.97	255.129	255.161	255.193	255.225
Last host	255.30	255.62	255.94	255.126	255.158	255.190	255.222	255.254
Broadcast	255.31	255.63	255.95	255.127	255.159	255.191	255.223	255.255

Subnetting in Your Head: Class B Addresses

Are you nuts? Subnet Class B addresses in our heads? It's actually easier than writing it out—I'm not kidding! Let me show you the steps:

1. What subnet and broadcast address is the IP address 172.16.10.33 255.255.255.224 (/27) a member of?

   The interesting octet is the fourth octet. 256 − 224 = 32. 32 + 32 = 64. Bingo: 33 is between 32 and 64. However, remember that the third octet is considered part of the subnet, so the answer is the 10.32 subnet. The broadcast is 10.63, because 10.64 is the next subnet. That was a pretty easy one.

2. What subnet and broadcast address is the IP address 172.16.66.10 255.255.192.0 (/18) a member of?

   The interesting octet is the third octet instead of the fourth octet. 256 − 192 = 64. 0, 64, 128. The subnet is 172.16.64.0. The broadcast must be 172.16.127.255 because 128.0 is the next subnet.

Notice in the last example I started counting at zero. This is called *ip subnet-zero*. It allows us to use the zero subnet as our first subnet. This may or may not be enabled on your router. If it is not enabled, then you cannot start counting subnets at zero. Most routers, if not all routers these days, support ip subnet-zero.

3. What subnet and broadcast address is the IP address 172.16.50.10 255.255.224.0 (/19) a member of?

   256 − 224 = 0, 32, 64 (remember, we always start counting at zero). The subnet is 172.16.32.0, and the broadcast must be 172.16.63.255 because 64.0 is the next subnet.

4. What subnet and broadcast address is the IP address 172.16.46.255 255.255.240.0 (/20) a member of?

   256 − 240 = 16. The third octet is interesting to us. 0, 16, 32, 48. This subnet address must be in the 172.16.32.0 subnet, and the broadcast must be 172.16.47.255 because 48.0 is the next subnet. So, yes, 172.16.46.255 is a valid host.

5. What subnet and broadcast address is the IP address 172.16.45.14 255.255.255.252 (/30) a member of?

   Where is the interesting octet? 256 − 252 = 0, 4, 8, 12, 16 (in the fourth octet). The subnet is 172.16.45.12, with a broadcast of 172.16.45.15 because the next subnet is 172.16.45.16.

6. What is the subnet and broadcast address of the host 172.16.88.255/20?

   What is a /20? If you can't answer this, you can't answer this question, can you? A /20 is 255.255.240.0, which gives us a block size of 16 in the third octet; and because no subnet bits are on in the fourth octet, the answer is always 0 and 255 in the fourth octet. 0, 16, 32, 48, 64, 80, 96...bingo. 88 is between 80 and 96, so the subnet is 80.0 and the broadcast address is 95.255.

7. A router receives a packet on an interface with a destination address of 172.16.46.191/26. What will the router do with this packet?

Discard it. Do you know why? 172.16.46.191/26 is a 255.255.255.192 mask, which gives us a block size of 64. Our subnets are then 0, 64, 128, 192. 191 is the broadcast address of the 128 subnet, so a router, by default, will discard any broadcast packets.

 Hey, what happened to class A subnetting? Subnetting Class A networks is covered in Appendix A, as well as more written labs. You need all the practice you can get! So head on over to Appendix A when you get done with this chapter.

Troubleshooting IP Addressing

Troubleshooting IP addressing is obviously an important skill because running into trouble somewhere along the way is pretty much a sure thing, and it's going to happen to you. No—I'm not a pessimist; I'm just keeping it real. Because of this nasty fact, it will be great when you can save the day because you can both figure out (diagnose) the problem and fix it on an IP network whether you're at work or at home!

Let's use Figure 8.3 as an example of your basic IP trouble—poor Sally can't log in to the Windows server. Do you deal with this by calling the Microsoft team to tell them their server is a pile of junk and causing all your problems? Probably not such a great idea—let's first double-check our network instead. Check out Figure 8.3.

FIGURE 8.3   Basic IP troubleshooting

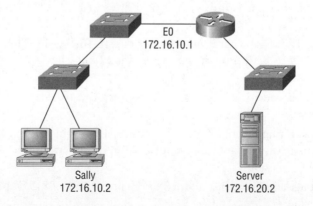

Okay, let's get started by going over the basic troubleshooting steps. They're pretty simple, but important nonetheless. Pretend you're at a customer host and they're complaining that they can't communicate to a server that just happens to be on a remote network:

1. Open a DOS window, and ping 127.0.0.1. This is the diagnostic, or loopback, address, and if you get a successful ping, your IP stack is considered to be initialized. If it fails, then you have an IP stack failure and need to reinstall TCP/IP on the host:

```
C:\>ping 127.0.0.1
Pinging 127.0.0.1 with 32 bytes of data:
Reply from 127.0.0.1: bytes=32 time<1ms TTL=128
Reply from 127.0.0.1: bytes=32 time<1ms TTL=128
Reply from 127.0.0.1: bytes=32 time<1ms TTL=128
Reply from 127.0.0.1: bytes=32 time<1ms TTL=128
Ping statistics for 127.0.0.1:
    Packets: Sent = 4, Received = 4, Lost = 0 (0% loss),
Approximate round trip times in milli-seconds:
    Minimum = 0ms, Maximum = 0ms, Average = 0ms
```

If you ping the loopback address and receive an "unable to contact IP driver, error code 2", you need to reinstall the TCP/IP protocol suite on the host.

2. From the DOS window, ping the IP address of the local host. If that's successful, your Network Interface Card (NIC) is functioning. If it fails, there is a problem with the NIC. Success here doesn't mean that a cable is plugged into the NIC, only that the IP protocol stack on the host can communicate to the NIC (via the LAN driver):

```
C:\>ping 172.16.10.2
Pinging 172.16.10.2 with 32 bytes of data:
Reply from 172.16.10.2: bytes=32 time<1ms TTL=128
Reply from 172.16.10.2: bytes=32 time<1ms TTL=128
Reply from 172.16.10.2: bytes=32 time<1ms TTL=128
Reply from 172.16.10.2: bytes=32 time<1ms TTL=128
Ping statistics for 172.16.10.2:
    Packets: Sent = 4, Received = 4, Lost = 0 (0% loss),
Approximate round trip times in milli-seconds:
    Minimum = 0ms, Maximum = 0ms, Average = 0ms
```

3. From the DOS window, ping the default gateway (router). If the ping works, it means that the NIC is plugged into the network and can communicate on the local network. If it fails, you have a local physical network problem that could be anywhere from the NIC to the router:

```
C:\>ping 172.16.10.1
Pinging 172.16.10.1 with 32 bytes of data:
```

```
Reply from 172.16.10.1: bytes=32 time<1ms TTL=128
Reply from 172.16.10.1: bytes=32 time<1ms TTL=128
Reply from 172.16.10.1: bytes=32 time<1ms TTL=128
Reply from 172.16.10.1: bytes=32 time<1ms TTL=128
Ping statistics for 172.16.10.1:
    Packets: Sent = 4, Received = 4, Lost = 0 (0% loss),
Approximate round trip times in milli-seconds:
    Minimum = 0ms, Maximum = 0ms, Average = 0ms
```

4. If steps 1 through 3 were successful, try to ping the remote server. If that works, then you know that you have IP communication between the local host and the remote server. You also know that the remote physical network is working:

```
C:\>ping 172.16.20.2
Pinging 172.16.20.2 with 32 bytes of data:
Reply from 172.16.20.2: bytes=32 time<1ms TTL=128
Reply from 172.16.20.2: bytes=32 time<1ms TTL=128
Reply from 172.16.20.2: bytes=32 time<1ms TTL=128
Reply from 172.16.20.2: bytes=32 time<1ms TTL=128
Ping statistics for 172.16.20.2:
    Packets: Sent = 4, Received = 4, Lost = 0 (0% loss),
Approximate round trip times in milli-seconds:
    Minimum = 0ms, Maximum = 0ms, Average = 0ms
```

If the user still can't communicate with the server after steps 1 through 4 are successful, you probably have some type of name resolution problem and need to check your Domain Name System (DNS) settings. But if the ping to the remote server fails, then you know you have some type of remote physical network problem and need to go to the server and work through steps 1 through 3 until you find the snag.

Before we move on to determining IP address problems and how to fix them, I just want to mention some basic yet handy DOS commands that you can use to help troubleshoot your network from both a PC and a Cisco router (the commands might do the same thing, but they are implemented differently):

Packet InterNet Groper (ping)   Uses an Internet Control Message Protocol (ICMP) echo request and replies to test if a host IP stack is initialized and alive on the network.

traceroute   Displays the list of routers on a path to a network destination by using TTL time-outs and ICMP error messages. This command will not work from a DOS prompt.

tracert   Same command as traceroute, but it's a Microsoft Windows command and will not work on other devices, like a Cisco router or Unix box.

arp -a   Displays IP-to-MAC-address mappings on a Windows PC.

ipconfig /all   Used only from a DOS prompt. Shows you the PC network configuration.

Once you've gone through all these steps and used the appropriate DOS commands, if necessary, what do you do if you find a problem? How do you go about fixing an IP address configuration error? That's exactly what you're going to learn about next—how to determine specific IP address problems and what you can do to fix them.

Determining IP Address Problems

It's common for a host, router, or other network device to be configured with the wrong IP address, subnet mask, or default gateway. Because this happens way too often, I'm going to teach you how to both determine and fix IP address configuration errors.

Once you've worked through the four basic steps of troubleshooting and determined there's a problem, you obviously then need to find and fix it. It really helps to draw out the network and IP addressing scheme. If it's already done, consider yourself lucky and go buy a lottery ticket, because although it should be done, it rarely is. And if it is, it's usually outdated or inaccurate anyway. Typically it is not done, and you'll probably just have to bite the bullet and start from scratch.

Once you have your network accurately drawn out, including the IP addressing scheme, you need to verify each host's IP address, mask, and default gateway address to determine the problem. (I'm assuming that you don't have a physical problem or that if you did, you've already fixed it.)

Let's check out the example illustrated in Figure 8.4. A user in the sales department calls and tells you that she can't get to Server A in the marketing department. You ask her if she can get to Server B in the marketing department, but she doesn't know because she doesn't have rights to log on to that server. What do you do?

FIGURE 8.4   IP address problem 1

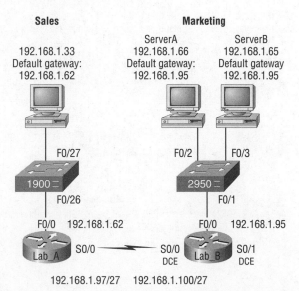

You ask the client to go through the four troubleshooting steps that you learned about in the preceding section. Steps 1 through 3 work, but step 4 fails. By looking at the figure, can you determine the problem? Look for clues in the network drawing. First, the WAN link between the Lab_A router and the Lab_B router shows the mask as a /27. You should already know that this mask is 255.255.255.224 and then determine that all networks are using this mask. The network address is 192.168.1.0. What are our valid subnets and hosts? 256 – 224 = 32, so this makes our subnets 32, 64, 96, 128, etc. So, by looking at the figure, you can see that subnet 32 is being used by the sales department, the WAN link is using subnet 96, and the marketing department is using subnet 64.

Now you've got to determine what the valid host ranges are for each subnet. From what you learned at the beginning of this chapter, you should now be able to easily determine the subnet address, broadcast addresses, and valid host ranges. The valid hosts for the Sales LAN are 33 through 62—the broadcast address is 63 because the next subnet is 64, right? For the Marketing LAN, the valid hosts are 65 through 94 (broadcast 95), and for the WAN link, 97 through 126 (broadcast 127). By looking at the figure, you can determine that the default gateway on the Lab_B router is incorrect. That address is the broadcast address of the 64 subnet, so there's no way it could be a valid host.

Did you get all that? Maybe we should try another one, just to make sure. Figure 8.5 shows a network problem. A user in the Sales LAN can't get to ServerB. You have the user run through the four basic troubleshooting steps and find that the host can communicate to the local network but not to the remote network. Find and define the IP addressing problem.

FIGURE 8.5   IP address problem 2

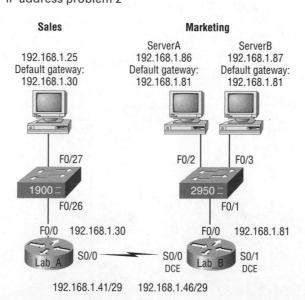

If you use the same steps used to solve the last problem, you can see first that the WAN link again provides the subnet mask to use— /29, or 255.255.255.248. You need to determine what the valid subnets, broadcast addresses, and valid host ranges are to solve this problem.

The 248 mask is a block size of 8 (256 − 248 = 8), so the subnets both start and increment in multiples of 8. By looking at the figure, you see that the Sales LAN is in the 24 subnet, the WAN is in the 40 subnet, and the Marketing LAN is in the 80 subnet. Can you see the problem yet? The valid host range for the Sales LAN is 25–30, and the configuration appears correct. The valid host range for the WAN link is 41–46, and this also appears correct. The valid host range for the 80 subnet is 81–86, with a broadcast address of 87 because the next subnet is 88. ServerB has been configured with the broadcast address of the subnet.

Okay, now that you can figure out misconfigured IP addresses on hosts, what do you do if a host doesn't have an IP address and you need to assign one? What you need to do is look at other hosts on the LAN and figure out the network, mask, and default gateway. Let's take a look at a couple of examples of how to find and apply valid IP addresses to hosts.

You need to assign a server and router IP addresses on a LAN. The subnet assigned on that segment is 192.168.20.24/29, and the router needs to be assigned the first usable address and the server the last valid host ID. What are the IP address, mask, and default gateway assigned to the server?

To answer this, you must know that a /29 is a 255.255.255.248 mask, which provides a block size of 8. The subnet is known as 24, the next subnet in a block of 8 is 32, so the broadcast address of the 24 subnet is 31, which makes the valid host range 25–30:

Server IP address: 192.168.20.30

Server mask: 255.255.255.248

Default gateway: 192.168.20.25 (router's IP address)

As another example, let's take a look at Figure 8.6 and solve this problem.

FIGURE 8.6   Find the valid host.

RouterA

E0: 192.168.10.33/27

HostA

Look at the router's IP address on Ethernet0. What IP address, subnet mask, and valid host range could be assigned to the host?

The IP address of the router's Ethernet0 is 192.168.10.33/27. As you already know, a /27 is a 224 mask with a block size of 32. The router's interface is in the 32 subnet. The next subnet is 64, so that makes the broadcast address of the 32 subnet 63 and the valid host range 33–62:

Host IP address: 192.168.10.34–62 (any address in the range except for 33, which is assigned to the router)

Mask: 255.255.255.224

Default gateway: 192.168.10.33

Figure 8.7 shows two routers with Ethernet configurations already assigned. What are the host addresses and subnet masks of hosts A and B?

FIGURE 8.7   Find the valid host #2

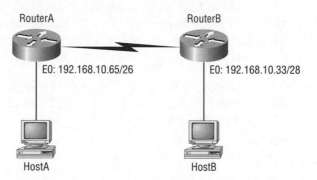

RouterA has an IP address of 192.168.10.65/26 and RouterB has an IP address of 192.168.10.33/28. What are the host configurations? RouterA Ethernet0 is in the 192.168.10.64 subnet, and RouterB Ethernet0 is in the 192.168.10.32 network:

Host A IP address: 192.168.10.66–126

Host A mask: 255.255.255.192

Host A default gateway: 192.168.10.65

Host B IP address: 192.168.10.34–46

Host B mask: 255.255.255.240

Host B default gateway: 192.168.10.33

Just a couple more examples, and then this section is history. Hang in there!

Figure 8.8 shows two routers; you need to configure the S0/0 interface on RouterA. The network assigned to the serial link is 172.16.17.0/22. What IP address can be assigned?

First, you must know that a /22 CIDR is 255.255.252.0, which makes a block size of 4 in the third octet. Because 17 is listed, the available range is 16.1 through 19.254; so, for example, the IP address S0/0 could be 172.16.18.255 because that's within the range.

FIGURE 8.8   Find the valid host address #3

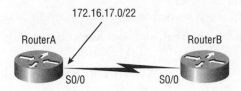

Okay, last one! You have one Class C network ID, and you need to provide one usable subnet per city while allowing enough usable host addresses for each city specified in Figure 8.9. What is your mask?

FIGURE 8.9   Find the valid subnet mask

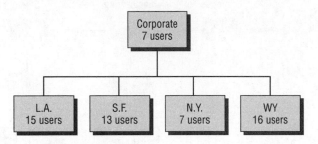

Actually, this is probably the easiest thing you've done all day! I count 5 subnets needed, and the Wyoming office needs 16 users (always look for the network that needs the most hosts). What block size is needed for the Wyoming office? 32. (Remember, you cannot use a block size of 16 because you always have to subtract 2!) What mask provides you with a block size of 32? 224. Bingo! This provides 8 subnets, each with 30 hosts.

Introduction to Network Address Translation (NAT)

Similar to Classless Inter-Domain Routing (CIDR), the original intention for NAT was to slow the depletion of available IP address space by allowing many private IP addresses to be represented by some smaller number of public IP addresses.

Since then, it's been discovered that NAT is also a useful tool for network migrations and mergers, server load sharing, and creating "virtual servers." So in this section, I'm going to describe the basics of NAT functionality and the terminology common to NAT.

At times, NAT really decreases the overwhelming amount of public IP addresses required in your networking environment. And NAT comes in very handy when two companies that have duplicate internal addressing schemes merge. NAT is also great to have around when an organization changes its ISP and the networking manager doesn't want the hassle of changing the internal address scheme.

Here's a list of situations when it's best to have NAT on your side:

- You need to connect to the Internet, and your hosts don't have globally unique IP addresses.

- You change to a new ISP that requires you to renumber your network.

- You need to merge two intranets with duplicate addresses.

You typically use NAT on a border router. For an illustration of this, see Figure 8.10, where NAT would be configured on the Corporate router.

FIGURE 8.10   Where to configure NAT

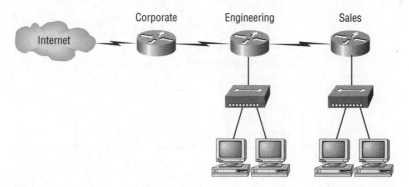

Now you may be thinking, "NAT's totally cool. It's the grooviest, greatest network gadget, and I just gotta have it." Well, hang on a minute. There are truly some serious snags related to NAT use. Oh, don't get me wrong: It really can save you sometimes, but there's a dark side you need to know about, too. For a visual of the pros and cons linked to using NAT, check out Table 8.3.

TABLE 8.3   Advantages and Disadvantages of Implementing NAT

Advantages	Disadvantages
Conserves legally registered addresses	Translation-introduces switching path delays
Reduces address overlap occurrences	Loss of end-to-end IP traceability
Increases flexibility when connecting to the Internet	Certain applications will not function with NAT enabled
Eliminates address renumbering as the network changes	

Types of Network Address Translation

In this section, I'm going to go over the three types of NAT with you:

Static NAT (SNAT)   This type of NAT is designed to allow one-to-one mapping between local and global addresses. Keep in mind that the static version requires you to have one real Internet IP address for every host on your network.

Dynamic NAT   This version gives you the ability to map an unregistered IP address to a registered IP address from a pool of registered IP addresses. You don't have to statically configure your router to map an inside to an outside address as you would using static NAT, but you do have to have enough real, bona-fide IP addresses for everyone who's going to be sending packets to and receiving them from the Internet.

Overloading   This is the most popular type of NAT configuration. Understand that overloading really is a form of dynamic NAT that maps multiple unregistered IP addresses to a single registered IP address—many-to-one—by using different ports. Now, why is this so special? Well, because it's also known as Port Address Translation (PAT). And by using PAT (NAT Overload), you get to have thousands of users connect to the Internet using only one real global IP address—pretty slick, yeah? Seriously, NAT Overload is the real reason we haven't run out of valid IP address on the Internet. Really—I'm not joking.

NAT Names

The names we use to describe the addresses used with NAT are pretty simple. Addresses used after NAT translations are called *global* addresses. These are usually the public addresses used on the Internet; but remember, you don't need public addresses if you aren't going on the Internet.

Local addresses are the ones we use before NAT translation. So, the inside local address is actually the private address of the sending host that's trying to get to the Internet, while the outside local address is the address of the destination host. The latter is usually a public address (web address, mail server, and so on) and is how the packet begins its journey.

After translation, the inside local address is then called the *inside global address*, and the outside global address then becomes the name of the destination host. Check out Table 8.4, which lists all this terminology, for a clear picture of the various names used with NAT.

TABLE 8.4   NAT Terms

Name	Meaning
Inside local	Name of the inside source address before translation
Outside local	Name of the destination host before translation
Inside global	Name of the inside host after translation
Outside global	Name of the outside destination host after translation

How NAT Works

Okay, now it's time to look at how this whole NAT thing works. I'm going to start by using Figure 8.11 to describe the basic translation of NAT.

FIGURE 8.11   Basic NAT translation

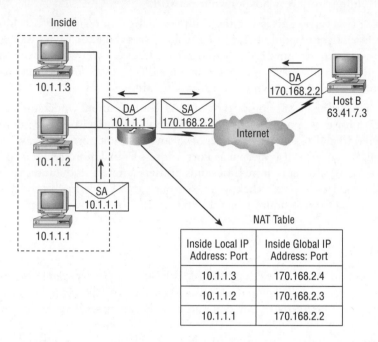

In the example shown in Figure 8.11, host 10.1.1.1 sends an outbound packet to the border router configured with NAT. The router identifies the IP address as an inside local IP address destined for an outside network, translates the address, and documents the translation in the NAT table.

The packet is sent to the outside interface with the new translated source address. The external host returns the packet to the destination host, and the NAT router translates the inside global IP address back to the inside local IP address using the NAT table. This is as simple as it gets.

Let's take a look at a more complex configuration using overloading, or what is also referred to as PAT. I'll use Figure 8.12 to demonstrate how PAT works.

With overloading, all inside hosts get translated to one single IP address; hence the term *overloading*. Again, the reason we have not run out of available IP addresses on the Internet is because of overloading (PAT).

Take a look at the NAT table in Figure 8.12 again. In addition to the inside local IP address and outside global IP address, we now have port numbers. These port numbers help the router identify which host should receive the return traffic.

Port numbers are used at the Transport layer to identify the local host in this example. If we had to use IP addresses to identify the source hosts, that would be called *static NAT*, and we would run out of addresses. PAT allows us to use the Transport layer to identify the hosts, which in turn allows us to use (theoretically) up to 65,000 hosts with one real IP address.

You're done, the diva has sung, the chicken has crossed the road…whew! Okay, take a good break, and then come back and go through the written labs and review questions.

FIGURE 8.12 NAT overloading example (PAT)

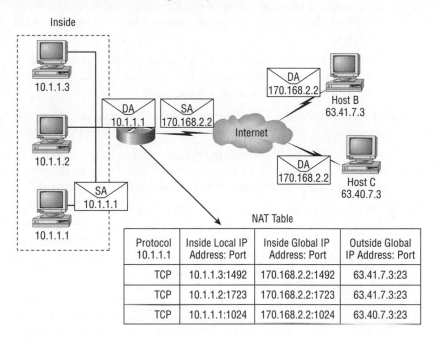

Protocol 10.1.1.1	Inside Local IP Address: Port	Inside Global IP Address: Port	Outside Global IP Address: Port
TCP	10.1.1.3:1492	170.168.2.2:1492	63.41.7.3:23
TCP	10.1.1.2:1723	170.168.2.2:1723	63.41.7.3:23
TCP	10.1.1.1:1024	170.168.2.2:1024	63.40.7.3:23

Summary

Did you read Chapters 7 and 8 and understand everything on the first pass? If so, that is fantastic—congratulations! The thing is, you probably got lost a couple of times—and as I told you, that's what usually happens, so don't stress. Don't feel bad if you have to read each chapter more than once, or even 10 times, before you're truly good to go.

This chapter provided you with an important understanding of IP subnetting. After reading this chapter, you should be able to subnet IP addresses in your head.

You should also understand the basic troubleshooting methods. You must remember the four steps you take when trying to narrow down exactly where a network/IP addressing problem is and then know how to proceed systematically in order to fix it. In addition, you should be able to find valid IP addresses and subnet masks by looking at a network diagram.

I finished this chapter with an introduction to Network Address Translation. I discussed the difference between static and dynamic NAT, and NAT overloading.

Exam Essentials

Remember the steps to subnet in your head.   Understand how IP addressing and subnetting work. First, determine your block size by using the 256-subnet mask math. Then, count your subnets and determine the broadcast address of each subnet—it is always the number right before the next subnet. Your valid hosts are the numbers between the subnet address and the broadcast address.

Understand the various block sizes.   This is an important part of understanding IP addressing and subnetting. The valid block sizes are always 4, 8, 16, 32, 64, 128, and so on. You can determine your block size by using the 256-subnet mask math.

Remember the four diagnostic steps.   The four simple steps for troubleshooting are ping the loopback address, ping the NIC, ping the default gateway, and ping the remote device.

You must be able to find and fix an IP addressing problem.   Once you go through the four troubleshooting steps, you should be able to determine the IP addressing problem by drawing out the network and finding the valid and invalid hosts addressed in your network.

Understand basic NAT terminology.   You want to know the difference between inside local and inside global. Inside local is before translation, and inside global is after translation. Inside global is defined as a registered address that represents an inside host to an outside network. You should also understand PAT and how it works by mapping multiple private IP addresses to a single registered IP address by using different port numbers.

Written Labs

Write the subnet, broadcast address, and valid host range for Question 1 through Question 6:

1. 192.168.100.25/30

2. 192.168.100.37/28

3. 192.168.100.66/27

4. 192.168.100.17/29

5. 192.168.100.99/26

6. 192.168.100.99/25

7. You have a Class B network and need 29 subnets. What is your mask?

8. What is the broadcast address of 192.168.192.10/29?

9. How many hosts are available with a Class C /29 mask?

10. What is the subnet for host ID 172.16.3.65/23?

   (The answers to the written labs can be found following the answers to the Review Questions for this chapter.)

Review Questions

1. What is the maximum number of IP addresses that can be assigned to hosts on a local subnet that uses the 255.255.255.224 subnet mask?

   A. 14

   B. 15

   C. 16

   D. 30

   E. 31

   F. 62

2. You have a class A host of 10.0.0.110/25. It needs to communicate to a host with an IP address of 10.0.0.210/25. Which of the following devices do you need to use in order for these hosts to communicate?

   A. A layer 2 switch

   B. Router

   C. DNS server

   D. Hub

3. What is the subnetwork address for a host with the IP address 200.10.5.68/28?

   A. 200.10.5.56

   B. 200.10.5.32

   C. 200.10.5.64

   D. 200.10.5.0

4. The network address of 172.16.0.0/19 provides how many subnets and hosts?

   A. 7 subnets, 30 hosts each

   B. 7 subnets, 2,046 hosts each

   C. 7 subnets, 8,190 hosts each

   D. 8 subnets, 30 hosts each

   E. 8 subnets, 2,046 hosts each

   F. 8 subnets, 8,190 hosts each

5. You receive a call from a user that is complaining that they cannot get on the Internet. You have them verify their IP address, mask, and default gateway. The IP address is 10.0.37.144, with a subnet mask of 255.255.254.0. The default gateway is 10.0.38.1. What is the problem?

   A. Invalid IP address

   B. Invalid subnet mask

   C. gateway IP is incorrect

   D. IP address and mask are not compatible.

6. If a host on a network has the address 172.16.45.14/30, what is the subnetwork this host belongs to?

    A. 172.16.45.0

    B. 172.16.45.4

    C. 172.16.45.8

    D. 172.16.45.12

    E. 172.16.45.16

7. On a network, which mask should you use on point-to-point WAN links in order to reduce the waste of IP addresses?

    A. /27

    B. /28

    C. /29

    D. /30

    E. /31

8. On which of the following devices are you most likely to be able to implement NAT?

    A. Hub

    B. Ethernet switch

    C. Router

    D. Bridge

9. You have an interface on a router with the IP address of 192.168.192.10/29. Including the router interface, how many hosts can have IP addresses on the LAN attached to router interface?

    A. 6

    B. 8

    C. 30

    D. 62

    E. 126

10. When configuring the IP settings on a computer on one subnet to ensure it can communicate with a computer on another subnet, which of the following is desirable?

    A. Configure the computer with the same default gateway as the other computer.

    B. Configure the computer with the same subnet mask as the other computer.

    C. Configure the computer with a default gateway that matches the IP address of the router's interface that is attached to the same subnet as the computer.

    D. Configure the computer with a subnet mask that matches the IP address of the router's interface that is attached to the same subnet as the computer.

You have an interface on a router with the IP address of 192.168.192.10/29. What is the broadcast address the hosts will use on this LAN?

A. 192.168.192.15

B. 192.168.192.31

C. 192.168.192.63

D. 192.168.192.127

E. 192.168.192.255

12. What is the highest usable address on the 172.16.1.0/24 network?

A. 172.16.1.255

B. 172.16.1.254

C. 172.16.1.253

D. 172.16.1.23

13. A network administrator is connecting hosts A and B directly through their Ethernet interfaces, as shown in the illustration. Ping attempts between the hosts are unsuccessful. What can be done to provide connectivity between the hosts? (Choose two.)

IP Address: 192.168.1.20   IP Address: 192.168.1.201
Mask 255.255.255.240   Mask 255.255.255.240

A. A crossover cable should be used in place of the straight-through cable.

B. A rollover cable should be used in place of the straight-though cable.

C. The subnet masks should be set to 255.255.255.192.

D. A default gateway needs to be set on each host.

E. The subnet masks should be set to 255.255.255.0.

14. If an Ethernet port on a router were assigned an IP address of 172.16.112.1/25, what would be the subnet address of this host?

A. 172.16.112.0

B. 172.16.0.0

C. 172.16.96.0

D. 172.16.255.0

E. 172.16.128.0

15. Using the illustration in question 16, what would be the IP address of E0 if you were using the eighth subnet? The network ID is 192.168.10.0/28, and you need to use the last available IP address in the range. The 0 subnet should not be considered valid for this question.

   A. 192.168.10.142

   B. 192.168.10.66

   C. 192.168.100.254

   D. 192.168.10.143

   E. 192.168.10.126

16. Using the following illustration, what would be the IP address of E0 if you were using the first subnet? The network ID is 192.168.10.0/28, and you need to use the last available IP address in the range. Again, the zero subnet should not be considered valid for this question.

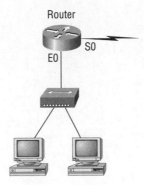

   A. 192.168.10.24

   B. 192.168.10.62

   C. 192.168.10.30

   D. 192.168.10.127

17. If you are forced to replace a router that has failed to the point that you are unable to access its current configuration to aid in setting up interface addresses on the new router, which of the following can you reference for assistance?

   A. The default-gateway settings on computers from each subnet that the old router interconnected.

   B. The router's configuration that was periodically cached on the DHCP server.

   C. The router's configuration that was periodically cached on the DNS server.

   D. The new router will auto-configure itself with the correct settings.

18. You have a network with a subnet of 172.16.17.0/22. Which of the following is a valid host address?

    A. 172.16.17.1 255.255.255.252

    B. 172.16.0.1 255.255.240.0

    C. 172.16.20.1 255.255.254.0

    D. 172.16.16.1 255.255.255.240

    E. 172.16.18.255 255.255.252.0

    F. 172.16.0.1 255.255.255.0

19. Your router has the following IP address on Ethernet0: 172.16.2.1/23. Which of the following can be valid host IDs on the LAN interface attached to the router? (Choose two.)

    A. 172.16.0.5

    B. 172.16.1.100

    C. 172.16.1.198

    D. 172.16.2.255

    E. 172.16.3.0

    F. 172.16.3.255

20. You have one IP address provided from your ISP with a /30 mask. However, you have 300 users that need to access the Internet. What technology will you use to implement a solution?

    A. PAT

    B. VPN

    C. DNS

    D. LANs

Answers to Review Questions

1. **D.** A /27 (255.255.255.224) is 3 bits on and 5 bits off. This provides 8 subnets, each with 30 hosts. Does it matter if this mask is used with a Class A, B, or C network address? Not at all. The number of host bits would never change.

2. **B.** Don't freak because this is a class A. What is your subnet mask? 255.255.255.128. Regardless of the class of address, this is a block size of 128 in the fourth octet. The subnets are 0 and 128. The 0 subnet host range is 1-126, with a broadcast address of 127. The 128 subnet host range is 129-254, with a broadcast address of 255. You need a router for these two hosts to communicate because they are in differenet subnets.

3. **C.** This is a pretty simple question. A /28 is 255.255.255.240, which means that our block size is 16 in the fourth octet. 0, 16, 32, 48, 64, 80, and so on. The host is in the 64 subnet.

4. **F.** A CIDR address of /19 is 255.255.224.0. This is a Class B address, so that is only 3 subnet bits, but it provides 13 host bits, or 8 subnets, each with 8,190 hosts.

5. **C.** The host ID of 10.0.37.144 with a 255.255.254.0 mask is in the 10.0.36.0 subnet (yes, you need to be able to subnet in this exam!). The third octet has a block size of two, so the next subnet is 10.0.38.0, which makes the broadcast address 10.0.37.255. The default gateway address of 10.0.38.1 is not in the same subnet as the host. Even though this is a Class A address, you still should easily be able to subnet this because you look more at the subnet mask and find your interesting octet, which is the third octet in this question. 256-254 = 2. Your block size is 2. Class A subnetting is covered in Appendix A.

6. **D.** A /30, regardless of the class of address, has a 252 in the fourth octet. This means we have a block size of 4, and our subnets are 0, 4, 8, 12, 16, and so on. Address 14 is obviously in the 12 subnet.

7. **D.** A point-to-point link uses only two hosts. A /30, or 255.255.255.252, mask provides two hosts per subnet.

8. **C.** Devices with Layer 3 awareness, such as routers and firewalls, are the only ones that can manipulate the IP header in support of NAT.

9. **A.** A /29 (255.255.255.248), regardless of the class of address, has only 3 host bits. Six hosts is the maximum number of hosts on this LAN, including the router interface.

10. **C.** A computer should be configured with an IP address that is unique throughout the reachable internetwork. It should be configured with a subnet mask that matches that of all other devices on its local subnet, but not necessarily one that matches the mask used on any other subnet. It should also be configured with a default gateway that matches its local router's interface IP address.

11. **A.** A /29 (255.255.255.248) has a block size of 8 in the fourth octet. This means the subnets are 0, 8, 16, 24, and so on. 10 is in the 8 subnet. The next subnet is 16, so 15 is the broadcast address.

12. B. A 24-bit mask, or prefix length, indicates the entire fourth octet is used for host identification. In a special case, such as this, it is simpler to visualize the all-zeros value (172.16.1.0) and the all-ones value (172.16.1.255). The highest usable address, the last one before the all-ones value, is 172.16.1.254.

13. A, E. First, if you have two hosts directly connected, as shown in the graphic, then you need a crossover cable. A straight-through cable won't work. Second, the hosts have differ- ent masks, which puts them in different subnets. The easy solution is just to set both masks to 255.255.255.0 (/24).

14. A. A /25 mask is 255.255.255.128. Used with a Class B network, the third and fourth octets are used for subnetting with a total of 9 subnet bits: 8 bits in the third octet and 1 bit in the fourth octet. Because there is only 1 bit in the fourth octet, the bit is either off or on—which is a value of 0 or 128. The host in the question is in the 0 subnet, which has a broadcast address of 127 because 128 is the next subnet.

15. A. A /28 is a 255.255.255.240 mask. Let's count to the ninth subnet (we need to find the broadcast address of the eighth subnet, so we need to count to the ninth subnet). Starting at 16 (remember, the question stated that we will not use subnet 0, so we start at 16, not 0), 16, 32, 48, 64, 80, 96, 112, 128, 144. The eighth subnet is 128, and the next subnet is 144, so our broadcast address of the 128 subnet is 143. This makes the host range 129–142. 142 is the last valid host.

16. C. A /28 is a 255.255.255.240 mask. The first subnet is 16 (remember that the question stated not to use subnet 0), and the next subnet is 32, so our broadcast address is 31. This makes our host range 17–30. 30 is the last valid host.

17. A. The best method here is to check the configuration of devices that were using the old router as a gateway to the rest of the internetwork. Routers do not periodically cache their configurations to servers of any sort. You might have copied the old router's configuration to a TFTP server or the like; but failing that, you will have to rebuild the configuration from scratch, which might well be much more than interface addresses. Therefore, keeping a copy of the router's current configuration somewhere other than on the router is a wise choice. Routers don't auto-configure themselves; we wouldn't want them to.

18. E. A Class B network ID with a /22 mask is 255.255.252.0, with a block size of 4 in the third octet. The network address in the question is in subnet 172.16.16.0 with a broadcast address of 172.16.19.255. Only option E even has the correct subnet mask listed, and 172.16.18.255 is a valid host.

19. D, E. The router's IP address on the E0 interface is 172.16.2.1/23, which is a 255.255.254.0. This makes the third octet a block size of 2. The router's interface is in the 2.0 subnet, and the broadcast address is 3.255 because the next subnet is 4.0. The valid host range is 2.1 through 3.254. The router is using the first valid host address in the range.

20. A. Network Address Translation can allow up to 65,000 hosts to get onto the Internet with one IP address by using Port Address Translation (PAT).

Answers to Written Labs

Write the subnet, broadcast address, and valid host range for Question 1 through Question 6:

1. 192.168.100.25/30. A /30 is 255.255.255.252. The valid subnet is 192.168.100.24, broadcast is 192.168.100.27, and valid hosts are 192.168.100.25 and 26.

2. 192.168.100.37/28. A /28 is 255.255.255.240. The fourth octet is a block size of 16. Just count by 16s until you pass 37. 0, 16, 32, 48. The host is in the 32 subnet, with a broadcast address of 47. Valid hosts are 33–46.

3. 192.168.100.66/27. A /27 is 255.255.255.224. The fourth octet is a block size of 32. Count by 32s until you pass the host address of 66. 0, 32, 64. The host is in the 64 subnet, broadcast address of 95. The valid host range is 65–94.

4. 192.168.100.17/29. A /29 is 255.255.255.248. The fourth octet is a block size of 8. 0, 8, 16, 24. The host is in the 16 subnet, broadcast of 23. Valid hosts are 17–22.

5. 192.168.100.99/26. A /26 is 255.255.255.192. The fourth octet has a block size of 64. 0, 64, 128. The host is in the 64 subnet, broadcast of 127. Valid hosts are 65–126.

6. 192.168.100.99/25. A /25 is 255.255.255.128. The fourth octet is a block size of 128. 0, 128. The host is in the 0 subnet, broadcast of 127. Valid hosts are 1–126.

7. A default Class B is 255.255.0.0. A Class B 255.255.255.0 mask is 256 subnets, each with 254 hosts. We need fewer subnets. If we use 255.255.240.0, this provides 16 subnets. Let's add one more subnet bit. 255.255.248.0. This is 5 bits of subnetting, which provides 32 subnets. This is our best answer, a /21.

8. A /29 is 255.255.255.248. This is a block size of 8 in the fourth octet. 0, 8, 16. The host is in the 8 subnet, and broadcast is 15.

9. A /29 is 255.255.255.248, which is 5 subnet bits and 3 host bits. This is only 6 hosts per subnet.

10. A /23 is 255.255.254.0. The third octet is a block size of 2. 0, 2, 4. The subnet is in the 16.2.0 subnet; the broadcast address is 16.3.255.

Chapter

9

Introduction to IP Routing

✓ **1.6 Explain the purpose and properties of routing**

- IGP vs. EGP

- Static vs. dynamic

- Next hop

- Understanding routing tables and how they pertain to
  path selection

IP routing is the process of moving packets from one network to another network using routers. The IP routing process is a super-important subject to understand because it pertains to all routers and configurations that use IP.

Before you read this chapter, you need to understand the difference between a routing protocol and a routed protocol. A *routing protocol* is a tool used by routers to dynamically find all the networks in the internetwork, as well as to ensure that all routers have the same routing table. Basically, a routing protocol determines the path of a packet through an internetwork. Examples of routing protocols are Routing Information Protocol (RIP), RIPv2, Enhanced Interior Gateway Routing Protocol (EIGRP), and Open Shortest Path First (OSPF).

Once all routers know about all networks, a *routed protocol* can be used to send user data (packets) through the established internetwork. Routed protocols are assigned to an interface and determine the method of packet delivery. Examples of routed protocols are Internet Protocol (IP) and IPv6.

In this chapter, I'm going to describe IP routing with routers. I will explain, in a step-by-step fashion, the IP routing process. I will also explain static and dynamic routing on a conceptual level, with more details about dynamic routing in Chapter 10, "Routing Protocols."

For up-to-the-minute updates for this chapter, please see www.lammle.com or www.sybex.com/go/comptianetwork+studyguide.

Routing Basics

Once you create an internetwork by connecting your wide area networks (WANs) and local area networks (LANs) to a router, you then need to configure logical network addresses, such as IP addresses, to all hosts on the internetwork so that they can communicate via routers across that internetwork.

In IT, routing essentially refers to the process of taking a packet from one device and sending it through the network to another device on a different network. Routers don't really care about hosts—they only care about networks and the best path to each network. The logical network address of the destination host is used to get packets to a network through a routed network, and then the hardware address of the host is used to deliver the packet from a router to the correct destination host.

If your network has no routers, then it should be apparent that, well, no... you are not routing. But if you do have them, they're there to route traffic to all the networks in your internetwork. To be capable of routing packets, a router must know at least the following information:

- Destination address
- Neighbor routers from which it can learn about remote networks
- Possible routes to all remote networks
- The best route to each remote network
- How to maintain and verify routing information

The router learns about remote networks from neighbor routers or from an administrator. The router then builds a *routing table* (a map of the internetwork) that describes how to find the remote networks. If a network is directly connected, then the router already knows how to get to it.

If a network isn't directly connected to the router, the router must use one of two ways to learn how to get to it. One way is called *static routing*, which can be a ton of work because it requires someone to hand-type all network locations into the routing table. The other way is known as dynamic routing.

In *dynamic routing*, a protocol on one router communicates with the same protocol running on neighbor routers. The routers then update each other about all the networks they know about and place this information into the routing table. If a change occurs in the network, the dynamic routing protocols automatically inform all routers about the event. If static routing is used, the administrator is responsible for updating all changes by hand into all routers. Understandably, in a large network, it's common to find that a combination of both dynamic and static routing is being used.

Before we jump into the IP routing process, let's take a look at a simple example that demonstrates how a router uses the routing table to route packets out of an interface. We'll be going into a more detailed study of this process in a minute.

Figure 9.1 shows a simple two-router network. Lab_A has one serial interface and three LAN interfaces

Looking at Figure 9.1, can you figure out which interface Lab_A will use to forward an IP datagram to a host with an IP address of 10.10.10.10?

By using the command show ip route, we can see the routing table (map of the internetwork) that router Lab_A will use to make all forwarding decisions:

```
Router_A#show ip route
[output cut]
Gateway of last resort is not set
C       10.10.10.0/24 is directly connected, FastEthernet0/0
C       10.10.20.0/24 is directly connected, FastEthernet0/1
C       10.10.30.0/24 is directly connected, FastEthernet0/2
C       10.10.40.0/24 is directly connected, Serial 0/0
```

FIGURE 9.1   A simple routing example

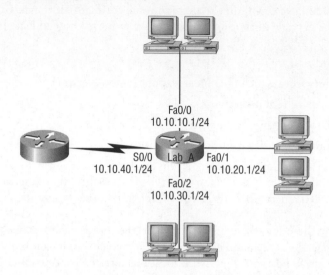

The C in the routing table output means that the networks listed are "directly connected"; and until we add a routing protocol—something like RIP, EIGRP, and so on—to the routers in our internetwork, or use static routes, we'll have only directly connected networks in our routing table.

So, let's get back to the original question: By looking at the figure and the output of the routing table, can you tell what Lab_A will do with a received packet that has a destination IP address of 10.10.10.10? If you answered, "The router will packet-switch the packet to interface FastEthernet 0/0, and this interface will then frame the packet and send it out on the network segment," you're right.

Just because we can, let's look at another example. Based on the output of the next routing table, which interface will a packet with a destination address of 10.10.10.14 be forwarded from?

```
Router_A#sh ip route
[output cut]
Gateway of last resort is not set
C       10.10.10.16/28 is directly connected, FastEthernet0/0
C       10.10.10.8/29 is directly connected, FastEthernet0/1
C       10.10.10.4/30 is directly connected, FastEthernet0/2
C       10.10.10.0/30 is directly connected, Serial 0/0
```

First, you can see that the network is subnetted and that each interface has a different mask. And I have to tell you, you positively can't answer this question if you can't subnet—no way! Here's the answer: 10.10.10.14 would be a host in the 10.10.10.8/29 subnet connected to the FastEthernet0/1 interface. Don't freak if this one left you staring vacantly. Instead, if you're struggling, go back and reread Chapter 8, "IP Subnetting, Troubleshooting IP, and Introduction to NAT," until you get it. This should then make perfect sense to you.

When the routing tables of all routers in the network are complete (because they include information about all the networks in the internetwork), they are considered *converged* or in steady state. This is covered in more detail in Chapter 10.

Now, let's get into this process in more detail.

The IP Routing Process

The IP routing process is actually pretty simple, and it doesn't change, regardless of the size of your network. I'm going to use Figure 9.2 to give you a picture of this step-by-step process. The question I'm asking is: What happens when Host_A wants to communicate with Host_B on a different network? I'll go through how to answer that question by breaking down the process with headings to make it easier to understand. First, check out Figure 9.2.

FIGURE 9.2 IP routing example using two hosts and one router

Okay—here you can see that a user on Host_A pings Host_B's IP address. Routing doesn't get any simpler than this, but it still involves a lot of steps. Let's work through them.

A packet is created on the host:

1. Internet Control Message Protocol (ICMP) creates an echo request payload (which is just the alphabet in the data field).

2. ICMP hands that payload to IP, which then creates a packet. At a minimum, this packet contains an IP source address, an IP destination address, and a Protocol field with 01h. (Remember that Cisco likes to use *0x* in front of hex characters, so this could look like 0x01.) All of that tells the receiving host whom it should hand the payload to when the destination is reached. In this example, it's ICMP.

The packet is forwarded:

3. After the packet is created, IP determines whether the destination IP address is on the local network or a remote one.

4. Because IP has discovered that this is a remote request, the packet needs to be sent to the default gateway so the packet can be routed to the correct remote network. The Registry in Windows is parsed to find the configured default gateway.

5. The default gateway of host 172.16.10.2 (Host_A) is configured to 172.16.10.1.
    For this packet to be sent to the default gateway, the hardware address of the rout-
    er's interface Ethernet 0 (configured with the IP address of 172.16.10.1) must be
    known. Why? So the packet can be handed down to the Data Link layer, framed,
    and sent to the router's interface that's connected to the 172.16.10.0 network.
    Because hosts only communicate via hardware addresses on the local LAN, it's
    important to recognize that for Host_A to communicate to Host_B, it has to send
    packets to the Media Access Control (MAC) address of the default gateway on the
    local network.

 MAC addresses are always local on the LAN and never go through and
past a router.

6. The Address Resolution Protocol (ARP) cache of the host is checked to see whether
    the IP address of the default gateway has already been resolved to a hardware
    address. If it has, the packet is then free to be handed to the Data Link layer for
    framing. (The hardware-destination address is also handed down with that packet.)
    To view the ARP cache on your host, use the following command:

```
C:\>arp -a
Interface: 172.16.10.2 --- 0x3
  Internet Address      Physical Address      Type
  172.16.10.1           00-15-05-06-31-b0     dynamic
```

If the hardware address isn't already in the ARP cache of the host, an ARP broadcast
is sent out onto the local network to search for the hardware address of 172.16.10.1.
The router responds to that request and provides the hardware address of Ethernet 0,
and the host caches this address.

7. After the packet and destination hardware address have been handed to the Data
    Link layer, the LAN driver is used to provide media access via the type of LAN being
    used (in this example, it's Ethernet). A frame is then generated, encapsulating the
    packet with control information. Within that frame are the hardware-destination and
    source addresses plus, in this case, an Ether-Type field that describes the Network
    layer protocol that handed the packet to the Data Link layer—in this instance, IP.
    At the end of the frame is something called a Frame Check Sequence (FCS) field that
    houses the result of the cyclic redundancy check (CRC). The frame would look some-
    thing like what I've detailed in Figure 9.3. It contains Host_A's hardware (MAC)
    address and the hardware-destination address of the default gateway. Importantly, it
    does not include the remote host's MAC address—remember that!

FIGURE 9.3   Frame used from Host_A to the Lab_A router when Host_B is pinged

Destination MAC (routers E0 MAC address)	Source MAC (Host_A MAC address)	Ether-Type field	Packet	FCS (CRC)

8. When the frame is completed, it's handed down to the Physical layer to be placed onto the physical medium one bit at a time. In this example, the physical medium is twisted-pair wire.

The router receives the packet:

9. Every device within the collision domain receives these bits and builds the frame. They each run a CRC and check the answer in the FCS field. If the answers don't match, the frame is discarded. But if the CRC matches, then the hardware-destination address is checked to see if it matches too (in this example, it's the router's interface, Ethernet 0). If it's a match, then the Ether-Type field is checked to find the protocol used at the Network layer.

10. The packet is pulled from the frame, and what is left of the frame is discarded. The packet is then handed to the protocol listed in the Ether-Type field—it's given to IP.

The router routes the packet:

11. IP receives the packet and checks the IP destination address. Because the packet's destination address doesn't match any of the addresses configured on the receiving router, the router will look up the destination IP network address in its routing table.

12. The routing table must have an entry for the network 172.16.20.0, or the packet will be discarded immediately and an ICMP message will be sent back to the originating device with a destination-network-unreachable message.

13. If the router does find an entry for the destination network in its table, the packet is switched to the exit interface—in this example, interface Ethernet 1. The following output displays the Lab_A router's routing table. The C means "directly connected." No routing protocols are needed in this network because all networks (all two of them) are directly connected:

```
Lab_A>sh ip route
Codes:C - connected,S - static,I - IGRP,R - RIP,M - mobile,B -
   BGP, D - EIGRP,EX - EIGRP external,O - OSPF,IA - OSPF inter
   area, N1 - OSPF NSSA external type 1, N2 - OSPF NSSA external
type 2, E1 - OSPF external type 1, E2 - OSPF external type 2,
E - EGP,i - IS-IS, L1 - IS-IS level-1, L2 - IS-IS level-2, ia
   - IS-IS intearea * - candidate default, U - per-user static
   route, o - ODR P - periodic downloaded static route

Gateway of last resort is not set

     172.16.0.0/24 is subnetted, 2 subnets
C        172.16.10.0 is directly connected, Ethernet0
C        172.16.20.0 is directly connected, Ethernet1
```

14. The router packet-switches the packet to the Ethernet 1 buffer.

15. Now that the Packet is in the Ethernet 1 buffer, IP needs to know the hardware address of the destination host and first checks the ARP cache. If the hardware address of Host_B has already been resolved and is in the router's ARP cache, then the packet and the hardware address are handed down to the Data Link layer to be framed. Let's take a look at the ARP cache on the Lab_A router by using the show ip arp command:

```
Lab_A#sh ip arp
Protocol  Address       Age(min)  Hardware Addr    Type   Interface
Internet  172.16.20.1   -         00d0.58ad.05f4   ARPA   Ethernet1
Internet  172.16.20.2   3         0030.9492.a5dd   ARPA   Ethernet1
Internet  172.16.10.1   -         00d0.58ad.06aa   ARPA   Ethernet0
Internet  172.16.10.2   12        0030.9492.a4ac   ARPA   Ethernet0
```

Okay—the dash (-) means that this is the physical interface on the router. From this output, we can see that the router knows the 172.16.10.2 (Host_A) and 172.16.20.2 (Host_B) hardware addresses. Cisco routers will keep an entry in the ARP table for 4 hours. But if the hardware address hasn't already been resolved, the router then sends an ARP request out E1 looking for the hardware address of 172.16.20.2. Host_B responds with its hardware address, and the packet and hardware-destination address are both sent to the Data Link layer for framing.

16. The Data Link layer creates a frame with the destination and source hardware address, Ether-Type field, and FCS field at the end. The frame is handed to the Physical layer to be sent out on the physical medium one bit at a time.

Finally, the remote host receives the packet:

17. Host_B receives the frame and immediately runs a CRC. If the result matches what's in the FCS field, the hardware-destination address is then checked. If the host finds a match, the Ether-Type field is then checked to determine the protocol that the packet should be handed to at the Network layer—IP, in this example.

18. At the Network layer, IP receives the packet and checks the IP destination address. Because there's finally a match made, the Protocol field is checked to find out whom the payload should be given to.

19. The payload is handed to ICMP, which understands that this is an echo request. ICMP responds to this by immediately discarding the packet and generating a new payload as an echo reply.

The destination host becomes a source host:

20. A packet is created, including the source and destination addresses, Protocol field, and payload. The destination device is now Host_A.

21. IP checks to see whether the destination IP address is a device on the local LAN or on a remote network. Because the destination device is on a remote network, the packet needs to be sent to the default gateway.

22. The default gateway IP address is found in the Registry of the Windows device, and the ARP cache is checked to see whether the hardware address has already been resolved from an IP address.

23. After the hardware address of the default gateway is found, the packet and destination hardware addresses are handed down to the Data Link layer for framing.

24. The Data Link layer frames the packet of information and includes the following in the header:

- The destination and source hardware addresses
- The Ether-Type field with 0x0800 (IP) in it
- The FCS field with the CRC result in tow

25. The frame is now handed down to the Physical layer to be sent out over the network medium one bit at a time.

Time for the router to route another packet:

26. The router's Ethernet 1 interface receives the bits and builds a frame. The CRC is run, and the FCS field is checked to make sure the answers match.

27. When the CRC is found to be okay, the hardware-destination address is checked. Because the router's interface is a match, the packet is pulled from the frame, and the Ether-Type field is checked to see which protocol at the Network layer the packet should be delivered to.

28. The protocol is determined to be IP, so it gets the packet. IP runs a CRC check on the IP header first and then checks the destination IP address.

NOTE   IP does not run a complete CRC the way the Data Link layer does—it only checks the header for errors.

Because the IP destination address doesn't match any of the router's interfaces, the routing table is checked to see whether it has a route to 172.16.10.0. If it doesn't have a route over to the destination network, the packet will be discarded immediately. (This is the source point of confusion for a lot of administrators—when a ping fails, most people think the packet never reached the destination host. But as we see here, that's not *always* the case. All it takes is just one of the remote routers to be lacking a route back to the originating host's network and—*poof!*—the packet is dropped on the *return trip*, not on its way to the host.)

TIP   Just a quick note to mention that when (if) the packet is lost on the way back to the originating host, you will typically see a request-timed-out message because it is an unknown error. If the error occurs because of a known issue, such as a route that is not in the routing table on the way to the destination device, you will see a destination-unreachable message. This should help you determine if the problem occurred on the way to the destination or on the way back.

29. In this case, the router does know how to get to network 172.16.10.0—the exit interface is Ethernet 0—so the packet is switched to interface Ethernet 0.

30. The router checks the ARP cache to determine whether the hardware address for 172.16.10.2 has already been resolved.

31. Because the hardware address to 172.16.10.2 is already cached from the originating trip to Host_B, the hardware address and packet are handed to the Data Link layer.

32. The Data Link layer builds a frame with the hardware-destination address and hardware-source address and then puts IP in the Ether-Type field. A CRC is run on the frame, and the result is placed in the FCS field.

33. The frame is then handed to the Physical layer to be sent out onto the local network one bit at a time.

The original source host, now the destination host, receives the reply packet:

34. The destination host receives the frame, runs a CRC, checks the hardware-destination address, and looks in the Ether-Type field to find out whom to hand the packet to.

35. IP is the designated receiver, and after the packet is handed to IP at the Network layer, IP checks the protocol field for further direction. IP finds instructions to give the payload to ICMP, and ICMP determines the packet to be an ICMP echo reply.

36. ICMP acknowledges that it has received the reply by sending an exclamation point (!) to the user interface. ICMP then attempts to send four more echo requests to the destination host.

You've just been introduced to "Todd's 36 easy steps to understanding IP routing." The key point to understand here is that if you had a much larger network, the process would be the *same*. In a really big internetwork, the packet just goes through more hops before it finds the destination host.

It's super-important to remember that when Host_A sends a packet to Host_B, the destination hardware address used is the default gateway's Ethernet interface. Why? Because frames can't be placed on remote networks—only local networks. So packets destined for remote networks must go through the default gateway.

Let's take a look at Host_A's ARP cache now by using the arp -a command from the DOS prompt:

```
C:\ >arp -a
Interface: 172.16.10.2 --- 0x3
  Internet Address       Physical Address        Type
  172.16.10.1            00-15-05-06-31-b0       dynamic
  172.16.20.1            00-15-05-06-31-b0       dynamic
```

Did you notice that the hardware (MAC) address that Host_A uses to get to Host_B is the Lab_A E0 interface? Hardware addresses are *always* local, and they never pass a router's interface. Understanding this process is as important to internetworking as breathing air is to you, so carve this into your memory!

Testing Your IP Routing Understanding

I want to make sure you understand IP routing, because it's really that important. So, I'm going to use this section to test your understanding of the IP routing process by having you look at a couple of figures and answer some very basic IP routing questions.

Figure 9.4 shows a LAN connected to RouterA, which is, in turn, connected via a WAN link to RouterB. RouterB has a LAN connected with an HTTP server attached. Take a look.

FIGURE 9.4   IP routing example 1

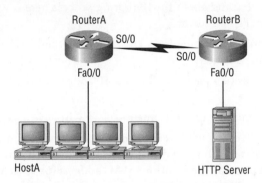

The critical information you need to glean from this figure is exactly how IP routing will occur in this example. Okay—we'll cheat a bit. I'll give you the answer, but then you should go back over the figure and see if you can answer example 2 without looking at my answers:

1. The destination address of a frame, from HostA, will be the MAC address of the F0/0 interface of the RouterA router.

2. The destination address of a packet will be the IP address of the network interface card (NIC) of the HTTP server.

3. The destination port number in the segment header will have a value of 80.

That example was a pretty simple one, and it was also very to the point. One thing to remember is that if multiple hosts are communicating to the server using HTTP, they must all use a different source-port number. That is how the server keeps the data separated at the Transport layer.

Let's mix it up a little and add another internetworking device into the network and then see if you can find the answers. Figure 9.5 shows a network with only one router but two switches.

FIGURE 9.5   IP routing example 2

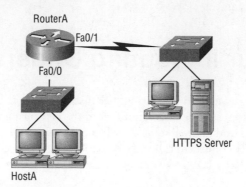

What you want to understand about the IP routing process here is what happens when HostA sends data to the HTTPS server:

1. The destination address of a frame from HostA will be the MAC address of the F0/0 interface of the RouterA router.

2. The destination address of a packet will be the IP address of the NIC of the HTTPS server.

3. The destination port number in the segment header will have a value of 443.

Notice that neither switch was used as either a default gateway or another destination. That's because switches have nothing to do with routing. I wonder how many of you chose the switch as the default gateway (destination) MAC address for HostA? If you did, don't feel bad—just take another look with that fact in mind. It's very important to remember that the destination MAC address will always be the router's interface—if your packets are destined for outside the LAN, as they were in these last two examples.

Static and Dynamic Routing

How does a router send packets to remote networks when the only way it can send them is by looking at the routing table to find out how to get to the remote networks? And what happens when a router receives a packet for a network that isn't listed in the routing table? It doesn't send a broadcast looking for the remote network—the router just discards the packet. Period.

There are several ways to configure the routing tables to include all the networks so that packets will be forwarded. Understand that what's best for one network isn't necessarily what's best for another. Knowing about and being able to recognize the different types of routing will really help you come up with the best solution for your specific environment and business requirements.

Looking at Figure 9.6, we can see that we can configure a router either with static or dynamic routing. If we choose static routing, then we have to go to each router and type in each network and the path that IP will use to send packets. However, static routing does not scale well in large networks, but dynamic routing does because network routes are automatically added to the routing table via the routing protocol.

FIGURE 9.6   Routing options

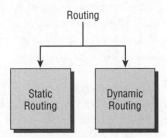

Dynamic routing protocols break up into many different categories or types of protocols, as shown in Figure 9.7. The first split in the dynamic protocol branch is the division of interior gateway protocols (IGPs) and exterior gateway protocols (EGPs). We are going to talk about each protocol and category in the next few sections, but for now the difference between IGP and EGP is interior or exterior routing of an autonomous system (AS).

FIGURE 9.7   Dynamic routing options

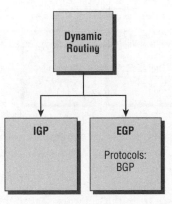

An *autonomous system* is a collection of networks or subnets that are in the same administrative domain. This is another way of saying an administrative domain is within your company's network, and you control or administer all the subnets that are within it. You control and set the policy for what happens in the network or autonomous system. I hope you can now see that an IGP operates and routes within an AS and an EGP works outside or between more than one AS.

The most popular protocol for an EGP is Border Gateway Protocol (BGP), which is typically used by ISPs or really large corporations. As an administrator of a small-to-medium-size network, you'll probably never use BGP. (BGP will be discussed in Chapter 10.)

Now that we have that out of the way, let's talk about all the great things that dynamic routing protocols do for us. The thing that comes to mind first is the amount of time and energy we save configuring routers. We won't have to go to every single router and define for it, with a static route, what and where every destination network is. If that was the only way to configure routing, there would probably be a lot fewer of us interested in doing this for a living. Thankfully, we have routing protocols that do much of the work for us. We still have to know what the routing protocols are going to do and how they will do it, but the protocols will take care of most of the updating and sending information to each other.

That is the end of the EGP branch of the tree, but the IGP branch continues to split out as we go down further. Looking at Figure 9.8, with the IGP split, you can see that there are two primary categories: Distance Vector (DV) and Link State (LS) routing protocols.

FIGURE 9.8   DV and LS routing protocols

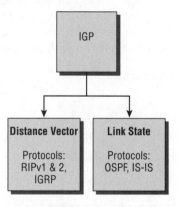

No worries—I'm going to discuss all of these types of protocols in the next chapters. But in the Distance Vector category, for example, we have RIP and Interior Gateway Routing Protocol (IGRP). Under the Link State category are OSPF and Intermediate System-to-Intermediate System (IS-IS).

Now, in Figure 9.9, you can see from the diagram that there is a third category: the Hybrid Protocol category.

The only protocol under this category is EIGRP. It is Cisco proprietary and uses the features of both DV and LS.

Okay, now that we have a handle on IP routing, let's move onto Chapter 10 and discuss the IGP routing protocols introduced in this chapter.

FIGURE 9.9   Hybrid routing

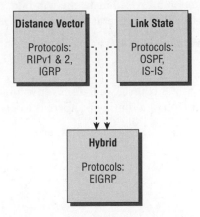

Summary

This chapter covered IP routing in detail. It's extremely important that you really understand the basics we covered in this chapter because everything that's done on a router typically will have some type of IP routing configured and running.

You learned in this chapter how IP routing uses frames to transport packets between routers and to the destination host. Understanding the process of how packets and frames traverse a network is critical to your fundamental understanding of IP routing.

After I covered the basics of IP routing, I went through some examples to test your understanding and help you really bring in the importance of routing that you need. I finished the chapter with an introduction to static and dynamic routing, explained IGP and EGP, as well as the difference between Distance Vector and Link State routing protocols. In the next chapter, we'll continue with dynamic routing by discussing the various dynamic routing protocols.

Exam Essentials

Understand the basic IP routing process.   You need to remember that the frame changes at each hop but that the packet is never changed or manipulated in any way until it reaches the destination device.

Understand that MAC addresses are always local.   A MAC (hardware) address will only be used on a local LAN. It will never pass a router's interface.

Understand that a frame carries a packet to only two places.   A frame uses MAC (hardware) addresses to send a packet on a LAN. The frame will take the packet to either a host on the LAN or a router's interface if the packet is destined for a remote network.

Remember the difference between static and dynamic routing.   Static routing is where you, as the administrator, by hand, add every route into every routing table on every router on the network. This is as much work as it sounds like, which is why we use dynamic routing protocols that do the work for us. Of course, we'll discuss dynamic routing protocols more in the next chapter, but the main job of a routing protocol is to update routing tables.

Written Lab

Write the answers to the following questions:

1.   True/False: RIPv2 is a hybrid routing protocol.

2.   True/False: RIPv1 is a Link State routing protocol.

3.   True/False: EIGRP is a non-proprietary routing protocol.

4.   True/False: EIGRP is harder to configure than RIP.

5.   You need a routing protocol that can be run in a very large network with routers from multiple vendors. What routing protocol would be your best choice?

6.   Which type of routing would you configure on a router if you needed to use as little router overhead and CPU processing as possible?

7.   You are trying to reach a server on another subnet. What will be the destination hardware address of a frame sent from your host?

8.   You are trying to reach a server on another subnet. What will be the destination IP address of a packet sent from your host?

9.   A server has received a frame from your remote host. What will be the source hardware address of the frame?

10. A server has received a packet from your remote host. What will be the destination IP address of the packet?

(The answers to the Written Lab can be found following the answers to the Review Questions for this chapter.)

Review Questions

1. Which is not a routing protocol?

   A. RIP

   B. RIPv2

   C. RIPv3

   D. EIGRP

2. Which of these best describes dynamic routing?

   A. All network addresses must be hand-typed into the routing table.

   B. Only a portion of the network address must be hand-typed into the routing table.

   C. Routing tables are updated automatically when changes occur in the network.

   D. A and B

3. Which is true regarding dynamic routing?

   A. Static routes are best in large networks thus better to use then dynamic routing protocols.

   B. Static routes are automatically added to the routing table, dynamic routes must be added by hand

   C. You must use a DNS and WINS server when configuring dynamic routing

   D. Dynamic routes are automatically added to the routing table

4. Which of the following is true for MAC addresses?

   A. MAC addresses are never local on the LAN and always pass through a router.

   B. MAC addresses are always local on the LAN and never go through or past a router.

   C. MAC addresses will always be the IP address of Fa0/0 interface.

   D. None of the above

5. The time required by protocols to update their forwarding tables after changes have occurred are called what?

   A. Name resolution

   B. Routing

   C. Convergence

   D. ARP resolution

6. What command would be used to view the ARP cache on your host?

   A. `C:\ >show ip route`

   B. `C:\ >show ip arp`

   C. `C:\ >show protocols`

   D. `C:\ >arp -a`

7. What happens when a router receives a packet for a network that isn't listed in the routing table?

    A. It forwards the packet to the next available router.

    B. It holds the packet until the address is updated in the routing table.

    C. The router will use RIP to inform the host that it can't send the packet.

    D. None of the above

8. Which of the following is not a Distance Vector protocol?

    A. RIPv1

    B. RIPv2

    C. OSPF

    D. IGRP

9. Which two of the following are Link State protocols?

    A. RIPv1

    B. RIPv2

    C. OSPF

    D. IS-IS

    E. IGRP

10. Which of the following is a hybrid routing protocol?

    A. RIPv2

    B. EIGRP

    C. IS-IS

    D. IGRP

11. What does the acronym IGRP stand for?

    A. Interior Gateway Routing Protocol

    B. Inside Gateway Redundancy Protocol

    C. Interior Group Reliability Protocol

    D. Interior Gateway Redundancy Protocol

12. What EGP protocol is used on the Internet?

    A. GGP

    B. EGP

    C. BGP

    D. IGP

13. What are the two categories of IGP protocols?

  A. Link State

  B. Static

  C. Distance Vector

  D. EGP

14. What two pieces of information does a router require to make a routing decision?

  A. Destination network (address)

  B. Destination MAC address

  C. Application layer protocol

  D. Neighbor router

15. Where does a frame have to carry a packet if it is destined for a remote network?

  A. Default gateway

  B. Neighbor host

  C. Switch

  D. Hub

16. Where along the IP routing process does a packet get changed?

  A. Router

  B. Host A

  C. Destination device

  D. Host B

17. When all routers in a network agree about the path from one point to another, the network is said to be what?

  A. Dynamic

  B. Static

  C. Secure

  D. Converged

18. What type of request must a client send if it does not know the destination MAC address?

  A. ARP broadcast

  B. Multicast

  C. ICMP redirect

  D. Reverse ARP

19. You need to perform maintenance on a router in your corporate office. It is important that the network does not go down. What can you do to accomplish your goal?

   A. Configure BGP on the router

   B. Implement NAT on the router

   C. Configure a static route on the router that temporarily re-routes traffic through another office

   D. Implement convergence on the router

20. When are you most likely to see a request-timed-out message?

   A. When an unknown error has occurred

   B. When you have used the `arp -a` command incorrectly

   C. When a known error has occurred

   D. When you are using a hybrid routing protocol

Answers to Review Questions

1. C. Yup, you got it. RIP, RIPv2, and EIGRP are all examples of routing protocols.

2. C. In dynamic routing, routers update each other about all the networks they know about and place this information into the routing table. This is possible because a protocol on one router communicates with the same protocol running on neighbor routers. If changes occur in the network, a dynamic routing protocol automatically informs all routers about the event.

3. D. Dynamic routing scales well in large networks and routes are automatically added into the routing table. Static routing is done by hand, one route at a time into each router.

4. B. Media Access Control (MAC) addresses are always local on the LAN and never go through and past a router.

5. C. Routing convergence is the time required by the routing protocols to update the routing tables (forwarding tables) on all routers in the network.

6. D. The `arp -a` command will show the ARP cache on your host.

7. D. Hope you answered D! A router will not send a broadcast looking for the remote network—the router will discard the packet.

8. C. RIPv1 and 2 and IGRP are all Distance Vector (DV) protocols. Routers using a DV protocol send all or parts of their routing table in a routing-update message at a regular interval to each of their neighbor routers.

9. C, D. Open Shortest Path First (OSPF) and Intermediate System-to-Intermediate System (IS-IS) are Link State (LS) routing protocols.

10. B. The only protocol you could select is Enhanced Interior Gateway Routing Protocol (EIGRP).

11. A. Interior Gateway Routing Protocol is a DV interior gateway protocol.

12. C. Border Gateway Protocol (BGP) is the most popular choice for ISPs or really large corporations.

13. A, C. Distance Vector (DV) and Link State (LS) are the two routing protocols to remember.

14. A, D. A frame uses MAC addresses to send a packet on the LAN. The frame will take the packet to either a host on the LAN or a router's interface if the packet is destined for a remote network.

15. A. I hope you said A! Packets specifically have to be carried to a router in order to be routed through a network.

16. C. Remember that the frame changes at each hop but that the packet is never changed in any way until it reaches the destination device.

17. D. When the routing table are complete because they include information about all networks in the internetwork, they are considered converged.

18. A. This is step 6 in the IP routing process. If the hardware address isn't in the ARP cache of the host, an ARP broadcast is sent out onto the local network to search for the hardware address.

19. C. The best answer would be to re-route traffic using a temporary static route until the maintenance is complete on the router.

20. A. You are most likely to see a request-timed-out message when (if) a packet is lost on the way back to the originating host for an unknown error. Remember, if the error occurs because of a known issue, you are likely to see a destination-unreachable message.

Answers to Written Lab

1. False. RIP and RIPv2 are both Distance Vector protocols.

2. False. RIP and RIPv2 are both Distance Vector protocols.

3. False. EIGRP is a Cisco proprietary routing protocol.

4. False. EIGRP has basically the same configuration as RIP.

5. RIP does not work well in large networks, so OSPF would be the best answer. EIGRP is not the answer because it only runs on Cisco routers.

6. Static routing

7. The MAC address of your default gateway (router)

8. The IP address of the server

9. The MAC address of the router sending the frame to the server

10. The IP address of the server

Chapter

10

Routing Protocols

THE FOLLOWING COMPTIA NETWORK+ EXAM OBJECTIVES ARE COVERED IN THIS CHAPTER:

✓ **1.5 Identify common IPv4 and IPv6 routing protocols**

- Link state
    - OSPF
    - IS-IS
- Distance vector
    - RIP
    - RIPv2
    - BGP
- Hybrid
    - EIGRP

✓ **1.6 Explain the purpose and properties of routing**

- Explain convergence (steady state)

Routing protocols are critical to a network's design. This chapter focuses on dynamic routing protocols. Dynamic routing protocols run only on routers that use them in order to discover networks and update their routing tables. Using dynamic routing is easier on you, the system administrator, than the labor-intensive, manually achieved, static routing method is, but it'll cost you in terms of router CPU processes and bandwidth on the network links.

The reason for the poor bandwidth economy is that a routing protocol defines the set of rules used by a router when it communicates routing information between its neighbor routers, and the router and its routing protocol need bandwidth to accomplish that.

In this chapter, I'm going to give you all the basic information you need to know about routing protocols so you can choose the correct one for each network you work on and/or design.

For up-to-the-minute updates for this chapter, please see www.lammle.com or www.sybex.com/go/comptianetwork+studyguide.

Routing Protocol Basics

Because getting a solid visual can really help people learn, I'm going to get you started by combining the last few figures used in Chapter 9, "Introduction to Routing." This way, you can get the big picture and really understand how routing works. Figure 10.1 shows the complete routing tree that I broke up piece by piece at the end of Chapter 9.

As I touched on in Chapter 9, there are two types of routing protocols used in internetworks: interior gateway protocols (IGPs) and exterior gateway protocols (EGPs). IGPs are used to exchange routing information with routers in the same *autonomous system (AS)*. An AS is a collection of networks under a common administrative domain, which simply means that all routers sharing the same routing table information are in the same AS. EGPs are used to communicate between multiple ASs. A nice example of an EGP would be Border Gateway Protocol (BGP), which really is beyond the scope of this book; I'll briefly describe it in this chapter anyway because there is a small objective about it on the exam. And no worries, we'll continue our discussion of IGPs too.

There are a few key points about routing protocols that I think it would be a good idea to talk over before getting deeper into the specifics of each one. First on the list is something known as an administrative distance.

FIGURE 10.1   Routing flow tree

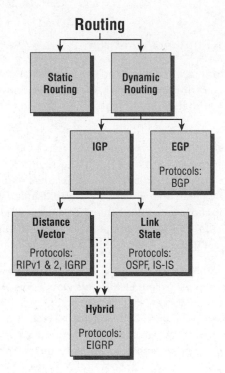

Administrative Distances

The *administrative distance (AD)* is used to rate the trustworthiness of routing information received on one router from its neighboring router. An AD is an integer from 0 to 255, where 0 equals the most trusted route and 255 the least. A value of 255 essentially means, "No traffic is allowed to be passed via this route."

If a router receives two updates listing the same remote network, the first thing the router checks is the AD. If one of the advertised routes has a lower AD than the other, the route with the lower AD is the one that will get placed in the routing table.

If both advertised routes to the same network have the same AD, then routing-protocol metrics like *hop count* or the amount of bandwidth of the lines will be used to find the best path to the remote network. And as it was with the AD, the advertised route with the lowest metric will be placed in the routing table. But if both advertised routes have the same AD as well as the same metrics, then the routing protocol will *load-balance* to the remote network. To perform load balancing, a router will send packets down each link to test for the best one.

Real World Scenario

Why Not Just Turn on all Routing Protocols?

There have been many customers who have hired me because all their employees were complaining about the slow, intermittent network. Many times, I have found that the administrators did not truly understand routing protocols and just enabled them all on every router.

This may sound laughable, but it is true. When an administrator tried to disable a routing protocol, such as Routing Information Protocol (RIP), they would receive a call that part of the network was not working. First, understand that because of default ADs, although every routing protocol was enabled, only Enhanced Interior Gateway Routing Protocol (EIGRP) would show up in most of the routing tables. This meant that Open Shortest Path First (OSPF), *Intermediate System-to-Intermediate System (IS-IS),* and *RIP* would be running in the background but just using up bandwidth and routing process, slowing the routers almost to a crawl.

By disabling all the routing protocols except EGIRP (this would only work on an all-Cisco router network), the network improved at least 30%. In addition, finding the routers that were configured only for RIP and enabling EIGRP solved the calls from users complaining that the network was down when RIP was disabled on the network. Last, I replaced the core routers with better routers with more memory, enabling faster, more efficient routing and raising the network response time to a total of 50%.

Table 10.1 shows the default ADs that a router uses to decide which route to take to a remote network:

TABLE 10.1   Default Administrative Distances

Route Source	Default AD
Connected interface	0
Static route	1
EIGRP	90
IGRP	100
OSPF	110

TABLE 10.1 Default Administrative Distances *(continued)*

Route Source	Default AD
RIP	120
External EIGRP	170
Unknown	255 (this route will never be used)

Understand that if a network is directly connected, the router will always use the interface connected to that network. Also good to know is that if you configure a static route, the router will believe that route to be the preferred one over any other routes it learns about dynamically. You can change the ADs of static routes, but by default, they have an AD of 1. That's only one place above zero, so you can see why a static route's default AD will always be considered the best by the router.

This means that if you have a static route, a RIP-advertised route, and an IGRP-advertised route listing the same network, then by default, the router will always use the static route unless you change the AD of the static route.

Classes of Routing Protocols

The three classes of routing protocols introduced in Chapter 9, and shown in Figure 10.1, are as follows:

Distance vector The *distance-vector protocols* find the best path to a remote network by judging—you guessed it—distance. Each time a packet goes through a router, it equals something we call a *hop*. The route with fewest hops to the network is determined to be the best route. The vector indicates the direction to the remote network. RIP, RIPv2, and Interior Gateway Routing Protocol (IGRP) are distance-vector routing protocols. These protocols send the entire routing table to all directly connected neighbors.

Link state Using *link-state protocols*, also called *shortest-path-first protocols*, the routers each create three separate tables. One of these tables keeps track of directly attached neighbors, one determines the topology of the entire internetwork, and one is used as the actual routing table. Link-state routers know more about the internetwork than any distance-vector routing protocol. OSPF and IS-IS are IP routing protocols that are completely link state. Link-state protocols send updates containing the state of their own links to all other routers on the network.

Hybrid A *hybrid protocol* uses aspects of both distance vector and link state, and at this writing, there's only one—EIGRP. It happens to be a Cisco proprietary protocol, meaning that it will only run on Cisco equipment. So if you have a multi-vendor environment, by default, this won't work for you.

I want you to understand that there's no one set way of configuring routing protocols for use in every situation. This is something you really have to do on a case-by-case basis. Even though this might seem a little intimidating, if you understand how each of the different routing protocols works, I promise you'll be capable of making good, solid decisions that will truly meet the individual needs of any business!

Distance-Vector Routing Protocols

Okay—the distance-vector routing algorithm passes complete routing-table contents to neighboring routers, which then combine the received routing-table entries with their own routing tables to complete the router's routing table. This is called *routing by rumor*, because a router receiving an update from a neighbor router believes the information about remote networks without finding out for itself if it actually is correct.

It's possible to have a network that has multiple links to the same remote network, and if that's the case, the AD of each received update is checked first. As I said, if the AD is the same, the protocol will then have to use other metrics to determine the best path to use to get to that remote network.

Distance vector uses only hop count to determine the best path to a network. If a router finds more than one link with the same hop count to the same remote network, it will automatically perform what's known as *round-robin load balancing*.

It's important to understand what a distance-vector routing protocol does when it starts up. In Figure 10.2, the four routers start off with only their directly connected networks in their routing table. After a distance-vector routing protocol is started on each router, the routing tables are then updated with all route information gathered from neighbor routers:

FIGURE 10.2   The internetwork with distance-vector routing

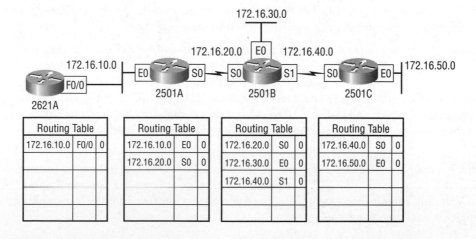

As you can see in Figure 10.2, each router has only the directly connected networks in each of their routing tables. Each router sends its complete routing table, which includes the network number, exit interface, and hop count to the network, out to each active interface.

Now, in Figure 10.3, the routing tables are complete because they include information about all the networks in the internetwork. They are considered *converged*. Usually, data transmission will cease while routers are converging—a good reason in favor of fast convergence time! In fact, one of the main problems with RIP is its slow convergence time.

FIGURE 10.3   Converged routing tables

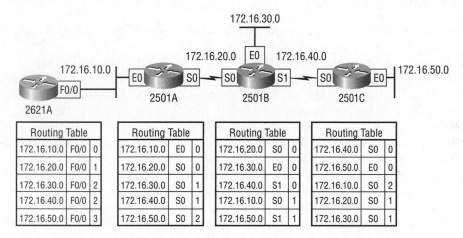

Okay, as you can see in Figure 10.3, once all the routers have converged, the routing table in each router keeps information about three important things:

- The remote network number
- The interface that the router will use to send packets to reach that particular network
- The hop count, or metric, to the network

 Remember! Routing convergence time is the time required by protocols to update their forwarding tables after changes have occurred.

Let's start discussing dynamic routing protocols with one of the oldest routing protocol that is still in existence today.

Routing Information Protocol (RIP)

RIP is a true distance-vector routing protocol. It sends the complete routing table out to all active interfaces every 30 seconds. RIP uses only one thing to determine the best way to a remote network—the hop count. And because it has a maximum allowable hop count of 15 by default, a hop count of 16 would be deemed unreachable. This means that although

RIP works fairly well in small networks, it's pretty inefficient on large networks with slow WAN links, or on networks populated with a large number of routers.

RIP version 1 uses only *classful routing*, which means that all devices in the network must use the same subnet mask. This is because RIP version 1 doesn't send updates with subnet mask information in tow. RIP version 2 provides something called *prefix routing* and does send subnet mask information with the route updates. Doing this is called *classless routing*.

RIP Version 2 (RIPv2)

Let's spend a couple of minutes discussing RIPv2 before we move into the distance-vector, Cisco-proprietary routing protocol EIGRP.

RIP Version 2 is mostly the same as RIP Version 1. Both RIPv1 and RIPv2 are distance-vector protocols, which means that each router running RIP sends its complete routing tables out all active interfaces at periodic time intervals. Also, the timers and loop-avoidance schemes are the same in both RIP versions (that is, holddown timers and split horizon rule). Both RIPv1 and RIPv2 are configured as classful addressing (but RIPv2 is considered classless because subnet information is sent with each route update), and both have the same AD (120).

But there are some important differences that make RIPv2 more scalable than RIPv1. And I've got to add a word of advice here before we move on; I'm definitely not advocating using RIP of either version in your network. But because RIP is an open standard, you can use RIP with any brand of router. You can also use OSPF because OSPF is an open standard as well.

Table 10.2 discusses the differences between RIPv1 and RIPv2.

TABLE 10.2   RIPv1 vs. RIPv2

RIPv1	RIPv2
Distance vector	Distance vector
Maximum hop count of 15	Maximum hop count of 15
Classful	Classless
Broadcast based	Uses Multicast 224.0.0.9
No support for VLSM	Supports VLSM networks
No authentication	Allows for MD5 authentication
No support for discontiguous networks	Supports discontiguous networks

RIPv2, unlike RIPv1, is a classless routing protocol (even though it is configured as classful, like RIPv1), which means that it sends subnet mask information along with the route updates. By sending the subnet mask information with the updates, RIPv2 can support Variable Length Subnet Masks (VLSMs), which are described in the next section, as well as the summarization of network boundaries.

VLSM and Discontiguous Networks

VLSM is classless, meaning that the routing protocol sends subnet-mask information with the route updates. The reason it's good to do this is to save address space. If we didn't use a routing protocol that supports VLSMs, then every router interface, every node (PC, printer, server, and so on), would have to use the same subnet mask.

As the name suggests, with VLSMs we can have different subnet masks for different router interfaces. Check out Figure 10.4 to see an example of why classful network designs are inefficient.

FIGURE 10.4   Typical classful network

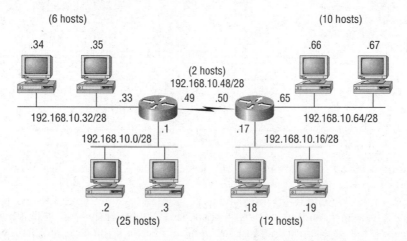

Looking at this figure, you'll notice that we have two routers, each with two LANs and connected together with a WAN serial link. In a typical classful network design example (RIP or IGRP routing protocol), you could subnet a network like this:

192.168.10.0 = Network

255.255.255.240 (/28) = Mask

Our subnets would be (you know this part, right?) 0, 16, 32, 48, 64, 80, and so on. This allows us to assign 16 subnets to our internetwork. But how many hosts would be available on each network? Well, as you probably know by now, each subnet provides only 14 hosts. This means that each LAN has 14 valid hosts available—one LAN doesn't even have enough addresses needed for all the hosts! But the point-to-point WAN link also has 14 valid hosts. It's too bad we can't just nick some valid hosts from that WAN link and give them to our LANs.

All hosts and router interfaces have the same subnet mask—again, this is called classful routing. And if we want this network to be more efficient, we definitely need to add different masks to each router interface.

But there's still another problem—the link between the two routers will never use more than two valid hosts! This wastes valuable IP address space, and it's the big reason I'm talking to you about VLSM networking.

Now let's take Figure 10.4 and use a classless design...which will become the new network shown in Figure 10.5. In the previous example, we wasted address space—one LAN didn't have enough addresses because every router interface and host used the same subnet mask. Not so good.

FIGURE 10.5 Classless network design

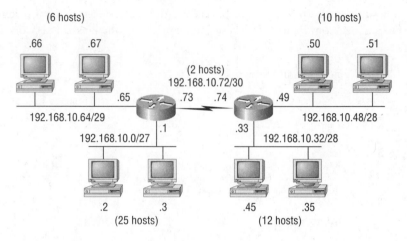

What would be good is to provide only the needed number of hosts on each router interface, meaning VLSMs.

So, if we use a /30 on our WAN links and a /27, /28, and /29 on our LANs, we'll get 2 hosts per WAN interface, and 30, 14, and 6 hosts per LAN interface—nice! This makes a huge difference—not only can we get just the right number of hosts on each LAN, we still have room to add more WANs and LANs using this same network.

Remember, in order to implement a VLSM design on your network, you need to have a routing protocol that sends subnet-mask information with the route updates. This would be RIPv2, EIGRP, or OSPF. RIPv1 and IGRP will not work in classless networks and are considered classful routing protocols.

By using a VLSM design, you do not necessarily make your network run better, but you can save a lot of IP addresses.

Now, what's a discontiguous network? It's one that has two or more subnetworks of a classful network connected together by different classful networks. Figure 10.6 displays a typical discontiguous network.

The subnets 172.16.10.0 and 172.16.20.0 are connected together with a 10.3.1.0 network. By default, each router thinks it has the only 172.16.0.0 classful network.

It's important to understand that discontiguous networks just won't work with RIPv1 or IGRP at all. They don't work by default on RIPv2 or EIGRP either, but discontiguous networks do work on OSPF networks by default because OSPF does not auto-summarize like RIPv2 and EIGRP.

FIGURE 10.6   A discontiguous network

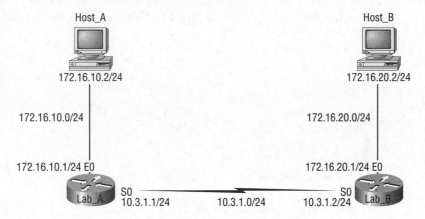

EIGRP

EIGRP is a classless, enhanced distance-vector protocol that gives us a real edge over another Cisco proprietary protocol, IGRP. That's basically why it's called Enhanced IGRP. IGRP is an older routing protocol and no longer supported by Cisco.

EIGRP uses the concept of an autonomous system to describe the set of contiguous routers that run the same routing protocol and share routing information. But unlike IGRP, EIGRP includes the subnet mask in its route updates. And as you now know, the advertisement of subnet information allows us to use VLSMs when designing our networks.

EIGRP is referred to as a *hybrid routing protocol* because it has characteristics of both distance-vector and link-state protocols. For example, EIGRP doesn't send link-state packets as OSPF does; instead, it sends traditional distance-vector updates containing information about networks plus the cost of reaching them from the perspective of the advertising router. But EIGRP has link-state characteristics as well—it synchronizes routing tables between neighbors at startup and then sends specific updates only when topology changes occur. This makes EIGRP suitable for very large networks.

There are a number of powerful features that make EIGRP a real standout from RIP, RIPv2, and other protocols. The main ones are listed here:

- Support for IP and IPv6 (and some other useless routed protocols) via protocol-dependent modules

- Considered classless (same as RIPv2 and OSPF)

- Support for VLSM / Classless Inter-Domain Routing (CIDR)
- Support for summaries and discontiguous networks
- Efficient neighbor discovery
- Communication via Reliable Transport Protocol (RTP)
- Best path selection via *Diffusing Update Algorithm (DUAL)*

Another great feature of EIGRP is that it's simple to configure and turn on like a distance-vector protocol, but it keeps track of more information than distance vector does. It creates and maintains additional tables instead of just one table as distance-vector routing protocols do.

These tables are called the *neighbor table*, *topology table*, and routing table, as shown in Figure 10.7.

FIGURE 10.7   EIGRP tables

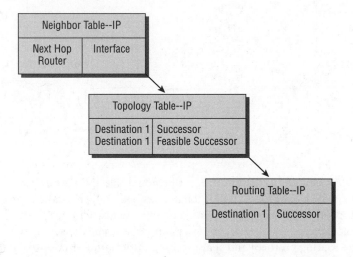

Neighbor table   Each router keeps state information about adjacent neighbors. When a newly discovered neighbor is learned about, the address and interface of that neighbor are recorded, and the information is held in the neighbor table and stored in RAM. Sequence numbers are used to match acknowledgments with update packets. The last sequence number received from the neighbor is recorded so that out-of-order packets can be detected.

Topology table   The topology table is populated by the neighbor table, and the best path to each remote network is found by running DUAL. The topology table contains all destinations advertised by neighboring routers, holding each destination address and a list of neighbors that have advertised the destination. For each neighbor, the advertised metric, which comes only from the neighbor's routing table, is recorded. If the neighbor is advertising this destination, it must be using the route to forward packets.

Feasible successor (backup routes)   A *feasible successor* is a path whose reported distance is less than the feasible (best) distance, and it is considered a backup route. EIGRP will keep up to six feasible successors in the topology table. Only the one with the best metric (the successor) is copied and placed in the routing table.

Successor (routes in a routing table)   A *successor route* (think successful!) is the best route to a remote network. A successor route is used by EIGRP to forward traffic to a destination and is stored in the routing table. It is backed up by a feasible successor route that is stored in the topology table—if one is available.

By using the feasible distance and having feasible successors in the topology table as backup links, the network can converge instantly, and updates to any neighbor only consist of traffic sent from EIGRP. All of these things make for a very fast, scalable, fault-tolerant routing protocol.

Border Gateway Protocol (BGP)

In a way, you can think of *Border Gateway Protocol (BGP)* as the heavyweight of routing protocols. In fact, it just happens to be the core routing protocol of the Internet. And it's not exactly breaking news that Internet has become a vital resource in so many organizations is it? No—but this growing dependence has resulted in redundant connections to many different ISPs.

This is where BGP comes in. The sheer onslaught of multiple connections would totally overwhelm other routing protocols like OSPF, which I am going to talk about in the next section. BGP is essentially an alternative to using default routes for controlling path selections.

Because the Internet's growth rate shows no signs of slowing, ISPs use BGP for its ability to make classless routing and summarization possible. These capabilities help to keep routing tables smaller and more efficient at the ISP core.

BGP is used for IGPs to communicate ASs together, as shown in Figure 10.8.

FIGURE 10.8   Border Gateway Protocol (BGP)

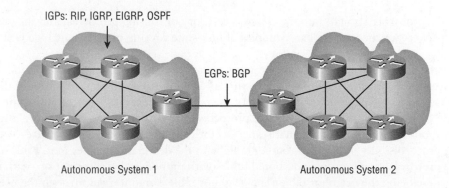

An autonomous system is a collection of networks under a common administrative domain. IGPs operate within an autonomous system, and EGPs connect different autonomous systems.

So yes, very large private IP networks can make use of BGP. Let's say you wanted to join a number of large OSPF networks together. Because OSPF just couldn't scale up enough to handle such a huge load, you would go with BGP instead to connect the ASs together. Another situation in which BGP would come in really handy would be if you wanted to multi-home a network for better redundancy, either to a multiple access point of a single ISP, or to multiple ISPs.

Internal routing protocols are employed to advertise all available networks; including the metric necessary to get to each of them. BGP is a personal favorite of mine because its routers exchange path vectors that give you detailed information on the BGP AS numbers, hop by hop, (called an AS-Path), required to reach a specific destination network.

And BGP also tells you about any/all networks reachable at the end of the path. These factors are the biggest differences you need to remember about BGP. Unlike IGPs that simply tells you how to get to a specific network, BGP gives you the big picture on exactly what's involved in getting to an AS, including the networks located in that AS, itself.

And there's more to that "BGP big picture" —this protocol carries information like the network prefixes found in the AS, and includes the IP address needed to get to the next AS, (the next-hop attribute). It even gives you the history on how the networks at the end of the path were introduced into BGP in the first place, known as the origin code attribute.

All of these traits are what makes BGP so useful for constructing a graph of loop-free autonomous systems, for identifying routing policies, and enabling us to create and enforce restrictions on routing behavior based upon the AS path –sweet!

Link-State Routing Protocols

Link-state protocols also fall into the classless category of routing protocols, and they work within packet-switched networks. Examples of link-state routing protocols include OSPF and IS-IS.

Remember, in order to be a classless routing protocol, the subnet-mask information must be carried with the routing update so that all neighbor routers know the cost of the network route that's being advertised. One of the biggest differences between link-state and distance-vector protocols is that link-state protocols learn and maintain much more information about the internetwork than distance-vector routing protocols do. Distance-vector routing protocols only maintain a routing table with the destination routes in it. Link-state routing protocols maintain two additional tables with more detailed information, with the first of these being the neighbor table. The neighbor table is maintained through the use of *hello packets* that are exchanged by all routers to determine which other routers are available to exchange routing data with. All routers that can share routing data are stored in the neighbor table.

The second table maintained is the topology table, which is built and sustained through the use of Link State Advertisements or Packets (LSAs or LSPs, depending on the protocol). In the topology table, you'll find a listing for every destination network, plus every neighbor (route) that it can be reached through. Essentially, it's a map of the entire internetwork.

Once all of that raw data is shared and each one of the routers has the data in its topology table, then the routing protocol runs the Shortest Path First (SPF) algorithm to compare it all and determine the best paths to each of the destination networks.

Open Shortest Path First (OSPF)

Open Shortest Path First (OSPF) is an open standard routing protocol that's been implemented by a wide variety of network vendors, including Cisco. OSPF works by using the *Dijkstra algorithm*. First, a shortest-path tree is constructed, and then the routing table is populated with the resulting best paths. OSPF converges quickly (although not as fast as EIGRP), and it supports multiple, equal-cost routes to the same destination. Like EIGRP, it supports both IP and IPv6 routed protocols; but OSPF must maintain a separate database and routing table for each, meaning you're basically running two routing protocols if you are using IP and IPv6 with OSPF.

OSPF provides the following features:

- Consists of areas and autonomous systems
- Minimizes routing update traffic
- Allows scalability
- Supports VLSM/CIDR
- Has unlimited hop count
- Allows multi-vendor deployment (open standard)

OSPF is the first link-state routing protocol that most people are introduced to, so it's good to see how it compares to more traditional distance-vector protocols like RIPv2 and RIPv1. Table 10.3 gives you a comparison of these three protocols:

TABLE 10.3 OSPF and RIP Comparison

Characteristic	OSPF	RIPv2	RIPv1
Type of protocol	Link state	Distance vector	Distance vector
Classless support	Yes	Yes	No
VLSM support	Yes	Yes	No
Auto-summarization	No	Yes	Yes
Manual summarization	Yes	No	No

TABLE 10.3 OSPF and RIP Comparison *(continued)*

Characteristic	OSPF	RIPv2	RIPv1
Discontiguous support	Yes	Yes	No
Route propagation	Multicast on change	Periodic multicast	Periodic broadcast
Path metric	Bandwidth	Hops	Hops
Hop-count limit	None	15	15
Convergence	Fast	Slow	Slow
Peer authentication	Yes	Yes	No
Hierarchical network	Yes (using areas)	No (flat only)	No (flat only)
Updates	Event triggered	Route table updates	Route table updates
Route computation	Dijkstra	Bellman-Ford	Bellman-Ford

OSPF has many features beyond the few I've listed in Table 10.3, and all of them contribute to a fast, scalable, and robust protocol that can be actively deployed in thousands of production networks.

OSPF is supposed to be designed in a hierarchical fashion, which basically means that you can separate the larger internetwork into smaller internetworks called *areas*. This is definitely the best design for OSPF.

The following are reasons you really want to create OSPF in a hierarchical design:

- To decrease routing overhead
- To speed up convergence
- To confine network instability to single areas of the network

Pretty sweet benefits! But you have to earn them—OSPF is more elaborate and difficult to configure in this manner.

Figure 10.9 shows a typical OSPF simple design. Notice how each router connects to the backbone—called area 0, or the backbone area. OSPF must have an area 0, and all other areas should connect to this area. Routers that connect other areas to the backbone area within an AS are called Area Border Routers (ABRs). Still, at least one interface of the ABR must be in area 0.

OSPF runs inside an autonomous system, but it can also connect multiple autonomous systems together. The router that connects these ASs is called an *Autonomous System Border Router (ASBR)*. Typically, in today's networks, BGP is used to connect between ASs, not OSPF.

FIGURE 10.9 OSPF design example

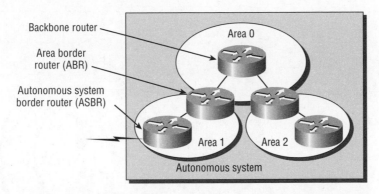

Ideally, you would create other areas of networks to help keep route updates to a minimum and to keep problems from propagating throughout the network. But that's beyond the scope of this chapter. Just make note of it for your future networking studies.

Intermediate System to Intermediate System (IS-IS)

IS-IS is an IGP, meaning that it's intended for use within an administrative domain or network, not for routing between ASs. That would be a job that an EGP, such as BGP, which we just covered, would handle instead.

IS-IS is a link-state routing protocol, meaning that it operates by reliably flooding topology information throughout a network of routers. Each router then independently builds a picture of the network's topology, just like OSPF does. Packets or datagrams are forwarded based on the best topological path through the network to the destination.

Figure 10.10 shows an IS-IS network and the terminology used with IS-IS.

Here are the definitions for the IS-IS network shown in Figure 10.10:

L1   Level 1 intermediate systems route within an area. When the destination is outside an area, they route toward a Level 2 system.

L2   Level 2 intermediate systems route between areas and toward other ASs.

The difference between IS-IS and OSPF is that IS-IS only uses Connectionless Network Service (CLNS) to provide connectionless delivery of data packets between routers. OSPF uses IP to communicate between routers instead.

An advantage to having CLNS around is that it can easily send information about multiple routed protocols (IP and IPv6), and as I already mentioned, OSPF must maintain a completely different routing database for IP and IPv6, respectively, for it to be able to send updates for both protocols.

IS-IS supports the most important characteristics of OSPF and EIGRP because it supports VLSM and also because it converges quickly. Each of these three protocols has advantages and disadvantages, but it's these two shared features that make any of them scalable and appropriate for supporting the large-scale networks of today.

FIGURE 10.10 IS-IS Network Terminology

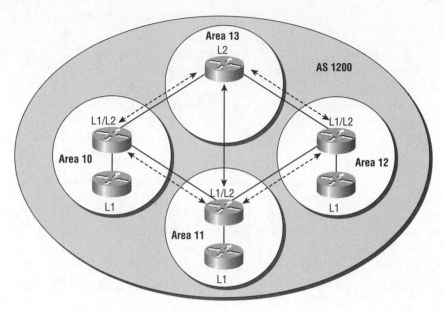

One last thing—even though it's not as common, IS-IS, although comparable to OSPF, is actually preferred by ISPs because of its ability to run IP and IPv6 without creating a separate database for each protocol like OSPF does. That single feature makes it more efficient in very large networks.

IPv6 Routing Protocols

Most of the routing protocols we've already discussed have been upgraded for use in IPv6 networks. Also, many of the functions and configurations that we've already learned will be used in almost the same way as they're used now. Knowing that broadcasts have been eliminated in IPv6, it follows that any protocols that use entirely broadcast traffic will go the way of the dodo—but unlike the dodo, it'll be good to say goodbye to these bandwidth-hogging, performance-annihilating little gremlins!

The routing protocols that we'll still use in v6 got a new name and a facelift. Let's talk about a few of them now.

First on the list is RIPng (next generation). Those of you who have been in IT for a while know that RIP has worked very well for us on smaller networks, which happens to be the reason it didn't get whacked and will still be around in IPv6. And we still have EIGRPv6 because it already had protocol-dependent modules and all we had to do was add a new one to it for the IPv6 protocol. Rounding out our group of protocol survivors is OSPFv3—that's not a typo, it really is v3. OSPF for IPv4 was actually v2, so when it got its upgrade to IPv6, it became OSPFv3.

RIPng

To be honest, the primary features of RIPng are the same as they were with RIPv2. It is still a distance-vector protocol, has a max hop count of 15, and uses split horizon, poison reverse, and other loop avoidance mechanisms, but it now uses UDP port 521.

And it still uses multicast to send its updates, too; but in IPv6, it uses FF02::9 for the transport address. This is actually kind of cool because in RIPv2, the multicast address was 224.0.0.9, so the address still has a 9 at the end in the new IPv6 multicast range. In fact, most routing protocols got to keep a little bit of their IPv4 identities like that.

But of course, there are differences in the new version, or it wouldn't be a new version, would it? We know that routers keep the next-hop addresses of their neighbor routers for every destination network in their routing table. The difference is that with RIPng, the router keeps track of this next-hop address using the link-local address, not a global address. So just remember that RIPng will pretty much work the same way as with IPv4.

EIGRPv6

As with RIPng, EIGRPv6 works much the same as its IPv4 predecessor does—most of the features that EIGRP provided before EIGRPv6 will still be available.

EIGRPv6 is still an advanced distance-vector protocol that has some link-state features. The neighbor-discovery process using hellos still happens, and it still provides reliable communication with a reliable transport protocol that gives us loop-free fast convergence using DUAL.

Hello packets and updates are sent using multicast transmission; and as with RIPng, EIGRPv6's multicast address stayed almost the same. In IPv4 it was 224.0.0.10; in IPv6, it's FF02::A (A = 10 in hexadecimal notation).

Last to check out in our group is what OSPF looks like in the IPv6 routing protocol.

OSPFv3

The new version of OSPF continues the trend of the routing protocols having many similarities with their IPv4 versions.

The foundation of OSPF remains the same—it is still a link-state routing protocol that divides an entire internetwork or autonomous system into areas, making a hierarchy.

Adjacencies (neighbor routers running OSPF) and next-hop attributes now use link-local addresses, and OSPFv3 still uses multicast traffic to send its updates and acknowledgements, with the addresses FF02::5 for OSPF routers and FF02::6 for OSPF-designated routers. These new addresses are the replacements for 224.0.0.5 and 224.0.0.6, respectively, which were used in OSPFv2.

With all this routing information behind you, it's time to go through some review questions and then move on to learning all about switching in the next chapter.

Summary

This chapter covered the basic routing protocols that you may find on a network today. Probably the most common routing protocols you'll run into are RIP, OSPF, and EIGRP.

I covered RIP, RIPv2, the differences between the two RIP protocols, EIGRP, and BGP in the distance-vector section of this chapter.

I finished by discussing OSPF and IS-IS and when you would possibly see each one in a network.

Exam Essentials

Remember the differences between RIPv1 and RIPv2.   RIPv1 sends broadcasts every 30 seconds and has an AD of 120. RIPv2 sends multicasts (224.0.0.9) every 30 seconds and also has an AD of 120. RIPv2 sends subnet mask information with the route updates, which allows it to support classless networks and discontiguous networks. RIPv2 also supports authentication between routers, and RIPv1 does not.

Know EIGRP features.   EIGRP is a classless, advanced distance-vector protocol that supports IP, IPX, AppleTalk, and now IPv6. EIGRP uses a unique algorithm called DUAL to maintain route information, and it uses RTP to communicate with other EIGRP routers reliably.

Compare OSPF and RIPv1.   OSPF is a link-state protocol that supports VLSM and classless routing; RIPv1 is a distance-vector protocol that does not support VLSM and supports only classful routing.

Written Lab

1. The default administrative distance of RIP is_____.

2. The default administrative distance of EIGRP is_____.

3. The default administrative distance of RIPv2 is_____.

4. The default administrative distance of a static route is?

5. What is the version or name of RIP that is used with IPv6?

6. What is the version or name of OSPF that is used with IPv6?

7. What is the version or name of EIGRP that is used with IPv6?

8. When would you use BGP?

9. When could you use EIGRP?

10. Is BGP considered link state or distance vector?

(The answers to the Written Lab can be found following the answers to the Review Questions for this chapter.)

Review Questions

1. Which of the following protocols support VLSM, summarization, and discontiguous networking? (Choose three.)
   A. RIPv1
   B. IGRP
   C. EIGRP
   D. OSPF
   E. BGP
   F. RIPv2

2. Which of the following are considered distance-vector routing protocols? (Choose two.)
   A. OSPF
   B. RIP
   C. RIPv2
   D. IS-IS

3. Which of the following are considered link-state routing protocols? (Choose two.)
   A. OSPF
   B. RIP
   C. RIPv2
   D. IS-IS

4. Which of the following is considered a hybrid routing protocol?
   A. OSPF
   B. BGP
   C. RIPv2
   D. IS-IS
   E. EIGRP

5. Why would you want to use a dynamic routing protocol instead of using static routes?
   A. Less overhead on the router
   B. Dynamic routing is more secure
   C. Dynamic routing scales to larger networks
   D. The network runs faster

6. Which of the following is a vendor-specific routing protocol?

   A. IGRP

   B. OSPF

   C. RIPv1

   D. EIGRP

   E. IS-IS

7. RIP has a long convergence time and users have been complaining of response time when a router goes down and RIP has to reconverge. Which can you implement to improve convergence time on the network?

   A. Replace RIP with static routes

   B. Update RIP to RIPv2

   C. Update RIP to OSPF using Link State

   D. Replace RIP with BGP as an exterior gateway protocol

8. What is the administrative distance of OSPF?

   A. 90

   B. 100

   C. 110

   D. 120

9. Which of the following protocols will advertise routed IPv6 networks?

   A. RIP

   B. RIPng

   C. OSPFv2

   D. EIGRPv3

10. What is the difference between static and dynamic routing?

    A. You use static routing in large, scalable networks

    B. Dynamic routing is used by a DNS server

    C. Dynamic routes are added automatically

    D. Static routes are added automatically

11. Which routing protocol has a maximum hop count of 15?

    A. RIPv1

    B. IGRP

    C. EIGRP

    D. OSPF

12. Which of the following describes routing convergence?

    A. The time it takes for your VPN to connect

    B. The time required by protocols to update their forwarding tables after changes have occurred

    C. The time required for IDS to detect an attack

    D. The time required by switches to update their link status and go into forwarding state

13. What routing protocol is typically used to connect AS's on the Internet?

    A. IGRP

    B. RIPv2

    C. BGP

    D. OSPF

14. RIPv2 sends out its routing table every 30 seconds just like RIPv1, but it does so more efficiently. What type of transmission does RIPv2 use to accomplish this task?

    A. Broadcasts

    B. Multicasts

    C. Telecast

    D. None of the above

15. Which routing protocols have an administrative distance of 120? (Choose two.)

    A. RIPv1

    B. RIPv2

    C. EIGRP

    D. OSPF

16. Which of the following routing protocols uses AS-Path as one of the methods to build the routing tables?

    A. OSPF

    B. IS-IS

    C. BGP

    D. RIP

    E. EIGRP

17. Which IPv6 routing protocol uses UDP port 521?

    A. RIPng

    B. EIGRPv6

    C. OSPFv3

    D. IS-IS

18. What EIGRP information is held in RAM and maintained through the usage of hello and update packets? (Select all that apply.)

    A. DUAL table

    B. Neighbor table

    C. Topology table

    D. Successor route

19. Which is true regarding EIGRP successor routes?

    A. Successor routes are saved in the neighbor table.

    B. Successor routes are stored in the DUAL table.

    C. Successor routes are used only if the primary route fails.

    D. A successor route is used by EIGRP to forward traffic to a destination.

20. Which of the following uses only hop count as a metric to find the best path to a remote network?

    A. RIP

    B. EIGRP

    C. OSPF

    D. BGP

Answers to Review Questions

1. C, D, F. RIPv1 and IGRP are true distance-vector routing protocols and can't do much, really—except build and maintain routing tables and use a lot of bandwidth! RIPv2, EIGRP, and OSPF build and maintain routing tables, but they also provide classless routing, which allows for VLSM, summarization, and discontiguous networking.

2. B, C. RIP and RIPv2 are distance-vector routing protocols. OSPF and IS-IS are link state.

3. A, D. RIP and RIPv2 are distance-vector routing protocols. OSPF and IS-IS are link state.

4. E. RIP and RIPv2 are distance-vector routing protocols. OSPF and IS-IS are link state. EIGRP uses qualities from both distance vector and link state to create a hybrid routing protocol.

5. C. Dynamic routing is typically used in today's networks because it scales to larger networks and takes less administrative work.

6. D. EIGRP is called a hybrid routing protocol because it uses the characteristics of both distance-vector and link-state routing protocols. However, EIGRP can be run only on Cisco routers and is not vendor neutral.

7. C. Static routes may be a good solution, but remember they are not dynamic and if a piece of equipment goes down, new routes to remote networks will not automatically update, so OSPF is the best answer. It dynamically will update the routing tables with faster convergence then RIP.

8. C. The administrative distance (AD) is a very important parameter in a routing protocol. The lower the AD, the more trusted the route. If you have IGRP and OSPF running, by default IGRP routes would be placed in the routing table because IGRP has a lower AD of 100. OSPF has an AD of 110. RIPv1 and RIPv2 both have an AD of 120, and EIGRP is the lowest, at 90.

9. B. The routing protocols that have been upgraded to advertise IPv6 routes are RIPng, OSPFv3, and EIGRPv6. IS-IS can advertise IPv6 routes as well, but no upgrade was needed for IS-IS.

10. C. Dynamic routing protocols, like RIP, EIGRP and OSPF automatically add route updates to the routing table. Static routes must be added by hand.

11. A. The distance-vector protocols RIPv1 and RIPv2 both have a maximum hop count of 15 (remember, 16 is unreachable). IGRP and EIGRP have a hop count of 255, and OSPF doesn't have a maximum hop count.

12. B. Convergence time happens in many protocols, for many devices, by routing convergence is the time for all routers to update their routing tables (forwarding tables).

13. C. BGP is the routing protocol used to connect autonomous systems together on the Internet for its ability to make classless routing and summarization possible. These capabilities help to keep routing tables smaller and more efficient at the ISP core.

14. B. RIPv1 sends broadcasts every 30 seconds and has an AD of 120. RIPv2 sends multicasts (224.0.0.9) every 30 seconds and also has an AD of 120. RIPv2 sends subnet-mask information with the route updates, which allows it to support classless networks and discontiguous networks. RIPv2 also supports authentication between routers; RIPv1 does not.

15. A, B. Both RIPv1 and RIPv2 have an AD of 120. EIGRP has an AD of 90.

16. C. Border Gateway Protocol (BGP) attributes include the IP address to get to the next AS (the next-hop attribute) as well as an indication of how the networks at the end of the path were introduced into BGP (the origin code attribute). The AS path information is useful to construct a graph of loop-free autonomous systems and is used to identify routing policies so that restrictions on routing behavior can be enforced based on the AS path.

17. A. RIPng has many of the same features as RIPv2: It's a distance-vector protocol; it has a max hop count of 15; and it uses split horizon, poison reverse, and other loop-avoidance mechanisms. And it still uses multicast to send its updates too; but in IPv6, it uses FF02::9 for the transport address. For RIPv2, the multicast address was 224.0.0.9, so the address still has a 9 at the end in the new IPv6 multicast range.

18. B, C. EIGRP holds three tables in RAM: neighbor, topology, and routing. The neighbor and topology tables are built and also maintained with the use of hello packets.

19. D. A successor route is used by EIGRP to forward traffic to a destination and is stored in the routing table. It is backed up by a feasible successor route that is stored in the topology table—if one is available. Remember that all routes are in the topology table.

20. A. RIP and RIPv2 uses only hop count as a metric, with a maximum of 15 hops, to find the best path to a remote network.

Answers to Written Lab

1. 120

2. 90

3. 120

4. 1

5. RIPng (Next Generation). I wonder how many of you answered RIPv3?

6. OSPFv3

7. EIGRPv6

8. To connect two autonomous systems (ASs) together

9. If all your routers were Cisco routers

10. Distance vector

Chapter

11

Switching and Virtual LANs (VLANs)

THE FOLLOWING COMPTIA NETWORK+ EXAM OBJECTIVES ARE COVERED IN THIS CHAPTER:

✓ **3.3 Explain the advanced features of a switch**

- PoE
- Spanning tree
- VLAN
- Trunking
- Port mirroring
- Port authentication

Layer 2 switching is the process of using the hardware addresses of devices on a LAN to segment a network. Because you've got the basic ideas down, I'm now going to focus on the more in depth particulars of Layer 2 switching and how it works.

You already know that switching breaks up large collision domains into smaller ones and that a collision domain is a network segment with two or more devices sharing the same bandwidth. A hub network is a typical example of this type of technology. But because each port on a switch is actually its own collision domain, you can create a much better Ethernet LAN network by simply replacing your hubs with switches!

Switches truly have changed the way networks are designed and implemented. If a pure switched design is properly implemented, it will result in a clean, cost-effective, and resilient internetwork. In this chapter, we'll survey and compare how networks were designed before and after switching technologies were introduced.

Routing protocols like RIP, which you learned about in Chapter 10, "Routing Protocols," employ processes for preventing network loops from occurring at the Network layer. This is all good, but if you have redundant physical links between your switches, routing protocols won't do a thing to stop loops from occurring at the Data Link layer. That's exactly the reason Spanning Tree Protocol was developed—to put a stop to loops taking place within a Layer 2 switched network. The essentials of this vital protocol, as well as how it works within a switched network, are some of the important subjects that we'll cover thoroughly in this chapter.

And to finish up this chapter, you're going to learn exactly what a VLAN is and how VLAN memberships are used in a switched network, as well as how trunking is used to send information from all VLANs across a single link. Good stuff!

For up-to-the-minute updates for this chapter, please see www.lammle.com or www.sybex.com/go/comptianetwork+studyguide.

Networking Before Layer 2 Switching

Because knowing the history of something really helps with understanding why things are the way they are today, I'm going to go back in time a bit and talk about the condition of networks before switches, and the part switches have played in the evolution of corporate LANs by helping to segment them. For a visual of how a typical network design looked before LAN switching, check out the network in Figure 11.1.

FIGURE 11.1   A network, before switching

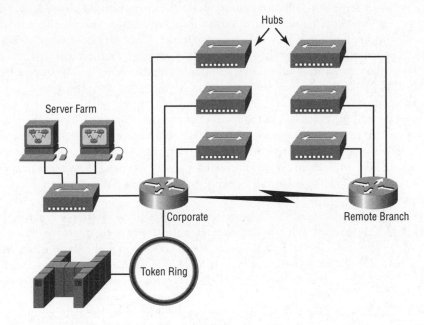

The design in Figure 11.1 was called a *collapsed backbone* because all the hosts involved had to go to the corporate backbone in order to reach any network services—both LAN and mainframe.

Going back even further, before networks like the one shown in Figure 11.1 had physical segmentation devices such as routers and hubs, there was the mainframe network. This type of network comprised mainframe controllers made by IBM, Honeywell, Sperry, DEC, and so on and dumb terminals that connected into the controller(s). Any remote sites were connected to the mainframe with bridges.

And then the PC began its rise to stardom, and the mainframe was connected to the Ethernet or to a Token Ring LAN where the servers were installed. These servers were usually OS/2 or LAN Manager because this was "pre-NT." Each floor of a building ran either coax or twisted-pair wiring to the corporate backbone, which was then connected to a router. PCs ran an emulating software program that allowed them to connect to mainframe services, giving those PCs the ability to access services from the mainframe and LAN simultaneously. Eventually, the PC became robust enough to allow application developers to port applications more effectively than they ever could before—an advance that markedly reduced networking prices and enabled businesses to grow at a much faster rate.

Moving forward to when Novell rose to popularity in the late 1980s and early 1990s, OS/2 and LAN Manager servers were by and large replaced with NetWare servers. This made the Ethernet network even more popular because that's what Novell 3.*x* servers used to communicate with client/server software.

So basically, that's the story about how the network in Figure 11.1 came into being. But soon, a big problem arose with this configuration. As the corporate backbone grew and grew, network services became slower and slower. A big reason for this was because at the same time this huge burst in growth was taking place, LAN services began to require even faster response times. This resulted in networks becoming totally saturated and overwhelmed. Everyone was dumping the dumb terminals used to access mainframe services in favor of those slick new PCs so they could more easily connect to the corporate backbone and network services.

And all this was taking place before the Internet's momentous popularity, so everyone in the company needed to access the corporate network's own, internal services. Without the Internet, all network services were internal, meaning that they were exclusive to the company network. As you can imagine, this situation created a screaming need to segment that single, humongous, and now plodding corporate network, which was connected together with sluggish old routers.

How was this issue addressed? Well, at first, Cisco responded by simply creating faster routers (no doubt about that); but still more segmentation was needed, especially on the Ethernet LANs. The invention of Fast Ethernet was a very good and helpful thing, yet it too fell short of solving that network segmentation need. But devices called *bridges* did provide relief, and they were first used in the networking environment to break up collision domains.

Sounds good, but only so much—bridges were sorely limited by the number of ports and other network services they could provide, and that's when Layer 2 switches came to the rescue. These switches saved the day by breaking up collision domains on each and every port—like a bridge—but switches could provide hundreds of ports! This early, switched LAN looked like the network pictured in Figure 11.2.

As you can see here, each hub was placed into a switch port—an innovation that vastly improved the network. So now, instead of each building being crammed into the same collision domain, each hub became its own separate collision domain. Yet still, as is too often the case, there was a catch—switch ports were still very new and therefore, superexpensive. Because switches were so cost prohibitive, simply adding a switch into each floor of the building just wasn't going to happen—at least, not yet. But thanks to whomever you choose to thank for these things, the switch price tag has dropped dramatically; now, having every one of your users plugged into a switch port is a really good solution, and cost-effective too!

So there it is—if you're going to create a network design and implement it, including switching services is a must.

A typical, contemporary, and complete switched network design/implementation would look something like Figure 11.3.

"But wait—there's still a router in there!" you say. Yes, it's not a mirage—there *is* a router in there. But its job has changed quite a bit. Instead of performing physical segmentation, it now creates and handles logical segmentation. Those logical segments are called VLANs; and no worries, I promise to explain them thoroughly throughout the rest of this chapter.

FIGURE 11.2   The first switched LAN

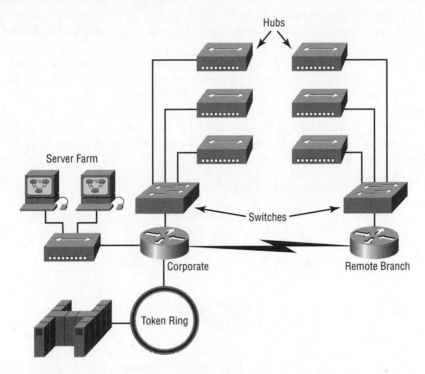

FIGURE 11.3   The typical switched network design

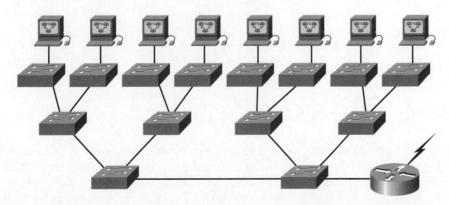

Switching Services

Unlike bridges, which use software to create and manage a filter table, switches use *application-specific integrated circuits (ASICs)* to accomplish this. Even so, it's still okay to think of a Layer 2 switch as a multiport bridge because their basic reason for being is the same: to break up collision domains.

Layer 2 switches and bridges are faster than routers because they don't take up time looking at the Network-layer header information. Instead, they look at the frame's hardware addresses before deciding to forward, flood, or drop the frame.

Switches create private, dedicated collision domains and provide independent bandwidth on each port, unlike hubs. Figure 11.4 shows five hosts connected to a switch—all running 10Mbps half-duplex to the server. Unlike with a hub, each host has 10Mbps of dedicated communication to the server:

FIGURE 11.4   Switches create private domains.

10Mbps Half-duplex links

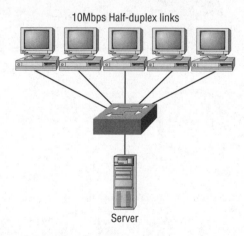

Server

Layer 2 switching provides the following benefits:

- Hardware-based bridging (ASIC)
- Wire speed
- Low latency
- Low cost

What makes Layer 2 switching so efficient is that no modification to the data packet takes place. The device reads only the frame encapsulating the packet, which makes the switching process considerably faster and less error-prone than routing processes.

And if you use Layer 2 switching for both workgroup connectivity and network segmentation (breaking up collision domains), you can create a flatter network design with more network segments than you can with traditional routed networks.

Plus, Layer 2 switching increases bandwidth for each user because, again, each connection (interface) into the switch is its own collision domain. This feature makes it possible for you to connect multiple devices to each interface—very cool.

Coming up, we'll dive deeper into the Layer 2 switching technology.

Limitations of Layer 2 Switching

Because people usually toss Layer 2 switching into the same category as bridged networks, we also tend to think it has the same hang-ups and issues that bridged networks do. Keep in mind that bridges are good and helpful things if we design the network correctly, keeping our devices' features as well as their limitations in mind. To end up with a solid design that includes bridges, there are two really important things to consider:

- You absolutely have to break up the collision domains properly.

- A well-oiled, functional bridged network is one where its users spend 80 percent of their time on the local segment.

Okay—so bridged networks break up collision domains; but remember, that network is really still just one big broadcast domain. Neither Layer 2 switches nor bridges break up broadcast domains by default—something that not only limits your network's size and growth potential but can also reduce its overall performance!

Broadcasts and multicasts, along with the slow convergence time of spanning trees, can give you some major grief as your network grows. These are the big reasons Layer 2 switches and bridges just can't completely replace routers (Layer 3 devices) in the internetwork.

Bridging vs. LAN Switching

It's true—Layer 2 switches really are pretty much just bridges that give us a lot more ports. But the comparison doesn't end there. Here's a list of some significant differences and similarities between bridges and switches that you need to keep in mind:

- Bridges are software based, whereas switches are hardware based because they use ASIC chips to help make filtering decisions.

- A switch can be viewed as a multiport bridge.

- There can be only one spanning-tree instance per bridge, whereas switches can have many. (I'm going to tell you all about spanning trees in a bit.)

- Switches have a higher number of ports than most bridges.

- Both bridges and switches forward Layer 2 broadcasts.

- Bridges and switches learn MAC addresses by examining the source address of each frame received.

- Both bridges and switches make forwarding decisions based on Layer 2 addresses.

Three Switch Functions at Layer 2

There are three distinct functions of Layer 2 switching—you need to know these! They are:

- Address learning
- Forward/filter decisions
- Loop avoidance

The next three sections cover these functions in detail.

Address Learning

Layer 2 switches and bridges are capable of *address learning*; that is, they remember the source hardware address of each frame received on an interface and enter this information into a MAC database known as a *forward/filter table*. But first things first—when a switch is initially powered on, the MAC forward/filter table is empty, as shown in Figure 11.5.

FIGURE 11.5   Empty forward/filter table on a switch

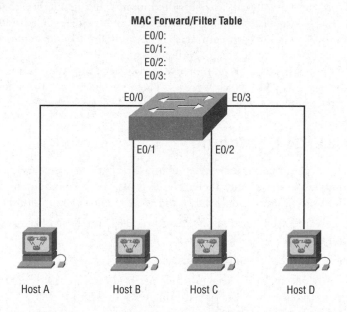

When a device transmits, and an interface receives a frame, the switch places the frame's source address in the MAC forward/filter table, which allows it to remember which interface the sending device is located on. The switch then has no choice but to flood the network with this frame out of every port except the source port because it has no idea where the destination device is actually located.

If a device answers this flooded frame and sends a frame back, then the switch will take the source address from that frame and place that MAC address in its database as well, thereby associating the newly discovered address with the interface that received the frame. Because the switch now has both of the relevant MAC addresses in its filtering table, the two devices can make a point-to-point connection. The switch doesn't need to flood the frame as it did the first time because now the frames can and will be forwarded only between the two devices recorded in the table. This is exactly the thing that makes Layer 2 switches better than hubs, because in a hub network, all frames are forwarded out all ports every time—no matter what. This is because hubs just aren't equipped to collect, store, and draw upon data in a table like a switch is. Figure 11.6 shows the processes involved in building a MAC database.

FIGURE 11.6 How switches learn hosts' locations

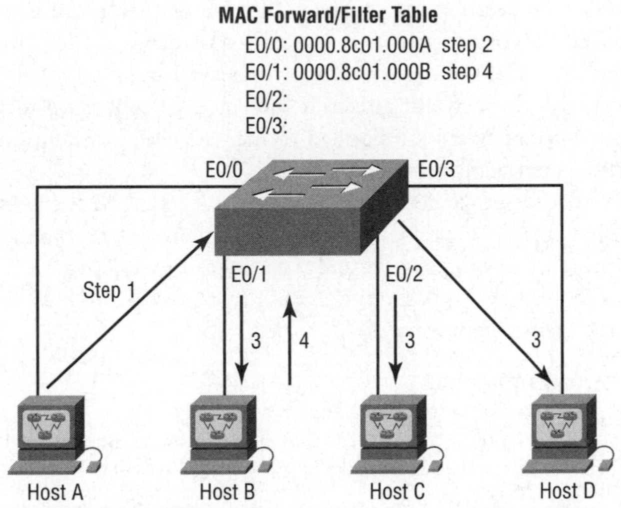

In this figure, you can see four hosts attached to a switch. When the switch is powered on, it has nothing in its MAC address forward/filter table (just as in Figure 11.6). But when the hosts start communicating, the switch places the source hardware address of each frame in the table along with the port that the frame's address corresponds to.

Let me give you a step-by-step example of how a forward/filter table becomes populated:

1. Host A sends a frame to Host B. Host A's MAC address is 0000.8c01.000A; Host B's MAC address is 0000.8c01.000B.

2. The switch receives the frame on the E0/0 interface and places the source address in the MAC address table.

3. Because the destination address is not in the MAC database, the frame is forwarded out all interfaces—except the source port.

4. Host B receives the frame and responds to Host A. The switch receives this frame on interface E0/1 and places the source hardware address in the MAC database.

5. Host A and Host B can now make a point-to-point connection, and only the two devices will receive the frames. Hosts C and D will not see the frames, nor are their MAC addresses found in the database because they haven't yet sent a frame to the switch.

Oh, by the way, it's important to know that if Host A and Host B don't communicate to the switch again within a certain amount of time, the switch will flush their entries from the database to keep it as current as possible.

Forward/Filter Decisions

When a frame arrives at a switch interface, the destination hardware address is compared to the forward/filter MAC database and the switch makes a *forward/filter decision*. In other words, if the destination hardware address is known (listed in the database), the frame is only sent out the specified exit interface. The switch will not transmit the frame out any interface except the destination interface. Not transmitting the frame preserves bandwidth on the other network segments and is called *frame filtering*.

But as I mentioned earlier, if the destination hardware address isn't listed in the MAC database, then the frame is flooded out all active interfaces except the interface the frame was received on. If a device answers the flooded frame, the MAC database is updated with the device's location—its particular interface.

So by default, if a host or server sends a broadcast on the LAN, the switch will flood the frame out all active ports except the source port. Remember, the switch creates smaller collision domains, but it's still one large broadcast domain by default.

In Figure 11.7, you can see Host A sending a data frame to Host D. What will the switch do when it receives the frame from Host A?

FIGURE 11.7   Forward/filter table

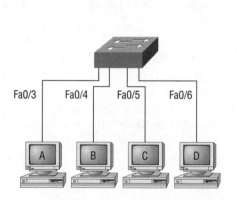

```
Switch#sh mac address-table
Vlan    Mac Address      Ports
----    -----------      -----
   1    0005.dccb.d74b   Fa0/4
   1    000a.f467.9e80   Fa0/5
   1    000a.f467.9e8b   Fa0/6
```

If you answered that because Host A's MAC address is not in the forward/filter table, the switch will add the source address and port to the MAC address table, and then forward the frame to Host D, you're halfway there. If you also came back with, "If Host D's MAC address was not in the forward/filter table, the switch would have flooded the frame out all ports except for port Fa0/3," then congratulations—you nailed it!

Let's take a look at the output of a show mac address-table command as seen from a Cisco Catalyst switch (the MAC address table works pretty much exactly the same on all brands of switches):

```
Switch#sh mac address-table
Vlan    Mac Address       Type        Ports
----    -----------       --------    -----
  1     0005.dccb.d74b    DYNAMIC     Fa0/1
  1     000a.f467.9e80    DYNAMIC     Fa0/3
  1     000a.f467.9e8b    DYNAMIC     Fa0/4
  1     000a.f467.9e8c    DYNAMIC     Fa0/3
  1     0010.7b7f.c2b0    DYNAMIC     Fa0/3
  1     0030.80dc.460b    DYNAMIC     Fa0/3
  1     0030.9492.a5dd    DYNAMIC     Fa0/1
  1     00d0.58ad.05f4    DYNAMIC     Fa0/1
```

Okay—now suppose the preceding switch received a frame with the following MAC addresses:

Source MAC: **0005.dccb.d74b**

Destination MAC: **000a.f467.9e8c**

How will the switch handle this frame? The right answer is that the destination MAC address will be found in the MAC address table, and the frame will be forwarded out Fa0/3 only. Remember that if the destination MAC address is not found in the forward/filter table, it will forward the frame out all ports of the switch looking for the destination device.

Now that you can see the MAC address table and how switches add hosts' addresses to the forward filter table, how do you stop switching loops if you have multiple links between switches? Let's talk about this possible problem in more detail.

Loop Avoidance

Redundant links between switches can be a wise thing to implement because they help prevent complete network failures in the event that one link stops working.

But it seems like there's always a down side—even though redundant links can be extremely helpful, they often cause more problems than they solve. This is because frames can be flooded down all redundant links simultaneously, creating network loops as well as other evils. Here are a few of the problems you can be faced with:

- If no *loop avoidance* schemes are put in place, the switches will flood broadcasts endlessly throughout the internetwork. This is sometimes referred to as a *broadcast storm*. (In real life, it's often referred to in less polite ways that we're not permitted to repeat in print!) Figure 11.8 illustrates how a broadcast can be propagated throughout the network. Pay special attention to how a frame is continually being flooded through the internetwork's physical network media.

FIGURE 11.8   Broadcast storm

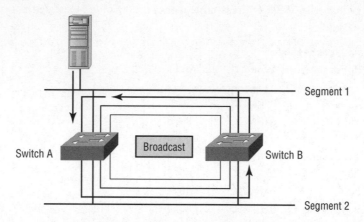

- What you see here is that a device can receive multiple copies of the same frame because that frame can arrive from different segments at the same time. Figure 11.9 demonstrates how a whole bunch of frames can arrive from multiple segments simultaneously. The server in the figure sends a unicast frame to Router C. Because it's a unicast frame, Switch A forwards the frame, and Switch B provides the same service—it forwards the unicast. This is bad because it means that Router C receives that unicast frame twice, causing additional overhead on the network.

FIGURE 11.9   Multiple frame copies

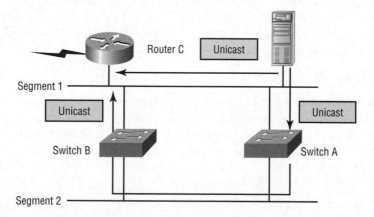

- You may have thought of this one: The MAC address filter table could be totally confused about the device's location because the switch can receive the frame from more than one link. Worse, the bewildered switch could get so caught up in constantly updating the MAC filter table with source hardware-address locations that it might fail to forward a frame! This is called *thrashing* the MAC table.

- One of the nastiest things that can happen is having multiple loops propagating throughout a network. This means you end up with loops occurring within other loops; and if a broadcast storm happened at the same time, the network wouldn't be able to perform frame switching at all—it's toast!

All of these problems spell disaster (or something like it) and are decidedly ugly situations that just must be avoided or at least fixed somehow. That's where the Spanning Tree Protocol comes into the game. It was developed to solve each and every one of the problems I just told you about.

Spanning Tree Protocol (STP)

Once upon a time, a company called Digital Equipment Corporation (DEC) was purchased and renamed Compaq. But before that happened, DEC created the original version of *Spanning Tree Protocol (STP)*. The IEEE later created its own version of STP called 802.1D. Yet again, it's not all clear skies—by default, most switches run the IEEE 802.1D version of STP, which isn't compatible with the DEC version. The good news is that there is a new industry standard called 802.1w, which is faster, but not enabled by default on any switches.

To begin with, STP's main task is to stop network loops from occurring on your Layer 2 network (bridges or switches). It achieves this feat by vigilantly monitoring the network to find all links and making sure that no loops occur by shutting down any redundant ones. STP uses the *spanning-tree algorithm (STA)* to first create a topology database and then search out and destroy redundant links. With STP running, frames will be forwarded only on the premium, STP-picked links. Switches transmit Bridge Protocol Data Units (BPDUs) out all ports so that all links between switches can be found.

NOTE   STP is a Layer 2 protocol that is used to maintain a loop-free switched network.

STP is necessary in networks such as the one shown in Figure 11.10.

FIGURE 11.10   A switched network with switching loops

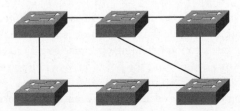

In Figure 11.10, you see a switched network with a redundant topology (switching loops). Without some type of Layer 2 mechanism to stop network loops, we would fall victim to the problems I discussed previously: broadcast storms and multiple frame copies.

Understand that the networking Figure 11.10 would actually sort of work, albeit extremely slowly. This clearly demonstrates the danger of switching loops. And to make matters worse, it can be super hard to find this problem once it starts!

Spanning-Tree Port States

The ports on a bridge or switch running STP can transition through five different states:

Blocking   A blocked port won't forward frames; it just listens to BPDUs and will drop all other frames. The purpose of the blocking state is to prevent the use of looped paths. All ports are in blocking state by default when the switch is powered up.

Listening   The port listens to BPDUs to make sure no loops occur on the network before passing data frames. A port in listening state prepares to forward data frames without populating the MAC address table.

Learning   The switch port listens to BPDUs and learns all the paths in the switched network. A port in learning state populates the MAC address table but doesn't forward data frames. Forward delay means the time it takes to transition a port from listening to learning mode. It's set to 15 seconds by default.

Forwarding   The port sends and receives all data frames on the bridged port. If the port is still a designated or root port at the end of the learning state, it enters the forwarding state.

Disabled   A port in the disabled state (administratively) does not participate in the frame forwarding or STP. A port in the disabled state is virtually nonoperational.

Switches populate the MAC address table in learning and forwarding modes only.

Switch ports are usually in either the blocking or forwarding state. A forwarding port is one that has been determined to have the lowest (best) cost to the root bridge. But when and if the network experiences a topology change because of a failed link or when someone adds a new switch into the mix, you'll find the ports on a switch in the listening and learning states.

As I mentioned, blocking ports is a strategy for preventing network loops. Once a switch determines the best path to the root bridge, all other redundant ports will be in blocking mode. Blocked ports can still receive BPDUs—they just don't send out any frames.

If a switch determines that a blocked port should now be the designated, or root port, say, because of a topology change, it will respond by going into listening mode and check all the BPDUs it receives to ensure it won't create a loop once the port goes back into forwarding mode.

STP Convergence

Convergence is what happens when all the ports on bridges and switches have transitioned to either forwarding or blocking modes. During this phase, no data will be forwarded until the convergence event is complete. Plus, before data can begin being forwarded again, all devices must be updated. Yes—you read that right: When STP is converging, all host data stops transmitting! So if you want to remain on speaking terms with your network's users (or remain employed for any length of time), you positively must make sure that your switched network is physically designed really well so that STP can converge quickly and painlessly.

Figure 11.11 demonstrates some really great ways to design and implement your switched network so that STP converges efficiently.

FIGURE 11.11   An optimal hierarchical switch design

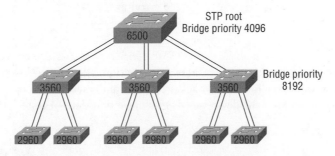

Create core switch as STP root for fastest STP convergence

Convergence is truly important because it ensures that all devices are in either the forwarding or blocking mode. But as I've drilled into you, it does cost you some time. It usually takes 50 seconds to go from blocking to forwarding mode, and I don't recommend changing the default STP timers. (You can adjust those timers if you really have to.) By creating your physical switch design in a hierarchical manner, as shown in Figure 11.11, you can make your core switch the STP root. This makes everyone happy because it makes STP convergence happen fast.

Because the typical spanning-tree topology's time to convergence from blocking to forwarding on a switch port is 50 seconds, it can create time-out problems on your servers or hosts—like, when you reboot them. To address this hitch, you can disable spanning tree on individual ports.

Virtual LANs (VLANs)

I know I keep telling you this, but I've got to be sure you never forget it, so here I go one last time: By default, switches break up collision domains, and routers break up broadcast domains. Okay, I feel better! Now we can move on.

In contrast to the networks of yesterday, which were based on collapsed backbones, today's network design is characterized by a flatter architecture—thanks to switches. So now what? How do we break up broadcast domains in a pure switched internetwork? By creating a Virtual Local Area Network (VLAN), that's how!

A VLAN is a logical grouping of network users and resources connected to administratively defined ports on a switch. When you create VLANs, you gain the ability to create smaller broadcast domains within a Layer 2 switched internetwork by assigning the various ports on the switch to different subnetworks. A VLAN is treated like its own subnet or broadcast domain, meaning that frames broadcasted onto the network are only switched between the ports logically grouped within the same VLAN.

So, does this mean we no longer need routers? Maybe yes, maybe no—it really depends on what your specific goals and needs are. By default, hosts in a specific VLAN can't communicate with hosts that are members of another VLAN; so if you want inter-VLAN communication, the answer is yes, you still need a router.

VLAN Basics

Figure 11.12 shows how Layer 2 switched networks are typically designed—as flat networks. With this configuration, every broadcast packet transmitted is seen by every device on the network regardless of whether the device needs to receive that data or not.

FIGURE 11.12   Flat network structure

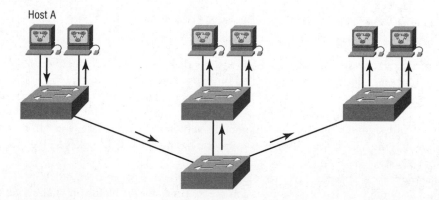

By default, routers allow broadcasts to occur only within the originating network, whereas switches forward broadcasts to all segments. Oh, and by the way, the reason it's called a *flat network* is because it's one *broadcast domain*, not because the actual design is physically flat. In Figure 11.12, you can see Host A sending out a broadcast, and all ports on all switches forwarding it—all except the port that originally received it.

Now check out Figure 11.13. It pictures a switched network and shows Host A sending a frame with Host D as its destination. What's important to get out of this figure is that the frame is only forwarded out of the port where Host D is located. This is a huge improvement over the old hub networks, unless having one collision domain by default is what you really want. (I'm guessing not!)

FIGURE 11.13   The benefit of a switched network

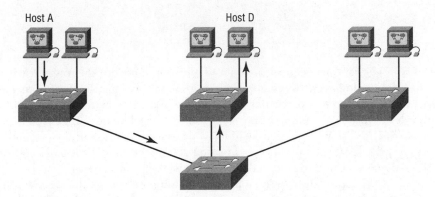

Okay—you already know that the coolest benefit you gain by having a Layer 2 switched network is that it creates an individual collision domain segment for each device plugged into each port on the switch. This scenario frees us from Ethernet's inherent distance constraints, enabling us to build larger networks. But as is often the case, new advances bring new challenges with them. One of the biggest is that the greater the number of users and devices, the more broadcasts and packets each switch must handle.

And of course, the all-important issue of security and its demands also must be considered, while simultaneously becoming more complicated! VLANs present a security challenge because by default, within the typical Layer 2 switched internetwork, all users can see all devices. And you can't stop devices from broadcasting, plus you can't stop users from trying to respond to broadcasts. This means your security options are dismally limited to placing passwords on your servers and other devices.

To understand how a VLAN looks to a switch, it's helpful to begin by first looking at a traditional network. Figure 11.14 shows how a network used to be created using hubs to connect physical LANs to a router.

FIGURE 11.14   Physical LANs connected to a router

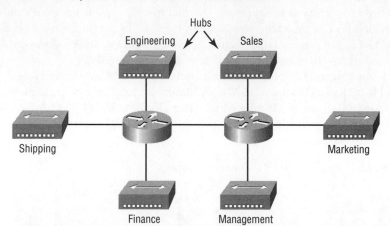

Here you can see that each network is attached with a hub port to the router (each segment also has its own logical network number even though this isn't obvious looking at the figure). Each host attached to a particular physical network has to match that network's number in order to be able to communicate on the internetwork. Notice that each department has its own LAN, so if we needed to add new users to, let's say, Sales, we would just plug them into the Sales LAN and they would automatically be part of the Sales collision and broadcast domain. This design actually did work well for many years.

But there was one major flaw: What happens if the hub for Sales is full and we need to add another user to the Sales LAN? Or, what do we do if there's no more physical space where the Sales team is located for a new employee? Hmmm, well, let's say there just happens to be plenty of room over in the Finance section of the building. That new Sales team member will just have to sit on the same side of the building as the Finance people, and we'll just plug the poor soul into the hub for Finance. Simple right?

So wrong! Doing this obviously makes the new user part of the Finance LAN, which is very bad for many reasons. First and foremost, we now have a major security issue. Because the new Sales employee is a member of the Finance broadcast domain, the newbie can see all the same servers and access all network services that the Finance folks can. Second, for this user to access the Sales network services they need to get their job done, they would have to go through the router to log in to the Sales server—not exactly efficient.

Now, let's look at what a switch accomplishes for us. Figure 11.15 demonstrates how switches come to the rescue by removing the physical boundary to solve our problem. It also shows how six VLANs (numbered 2 through 7) are used to create a broadcast domain for each department. Each switch port is then administratively assigned a VLAN membership, depending on the host and which broadcast domain it's placed in.

So now, if we needed to add another user to the Sales VLAN (VLAN 7), we could just assign the port to VLAN 7 regardless of where the new Sales team member is physically located—nice! This illustrates one of the sweetest advantages to designing your network with VLANs over the old collapsed backbone design. Now, cleanly and simply, each host that needs to be in the Sales VLAN is merely assigned to VLAN 7.

FIGURE 11.15 Switches removing the physical boundary

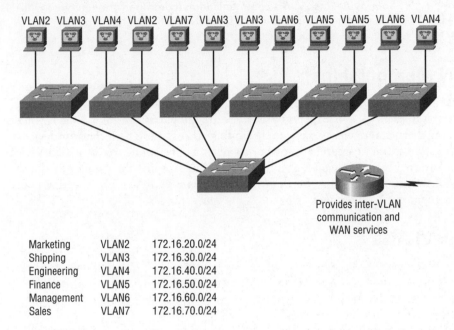

Marketing	VLAN2	172.16.20.0/24
Shipping	VLAN3	172.16.30.0/24
Engineering	VLAN4	172.16.40.0/24
Finance	VLAN5	172.16.50.0/24
Management	VLAN6	172.16.60.0/24
Sales	VLAN7	172.16.70.0/24

Notice that I started assigning VLANs with VLAN number 2. The number is irrelevant, but you might be wondering what happened to VLAN 1. Well, that VLAN is an administrative VLAN, and even though it can be used for a workgroup, Cisco recommends that you use it for administrative purposes only. You can't delete or change the name of VLAN 1; and by default, all ports on a switch are members of VLAN 1 until you actually do change them.

Now, because each VLAN is considered a broadcast domain, it's got to also have its own subnet number (refer again to Figure 11.15). And if you're also using IPv6, then each VLAN must also be assigned its own IPv6 network number. So you don't get confused, just keep thinking of VLANs as separate subnets or networks.

Let's get back to that "because of switches, we don't need routers anymore" misconception. When looking at Figure 11.15, you can see that there are seven VLANs, or broadcast domains, counting VLAN 1.The hosts within each VLAN can communicate with each other but not with anything in a different VLAN because the hosts in any given VLAN "think" that they're actually in a collapsed backbone, as illustrated in Figure 11.14.

So what handy little device do you think we need to enable the hosts in Figure 11.15 to communicate to a host or host on a different VLAN? You guessed it—a router! Those hosts absolutely need to go through a router, or some other Layer 3 device, just as they do when they're configured for internetwork communication (as shown in Figure 11.14). It works the same way it would if we were trying to connect different physical networks. Communication between VLANs must go through a Layer 3 device. So don't expect mass router extinction anytime soon!

To provide inter-VLAN communication (communication between VLANs), you need to use a router, or a layer-3 switch.

VLAN Memberships

Most of the time, VLANs are created by a system administrator who proceeds to assign switch ports to each VLAN. VLANs of this type are known as *static VLANs*. If you don't mind doing a little more work when you begin this process, assign all the host devices' hardware addresses into a database so your switches can be configured to assign VLANs dynamically anytime you plug a host into a switch. I hate saying things like "obviously," but obviously, this type of VLAN is known as a *dynamic VLAN*. I'll be covering both static and dynamic VLANs next.

Static VLANs

Creating static VLANs is the most common way to create a VLAN, and one of the reasons for that is because static VLANs are the most secure. This security stems from the fact that any switch port you've assigned a VLAN association to will always maintain it unless you change the port assignment manually.

Static VLAN configuration is pretty easy to set up and supervise, and it works really well in a networking environment where any user movement within the network needs to be controlled. It can be helpful to use network management software to configure the ports, but you don't have to use it if you don't want to.

In Figure 11.15, each switch port was configured manually with a VLAN membership based on which VLAN the host needed to be a member of—remember, the device's actual physical location doesn't matter one bit. Which broadcast domain your hosts become members of is purely up to you. And again, remember that each host also has to have the correct IP address information. For instance, you must configure each host in VLAN 2 into the 172.16.20.0/24 network for them to become members of that VLAN. It's also a good idea to keep in mind that if you plug a host into a switch, you have to verify the VLAN membership of that port. If the membership is different than what's needed for that host, the host won't be able to gain access to the network services that it needs, such as a workgroup server.

Static access ports are either manually assigned to a VLAN or assigned through a RADIUS server for use with IEEE 802.1x.

Dynamic VLANs

On the other hand, a dynamic VLAN determines a host's VLAN assignment automatically. Using intelligent management software, you can base VLAN assignments on hardware (MAC) addresses, protocols, or even applications that work to create dynamic VLANs.

For example, let's say MAC addresses have been entered into a centralized VLAN management application, and you hook up a new host. If you attach it to an unassigned switch port, the VLAN management database can look up the hardware address and both assign and configure the switch port into the correct VLAN. Needless to say, this makes management and configuration much easier because if a user moves, the switch will simply assign them to the correct VLAN automatically. But here again, there's a catch—initially, you've got to do a lot more work setting up the database. It can be very worthwhile, though!

And here's some more good news: You can use the VLAN Management Policy Server (VMPS) service to set up a database of MAC addresses to be used for the dynamic addressing of your VLANs. The VMPS database automatically maps MAC addresses to VLANs.

Identifying VLANs

Know that switch ports are Layer 2–only interfaces that are associated with a physical port. A switch port can belong to only one VLAN if it is an access port or all VLANs if it is a trunk port. You can manually configure a port as an access or trunk port, or you can let the Dynamic Trunking Protocol (DTP) operate on a per-port basis to set the switch port mode. DTP does this by negotiating with the port on the other end of the link.

Switches are definitely pretty busy devices. As frames are switched throughout the network, they've got to be able to keep track of all the different types plus understand what to do with them depending on the hardware address. And remember—frames are handled differently according to the type of link they're traversing.

There are two different types of links in a switched environment: access ports and trunk ports.

Access Ports

An access port belongs to and carries the traffic of only one VLAN. Traffic is both received and sent in native formats with no VLAN tagging whatsoever. Anything arriving on an access port is simply assumed to belong to the VLAN assigned to the port. So, what do you think will happen if an access port receives a tagged packet, like IEEE 802.1Q tagged? Right—that packet will simply be dropped. But why? Well, because an access port doesn't look at the source address, so tagged traffic can be forwarded and received only on trunk ports. With an access link, this can be referred to as the *configured VLAN* of the port. Any device attached to an *access link* is unaware of a VLAN membership—the device just assumes it's part of the same broadcast domain, but it doesn't have the big picture, so it doesn't understand the physical network topology at all.

Another good thing to know is that switches remove any VLAN information from the frame before it's forwarded out to an access-link device. Remember that access-link devices can't communicate with devices outside their VLAN unless the packet is routed. And you can only create a switch port to be either an access port or a trunk port—not both. So you've got to choose one or the other and know that if you make it an access port, that port can be assigned to one VLAN only.

You plug a host into a switch port and users are unable to access any server resources. The two typical reasons this happens is because the port is in the wrong VLAN membership or STP has shut down the port because STP thought there was possibly a loop.

Trunk Ports

Believe it or not, the term *trunk port* was inspired by the telephone system trunks that carry multiple telephone conversations at a time. So it follows that trunk ports can similarly carry multiple VLANs at a time.

A *trunk link* is a 100- or 1000-Mbps point-to-point link between two switches, between a switch and router, or even between a switch and server, and it carries the traffic of multiple VLANs—from 1 to 4,094 at a time.

Trunking can be a real advantage because with it, you get to make a single port part of a whole bunch of different VLANs at the same time. This is a great feature because you can actually set ports up to have a server in two separate broadcast domains simultaneously so your users won't have to cross a Layer 3 device (router) to log in and access it. Another benefit of trunking comes into play when you're connecting switches. Trunk links can carry various amounts of VLAN information across the link; but by default, if the links between your switches aren't trunked, only information from the configured VLAN will be switched across that link.

Check out Figure 11.16. It shows how the different links are used in a switched network. All hosts connected to the switches can communicate to all ports in their VLAN because of the trunk link between them. Remember, if we used an access link between the switches, this would allow only one VLAN to communicate between switches. As you can see, these hosts are using access links to connect to the switch, so they're communicating in one VLAN only. That means that without a router, no host can communicate outside its own VLAN, but the hosts can send data over trunked links to hosts on another switch configured in their same VLAN.

Okay—it's finally time to tell you about the VLAN identification methods.

VLAN Identification Methods

VLAN identification is what switches use to keep track of all those frames as they're traversing a switch fabric. It's how switches identify which frames belong to which VLANs, and there's more than one trunking method.

FIGURE 11.16   Access and trunk links in a switched network

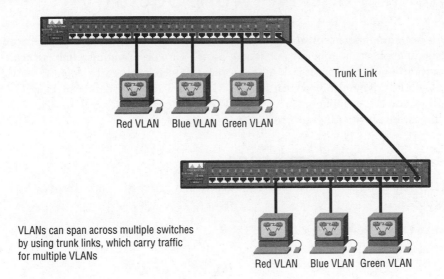

Red VLAN   Blue VLAN   Green VLAN

Trunk Link

VLANs can span across multiple switches
by using trunk links, which carry traffic
for multiple VLANs

Red VLAN   Blue VLAN   Green VLAN

Inter-Switch Link (ISL)

Inter-Switch Link (ISL) is a way of explicitly tagging VLAN information onto an Ethernet frame. This tagging information allows VLANs to be multiplexed over a trunk link through an external encapsulation method (ISL), which allows the switch to identify the VLAN membership of a frame over the trunked link.

By running ISL, you can interconnect multiple switches and still maintain VLAN information as traffic travels between switches on trunk links. ISL functions at Layer 2 by encapsulating a data frame with a new header and cyclic redundancy check (CRC).

Of note is that this is proprietary to Cisco switches, and it's used for Fast Ethernet and Gigabit Ethernet links only. *ISL routing* is pretty versatile and can be used on a switch port, on router interfaces, and on server interface cards to trunk a server.

IEEE 802.1Q

Created by the IEEE as a standard method of frame tagging, IEEE 802.1Q actually inserts a field into the frame to identify the VLAN. If you're trunking between a Cisco switched link and a different brand of switch, you've got to use 802.1Q for the trunk to work.

And it works like this: You first designate each port that you want to be a trunk port with 802.1Q encapsulation. The ports must be assigned a specific VLAN ID, which makes them part of the native VLAN in order for them to communicate. The ports that populate the same trunk create a group with this native VLAN, and each port gets tagged with an identification number reflecting that status, again the default being VLAN 1. The native VLAN allows the trunks to carry information that was received without any VLAN identification or frame tag.

Switching and Network Security

Security is becoming more critical to us every day, so just how do you stop people from simply plugging a host into one of your switch ports—or worse, adding a hub, switch, or access point into the Ethernet jack in their office? Remember that, by default, MAC addresses will just dynamically appear in your MAC forward/filter database. Here I describe how you can ensure port security, and how you can take control of each port to provide better security for your network resources.

Port Security/Authentication

Figure 11.17 illustrates how a host plugged into a switch can restrict port security by MAC address.

FIGURE 11.17   Port security

Unauthorized MAC address—
access denied   0010.f6b3.d000

There are a few ways to ensure port security on your switches. The first solution is to simply implement port security on each switch. This works great if you have only a few switches, but what if your network is huge and populated with dozens—maybe even hundreds—of switches? I don't think I have to tell you that this would be crazy to maintain.

But if you're dealing with a whole bunch of switches—Cisco switches or any other flavor—you can create port security on all of them by using 802.1x authentication, as shown in Figure 11.18.

Of note here is that all the clients must be authenticated through the server before they're connected through the switch to the network. And relax—I'm going to cover 802.1x authentication in Chapter 13, "Authentication and Access Control."

How VLANs Enhance Network Security

As described at the beginning of this chapter, a flat internetwork's security used to be tackled by connecting hubs and switches together with routers. So basically, it was the router's job to maintain security. This arrangement was pretty ineffective for several reasons. First, anyone connecting to the physical network could access the network resources located on that particular physical LAN. Second, all anyone had to do to observe any and all traffic happening in that network was to simply plug a network analyzer into the hub. And similar to that last vile fact, users could join a workgroup by just plugging their workstations into the existing hub. That's about as secure as an open barrel of honey in a bear enclosure!

FIGURE 11.18   Using 802.1x authentication on your switch

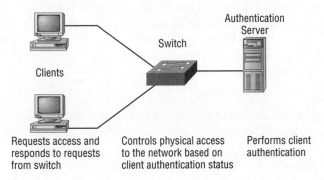

Security is one of the many capabilities and features that make VLANs so very cool. If you take the time to build them and create multiple broadcast groups, you get total control over each port and user in return. So the days when anyone could just plug their workstations into any switch port and gain access to network resources are history. Using VLANs gives you control of each port plus whatever resources that port can access.

Oh, and it doesn't end there, my friends, because VLANs can be created in accordance with the network resources a given user requires, and switches can be configured to inform a network management station of any unauthorized access to network resources. Talk about empowerment! And if you need inter-VLAN communication, you can implement restrictions on a router to make that happen too. Plus, you get to place restrictions on hardware addresses, protocols, and applications. *Now* we're talking security—the honey barrel is sealed, shrouded in razor wire, and made of solid titanium.

Two Additional Advanced Features of Switches

Switches really expand our flexibility when designing our networks. The features that we need to cover for the CompTIA Network+ objectives are as follows:

- Power over Ethernet (PoE)
- Port Mirroring/Spanning

Power over Ethernet (PoE)

Power over Ethernet (PoE) technology describes a system for transmitting electrical power, along with data, to remote devices over standard twisted-pair cable in an Ethernet network. This technology is useful for powering IP telephones (Voice over IP (VoIP)), wireless LAN access points, network cameras, remote network switches, embedded computers, and other appliances—situations where it would be inconvenient, expensive, and possibly not even feasible to supply power separately. A reason for this is because the main wiring usually must be done by qualified and/or licensed electricians for legal and/or insurance mandates.

The IEEE has created a standard for PoE called 802.3af. This standard describes how a powered device is detected and also defines two methods of delivering Power over Ethernet to that particular powered device.

> The IEEE has formed a new working group to develop the 802.3at standard or PoE Plus, with the goal of boosting the amount of power that PoE can deliver.

This process happens one of two ways: either by receiving the power from an Ethernet port on a switch, or other capable device, or via a power injector. And you can't use both approaches to get the job done. This can lead to serious trouble, so be aware before connecting!

 Real World Scenario

PoE

It would be unusual for me not to design a network around PoE. Most of my consulting work is wireless networking, including large outdoor wireless MESH networks (which I discuss more in Chapter 12, "Wireless Networking"). When I design the network, I order equipment based on the amount of power needed to run the network, knowing I'll have only a few electrical outlets, or even no outlets if all my equipment is outside. This means that all my switches must run PoE to my access points and wireless bridges and must do this for long distances.

In order for me to accomplish this, I need to order the more expensive, large-scale, enterprise switches. If you have devices that need PoE but do not have long-distance connections, you can use lower-end switches, but you must verify that they provide the right amount of power. There was a customer who called me because their network access points were going up and down. The bottom line is that they had purchased less expensive switches and the power was not enough to run the equipment. They ended up buying all new switches. So, before you buy a PoE switch, verify that the switch provides the right power you need for your environment.

Figure 11.19 shows an example of a switch that provides PoE to any PoE-capable device.

As I just said, if you don't have a switch with PoE, then you can use a power injector. Figure 11.20 shows a picture of a typical power injector physically installed in a network.

FIGURE 11.19   Switched Ethernet ports can provide power to devices.

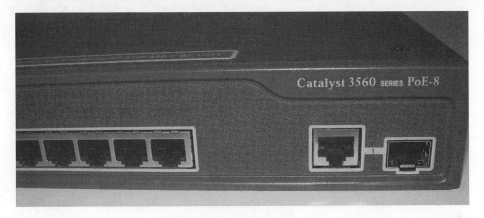

FIGURE 11.20   An external power injector used for PoE

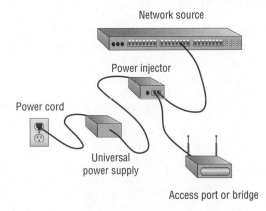

 WARNING   Use caution when using an external power injector! Take the time to make sure the power injector provides the proper voltage level for which your device was manufactured.

Because most higher-end switches provide PoE, we don't need to worry about injectors; but if you are adding a wireless bridge into an existing network that has switches without PoE, you need to add a power injector. Figure 11.21 shows a power injector used for a wireless bridge.

Let's discuss how we would troubleshoot a network that has a switch in the LAN instead of a hub.

FIGURE 11.21   Wireless-bridge power injector

FIGURE 11.21   Wireless-bridge power injector

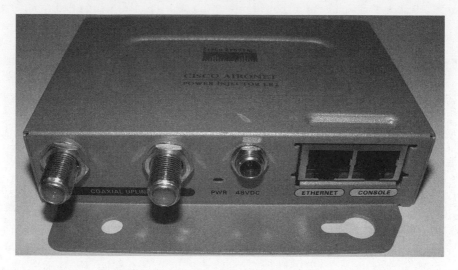

Port Mirroring/Spanning

Port mirroring, also called *Switch Port Analyzer (SPAN)*, allows you to sniff traffic on a network when using a switch. In Figure 11.22, you can see how a typical switch will read the forward/filter table and only send traffic out the destination port (this is the whole idea of using a switch, so this is good!).

FIGURE 11.22   Switches send frames out only the destination port.

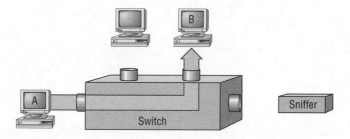

All good, but a problem with this arises when you need to sniff traffic on the network. Figure 11.22 illustrates this issue and a solution to it. In it, you can see that the sniffer isn't seeing data coming from Host A to Host B. To solve this little snag, you can temporarily place a hub between Host A and Host B, as demonstrated in Figure 11.23.

This method will allow you to see the frames sent from Host A to Host B; but the bad news is that by doing this, you'll bring down the network temporarily.

The port-mirroring option allows you to place a port in spanning mode so that every frame from Host A is captured by both Host B and the sniffer, as shown in figure 11.24.

FIGURE 11.23   Place a hub between two hosts to troubleshoot.

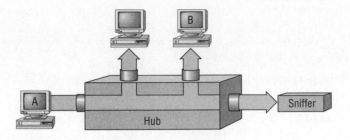

FIGURE 11.24   Port mirroring

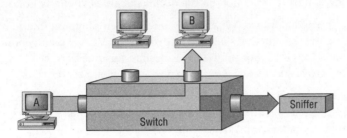

Do be careful when using port mirroring, because it can cause a lot of overhead on the switch and possibly crash your network. So, it's a good idea to use this feature at strategic times and only for short periods if possible.

Summary

In this chapter, I talked about the differences between switches and bridges and how they both work at Layer 2 and create a MAC address forward/filter table in order to make decisions about whether to forward or flood a frame.

I also discussed problems that can occur if you have multiple links between bridges (switches) and how to solve these problems by using the Spanning Tree Protocol (STP).

This chapter also introduced you to the world of Virtual LANs and described how switches can use them. We talked about how VLANs break up broadcast domains in a switched internetwork—a very important, necessary thing because Layer 2 switches only break up collision domains and by default, all switches make up one large broadcast domain. I also described access links to you and went over how trunked VLANs work across a Fast Ethernet link.

Trunking is a crucial technology to understand well when you're dealing with a network populated by multiple switches that are running several VLANs.

Exam Essentials

Remember the three switch functions. Address learning, forward/filter decisions, and loop avoidance are the functions of a switch.

Understand the main purpose of the Spanning Tree Protocol in a switched LAN. The main purpose of STP is to prevent switching loops in a network with redundant switched paths.

Remember the states of STP. The purpose of the blocking state is to prevent the use of looped paths. A port in the listening state prepares to forward data frames without populating the MAC address table. A port in the learning state populates the MAC address table but doesn't forward data frames. A port in the forwarding state sends and receives all data frames on the bridged port. Last, a port in the disabled state is virtually nonoperational.

Remember to check a switch port's VLAN assignment when plugging in a new host. If you plug a new host into a switch, then you must verify the VLAN membership of that port. If the membership is different than what is needed for that host, the host will not be able to reach the needed network services, such as a workgroup server.

Understand what PoE provides. Power over Ethernet was created to provide power to devices that are connected to a switch port but that are not in a place that has a power outlet—for example, an access point in a ceiling.

Written Lab

In this section, write the answers to the following questions:

1. VLANs break up _____ domains in a Layer 2 switched network.

2. Switches, by default, only break up _____ domains.

3. What does trunking provide?

4. You need to power a device, such as an access point or IP phone. What protocol can provide power to these devices over an Ethernet cable?

5. You plug a host into a switch port, but the user can't get to the services it needs. What is probably the problem?

6. If a destination MAC address is not in the forward/filter table, what will the switch do with the frame?

7. What are the three switch functions at Layer 2?

8. If a frame is received on a switch port and the source MAC address is not in the forward/filter table, what will the switch do?

9. What is used at Layer 2 to prevent switching loops?

10. You need to implement a separate network for contractors and guests working at your office. Which technology should you implement?

(The answers to Written Lab can be found following the answers to the Review Questions for this chapter.)

Review Questions

1. You want to improve network performance by increasing the bandwidth available to hosts and limiting the size of the broadcast domains. Which of the following options will achieve this goal?

   A. Managed hubs

   B. Bridges

   C. Switches

   D. Switches configured with VLANs

2. The types of ports that can found on a switch are_____ and _____. (Choose two.)

   A. VLAN Trunk Protocol

   B. Access

   C. 802.1Q

   D. Trunk

3. Which switching technology reduces the size of a broadcast domain?

   A. ISL

   B. 802.1Q

   C. VLANs

   D. STP

4. Which of the following are the IEEE version of STP? (Choose 2)

   A. 802.1x

   B. VLANs

   C. 802.1d

   D. 802.11

   E. 802.1w

5. You connect a host to a switch port, but the new host cannot log into the server that is plugged into the same switch. What could the problem be? (Choose two.)

   A. The router is not configured for the new host.

   B. The STP configuration on the switch is not updated for the new host.

   C. The host has an invalid MAC address.

   D. The switch port the host is connected to is not configured to the correct VLAN membership.

   E. The STP shut down the port

6. Which of the following are benefits of VLANs? (Choose three.)

    A. They increase the size of collision domains.

    B. They allow logical grouping of users by function.

    C. They can enhance network security.

    D. They increase the size of broadcast domains while decreasing the number of collision domains.

    E. They simplify switch administration.

    F. They increase the number of broadcast domains while decreasing the size of the broadcast domains.

7. Which of the following is a Layer 2 protocol used to maintain a loop-free network?

    A. VTP

    B. STP

    C. RIP

    D. CDP

8. What is the result of segmenting a network with a bridge (switch)? (Choose two.)

    A. It increases the number of collision domains.

    B. It decreases the number of collision domains.

    C. It increases the number of broadcast domains.

    D. It decreases the number of broadcast domains.

    E. It makes smaller collision domains.

    F. It makes larger collision domains.

9. You connect your host to a switch that is running network analyses software. However, you are not seeing any packets from the server. What do you need to implement on the switch to see all the packet information?

    A. VLANs

    B. STP

    C. Port Mirroring

    D. Authentication

10. Which of the following features of a switch will allow two switches to pass network information?

    A. PoE

    B. VLANs

    C. Trunking

    D. STP

11. What are the distinct functions of Layer 2 switching that increase available bandwidth on the network? (Choose three.)

    A. Address learning

    B. Routing

    C. Forwarding and filtering

    D. Creating network loops

    E. Loop avoidance

    F. IP addressing

12. Which of the following statements is true?

    A. A switch creates a single collision domain and a single broadcast domain. A router creates a single collision domain.

    B. A switch creates separate collision domains but one broadcast domain. A router provides a separate broadcast domain.

    C. A switch creates a single collision domain and separate broadcast domains. A router provides a separate broadcast domain as well.

    D. A switch creates separate collision domains and separate broadcast domains. A router provides separate collision domains.

13. What does a switch do when a frame is received on an interface and the destination hardware address is unknown or not in the filter table?

    A. Forwards the switch to the first available link

    B. Drops the frame

    C. Floods the network with the frame looking for the device

    D. Sends back a message to the originating station asking for a name resolution

14. If a switch receives a frame, and the source MAC address is not in the MAC address table but the destination address is, what will the switch do with the frame?

    A. Discard it and send an error message back to the originating host

    B. Flood the network with the frame

    C. Add the source address and port to the MAC address table and forward the frame out the destination port

    D. Add the destination to the MAC address table and then forward the frame

15. Which of the following help isolate network traffic?

    A. hubs

    B. VLANs

    C. Repeaters

    D. Hosts

16. When is STP said to be converged? (Choose two.)

    A. When all ports are in the forwarding state

    B. When all ports are in the blocking state

    C. When all ports are in the Listening state

    D. When all ports are in the Learning state

17. In which two states is the MAC address table populated with addresses?

    A. Blocked

    B. Listening

    C. Learning

    D. Forwarding

18. You have multiple departments all connected to switches, with cross-over cables connecting the switches together. However, response time on the network is still very slow because you have upgraded from hubs to switches. What technology should you implement to improve response time on the networks?

    A. STP

    B. VLANs

    C. Convergence

    D. OSPF

19. Why are switches better than hubs in your network by default?

    A. Because they break up broadcast commands by default

    B. Because each port on a switch is a broadcast domain

    C. Because each port on a switch is a collision domain

    D. Because all ports on a hub are broken into broadcast domains by default

20. What is a disadvantage of using port spanning?

    A. It breaks up broadcast domains on all ports

    B. It can create overhead on the switch

    C. It makes the switch one large collision domain

    D. It makes the switch fast between only two ports instead of all ports

Answers to Review Questions

1. D. By creating and implementing VLANs in your switched network, you can break up broadcast domains at Layer 2. For hosts on different VLANs to communicate, you must have a router or Layer 3 switch.

2. B, D. Hosts are connected to a switch and are members of one VLAN. This is called an access port. Trunk links connect between switches and pass information about all VLANs.

3. C. Virtual LANs break up broadcast domains in Layer 2 switched internetworks.

4. C, E. 802.1d and 802.1w are both IEEE STP versions, with 802.1w being the latest and greatest version.

5. D, E. the best answers are that the VLAN membership for the port is configured incorrectly and that STP shut down the port.

6. B, C, F. VLANs break up broadcast domains in a switched Layer 2 network, which means smaller broadcast domains. They allow configuration by logical function instead of physical location and can create some security if configured correctly.

7. B. The Spanning Tree Protocol is used to stop switching loops in a switched network with redundant paths.

8. A, E. Bridges break up collision domains, which would increase the number of collision domains in a network and also make smaller collision domains.

9. C. In order to see all frames that pass through the switch and read the packets with a network analyzer, you need to enable port mirroring on the port your diagnostic host is plugged into.

10. C. Trunking allows switches to pass information about many or all VLANs configures on the switches.

11. A, C, E. Layer 2 features include address learning, forwarding and filtering of the network, and loop avoidance.

12. B. Switches break up collision domains, and routers break up broadcast domains.

13. C. Switches flood all frames that have an unknown destination address. If a device answers the frame, the switch will update the MAC address table to reflect the location of the device.

14. C. Because the source MAC address is not in the MAC address table, the switch will add the source address and the port it is connected to into the MAC address table and then forward the frame to the outgoing port.

15. B. Virtual LANs help isolate network traffic by breaking up broadcast domains in a layer-2 switched network.

16. A, B. The sequence of steps for STP convergence is, by default, blocking, listening, learning, and forwarding. When all ports are in either the blocking or forwarding state, STP is converged.

17. C, D. In the blocked and listening states, the MAC address table is not learning. Only in the learning and forwarding states is the MAC address table learning MAC addresses and populating the MAC address table.

18. B. Switches break up collision domains by default, but the network is still one large broadcast domain. In order to break up broadcast domains in a Layer 2 switched network, you need to create Virtual LANs.

19. C. Hubs create one collision domain and one broadcast domain. Switches break up collision domains but the network is one large broadcast domain by default.

20. B. Be careful when using port mirroring/spanning on a switch because it can cause a lot of overhead on the switch and possibly crash your network. So, it's a good idea to use this feature at strategic times and only for short periods if possible.

Answers to Written Lab

1. Broadcast

2. Collision

3. Trunking allows you to make a single port part of multiple VLANs at the same time.

4. Power over Ethernet (PoE)

5. The VLAN port membership is set wrong.

6. Flood the frame out all ports except the port it was received on

7. Address learning, filtering, and loop avoidance

8. It will add the source MAC address to the forward/filter table.

9. Spanning Tree Protocol (STP)

10. Create a VLAN for Contractor and another VLAN for guests

Chapter

12

Wireless Technologies

THE FOLLOWING COMPTIA NETWORK+ EXAM OBJECTIVES ARE COVERED IN THIS CHAPTER:

✓ **1.7 Compare the characteristics of wireless communication standards**

- 802.11 a/b/g/n

  - Speeds

  - Distance

  - Channels

  - Frequency

- Authentication and encryption

  - WPA

  - WEP

  - RADIUS

  - TKIP

✓ **3.4 Implement a basic wireless network**

- Install client

- Access point placement

- Install access point

  - Configure appropriate encryption

  - Configure channels and frequencies

  - Set ESSID and beacon

- Verify installation

Sipping coffee at a café or hanging out in an airport until they finally fix the plane you're waiting to board no longer requires reading actual papers and magazines to avoid numbing boredom and kill time. Now, you can just connect to the local wireless network and catch up on your emails, blog, do a little gaming—maybe even get some work done! It's come to the point that many of us wouldn't even think of checking into a hotel that doesn't offer this important little amenity. So clearly, those of us already in or wishing to enter the IT field better have our chops down regarding wireless network components and their associated installation factors, right? (Answer: a resounding YES!)

With that established, here's a great starting point... If you want to understand the basic wireless LANs (WLANs) most commonly used today, just think 10BaseT Ethernet with hubs. What this means is that our WLANs typically run half-duplex communication—everyone is sharing the same bandwidth, and only one user is communicating at a time. This isn't necessarily bad, it's just not good enough. Because most people rely upon wireless networks today, it's critical that they evolve faster than greased lightening to keep up with our rapidly escalating needs. The good news is that this is actually happening—and it even works securely!

The goal in this chapter is to introduce you to wireless networks and the technologies in use today. I'll also cover the various components used, the IEEE 802.11 standards, wireless installation, and of course, wireless security.

For up-to-the-minute updates for this chapter, please see www.lammle.com or www.sybex.com/go/comptianetwork+studyguide.

Introduction to Wireless Technology

Transmitting a signal using the typical 802.11 specifications works a lot like it does with a basic Ethernet hub: They're both two-way forms of communication, and they both use the same frequency to both transmit and receive, often referred to as *half-duplex* as mentioned in the chapter introduction. Wireless LANs (WLANs) use radio frequencies (RFs) that are radiated into the air from an antenna that creates radio waves. These waves can be absorbed, refracted, or reflected by walls, water, and metal surfaces, resulting in low signal strength. So because of this innate vulnerability to surrounding environmental factors, it's pretty apparent that wireless will never offer us the same robustness as a wired network can, but that still doesn't mean we're not going to run wireless. Believe me, we definitely will!

We can increase the transmitting power, and we'd be able to gain a greater transmitting distance; but doing so can create some nasty distortion, so it has to be done carefully. By using higher frequencies, we can attain higher data rates, but this is, unfortunately, at the cost of decreased transmitting distances. And if we use lower frequencies, we get to transmit greater distances but at lower data rates. This should make it pretty clear to you that understanding all the various types of WLANs you can implement is imperative to creating the LAN solution that best meets the specific requirements of the unique situation you're dealing with.

Also important to note is the fact that the 802.11 specifications were developed so that there would be no licensing required in most countries—to ensure the user the freedom to install and operate without any licensing or operating fees. This means that any manufacturer can create wireless networking products and sell them at a local computer store or wherever. It also means that all our computers should be able to communicate wirelessly without configuring much, if anything at all.

Various agencies have been around for a very long time to help govern the use of wireless devices, frequencies, standards, and how the frequency spectrums are used. Table 12.1 shows the current agencies that help create, maintain, and even enforce wireless standards worldwide.

TABLE 12.1   Wireless Agencies and Standards

Agency	Purpose	Web Site
Institute of Electrical and Electronics Engineers (IEEE)	Creates and maintains operational standards	www.ieee.org
Federal Communications Commission (FCC)	Regulates the use of wireless devices in the U.S.	www.fcc.gov
European Telecommunications Standards Institute (ETSi)	Chartered to produce common standards in Europe	www.etsi.org
Wi-Fi Alliance	Promotes and tests for WLAN interoperability	www.wi-fi.com
WLAN Association (WLANA)	Educates and raises consumer awareness regarding WLANs	www.wlana.org

Because WLANs transmit over radio frequencies, they're regulated by the same types of laws used to govern things like AM/FM radios. In the United States, it's the Federal Communications Commission (FCC) that regulates the use of wireless LAN devices, and the Institute of Electrical and Electronics Engineers (IEEE) takes it from there and creates standards based on what frequencies the FCC releases for public use.

The FCC has released three unlicensed bands for public use: 900MHz, 2.4GHz, and 5GHz. The 900MHz and 2.4GHz bands are referred to as the Industrial, Scientific, and Medical (ISM) bands, and the 5GHz band is known as the Unlicensed National Information Infrastructure (UNII) band. Figure 12.1 shows where the unlicensed bands sit within the RF spectrum.

FIGURE 12.1 Unlicensed frequencies

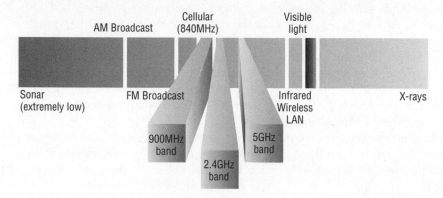

So it follows that if you opt to deploy wireless in a range outside of the three public bands shown in Figure 12.1, you need to get a specific license from the FCC to do so. Once the FCC opened the three frequency ranges for public use, many manufacturers were able to start offering myriad products that flooded the market, with 802.11b/g being the most widely used wireless network found today.

Figure 12.2 shows the WLAN history that is important to us. Although wireless transmissions date back many, many years, the type we really care about is wireless as related to WLANs starting in the 1990s. Use of the ISM band started in early 1990, and it's deployed today in multiple environments, including outdoor links, mesh networks, office buildings, healthcare, warehousing, and homes.

FIGURE 12.2 Wireless LAN history

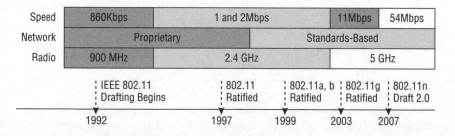

The Wi-Fi Alliance grants certification for interoperability among 802.11 products offered by various vendors. This certification provides a sort of comfort zone for the users purchasing the many types of products, although in my personal experience, it's just a whole lot easier if you buy all your access points from the same manufacturer.

In the current U.S. WLAN market, there are several accepted operational standards and drafts created and maintained by the IEEE. We'll now take a look at these standards and then talk about how the most commonly used standards work.

The 802.11 Standards

Taking off from what you learned in Chapter 1, "Introduction to Networks," wireless networking has its own 802 standards group—remember, Ethernet's committee is 802.3. Wireless starts with 802.11, and there are various other up-and-coming standard groups as well, like 802.16 and 802.20. And even cellular networks are becoming huge players in our wireless experience. But for now, we're going to concentrate on the 802.11 standards committee and subcommittees.

IEEE 802.11 was the first, original standardized WLAN at 1 and 2Mbps. It runs in the 2.4GHz radio frequency. It was ratified in 1997, although we didn't see many products pop up until around 1999 when 802.11b was introduced. All the committees listed in Table 12.2 made amendments to the original 802.11 standard except for 802.11F and 802.11T, which produced stand-alone documents.

TABLE 12.2   802.11 Committees and Subcommittees

Committee	Purpose
IEEE 802.11a	54Mbps, 5GHz standard
IEEE 802.11b	Enhancements to 802.11 to support 5.5 and 11Mbps
IEEE 802.11c	Bridge operation procedures; included in the IEEE 802.1D standard
IEEE 802.11d	International roaming extensions
IEEE 802.11e	Quality of service
IEEE 802.11F	Inter-Access Point Protocol
IEEE 802.11g	54Mbps, 2.4GHz standard (backward compatible with 802.11b)
IEEE 802.11h	Dynamic Frequency Selection (DFS) and Transmit Power Control (TPC) at 5Ghz
IEEE 802.11i	Enhanced security
IEEE 802.11j	Extensions for Japan and U.S. public safety
IEEE 802.11k	Radio resource measurement enhancements

TABLE 12.2   802.11 Committees and Subcommittees *(continued)*

Committee	Purpose
IEEE 802.11m	Maintenance of the standard; odds and ends
IEEE 802.11n	Higher throughput improvements using multiple input, multiple output (MIMO) antennas
IEEE 802.11p	Wireless Access for the Vehicular Environment (WAVE)
IEEE 802.11r	Fast roaming
IEEE 802.11s	ESS Extended Service Set Mesh Networking
IEEE 802.11T	Wireless Performance Prediction (WPP)
IEEE 802.11u	Internetworking with non-802 networks (cellular, for example)
IEEE 802.11v	Wireless network management
IEEE 802.11w	Protected management frames
IEEE 802.11y	3650–3700 operation in the U.S.

 One type of wireless networking that doesn't get a whole lot of attention is infrared wireless. Infrared wireless uses the same basic transmission method as many television remote controls—that's right, infrared technology. Infrared is used primarily for short distance, point-to-point communications, like those between a peripheral and a PC, with the most widely used for peripherals being the IrDA standard.

Okay, now let's discuss some important specifics of the most popular 802.11 WLANs.

2.4GHz (802.11b)

First on the menu is the 802.11b standard. It was the most widely deployed wireless standard, and it operates in the 2.4GHz unlicensed radio band that delivers a maximum data rate of 11Mbps. The 802.11b standard has been widely adopted by both vendors and customers who found that its 11Mbps data rate worked pretty well for most applications. But now that 802.11b has a big brother (802.11g), no one goes out and just buys an 802.11b card or access point anymore—why would you buy a 10Mbps Ethernet card when you can score a 10/100 Ethernet card for the same price?

An interesting thing about all Cisco 802.11 WLAN products is that they have the ability to data-rate-shift while moving. This allows the person operating at 11Mbps to shift to 5.5Mbps, then 2Mbps, and finally still communicate farthest from the access point at 1Mbps. And furthermore, this rate shifting happens without losing connection and with no interaction from the user. Rate shifting also occurs on a transmission-by-transmission basis. This is important because it means that the access point can support multiple clients at varying speeds depending upon the location of each client.

The problem with 802.11b lies in how the Data Link layer is dealt with. In order to solve problems in the RF spectrum, a type of Ethernet collision detection was created called *Carrier Sense Multiple Access with Collision Avoidance (CSMA/CA)*. To get a clear picture of this, check out Figure 12.3.

FIGURE 12.3   802.11b CSMA/CA

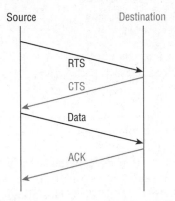

CSMA/CA is also called a *Request to Send, Clear to Send (RTS/CTS)* because of the way that hosts must communicate to the access point (AP). For every packet sent, an RTS/CTS and acknowledgment must be received, and because of this rather cumbersome process, it's kind of hard to believe it all actually works!

2.4GHz (802.11g)

The 802.11g standard was ratified in June 2003 and is backward compatible to 802.11b. The 802.11g standard delivers the same 54Mbps maximum data rate as you'll find in the 802.11a range but runs in the 2.4GHz range—the same as 802.11b.

Because 802.11b/g operates in the same 2.4GHz unlicensed band, migrating to 802.11g is an affordable choice for organizations with existing 802.11b wireless infrastructures. Just keep in mind that 802.11b products can't be "software upgraded" to 802.11g. This limitation is because 802.11g radios use a different chipset in order to deliver the higher data rate.

But still, much like Ethernet and Fast Ethernet, 802.11g products can be commingled with 802.11b products in the same network. Yet, for example, and completely unlike Ethernet, if you have four users running 802.11g cards and one user starts using an 802.11b card, everyone connected to the same access point is then forced to run the 802.11b CSMA/CA method—an ugly fact that really makes throughput suffer badly. So to optimize performance, it's recommended that you disable the 802.11b-only modes on all your access points.

To explain this further, 802.11b uses a *modulation technique* called *Direct Sequence Spread Spectrum (DSSS)* that's just not as robust as the *Orthogonal Frequency Division Multiplexing* (OFDM) modulation used by both 802.11g and 802.11a (modulation techniques will be discussed later in this chapter). 802.11g clients using OFDM enjoy much better performance at the same ranges as 802.11b clients do, but—and remember this—when 802.11g clients are operating at the 802.11b rates (11, 5.5, 2, and 1Mbps), they're actually using the same modulation 802.11b does.

Figure 12.4 shows the 14 different channels (each 22Mhz wide) that the FCC released in the 2.4GHz range.

FIGURE 12.4   ISM 2.4GHz channels

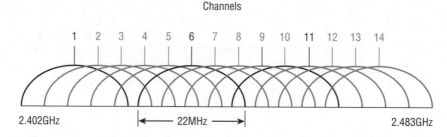

In the U.S., only 11 channels are configurable, with channels 1, 6, and 11 being non-overlapping. This allows you to have three access points in the same area without experiencing interference. You must be aware of the channels when installing AP's in a large environment so you do not overlap channels. Make sure that each channel is not overlapping the same channel number! If you configure one AP with channel 1, then the next AP would be configured in channel 11, the channel farthest from that configured on the first AP.

5GHz (802.11a)

The IEEE ratified the 802.11a standard in 1999, but the first 802.11a products didn't begin appearing on the market until late 2001—and boy, were they pricey! The 802.11a standard delivers a maximum data rate of 54Mbps with 12 non-overlapping frequency channels. Figure 12.5 shows the UNII bands.

FIGURE 12.5   UNII 5GHz band has 12 non-overlapping channels (U.S.).

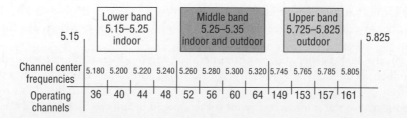

Operating in the 5GHz radio band, 802.11a is also immune to interference from devices that operate in the 2.4GHz band, like microwave ovens, cordless phones, and Bluetooth devices. 802.11a isn't backward compatible with 802.11b because they are different frequencies, so you don't get to just "upgrade" part of your network and expect everything to work together in perfect harmony. But no worries—there are plenty of dual-radio devices that will work in both types of networks. A definite plus for 802.11a is that it can work in the same physical environment without interference from 802.11b users.

Similar to the 802.11b radios, all 802.11a products also have the ability to data-rate-shift while moving. The 802.11a products allow the person operating at 54Mbps to shift to 48Mbps, 36Mbps, 24Mbps, 18Mbps, 12Mbps, and 9Mbps, and finally still communicate farthest from the AP at 6Mbps.

There's also an extension to the 802.11a specifications called 802.11h, which is described next.

5GHz (802.11h)

The FCC added 11 new channels in February 2004; and now, in 2008, we finally get to begin using these channels based on manufacturers' releases of more 802.11a 5GHz products. This means that we gain access to up to 23 non-overlapping channels! And there are even two new features to the 5GHz radio that are part of the 802.11h specification: *Dynamic Frequency Selection (DFS)* and *Transmit Power Control (TPC).*

Dynamic Frequency Selection (DFS)   This cool feature continuously monitors a device's operating range for any radar signals that are allowed to operate in portions of the 5GHz band as well as 802.11a before transmitting. If DFS discovers any radar signals, it'll either abandon the occupied channel or mark it as unavailable to prevent interference from occurring on the WLAN.

Transmit Power Control (TPC)   Even though it's been employed by the mobile phone industry for a long time, this technology has some handy new uses. You can set the client machine's adapter and the access point's transmit power to cover various size ranges—a feature that's useful for many reasons. For one, setting the access point's transmit power to 5mW reduces cell range, which works great if you've got a compact area with high-density usage.

Further advantages include the fact that TPC enables the client and the access point to communicate. This means the client machine can fine-tune its transmit power dynamically so it uses just enough energy to preserve its connection to the access point, conserve its battery power, plus reduce interference on the neighboring WLAN cells—sweet!

2.4GHz/5GHz (802.11n)

802.11n builds on previous 802.11 standards by adding *Multiple-Input Multiple-Output (MIMO),* which employs multiple transmitters and receiver antennas to increase data throughput. 802.11n can have up to eight antennas, but most of today's access points use four. These are sometimes referred to as *smart antennas*, and if you did have four of them, two would be used for transmitting simultaneously with the other two receiving simultaneously. This setup would allow for much higher data rates than 802.11a/b/g. In fact, the marketing people claim it will provide about 250Mbps; but personally, I'm not buying it. I just don't believe that's what our actual throughput levels can be; and even if what they're saying is true, exactly how would that help if all you've got is a 1 or 2Mbps cable or DSL connection to the Internet?

Keep in mind that the 802.11n standard hasn't yet been ratified and isn't expected to be until sometime in 2009. This means that the products on the shelf today are proprietary, and they are called *pre-N* products. In some large, outdoor Cisco proprietary networks that I'm currently working on, the Cisco "N" products work great. But keep in mind that all the devices are Cisco, and the network won't tolerate other vendor's products working within it—at least, not today.

 802.11n allows for communication at both the 2.4Ghz and 5Ghz frequencies by using channel bonding.

Listed next are some of the primary components of 802.11n that give people reason to say 802.11n has greater reliability and predictability:

40Mhz channels 802.11g and 802.11a use 20Mhz channels and tones on the sides of each channel are not used to protect the main carrier, which means that 11Mbps are unused or wasted. 802.11n aggregates two carriers to double the speed from54Mbps to 108, plus the 11Mbps that we gain from not wasting the side tones = 119Mbps.

MAC Efficiency 802.11 protocols require acknowledgment of each and every frame. 802.11n can pass many packets before an acknowledgment is required which saves you on overhead. This is called *block acknowledgment.*

Multiple-Input Multiple-Output (MIMO) Several frames are sent by several antennae over several paths and are then recombined by another set of antennae to optimize throughput and multipath resistance. This is called *spatial multiplexing.*

So What Is Wi-Fi?

You may have seen products that are 802.11 compliant with a small sticker on them that says "Wi-Fi." You might be able to guess that this rather odd phrase stands for Wireless Fidelity, but you may not know what its implications are. Simply put, that sticker indicates that the product in question has passed certification testing for 802.11 interoperability by the Wi-Fi Alliance. This nonprofit group was formed to ensure that all 802.11a/b/g/n wireless devices would communicate seamlessly. So, Wi-Fi is a good thing.

Comparing 802.11 Standards

Okay—before I move on to wireless installations, take at look at Figure 12.6, which lists the years each standard was ratified, the frequency of each, the number of non-overlapping channels, the physical layer transmission technique and the data rates for each of the IEEE standards in use today.

FIGURE 12.6   Standards for spectrums and speeds

	802.11	802.11b	802.11a	802.11g		802.11n
Ratified	1997	1999	1999	2003		Not Ratified
Frequency Band	2.4GHz	2.4GHz	5GHz	2.4GHz		2.4GHz, 5GHz
No. of Channels	3	3	Up to 23	3		Varies
Transmission	IR, FHSS, DSSS	DSSS	OFDM	DSSS	OFDM	DSSS, CCK, OFDM
Data Rates (Mbps)	1, 2	1, 2, 5.5, 11	6, 9, 12, 18, 24, 36, 48, 54	1, 2, 5.5, 11	6, 9, 12, 18, 24, 36, 48, 54	100+

I mentioned earlier that 802.11b runs DSSS, whereas 802.11g and 802.11a both run the OFDM modulation technique. Let's take a closer look at these different modulation techniques used in today's networks.

Wireless LAN Modulation Techniques

I'm not going to go into a complete discourse of the technical workings of the wireless modulation techniques because doing so is beyond the scope of the objectives of the Network + exam and, therefore, this study guide. But it's still important for you to be aware of how these techniques match their corresponding 802.11 standards.

Direct-Sequence Spread Spectrum (DSSS)

First, there's DSSS. It's one of the modulation techniques specified by the original IEEE 802.11 standard and also happens to be the one chosen for use in the widely accepted IEEE 802.11b standard. IEEE 802.11 uses Differential Binary Phase Shift Keying (DBPSK) for 1Mbps DSSS, and Differential Quadrature Phase Shift Keying (DQPSK) for 2Mbps DSSS. The DSSS defined in IEEE 802.11b uses the Complementary Code Keying (CCK) modulation technique that gives us both 5.5Mbps and 11Mbps data rates. The cool thing is that all three modulation schemes are compatible and can coexist by using 802.11-standardized rate-switching procedures. Also important is that DSSS creates a redundant bit pattern for each bit that's transmitted, increasing DSSS's resistance to interference. A nice benefit of this is that if any bits in the bit pattern are damaged in transmission, you've got a chance at recovering the original data from the redundant bits.

Frequency-Hopping Spread Spectrum (FHSS)

Even though it's the original modulation technique specified by the IEEE 802.11 standard, *Frequency-Hopping Spread Spectrum (FHSS)* isn't the technique of choice for either vendors or the 802.11 working group. A big reason for this is because so few vendors support FHSS in 802.11 products, DSSS has become the favored flavor instead. Plus, continued developments within 802.11 also favor DSSS.

FHSS modulates the data signal with a carrier signal that changes (hops) in a random but, over time, predictable sequence of frequencies. These changes also occur over a wide frequency band, with a spreading, or hopping, code establishing the transmission frequencies used. The receiver is set to the same code, allowing it to listen to the incoming signal at the right time and frequency so it can receive the signal properly. Manufacturers use 75 or more frequencies per transmission channel. The maximum *dwell time* (time spent during a hop at a particular frequency) has been established by the FCC at 400ms.

Orthogonal Frequency Division Multiplexing (OFDM)

802.11a/g uses OFDM with a system of 52 carriers (sometimes referred to as *subcarriers*) that are modulated by BPSK or QPSK. OFDM's spread-spectrum technique distributes the data over these 52 carriers, which are spaced apart at precise frequencies. This spacing approach helps prevent demodulators from seeing frequencies other than their own. OFDM is resistant to RF interference, and it presents lower multipath distortion—big reasons why we use it in our higher-speed wireless networks.

Range Comparisons

Now let's take a look at Figure 12.7, which delimits the range comparisons of each 802.11 standard and shows these different ranges using an indoor open-office environment as a factor. (We'll be using default power settings.)

FIGURE 12.7   Range comparisons of 802.11 standards

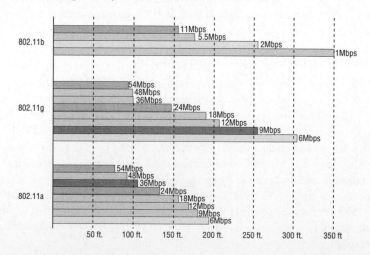

You can see that to get the full 54Mbps benefit of both 802.11a and 802.11g, you need to be between 50 feet and 100 feet (at the furthest) away, and likely even less if there happen to be any obstructions between the client and the access point.

Wireless Network Components

Though it might not seem this way to you right now, wireless networks are less complex than their wired cousins because they require fewer components. To make a wireless network work properly, all you really need are two main devices: a wireless access point and a wireless NIC. This also makes it a lot easier to install a wireless network because basically, you just need an understanding of these two components in order to do so.

Wireless Access Points

You'll find a central component—like a hub or switch—in the vast majority of wired networks that serves to connect hosts together and allow them to communicate with each other. It's the same idea with wireless networks. They also have a component that connects all wireless devices together, only that device is known as a *wireless access point (WAP),* or just AP. Wireless access points have at least one antenna (sometimes two for better reception—called *diversity*) and a port to connect them to a wired network. Figure 12.8 shows an example of a typical wireless access point.

FIGURE 12.8   A wireless access point

You can even think of an AP as a bridge between the wireless clients and the wired network. In fact, an AP can be used as a wireless bridge (depending on the settings) to bridge two wired network segments together.

In addition to the stand-alone AP, there is another type of AP that includes a built-in router, which you can use to connect both wired and wireless clients to the Internet (the most popular home brand being Linksys).

These devices are usually known as (surprise) wireless routers. They're usually employed as Network Address Translation (NAT) servers by using the one ISP-provided global IP address to multiplex numerous local IP addresses that are generally doled out to inside clients by the wireless router from a pool within the 192.168.x.x range. What's cool about this is that you don't have to make any changes your service with the ISP in order to increase the number of devices that can simultaneously access the Internet!

Wireless Network Interface Card (NIC)

Every host that wants to connect to a wireless network needs a *wireless network interface card (NIC)* to do so. Basically, a wireless NIC does the same job as a traditional NIC; but instead of having a socket to plug some cable into, the wireless NIC has a radio antenna. In addition to the different types of wireless networking (I'll talk about those in a minute), wireless NICs (like other NICs) can also differ in the type of connection they use to connect to the host computer.

Figure 12.9 shows an example of a wireless NIC.

FIGURE 12.9 A wireless NIC

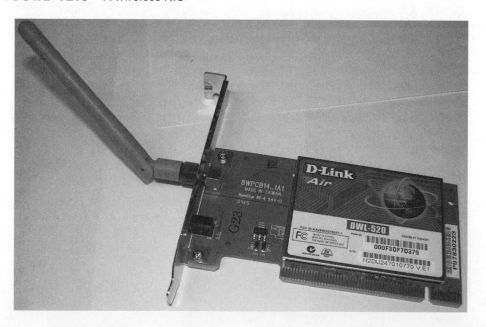

The wireless card shown in Figure 12.9 is used in a desktop PC. There are many various options for laptops as well. Most new laptops have wireless cards built into the motherboard.

> These days, it's pretty rare to use an external wireless client card because all laptops come with them built in, and desktops can be ordered with them too. But it's good to know that you can still buy the client card shown in Figure 12.9. Typically, you would use cards like the one shown in the figure for areas of poor reception, because they can have better range—depending on the antenna you use.

Wireless Antennas

Wireless antennas act as both transmitters and receivers. There are two broad classes of antennas on the market today: *Omni directional* (or point-to-multipoint) and *directional*, or *Yagi* (or point-to-point). Yagi antennas usually provide greater range than Omni antennas of equivalent gain. Why? Because Yagis focus all their power in a single direction, whereas Omnis must disperse the same amount of power in all directions at the same time. A downside to using a directional antenna is that you've got to be much more precise when aligning communication points. This is why a Yagi is really only a good choice for point-to-point bridging of access points. It's also why most APs use Omnis, because often, clients and other APs could be located in any direction at any given moment.

To get a picture of this, think of the antenna on your car. Yes, it's a non-networking example, but it's still a good one because it clarifies the fact that your car's particular orientation doesn't affect the signal reception of whatever radio station you happen to be listening to. Well, most of the time, anyway. If you're in the Boonies, you're out of range—something that also applies to the networking version of Omnis.

The television aerials that *some* of us are old enough to remember rotating into a specific direction for a certain channel (how many of you labeled your set-top antenna dial for the actual TV stations you could receive?) are examples of Yagi antennas. Believe it or not, they still look the same to this day!

Both Omnis and Yagis are rated according to their signal gain with respect to an actual or theoretical laboratory reference antenna. These ratings are relative indicators of the corresponding production antenna's range. Range is also affected by the bit rate of the underlying technology, with higher bit rates extending shorter distances. Remember, a Yagi will always have a longer range than an equivalently rated Omni, but as I said, the straight-line Yagi will be very limited in its coverage area.

Both antennas are also rated in units of decibel isotropic (dBi) or decibel dipole (dBd), based on the type of reference antenna (isotropic or dipole) of equivalent frequency that was initially used to rate the production antenna. A positive value for either unit of measure represents a gain in signal strength with respect to the reference antenna. *Webster's* defines *isotropic* as "exhibiting properties (as velocity of light transmission) with the same values when measured along axes in all directions." Isotropic antennas are not able to be produced in reality, but their properties can be engineered from antenna theory for reference purposes.

As a practical example, I'm going to use the Cisco Systems series of Aironet Access Point (indoor) and Bridge (outdoor) antennas. Table 12.3 describes the effect that gain ratings and attempted bit rates have on range limitations.

TABLE 12.3   Wireless Antenna Types and Ranges

Model	Gain	Indoor Range at 1Mbps	Indoor Range at 11Mbps	Outdoor Range at 2Mbps	Outdoor Range at 11Mbps
AIR-ANT2410Y-R	10dBi	800ft	230ft	Not specified	Not specified
AIR-ANT1728	5.2dBi	497ft	142ft	Not specified	Not specified
AIR-ANT4941	2.2dBi	350ft	130ft	Not specified	Not specified
AIR-ANT2506	5.2dBi	Not specified	Not specified	5,000ft	1,580ft
AIR-ANT24120	12dBi	Not specified	Not specified	24,288ft	7,392ft

It's pretty much a given that antennas operating with frequencies below 1GHz are measured in dBd while those operating above 1GHz are measured in dBi. But because this rule doesn't always work definitively, sometimes we have to compare the strength of one antenna measured in dBd with another measured in numerically equivalent dBi, in order to determine which one is stronger. This is exactly why it's important to know that a particular numerical magnitude of dBd is more powerful than the same numerical magnitude of dBi.

I know this sounds pretty complicated, but because the relationship between these two values is linear, it really makes the conversion a lot easier than you might think. Here's how it works: At the same operating frequency, a dipole antenna has about 2.2dB gain over a 0dBi theoretical isotropic antenna, which means you can easily convert from dBd to dBi by adding 2.2 to the dBd rating. Conversely, subtract 2.2 from the dBi rating, and you get the equivalent dBd rating.

Okay—armed with what you've learned about the difference between Omni and Yagi antennas and the difference between dBd and dBi gain ratings, you should be able to compare the relative range of transmission of one antenna with respect to another based on a combination of these characteristics. For example, the following four antenna ratings are given in relative order from greatest to least range:

- 7dBd Yagi (equivalent to a 9.2dBi Yagi)

- 7dBi Yagi (longer range than 7dBi Omni)

- 4.8dBd Omni (equivalent to a 7dBi Omni)

- 4.8dBi Omni (equivalent to a 2.6dBd Omni)

If you are having an intermittent problem with hosts connecting to the wireless network and varying signal strengthens at different locations, check your antennae location in the office or warehouse to make sure you are getting the best coverage possible.

So now that you understand the basic components involved in a wireless network, it's time to learn about the standards we use in our everyday home and corporate wireless networks and about the different ways that they're actually installed.

Installing a Wireless Network

Let's say you just bought a wireless NIC and a WAP for your laptop. What's next? Well, that all depends on the type of installation you want to create with your new toys. There are two main installation types: ad hoc and infrastructure mode, and each 802.11 wireless network device can be installed in one of these two modes, also called *service sets*.

Ad hoc Mode: Independent Basic Service Set (IBSS)

This is the easiest way to install wireless 802.11 devices. In this mode, the wireless NICs (or other devices) can communicate directly without the need for an AP. A good example of this is two laptops with wireless NICs installed. If both cards were set up to operate in ad hoc mode, they could connect and transfer files as long as the other network settings, like protocols, were set up to enable this as well. We'll also call this an *independent basic service set (IBSS)*, which is created as soon as two wireless devices communicate.

Okay—to set up a basic ad hoc wireless network, all you need are two wireless NICs and two computers. First (assuming they aren't built in), install the cards into the computers according to the manufacturer's directions. During the software installation, you'll be asked if you want to set up the NIC in ad hoc mode or infrastructure mode. For an ad hoc network, you would obviously go with the ad hoc mode setting. Once that's done, all you've got to do is bring the computers within range (90–100m) of each other, and voila—they'll "see" each other and be able to connect to each other.

Figure 12.10 shows an example of an ad hoc wireless network. (Note the absence of an access point).

An ad hoc network would not scale well and really is not recommended due to collision and organization issues. With the low costs of APs, this type of network is just not needed today.

FIGURE 12.10   A wireless network in ad hoc mode

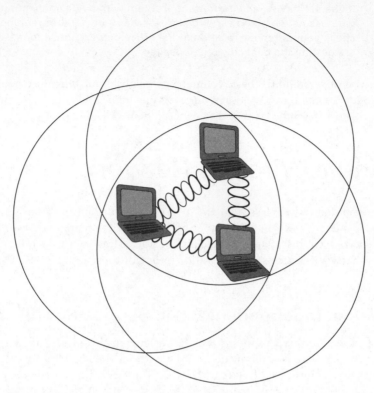

Infrastructure Mode: Basic Service Set (BSS)

The most common use of wireless networking equipment is to give us the wireless equivalent of a wired network. To do this, all 802.11 wireless equipment has the ability to operate in what's known as infrastructure mode, also referred to as a *Basic Service Set (BSS)*, that's provided by an AP. The term Basic Service Area (BSA) is also used at times to define the area managed by the AP, but BSS is the most common term that's used to define the cell area.

In infrastructure mode, NICs only communicate with an access point instead of directly with each other as they do when they're in ad hoc mode. All communication between hosts, plus any wired portion of the network must go through the access point. A really important fact to remember is that in this mode, wireless clients actually appear to the rest of the network as though they were standard, wired hosts.

Figure 12.11 shows a typical infrastructure mode wireless network. Pay special attention to the access point and the fact that it's also connected to the wired network. This connection from the access point to the wired network is called the *Distribution System (DS)*.

FIGURE 12.11   A wireless network in infrastructure mode

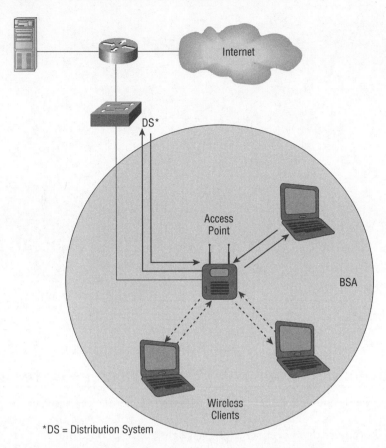

*DS = Distribution System

When you configure a client to operate in wireless infrastructure mode, you need to understand a couple of basic wireless concepts—namely, SSID and security. The *Security Set Identifier (SSID)* refers to the unique 32-character identifier that represents a particular wireless network and defines the basic service set. (By the way, a lot of people use the terms SSID and BSS interchangeably, so don't let that confuse you!) All devices involved in a particular wireless network must be configured with the same SSID.

Good to know is that if you set all your access points to the same SSID, mobile wireless clients can roam around freely within the same network. Doing this creates an *Extended Service Set (ESS)* and provides more coverage then a single access point. Figure 12.12 shows two APs configured with the same SSID in an office, thereby creating the ESS network.

For users to be able to roam throughout the wireless network—from AP to AP without losing their connection to the network—all APs must overlap by 10% of their signal or more. To make this happen, be sure the channels on each AP are set differently; and remember, in an 802.11b/g network, there are only three non-overlapping channels (1, 6, 11), so careful design is super important here!

FIGURE 12.12   Extended Service Set (ESS)

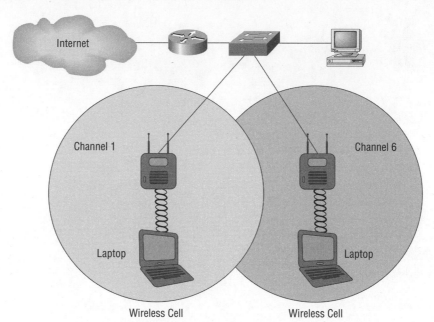

Design Considerations with Large Wireless Networks

As more vendors migrate to a mesh hierarchical design, and as larger networks are built using lightweight access points (managed by a controller), you can see that we really need a standardized protocol that governs how lightweight access points communicate with WLAN systems. This is exactly the role filled by one of the Internet Engineering Task Force's (IETF's) latest draft specification, Lightweight Access Point Protocol (LWAPP).

Mesh networking infrastructure is decentralized and comparably inexpensive for all the nice amenities it provides because each host only needs to transmit as far as the next host. Hosts act as repeaters to transmit data from nearby hosts to peers that are too far away for a manageable cabled connection. This results in a network that can span a really large distance, especially over rough or difficult terrain.

Another thing that's really important to consider when installing a wireless network is signal degradation, which will be discussed shortly.

Mesh and Lightweight Access Port Protocol (LWAPP)

Remember that mesh is a network topology in which devices are connected with many redundant connections between hosts nodes (See Chapter 1 for a review of this topology), and we can use this topology to our advantage in large wireless installations. Figure 12.13 shows a large meshed environment using Cisco 1520 APs (outdoor managed APs) to "umbrella" an outdoor area with wireless connectivity.

FIGURE 12.13   Typical large mesh outdoor environment

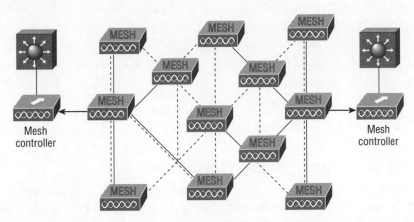

Mesh
controller

Mesh
controller

Oh, and did I mention that mesh networks also happen to be extremely reliable? Because each host can potentially be connected to several other hosts, if one of them drops out of the network because of hardware failure or something, its neighbors simply find another route. So you get extra capacity and fault tolerance automatically by adding more hosts.

Wireless mesh connections between AP hosts are formed with a radio, providing many possible paths from a single host to other hosts. Paths through the mesh network can change in response to traffic loads, radio conditions, or traffic prioritization.

At this time, mesh networks just aren't a justifiable solution for home use or small companies on a budget. As the saying goes, "If you have to ask…" As with most things in life, the more bells and whistles, the more it costs, and mesh networks are no exception!

Signal Degradation

Something that's really important to consider when installing a wireless network is signal degradation. Because the 802.11 wireless protocols use radio frequencies, the signal strength varies according to many factors. The weaker the signal, the less reliable the network connection will be, and so the less usable as well. (Think, dropped calls!) Some key factors that affect signal strength are

Distance   Okay, this one is definitely on the obvious side—the farther away from the WAP you get, the weaker the signal you get. Most APs have a very limited maximum range that equals less than 100m for most systems. You can extend this range to some degree using amplifiers or repeaters or even by using different antennas.

Walls and other barriers   Also easy to imagine is the fact that the more walls and other office barriers a wireless signal has to pass through, the more attenuated (reduced) the signal becomes. Also, the thicker the wall, the more it interrupts the signal. So in an indoor office area with lots of walls, the range of your wireless network could be as low as 25 feet!

Protocols used   This one isn't so apparent, but it certainly is a factor that affects, and can even determine, the range of a wireless LAN. The various wireless 802.11 protocols have different maximum ranges. As discussed earlier, in Figure 12.6, the maximum effective range varies quite a bit depending on the 802.11 protocol used. For example, if you have a client running the 802.11g protocol, but it connects to an AP running only the 802.11b protocol, you'll only get a throughput of 11Mbps to the client.

Interference   The final factor that affects wireless performance is outside interference. Because 802.11 wireless protocols operate in the 900MHz, 2.4GHz, and 5GHz ranges, interference can come from many sources. These include other wireless devices like Bluetooth, cordless telephones, cell phones, other wireless LANs, and any other device that transmits a radio frequency (RF) near the frequency bands that 802.11 protocols use. Even microwave ovens—a huge adversary of 802.11b and 802.11g—can be serious culprits!

Installing and Configuring Hardware

As I said earlier, installing 802.11 equipment is actually fairly simple—remember that there are really only two main types of components in 802.11 networks: APs and NICs. Wireless NIC installation is just like installing any other network card; but nowadays, most, if not all, laptops have wireless cards preinstalled, and that's as easy as it gets! And just like connecting an Ethernet card to a LAN switch, you need the wireless network card to connect to an access point.

The AP installation can be fairly simple as well. Take it out of the box, connect the antenna(e) if necessary, connect the power, and then place the AP where it can reach the highest number of clients. This last part is probably the trickiest, but it really just involves a little common sense and maybe a bit of trial and error. Knowing that walls obstruct the signal means putting the AP out in the open—even indoors—works better. And you also know it should be placed away from sources of RF interference, so putting it next to the microwave or phone system is probably a really bad idea too. Near a metal filing cabinet is also not so good. So just experiment and move your AP around to find the spot that gives you the best signal strength for all the clients that need to use it.

Okay—now that you have the hardware installed, it's time to configure it, right? Let's get started...

No worries—configuring your AP and NIC to work together isn't as tricky as it sounds. Most wireless equipment is designed to work almost without configuration; so, by default, you can pretty much turn things on and start working. The only things you need to configure are customization settings (name, network address, and so on) and security settings, and even these aren't required. But because I do highly recommend configuring them, I'll take you through that now.

NIC Configuration

Both Windows XP and Vista (as well as Server 2003/2008) include software to automatically configure a wireless connection, and they do so automatically when you install a wireless NIC. Let's discuss both XP and Vista installations:

1. The first time you reboot an XP machine after the installation of the NIC, you'll see a screen like the one shown in Figure 12.14. (This is the Windows wireless configuration screen.) From this screen, you can see any available wireless networks and configure how a computer connects to them.

2. You can then configure several of the properties for how this wireless NIC connects to a particular wireless network, using the following options as shown on the wireless network configuration screen:

> **Use Windows to Configure My Wireless Settings**   This check box determines whether Windows XP will configure the wireless settings. When it's unchecked, Windows XP will need an external program to configure how it connects to a wireless network, as is the case with some wireless NICs that have their own software program for this purpose. It is usually best to let Windows XP manage your wireless settings.

> **Available Networks**   This list shows of all the wireless networks within range, with each of the networks listed by their SSID. From this list, you can choose which network you wish to connect to, and you can then configure how your workstation connects by clicking the Configure button. If you don't see the wireless network you are looking for, and you are in range, try clicking the Refresh button.

FIGURE 12.14   Windows XP wireless configuration screen

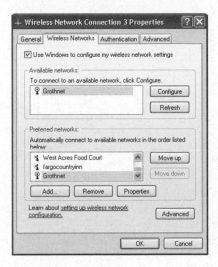

> **Preferred Networks**   This list details any wireless networks you have connected to before and want to connect to again automatically. If there is more than one wireless network in range, this list determines the order in which the workstation will try to connect to them. You can change this order using the Move Up and Move Down buttons.

3. In addition to the general configuration, you may have to configure the encryption for the connection (if the wireless connection you are using requires it). To set up how your workstation uses encryption for a particular connection, from the screen shown in Figure 12.14, click the SSID of the wireless network you want to configure, and then click Configure. You will then see the screen shown in Figure 12.15.

Proceeding from this screen, you can configure several parameters for the specific connection:

Network Name If for some reason the SSID of the AP changes, you can change the name of the AP you're connecting to in this field. All you need to do is delete the old one and type in the new name. This is also the area where you add an SSID name if the AP is not broadcasting the name, so the client can find the AP.

Wireless Network Key (WEP) This section contains all the parameters for config-uring encryption for this particular connection. If the network you are connecting to uses *Wired Equivalent Privacy (WEP)* encryption, this is the section where you will click the check boxes and configure how the wireless connection uses WEP, the key it uses, and what type of key it is (I'll cover WEP in the section on security at the end of this chapter). The following parameters are in this section:

FIGURE 12.15 Configuring encryption

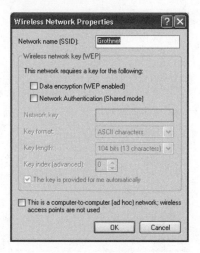

Data Encryption (WEP Enabled) If the network uses a key to encrypt data sent over the network, you should definitely make sure this box is checked (even though it is by default). You'll then need to specify the key in the box labeled Network Key, as well as specify what type of key it is (ASCII or hex) by selecting the appropriate item from the drop-down list.

Network Authentication (Shared Mode) If your AP uses shared mode authentication, you've got to check this box to ensure your workstation will authenticate to the AP using the shared key. The key can be provided automatically by the AP during the response to the initial request. If this is the case, you simply check the box labeled The Key Is Provided for Me Automatically, which happens to be the default. Otherwise, just uncheck it and enter the key and related information in the appropriate boxes.

This Computer Is a Computer-to-Computer (Ad Hoc) Network   Check this check box if you're connecting to another computer instead of an access point (not recommended, remember?).

4. Once you have changed any settings you need to, click OK to save the changes and finish the configuration.

Configuring a Vista client is pretty simple unless, well, it doesn't work. Should the latter happen, you can indeed spend a long time searching for the answer!

1. To find a wireless network, go to Control Panel, Network and Sharing Center, and then to Connect to a Network. If all is well, you'll get a screen similar to this one:

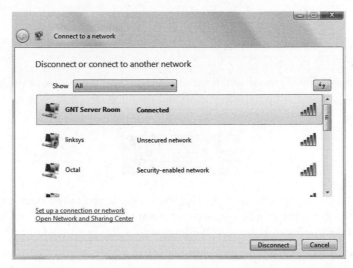

2. Double-click the Network you want to join, and click Connect Anyway if it is an unsecured network. You'll then get a screen showing that it's trying to connect:

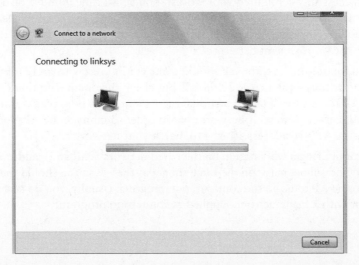

3. If you're using security, the AP will ask you for your credentials. If not, the next screen should be this one—again, if it works:

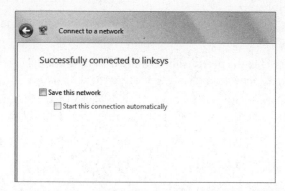

This screen is definitely what we all want to see. Now, take a look at the lower-right corner of your Vista window, and you should see an icon of two PCs with a globe, as shown in at right on this screen:

This means you are connected to the wireless network and to the Internet. If you do not see the globe in the middle of the two network devices, it means you're connected to your wireless network but not to the Internet.

4. Check your TCP/IP settings to troubleshoot if you are not connected to the Internet.

AP Configuration

Once you've successfully configured your workstation(s), it's time to move on and configure the AP. There are literally hundreds of different APs out there, and of course, each uses a different method to configure its internal software. The good news is that for the most part, they all follow the same general patterns:

1. First of all, out of the box, the AP should come configured with an IP address that's usually something similar to 192.168.1.1. But check the documentation that comes with the AP to be sure. You can just take the AP out of its box, plug it into a power outlet, and connect it to your network; but in order to manage the AP, you've got to configure the AP's IP address scheme to match your network's.

2. Start by configuring a workstation on the wired network with an IP address (192.168.1.2 or similar) and subnet mask on the same subnet as the AP's. You should then be able to connect to the AP to begin the configuration progress. Usually, you do this via a web browser or with a manufacturer-supplied configuration program.

3. Once you have successfully connected to the AP, you then get to configure its parameters.

Following are the minimum parameters common to APs that you should configure for your AP to work properly (remember, typically, an AP works right out of the box, but it is insecure too!).

SSID   As I talked about earlier, this is the name of the wireless network that your AP will advertise. If this new AP is to be part of an existing wireless network, it needs to be configured with the same SSID as the existing network. In a network with only one AP, you can think of the SSID as the "name" of the AP.

AP IP addresses   Remember—even though most APs come preconfigured with an IP address, it may not be one that matches the wired network's IP addressing scheme. So it follows that you should configure the AP's IP addresses (including the address, subnet mask, and default gateway addresses) to match the wired network you want it connected to. An AP does not need an IP address to work in your network. The IP address of the AP is used only to manage the AP.

Operating mode (Access Point or Bridging)   Access points can operate in one of two main modes: *Access Point mode* or *Bridging mode*. Access Point mode allows the AP to operate as a traditional access point to allow a wireless client transparent access to a wired network. Alternatively, two APs set to Bridging mode provide a wireless bridge between two wired network segments.

Password   Every access point has some kind of default password that's used to access the AP's configuration. For security reasons, it's a good idea to change this as soon as you can to connect to and configure the AP.

Wireless channel   802.11 wireless networks can operate on different channels to avoid interference. Most wireless APs come set to work on a particular channel from the factory, so for security reasons, you should also change this as soon as you can.

WEP/WPA   Although it isn't a requirement per se, I definitely recommend enabling security right from the start as soon as you turn on the AP. WEP and Wi-Fi Protected Access (WPA) allow data to be encrypted before it's sent over the wireless connection, and all configuring it entails is to enable it and pick a key to be used for the connections. Simple, easy-to-configure security is certainly worth your time!

So here's what you do: First, you'll be asked to enter one or more human-readable passphrases called *shared keys*—secret passwords that won't ever be sent over the wire. After entering each one, you'll generally click a button to initiate a one-way hash to produce a WEP key of a size related to the number of bits of WEP encryption you want. Entering the same passphrase on a wireless client causes the hash (not the passphrase) to be sent from the wireless client to the AP during a connection attempt. Most configuration utilities allow you to create multiple keys in case you want to grant someone temporary access to the network, but you still want to keep the primary passphrase a secret. You can just delete the key you enabled to permit temporary access after you don't need it anymore without affecting access by any primary LAN participants.

Here's an example of connecting to a Linksys access point (not a Linksys wireless router, which is a different device):

1. The first screen shows that I've connected using HTTP to configure the device. The IP address of the Linksys AP is 192.168.1.245. If it was a Linksys wireless router instead—the typical home DSL/cable modem wireless connection device around today—than the address would be 192.168.1.1.

2. As you can see, there's no username required, and the password is just "admin." As I mentioned, be sure not to leave this login configuration at the default! Once I click OK, I get taken to a screen where I can change my IP address:

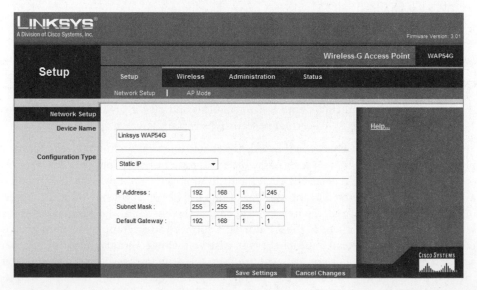

3. It is not vitally important that an AP have an IP address, but it comes in handy for management purposes. But you can change the IP address as well as the device name from this screen if you want to. I clicked the Wireless tab on top and received this screen:

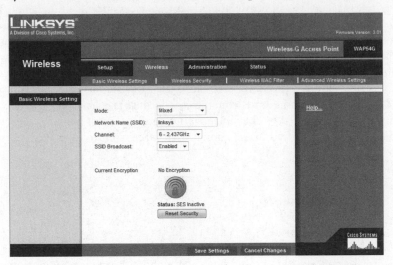

4. From here, you can set the device to run b/g or just g—even Mixed mode, which happens to be the default. You can also change the SSID from Linksys to another name, and I highly recommend doing this. The AP channel can be also be changed, and you can turn off the AP beacons as well—which, again, is recommended (if you do this, you have to set the new SSID name in each of your clients!). Last, you can see that by default, there's no encryption. Click the Wireless Security tab, and you'll get this screen:

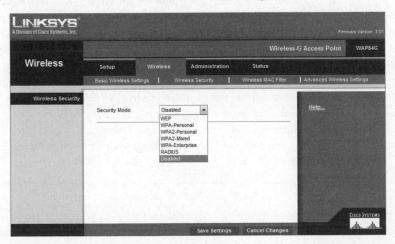

5. You can see from the pull-down menu that security is set to Disabled by default, but you can choose from various wireless security options.

I'll talk about security next.

Wireless Security

Okay—so wireless security is basically nonexistent on access points and clients. The original 802.11 committee just didn't imagine that wireless hosts would one day outnumber bounded media hosts, but that's actually where we're headed now. Also unfortunately, just like with the IPv4 routed protocol, engineers and scientists didn't include security standards that are robust enough to work in a corporate environment. So we're left with proprietary solution add-ons to aid us in our quest to create a secure wireless network. And no—I'm not sitting here bashing the standards committees, because the security problems we're experiencing were also created by the U.S. government because of export issues with its own security standards. Our world is a complicated place, so it follows that our security solutions would have to be as well.

 Real World Scenario

War Driving

It's a fact—wireless networks are pretty much everywhere these days. You can get your hands on a wireless access point for less than $100.00, and they're flying off the shelves. You can find APs in public places like shopping malls, coffee shops, airports, and hotels; and in some cities, you can just hang out in a downtown area and zero in on a veritable menu of APs operating in almost every nearby business.

Predictably, this proliferation of APs has led to a new hobby for those with enough skill: It's called *war driving*. Not for the technologically challenged, war driving involves driving around in a car with a laptop, a wireless NIC, and a high-gain antenna, trying to locate open APs. If one with high-speed Internet access is found, it's like hitting the jackpot. People do this aided by various software programs and Global Positioning Systems (GPSs) to make their game even easier. But it's not always innocent—war drivers can be a serious security threat because they can potentially access anything on your wireless LAN, as well as anything it's attached to! Even though they're not a sinister threat most of the time, realize that in the very least, they're consuming precious resources from your network. So, if you happen to notice unusually slow-moving vehicles outside your home or business—especially those with computer equipment inside—know that you're the potential target of a war driver.

A good place to start discussing Wi-Fi security is by talking about the standard basic security that was incorporated into the original 802.11 standards and why those standards are still way too flimsy and incomplete to help us create a secure wireless network relevant to today's challenges.

Open Access

All Wi-Fi Certified wireless LAN products are shipped in "open-access" mode, with their security features turned off. Although open access or no security may be appropriate and acceptable for public hot spots such as coffee shops, college campuses, and maybe airports, it's definitely not an option for an enterprise organization, and it's probably not even adequate for your private home network.

With what I've told you so far, I'm sure you agree that security needs to be enabled on wireless devices during their installation in enterprise environments. Yet surprisingly, many companies actually don't enable any WLAN security features. Obviously, the companies that do this are exposing their networks to tremendous risk.

The reason that the products are shipped with open access is so that any person who knows absolutely nothing about computers can just buy an access point, plug it into their cable or DSL modem, and voilà—they're up and running. It's marketing, plain and simple, and simplicity sells.

Service Set Identifiers (SSIDs), Wired Equivalent Privacy (WEP), and Media Access Control (MAC) Address Authentication

What the original designers of 802.11 did to create basic security was to include the use of SSIDs, open or shared-key authentication, static WEP, and optional *Media Access Control (MAC) authentication*. Sounds like a lot, but none of these really offer any type of serious security solution—all they may be close to adequate for is use on a common home network. But we'll go over them anyway.

SSID is a common network name for the devices in a WLAN system that create the wireless LAN. An SSID prevents access by any client device that doesn't have the SSID. The thing is, by default, an access point broadcasts its SSID in its beacon many times a second. And even if SSID broadcasting is turned off, a bad guy can discover the SSID by monitoring the network and just waiting for a client response to the access point. Why? Because, believe it or not, that information, as regulated in the original 802.11 specifications, must be sent in the clear—how secure!

> If you cannot see an AP when trying to perform a site survey, verify that the AP has SSID beaconing enabled or not.

Two types of authentication were specified by the IEEE 802.11 committee: open and shared-key authentication. Open authentication involves little more than supplying the correct SSID—but it's the most common method in use today. With shared-key authentication, the access point sends the client device a challenge-text packet that the client must then encrypt with the correct WEP key and return to the access point. Without the correct key, authentication will fail and the client won't be allowed to associate with the access point.

But shared-key authentication is still not considered secure because all an intruder has to do to get around this is detect both the clear-text challenge and the same challenge encrypted with a WEP key and then decipher the WEP key. Surprise—shared key isn't used in today's WLANs because of clear-text challenge.

With open authentication, even if a client can complete authentication and associate with an access point, the use of WEP prevents the client from sending and receiving data from the access point unless the client has the correct WEP key. A WEP key is composed of either 40 or 128 bits, and in its basic form, it's usually statically defined by the network administrator on the access point and all clients that communicate with that access point. When static WEP keys are used, a network administrator must perform the time-consuming task of entering the same keys on every device in the WLAN. Obviously, we now have fixes for this because tackling this would be administratively impossible in today's huge corporate wireless networks!

Last, client MAC addresses can be statically typed into each access point, and any of them that show up without that MAC addresses in the filter table will be denied access. Sounds good, but of course all MAC layer information must be sent in the clear—anyone equipped with a free wireless sniffer can just read the client packets sent to the access point and spoof their MAC address.

 If you cannot connect to an AP and you've verified that your DHCP configuration and WEP key are correct, check the MAC address filtering on the AP.

WEP can actually work if administered correctly. But basic static WEP keys are no longer a viable option in today's corporate networks without some of the proprietary fixes that run on top of it.

So, what should you use today? The answer lies in the size of your wireless network and how tight your security needs to be. Let's discuss this further now.

Remote Authentication Dial In User Service (RADIUS)

Remote Authentication Dial In User Service (RADIUS) is a networking protocol that offers us several security benefits: authorization, centralized access, and accounting supervision regarding the users and/or computers that connect to and access our network's services. Once RADIUS has been authenticated, it allows us to specify the type of rights a user or workstation has, plus control what it, or they, can do within the network. It also creates a record of all access attempts and actions. The provision of Authentication, Authorization, and Accounting is called AAA (spoken just like the automobile insurance company: "Triple A").

RADIUS has risen to stardom because of its AAA features and is often employed by ISPs, web servers, wireless networks, APs, as well as network ports—basically, by anybody who wants or needs a AAA server. And these servers are only becoming more critically important in large corporate environments because they offer security for wireless networks. From the Linksys security screen shown earlier, you can see that RADIUS is an available option. If you choose it, you'll be asked for the IP address of the RADIUS server so the AP can send authentication packets.

Figure 12.16 shows how the AP becomes an authenticator when you choose the RADIUS authentication method.

Now, packets must pass through the AP until the user and or host gets authenticated by the RADIUS server.

FIGURE 12.16   RADIUS authentication server

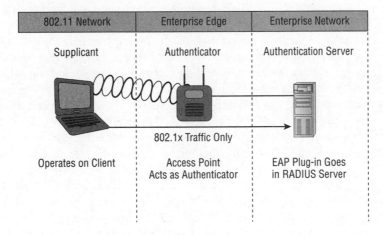

Temporal Key Integrity Protocol (TKIP)

Put up a fence, and it's only a matter of time until bad guys find a way over, around, and through it. And true to form, they indeed found ways to get through WEP's defenses, leaving our Wi-Fi networks vulnerable—stripped of their Data Link layer security! So someone had to come to the rescue. In this case, it happened to be the IEEE 802.11i task group and the Wi-Fi Alliance, joining forces for the cause. They came up with a solution called Temporal Key Integrity Protocol (TKIP). The Wi-Fi Alliance unveiled it back in late 2002 and introduced it as *Wi-Fi Protected Access (WPA)*. This little beauty even saved us lots of money because TKIP—say this like, "tee kip"—didn't make us upgrade all our legacy hardware equipment in order to use it. Then, in the summer of 2004, the IEEE put their seal of approval on its final version and added even more defensive muscle with goodies like 802.1X and AES-CCMP (AES-Counter Mode CBC-MAC Protocol) upon publishing IEEE 802.11i-2004. The Wi-Fi Alliance responded positively by embracing the now-complete specification and dubbing it WPA2 for marketing purposes.

A big reason that TKIP doesn't require buying new hardware to run is because it really just kind of a wraps around the pre-existing WEP encryption key (which was way too short) and upgrades it a whole lot to a much more impenetrable 128-bit encryption. Another reason for TKIP's innate compatibility is that both its encryption mechanism and the RC4 algorithm used to power and define WEP, respectively, remained the same.

But there are still significant differences that help make it the seriously tough shield it is, one of them being that it actually changes each packet's key. Let me explain... Packet keys are made up of three things: a base key, the transmitting device's MAC address, and the packet's serial number. It's an elegant design because although it doesn't place a ton of stress on workstations and APs, it serves up some truly formidable cryptographic force. Here's how it works: Remember the packet serial number part of the transmission key? Well, it's not just your average serial number; it's special—very special.

TKIP-governed transmission ensures that each packet gets its very own 48-bit serial number, which is augmented with a sequence number whenever a new packet gets sent out and which not only serves as part of the key, but also acts as the initialization vector. And the good news doesn't end there—because each packet is now uniquely identified, the collision attacks that used to happen using WEP are also history. Plus, the fact that part of the packet's serial number is also the initialization vector prevents something called *replay attacks*. It takes an ice age for a 48-bit sequence repeat, so replaying packets from some past wireless connection is just not going to happen; those "recycled" packets won't be in sequence, but they will be identified, thus preventing the attack.

Okay—now for what may be the truly coolest thing about TKIP keys: the base key. Because each base key that TKIP creates is unique, no one can recycle a commonly known key over and over again to gain access to a formerly vulnerable WEP wireless LAN. This is because TKIP throws the base key into the mix when it assembles each packet's unique key, meaning that even if a device has connected to a particular access point a bunch of times, it won't be permitted access again unless it has a completely new key granting it permission.

Even the base key itself is a fusion of something called *nonces*—an assortment of random numbers gleaned from the workstation, the access point, and each of these devices' MAC addresses, referred to as a *session secret*. So basically, if you've got IEEE 802.1X authentication working for you, rest assured that a session secret absolutely will be transmitted securely to the each machine every time it initiates connect to the wireless LAN by the authentication server. Unless you're using pre-shared keys, that is, because if you happen to be using these, that important session secret always remains the same. Using TKIP with pre-shared keys is kind of like closing an automatically locking security door but not enabling its security settings and alarm—anyone who knows where the secret latch is can get right in!

Wi-Fi Protected Access (WPA) or WPA 2 Pre-Shared Key

These are both essentially another form of basic security that's really just an add-on to the specifications. Even though you can totally lock the vault, as I mentioned in the previous section, WPA/WPA2 Pre-Shared Key (PSK) is a better form of wireless security than any other basic wireless security method I've talked about so far. And note that I did say *basic*!

Wi-Fi Protected Access (WPA) is a standard developed by the Wi-Fi Alliance, formerly known as Wireless Ethernet Compatibility Alliance (WECA). WPA provides a standard for authentication and encryption of WLANs that's intended to solve known security problems. The standard takes into account the well-publicized AirSnort and man-in-the-middle WLAN attacks. So of course we use WPA2 to help us with today's security issues.

The PSK verifies users via a password or identifying code (also called a *passphrase*) on both the client machine and the access point. A client gains access to the network only if its password matches the access point's password. The PSK also provides keying material that TKIP or Advanced Encryption Standard (AES) uses to generate an encryption key for each packet of transmitted data.

Although more secure than static WEP, PSK still has a lot in common with static WEP in that the PSK is stored on the client station and can be compromised if the client station is lost or stolen (even though finding this key isn't all that easy to do). It's a definite recommendation to use a strong PSK passphrase that includes a mixture of letters, numbers, and non-alphanumeric characters. With WPA, it's still actually possible to specify the use of dynamic encryption keys that change each time a client establishes a connection.

 The benefit of WPA over static WEP key is that WPA can change dynamically while the system is used.

WPA is a step toward the IEEE 802.11i standard and uses many of the same components, with the exception of encryption—802.11i (WPA2) uses AES-CCMP encryption. The IEEE 802.11i standard replaced WEP with a specific mode of AES known as the CCMP, as mentioned in the above section. This allows AES-CCMP to provide both data confidentiality (encryption) and data integrity.

 The highest level of wireless encryption you can run is WPA2-AES.

The following screen shows that if you choose WPA-2 Personal on the Linksys AP, you can then enter your passphrase—it's really called WPA2-Pre-Shared Key, but whatever:

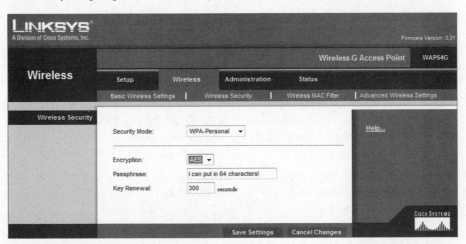

You have a choice of TKIP or AES as the encryption, and by the way, you can choose up to a 64-character key—pretty tight!

WPA's mechanisms are designed to be implementable by current hardware vendors, meaning that users should be able to implement WPA on their systems with only a firmware/software modification.

 The IEEE 802.11i standard has been sanctioned by WPA and is called WPA version 2.

Summary

Like rock 'n' roll, wireless technologies are here to stay. And for those of us who have come to depend on wireless technologies, it's actually pretty hard to imagine a world without wireless networks—what did we do before cell phones?

So we began this chapter by exploring the essentials and fundamentals of how wireless networks function.

Springing off that foundation, I then introduced you to the basics of wireless radio frequencies (RF) and the IEEE standards. We discussed 802.11 from its inception through its evolution to current and near future standards and talked about the subcommittees who create these standards.

All of this led into a discussion of wireless security—or, rather non-security for the most part—which we went over in detail.

We finished the chapter by bringing you up to speed on TKIP and WPA/WPA 2 security solutions—important tools used to protect the wireless LANs of today.

Exam Essentials

Understand the IEEE 802.11a specification.   802.11a runs in the 5GHz spectrum, and if you use the 802.11h extensions, you have 23 non-overlapping channels. 802.11a can run up to 54Mbps, but only if you are less than 50 feet from an access point.

Understand the IEEE 802.11b specification.   IEEE 802.11b runs in the 2.4GHz range and has three non-overlapping channels. It can handle long distances, but with a maximum data rate of up to 11Mpbs.

Understand the IEEE 802.11g specification.   IEEE 802.11g is 802.11b's big brother and runs in the same 2.4GHz range, but it has a higher data rate of 54Mbps if you are less than 100 feet from an access point.

Remember the Wireless LAN modulation techniques.   Direct-Sequence Spread Spectrum (DSSS) is the most widely used modulation technique, but has speeds only to 11Mbps. Frequency-Hopping Spread Spectrum (FHSS), although it is used in wireless devices like Bluetooth, isn't the technique of choice for either vendors or the 802.11 working group. To get the higher speeds needed in today's WLANs, we use Orthogonal Frequency Division Multiplexing (OFDM) in 802.11g and 802.11a networks.

Understand how WPA works in a WLAN.   Wi-Fi Protected Access (WPA) is the security of choice in today's home and corporate networks. It provides both authentication and encryption (either TKIP or AES); the latest version is WPA2.

Written Lab

In this section, write the answers to the following wireless questions:

1. What is the maximum data rate of IEEE 802.11b?

2. What is the maximum data rate of IEEE 802.11g?

3. What is the maximum data rate of IEEE 802.11a?

4. What is the frequency range of IEEE 802.11b?

5. What is the frequency range of IEEE 802.11g?

6. What is the frequency range of IEEE 802.11a?

7. APs come set up with what type of security enabled by default?

8. Why would we use WPA instead of basic WEP?

9. Which IEEE committee has been sanctioned by WPA and is called WPA 2?

10. The IEEE 802.11b/g basic standard has how many non-overlapping channels?

   (The answers to Written Lab can be found following the answers to the Review Questions for this chapter.)

Review Questions

1. You need to install wireless Internet access in an open warehouse environment. After installing the equipment the technician notices varying signal strengths throughout the warehouse.

   A. Turn on broadcast key rotation

   B. Change the encryption method used on all the AP's

   C. Change the antenna placement

   D. Use channel bonding

   E. Use channel shaping

2. What is the frequency range of the IEEE 802.11a standard?

   A. 2.4Gbps

   B. 5Gbps

   C. 2.4GHz

   D. 5GHz

3. What is the frequency range of the IEEE 802.11g standard?

   A. 2.4Gbps

   B. 5Gbps

   C. 2.4GHz

   D. 5GHz

4. Which devices can interfere with the operation of a wireless network because they operate on similar frequencies? (Choose two.)

   A. Copier

   B. Microwave oven

   C. Toaster

   D. Cordless phone

   E. IP phone

   F. AM radio

5. Which wireless standard allows you to channel bond to increase bandwidth and uses both the 2.4Ghz and 5Ghz frequencies?

   A. 802.11b

   B. 802.11g

   C. 802.11a

   D. 802.11n

6. How many non-overlapping channels are available with 802.11b?

   A. 3

   B. 12

   C. 23

   D. 40

7. How many non-overlapping channels are available with 802.11a?

   A. 3

   B. 12

   C. 23

   D. 40

8. What is the maximum data rate for the 802.11a standard?

   A. 6Mbps

   B. 11Mbps

   C. 22Mbps

   D. 54Mbps

9. You need to install wireless on multiple floors of a large building and maintenance area. What is your first concern before installing the AP's?

   A. Authentication

   B. Encryption

   C. Channel Overlap

   D. AP configuration

10. What is the maximum data rate for the 802.11b standard?

   A. 6Mbps

   B. 11Mbps

   C. 22Mbps

   D. 54Mbps

11. You connect a new host to your companies wireless network. The host is set to receive a DHCP address and the WEP key is entered correctly, however, the host cannot connect to the network. What can the problem be?

   A. DNS is not configured on the host

   B. MAC filtering is enabled on the AP

   C. The network has run out of wireless connections

   D. The host is enabled to run 802.11b and 802.11g

12. Which is the highest encryption that WPA2 can use?

   A. AES-CCMP

   B. PPK via IV

   C. PSK

   D. TKIP/MIC

13. Which additional configuration step is necessary in order to connect to an access point that has SSID broadcasting disabled?

   A. Set the SSID value in the client software to public.

   B. Configure open authentication on the AP and the client.

   C. Set the SSID value on the client to the SSID configured on the AP.

   D. Configure MAC address filtering to permit the client to connect to the AP.

14. Which spread-spectrum technology does the 802.11b standard define for operation?

   A. IR

   B. DSSS

   C. FHSS

   D. DSSS and FHSS

   E. IR, FHSS, and DSSS

15. Which wireless LAN design ensures that a mobile wireless client will not lose connectivity when moving from one access point to another?

   A. Using adapters and access points manufactured by the same company

   B. Overlapping the wireless cell coverage by at least 10%

   C. Configuring all access points to use the same channel

   D. Utilizing MAC address filtering to allow the client MAC address to authenticate with the surrounding APs

16. You have installed a point-to-point connection using wireless bridges and omni-directional antennas between two buildings. The throughput is low. What can you do to improve the link?

   A. Replace the bridges with AP's

   B. Replace the omni-directional antennas with Yagi's

   C. Configure 802.11a on the links

   D. Install amps to boost the signal

17. What does Extended Service Set ID mean (ESS)?

   A. That you have more than one access point, and they are in the same SSID connected by a distribution system

   B. That you have more than one access point, and they are in separate SSIDs connected by a distribution system

   C. That you have multiple access points, but they are placed physically in different buildings

   D. That you have multiple access points, but one is a repeater access point

18. What is one reason that WPA encryption is preferred over WEP?

   A. A WPA key is longer and requires more special characters than the WEP key.

   B. The access point and the client are manually configured with different WPA key values.

   C. WPA key values remain the same until the client configuration is changed.

   D. The values of WPA keys can change dynamically while the system is used.

19. How wide are the channels used in 802.11n in order to gain the large bandwidth that the specification provides?

   A. 22MHz

   B. 20Mhz

   C. 40Mhz

   D. 100Mhz

20. 802.11n uses MIMO. How does this optimize throughput to gain the high speed advantage that 802.11n provides?

   A. By specifying an acknowledgment of each and every frame, 802.11n provides better overhead.

   B. Several frames are sent by several antennae over several paths and are then recombined by another set of antennae.

   C. One frame at a time is sent, but faster than in 802.11g because multiple antennas are used (multiple-in, multiple-out).

   D. MIMO packs smaller packets into a single unit, which improves throughput.

Answers to Review Questions

1. C. It is imperative that a good site survey is completed before installing your wireless network. Trying various types of antennas and their placements is the key to covering the whole wireless area.

2. D. The IEEE 802.11a standard runs in the 5GHz RF range.

3. C. The IEEE 802.11b and IEEE 802.11g both run in the 2.4GHz RF range.

4. B, D. If you are running 802.11b/g frequency, which most networks are, then you can receive interference from microwave ovens and cordless phones.

5. D. 802.11n uses channel bonding of both the 2.4Ghz range and the 5Ghz range to get increased bandwidth of over 100Mbps.

6. A. The IEEE 802.11b and g standards provide three non-overlapping channels.

7. B. The IEEE 802.11a standard provides up to 12 non-overlapping channels, or up to 23 if you add the 802.11h standard.

8. D. The IEEE 802.11a standard provides a maximum data rate of up to 54Mbps.

9. C. If you have a large area to cover with wireless, you need to be concerned with channel overlap.

10. B. The IEEE 802.11b standard provides a maximum data rate of up to 11Mbps.

11. B. If everything is correctly configured on the host, then MAC filtering would stop the host from connecting to the AP. If you try and connect and can't, check the AP's settings.

12. A. The IEEE 802.11i standard replaced Wired Equivalent Privacy (WEP) with a specific mode of the Advanced Encryption Standard (AES) known as the Counter Mode Cipher Block Chaining-Message Authentication Code (CBC-MAC) protocol. This allows AES-CCMP to provide both data confidentiality (encryption) and data integrity.

13. C. If you disable SSID broadcasting, which you should, then you must configure the SSID name on the clients that need to connect to the AP.

14. B. The IEEE 802.11b standard uses Direct Sequence Spread Spectrum (DSSS). If you are running 802.11g, it uses Orthogonal Frequency Division Multiplexing (OFDM).

15. B. If you are running an Extended Service Set (meaning more than one AP with the same SSID name), you need to overlap the cell coverage by 10% or more so clients will not drop out while roaming.

16. B. You need to use directional antennas, like a Yagi, in order to get the best signal between antennas.

17. A. Extended Service Set ID means that you have more than one access point, they all are set to the same SSID, and they are all connected together in the same VLAN or distribution system so users can roam.

18. D. WPA is cool because it is easy to configure and works great. Type in a passphrase (assuming you're using Pre-Shared Key), and you're done. Plus you have great security because the keys change dynamically.

19. C. 802.11n uses two 20MHz-wide channels to create a 40Mhz-wide channel, which provides over 100Mbps wireless.

20. B. 802.11n MIMO sends multiple frames by several antennae over several paths. The frames are then recombined by another set of antennae to optimize throughput and multi-path resistance. This is called spatial multiplexing.

Answers to Written Lab

1. 11Mbps

2. 54Mbps

3. 54Mbps

4. 2.4GHz

5. 2.4GHz

6. 5GHz

7. None

8. The values of WPA keys can change dynamically while the system is used.

9. The IEEE 802.11i standard has been sanctioned by WPA and is called WPA version 2.

10. Three

Chapter

13

Authentication and Access Control

THE FOLLOWING COMPTIA NETWORK+ EXAM OBJECTIVES ARE COVERED IN THIS CHAPTER:

✓ **6.3 Explain the methods of network access security**

✓ **Filtering:**

- ACL
    - MAC filtering
    - IP filtering
- Tunneling and encryption
    - SSL VPN
    - VPN
    - L2TP
    - PPTP
    - IPSEC
- Remote Access
    - RAS
    - RDP
    - PPPoE
    - PPP
    - VNC
    - ICA

✓ **6.4 Explain methods of user authentication**

- PKI
- Kerberos
- AAA
    - RADIUS
    - TACACS+
- Network access control
    - 802.1x
- CHAP
- MS-CHAP
- EAP

So far, you've learned a lot about networking standards and related technologies, and even how to make computers and devices communicate so you can get a network up and running. But there's more—today, because network security is absolutely critical, I'm going to equip you with the knowledge you need to keep your network safe from intruders.

Yes, communication and accessing the information you need is all good, but knowing exactly who it is at the other end of the connection is vital. This means you need ways to confirm that the person or computer at the other end of the connection is really supposed to be accessing the resource it's trying to, and even whether the resources or entities that you're contacting are really who and what they appear to be. Seriously, if you don't have network security firmly in place, you're flying dangerously blind—you could be inadvertently exposing critical data to people who have no right to see that information and may even intend to exploit it in a big way! So, in this chapter, we'll focus on some very important pieces of the security puzzle; two of the first things on our list are security filtering and user authentication.

For up-to-the-minute updates for this chapter, please see www.lammle.com or www.sybex.com/go/comptianetwork+studyguide.

Security Filtering

How do we know who's really at the other end of our connections? The answer to that may seem simple enough because the computer or person on the other end has to identify him/her/itself, right? Wrong! That's just not good enough, because people—especially hackers—lie, so it's totally naïve to assume that the person or computer on the other end of the line is who they're claiming to be. Sad but true: hackers use the many tools out there today with the precise goal of convincing us they're someone else, and way too many of us have been, or know of someone who has been, a victim of identity theft thanks to bad guys with the right spoofing software in hand.

This means it's imperative to control who or what can get into our network by identifying the specific computers and individuals that have the right to gain access to it and its resources. But how do we do this? Well, for starters, I'm going to cover some basic ways to safely allow in the computers you want to access to your network, plus ways to keep out the ones you don't.

The first line of defense is something called *security filtering*, which broadly refers to ways to let people securely access your resources. This process is twofold and includes ensuring that only authorized computers get to enter your network, and making sure data you're sending back and forth between networks is secured so it can't be intercepted and translated by bad guys.

Access Control Lists

It's rare to find a network around these days that isn't connected to the Internet. The Internet is clearly a public internetwork that anyone can connect to, but your company's or personal network is, and should definitely be, a private one. The catch here is that every time you connect to the Internet (where everyone is welcome) from a private network, you're instantly vulnerable to security break-ins. This is where something we call a *firewall* comes into play. Firewalls are basically tools that you can implement to prevent any unauthorized users roaming around on public networks from gaining access to your private network.

> I'll be covering the different types of firewalls, plus the skinny on exactly how they work, in Chapter 15, "Physical and Hardware Security." For now, understand that firewalls can either be stand-alone devices or combined with another hardware device like a server or a router. And although firewalls can use a lot of various technologies to restrict information flow, their primary weapon is known as an *access control list* (ACL).

ACLs typically reside on routers to determine which devices are allowed to access them based on the requesting device's Internet Protocol (IP) address. Oh, and just so you know, ACLs have been around for decades and have other uses apart from firewalls.

Figure 13.1 demonstrates how ACLs prevent users on Network B from accessing Network A

FIGURE 13.1 Two networks with an ACL-enabled router

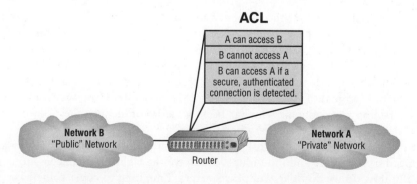

Okay, what we see here is that users in Network A can pass through the router into Network B. This means that an IP spoofing attack, when someone pretends to have a network address on the inside of a firewall to gain network access, can still happen if a user in Network B pretends to be located in Network A. We'll go over things like IP spoofing more thoroughly in Chapter 14, "Network Threats and Mitigation," but for now, let's get back to ACLs.

You can create a wide array of ACLs, from the very simple to the highly complex, depending on exactly what you want to have them do for you. One example is placing separate inbound and outbound ACLs on a router to ensure that the data that's leaving your network comes from a different source than the data that's coming into it.

When configuring ACLs between the Internet and your private network to mitigate security problems, it's a good idea to include these four conditions:

- Deny any addresses from your internal networks.
- Deny any local host addresses (127.0.0.0/8).
- Deny any reserved private addresses.
- Deny any addresses in the IP multicast address range (224.0.0.0/4).

None of these addresses should ever be allowed to enter your internetwork.

Most of the time, it's wise to configure ACLs so that they'll allow or deny access based on the IP address of the source or destination device. ACLs that filter network traffic this way are commonly called *port ACLs* because the ports on your router are where they're implemented. If your network is running a protocol other than Transmission Control Protocol/Internet Protocol (TCP/IP), you can filter traffic based on a Media Access Control (MAC), or hardware, address instead of an IP address. You can still use a MAC address–based ACL if you're running TCP/IP, but keep in mind that it's a lot easier to deal with IP addresses than MAC addresses. Another point to remember is that even though most firewalls and routers will allow you to create both IP-based and MAC-based ACLs, doing so can create an exceptionally ugly situation where access is denied when it really shouldn't be.

Tunneling

Just thinking about the huge amount of sensitive data bouncing all over the Internet 24/7 makes me want to scream the word *security*! It's seriously clear that we need it almost as much as air. Worse, most of that data is sent out over the Internet without any encryption or security. But at least not the really sensitive stuff, which should be sent via one of several different security protocols available today—phew. These vital protocols are really sets of conditions or rules that define how a secure connection is maintained when we send sensitive data through an unsecure medium like the Internet or a wireless connection. Before talking about the security protocols that the Network+ exam is likely to quiz you on, I'd like to define a few terms.

The first is a concept called *tunneling*, which basically means encapsulating one protocol within another to ensure that a transmission is secure. Here's an example. The lion's share of us use IP, known as a *payload protocol*, which can be encapsulated within a *delivery protocol* like Internet Protocol Security (IPSec); if you took a look at these packets individually, you would see that they're encrypted. If you look at the process as a whole, it appears literally that a point-to-point tunnel is created on the Internet, as Figure 13.2 illustrates. (Make a note to yourself that usually, the tunneled protocol is running at a higher layer in the OSI model than the payload protocol, but not always.)

FIGURE 13.2   A tunnel through the Internet

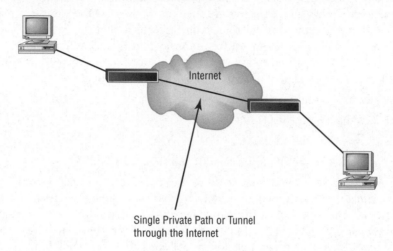

Single Private Path or Tunnel
through the Internet

The Network+ exam will test your understanding of the following tunneling protocols:

- Virtual Private Network (VPN)
- Secure Sockets Layer (SSL)
- Secure Sockets Layer Virtual Private Network (SSL VPN)
- Layer 2 Tunneling Protocol (L2TP)
- Point to Point Tunneling Protocol (PPTP)
- Internet Protocol Security (IPSec)

Let's dig in and take a detailed look at each one now.

Virtual Private Network (VPN)

I discussed this back in Chapter 1, but let's add a bit more information here. Remember that the reason we use a VPN is so that our host will traverse an insecure network (Internet) and become local to the remote network. A good example would be, say, a corporate secure local area network (LAN) or virtual LAN (VLAN) connected to by remote host machines over the Internet accessing the company's secure servers.

Types of VPNs are named based on the kind of role they play in a real-world business situation. There are three different categories of VPNs:

Remote access VPNs   *Remote access VPNs* allow remote users like telecommuters to securely access the corporate network wherever and whenever they need to. (This is the

type of VPN access I used as an example back in Chapter 1, "Introduction to Networks.").
It is typical that users can connect to the Internet but not to the office via their VPN client
because they don't have the correct VPN address and password. This is the most common
problem and one you should always check first.

Site-to-site VPNs *Site-to-site VPNs*, or intranet VPNs, allow a company to connect its
remote sites to the corporate backbone securely over a public medium like the Internet instead
of requiring more expensive wide area network (WAN) connections like frame relay.

Extranet VPNs *Extranet VPNs* allow an organization's suppliers, partners, and customers
to be connected to the corporate network in a limited way for business-to-business (B2B)
communications.

SSL and SSL VPN

Next on the list is *Secure Sockets Layer (SSL)*. This security protocol was developed by
Netscape to work with its browser. It's based on Rivest, Shamir, and Adleman (RSA)
public-key encryption and used to enable secure Session-layer connections over the Internet between a web browser and a web server. SSL is service independent; meaning a lot of
different network applications can be secured with it—a famous one being the ubiquitous
HTTP Secure (HTTPS) protocol. As time marched on, SSL was merged with other Transport layer security protocols to form a new protocol called Transport Layer Security (TLS).
Figure 13.3 shows the SSL connection process

FIGURE 13.3 The SSL connection process

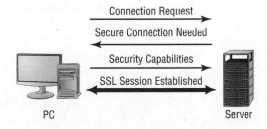

SSL VPN is really the process of using SSL to create a Virtual Private Network (VPN).
A VPN is a secured connection between two systems that would otherwise have to connect
to each other through a non-secured network. Here's what I mean. Even though I'd never
really let this happen, let's just say I could connect to the servers in my corporate office
through the Internet like, snap! You know by now that this would be a very bad thing
because the Internet is far from secure, right? But if I connected to those servers using a
VPN with a tunneling protocol instead, anything I send from my PC to my corporate office
would be locked up nice and securely.

Plus, VPNs also come in handy for data that's being sent within a private network that you
probably wouldn't want everyone on that network to be able to see. Maybe you want a few
specific computers on the intranet to be able to communicate with each other securely—like

say, the computers used by your top finance people. You wouldn't necessarily want that data just sent off in the clear to be viewed by the office gossip, now would you? No way. So, you can put those finance folks on a VPN that's just like having them on their own little private, secure subnetwork. Plus, what's even cooler about this setup is that the members of your intranet's VPN can still communicate with everyone else whenever they want; they just won't be doing that securely—nice solution!

L2TP

Next, we have the *Layer 2 Tunneling Protocol (L2TP)*, which was created by the Internet Engineering Task Force (IETF). It comes in handy for supporting non-TCP/IP protocols in VPNs over the Internet. L2TP is actually a combination of Microsoft's Point-to-Point Tunneling Protocol (PPTP) and Cisco's Layer 2 Forwarding (L2F) technologies. A nice L2TP feature is that because it works way down there at the Data Link layer (Layer 2) of the OSI model, it can support tons of protocols beyond just TCP/IP—a couple of biggies being Internetwork Packet Exchange (IPX) and AppleTalk. It's a really great tool to implement if you happen to have two non-TCP/IP networks that need to be connected via the Internet.

PPTP

I just mentioned *Point to Point Tunneling Protocol (PPTP)*, and even though I said, "Microsoft's PPTP," this security protocol was really developed jointly by Microsoft, Lucent Technologies, 3COM, and a few other companies. Oh, and it's not actually sanctioned by the IETF, but that doesn't mean it doesn't work. PPTP acts by combining an unsecured Point to Point Protocol (PPP) session with a secured session using the *Generic Routing Encapsulation (GRE) protocol.*

Because PPTP uses two different protocols, it actually opens up two different network sessions: so be warned, it can give you some grief when passing through a router. This is a big reason you won't find it around much nowadays. Another reason it's going the way of the dinosaurs is that it originally gained popularity because it was the first VPN protocol to be supported by Microsoft's dial-up networking services, and not too many of us depend on dial-up to get to the Internet anymore. As if these aren't reasons enough for PPTP's impending extinction, it's also not that secure. In fact, as you'd probably expect from a first-generation security protocol, it's now really vulnerable to spoofing attacks, which is why it's pretty much been replaced by L2TP and IPSec.

 PPTP is a VPN protocol that runs over port 1723 and allows encryption to be done at the Application (data) level. It is important to remember for the CompTIA Network+ objectives that PPTP is a protocol that allows secure access to a VPN.

IPSec

On the other hand, IP Security (IPSec) was designed by the IETF for providing authentication and encryption over the Internet. It works at the Network layer of the OSI model (Layer 3) and secures all applications that operate in the layers above it. Because it's sanctioned by the IETF and designed to work with IPv4 and IPv6, it's got a huge amount of industry support, so it's the standard for VPNs on the Internet today.

The two major protocols you'll find working in IPSec are the *Authentication Header (AH)* and *Encapsulating Security Payload (ESP)*. AH serves up authentication services only—no encryption—but ESP provides both authentication and encryption abilities.

 The AH protocol within IPSec isn't compatible with networks running Network Address Translation (NAT).

IPSec works in two modes: transport mode and tunneling mode. Transport mode is the simpler of the two because all it does is create a secure IP connection between two hosts. The data is protected by authentication and/or encryption, but in this mode, a tunnel isn't created. Figure 13.4 illustrates a TCP/IP packet and a TCP/IP packet in transport mode using AH.

FIGURE 13.4   TCP/IP packet in IPSec transport mode with AH

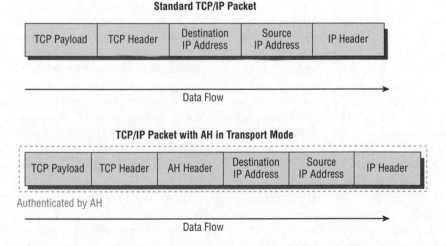

On the other hand, in tunnel mode, the complete packet is encapsulated within IPSec, which makes sense if you think about what's really going on inside a VPN. And because ESP gives us both authentication and encryption, it's more commonly used to create secure tunnels. Figure 13.5 first shows a TCP/IP packet and then depicts one using ESP in tunnel mode.

You can see here that when data is tunneled in this way, hackers can't even see what transport protocol you're using, let alone decipher the data you're transmitting.

FIGURE 13.5   TCP/IP packet in IPSec tunnel mode with ESP

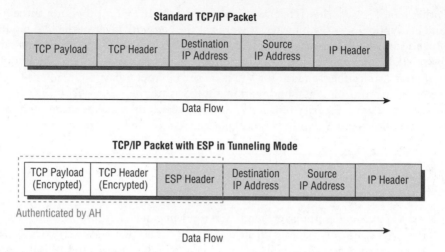

Encryption

Sometimes, like it or not, sending out corporate financial and other types of sensitive and data over the Internet just can't be avoided. This is why being able to hide or encode that data with encryption technologies is so vital for shielding it from the prying eyes of a company's competitors, identity thieves—anyone who wants to take a look. Without encryption, our sensitive files and information are essentially being paraded on full display as the data courses over the Internet.

Encryption works by running the data (which when encoded is represented as numbers) through a special encryption formula called a *key* that the designated sending and receiving devices both "know." When encrypted data arrives at its specified destination, the receiving device uses that key to decode the data back into its original form.

Back in 1979, the NSA classified encryption tools and their associated formulas as munitions, so it's overseen their regulation ever since. The dangerous possibility that hostile nations, terrorists, and criminals may use encrypted communications to plan crimes and go undetected is the compelling reason for doing so. It's also the reason that we're only allowed to export weak encryption methods that are no match for those designed commercially overseas.

This brings up an important question: Exactly how do we measure an encryption algorithm's strength? One way to do that is to measure its bit strength. Until 1998, only software with 40-bit strength or less could be exported; but today, the bar has been raised to 64-bit strength. And by the way, exporting any software with a key length greater than 64 bits is subject to review by the Export Administration Regulations (EAR) required by the U.S. Department of Commerce Bureau of Industry and Security. This doesn't include exporting to every country because some—like most of those in Western Europe plus Canada, Australia, and Japan—are countries we trust with the technology. But if you happen to be curious or just want to be really careful, check out the current regulations at `www.access.gpo.gov/bis/index.html`. Remember, these regulations aren't there to make life a hassle; they're in place to protect us. The greater the number of bits that are encrypted, the tougher it is to crack the code.

 Clearly, the security of monetary transfers is extremely important. The NSA does allow U.S. banks to use more secure encryption methods for this reason, and to ensure that they communicate very securely with their overseas branches, customers, and affiliates.

Encrypting passwords being sent from a workstation to a server at login is the most basic need for internal networks, and it's done automatically by most network operating systems today. But legacy utilities like File Transfer Protocol (FTP) and Telnet don't have the ability to encrypt passwords. Most email systems also give users the option to encrypt individual (or all) email messages, and third-party software packages like Pretty Good Privacy (PGP) are used by any email systems that don't come with encryption abilities of their own. And you already know how critical encryption is for data transmission over VPNs. Last but not least, encryption capability is clearly very important for e-commerce transactions, online banking, and investing.

I mentioned this earlier, but I didn't tell you exactly what it is: an encryption key is essentially a table or formula that defines a specific character in the data that translates directly to the key. Encryption keys come in two flavors: public and private. I'm going to tell you how each one is used next.

Private Encryption Keys

Private keys are commonly referred to as *symmetrical keys*. Using private-key encryption, both the sender and receiver have the same key and use it to encrypt and decrypt all messages, just as I described earlier. The downside of this technique is that it makes hard to initiate communication the first time—how do you securely transmit the private key to each user? You jump this hurdle by using public keys, and I'll get to those in a minute. First, there are a few more things you need to know about private keys.

The Data Encryption Standard (DES)

Kudos go to IBM for coming up with one of the most widely used private-key systems: *Data Encryption Standard (DES)*. It was made a standard back in 1977 by the U.S government. If you want, you can look it up in the Federal Information Processing Standards Publication 46-2 (FIPS 46-2).

Basically, DES uses lookup and table functions, and it actually works much faster than public-key systems. It uses 56-bit private keys. RSA Data Systems once issued a challenge to see if anyone could break the key. A group of Internet users worked together to attempt the task, with each member dealing with a portion of the 72 quadrillion possible combinations. They succeeded and cracked the key in June 1997, after searching only 18 quadrillion keys. Their prize? Knowing they had succeeded when they read a plain-text message that said, "Strong cryptography makes the world a safer place."

Back in the day, DES was a great security standard, but its 56-bit key length has proved to be too short. As I said, the key was first cracked in June of 1997 a year later, one was cracked in just 56 hours; and in January 1999, a DES key was broken in a blazing 22 hours and 15 minutes! Not exactly secure, right? We definitely needed something stronger.

Triple Data Encryption Standard (3DES)

That's when *Triple Data Encryption Standard (3DES*, also referred to as TDES) came into its glory. Originally developed in the late 1970s, it became the recommended method of implementing DES encryption in 1999. As its name implies, 3DES is essentially three DES encryption methods combined into one.

So 3DES encrypts three times, and it allows us to use one, two, or three separate keys. Clearly, going with only one key is the most unsecure, and opting to use all three keys gives you the highest level of security. Three-key TDES has a key length of 168 bits (56 times 3), but due to a complex type of attack known as *meet-in-the-middle* it really provides only 112 bits of security. It gets worse farther down the food chain—even though the two-key version has a key size of 112 bits, it actually arms you with only 80 bits of effective security.

Another problem with 3DES is that it's slow. No one likes that, so the National Institute of Standards and Technology (NIST) believes that 3DES will only be an effective encryption standard until sometime around 2030. Even now, it's being phased out in favor of faster methods like AES.

The Advanced Encryption Standard (AES)

The *Advanced Encryption Standard (AES*, also known as Rijndael) has been the "official" encryption standard in the United States since 2002. It specifies key lengths of 128, 192, or 256 bits.

The United States government has determined that 128-bit security is adequate for things like secure transactions and all materials deemed Secret, but all Top Secret information must be encoded using 192- or 256-bit keys.

The good news is that the AES standard has proven amazingly difficult to crack. Those who try use a popular method involving something known as a *side channel attack*. This means that instead of going after the cipher directly, they attempt to gather the information they want from the physical implementation of a security system. Hackers attempt to use power consumption, electromagnetic leaks, or timing information (like the number of processor cycles taken to complete the encryption process) to give them critical clues about how to break the AES system. Although it's true that attacks like these are possible to pull off, they're not really practical to clinch over the Internet.

Public Key Encryption

Public key encryption uses the *Diffie-Hellman algorithm*, which employs a public key and a private key to encrypt and decrypt data. It works like this: The sending machine uses the receiver's public key (which is publicly known) to encrypt a message. The receiver then decrypts the message with their own private key. It's a one-way communication, but if the receiver wants to send a return message, it does so via the same process. If the original sender doesn't have a public key, the message can still be sent with a digital certificate that's often called a *digital ID*, which verifies the sender of the message.

Figure 13.6 shows public-key-encrypted communication between User X and User Y

Here's a cool factoid for you—*Diffie-Hellman* refers to all public-key algorithms. Whitfield Diffie and Martin Hellman from the Stanford Research Institute invented public-key encryption. They introduced the dual-key concept in their 1976 paper, "New Directions in Cryptography."

FIGURE 13.6   Public-key encryption

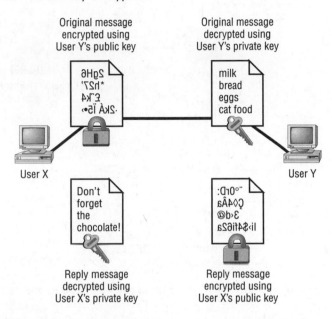

RSA Data Security

Rivest, Shamir, and Adleman (RSA) encryption is a public-key algorithm named after the three scientists from MIT who created it. They formed a commercial company in 1977 to develop asymmetric keys and nailed several U.S. patents. Their encryption software is used today by Netscape.

For more information about RSA Data Security, go to www.rsa.com.

Pretty Good Privacy (PGP)

In the early 1990s, Phil Zimmerman (also from MIT) wrote most of the code for this freely available version of public-key encryption designed to encrypt data for email transmission. Zimmerman basically compared email to postcards, because anyone can read email messages traversing the Internet just like postcards traveling through the postal service. By contrast, he compared an encrypted message to a letter mailed inside an envelope. Figure 13.7 shows the PGP encryption system.

FIGURE 13.7 The PGP encryption system

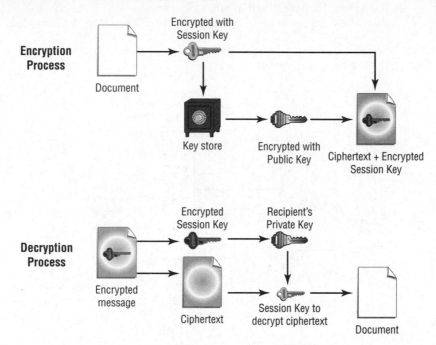

Zimmerman distributed the software for personal use only; and as the name implies, it's really pretty good security.

RSA Data Security and the U.S. federal government both had a problem with Zimmerman's product—the RSA complained about patent infringement, and the government actually decided to prosecute Zimmerman for exporting munitions-grade software. The government eventually dropped the charges, and now a licensing fee is paid to RSA; so today, PGP and other public-key-related products are readily available.

Don't let the name fool you! PGP is a highly secure encryption standard.

Remote Access

Think of remote access as a telecommuting tool, because it's used by companies to allow employees to connect to the internal network and access resources that aren't in the office. Remote access is great for users who work from home or travel frequently; but clearly, to a stalking hacker, an unsecured remote-access connection is like stealing candy from a baby.

Using remote access requires a server configured to accept incoming calls and also requires remote-access software to be installed on the client. Microsoft Windows operating systems since Windows 95 have had remote-access client software built in, and there are many third-party remote access clients available as well. Several different methods exist to create remote-access connections.

RAS

Remote Access Services (RAS) is not a protocol but refers to the combination of hardware and software required to make a remote-access connection. The term was popularized by Microsoft when the company began referring to its Windows NT–based remote-access tools under this name. Users would dial in via a modem, be authenticated by the server, and then be asked for their username and password just as if they were on the local network. Once logged in, users had access to data on the internal network just as if they were logged in locally. Figure 13.8 gives you an idea of what this would look like.

FIGURE 13.8 A typical remote-access connection between a remote user and a server

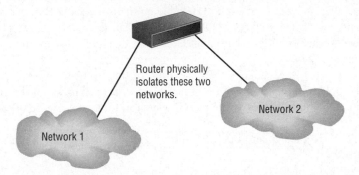

RAS itself was not secure; but there are options within RAS to include a secure protocol for tunneling, such as PPTP, and for authentication, such as Microsoft Challenge Handshake Authentication Protocol (MS-CHAP) and Extensible Authentication Protocol (EAP). RAS is versatile because it supports several other network protocols in addition to TCP/IP.

RDP

Remote Desktop Protocol (RDP) allows users to connect to a computer running Microsoft's Terminal Services, but a remote computer must have the right kind of client software installed for this to happen. Most Windows–based operating systems include an RDP client, and so do most other major operating systems like Linux, Solaris, and Mac OS X. Microsoft's RDP client software is called either Remote Desktop Connection (RDC) or Terminal Services Client (TSC).

After establishing a connection, the user sees a *terminal window* that's basically a preconfigured window that looks like a Windows or other operating system's desktop. From there, the user on the client computer can access applications and files available to them by using the remote desktop.

The most current version of RDP is RDP 6.1, released in February 2008. When logged in using RDP, clients are able to access local files and printers from the remote desktop just as if they were logged into the network. RDP offers 128-bit encryption using the RC4 encryption algorithm and also offers TLS 1.0 support.

PPP

Point to Point Protocol (PPP) is a Layer 2 protocol that provides authentication, encryption, and compression services to clients logging in remotely. ISPs use PPP a lot to authenticate clients dialing in with a modem and a DSL or cable modem. Many network servers that provide remote-access services (such as RAS) can also use PPP as an authentication protocol.

PPPoE

Point to Point Protocol over Ethernet (PPPoE) is an extension of PPP. Its purpose is to encapsulate PPP frames within Ethernet frames.

The need for PPPoE was born out of the need to deal with the massive increase in high-speed Internet connections. Service providers offering customers high-speed access using Asymmetric Digital Subscriber Line (ADSL) or cable modems needed a way to offer the authentication and encryption services of PPP. A Remote Authentication Dial In User Service (RADIUS) server—something I'll get into a bit later in this chapter—is commonly used to manage PPPoE connections.

PPPoE works in two stages: discovery and session. In the discovery phase, the MAC addresses of each of the connection's end points are given to each other so that a secure PPP connection can be made. During this phase, a session ID is also created that's used to facilitate further data transmission during the session. When the MAC addresses of each end point are known to each other, a point-to-point connection is created; the session stage begins at this time.

VNC

Virtual Network Computing (VNC) is a graphical desktop-sharing system. It uses the remote frame buffer (RFB) protocol to allow you to remotely control a computer that's at another location. When you do this, whatever you're doing on your keyboard and mouse is transmitted over the network to a specific computer, and the graphics are transmitted back to you accordingly. One of the best features of VNC is that it's platform independent—as long as the client has a VNC viewer installed, it can connect to a VNC server regardless of the type of operating system running on the other machine. Also, more than one VNC client can connect to a VNC server at the same time—cool!

These are exactly the capabilities that make VNC such a great tool for troubleshooting computers remotely. In fact, it's the most common thing that VNC is used for today. Here's an example: Let's say you work at the help desk, and a user calls you saying they've got a problem with their workstation in some other part of the building. Using VNC, you can connect to that workstation remotely, take control of the machine, troubleshoot the issue, and fix it. This is all good, but there's one drawback associated with VNC: the RFB protocol it uses just isn't secure. But this problem can be resolved by tunneling VNC through a secure protocol like SSH or even a VPN connection.

ICA

Independent Computing Architecture (ICA) is a protocol designed by Citrix Systems to provide communication between servers and clients. The most common application that uses ICA is Citrix's WinFrame, which administrators can use to set up Windows applications on a Windows–based server and then use to allow clients with virtually any operating system to access those applications. Client computers running Linux, UNIX, or Mac OSs can access Windows–based applications with the help of WinFrame, giving network administrators all kinds of flexibility with client operating systems. But again, there's a downside—connections like these tend to be slow because of the huge amount of translation that's required to enable the client and server to communicate with each other properly.

Managing User Account and Password Security

A whole bunch of authentication schemes are used today, and although it's important to know about these different schemes and how they work, all that knowledge doesn't equal power if your network's users aren't schooled on how to manage their account names and passwords correctly. This is because if bad guys get their hands on usernames and passwords, it gives them a way to get into your network. Worse, if a hacker gains the administrator account name and password for your network, it doesn't matter what authentication protocol or server you're using—that hacker isn't just going to get in, they're going to get in armed with the escalated rights that type of account allows, meaning they can do some serious damage.

With that in mind, let's get into some solid ways to manage user accounts and passwords, and follow that up by talking about the key authentication methods in use today.

Usernames and passwords are vital to network security because their whole purpose is to control initial access to it. Even if the system administrator assigns individuals their usernames and passwords, users can and do often change them; so, you need to make sure your network's users know the difference between a good password and a bad one and how to keep their passwords safe from theft.

I'm going to cover the important security issues related to user accounts and passwords, including resource-sharing models and user account and password management in this section.

Network Resource-Sharing Security Models

You can secure files that are shared over the network in two ways:

- At the share level
- At the user level

Although user-level security is the preferred way to go because it gives you a lot more control over files, implementing share-level security is a whole lot easier to manage. Let's take a look at these two security models and their features.

Share-Level Security

Opting for share-level security makes you the god of assigning passwords to individual files or other network resources like printers instead of assigning rights to individual users. You then give these passwords to all users who need access to specific resources. The problem is, these resources are visible from anywhere in the network, and any user who knows the password for a particular network resource can make changes to it; and, worse, this security method gives the network support staff no way of knowing exactly who is manipulating each resource. This means that share-level security is really practical to use only in smaller networks where resources are more easily tracked.

It also means that because of its limitations, we don't use it very much any more. Yes, it's easy to set up, but it's a nightmare to manage if you have more than about ten computers; and for all that hassle, it's still impossible to track who accessed what resources. Basically, it's just a pretty weak solution.

User-Level Security

In a network that uses user-level security, rights to network resources like files, directories, and printers get assigned to specific users who gain access to them through individually assigned usernames and passwords. This means that only users who have a valid username and password that's assigned the appropriate rights to network resources can see and access those resources. User-level security gives you a lot more control over who's accessing which resources, but only if users don't share their usernames and passwords with others. This happens to be the most popular method for securing files, and it's used by most operating systems today.

Managing User Accounts

Okay—so your first step in managing access to network resources is through user accounts and the rights you assign to the network resources. Sys admins usually maintain user accounts on a daily basis, doing things like renaming accounts and setting the number of simultaneous connections. You can also specify where users can log in, how often, and when; plus, you can adjust how often their passwords expire and delimit when their accounts expire as well.

Disabling Accounts

This is important, so remember it—when a user leaves the organization, you have these three options:

- Leave the account in place.
- Delete the account.
- Disable the account.

The first option is not so good because if you just leave the account in place, anyone (including the user to whom it belonged) can still log in as that user if they know the password. This is clearly very bad security, but deleting the account presents its own set of problems too. If you delete an account and then create a new one, the numeric ID associated with that user (UID in UNIX, SID in Windows Servers) will be lost; and it's through this magic number that passwords and rights to network resources are associated with the user account. This can be a good thing—but if you create a new user account with the same name as the one you deleted, the identification number of the new account will be different from the old one, so none of its settings will be there for the new account.

This means that disabling an account until you've made a decision about what should happen to it is your best bet, because you'll probably just want to rename the account when someone new is hired. When you disable an account, it still exists, but no one can use it to log in. Another good time to disable an account is when someone leaves for an extended period, like for maternity/paternity leave or other medical reasons, or goes on sabbatical.

Because it's really common for companies today to have contract and temporary employees, you need to know how to manage temporary accounts that will be used for only a short time and then disabled.

Managing these accounts is easy—you just set the account to expire on the employee's expected last day of work.

Setting Up Anonymous Accounts

Anonymous accounts allow only extremely limited access for a large number of users who all log in with the same username—for instance, Anonymous or Guest. These logins are frequently used to access FTP files; you gain access when you log in with the username Anonymous and enter your email address as the password.

Sometimes people don't use their real email addresses. If you really want to know where a user is located on the Internet, use third-party software to verify IP addresses and Internet domain names.

It's obviously a very bad idea to use anonymous accounts for regular network access—you just can't track them. All Windows Server products from Windows NT on come with the anonymous account Guest disabled, and it's usually a good thing to leave it that way. During times that you want to enable that account, like at a public kiosk, make sure you carefully manage what the Guest account is able to access by implementing strict group policies.

Some web servers create an Internet user account to allow anonymous access to the website through which a user is allowed to access the web server over the network. The password is always blank, and you never see a request to log in to the server because it's done automatically. Without this kind of account, no one would be able to access your web pages.

Do not rename the Internet user account or set a password, because if you do so, the general public won't be able to view your website. If you want to secure documents, use a separate secure HTTP or Windows Server.

Limiting Connections

There is a good reason you want to limit how many times a user can connect to the network. Users should normally be logged in to the network for one instance, because they can only be in one place at a time. So if your system is telling you that someone is logged in from more than one place, it's probably because someone else is using their account. By limiting simultaneous connections to one, only a single user at a single workstation can gain access to the network using a specific user account. But there are times that some users need to log in multiple times to use certain applications or perform certain tasks; and if so, you can allow that specific user to have multiple concurrent connections.

You may also want to limit the specific location from which a user logs in, because most of the time, your users will be logging on to the network only from their own workstations. This makes sense, but this rule isn't usually enforced because sometimes users move around without taking their computers with them, or they log in at someone else's station to get their jobs done. So unless you require super-tight security, imposing this rule can really complicate your job because it requires a lot of administration. Windows Server products can limit which station(s) a user is allowed to log in from, but they don't do so by default. Another Windows Server default feature is that average users aren't allowed to log in at the Server console because they shouldn't be working directly on a server. They can do some serious damage accidentally!

Renaming the Maintenance Account

Network operating systems automatically give the network maintenance (or administration) account a default name. On Windows Servers, it's (surprise) Administrator, and in UNIX it's Root. So it should be crystal clear that if you don't change this account name, bad guys already have half the information they need to break in to your network. The only thing they're missing is the password—yikes!

By all means, rename that account to something cool and creative that you'll remember but that would be really hard for someone to guess—and don't write it on a post-it and stick it to the server. Here's a "do not use" list of names:

- Admin
- Administrator
- Analyst
- Audit
- Comptroller
- Controller
- Manager
- Root
- Super
- Superuser
- Supervisor

- Wizard
- Any variation on the above

Managing Passwords

Like any other aspect of network security, passwords must be managed; and doing that involves ensuring that all passwords for user accounts follow security guidelines so bad guys can't easily guess or crack them. You've also got to implement certain features of your network operating system to prevent unauthorized access.

    Basically, a strong password is some combination of alphanumeric and special characters that's easy for you to remember but really hard for someone else to guess. Like server account names, they should never be written down and stuck into your desk or onto your computer. Unfortunately, this only happens in a perfect world—users invariably try to make things easy on themselves by choosing passwords that are so simple to guess, you'd have to be seriously mentally challenged not to be able to. Let's look at some characteristics of strong passwords.

Minimum Length

Strong passwords should be at least eight characters (the more, the merrier), but they shouldn't be any longer than 15 characters to make them easier to remember. You absolutely must specify a minimum length for passwords, because a short password is easily cracked—after all, there are only so many combinations of three characters, right? The upper limit depends on the capabilities of your operating system and the ability of your users to remember complex passwords. Here's what I call "The Weak List" for passwords—never use them!

- The word *password* (not kidding—people actually do this!)
- Proper names
- Your pet's name
- Your spouse's name
- Your children's names
- Any word in the dictionary
- A license plate number
- Birth dates
- Anniversary dates
- Your username
- The word *server*
- Any text or label on the PC or monitor
- Your company's name
- Your occupation
- Your favorite color
- Any of the above with a leading number

- Any of the above with a trailing number
- Any of the above spelled backward

There are more, but you get the idea, and these really are the most commonly used brainless passwords.

 Real World Scenario

Security Audits

A great way to begin a basic security audit to get a feel for any potential threats to your network is to simply take a walk through the company's halls and offices. I've done this a lot, and it always pays off, because invariably I happen upon some new and different way that people are trying to "beat the system" regarding security. This doesn't necessarily indicate that a given user is trying to cause damage on purpose; it's just that following the rules can be a little inconvenient—especially when it comes to adhering to strict password policies. Your average user just doesn't get how important their role is in maintaining the security of the network (maybe even their job security as well) by sticking to the network's security policy, so you have to make sure they do.

Think about it. If you can easily discover user passwords just by taking a little tour of the premises, so can a bad guy; and once someone has a username and a password, it's pretty easy to hack into resources. I wasn't kidding about people slapping stickies with their usernames and/or passwords right on their monitors—this happens a lot more than you would think. Some users, thinking they're actually being really careful, glue them to the back of their keyboards instead; but you don't have to be James Bond to think about looking there either, right? People wouldn't think of leaving their cars unlocked with the windows down and the keys in the ignition, but that's exactly what they're doing by leaving sensitive info anywhere on or near their workstations.

Even though it might not make you Mr. or Ms. Popularity when you search workspaces or even inside desks for any notes with interesting or odd words written on them, do it anyway. People will try to hide these goodies anywhere. Or sometimes, not so much. I kid you not—I had a user who actually wrote his password on the border of his monitor with a Sharpie; and when his password expired, he just crossed it off and wrote the new one underneath it (sheer genius!). But my personal favorite was when I glanced at this one guy's keyboard and noticed that some of the letter keys had numbers written on them. All you had to do was follow the numbers that (surprise!) led straight to his password. Oh sure—he'd followed policy to the, ahem, letter by choosing random letters and numbers, but a lot of good that did—he had to draw himself a little map in plain sight on his keyboard to remember the password.

So, like it or not, you've got to walk your beat to find out if users are managing their accounts properly. If you find someone doing things the right way, praise them for it openly. If not, it's time for more training—or maybe worse, termination.

Using Characters to Make a Strong Password

The good news is that solid passwords don't have to be in ancient Mayan to be hard to crack. They just need to include a combination of numbers, letters, and special characters—that's it. Special characters aren't letters or numbers, but symbols like $ % ^ # @). Here's an example of a strong password: tqbf4#jotld. Looks like gibberish; but remember that famous sentence, "The quick brown fox jumped over the lazy dog"? Well, this particular password uses the first letter of each word in that sentence with a 4# thrown in the middle of it. Sweet—solid and easy to remember. You can do this with favorite quotes, song lyrics, and so on, with a couple of numbers and symbols stuck in the middle. Just make sure you don't sing the song or quote Shakespeare every time you log in!

If you want to test the strength of passwords to make sure they're nice and tight, you can use auditing tools like crack programs that try to guess passwords. Clearly, if that program has a really tough time or even fails to crack the password, you've got a good one. By the way, don't just use a regular word preceded by or ending with a special character, because good crack programs strip off the leading and trailing characters during decryption attempts.

Password-Management Features

All network operating systems include built-in features for managing passwords to help ensure that your system remains secure and that passwords cannot be easily hacked with crack programs. These features usually include automatic account lockouts and password expiration.

Automatic Account Lockouts

Hackers, and even people who forget their passwords, usually try to log in by guessing passwords. This is why most network operating systems will lock you out after a few unsuccessful attempts. Some will even disable the account. Once that happens, the user won't be able to log in to that account even if they enter the correct password. This feature prevents a potential hacker from running an automated script to crack account passwords by continuously attempt logins using different character combinations.

When an account is on lockdown, guards—I mean, network staff—will have to unlock the account if the network operating system doesn't unlock it after a preset period. In any high-security network, it's a good idea to require an administrator to manually unlock every locked account instead of setting the network operating system to do it automatically. This way, the administrator will be sure to know about any possible security breaches.

WARNING   Be careful not to lock yourself out. With many network operating systems, only administrators can reset passwords, so if you happen to be the administrator and you lock yourself out, only another administrator can unlock your account. Embarrassing, yes, but what If you're the only administrator? You're in trouble then, because even though many network operating system vendors do have solutions to this humiliating little problem, the cost of that solution isn't going to be cheap!

It's good to know that Windows-based servers allow you to configure accounts to be locked out after a number of bad login attempts, but the default Administrator account is exempt from this happening. This might sound convenient for you, but it's actually a security risk. You should definitely rename this account, and it's also a good idea not to use it for day-to-day administration. Create a new administrator account (with a different name, of course), and use it for administrative purposes instead.

Password Expiration and Password Histories

Unlike a good wine, even really good passwords don't age well over time; they just become more likely to be cracked. This is why it's good to set passwords so that they expire after a specific amount of time. Most organizations set up passwords to expire every 30–45 days, after which the network's users all must reset their passwords either immediately or during a preset grace period. The grace period is usually limited to a specific number of login attempts, or it may allow a couple of days.

By default, each network operating system delimits a specific password-expiration period that bad guys usually know about. So, make sure you reset that time period to something other than the default that works in accord with your security policy.

Older network operating systems allowed users to reset their passwords back to their original form after using an intermediary password for a while, but today's network operating systems prevent this by employing password histories that consist of a record of the past several passwords used by a specific user. This record prevents you from using any password that's stored in the password history. If you try, the password will fail, and the operating system will then request a password change. What this means to you, the sys admin, is that if your security policy dictates that passwords be reset every two weeks, you should make sure your password history can hold at least 20 passwords.

By the way, your more experienced users know about this history feature; and because coming up with a really tight password takes a little thought, when savvy users create ones they really like, they may have a hard time letting go. Maybe they just want to avoid the hassle of creating a tight new password and remembering it, so they'll try to find ways to get out of doing that by getting around the password-history feature. For instance, I knew one guy who actually admitted that he just changed his password as many times as it took to defeat the history log and then changed it one last time to his beloved, original password—all of which took him only about five minutes to accomplish.

You can force users to change their passwords to ones that are unique, because the latest operating systems require unique passwords and can, depending on the network operating system, store more than 20 passwords. This feature makes it a whole lot harder to revert to any previous passwords. But it's still possible for users to beat the system, so don't rely completely on it.

User-Authentication Methods

There are a number of authentication systems in use today, but I'm going to focus on the ones you're likely to be confronted with on the Network+ exam.

Public Key Infrastructure (PKI)

Public Key Infrastructure (PKI) is a system that links users to public key that verifies the user's identity by using a *certificate authority (CA)*. Think of a CA as an online notary public—an organization that's responsible for validating user IDs and issuing unique identifiers to confirmed individuals to certify that their identity can really be trusted. Figure 13.9 shows how the CA process works in relation to two users.

FIGURE 13.9   The certificate authority process

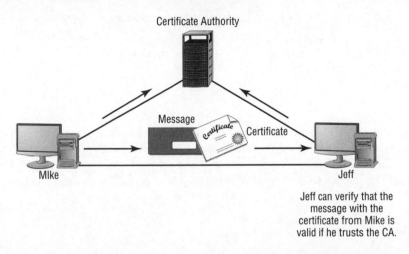

PKI allows people to communicate with each other with confidence that they're talking to who they think they are, to establish confidentiality and ensure message integrity without knowing anything about the other party prior to the conversation. It's also used to verify the digital signature of a public key's owner.

Public-key encryption operates through asymmetric cryptography, meaning that a different key is used to encrypt and decrypt the message, respectively. Symmetric cryptography uses the same key to encrypt and decrypt, so it's a lot less secure. Here's how it works. If I sent you a message using PKI, I'd use your public key to encrypt the message. When you received the message, you would use your private key, which is theoretically the only thing that can be used to decrypt the message back into something humanly readable. If a digital signature was required, you would sign the document with your private key, and anyone with access to your public key would be able to verify that the signature was truly yours. So clearly, you should be the only one who has access to your private key. Figure 13.10 illustrates what I just described.

FIGURE 13.10   PKI in action

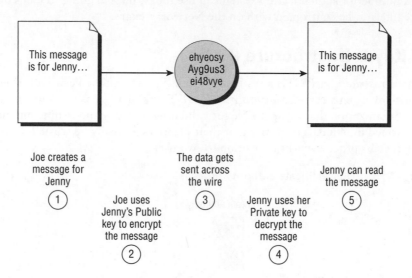

Public Key Encryption at work

This type of authentication is used a lot in websites that perform transactions. You've probably experienced shopping online and having an error message pop up, notifying you that a certain site's certificate or key has expired and asking if you want to proceed with the transaction. If you do, it's time to rethink things—you're probably way too trusting. Just say no!

Kerberos

Kerberos, created at MIT, isn't just a protocol, it's an entire security system that establishes a user's identity when they first log on to a system that's running it. It employs strong encryption for all transactions and communication, and it's readily available. The source code for Kerberos can be freely downloaded from lots of places on the Internet.

Kerberos works by issuing tickets to users who log in, kind of like going to an amusement park—as long as you've got your ticket to ride, you're good to go. Even though the tickets expire quickly, they're automatically refreshed as long as you remain logged in. Because of this refresh feature, all systems participating in a Kerberos domain must have synchronized clocks. This synchronicity requires a bit to set up, the real negative hits happen if you have only one Kerberos authentication server—if it goes down, no one can log in to the network! So, when running Kerberos, having redundant servers is clearly vital. You should also know that because all users' secret keys are stored in one centralized database, if that's compromised, you've got a security tsunami on your hands. Figure 13.11 shows Kerberos in action.

FIGURE 13.11 The Kerberos authentication process

Authentication, Authorization, and Accounting (AAA)

In computer security speak, *AAA* (triple A, like the auto club) refers to authentication, authorization, and accounting. *AAAA* is a more robust version that adds auditing into the mix. AAA and AAAA aren't really protocols; instead, they're systematized, conceptual models for managing network security through one central location. Two common implementations of AAA are RADIUS and TACACS+.

RADIUS

Although its name implies it, the *Remote Authentication Dial-In User Service (RADIUS)* is not a dial-up server. Like pretty much everything else, it originated that way, but it's evolved into more of a verification service. Today, RADIUS is an authentication and accounting service that's used for verifying users over various types of links, including dial-up. Many ISPs use a RADIUS server to store the usernames and passwords of their clients in a central spot through which connections are configured to pass authentication requests. RADIUS servers are client-server based authentication and encryption services maintaining user profiles in a central database.

RADIUS is also used in firewalls. Purposed this way, when a user wants to access a particular TCP/IP port, they must provide a username and a password. The firewall then contacts the RADIUS server to verify the credentials given. If successful, the user is granted access to that port.

 RADIUS is an authentication server that allows for domain level authentication on both wired and wireless network.

TACACS+

The *Terminal Access Controller Access-Control System Plus (TACACS+)* protocol is an alternative AAA method to RADIUS. Although based on its name you would think it's an extension of the TACACS protocol (and in some ways it is), but the two definitely are not compatible.

Here are two major differences between TACACS+ and RADIUS:

- RADIUS combines user authentication and authorization into one profile, but TACACS+ separates the two.

- TACACS+ utilizes the connection-based TCP protocol, but RADIUS uses UDP instead.

Even though both are commonly used today, because of these two reasons TACACS+ is considered more stable and secure than RADIUS. The process is very similar for all user-authentication methods, but TACACS+ and AAAA services include that nice extra accounting benefit.

Figure 13.12 shows how TACACS+ works.

FIGURE 13.12   TACACS+ login and logout sequence

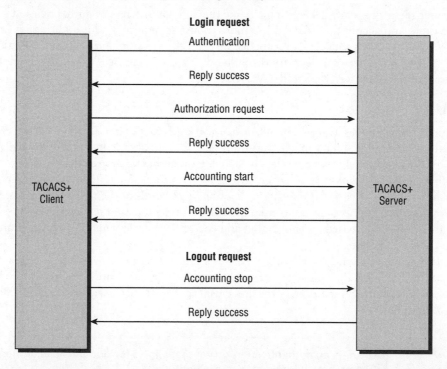

Okay—just to clarify things, in the IT world, *accounting* has nothing to do with money. Here's what I mean: When a TACACS+ session is closed, the information in the following list is logged, or accounted for. This isn't a complete list, it's just meant to give you an idea of the type of accounting information that TACACS+ gathers:

- Connection start time and stop time
- The number of bytes sent and received by the user
- The number of packets sent and received by the user
- The reason for the disconnection

The only time the account feature has anything to do with money is if your service provider is charging you based on the amount of time you've spent logged in, or for the amount of data sent and received.

Network Access Control (NAC)

Network Access Control (NAC) is a method of securing network hosts before they're allowed to access the network. The most common implications for NAC are in wireless networking, where nodes are often added to and removed from the network freely. One of the most common forms of NAC is IEEE 802.1x.

Even the Institute of Electrical and Electronics Engineers (IEEE) recognizes the potential security holes in wireless networking, so it came up with the *IEEE 802.1x* standard as a way to authenticate wireless users. 802.1x is an open framework that's designed to support multiple authentication schemes. Before a client, called a *supplicant* in 802.1x speak, can communicate on a wireless network, it asks the access point, or *authenticator* for permission to join, and then provides its credentials. The access point passes those credentials to a centralized authentication server that sends back an accept message to the access point if the authentication is accepted. Only then will the access point allow a user to connect to the wireless network.

Challenge Handshake Authentication Protocol (CHAP)

The *Challenge Handshake Authentication Protocol (CHAP)* is a secure authentication protocol because with CHAP, the username and password never cross the wire. Instead, both the client and server are configured with the same text phrase that's known as a *shared secret*. When a client sends out an authentication request, the server responds by sending a random value called a *nonce* plus an ID value back to the client. The client takes these two strings, sequences them with the shared secret, and then generates a one-way hash value using the Message-Digest algorithm 5 (MD5) encryption algorithm. This hash value is transmitted back to the server, which performs the same algorithm using the same values and shared secret. The server basically compares the hash value that it's received from the client with the hash value it has calculated, and if they match, the client gets to be authenticated. I know this sounds pretty complicated, so let me give you a visual demonstration of how CHAP works in Figure 13.13.

FIGURE 13.13   CHAP authentication process

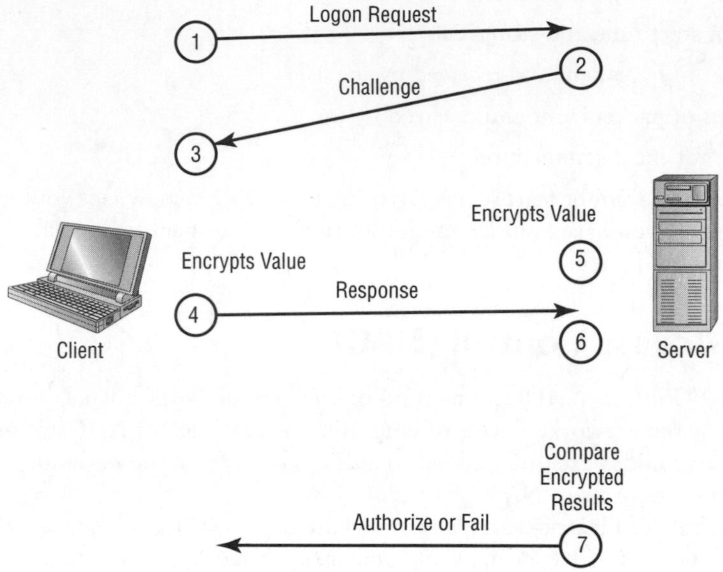

Logon Request

Challenge

Encrypts Value

Encrypts Value

Response

Client

Server

Compare
Encrypted
Results

Authorize or Fail

> CHAP has replaced the older Password Authentication Protocol (PAP) because PAP sends usernames and passwords in clear text and CHAP does not.

MS-CHAP

Microsoft has its own variation of CHAP known as *Microsoft Challenge Handshake Authentication Protocol (MS-CHAP)*. It works basically the same way as CHAP, except that unlike CHAP, which requires the shared secret to be stored locally in clear text, MS-CHAP encrypts the secret locally. And whereas CHAP provides authentication of the client by the server only, MS-CHAP version 2 is capable of mutual authentication so that the client can be sure the server is legitimate as well. Also, the encryption method used to generate the one-way hash in MS-CHAP is DES. Finally, and predictably, MS-CHAP doesn't work on Linux or other platforms—it's a Windows proprietary protocol.

Extensible Authentication Protocol (EAP)

Extensible Authentication Protocol (EAP) is an extension to PPP that provides a host of additional authentication methods for remote access clients. Some examples include smart cards, certificates, Kerberos, and biometric schemes like retinal scans and fingerprint and voice recognition. Although EAP itself doesn't allow for mutual authentication, enhanced forms of the protocol do. For example, EAP-TLS and EAP-TTLS, a tunneled version of EAP-TLS, create a secure tunnel through which password-based versions like EAP-MD5 can run.

Summary

In this chapter, you learned about the two most basic security concerns: security filtering and user authentication. First, we talked about how to allow remote computers to join your network and how to specify the way traffic leaves your network using access control lists. Then, you learned about various tunneling and encryption protocols like SSL, VPN, L2TP, PPTP, and IPSEC.

Moving on, we examined several of the ways used today to remotely access networks, including RAS, RDP, PPP, PPPoE, VNC, and ICA.

We wrapped things up by discussing solid user-account and password-management policies and why those policies are essential to maintaining tight security on your network. Finally, you learned about authentication methods like PKI, Kerberos, RADIUS, TACACS+, 802.1x, CHAP, MS-CHAP, and EAP—good stuff!

Exam Essentials

Know two ways you can filter traffic using an access control list.   Access control lists can filter traffic by IP address or MAC address.

Know which protocols can be used for tunneling and encryption of data.   Tunneling and encryption protocols include SSL, VPN, L2TP, PPTP, and IPSec.

Know which services allow you to remotely access computers across a network.   Remote-access services and protocols include RAS, RDP, PPP, PPPoE, VNC, and ICA.

Know different user-authentication protocols used on networks.   User-authentication protocols and systems include PKI, Kerberos, RADIUS, TACACS+, 802.1x, CHAP, MS-CHAP, and EAP.

Written Lab

In this section, write the answers to the following authentication and access-control questions:

1. What two types of addresses can access control lists filter?

2. Which encryption protocol works with both IPv4 and IPv6?

3. Which encryption protocol or standard allows you to create a virtual subnet on an intranet?

4. Which user-authentication method uses a public key and private key pair?

5. In an authentication system that uses private and public keys, who should have access to the private key?

6. Which authentication method relies on tickets to grant access to resources?

7. In computer security, what does AAA stand for?

8. Which network-access security method is commonly used in wireless networks?

9. Which user-authentication method is available only in an all-Windows environment?

10. Which user-authentication method utilizes the TCP protocol?

(The answers to the Written Lab can be found following the answers to the Review Questions for this chapter.)

Review Questions

1. To reduce the possibility of security break-ins from unauthorized users, which should be implemented?

    A. Packet sniffers

    B. Firewall

    C. Port scanners

    D. Intrusion detection system

2. What is the main difference between a private network and a public network?

    A. In a private network, everyone has access; in a public network, only authorized users have access.

    B. In a private network, only authorized users have access; in a public network, only authorized users have access.

    C. In a private network, only authorized users have access; in a public network, everyone that is connected has access.

    D. In a private network, everyone has access; in a public network, only the first 100 people have access.

3. You have a remote user that can connect to the Internet but not to the office via their VPN client. After determining the problem, which should be your next step?

    A. Have the client reboot their host

    B. Make sure the user has the correct VPN address and password

    C. Have the client reinstall their VPN software

    D. Reboot the router at the corporate office

4. Which IP Address should you deny into your internetwork?

    A. 126.10.10.0/8

    B. 168.0.0.0/8

    C. 128.0.0.0/8

    D. 127.0.0.0/8

5. Which of the following is a tunneling protocol?

    A. Layer 2 Tunneling Protocol (L2TP)

    B. Internet Protocol Security (IPSec)

    C. Secure Sockets Layer (SSL)

    D. All of the above

6. Which tunneling protocol is based on RSA public-key encryption?

   A. SSL

   B. L2TP

   C. IPSec

   D. SSL VPN

7. What is the minimum number of characters you should use when creating a secure password?

   A. 6

   B. 7

   C. 8

   D. 15

8. Which layer of the OSI model does IPSec operate in?

   A. Physical

   B. Network

   C. Transport

   D. Application

9. Which protocol works in both the transport mode and tunneling mode?

   A. SSL

   B. L2TP

   C. PPTP

   D. IPSec

10. Companies that want to ensure their data is secure during transit should follow what practice?

   A. Firewalls

   B. Encryption

   C. Data accounting

   D. Routing table

11. Which network utilities do not have the ability to encrypt passwords? (Select two.)

   A. FTP

   B. SSH

   C. Telnet

   D. SCP

12. To encode or read an encrypted message, what tool is necessary?

    A. Routing table

    B. Internet access

    C. Encryption key

    D. Email address

13. Which keys are known as symmetrical keys?

    A. Private

    B. Public

    C. Diffie-Hellman

    D. RSA

14. Which of the following is not a type of public-key encryption?

    A. Diffie-Hellman algorithm

    B. RSA Data Security

    C. Pretty Good Privacy (PGP)

    D. DES

15. Which of the following VPN protocols runs over port 1723 and allows encryption to be done at the data level, and allows secure access?

    A. RAS

    B. Radius

    C. PPPoE

    D. PPTP

16. At which stage of PPPoE are the MAC addresses of each of the end points of the connection given to each other so that a PPP connection can be made?

    A. Session

    B. Discovery

    C. Transport

    D. Final

17. A network administrator wanting to assign passwords to individual files, folders, or printers would implement which type of security?

    A. Building password

    B. Group password

    C. Share-level security

    D. User-level security

18. Which of the following authentication methods allows for domain level authentication on both wired and wireless networks?

   A. RADIUS

   B. TACACS+

   C. PKI

   D. RDP

19. Which user-client-server authentication software system combines user authentication and authorization into one central database and maintains user profiles?

   A. RADIUS

   B. TACACS+

   C. Kerberos

   D. PKI

20. Which of the following is not a Network Access Control method?

   A. CHAP

   B. 802.1x

   C. EAP

   D. ICA

Answers to Review Questions

1. B. A firewall protects a private network from unauthorized users on a public network.

2. C. On a private network, only authorized users have access to the data, versus a public network where everyone connected has access to the data.

3. B. After determining that the user has local network access, your next step would be to verify the VPN address and password.

4. D. To have good security on your network, deny any addresses from your internal networks, deny any local host addresses (127.0.0.0/8), deny any reserved private addresses, and deny any addresses in the IP multicast address range (224.0.0.0/4).

5. D. Tunneling is encapsulating one protocol within another protocol to complete a secure transmission. All of the above are tunneling protocols you should be aware of, as well as Secure Sockets Layer Virtual Private Network (SSL VPN) and Point to Point Tunneling Protocol (PPTP).

6. A. SSL is based on RSA public-key encryption and is used to provide secure Session layer connections over the Internet between a web browser and a web server.

7. C. The minimum length should be 8, and the maximum length should be 15. A strong password is a combination of alphanumeric and special characters that is easy for you to remember but difficult for someone else to guess.

8. B. IPSec works at the Network layer of the OSI model (Layer 3) and secures all applications that operate above it (Layer 4 and above). Additionally, because it was designed by the IETF and designed to work with IPv4 and IPv6, it has broad industry support and is quickly becoming the standard for VPNs on the Internet.

9. D. IPSec works in both transport mode and tunneling mode. In transport mode, a secure IP connection between two hosts is created. Data is protected by authentication or encryption (or both), but no tunnel is created. Tunnel mode encapsulates the entire packet within IPSec.

10. B. Companies that want to ensure their data is secure during transit should encrypt their data before transmission. Encryption is the process that encodes and decodes data.

11. A, C. Some older network utilities such as FTP and Telnet don't have the ability to encrypt passwords.

12. C. To encode a message and decode an encrypted message, you need the proper encryption key or keys. The encryption key is the table or formula that defines which character in the data translates to which encoded character.

13. A. Private keys are known as symmetrical keys. In private-key encryption technology, both the sender and receiver have the same key and use it to encrypt and decrypt all messages.

14. D. The Data Encryption Standard (DES) is not a type of public-key encryption.

15. D. PPTP is a VPN protocol that was created by Microsoft and uses port 1723 to encrypt data at the Application level.

16. B. PPPoE has only two stages: discovery and session. In the discovery phase, the MAC addresses of each of the end points of the connection are given to each other so that a secure PPP connection can be made.

17. C. This type of security is share-level security. You assign passwords to individual files or other network resources (such as printers) instead of assigning rights to users. All resources are visible from anywhere in the network, and any user who knows the password for a particular network resource can make changes to it.

18. A. RADIUS servers provide both authentication and encryption services and can combine these into one service. RADIUS can be used for allowing or denying access on both wired and wireless access at the domain level.

19. A. RADIUS combines user authentication and authorization into one centralized database and maintains user profiles.

20. D. Independent Computing Architecture (ICA) is a protocol designed by Citrix Systems to provide communication between servers and clients. ICA is a remote-access method.

Answers to Written Lab

1. IP addresses and MAC addresses

2. IPSec

3. SSL VPN

4. PKI

5. Only the owner of the key

6. Kerberos

7. Authentication, authorization, and accounting

8. 802.1*x*

9. MS-CHAP

10. TACACS+

Chapter

14

Network Threats and Mitigation

THE FOLLOWING COMPTIA NETWORK+ EXAM OBJECTIVES ARE COVERED IN THIS CHAPTER:

✓ **6.6 Identify common security threats and mitigation techniques**

- Security threats
  - DoS
  - Viruses
  - Worms
  - Attackers
  - Man in the middle
  - Smurf
  - Rogue access points
  - Social engineering (phishing)
- Mitigation techniques
  - Policies and procedures
  - User training
  - Patches and updates

It's true... You're not paranoid if they really *are* out to get you. Although "they" probably aren't after you, personally, your network—no matter the size—is seriously vulnerable, so it's wise to be very concerned about keeping it secure. Unfortunately, it's also true that no matter how secure you think your network is, it's a good bet that there are still some very real threats out there that could breach its security and totally cripple your infrastructure!

I'm not trying to scare you; it's just that networks, by their very nature, are not secure environments. Think about it—the whole point of a having a network is to make resources available to people who aren't at the same physical location as the network's resources. Because of this, it follows that you've got to open access to those resources to users whom you may not be able to identify. One network administrator I know referred to a server running a much-maligned network operating system as "a perfectly secure server until you install the NIC." You can see the dilemma here, right?

Okay, with all this doom and gloom, what's a network administrator to do? Well, the first line of defense is to know about the types of threats out there, because you can't do anything to protect yourself from something you don't know about. But once you understand the threats, you can then begin to design defenses to combat bad guys lurking in the depths of cyberspace just waiting for an opportunity to strike.

I'm going to introduce you to some of the more common security threats and teach you about the ways to mitigate them. I'll be honest—the information I'll be giving you in this chapter is definitely not exhaustive, because securing computers and networks is a huge task and there are literally hundreds of books on this subject alone. If you want to learn more about security on a much deeper level (and get another powerful certification in the process), get your hands on the *CompTIA Security+ Deluxe Study Guide* by Emmett Dulaney (Sybex, 2008).

For up-to-the-minute updates for this chapter, please see www.lammle.com or www.sybex.com/go/comptianetwork+studyguide.

Recognizing Security Threats

I'm not trying to freak you out, but I'm not exaggerating the dangers to your network security. Here's an example. Recently, I hooked up a friend's computer to a high-speed network connection from his phone company. He had antivirus software but no personal firewall in place yet, and before I could get that firewall set up (which usually takes about 10 minutes), he had 15 virus alerts pop up!

Although viruses are common threats that we hear about all the time, there are many other nasty things out there as well. Bad guys who create threats to a network generally have one of two purposes in mind: destruction or reconnaissance. They're seeking to destroy data or deny access, and maybe even nick information that you definitely don't want them to have. Some types of attacks can accomplish both, but they're usually combinations of simpler forms. In this section, we'll look at several common approaches that bad guys use to breach the security of our precious networks.

Denial of Service (DoS)

A *denial of service (DoS) attack* does exactly what it sounds like it would do—it prevents users from accessing the network and/or its resources. Today, DoS attacks are commonly launched against a major company's intranet and especially their websites. "Joe the Hacker" (formerly a plumber) thinks that if he can make a mess of, say, Microsoft's or Amazon's website, he's done that company some serious damage; and you know what? He's right!

Even though DoS attacks are nasty, strangely, hackers don't respect other hackers who execute them because they're really easy to deploy. It's true—even a pesky little 10-year-old can execute one and bring you to your knees. (That's just wrong!) This means that "real" bad guys have no respect for someone who uses DoS attacks, and they usually employ much more sophisticated methods of wreaking havoc on you instead. I guess it comes down to that "honor among thieves" thing. Still, know that even though a DoS-type attack won't gain the guilty party any esteemed status among "real" hackers, it still is not exactly a day at the beach to deal with.

Worse, DoS attacks come in a variety of flavors. Let's talk about some of them now.

The Ping of Death

Ping is primarily used to see whether a computer is responding to IP requests. Usually, when you ping a remote host, what you're really doing is sending four normal-sized Internet Control Message Protocol (ICMP) packets to the remote host to see if it's available. But during a *Ping of Death* attack, a humongous ICMP packet is sent to the remote host victim, totally flooding the victim's buffer and causing the system to reboot or helplessly hang there, drowning. It's good to know that patches are available for most operating systems to prevent a Ping of Death attack from working.

Smurf

Smurfs are happy little blue creatures that like to sing and dance, but a *Smurf attack* is far more nefarious. It's a version of a DoS attack that floods its victim with spoofed broadcast ping messages. I'll talk about spoofing in more detail later; for now, understand that it basically involves stealing someone else's IP address.

Here's how it works. The bad guy spoofs the intended victim's IP address and then sends a large number of pings (IP echo requests) to IP broadcast addresses. The receiving router responds by delivering the broadcast to all hosts on the network, and all the hosts on the network respond to the router with an IP echo reply—all of them at the same time. On a network with hundreds of hosts, this results in major network gridlock because all the machines are kept busy responding to each echo request. Figure 14.1 shows a Smurf attack in process.

FIGURE 14.1 Smurf attack in progress

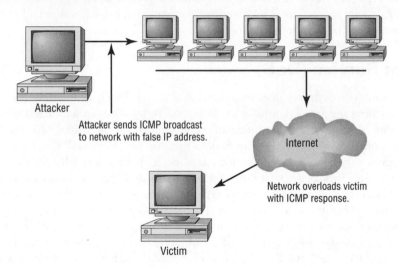

Fortunately, Smurf attacks aren't very common anymore because most routers are configured in a way that prevents them from forwarding broadcast packets to other networks. Plus, it's really easy to configure routers and hosts so they won't respond to ping requests directed toward broadcast addresses.

SYN Flood

A *SYN flood* is also a DoS attack that inundates the receiving machine with lots of meaningless packets. In normal communications, a workstation that wants to open a Transmission Control Protocol/Internet Protocol (TCP/IP) communication with a server sends a TCP/IP packet with the SYN flag set to 1. The server automatically responds to the request, indicating that it's ready to start communicating. SYN flags are only used to initiate new communications, so they don't get sent if you're in the middle of downloading a file. A new SYN packet is used only if you lose your connection and have to reestablish communication.

So, to initiate a SYN flood, a hacker sends a barrage of SYN packets. The receiving machine normally can't help itself and tries to respond to each SYN request for a connection and quickly depletes its resources trying to deal with the situation. This means that any further incoming connections to the victimized device will be rejected until it can respond to the barrage of connection requests it's already busy trying to deal with. Figure 14.2 shows an example of a simple DoS/SYN flood attack.

FIGURE 14.2   A sample DoS/SYN flood attack

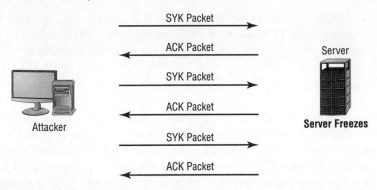

You can see that the preyed-upon machine can't respond to any other requests because its buffers are already overloaded, and it therefore rejects all packets requesting connections—even valid ones, which is the idea behind the attack. The good news is that patches to help guard against this type of attack are available for the various network operating systems today.

Tribe Flood Network (TFN) and Tribe Flood Network 2000 (TFN2K)

These nasty assaults are a bit more complex because they initiate synchronized DoS attacks from multiple sources and can target multiple devices. They're called *distributed denial of service (DDos) attacks* and also make use of IP spoofing. Figure 14.3 shows what a DDos attack would look like.

FIGURE 14.3   Distributed denial of service attack

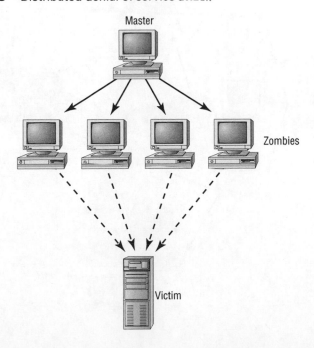

Stacheldraht

This is actually a mélange of techniques that translates from the German word for barbed wire. It basically incorporates TFN and adds a dash of encryption to the mix. The nightmare begins with a huge invasion at the root level, followed with a DoS attack finale.

Viruses

Viruses with catchy names like Chernobyl, Michelangelo, Melissa, I Love You, and Love Bug are probably the best-known threats to your computer's security because they get a lot of media coverage as they proliferate and cause tons of damage to legions of people. In their simplest form, viruses are basically little programs that cause a variety of very bad things to happen on your computer, ranging from merely annoying to totally devastating. They can display a message, delete files, or even send out huge amounts of meaningless data over a network to block legitimate messages. A key trait of viruses is that they can't replicate themselves to other computers or systems without a user doing something like opening an executable attachment in an email to propagate them. Figure 14.4 shows how fast a virus can spread through an email system.

FIGURE 14.4 An email virus spreading rapidly

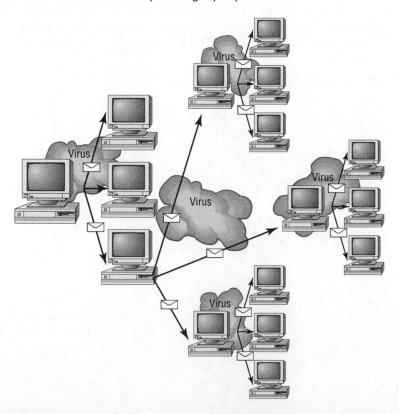

There are several different kinds of viruses, but the most popular ones are file viruses, macro (data file) viruses, and boot-sector viruses. Each type differs slightly in the way it works and how it infects your system. Predictably, many viruses attack popular applications like Microsoft Word, Excel, and PowerPoint because those programs are easy to use, so it's easy to create a virus for them. Unlike DoS attacks, writing a unique virus is considered a programming challenge, so the scoundrel who's able to come up with it not only gains respect from the hacking community but also gets to bask in the glow of the media frenzy that results from his or her creation and relish their 15 minutes of fame. This is also a big reason why viruses are becoming more and more complex and harder to eliminate.

Don't fall into the trap of thinking that just because you have a Mac, you don't need to worry about viruses. It's a common misconception that Mac operating systems are immune to viruses, but they're not. Today's Macs are really BSD Unix machines with a couple of proprietary programs running on top that provide users with a slick interface. And although it's true that more sophisticated programming skills are required to write viruses for Mac, BSD Unix, and Linux operating systems than for DOS-based operating systems like Windows, all operating systems are vulnerable to attacks. True, it's a lot easier for a bad guy to write malicious code for Windows machines; but the real reason few programmers spend their time creating viruses for Sun workstations and Macs is that there aren't nearly as many people using them. On the other hand, Windows machines are everywhere, so viruses written for them will clearly infect multitudes, giving bad guys who want to infect as many computers as possible a lot more bang for their evil programming buck!

File Viruses

A *file virus* attacks executable application and system program files like those ending in .COM, .EXE, and .DLL. These viruses do their damage by replacing some or all of the target program's code with their own. Only when the compromised file is executed can the virus do its dirty work. First, it loads itself into memory and waits to infect other executables, propagating its destructive effects throughout a system or network. A couple of well-known file viruses are Jerusalem and Nimda, which is actually an Internet worm that infects common Windows files and other files with extensions like .HTML, .HTM, and .ASP.

Macro Viruses

A macro is basically a script of commonly enacted commands used to automatically carry out tasks without requiring a user to initiate them. Some popular programs even give you the option of creating your own, personal scripts to perform tasks you do repeatedly in them in a single step instead of having to enter the individual commands one by one.

Similar to this, a *macro virus* uses something known as the Visual Basic macro-scripting language to perform nasty things in data files created with programs like those in the

Microsoft Office Suite. Because macros are so easy to write, they're really common and usually fairly harmless, but they can be super annoying! People frequently find them affecting the files they're working on in Microsoft Word and PowerPoint. Suddenly you can't save the file even though the Save function is working; or you can't open a new document, only a template. Like I said, these viruses won't crash your system, but they can ruin your day. Cap and Cap A are examples of macro viruses.

Boot-Sector Viruses

Boot-sector viruses work their way into the master boot record that's essentially the ground-zero sector on your hard disk where applications aren't supposed to live. When a computer boots up, it checks this area to find a pointer for its operating system. Boot-sector viruses overwrite your boot sector, making it appear as if there's no pointer to your operating system. You know you've got this type of virus when you power up the computer and get a Missing Operating System or Hard Disk Not Found error message. Monkey B, Michelangelo, Stoned, and Stealth Boot are a few examples of boot-sector viruses.

Multipartite Viruses

A *multipartite virus* is one that affects both the boot sector and files on your computer, making such a virus particularly dangerous and exasperatingly difficult to remove. Figure 14.5 gives you an idea how a multipartite virus works.

FIGURE 14.5   Multipartite virus

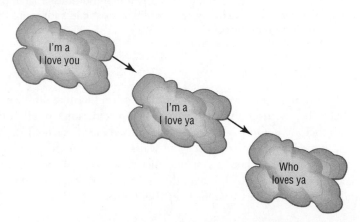

Anthrax and Tequila are both multipartite viruses. These viruses are so nasty that you might end up reformatting your computer if you get one. Although the anthrax virus was more of a hoax then a real virus, what is really interesting about the Tequila virus is that is does nothing until four months has passed after infection—it was no hoax!

Although many software companies can handle these, the best way to save your computer from a complete overhaul is to make sure you do not get a virus in the first place by using a good virus scan as well as Windows Defender (new on Vista and Server 2008).

Most of the viruses in one of these three categories infect your system through something known as a *Trojan Horse.* Just as Troy was successfully invaded by hiding troops inside a giant horse, a Trojan virus hides within other programs and is launched when the program it's lurking in starts up. DMSETUP.EXE and LOVE-LETTER-FOR-YOU.TXT.VBS are examples of known Trojan Horses. Displaying extensions for known file types can help spot naming tricks like these, but they're only a short list of the viruses out there. For a more complete inventory, see your antivirus software manufacturer's website.

Worms

Functionally, or not so much if your computer happens to have been infected with one, *worms* are a lot like viruses—only worse because they're much harder to stop. Worms can actively replicate without requiring you to do anything like open an infected file. Plus they can activate, propagate, and destroy all by themselves!

Attackers and Their Tools

The old adage "never talk to strangers" applies here, because you can't spot a hacker by looking at one. That quiet 15-year-old kid next door or the head of the P.T.A. could secretly be a criminal hacker (or *cracker*, in nerd-speak)—you just never know. But instead of living your life being suspicious of everyone you meet, it's much better to understand the ways and strategies bad guys use to infiltrate your defenses.

The interaction between a hacker and a network administrator can be anything from a harmless game of cat and mouse to a terrorist attack on national security. Either way, there's someone out there trying to break into or crash your system, and it's up to you to track and prevent the attacks.

Network attacks executed by an actual hacker are called *directed attacks*. For instance, a bad guy can use the WinNuke utility that I'll talk about soon to generate a packet and send it to a specific machine. On the other hand, viruses aren't usually directed attacks—instead they're just blindly copied from user to user.

I'll start by telling you about some common network attacks and then move on to cover the techniques used to prevent them from happening to you.

IP Spoofing

IP spoofing is the process of sending packets with a fake source address that makes it look like those packets actually originate from within the network that the hacker is trying to attack. This means that even a packet-filtering router is going to treat this packet as validly coming from within the network and pass it on. You need a firewall in place to prevent this type of packet from passing into your network. Figure 14.6 shows a hacker attempting an IP spoof with the spoofed IP address being denied access to the network by the firewall.

FIGURE 14.6   IP spoofing

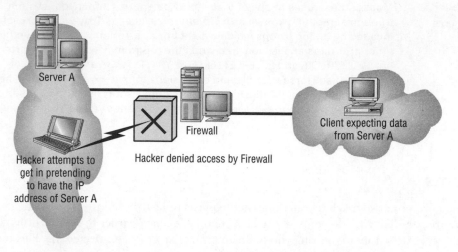

  Real World Scenario

Do We Really Need Firewalls?

Believe it or not, the honor system used to apply to the Internet, and it pretty much worked, so firewalls just weren't needed. Now, nothing could be further from the truth! Today, multitudes of companies have their entire corporate intranets connected to the Internet; plus, a legion of e-commerce sites like eBay, Amazon, and so on transfer seriously sensitive personal and financial data over the Internet. Corporate espionage and identity theft are currently the fastest growing crimes worldwide—evil deeds pulled off by bad guys lurking on the Net. So, we all need to practice "Safe Net," and one popular way to do that is by implementing firewalls on our networks.

Application-Layer Attacks

Application-layer attacks usually zero in on well-known holes in software that's running on our servers. Favorite targets include FTP, sendmail, and HTTP because the permissions level granted to these accounts is often privileged. This means that bad guys who break in not only gain access to your network but also get the added bonus of having privileged status while they're in there—yikes!

Active-X Attacks

A fairly new form of attack makes its way to your computer through ActiveX and Java programs (applets). These are miniature programs that run on a web server or that you download to your local machine. Most ActiveX and Java applets are safe, but some contain viruses, or snoop, or spyware programs. Snoop or spyware programs allow a hacker to look at everything on your hard drive from a remote location without you knowing about it, which is really bad; so be sure you properly configure the on-access component of your antivirus software to check and clean for these types of attacks.

Autorooters

You can think of autorooters as a kind of hacker automaton. Hackers use something called a *rootkit* to probe, scan, and then capture data on a strategically positioned computer that's poised to give them "eyes" into entire systems automatically. This is clearly very bad for you and your data. Note that this is typically how a cracker can attack a Mac or Unix box.

Backdoors

Backdoors are simply paths leading into a computer or network. From simple invasions to elaborate Trojan Horses, villains can use their previously placed inroads into a specific host or a network whenever they want to. That is, unless you can detect them and stop them in their tracks.

Network Reconnaissance

Before breaking into a network, bad guys gather all the information they can about it, because the more they know about the network, the better they can compromise it. This is called *network reconnaissance*. Hackers accomplish their objectives through methods like port scans, Domain Name Service (DNS) queries, and ping sweeps—even social engineering, or *phishing,* which I'll talk about in a bit.

Packet Sniffers

A *packet sniffer* is a software tool that can be incredibly effective in troubleshooting a problematic network but that can also be a hacker's friend. Here's how it works. A network adapter card is set to promiscuous mode so it will send all packets snagged from the network's Physical layer through to a special application to be viewed and sorted out. A packet sniffer can nick some highly valuable, sensitive data including, but not limited to, passwords and usernames, making such a tool a prize among identity thieves.

Password Attacks

Password attacks come in many flavors. Even though they can be achieved via more sophisticated types of attacks like IP spoofing, packet sniffing, and Trojan Horses, their sole purpose is to (surprise!) discover user passwords so the thief can pretend they're a valid user and then access that user's privileges and resources.

Brute-Force Attacks

A brute-force attack is another software-oriented attack that employs a program running on a targeted network that tries to log in to some type of shared network resource like a server. For the hacker, it's ideal if the accessed accounts have a lot of privileges because then the bad guys can form backdoors to use for gaining access later and bypass the need for passwords entirely.

Port-Redirection Attacks

A port-redirection attack requires a host machine the hacker has broken into and uses to get wonky traffic that normally wouldn't be allowed passage through a firewall.

Trust-Exploitation Attacks

Trust-exploitation attacks happen when someone exploits a trust relationship inside your network. For example, a company's perimeter network connection usually shelters important things like Simple Mail Transfer Protocol (SMTP), DNS, and HTTP servers, making the servers really vulnerable because they're all on the same segment.

Man-in-the-Middle Attacks

Interception! But it's not a football, it's a bunch of your network's packets—your precious data. A man-in-the-middle attack happens when someone intercepts packets intended for one computer and reads the data. A common guilty party could be someone working for your very own ISP using a packet sniffer and augmenting it with routing and transport protocols. Rogue ATM machines and even credit-card swipers are tools also increasingly used for this type of attack. Figure 14.7 shows a man-in-the-middle attack.

FIGURE 14.7   Man-in-the-middle attack

Client   Man in the Middle   Server

Rogue Access Points

Wireless network access has become quite common over the last several years, so properly securing a wireless network has become a critical task for most network administrators. With a wired network, you know where the cables start and stop; but with a wireless network, you're free from those bonds, which is great until someone you don't want is breathing *your* air.

A *rogue access point* is one that's been installed on a network without the administrator's knowledge. These can be unintentional—when a user innocently plugs a wireless router or wireless access point in to the end of a network cable in your building it is clearly unsecured, and so it's rogue. Of course, not all users—even valid ones on your network—are innocent, and they can also hook things up on purpose to facilitate an easy attack. Rogue access points are very useful to someone who wants to set up a man-in-the-middle attack.

Social Engineering (Phishing)

Hackers are more sophisticated today than they were 10 years ago, but then again so are network administrators. Because most of today's sys admins have secured their networks well enough to make it pretty tough for an outsider to gain access, hackers decided to try an easier route to gain information: they just asked the network's users for it.

Social engineering, or *phishing,* refers to the act of attempting to illegally obtain sensitive information by pretending to be a credible source. Common phishing tactics include emails, phone calls, or even starting up a conversation in person.

Some email phishing scams have made the news. There was this case where bad guys sent out a mass email that was all dressed up to appear as though the message actually came from a real bank. The email said that the bank had an issue with one of its servers, so they now required you to confirm your user-account information to verify that none of your data was lost. All you needed to do was click the link provided in the email and enter your information, and snap—your identity went poof! If you possess a working brain and someone you didn't know phoned and asked for your bank-account number, you certainly wouldn't give it to them, right? No way—but the same request, coming in the form of a really legitimate-looking email, seems more believable for some reason. This has become a popular phishing tool, notoriously used to separate people from anything from a few bucks to their entire identity. Be careful!

Oh, and speaking of phone calls… Let's say you get a call to your desk at work from "Joe" in IT. Joe says he's noticed some unusual activity on your network account and wants to check it out, but for security purposes he needs your permission first. So he proceeds to confirm your login, and then he tells you he needs to enter your password into the network tracker. He asks, "What's your password?" To protect yourself from this one, all you need to do is confirm *his* information and verify it with your IT department *before* you give him any of your data. You know by now that just because "Joe" knows your login doesn't mean he's on the up and up; even if "Joe" hangs up on you, you should still report the call to IT.

How did Joe get your login and telephone number? Remember network reconnaissance? First, because company phone directories are often on the Web, getting your phone number was easy. Even if it isn't published, maybe Joe did some earlier phishing by calling one of your co-workers and pretending to be a colleague at another site, and asked for your phone number. But what about the username? On most networks, your username is the same as your email address because that makes things easier for your sys admin. This means that knowing that information is probably just a good guess on the attacker's part. Maybe Joe the Hacker has gotten an email from someone at your company and knows what your email format is, plus some other information to help him figure out your network login. And even if the number on your caller ID when Joe called was an internal phone number, it doesn't mean a thing—remember IP spoofing? Well, you can do that with phone numbers too.

The golden rule is, don't ever give any of your information or anyone else's to anyone you're not absolutely sure should have it. And if they are someone who should have it, they probably already do, and they shouldn't be contacting you for it!

Understanding Mitigation Techniques

To be honest, I'm not going to go into detail about how to mitigate each and every one of the security threats I just talked about, not only because that would be outside the scope of this book, but also because the methods I am going to teach you will truly protect you from being attacked in general. You'll learn enough tricks to make all but the most determined bad guys give up on you and search for easier prey. Basically, think of this as a section on how to practice "Safe Net."

Safe networking techniques fall into three major categories: policies and procedures, training, and patches and upgrades. But before we go there, let's cover some of those general defense techniques I just referred to.

Okay—first know that there are three main ways to detect an intruder and defend yourself against one:

- Active detection, which involves constantly scanning the network for possible break-ins
- Passive detection, which involves logging all network events to a file
- Proactive defense methods, which involve using tools to shore up your network walls against attack

Active Detection

Active detection is analogous to a security guard walking the premises, rattling doors to make sure they're locked, and checking for intruders and any unusual activity. Similarly, there's special network software that searches for hackers attempting known attack methods and scans for the kind of suspicious activity and weird network traffic that hackers leave behind as they travel over the network. Some sophisticated active systems go a step further and take action by doing things like shutting down the communications sessions a bad guy is using, as well as emailing or paging you. Some security packages will even go as far as trying to cripple the computer the hacker is attacking from! Cisco's NetRanger, Memco's Session Wall, and Snort are all forms of active intrusion-detection software.

Passive Detection

Video cameras are a good example of passive intrusion-detection systems. Their counterparts in networking are files that log events that occur on the network. Tripwire for Unix systems is one of the earliest programs of this variety. Passive detection systems work by examining files and data and then calculating the checksums for each. These checksums are stored in a log file so that if the sys admin notices that a security breach has occurred on the network, they can access the log files to find clues about it.

Proactive Defense

A proactive defense is something you do or implement to ensure that your network is impenetrable. You can accomplish a lot through solid research and vigilant maintenance—you absolutely must stay current regarding any known security holes relevant to your type of network and the devices that populate it. You can use also tools like the unfortunately dubbed Security Administrator Tool for Analyzing Networks (SATAN) to find the holes in your security walls and plug them with software patches.

Clearly, before you can patch a hole, you've got to know it's there, right? This is why I said it's so important to stay current. Even better, stay a step ahead of bad guys by knowing your enemy's strategies, because the war against attackers is ever evolving—as soon as one hole is patched, bad guys will search for and find another vulnerability to exploit. And because patches usually take some time to develop, you can lose your shirt to a hacker in the interim. This is a big reason I'm saying it's a better idea for you to know thy enemy than to rely on patches and the like.

There is a host of great shareware and freeware available on the Internet today including Windows Defender, Spybot Search & Destroy, and Ad-Aware, as well as Windows Update.

Policies and Procedures

Every company should have written policies to effectively enable security on their computer networks. These policies should have the approval of the highest-ranking security or IT officer within the company, and they should address all aspects of the company network. Procedures should also be in place to determine the appropriate course of action in the event that there is a security breach. And all network administrators absolutely need to be thoroughly trained on all policies and procedures—no weak links.

All of this might sound a bit militaristic in nature, but it's truly necessary. Speaking of the military, though, the U.S. Department of Defense (DoD) has some really good standards that it wouldn't hurt you to keep in mind when setting up the security policies for your own network.

You can find the evaluation criteria for the DoD computer standards at http://www.niap-ccevs.org/cc-scheme/. In the past, this was known as the Rainbow Series (found at https://www.securecomputing.com/WBT/wbt-61/csec0001_r/module3/3mandatory.sb.html)because of the color of the books, but that's been replaced by the much less colorful Common Criteria Evaluation and Validation Scheme (CCEVS).

Security Policies

So what, exactly, is a *security policy*? Ideally, it should precisely define how security is to be implemented within an organization and include physical security, document security, and network security. Plus, you've got to make sure these forms of security are implemented completely and solidly, because if they aren't, your security policy will be a lot like a block of Swiss cheese—some areas are covered, but others are full of holes.

Before a network can be truly secure, the network support staff should post the part of the security policy that applies to employee conduct on bulletin boards, which should include things like forbidding posting any company and/or employee information that's not absolutely necessary—like, believe it or not, prohibiting anyone from sticking post-its with usernames and passwords on their computer screens. Really clean desks, audits, and recording email communications and, in some cases, phone calls, should also be requirements. And don't forget to post the consequences of not complying with the security policy, too.

Security Audit

Let me take a minute to explain all this a little more, beginning with security audits. A *security audit* is a thorough examination of your network that includes testing all its components to make sure everything is secure. You can do this internally, but you can also contract an audit with a third party if you want the level of security to be certified. A valid and verified consultant's audit is a good follow-up to an internal audit. One reason for having your network's security certified like this is that government agencies usually require it before they'll grant you contract work, especially if that work is considered confidential, secret, or top-secret.

Clean-Desk Policy

That clean-desk policy doesn't just end with "get rid of the crumbs from your last snack"; it means requiring that all potentially important documents like books, schematics, confidential letters, notes to self, and so on aren't left out in the open when someone's away from their desk. Instead, they're locked away, securely out of sight. And make sure it's clear that this rule applies to users' PC desktops, too. Policies like this apply to offices, laboratories, and workbenches as well as desks, and it's really important for employees who share workspaces and/or workstations.

It's super easy to nick something off someone's desk or screen. Because most security problems involve people on the inside, implementing and enforcing a clean-desk policy is a simple way to guard against security breaches.

 The International Computer Security Association (ICSA, www.icsa.net) reports that as many as 80 percent of all network break-ins occur from within the company and are carried out by employees, so protecting your data with a firewall is just the beginning of establishing network security.

It might sound really nit-picky, but for a clean-desk policy to be effective, users have to clean up their desks every time they walk away from them—without exception. The day someone doesn't will be the very day when some prospective tenant is being shown the building's layout, and a sensitive document suddenly disappears. You should make sure that workstations are locked to desks and do random spot checks once in a while to help enforce the policy. For obvious reasons, before company picnics and parties and before "bring your child to work day" are good times to do this.

The ICSA is a vendor-neutral organization that certifies the functionality of security products as well as makes recommendations on security in general.

Recording Equipment

Any recording equipment, like tape recorders, cell phones, and small-memory devices like USB flash memory keychains, can contain sensitive, confidential information, so a good security policy should prohibit their unauthorized presence and use.

Just walk into almost any large technology company, and you'll be immediately confronted with signs. A really common one is a camera with a circle surrounding it and a slash through the center of the circle. Read the text below the sign, and you'll be informed that you can't bring any recording devices onto the premises.

Here's a good example. The NSA has updated its policy to include prohibiting Furby dolls on government premises because they have reasonably sophisticated computers inside them complete with a digital recording device. The doll repeats what it hears at a certain interval of time, which is either cute or creepy, but pretty much harmless—maybe even protective—in a children's daycare center. Not so much at the NSA, though—no recording conversations there. Maybe, at least in some locations, it's not such a good idea for your company either.

Other Common Security Policies

So you get the idea—security policies can cover literally hundreds of items. Here are some common ones:

Notification   Security policies aren't much good if no one knows about them, right? So make sure you give users a copy of the security policy when you give them their usernames and passwords. It's also a good idea to have computers display a summarized version of the policy when any user attempts to connect. Here's an example: "Unauthorized access is prohibited and will be prosecuted to the fullest extent of the law." Remember—your goal is to close loopholes. One hacker actually argued that because a computer didn't tell him otherwise, anyone was free to connect to and use the system!

Equipment access   Disable all unused network ports so that any nonemployees who happen to be in the building can't connect a laptop to an unused port and gain access to the network. And don't forget to place all network equipment under lock and key.

Wiring   Your network's wires should never run along the floor where they can be easily accessed (or tripped over, getting you sued). Routers, switches, and concentrators should live in locked closets or rooms, with access to those rooms controlled by anything ranging from a good lock to a biometric access system, depending on the level of security your specific network and data require.

Door locks/swipe mechanisms   Be sure that only authorized people know the combination to the cipher lock on your data-center doors or that only the appropriate people have badges that allow access to the data center. Change lock combinations often, and never ever leave server room doors open or unlocked.

Badges   Require everyone to wear an ID badge, including contractors and visitors, and assign appropriate access levels to everyone.

Tracking   Require badge access to all entrances to buildings and internal computer rooms. Track and record all entry to and exits from these rooms.

Passwords   Reset passwords at least every month. Train everyone on how to create strong passwords. Set BIOS passwords on every client and server computer to prevent BIOS changes.

Monitor viewing   Place computer monitors strategically so that visitors or people looking through windows can't see them, and make sure unauthorized users/persons can't see security-guard stations and server monitors. Use monitor privacy screens if necessary.

Accounts   Each user should have their own, unique user account, and employees should never share user accounts. Even temporary employees should have their own account. Otherwise, you won't be able to isolate a security breach.

Testing   Review and audit your network security at least once a year.

Background checks   Do background checks on all network support staff. This may include calling their previous employers, verifying their college degrees, requiring a drug test, and checking for a criminal background.

Firewalls   Use a firewall to protect all Internet connections, and use the appropriate proxies and dynamic packet-filtering equipment to control access to the network. Your firewall should provide as much security as your company requires and that your budget allows.

Intrusion detection   Use intrusion-detection and logging software to discover security breaches, and be sure you're logging the events you want to monitor.

Cameras   Cameras should cover all entrances to the building and the entire parking lot. Be sure that cameras are in weather-proof and tamper-proof housings, and review the output at a security-monitoring office. Record everything on extended-length tape recorders.

Mail servers   Provide each person with their own email mailbox, and attach an individual network account to each mailbox. If several people need to access a mailbox, don't give all of them the password to a single network account. Instead, assign individual privileges to each person's network account so you can track activity down to a single person, even with a generic address like info@mycompany.com.

DMZ   Use a demilitarized zone (DMZ) for all publicly viewable servers, including web servers, FTP servers, and email relay servers. Figure 14.8 shows a common DMZ setup.

FIGURE 14.8   A common DMZ configuration

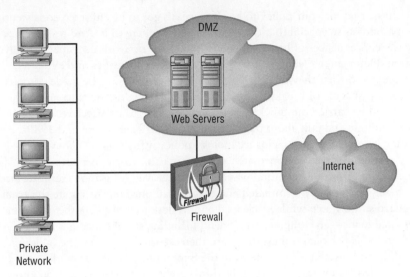

It is not advisable to put a DMZ outside the firewall, because any servers outside your firewall defeat the whole purpose having one, however, it is possible that you may see a DMZ outside the firewall in some networks.

Mail relay   Use a mail-relay server for email. Email traffic should never go straight to your production servers because that would enable a hacker to directly access your server as well. Use a relay server in a DMZ.

Patches   Make sure the latest security updates are installed after being properly tested on a nonproduction computer.

Backups   Store backup tape cartridges securely, not on a shelf or table within reach of someone working at the server. Lock tapes in a waterproof, fireproof safe, and keep at least some of your backups off site.

Modems   Do not ever allow desktop modems, because they allow users to get to the Internet without your knowledge. Restrict modem access to approved server-based modem pools.

Guards   If you need security guards, they shouldn't patrol the same station all the time. As people become familiar with an environment and situation, they tend to become less observant about that environment, so rotating guards to keep their concentration at the highest possible level makes a lot of sense. Clearly, guards are people who need breaks to ensure alertness, but make sure that all patrol areas are covered during shift changes, rotations, and breaks. Guards should also receive periodic training and testing to make sure they can recognize a threat and take appropriate action.

 WARNING   Believe it or not, covering all these bases still won't guarantee that your network or facility is secure. All of this is really just a starting point that's meant to point you in the right direction.

Breaking Policy

Okay—you know that for your policy to be effective it's got to be enforced consistently and completely. Nobody is so special that they don't have to adhere to it. And people have to understand the consequences of breaking policy, too. Your network users need to have a clearly written document, called a *security policy*, that fully identifies and explains what's expected of them and what they can and can't do. Plus, people must be made completely aware of the consequences of breaking the rules, and any penalties have to match the severity of the offense and be carried out quickly, if not immediately, to be effective.

Let's take a minute and talk about those penalties. As far back as the mid-1980s, employees were immediately terminated for major technology policy infractions. There was one guy from a large computer company who immediately got his pink slip when pornography was found on his computer's hard drive. The situation was handled decisively—his manager informed him that he was being immediately terminated and that he had one hour to vacate the premises. A security guard stood watch while he cleaned out his desk to make sure the employee only touched personal items—no computer equipment, including storage media—and when he had finished gathering his personal things, the guard then escorted him from the building.

Downloading and installing software from the Internet to your PC at work is not as major (depending on where you work), but from the things we've been over so far, you know that doing that can compromise security. Any Beta products, new software, and patches need to be tested by the IT department before anyone can use them, period! Here's an example. After an employee installed the untested Beta release of a web browser and rebooted their PC, the production Windows NT server at a national telephone company crashed. The resulting action was to revoke that employee's Internet FTP privileges for three months.

The Exit Interview

Sometimes, the importance of an employee's position and the amount of knowledge he or she has about the company and its systems requires an exit interview when they're terminated. It's done to minimize the risk of that employee being disgruntled and to attempt to ensure that they're leaving under the most favorable circumstances possible. The interview can include the IT manager, a human resources representative, a sys admin, and sometimes even security personnel.

When an employee leaves the company—whether they're quitting to move on to another job or being terminated—all company property needs to be turned in and logged. This includes things like company cell phones, pagers, toolkits, keys, badges, security tokens, models, and, obviously, all company documents.

And clearly, IT needs to disable all accounts immediately, including those for network access and voice mail, and remaining employees should be informed that the employee is leaving at this time as well. This is especially important when that employee has access to sensitive documents, because even if they're leaving under favorable conditions, they could still log in and copy data to take with them for their own use. For instance, salespeople can easily hurt a company by taking client information with them, and it has happened—a salesperson accessed his former company's voice-mail system and stole sales leads. So it's not just the obviously disgruntled ex-network administrator who could demolish your website after leaving that you need to be concerned about.

Security Procedures

A *security procedure* defines how to respond to any security event that happens on your network. Here's a short list.

- What to do when someone has locked themselves out of their account
- How to properly install or remove software on servers
- What to do if files on the servers suddenly appear to be "missing" or altered
- How to respond when a network computer has a virus
- Actions to take if it appears that a hacker has broken into the network
- Actions to take if there is a physical emergency such as a fire or flood

Security Training

This brings us to talking about the human element of network security. It's true that most of your users want to do the right thing to protect the company—and their jobs—from the prying eyes of hackers, but the problem is, people don't always know what the right thing to do is. That's why training is so vital. It can include classroom sessions and/or web-based training, but experience has shown me that actual classroom-based instruction works the best. It's also a good idea to have separate training classes for IT personnel and end users.

End-User Training

End-user training is pretty easy—it can take just an hour or so to bring employees up to speed. The "keep it short and simple" rule applies here, or you'll just end up with nap-time. This is a great time to include detailed security protocol training. But if you see eyes beginning to glaze over or hear anyone snoring, you might want to make security protocol training into a separate session because like I said, it's really important for the effectiveness of your security policy for everyone to know about and understand it. You can even use a year-end bonus or something else cool as a motivational reward for the employees who complete their training and test well on it.

And you've got to back up your training by providing your end users with hard-copy, printed reference manuals in case they forget something (which they will). Include things like

- Recommended policies for creating safe passwords
- The number to call if they've locked themselves out of their accounts
- What to do if they think someone is phishing for information
- What to do if they think their computer has a virus

Clearly, new employees to the company or division should be required to go through training, but requiring that everybody attend refresher courses is also a good idea. And don't hesitate to call a meeting if new threats arise or any sudden changes occur, to keep everyone up to date.

Administrator Training

Obviously, training sessions for your IT personnel have to be a lot more in-depth, because they'll be the ones who set up and configure policies, and they'll also be the first responders to any security emergency.

Some key things to cover with these people include every aspect of your security policy. And be sure they understand the correct ways to escalate issues in case of emergency. Reacting to a security emergency is pretty stressful, and you don't want your administrators to panic or feel isolated if one occurs. Making sure they know where their lifelines are and how to reach them quickly if they need backup will take off a lot of pressure when something nasty happens.

Patches and Upgrades

The operating systems and applications we use today are really just gigantic collections of computer code. Windows Vista has about 50 million lines of code, and Windows XP has 35–40 million lines of code. And if you look at the subsystems within Windows, you'll find that there are more than 50 dependency layers—processes that depend on other processes. Experts who work on developing Windows say that it typically takes someone about five years to fully learn two or three of these layers. So it's pretty easy to imagine that with that much code being created by a couple of thousand different people, sometimes a few things get mixed up—and that's the reason why there always seems to be a few holes, glitches, and bugs to fix.

The good news is, as operating systems and applications are released, their developers have a chance to catch and repair the problems they uncover. In addition, as hackers find and take advantage of vulnerabilities, software developers work to plug those holes. The repairs are usually released to the public as *patches* or *hot fixes*. To address large-scale issues or add major features and components to the program, companies release complete upgrades instead.

Here's where we get into the software side of security, which includes things like applying patches, hot fixes, and upgrades, plus how to choose and install the right third-party software to protect yourself against viruses.

Ensuring that your software is up to date is one of the best ways to protect against bad guys exploiting the security holes on your network.

Automatic Updates through Windows Update

It's really easy to get updates for Windows-based operating systems from Windows 2000 on, through Windows Update—a utility that's usually automatically installed when you install Windows. If you need to get more information, go to www.microsoft.com.

To ensure that Windows Update is enabled, go to your System properties (right-click My Computer and then choose Properties). You will see a screen similar to the one shown in Figure 14.9.

FIGURE 14.9   Automating Windows Update

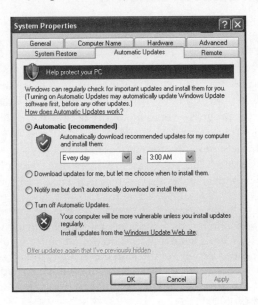

If you have Windows Update installed, it will periodically scan your system for the version of Windows components you already have installed and compare them to the most current versions available from Microsoft. If your software is out of date, a Windows Update dialog box will appear, asking if you want to install the software updates. If you click Continue, the installation will proceed in the background; you'll still be able to work in the foreground without skipping a beat.

Downloading Patches and Hot Fixes

If you don't have automatic update set up, you can download patches and hot fixes manually. A hot fix is just like a patch that updates software, but this term is reserved for a solution to potentially serious issues that could compromise your network and hosts. When a company like Microsoft has created a whole bunch of patches, hot fixes, and upgrades, it will put them together in a larger bundle called a *service pack*. For instance, you can download Windows XP Service Pack 3 (SP3) or Windows Vista SP1, which will update lots of components and address security, performance, and stability issues all at the same time. For the latest service pack for your Windows-based operating system or application, visit support.microsoft.com.

But let's say you think you have a smaller, specific issue, and you only want to download a patch for that particular problem. Maybe you're dealing with an issue with IPSec and you want to know about creating IPSec security filters in Windows XP. After surfing Microsoft's support site, you come across article KB914841 (support.microsoft.com/default .aspx?kbid=914841). (KB means Knowledge Base, and it's one way Microsoft organizes their support documents.) This article will give you background information as well as allow you to download hot fixes for the appropriate operating system you're running.

Updating Antivirus Components

A typical antivirus program consists of two components:

- The definition files
- The engine

The definition files list the various viruses, their types, and their footprints and tell you how to remove them. More than 100 new viruses are found in the wild each month, so it's easy to see that an antivirus program would be totally useless if it didn't keep up with all those emerging viruses.

The engine accesses the definition files (or database), runs virus scans, cleans the files, and notifies the appropriate people and accounts. Eventually, viruses become so sophisticated that a new engine, or even a whole new technology, is required to combat them effectively.

Heuristic scanning is a technology that allows an antivirus program to search for a virus even if there's no definition for it yet. The engine looks for suspicious activity of the kind that usually indicates the presence of a virus. But use such a tool with caution—if it's turned on, this scanning technique can mistake harmless or even necessary code that can give you some major grief.

For your antivirus program to work for you, you've got to upgrade, update, and scan in a specific order:

1. Upgrade the antivirus engine.
2. Update the definition files.
3. Create an antivirus emergency boot disk.
4. Configure and run a full on-demand scan.
5. Schedule monthly full on-demand scans.
6. Configure and activate on-access scans.
7. Make a new antivirus emergency boot disk monthly.
8. Get the latest update when fighting a virus outbreak.
9. Repeat all steps when you get a new engine.

I'm only going to cover the steps in this list that map to objectives of the Network+ exam, but looking into the others won't hurt and will give you some worthwhile knowledge.

Upgrading an Antivirus Engine

Okay—an antivirus engine is the core program that runs the scanning process and virus definitions are keyed to an engine version number. For example, a 3.*x* engine won't work with 4.*x* definition files. When the manufacturer releases a new engine, consider both the cost to upgrade and how much you'll benefit before buying it.

Before installing new or upgraded software, back up your entire computer system, including all your data.

Updating Definition Files

I'd recommend that you update your list of known viruses—called the *virus definition files* no less than weekly. You can do this manually or automatically through the manufacturer's website, and you can use a staging server within your company to download and distribute the updates or set up each computer to download updates individually.

Scanning for Viruses

An *antivirus scan* is the process that an antivirus program deploys to examine a computer suspected of having a virus, identify the virus, and then get rid of it. There are three types of antivirus scans, and to really make sure your system is clean, you should use a combination of the types I'm covering in this section:

On-demand scan   An *on-demand scan* is a virus scan initiated by you or an administrator that searches a file, a directory, a drive, or an entire computer but only checks the files you're currently accessing. I recommend doing this at least monthly, but you'll also want to do an on-demand scan

- When you first install the antivirus software
- When you upgrade the antivirus software engine
- Any time you suspect a virus outbreak

Before you initiate an on-demand scan, be sure that you have the latest virus definitions.

On-access scan   An on-access scan runs in the background when you open a file or use a program in situations like these:

- Insert a floppy disk or thumb drive
- Download a file with FTP
- Receive email messages and attachments
- View a web page

This kind of scan slows down the processing speed of other programs, but it's worth the inconvenience.

Emergency scan   During an emergency scan, only the operating system and the antivirus program are running. You initiate one of these scans when a virus has totally invaded your system and taken control of the machine. In this situation, insert your antivirus emergency boot disk and boot the infected computer from it. Then, scan and clean the entire computer.

If you don't have your boot disk, go to another, uninfected machine and create one from it. Another possibility is to use an emergency scan website like housecall.trendmicro.com, which allows you to scan your computer via a high-speed Internet access without using an emergency disk.

Fixing an Infected Computer

So what do you do if you know you've got a virus? First, you want to make sure to scan all potentially affected hard disks plus any external disks that could be infected. Establish a cleaning station, and quarantine the infected area. You'll have a really hard time doing this if anyone continues to use the computer while it is infected, so make sure all users in the infected area stop using their computers.

Then, remove all external memory devices from all disk drives and perform a scan and clean at the cleaning station. Update the virus definitions of any computers that are still operational. For the ones that aren't, or the ones that are still working but are infected, boot to an antivirus emergency boot disk. After you've done that, run a full scan and clean the entire system on all computers in the office space. With luck, you will be done before your users return from lunch.

WARNING   It's frustrating, but a lot of programs won't install unless you disable the on-access portion of your antivirus software. Clearly, this is dangerous if the program has a virus. If you want to be really safe, do an on-demand scan of the software before installing it. If things are all good, go ahead and disable on-access scanning during installation, and then reactivate it when the installation is complete.

Summary

Whew—this was a long chapter with a lot of good information in it. We talked about the dark side of computer networking: bad guys and the threats and attacks they use to victimize our systems and networks. You learned a lot about tactics like denial of service attacks, viruses, worms, social engineering, and other devious methods that hackers use. After that, you learned about ways to mitigate these threats and protect yourself by establishing policies and procedures, providing training, and ensuring that all your software is up to date. You also learned what to do about the ubiquitous problem of viruses. It's a lot to remember, I know; but believe me, you'll be really glad you're armed with this knowledge, because unfortunately, you'll probably deal with these threats sooner or later.

Exam Essentials

Know what types of threats can adversely affect your network.   Threats include denial of service attacks, viruses, worms, rogue access points, phishing, and various other attack methods employed by hackers.

Understand how attackers attempt to get information about your network.   Attackers have various methods they can use to gather information. Some of the most common reconnaissance tools are packet sniffers and social engineering.

Know how to keep your systems automatically updated.   Programs such as Windows Update can keep your operating systems current, which will reduce opportunities attackers have of exploiting your computers and network.

Know where to go to find downloadable software updates.   Check the manufacturer's website for the most current security information, patches, and updates.

Written Lab

In this section, write the answers to the following wireless questions:

1. The Ping of Death and SYN floods are examples of what types of attack?

2. How often should you update your virus definitions in your antivirus software?

3. What is the U.S. Department of Defense standard for individual computers?

4. What type of virus attacks executable programs?

5. What kind of tool could a hacker use to intercept traffic on your network?

6. What type of virus uses Microsoft's Visual Basic scripting language?

7. What is it called when someone intercepts traffic on your network that's intended for a different destination computer?

8. If someone installed a wireless router on your network without your knowledge, that would be called_____.

9. What software application can help automatically ensure that your Windows-based computers have the most current security patches?

10. The two different types of virus scans are _____.

(The answers to the Written Lab can be found following the answers to the Review Questions for this chapter.)

Review Questions

1. Which of the following is a type of denial of service attack?

    A. Ping of Death

    B. Stacheldraht

    C. SYN flood

    D. All of the above

2. Which is not a type of threat that can affect your network?

    A. Worm

    B. Phishing

    C. Access control list

    D. Rogue access point

3. Which type of virus impacts .COM, .EXE, and .DLL files?

    A. File viruses

    B. SYN flood

    C. Smurf

    D. Tribe Flood Network

4. Which type of virus uses the Visual Basic macro-scripting language to perform malicious or mischievous functions in data files?

    A. IP spoofing

    B. File

    C. Macro

    D. None of the above

5. Monkey B, Michelangelo, Stoned, and Stealth Boot are examples of which type of virus?

    A. IP spoofing

    B. Multipartite

    C. Macro

    D. Boot sector

6. Which type of virus affects both the boot sector and files on a computer?

    A. Mulipartite

    B. Macro

    C. Tribe Flood Network 2000 (TFN2K)

    D. Smurf

7. What is the main difference between a worm and a virus?
   - **A.** Worms require user action for replication.
   - **B.** Viruses do not require user intervention for replication.
   - **C.** Worms can replicate without user intervention.
   - **D.** None of the above

8. What kind of attack could a hacker use to target a network that tries to log in to some type of shared network resource?
   - **A.** Packet sniffers
   - **B.** Brute-force attack
   - **C.** Worm
   - **D.** Backdoor

9. What type of security threat allows an attacker to learn your password through the use of an email or phone call?
   - **A.** Phishing
   - **B.** Trust-exploration attack
   - **C.** Man-in-the-middle attack
   - **D.** Rogue access point

10. Which type of policy should be implemented to secure important company documents and materials when employees leave their workstations?
    - **A.** Clean housekeeping
    - **B.** Clean desk
    - **C.** Security audit
    - **D.** Proactive defense

11. If you implement a set of policies and procedures that define corporate information as confidential and then train employees on these procedures prevents what type of attack?
    - **A.** DoS
    - **B.** Man-in-the-middle attacks
    - **C.** Smurf
    - **D.** Social engineering

12. If an employee leaves a company voluntarily, what type of interview should be conducted?
    - **A.** Entrance
    - **B.** Application
    - **C.** Exit
    - **D.** Manager rating

13. What defines the appropriate response to a security event on a network?

    A. Implementing security procedures

    B. Installing a new router

    C. Turning off the network

    D. HR policy for dress code

14. What type of virus works its way into the master boot record and changes the pointer to your operating system?

    A. DoD virus

    B. Boot-sector virus

    C. File-system virus

    D. Macro virus

15. What process allows you to update your Windows-based operating system?

    A. Technet

    B. Windows Update

    C. Text message

    D. Hot fix

16. Why is it important to keep your system patched and up to date?

    A. To completely stop your need for security

    B. To increase the functionality of your applications

    C. To fix system vulnerabilities

    D. To make Windows completely safe and worry free

17. A network administrator wanting to assign passwords to network resources only would implement which type of security?

    A. Building password

    B. Group password

    C. Share-level security

    D. User-level security

18. Which type of scanning allows an antivirus program to search for a virus even if there is no definition for it?

    A. Update scan

    B. Signature-file scan

    C. Database scan

    D. Heuristic scan

19. What type of files need to be updated in order for your antivirus program to have the latest information about attacks and viruses?

    A. Definition files

    B. Email files

    C. .doc files

    D. .exe files

20. What type of scan can be done by an antivirus program?

    A. Emergency

    B. In-demand

    C. On-access

    D. All of the above

Answers to Review Questions

1. D. A denial of service (DoS) attack prevents users from accessing the system. All of the above are possible denial of service attacks.

2. C. Worms, phishing, and rogue access points are all threats that may adversely affect a network.

3. A. Answers B, C, and D are all DoS types, so the only real option is a file virus. A file virus attacks executable application and system program files.

4. C. A macro is a script of commonly enacted commands that are used to automatically perform operations without a user's intervention. Macro viruses are among the most common viruses; they affect the file you are working on, usually in Microsoft Word or PowerPoint.

5. D. These are all examples of boot-sector viruses that get into the master boot record. A boot-sector virus will overwrite the boot sector, thereby making it look as if there is no pointer to your operating system. When you power up the computer, you will see a Missing Operating System or Hard Disk Not Found error message.

6. A. A multipartite virus is one that affects both the boot sector and files on your computer.

7. C. A worm can actively replicate itself without user intervention, whereas a virus needs a user to open an application to activate and spread.

8. B. A brute-force attack is a software-related attack that employs a program running on a targeted network that tries to log in to some type of shared network resource like a server.

9. A. Social engineering or phishing refers to the act of attempting to illegally obtain sensitive information by pretending to be a credible source. Phishing usually takes one of two forms: an email or a phone call.

10. B. A clean-desk policy means that all important documents, such as books, schematics, confidential letters, and the like, are removed from the desk (and locked away) when employees leave their workstations.

11. D. It is important to train all employees that people will try and call and email them to gather information in order to attack the company. This is called phishing or social engineering.

12. C. The exit interview is the process in which employers ask employees who are leaving the company about their employment experience. The exit interview is used to minimize risks whether the employee is leaving under favorable circumstances or is being terminated.

13. A. A security procedure defines the appropriate response to a security event on your network.

14. B. You know you've got this type of virus when you power up the computer and get a Missing Operating System or Hard Disk Not Found error message.

15. B. Windows Update is a utility that is typically automatically installed when you install Windows. The update engine will periodically scan your system for the version of Windows components you have installed and compare them to the most current versions available from Microsoft. If your software is out of date, a Windows Update dialog box will appear, asking if you want to install the software updates.

16. C. With so much code written for applications or operating systems, developers go back after the initial release to fix any problems that are uncovered. These fixes are released as hot fixes or patches.

17. C. This type of security is share-level security. You assign passwords to individual files or other network resources (such as printers) instead of assigning rights to users. All resources are visible from anywhere in the network, and any user who knows the password for a particular network resource can make changes to it.

18. D. Heuristic scanning allows for this type of scanning. The engine looks for suspicious activity that might indicate a virus.

19. A. Every week, you need to update your list of known viruses—called the virus definition files. You can do this manually or automatically through the manufacturer's website. You can use a staging server within your company to download and then distribute the updates, or you can set up each computer to download updates.

20. D. An antivirus program examines the computer suspected of having a virus and eradicates any viruses it finds using any of these methods.

Answers to Written Lab

1. Denial of service (DoS)

2. Once per week

3. Trusted computer system

4. A file virus

5. Packet sniffer

6. A macro virus

7. Man-in-the-middle attack

8. A rogue access point

9. Windows Update

10. On-demand and on-access

Chapter

15

Physical and Hardware Security

THE FOLLOWING COMPTIA NETWORK+ EXAM OBJECTIVES ARE COVERED IN THIS CHAPTER:

✓ **6.1 Explain the function of hardware and software security devices**

- Network based firewall
- Host based firewall
- IDS
- IPS
- VPN concentrator

✓ **6.2 Explain common features of a firewall**

- Application layer vs. network layer
- Stateful vs. stateless
- Scanning services
- Content filtering
- Signature identification
- Zones

✓ **6.5 Explain issues that affect device security**

- Physical security
- Restricting local and remote access
- Secure methods vs. unsecure methods
  - SSH, HTTPS, SNMPv3, SFTP, SCP
  - TELNET, HTTP, FTP, RSH, RCP, SNMPv1/2

Finding a corporate network that isn't connected to the Internet would be pretty tough these days. Being connecting allows for a huge increase in productivity, and not having an online presence is akin to sheer oblivion in today's business environment. But as is often the case, advantages, even big ones, have a downside to them, and being hooked up to the Internet is no exception. Connecting our private network to a huge public one exposes you to some really major security risks, so we absolutely have to protect our networks from the very real threats of intrusion, corporate espionage, data and identity theft, and exploitation in general. To succeed at doing this, our networks need one or more security devices to control any traffic coming into and flowing out from them. We need things like firewalls and intrusion detection and/or prevention systems as much as we need any other form of security in our businesses and daily lives today—period.

These vital security methods are going to be the focus of this chapter. In it, I'll be covering the ins and outs of the protective networking measures and devices designed to shield and secure our network traffic, zooming in on the all-important firewalls because they're a ubiquitous and critical line of defense against the exploits of the all-too-common hackers who seek to compromise our corporate and personal network security.

I'll end this important chapter by going over the specific issues that can and do affect device security on your network. I'll discuss things you can do physically and logically to implement tight security, right down to choosing the best protocols to use for safe communication to the outside world.

For up-to-the-minute updates for this chapter, please see www.lammle.com or www.sybex.com/go/comptianetwork+studyguide.

Using Hardware and Software Security Devices

This heading may be a little misleading because it makes it sound like I'm going to talk about the differences between hardware and software security devices. But I'm not, because even though many firewalls and routers that contain proxy and/or firewall services brand themselves as hardware or software solutions, the fact is, most of these devices are really a combination of the two. For instance, there's software embedded within a hardware ROM chip to make the software harder to attack, but it still actually functions as software. So instead of focusing on the type of device, it makes a lot more sense to delve into exactly what it is that a device does and how it does it.

In medium to large enterprise networks, strategies for security usually include some combination of internal and perimeter routers plus firewall devices. Internal routers provide added security by screening traffic to the more vulnerable parts of a corporate network though a wide array of strategic *access lists*. You can see where each of these devices is found within a typical network in Figure 15.1.

FIGURE 15.1   A typical secured network

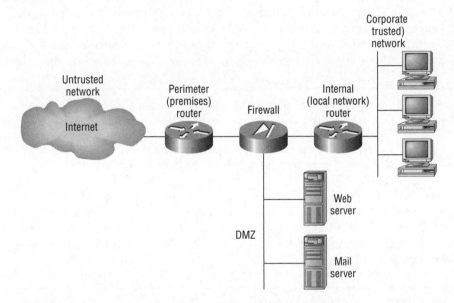

I'll use the terms *trusted network* and *untrusted network* throughout this chapter, so it's important that you can see where they are found in a typical secured network. The demilitarized zone (DMZ) can be global (real) Internet addresses or private addresses, depending on how you configure your firewall, but this is typically where you'll find the HTTP, Domain Name Service (DNS), email, and other Internet-type corporate servers. The DMZ is used to create a security zone that allows public traffic but the traffic is isolated from the company private network.

Instead of having routers, we can also use virtual local area networks (VLANs) with switches on the inside trusted network. Multilayer switches containing their own security features can sometimes replace internal (LAN) routers to provide higher performance in VLAN architectures.

Next, I'll talk about how these devices go about directing traffic between your *private network* that only authorized users have access to, and the *public network* part of the network that everyone connects to.

Defining Firewalls

Firewalls are usually a combination of hardware and software. The hardware part is usually a router, but it can also be a computer or a dedicated piece of hardware called a *black box* that has two Network Interface Cards (NICs) in it. One of the NICs connects to the public side, and the other one connects to the private side. The software part is configured to control how the firewall actually works to protect your network by scrutinizing each incoming and outgoing packet and rejecting any suspicious ones.

Firewalls generally allow only packets that pass specific security restrictions to get through; they can also permit, deny, encrypt, decrypt, and proxy all traffic that flows through, either between the public and private parts of a network or between different security domains, or zones, on a private network. The system administrator decides on and sets up the rules a firewall follows when deciding to forward data packets or reject them.

Just so you know, a Network+ certified system administrator rarely has the sophisticated knowledge required to design, install, and manage a firewall. The information I'm imparting to you here will give you the tools you need to understand the basic ways firewalls work and to help you to work effectively in an environment where a firewall is already installed.

Firewalls can be placed on top of an existing operating system or be self-contained. Conversely, black-box systems are proprietary and have external controls that aren't controlled by the operating system itself. If you opt to use a general-purpose server operating system to run your firewall, you can do that with Unix and Windows because both of these support third-party firewall products.

For networks with multiple Windows-based computers, any firewalls should be installed on a router that connects the private network to the Internet or to a Windows Server like Windows Server 2003 (2008 server can't route), rather than on clients like Vista or XP.

Clearly, if your firewalls aren't configured properly, they're not going to do you much good. Most of them are configured as default-deny, meaning that the only network connections allowed are the ones that have been specified to be. A proficient system administrator has to do this, and trust me, with the multitude of applications and ports involved in internal-external network communication, it's not all that easy! To make life easier, some people resort to trusting the default-allow option, where all traffic is allowed to pass through unless it's been specifically blocked. But doing this isn't exactly tight because it makes inadvertent network connections and security breaches much more likely to happen. Even though it might ease a little administrative pain, I don't recommend going with this method—ever.

Network-Based Firewalls

A *network-based firewall* is what companies use to protect their private network from public networks. The defining characteristic of this type of firewall is that it's designed to protect an entire network of computers instead of just one system, and it's usually a combination of hardware and software.

As you can imagine, protecting an entire network of computers from malicious attacks is quite the challenge. Most of the firewall features that I'm going to talk about in this chapter are designed with this goal in mind, although the technology is certainly applicable to host-based firewalls too.

Host-Based Firewalls

In contrast to a network-based firewall, a *host-based firewall* is implemented on a single machine so it only protects that one machine. This type of firewall is usually a software implementation, because you don't need any additional hardware in your personal computer to run it. All current Windows client operating systems come with Windows Firewall, which is a great example of a host-based solution.

If you hear someone say that host-based software solutions just aren't as secure as a separate hardware-based solution, they're pretty much right. This is because if you're running a dedicated black-box firewall and someone manages to hack in and disable it, your best-case scenario is a blown black box and a ruined firewall. Believe it or not, even if that happens, all the data on your internal network may still be safe if the bad guy wasn't able to get past everything. But if they were able to get all the way in, you could have some ugly consequences to deal with; if the hacker makes it through the often relatively flimsy software firewall running on your local computer, they could not only view and/or nick your files but also trash your entire system—yikes!

Still, it all comes down to how much security you really require. Unless you're the Director of the CIA or something, you probably don't need to go the extra mile and shell out for a dedicated black box if all you want to do is protect your personal computer from someone who's trying to hack their way in through your high-speed Internet connection.

Firewall Technologies

There's a whole bunch of firewall technologies, and they all differ in the way that they restrict information flow. Things like access control lists and dynamic packet filtering are often used as firewalls in their own right, or they can be implemented along with proxies and DMZs and other firewall technologies to build a serious, formidable system fortress.

Access Control Lists (ACL)

The first line of defense for any network that's connected to the Internet is what we call *access control lists (ACLs)*. These reside on your routers and determine by IP addresses which machines are allowed to use those routers and in what direction. ACLs have been around for decades and have some other really cool uses apart from firewalls. Figure 15.2 gives you a great demonstration of how ACLs can work to prevent users on Network B from accessing Network A.

FIGURE 15.2   Two networks with an ACL-enabled router

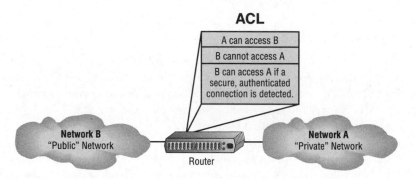

An important thing to note here is that data from users in Network A can still pass through the router into Network B. This means that a hacker executing an IP spoofing attack that makes it appear as though they're an IP address originating from inside the firewall can still gain access to Network B by pretending to be a valid user in Network A.

ACLs are essentially lists of conditions that categorize packets, so you can imagine how helpful they can be in helping you gain control over the network's traffic. One of the most common and easiest-to-understand ways that ACLs are used is for filtering unwanted packets when you're implementing security policies. You can set up the ACLs to make very specific decisions about regulating traffic patterns so that they'll allow only certain hosts to access web resources on the Internet while restricting others. With a solid combination of ACLs, network managers can arm themselves like Rambo and powerfully enforce pretty much any security policy they need to.

Chapter 14 discusses some of the security threats that ACLs can help mitigate. Those threats include the following:

- IP address spoofing, inbound
- IP address spoofing, outbound
- Denial of service (DoS) TCP SYN attacks, and blockading external attacks
- DoS TCP SYN attacks, using TCP intercept
- DoS Smurf attacks
- Filtering ICMP messages, inbound

- Filtering ICMP messages, outbound
- Filtering traceroute

You can even employ ACLs for situations that don't necessarily involve blocking packets—like using them to control which networks will or won't be advertised by dynamic routing protocols. The way you configure your ACL to do the latter is the same; you just apply it to a routing protocol instead of an interface. The only other difference here is that an ACL applied to a protocol is referred to as a *distribution list*, and it doesn't stop routing advertisements, it just controls their content. You can also use ACLs to categorize packets for queuing or quality of service (QoS)-type services and for controlling the types of traffic that can activate a pricey backup link.

So, how do you go about creating an ACL? Well, it's really a lot like programming a series of if-then statements: If a given condition is met, then a specific action happens; but if that explicit condition isn't met, nothing happens except that the next statement in the list is evaluated. Access-list statements are basically packet filters that packets are compared against, categorized by, and then acted on accordingly as directed. Once your list is built, it can be applied to either inbound or outbound traffic on any interface, causing the router to analyze every packet crossing that interface in the specified direction and take the appropriate action.

There are a few important rules by which packets are processed when being compared with an ACL:

- They're always compared with each line of the ACL in sequential order, always beginning with the first line, then proceeding to line 2, then line 3, and so on.

- They'll be compared with subsequent lines of the list until a match is made. Once the packet matches the condition on a line of the ACL, the packet is acted upon and no further comparisons take place.

- There is an implicit "deny" at the end of each ACL that says that if a packet doesn't match the condition on any of the lines in the ACL, it will be discarded.

Each of these rules has some powerful implications for filtering IP packets with ACLs, which is why creating an effective ACLs truly takes some practice!

There are two main types of ACLs:

Standard ACLs   These use only the source IP address in an IP packet as the condition test, so all decisions regarding a packet will be based on the source IP address. This means that standard ACLs basically permit or deny an entire suite of protocols without distinguishing between any of the myriad types of IP traffic like web, Telnet, UDP, and so on.

Extended ACLs   Extended ACLs go the distance and evaluate lots of the other fields in the Layer 3 and 4 headers of an IP packet. They can evaluate source and destination IP addresses, the protocol field in the Network layer header, and the port number at the Transport layer header. This gives extended ACLs the ability to enforce highly specific network traffic control conditions.

Once you create an ACL, it doesn't do much of anything until you apply it. Yes, it's there on the router, but it's inactive until you tell that router what to do with it. To use an ACL as a packet filter, you've got to apply it to the interface on the router exactly where you want the traffic filtered, and you've also got to specify the traffic's direction—inbound or outbound. This is because you probably want different controls in place for traffic leaving your network that's destined for the Internet than you want for traffic coming into your network from the Internet. Here's the difference:

Inbound ACLs   When an ACL is applied to inbound packets on an interface, those packets are processed through the ACL before being routed to the outbound interface. Any packets that are denied won't be routed because they'll be discarded before the routing process is completed.

Outbound ACLs   When an ACL is applied to outbound packets on an interface, those packets are routed to the outbound interface and then processed through the ACL before being queued.

Creating ACLs is great, but don't forget to apply them to an interface or they're not going to filter traffic. With that in mind, here's a list of rules to live by when configuring ACLs on interfaces from the Internet into your production network:

- Deny any addresses from your internal networks.
- Deny any local host addresses (127.0.0.0/8).
- Deny any reserved private addresses.
- Deny any addresses in the IP multicast address range (224.0.0.0/4).

These addresses should never, ever be allowed to enter your internetwork.

Demilitarized Zone (DMZ)

Most firewalls in use today implement something called a *demilitarized zone (DMZ)*, which, as its name implies, is a network segment that isn't public or local but halfway between the two. People outside your network primarily access your web servers, File Transfer Protocol (FTP) servers, and mail-relay servers; and because bad guys tend to go after these servers first, it's a good idea place them in the DMZ.

A standard DMZ setup typically (but not always) has two or three network cards in the firewall computer. The first goes to the Internet, the second one goes to the network segment where the commonly targeted servers exist that I recommended be placed in the DMZ, and the third connects to your intranet. As you can see in Figure 15.3, the E-Mmail server, the FTP server, and web server are all in the DMZ, so all critical servers live inside the firewall.

Understand that it is very possible to have a DMZ outside the firewall. Figure 15.3 shows an example of having the DMZ inside the firewall. Both options are available when building your intranets.

If you set things up like this, hackers who break into servers in the DMZ will only get to see public information—meaning your entire corporate network won't be compromised. Understand that email messages are still fairly vulnerable, but only the relay server can be accessed because all messages are stored and viewed on email servers inside the network.

FIGURE 15.3   A firewall with a DMZ

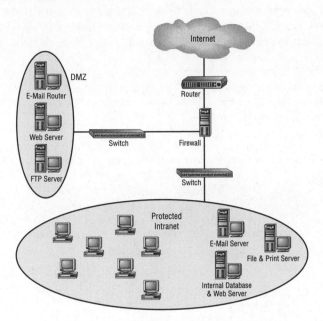

It is important to understand and remember that you need to administrate your DMZ. This is not a device you buy at the store and just connect, turn on, and forget it - you need to permit and deny the ports you want. If your company uses custom port numbers, you need to verify that the DMZ is allowing these ports through your server. This is easy to do by telneting to the DMZ server using the custom port number. If the server responds, you're good!

Protocol Switching

Protocol switching protects data on the inside of a firewall; and because Transmission Control Protocol/Internet Protocol (TCP/IP) is what the Internet runs on, most external attacks take direct aim at this protocol stack. In days gone by, protocol switching used to be pretty popular, but not so much anymore due to the greatly intensified power of firewall technology and the fact that TCP/IP is now the protocol of choice for all network communications. But if you did want to implement protocol switching, here are the two best ways to do it:

- Use a protocol other than TCP/IP on the internal network inside the firewall. IP-based attacks aimed at your development server just can't work if you use Internetwork Packet Exchange (IPX) on the internal-network side of a router, which gives you an automatic firewall.

- Use TCP/IP on both the internal network and the Internet, and use a different protocol like IPX in a dead zone between them. Basically, you'll have things set up to switch from IP to IPX in that dead zone and switch back to IP again once inside your network (IPv6 would work in this example as well, but IPX is a good example because no one would expect it).

Figure 15.4 demonstrates both of these strategies. Focus on the dead zone between two of the routers, and also notice that the only protocol on the inside of either router is IPX. This means that any TCP/IP packets coming in from the Internet can't pass through into the local network because of the difference in protocols used by each.

 Both of these methods only protect the external network. You still need a firewall to guard against attacks on your network's access point and protocol-switching device.

FIGURE 15.4   Protocol switching with and without a dead zone

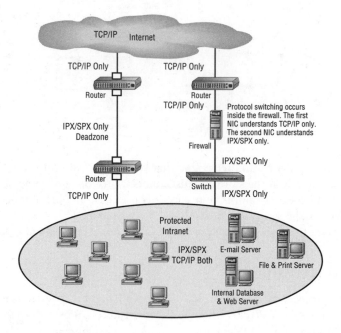

Dynamic Packet Filtering

Packet filtering refers to the ability of a router or a firewall to discard packets that don't meet the right criteria. Firewalls use *dynamic packet filtering* to ensure that the packets they forward match sessions initiated on their private side by something called a *dynamic state list* or *state table*, which keeps track of all communication sessions between stations from inside and outside the firewall. This list changes dynamically as sessions are added and deleted.

So with dynamic packet filtering, only packets for valid and current sessions are allowed to pass. Anyone trying to play back a communication session—for instance, a login to gain access—won't be able to do that if your firewall is using dynamic packet filtering with a dynamic state list, because the data they send isn't part of a currently valid session. The firewall will respond to an event like this by dropping all packets that don't correspond to a current session via the information in the dynamic state list. Let me clarify this. Say a computer in Network A requests a Telnet session with a server in Network B. The firewall in between the two keeps a log of the communication packets that are sent each way, and only packets that belong to the current session will be allowed back into Network A through that firewall.

Figure 15.5 depicts a failed attempt to infiltrate a network protected with a dynamic state list. Can you see that the hacker attempts to insert a packet into the communication stream but can't because they don't have the correct packet number? This is because the firewall was waiting for a specific order of packets, and the hacker's packet is out of sequence.

FIGURE 15.5   A hacker denied by a dynamic state list

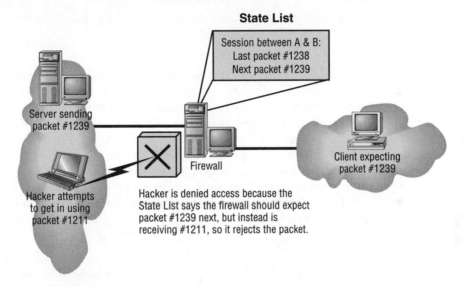

Proxy Services

Firewalls can also implement something called *proxy services*, which actually makes them *proxy servers*, or proxies for short. Proxies act on behalf of the whole network to completely separate packets from internal hosts and external hosts. Let's say an internal client sends a request to an external host on the Internet. That request will get to the proxy server first, where it will be examined, broken down, and handled by an application that will create a new packet requesting information from the external server. Figure 15.6 demonstrates this process. Make a note to self that this exchange occurs between applications at the Application layer of the OSI model.

FIGURE 15.6   A packet going to a proxy

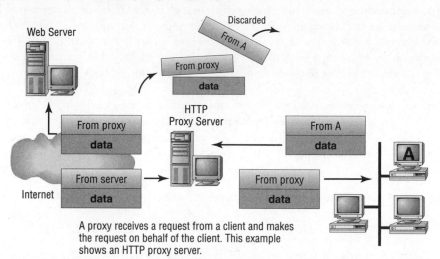

A proxy receives a request from a client and makes the request on behalf of the client. This example shows an HTTP proxy server.

Proxies make good firewalls because they dissect the entire packet so that each section of it can be scrutinized for invalid data at each and every layer of the OSI model; proxies look at everything from information in the packet header to the actual contents of the message. They can even examine attachments for viruses. As if all that isn't cool enough, proxies can also search messages for keywords that can indicate the source of a packet. That last little goodie is vital because you can use this type of searching to prevent sensitive information from escaping your organization along with the outbound data stream. If your sensitive documents contain a header or footer that includes something like *MyCompanyName Confidential*, you can set up your proxy server software to search for them. The only downside is that all that analysis will definitely degrade overall performance because it requires a lot more time than just checking state lists.

There are many types of proxy servers:

IP proxy   An *IP proxy* hides the IP addresses of all the devices on the internal network by exchanging its IP address for the address of any requesting station. This is good because you definitely don't want a hacker to know any IP addresses specific to your internal network, right? Even Internet web servers won't be able to determine the specific IP address from which they receive a request, because any and all communications appear to have originated from the proxy server—nice! These proxies are sometimes called *Network Address Translation (NAT)* proxies.

Web (HTTP) proxy   *Web proxies*, also called HTTP proxies, handle HTTP requests on behalf of the sending workstation. When these are implemented correctly, a client's web browser asks a web server on the Internet for a web page using an HTTP request. Because the browser is configured to make HTTP requests using an HTTP proxy, the browser sends the request to the proxy server. The proxy server changes the From address of the HTTP request to its own network address and sends it to the Internet web server. The response to the HTTP request goes directly to the proxy (because it replaced the sender's address with its own). The proxy server then replaces its address with the address of the original sender, and the response is delivered to the original sender.

The most popular implementation of a web proxy is a *proxy cache server.* This server receives an HTTP request from a web browser and then makes the request on behalf of the sending workstation. When the requested page is returned, the proxy server caches a copy of the page locally. The next time someone requests the same web page or Internet information, the page can be delivered from the local cache instead of the proxy server having to formulate a new request to the web server on the Internet. This speeds up web surfing for commonly accessed pages. Web proxies can also increase network security by filtering out content that is considered insecure, such as executables, scripts, or viruses.

FTP proxy   FTP proxies handle the uploading and downloading of files from a server on behalf of a workstation. An FTP proxy operates in a fashion similar to a web proxy. As with web proxies, FTP proxies can filter out undesirable content (viruses and the like).

SMTP proxy   SMTP proxies handle Internet email. Here, the actual contents of the packet and mail can be automatically searched. Any packets or messages that contain material that is not considered secure can be blocked. Many SMTP proxies allow network virus protection software to scan inbound mail.

Not every firewall falls into a simple category. Although firewalls used to typically work in one arena, today's firewalls offer multiple solutions within one box or software program. Firewalls that perform more than one type of filtering service are sometimes referred to as *hybrid firewalls*.

Firewalls at the Application Layer vs. the Network Layer

By now, you know all about the OSI model and remember that the Application layer is at the top of the heap and the Network layer is third up from the bottom. And as a rule of thumb, the higher you get in the OSI model, the more complex the interactions become. This rule holds true for discussions of firewalls that work at the Application layer versus those that work at the Network layer.

The first firewalls that were developed functioned solely at the Network layer, and the earliest of these were known as *packet-filter firewalls.* I covered packet filtering a bit earlier in this chapter; as a refresher, all it means is that the firewall looks at an incoming packet and applies it against the set of rules in the ACL(s). If the packet passes, it gets sent on. If not, the packet is dropped.

This type of filtering is pretty basic, because all the firewall considers is the individual packet. All that matters are the source and destination addresses, protocol, and port number. The firewall doesn't care whether that packet is stand-alone or part of another data stream. This process works fairly well for common protocols such as TCP and User Datagram Protocol (UDP), which communicate on predefined port numbers. People generally refer to two types of Network-layer firewalls: stateful and stateless.

Stateful vs. Stateless Network-Layer Firewalls

As I said in the last section, a basic packet filter doesn't care about whether the packet it is examining is stand-alone or part of a bigger message stream. That type of packet filter is said to be *stateless*, in that it does not monitor the status of the connections passing through it. Again, these work pretty well, but the firewall has no idea whether a packet is legitimate or possibly a rogue packet trying to sneak by. These types of firewalls tended to be susceptible to various DoS attacks and IP spoofing.

The one big advantage that a stateless firewall has over its stateful counterparts is that it uses less memory. Today, stateless firewalls are best used on an internal network where security threats are lower and there are few restrictions.

In contrast to a stateless firewall, a *stateful* firewall is one that keeps track of the various data streams passing through it. If a packet that is a part of an established connection hits the firewall, it's passed through. New packets are subjected to the rules as specified in the ACL. These types of firewalls are better at preventing network attacks that look to exploit existing connections, or DoS attacks.

A stateful firewall works by using the TCP three-way handshake. First, the client sends a packet with the SYN bit set to the firewall. The firewall interprets this as a new connection and passes the request to the appropriate service provider on the internal network. Next, the service responds with a packet that has both the SYN and ACK bits set. Finally, the client responds with a packet with only the ACK bit set. At that point, the connection is considered established, and the firewall will only allow packets in that have the same connection identification. The established connection is logged in the *state table*.

If there is no data on the connection for a specified period of time, the connection will time out in the state table. Any new communication will need to be reestablished based on the ACL rules.

 In a common DoS attack, the SYN flood, the attacker attempts to overload a firewall by spamming it with inordinate numbers of SYN requests. The firewall by default will keep sending SYN ACKs back, thereby preventing it from responding to legitimate connection requests. Many of today's firewalls can circumvent this problem by not responding to multiple SYN requests from the same host.

Stateful firewalls tend to be a bit slower at establishing connections than stateless ones because there is more to do. After the connection is established, though, stateful firewalls are usually faster because they just have to check the state table for the connection instead of comparing the packet against all the relevant ACLs. This is done via *stateful packet inspection*. Most stateful firewalls can also keep track of connections using connectionless protocols such as UDP.

 Real World Scenario

Firewall Challenges

You were just given a firewall for your network that was appropriated from a different part of your company, and you want to make sure hackers can't get in through that firewall on random ports. Fortunately for you, the firewall is default deny, so you don't have too many worries. You open up the ports for legitimate traffic, such as 80 for HTTP, 161 for Simple Network Management Protocol (SNMP), 21 for FTP, and so on. But users complain that they are unable to download files from the extranet using FTP. What happened?

FTP does work on port 21, but it also establishes connections on arbitrary high-number ports to complete its work. If those ports are not opened, FTP won't work. This is where a stateful firewall is handy. When FTP goes to open the new port number, the firewall will see that the data intended for the new port is part of the existing FTP connection and let the data pass through. Yet another reason why stateful firewalls are so much better than stateless ones!

Application-layer Firewalls

Although stateful firewalls are more powerful and secure than stateless ones, application-layer firewalls are even better. They work by inspecting more than just data in the IP header: They read data at the application layer. In other words, they will know whether a packet is FTP, SNMP, HTTP, or whatever application-layer protocol it is. The one major drawback is speed. Because these devices have to read more information than their network-layer counterparts, they do tend to be a bit slower. It's generally not enough that you'll notice, though, unless you have the reaction time of Superman.

One nice feature of application-layer firewalls is that they let you set proxy rules for multiple applications on the same firewall. As a proxy, the firewall processes all data between the two endpoints and drops all packets that are suspicious. In theory, a rogue packet will never reach the system on your internal network. Application-layer firewalls also handle complex protocols such as H.323, which is used for Voice over IP (VoIP), much better than their network-layer counterparts.

Scanning Services and Other Firewall Features

Most firewalls are capable of performing *scanning services*, which means that they scan different types of incoming traffic in an effort to detect problems. For example, firewalls can scan incoming HTTP traffic to look for viruses or spyware, or scan email looking for spam. You can often set scanning rules that will prevent users from downloading large files over a certain size. On Cisco routers, scanning is administered by the Content Security Control (CSC) and Security Services Module (SSM). Two categories of content are typically scanned: mail and web.

Table 15.1 shows some key default scanning settings within CSC SSM.

TABLE 15.1   Default Scanning Settings

Category	Protocol	Function
Mail	SMTP and POP3	Scans all scannable files in the email
Mail	SMTP and POP3	Rejects all messages larger than 15MB
Mail	SMTP	Rejects messages addressed to more than 100 recipients
Mail	SMTP	Cleans emails or attachments containing malware, and attaches a notification that the malware was deleted
Web	HTTP	Scans all file downloads
Web	HTTP	Scans webmail sites for AOL, MSN, Google, and Yahoo!
Web	FTP	Scans all file transfers
Web	HTTP and FTP	Skips scanning of files larger than 50MB; can also enable deferred scanning
Web	HTTP and FTP	Cleans files in which malware is detected; if the file cannot be cleaned, the file is deleted

The defaults give you a pretty good level of protection, but there may be instances where you want to change settings. For example, if you are concerned about bandwidth, then you can limit the size of files transferred via FTP or HTTP. If mail storage is an issue, then you can set the firewall to reject mail larger than 10MB.

Keep in mind, though, that by changing some settings, you are increasing your security risk. If you offer deferred scanning for large files, it will speed up the file transfer process but also introduce a security risk because the file will not be scanned as it's being transferred.

If you are having problems with large file transfers timing out on your network, it's possible that it's partially caused by the firewall scanning the files immediately. Offering deferred scanning can help fix the problem, but you also need to weigh the additional security risk.

Content Filtering

Content filtering is very closely related to scanning services, and on Cisco routers it's also provided by the CSC SSM. Specifically, *content filtering* means blocking data based on the content of the data rather than the source of the data. Most commonly, this is used to filter email and website access.

The reasons for using content filtering seem pretty obvious. Most companies have a zero-tolerance policy against hateful material or pornography. If a user on a company network uses that network to spread hate mail or porn, the company could be liable for damages in a lawsuit if they didn't take measures to prevent such actions. It's not only a moral thing but a legal thing, too.

Content filtering is also important in places like schools. It's doubtful that parents want their kids being able to stumble upon a porn site in the school library while researching a school project. Content filtering can block that site from being accessed so the problem never occurs. You can also find several parental-control software packages for home use that employ content filtering.

There are several ways to filter content; here are some of the more common categories used:

- Attachment (all attachments of a certain type, such as `.exe`, are blocked)
- Bayesian
- Content-encoding
- Email headers
- Language
- Phrases
- Proximity of words to each other
- URLs

Nearly all filtering methods use a combination of filters to protect users from improper content.

Signature Identification

Firewalls can also stop attacks and problems through a process called *signature identification*. Viruses that are known will have a signature, which is a particular pattern of data, within them. Firewalls (and antivirus programs) can use signatures to identify a virus and remove it. The same holds true for other software bugs such as worms and spyware.

Numerous network attacks have signatures as well. For example, if your router starts getting hit by large numbers of SYN requests, you may be at the beginning of a SYN flood attack. The inundation of SYN traffic is a signature of a SYN flood.

Zones

A *zone* is an individual area of the network that has been configured with a specific trust level. Firewalls are ideal devices to regulate the flow of traffic between zones. If you look back at Figure 15.3, this provides a good example of how zone levels could work. The Internet would be a zone with no trust or a low level of trust. The DMZ, located between the Internet and the internal network, could have a medium level of trust. The computers on the intranet would all be within a high trust zone. The higher the trust level, the less scrutiny you place on data coming from a computer in that zone.

Another way to look at zones is to understand how Internet Explorer deals with them. Figure 15.7 shows you what the Internet Options Security tab looks like. On this tab, you can see that there are four zones for which you can configure security levels: Internet, Local Intranet, Trusted Sites, and Restricted Sites. There are three default security levels for the Internet: High, Medium, and Low. Don't get this confused with the trust levels I talked about in the previous paragraph—they are basically opposites. If the security level is set to High, it means you have low trust.

FIGURE 15.7   Internet Options Security tab

A good way to ensure some security through your browser is to set the security level to Medium-high or High and leave it there. If there are sites that you download from frequently and that you trust, then you can put those sites into the Trusted Sites zone. Click Trusted Sites and then click the Sites button to get to the screen shown in Figure 15.8.

FIGURE 15.8   Adding a trusted site

Finally, you can customize the security level of any of the zones by clicking the Custom Level button near the bottom of the Internet Options window. This will take you to a screen similar to the one shown in Figure 15.9.

FIGURE 15.9   Custom security settings

Within the custom settings, you can specify behavior for .NET framework components, ActiveX controls and plug-ins, downloads, scripting, user authentication, and several other options. Most of the options have choices to disable, enable, or prompt you if you want to continue with that operation.

> Although Internet Explorer security options can help protect your computer, do not think of them as a replacement for a firewall. The best security systems are multi-faceted. You should have a firewall solution in place and then augment that with solid security measures on your local computer as well.

Intrusion-Detection and -Prevention Systems

If someone has broken into your network, how would you know? I mean, it's not like you're going to find broken windows or the door left wide open, right? Although it's true that you won't be dusting for prints, bad guys who break into networks still leave clues behind that can help you sleuth out their identities as well as how they gained access. A great tool for doing network detective work is known as an *Intrusion Detection System (IDS)*.

Firewalls are designed to block nasty traffic from entering your network, but IDS is more of an auditing tool: It keeps track of all activity on your network so you can see if someone has been trespassing. Because IDSs are a fairly new technology, people are busy developing ways to combine IDS technology with existing firewalls.

> An Intrusion Detection System does *not* replace a firewall on your network!

There are two ways IDS systems can detect attacks or intrusions. The first is based on the signature of an intrusion that's often referred to as a *misuse-detection IDS (MD-IDS)*, and it works by looking for fingerprints. That's right—I said fingerprints, which in this case means strange or abusive use of the network. IDS sends up an alarm only if it recognizes the fingerprints typical of attackers. The second approach looks for anomalies in network activity, or an *anomaly-detection IDS (AD-IDS)*. An AD-IDS basically watches for anything out of the ordinary; if it discovers fingerprints where there shouldn't be any, it will send out an alert. And a really cool feature is that it's known as a *smart system* because it learns on the go by keeping track of and building a history of network activity for norms to compare unusual activity to. Most IDSs today are a combination the two types of detection systems. Figure 15.10 shows an MD-IDS in action.

> An Intrusion Detection System cannot detect attacks within encrypted traffic.

FIGURE 15.10   An MD-IDS system in action

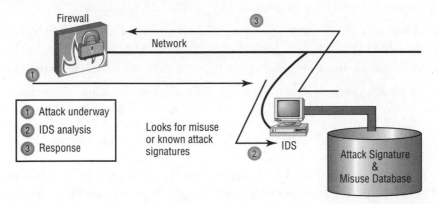

An IDS is a system made up of several components including one or more sensors to detect events, a console to control and configure the sensors and monitor events, and a database that records the events. These three elements can all be on the same device, or they can be implemented on multiple devices.

The two most common types of IDS implementations are network-based and host-based.

Network-Based IDS

By far the most common implementation of a detection system is a *network-based IDS (NIDS)*, where the IDS system is a separate device attached to the network via a machine like a switch or directly via a tap. Some IDSs are even capable of attaching to the network both outside and inside the firewall; this gives you the best security because you can see what is happening out in the wild and really nail exactly what's getting through your defenses. Figure 15.11 gives you an example of what this setup can look like.

FIGURE 15.11   An IDS connected to the network

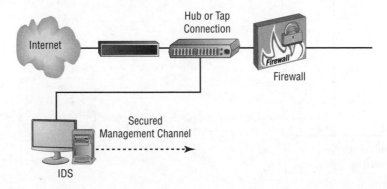

When your IDS detects an intrusion, it will respond to it either passively or actively. Passive responses are the easiest to configure and include the following:

Logging All activity to the intrusion is logged. The information gathered can be used to foil future attacks of the same type. Intrusions should always be logged.

Notification When an attack occurs, an IDS can send an alert to one or more administrators.

Shunning I'm not kidding about this one—you can sometimes just ignore the attack because it's possible it won't affect your network. For instance, if someone launches an attack designed to cripple a Microsoft Exchange email server at a network that's running Lotus Notes, you're all good, so why waste time doing anything about it? I would recommend recording the event, though.

Active responses mean taking immediate action. When an IDS moves to prevent an attack, it's often called a reactive system or an *Intrusion Protection System (IPS)*. Here are three common active responses:

Changing network configuration Let's say an attack comes in on port 21. Your IDS can close the port either temporarily or permanently. The downside is that if the IDS closes ports, legitimate traffic can't get through either, but it will definitely stop the attack. Figure 15.12 shows an example of closing port 80 (HTTP) for 60 seconds.

FIGURE 15.12 Shutting down port 80 for 60 seconds to stop an attack

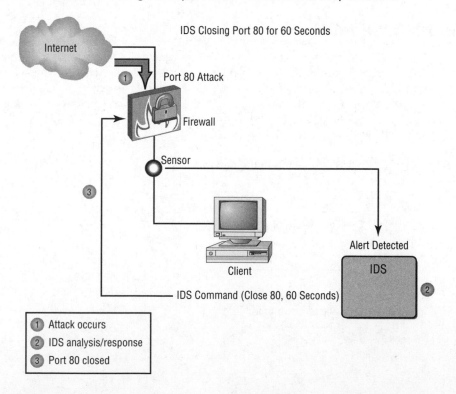

Terminating sessions   When the IDS detects an attack, it can force all sessions to close and restart, which will affect and delay legitimate traffic too, but not for long.

Deceiving the attacker   This one's the most fun because it tricks the bad guy into thinking their attack is really working when it's not. The system logs information, trying to pinpoint who's behind the attack and which methods they're using. This response requires something called a *honeypot,* typically a group of servers or maybe even access points, which the hacker is directed to; it's intended keep their interest long enough to gather enough information to identify them and their attack method, so you can prevent another attack in the future. Figure 15.13 demonstrates this.

FIGURE 15.13   Deceiving an attacker with a honeypot

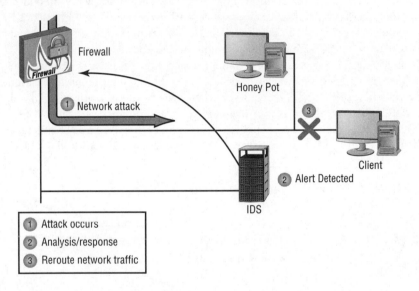

I am not endorsing using honeypots, just explaining the concept and how they work.

Host-Based IDS

In a *host-based IDS (HIDS),* software runs on one computer to detect abnormalities on that system alone by monitoring applications, system logs, and event logs—not by directly monitoring network traffic.

Systems like these are typically implemented on servers because they're a bear to manage if spread across several client computers on a network. Plus, if the IDS database is on the local computer and its data becomes compromised by an attack, the IDS data could be corrupted too.

Other types of IDSs are protocol-based (PIDS), which monitor traffic for one protocol on one server; application protocol-based (APIDS), which monitor traffic for a group of servers running the same application (such as SQL); and hybrid IDS, which combine one or more IDS technologies.

VPN Concentrators

A *VPN concentrator* is a device that creates remote access for virtual private networks (VPNs) either for users logging in remotely or for a large site-to-site VPN. In contrast to standard remote-access connections, remote-access VPNs often allow higher data throughput and provide encryption. Cisco produces VPN concentrators that support anywhere from 100 users up to 10,000 simultaneous remote-access connections.

Encryption for a remote-access VPN through a concentrator is usually handled by Internet Protocol Security (IPSec) or by Secure Sockets Layer (SSL), and user authentication can be achieved via Microsoft's Active Directory, Kerberos, Remote Authentication Dial In User Service (RADIUS), Rivest, Shamir, and Adleman (RSA), and digital certificates. Many VPN concentrators also have a built-in authentication server and allow ACLs to be implemented through them. In Figure 15.14, you can see where VPN concentrators are usually placed within a network setup.

FIGURE 15.14 VPN concentrator in a network

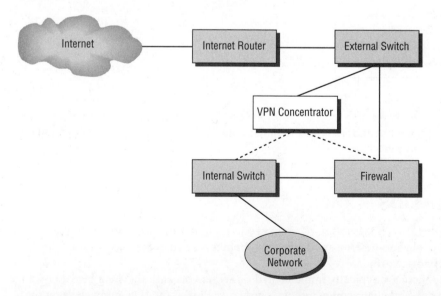

The dotted line indicates that you can opt to run your remote-access clients through the firewall before they're granted internal access, or you can just let the concentrator handle the security.

Understanding Problems Affecting Device Security

Through this whole chapter, I've been going on and on about the myriad devices we use to secure traffic coming into our networks and devices and the things we depend on to detect and prevent attacks on them. It's an important subject and one that you must solidly understand in order to be effective in networking. How to implement a tight security program requires working knowledge of these devices; but it doesn't end there, because there's always more you can know.

There happen to be a few more really significant and valuable concepts you should have a good grasp of when setting up and managing the security on your network. So that's the direction we're going to head in for the remainder of this chapter—we'll cover key issues you need to be aware of, including physical security and corresponding logical security structures, restricting access, and the types of protocols you should and should not use on your network.

Physical Security

Over the years, I've visited lots of different companies, large and small, public and private, and analyzed, advised, troubleshot, designed, and implemented their networks. Without fail, the system administrators I've met along the way have been really eager to tell me all about the security systems they have in place. "Look at this awesome firewall setup!" "Check out the cool group-policy structure we have!" "Watch how quickly our fault tolerance springs into action!" They're very proud, and rightly so, of what they've worked so hard to set up, because doing that isn't easy.

But interestingly, one of the things few people brag about is physical security—like it's some kind of afterthought. Maybe the server room has a locked door, maybe it doesn't. Maybe the right people's badges open that door, or maybe they don't. I guess that on a subconscious level, we tend to inherently trust the people working within the walls and focus our fears, suspicions, and ammo on mysterious outside forces that we're sure are incessantly trying to break in, steal data, or totally murder our networks. Some of the sharpest, most talented and savvy system administrators I've ever met still have a tendency to neglect inside security and reasonably monitor things going on within the building.

And there are some seriously vital things to nail down on the inside. For instance, does it really matter if your network has a secured subnet for the servers, with its own dedicated internal firewall? Definitely—I've actually found servers in racks like sitting ducks in a hallway right across from the lunch room. When I pointed out the fact that this was not so good, I was assured that it was only temporary until the server room construction was complete. I don't know about you, but for some reason, that didn't cut it and didn't make me feel anywhere near okay with the situation. At another company, I found the door to the server room propped open because otherwise "it got too hot in there." Because that toasty server room didn't exactly have a guard posted, anyone could just walk in and do whatever; the backup tapes were clearly marked and sitting there on a shelf—yikes! And don't even get me started about the heat. The bottom line is that if your system is not physically secured, you're basically sending out an open invitation to a Pandora's box of problems without even realizing it.

 Real World Scenario

Beware the Big Gulp

Several years ago when I was teaching a networking class, one of my best students issued me a challenge. He was proud of the security configuration on his server computer in the classroom and went so far as to tell me there was no way I could get to or damage any files on his system. He was really sure about that. Well, it just so happens I like a good challenge...

The students went off to lunch, and I stayed behind to work on a few things. While they were gone, I got out my handy Partition Magic diskette (I said this was a while ago) and popped it into his system. One reset button push later, I was in business. I wiped out the partitions on his hard drive and shut down the system.

When he came back from lunch, he looked a bit confused. He clearly remembered leaving his computer on; and upon booting up and playing around for a minute, he realized that his hard drive was gone. At first, he was more than a little angry at me for doing that, but then I asked him to give me a chance to prove a point—an important one. That is, when someone has access to your computer, they can do whatever they want. Yes, they might not be able to read your files (although I could have done that too), but they can still do a lot of damage. My tool of destruction was a partitioning program; but going back to that "servers out in the open across from the lunch room" situation, all it would take is a spilled soft drink to cause mass destruction. In any case, the data clearly was not safe, so physical security needs to be a top priority.

Physical Barriers

Your first objective is to keep people from physically getting to your equipment. Clearly, end users need to be able to get to their workstations, but only authorized personnel should be anywhere near your servers. The best way to do this is to have a dedicated, two-stage, air-conditioned server room with really secure doors and locks. Even better, your data center should have more than one form of physical security—preferably three. We call that a *multiple barrier system*. For instance, you could have a perimeter security system controlling access to the building as your first line of defense. The second would be a secured door to the computer room, and the third would be another security door to the server room itself. This is illustrated in Figure 15.15.

FIGURE 15.15   A three-layer security model

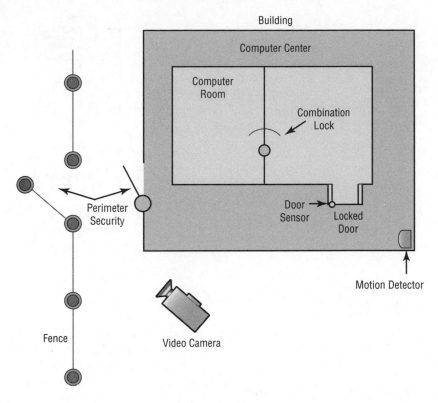

Security Zones

Your network probably has different security zones. Let's say your servers are in one zone and the clients are in another. Maybe your engineering department has its own zone. So why not have the same zones for physical access to the computers? Many companies today use magnetically encoded badges to control where employees are allowed to go inside the building. You may need a safety clearance and/or certification before you can go in the room where the pilot production machine lives. People should be cleared and certified before they're allowed in the server room as well.

Logical Security Configurations

Okay—now that you have your physical network locked down tight, it's time to review the security configuration of your network. The same concepts that apply to physical security apply here, too. First, you want to ensure that your network has an outside barrier and/or a perimeter defense. This is usually achieved by having a solid firewall, and it's best to have an IDS or IPS of some sort as well. Figure 15.16 shows what this might look like.

FIGURE 15.16 Network perimeter defense

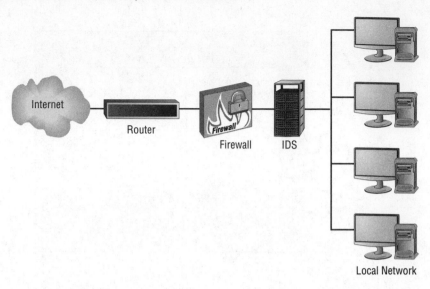

That may be enough for your network, but maybe not. Let's say that your network serves several distinct departments at your company. The engineering, accounting, and sales groups all have their own unique needs. What you can now do is divide up your internal network into smaller administrative zones by creating VLANs and using a DMZ. Maybe your network would logically look like the one shown in Figure 15.17.

FIGURE 15.17 Network divided into security zones

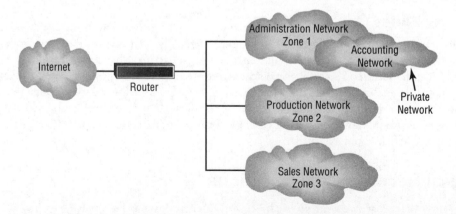

Finally, your network might be similar to the one shown earlier, but just larger. Maybe traffic is heavy, and you need to break up physical segments. Perhaps different groups are in different buildings or on different floors of a building, and you want to effectively segment them. There could be any number of reasons for you to "physically" separate your network into different groups, effectively partitioning your network by using multiple routers as shown in Figure 15.18.

FIGURE 15.18   Network divided into security zones

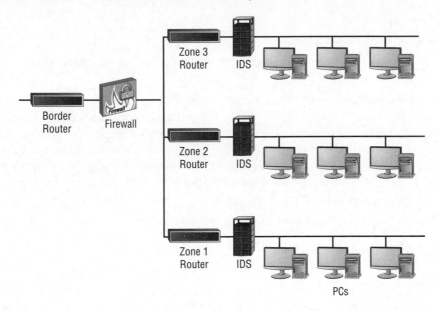

Restricting Local and Remote Access

Access control is a key part of any security program. I've already talked about physical security and logical security considerations, and now it's time to think about who can get on your network and how they do it.

When it comes to local access, only administrators should have the ability to log on to server consoles directly. In the world of Microsoft Server operating systems, the default setting is that only administrators can log on at the server—regular user accounts are prohibited from doing so. It's usually best to keep things this way, because ensuring that users don't have direct contact with the server is one really easy way to keep your physical security strong.

Remote access is an entirely different beast. You could work for a company that has a traveling sales force that needs to access data from the road, or one that has a work-from-home policy where users need remote access. Remote access is a great tool that helps increase productivity, but it also needs to be managed super-carefully. The first rule in securing remote access is to grant access to the network remotely only to those who absolutely need it. In most server operating systems, Windows 2003 and 2008 included, you must explicitly grant remote-access capability to user accounts.

WARNING   Never ever grant remote access to the Administrator account, because it's a huge security risk. Some accounts with administrative privileges may need remote-access capabilities, but those should be frugally limited and meticulously monitored for any suspicious activity whatsoever.

Access-Control Principles

When securing access to systems, whether local or remote, keep these important factors in mind:

Utilize implicit denies   An *implicit deny* is when a user is specifically locked out of a resource. Various Unix services have an .allow file and a .deny file that control access. If a given user isn't specifically mentioned in the .allow file, they are implicitly denied access to the service. It's much easier to grant a few people access through the .allow file than it is to manage long lists of people in a .deny file. In Windows, group policies are employed to manage the people who can specifically access certain services and resources.

Follow the least-privilege model   In a *least-privilege* model, users can only get to the bare minimum of resources they need access to, and their access level is always the lowest possible that still gives them the resources they need. For example, when you are setting permissions to a file such as a phone list, the administrator of that list would need to be able to modify the list, whereas everyone else should have read-only access. Don't give people more access then they absolutely need.

Separate out administrative duties   Separating administrative duties allows you to train junior administrators without giving them the keys to the kingdom. For instance, you can give a junior administrator's account the ability to reset user passwords and manage printers, but not the ability to access the SQL server or the email server. If you have a big IT department, separation of duties ensures that you know which administrators have access to the specific area you're managing. It's easier to control issues, and it nicely limits any finger-pointing.

Rotate administrator jobs   Make sure you have people cross-trained in various administrative aspects of your network. If you have a complex SQL server configuration, and the one person who knows SQL gets the plague when a major catastrophe hits, you could be in trouble. I mean, worst-case scenarios do happen; and, well, what if someone gets squished by a meteorite on the way to work? Yes, that's really not likely, but you get the point. Just make sure more than one person understands how each system works and can fill in just in case.

Access-Control Models

People use several predefined access-control models as references today. No, they aren't the exhaustive authority on access control, but they will give you a nice framework for an approach to securing your network. These models are as follows:

Mandatory Access Control   In the *Mandatory Access Control (MAC)* model, everyone's role regarding the network and related information access is set in stone. Users can't share information unless they are explicitly allowed to, and administrators must approve of and make any and all changes. This is the strictest and least flexible of the models, but it gives the administrator the most control. The downside to being a control freak is that it's really labor-intensive because all that work is left up to one person. So, using this model for anything but a small network could be a nightmare or even impossible.

Discretionary Access Control   Under a *Discretionary Access Control (DAC)* system, users get to have a say about who can access what data. Your users get lots of wiggle room, which means it's entirely possible that sensitive data could be shared inappropriately. In fact, a DAC system is actually the polar opposite of MAC; and if taken too far, it can result in a wide-open system that the administrator doesn't have much control over at all. Which network resources are shared, and who has access to them, is pretty much out of your hands. So unless you're naïve, super trusting, or really sure that your network's users are skilled and steadfastly honest, don't go with this one.

Role-Based Access Control   With *Role-Based Access Control (RBAC),* access to resources is granted based on the role the individual plays within the company. Think of RBAC as a hybrid between MAC and DAC—users get access based on who they are and what they need, and if they switch roles, they may gain new access but lose their old privileges.

Rule-Based Access Control   Just to make things confusing, RBAC can also refer to *Rule-Based Access Control*. In a rule-based approach, predefined security policies based on specific rules are used to determine network access. Whereas role-based defines needs based on the user's role, rule-based is more flexible: It assumes that users with the same roles may actually have different needs, and therefore, different rules may apply to them. A lot of operating systems today, like Windows Server 2008 and the various flavors of Unix, use a combination of role-based and rule-based access control for delimiting access to network resources—makes sense to me.

Secure and Unsecure Application Protocols

The kinds of application protocols you choose for communication on your network can have a huge impact on security. This is because a lot of the popular protocols in use today are inherently unsecure. They have no encryption built in, so anyone using a packet sniffer can intercept traffic and read your sensitive data. This may not be a problem for some transmissions, but I wouldn't feel all warm and fuzzy about my banking information being sent in plain-text across a telephone line, would you?

This is why I'm going to spend some time talking about two different types of protocols, beginning with a list of the unsecure variety. I'm not saying you should never use these, just that you need to be aware of their security limitations. I'll then list some popular secure protocols, most of which can be mapped to or even considered extensions of the unsecure protocols in the first group.

Unsecure Protocols

These are some widely used protocols that don't provide any security. Again, I'm not saying not to use them—just understand their limitations.

Telnet

Telnet is short for telecommunication network, and it's one of the oldest network protocols still in use today. It was developed to allow a user to log in remotely (or *telnet in*) to a Unix-based server, meaning that once you've telnetted in and logged in to the server, you can run commands on that server as if you were local to it.

Telnet was originally defined as RFC 15, and it operates on TCP port 23. It's not as popular as it used to be because it doesn't encrypt anything—including usernames and passwords. All you need is a packet sniffer to nick Telnet data, so it's only used in limited applications. Telnet is likely being used if your network still has any mainframe computers in it; it's also used for some Internet-based multiuser games because of its low overhead and fast speed.

HTTP

The ubiquitous *Hypertext Transfer Protocol (HTTP)* is the protocol of the World Wide Web. Although other protocols are used on the Internet, HTTP accounts for the lion's share of Internet traffic.

HTTP was developed as a joint effort between the World Wide Web Consortium (W3C) and the Internet Engineering Task Force (IETF). The most commonly referred-to HTTP standard is version 1.1, which was defined in 1999 as RFC 2616. By default, HTTP uses TCP port 80, but it can be configured to use alternate port numbers.

Resources are accessed via HTTP using *Uniform Resource Locators (URLs)*. Most of us in the developed world are familiar with URLs like www.lammle.com and www.comptia.org.

HTTP is totally unsecure, but it's a great example of a protocol you definitely want to use. When you're reading the news on cnn.com, security isn't the issue—loading all that information and multimedia quickly and efficiently is what's important. Additional security always slows things down, but there are ways to secure HTTP that I'll talk about soon.

FTP

File Transfer Protocol (FTP) is one of the most common protocols used to transfer files from one computer to another. If you've ever gone to a website and downloaded a file, chances are you used FTP. File downloads from websites can be accomplished via protocols like HTTP, but HTTP causes more overhead than FTP does, which makes it slower for downloading things. FTP is elegantly streamlined like a Thoroughbred for quick and easy downloading. The original RFC for FTP was RFC 114, which has been replaced by RFC 959.

FTP servers listen on TCP port 21 for incoming requests. TCP port 20 is also commonly used for data transmission, and FTP is famous (or infamous) for setting up connections on arbitrary higher-numbered ports called *dynamic ports*. If FTP is running in *active mode*, the client opens up the dynamic port, sends the FTP server the port number, and waits for the connection. In *passive mode*, the FTP server is the one that activates the dynamic port. For now, TCP port 21 is the one you need to remember.

Here's a list of some of the reasons FTP can give you grief:

- There is no security at all—passwords are sent in plain text.

- FTP uses multiple TCP connections on different ports, which can cause ugly problems with legacy firewalls.

- No data-integrity check is performed on the receiving side. If the file transfer is interrupted, the client technically has no way of knowing whether the transfer was completed.

- There is no ability to transfer timestamps or other file attributes like security permissions. All uploaded files are given a timestamp on the client that reflects when the transfer occurred.

Most FTP servers are set up as anonymous servers: To log in, you just enter anonymous (or ftp) as the username and then your email address as the password. You don't even have to enter your real email address, because verification will rarely happen. If you've downloaded via a website, the anonymous authentication was likely performed for you without you even knowing. FTP servers can be administratively secured so that usernames and passwords aren't just anonymous, but they'll still be transmitted in plain text.

If you do need to access an FTP server using a username and password, here's the context to easily do it through your web browser. In the Address bar, enter **ftp:// username:password@ftp.ftpsite.com/directory** where **username** and **password** are your username and password, **ftpsite.com** is the site you are accessing, and **directory** is the directory on the site you need access to, which may be optional.

rsh

Like many other legacy commands, *remote shell (rsh)* originated in the Unix world. It was released as part of the `rlogin` package in 1983 with version 4.2BSD. `rsh` is defined in RFC 1258 with `rlogin` and runs on TCP port 514.

Clients can use the `rsh` command to execute shell commands as though they're actually another user, and commonly, to execute shell commands on a remote computer. After the command is executed, `rsh` terminates the session. `rsh` is rarely used these days because it's been replaced by Secure Shell (SSH).

rcp

Remote copy (rcp) was introduced in the `rlogin` package along with `rsh`. It's a command used to remotely copy one file from one computer to another. Like `rsh`, it is unsecure, and like `rsh`, it's been replaced by the secure SSH.

SNMP (v1 and v2)

Simple Network Management Protocol (SNMP) is both a protocol and a set of standards for basic network management. The first RFC for SNMP, known as SNMPv1, was published in 1988 as RFC 1065, and the current standard is RFC 3411. SNMP allows administrators to collect information about devices on the network, including host computers, printers, hubs, routers, and switches; it uses UDP ports 161 and 162.

Here are some of the key components of the SNMP system:

- Network elements, also known as *managed objects*, are the devices on the network that are commonly tracked via SNMP.

- The *agent* is the software on the managed object that collects data about it.

- The *Network Management System (NMS)* is another name for the SNMP server. It executes applications that monitor and control managed objects. There can be more than one NMS on a network.

- The *Management Information Base (MIB)* is a database on the NMS that collects data from the individual agents on the network.

Examples of information collected by the agents include how much data has traveled through an interface (NIC) and how much traffic was transmitted per protocol. Other types of information indicate whether an action has occurred but don't keep track of how many times something has happened.

Even though SNMP was updated in 1999 to SNMPv2 (RFC 1441–RFC 1452), SNMPv2 still doesn't provide for secure data transmissions. Version 1 was particularly notorious for poor security because it transmitted authentication passwords (called *community strings*) in clear text on the network. Although version 2 includes a few improvements to both device management and security, it's still pretty vulnerable to packet sniffers, brute-force attacks, and IP spoofing.

Secure Protocols

These protocols have security built right in, and a lot of them are extensions of the protocols I just talked about. Keep in mind that although security slows down the transmission speed a bit, it's clearly well worth it if you need to protect your passwords and resources.

SSH

Secure Shell (SSH) is a protocol that was developed in 1995 and that allows two networked devices to exchange data using a secure channel. SSH was designed to be a replacement for Telnet and other unsecure remote shell programs such as `rlogin` and `rsh`. Technical details for SSH can be found in RFC 4252. SSH uses TCP port 22.

SSH provides encryption and uses public-key cryptography for authentication. The current version is SSH-2, which was originally designed in 1996 and proposed as an Internet standard in 2006. Open SSH is the most popular SSH implementation used today.

SSH can be used in conjunction with other secure file-management protocols such as `scp` and `sftp`. Finally, SSH is used to create tunnels for X11 applications, securely browse the Web through an encrypted proxy connection (using the SSH server as a proxy server), and create VPNs.

HTTPS

An extension to HTTP, *Hypertext Transfer Protocol over SSL (HTTPS)* is the current standard for creating secure HTTP sessions. When you go to a website that uses HTTPS, it's really still using HTTP with a couple of key differences. First, the port changes to TCP 443, and an additional encryption and authentication layer is added between the HTTP and TCP protocols.

WARNING   HTTPS essentially encrypts HTTP data over an SSL or Transport Layer Security (TLS) connection. Although this protects the transmissions from eavesdroppers, it does not protect the user from man-in-the-middle attacks.

For HTTPS to work, the web server you are connecting to must have a public key certificate signed by a certificate authority (CA). This certifies that the web server is actually the one it's claiming to be—if the certificate is expired, or if there are any other abnormalities when you try to make an HTTPS connection, you'll get a warning asking if you want to continue. If you do, it's at your own risk, because designing a site that looks exactly like a valid storefront is a popular scam today.

Even though HTTPS does a pretty good job of protecting the data being transmitted over the Web, it still has some very real vulnerabilities. Along with being susceptible to man-in-the-middle attacks, it has no provision for securing the data once it gets to the client computer. Security expert Gene Spafford once said that using HTTPS was like "using an armored truck to transport rolls of pennies between someone on a park bench and someone doing business from a cardboard box." That might sound a bit harsh, but understand that HTTPS isn't perfectly secure.

SFTP

An extension of the SSH protocol is the *Secure File Transfer Protocol (SFTP)*, which is designed to perform file transfers and remote file management. It can be used in place of FTP and employs TCP port 22. SFTP itself doesn't provide any authentication or security—those are left are up to SSH.

NOTE   Make no mistake—SFTP isn't FTP run over an SSH connection. That's creatively called "FTP over SSH," and it presents problems with creating secure tunnels because FTP creates dynamic ports to complete data transfers.

In contrast to the SCP protocol, SFTP is used for file-management tasks like pulling directory listings, using wildcards, and deleting remote files. As an added bonus, the SFTP protocol does not show plain-text passwords.

SCP

Secure Copy Protocol (SCP) is a descendent of the rcp protocol and is used to securely copy files from one system to another. Encryption is provided by SSH. SCP runs on TCP port 22.

SNMPv3

SNMPv3 provides the same features as SNMP versions 1 and 2, but it adds some important security elements like encryption, authentication, and message integrity. As of 2004, SNMPv3 is the current SNMP standard as defined by RFV 3411–RFC 3418. Earlier versions of SNMP are considered obsolete.

Summary

In this chapter, you learned a lot about physical and hardware security. We dove into this increasingly important subject by looking at one of the most useful network protection devices around: firewalls. You found out the differences between network-based versus host-based firewalls and then learned the specific ways that firewalls work to protect our data and networks by using access control lists (ACLs). You also learned about other key firewall topics like demilitarized zones (DMZs), protocol switching, packet filtering, and proxy services. I talked about how firewalls can operate at the Network layer or the Application layer of the OSI model. For those operating at the network level, there are stateful firewalls that keep track of the established connections passing through them and stateless firewalls that don't. Other services provided by firewalls include scanning services, signature identification, content filtering, and breaking your network up into security zones.

We then moved on and discussed two other vital hardware devices: Intrusion Detection and Prevention Systems and VPN concentrators. You learned that IDS devices can be network- or host-based, just like firewalls; but unlike firewalls, which block traffic based on specific rules, IDS and IPS systems allow traffic in and then initiate a reaction if any problems are detected. I also talked about something called an IPS, which is an IDS that can generate an active response when an intrusion is detected. We then covered VPN concentrators, which are specifically designed to allow several hundred—even several thousand—users to remotely access your network either through a secure connection or by setting up a virtual secure network between two locations.

You also discovered some often-overlooked aspects of physical security that can seriously affect your network. You now know that beyond a doubt, if people can get to your hardware, they can do damage to your infrastructure, intentionally or not. I showed you some ways to secure your network and gave you some tips and policies for restricting who can access resources and where they can access them from.

Finally, we talked about several Application-layer protocols and commands used in networking. I went over unsecure protocols like Telnet, HTTP, FTP, rsh, rcp, and SNMP, and finished up by briefing you on secure versions such as SSH, HTTPS, SNMPv3, SFTP, and RCP.

Exam Essentials

Understand the difference between a network-based firewall and a host-based firewall. A network-based firewall is a hardware device on the network or on a router that protects a group of computers. A host-based firewall is software installed on one individual machine, and it only protects that machine.

Understand how a firewall determines which traffic can pass through it.   Firewalls use access control lists (ACLs), which are sets of rules, to determine which traffic is allowed to pass through.

Remember where a DMZ can be placed   A demilitarized zone (DMZ) can be located outside a firewall, connected directly to the Internet. However, it can also be placed after the firewall. You need to remember that it can be placed in either location.

Understand what a proxy server is and what types of proxying are common.   A proxy server is a computer that makes and fulfills requests on behalf of another computer. Many firewalls can act as proxies. Common proxy services include IP proxy, web proxy, FTP proxy, and mail (SMTP) proxy.

Know which levels of the OSI model a firewall can operate on.   Firewalls work at the application layer or the network layer.

Understand the difference between stateful and stateless firewalls.   A stateful firewall keeps track of the established connections passing through it. When another packet is received that's part of an existing connection (part of a current state), the packet is passed without checking the ACLs. A stateless firewall examines each packet individually and does not track existing states. This makes it a bit slower and more susceptible to network attacks.

Know what types of services firewalls can provide.   Most firewalls provide scanning services, content filtering, signature identification, and the ability to segregate network segments into separate security zones.

Know the difference between an IDS and an IPS.   An Intrusion Detection System (IDS) monitors network traffic, looking for signs of an intrusion. Intrusions are detected by matching activity versus known signatures within the IDS's database. If an intrusion is detected, a passive response such as logging or notifying a network administrator is executed. An Intrusion Prevention System (IPS) is like an IDS, but with two key differences. First, it learns what is "normal" on the network and can react to abnormalities even if they're not part of the signature database. Second, it can issue an active response such as shutting down a port, resetting connections, or attempting to lull the attacker into a trap.

Know which application-layer protocols are not secure.   The unsecure list includes telnet, HTTP, FTP, rsh, rcp, and SNMP versions 1 and 2.

Know which application-layer protocols are secure.   The secure list includes SSH, HTTPS, SFTP, SCP, and SNMPv3.

Written Lab

In this section, write the answers to the following security questions:

1. Which type of security device employs a redirection device known as a honeypot?

2. Which type of firewall keeps track of existing connections passing through it?

3. If you wanted to ensure that your firewall could block inflammatory email, which type of service would you look for?

4. A firewall's list of rules that it uses to block traffic is called _____.

5. If you wanted to allow remote access to 500 users, which type of device is recommended?

6. If data from one of your subnets should be restricted from entering another subnet, the subnets should be configured as different _____.

7. Which unsecure protocol uses port 80 by default?

8. Which unsecure protocol utilizes arbitrary port numbers to complete its work?

9. What port number does Secure Shell (SSH) use by default?

10. Logging, notification, and shunning are what types of reactions from what type of security device?

(The answers to the Written Lab can be found following the answers to the Review Questions for this chapter.)

Review Questions

1. In general, firewalls work by _____.

   A. Rejecting all packets regardless of security restrictions

   B. Forwarding all packets regardless of security restrictions

   C. Allowing only packets that pass security restrictions to be forwarded

   D. None of the above

2. Which layer of the OSI model do software firewalls operate in? (Choose all that apply.)

   A. Application

   B. Presentation

   C. Physical

   D. Network

3. What is the main difference between a network-based firewall and a host-based firewall?

   A. A network-based firewall protects the Internet from attacks.

   B. A network-based firewall protects a network, not just a single host.

   C. A network-based firewall protects the network wires.

   D. A network-based firewall protects a CD from data loss.

4. What is one advantage that a stateless firewall has over its stateful counterparts?

   A. It's faster.

   B. It utilizes less memory.

   C. It's better at preventing network attacks.

   D. It works better on external networks.

5. A network administrator needs to filter unwanted packets when implementing the companies' security policies. What should be implemented to help exercise control over future network traffic?

   A. Access control list (ACL)

   B. Proxy server

   C. Intrusion Prevention System

   D. VPN concentrator

6. What is the benefit of using a firewall?

   A. Protects external users

   B. Protects external hardware

   C. Protects LAN resources

   D. Protects hardware from failure

7. Your company uses a custom TCP port number of 9080 that is hosted on your DMZ server. Users can no longer access a custom application that uses this port. You've verified that the firewall is permitting this TCP port. Which command can you use to verify the DMZ server is still accepting connections on TCP port 9080?

    A. ping

    B. telnet

    C. nbtstat

    D. netstat

    E. ipconfig

8. Which device can limit traffic on a network and allow access onto specific TCP/IP port numbers when security is a concern?

    A. Hub

    B. Firewall

    C. DNS

    D. Modem

9. Which is not a type of access control list (ACL)?

    A. Standard

    B. Extended

    C. Referred

    D. Outbound

10. A network administrator is creating an outbound ACL. Which of the following is not a general access-list guideline that should be followed when the network administrator is creating and implementing ACLs on the router?

    A. Use only one ACL per interface per protocol per direction.

    B. Place IP-extended ACLs as far away from the source as possible.

    C. Create ACLs and then apply them to an interface.

    D. Every list should have at least one `permit` statement or it will deny all traffic.

11. What is the best explanation for a DMZ?

    A. To separate a security zone for an IPS and IDS server

    B. To create a security zone for VPN terminations

    C. To create a security zone that allows public traffic but is isolated from the private inside network

    D. To create a security zone that allows private traffic but is isolated from the public network

12. Which of the following are types of services that firewalls can provide? (Choose all that apply.)

    A. Content filtering

    B. Segregate network segments

    C. Signature identification

    D. Scanning services

    E. All of the above

13. Which type of security device monitors network traffic, looking for signs of an intrusion?

    A. Intrusion Detection System

    B. Demilitarized zone (DMZ)

    C. Firewall

    D. VPN concentrator

14. Which of these application-layer protocols is not secure?

    A. SSH

    B. HTTP

    C. HTTPS

    D. SNMPv3

15. Which of these application-layer protocols is secure?

    A. SFTP

    B. RSH

    C. SNMPv1

    D. SNMPv2

16. Changing network configurations, terminating sessions, and deceiving the attacker are actions that can be taken from what type of security device?

    A. Access control list (ACL)

    B. Content filtering

    C. Security zones

    D. Intrusion Prevention System (IPS)

17. Which of the following are access-control principles that should be followed? (Choose all that apply.)

    A. Use implicit deny or allow.

    B. Follow the least-privilege model.

    C. Separate out administrative duties.

    D. Rotate administrator jobs.

    E. All of the above

18. Which protocol uses port 22 by default?

    A. Telnet

    B. FTP

    C. SSH

    D. HTTPS

19. A network administrator needs to transfer files from one computer to another. What protocol would most likely be used in this scenario?

    A. Telnet

    B. FTP

    C. HTTP

    D. RCP

20. What protocol can be used to transfer files and is similar to FTP but not secure?

    A. SCP

    B. SFTP

    C. SSH

    D. TFTP

Answers to Review Questions

1. C. Firewalls work by allowing only packets that pass security restrictions to be forwarded through the firewall. A firewall can also permit, deny, encrypt, decrypt, and proxy all computer traffic that flows through it; this can be between a public and private network or between different security domains (or zones) on a private network. You as the administrator set up the rules by which a firewall decides to forward or reject packets of data.

2. A, D. Firewalls work at the application layer or the network layer.

3. B. A *network-based firewall* is what companies use to protect their private network from public networks. The defining characteristic of this type of firewall is that it's designed to protect an entire network of computers as opposed to just one system. This is usually a combination of hardware and software. A *host-based firewall* is implemented on one machine and is designed to protect that machine only. Most often, this is implemented as software; no additional hardware is required in your personal computer to run a host-based firewall.

4. B. The one big advantage that a stateless firewall has over its stateful counterparts is that it uses less memory. Today, stateless firewalls are best if used on an internal network where security threats are lower and there are few restrictions.

5. A. ACLs allow routers to filter packets. These filters allow you, the administrator, to control the flow of packets through a network.

6. C. One of the benefits of using a firewall is that it helps protect LAN resources from unwanted attacks.

7. B. From any command prompt, or router prompt, you can telnet to the port number on the DMZ server to verify it is responding.

8. B. Firewalls, which use access-lists can permit or deny connections and types of traffic in or out of the network.

9. C. Standard, extended, and outbound are all types of ACL. Referred is not.

10. B. When configuring an ACL, you need to place IP-extended ACLs as close to the source as possible. Because extended ACLs can filter on very specific addresses and protocols, you don't want your traffic to traverse the entire network and then be denied. By placing this list as close to the source address as possible, you can filter traffic before it uses up your precious bandwidth.

11. C. A DMZ can be set up many different ways, but the best explanation is the DMZ is to separate and secure your inside network from the Internet well allowing hosts on the Internet to access your servers.

12. E. Most firewalls provide content filtering, signature identification, and the ability to segregate network segments into separate security zones. Most firewalls are also capable of performing scanning services, which means that they scan different types of incoming traffic in an effort to detect problems.

13. A. An Intrusion Detection System (IDS) monitors network traffic, looking for signs of an intrusion. Intrusions are detected by matching activity versus known signatures within the IDS's database. If an intrusion is detected, a passive response such as logging or notifying a network administrator is executed. An Intrusion Prevention System (IPS) is like an IDS, but with two key differences. First, it learns what is "normal" on the network and can react to abnormalities even if they aren't part of the signature database. Second, it can issue an active response such as shutting down a port, resetting connections, or attempting to lull the attacker into a trap.

14. B. HTTP is an Application-layer protocol that is not secure.

15. A. SFTP is an Application-layer protocol that is secure.

16. D. Changing network configurations, terminating sessions, and deceiving the attacker are all actions that can be taken by an IPS device.

17. E. All of these are common access-control principles that should be followed. An *implicit deny* is when a user is specifically locked out of a resource. In the *least-privilege* model, users only have access to the bare minimum of resources they need. Separating administrative duties allows you to train junior administrators without giving them full access. It is also a good idea to make sure you have people cross-trained in various administrative aspects of your network.

18. C. *Secure Shell (SSH)* uses port 22 by default. This protocol allows two networked devices to exchange data using a secure channel. SSH was designed to be a replacement for Telnet and other unsecure remote shell programs such as `rlogin` and `rsh`.

19. B. Although it's true that transferring files can be done using HTTP, HTTP has more overhead than FTP, which makes it slower for tasks such as downloading. FTP is streamlined specifically for this task.

20. D. Trivial File Transfer Protocol (TFTP) is a transfer protocol that does not provide any security. It has no password for authentication or login and no encryption for transfer security. It is useful for moving configuration and operating-system files onto and off of networking devices because it has low overhead and the software is easy to run. FTP by default isn't secure either, but it wasn't listed as a possible answer to the question.

Answers to Written Lab

1. Intrusion Prevention System

2. Stateful

3. Content filtering

4. Access Control List (ACL)

5. A VPN concentrator

6. Security zones

7. HTTP

8. FTP

9. 22

10. Passive reactions from an IDS

Chapter

16

Wide Area Networks

THE FOLLOWING COMPTIA NETWORK+ EXAM OBJECTIVES ARE COVERED IN THIS CHAPTER:

✓ **2.5 Categorize WAN technology types and properties**

- Type:
    - Frame relay
    - E1/T1
    - ADSL
    - SDSL
    - VDSL
    - Cable modem
    - Satellite
    - E3/T3
    - OC-x
    - Wireless
    - ATM
    - SONET
    - MPLS
    - ISDN BRI
    - ISDN PRI
    - POTS
    - PSTN
- Properties
    - Circuit switch
    - Packet switch
    - Speed
    - Transmission media
    - Distance

So what, exactly, is it that makes something a wide area network (WAN) instead of a local area network (LAN)? Well, there's obviously the distance thing, but these days, wireless LANs can cover some serious turf. What about bandwidth? Here again, some really big pipes can be had for a price in many places, so that's not it either. What the heck is it then?

One of the main ways a WAN differs from a LAN is that whereas you generally own a LAN infrastructure, you usually lease WAN infrastructure from a service provider. To be honest, modern technologies even blur this definition, but it still fits neatly into the context of CompTIA's Network+ exam objectives. Anyway, I've already talked about the data link that you usually own (Ethernet), but now we're going to find out about the kind you usually don't own—the type most often leased from a service provider.

You may already be familiar with T Series Connections, which are a type of leased-line connection that reserve or dedicate lines that provide paths between network segments. In addition to these, I'll also cover broadband services including the various flavors of *Digital Subscriber Lines* (DSL) and *cable modem* connectivity that most of us use to connect to the Internet from home.

We'll also talk about the different kinds of WAN connectivity that are achieved through other kinds of links and over different transmission media. WAN technologies run the gamut from short-range *Bluetooth* to the seriously long-distance coverage available through satellite transmissions. And not to be forgotten are the WAN protocols that are basically sets of rules that delimit how long-distance communication and connectivity should happen. I'll tell you about the not-so-modern technologies like *Integrated Services Digital Networks (ISDN), Frame Relay,* and *Asynchronous Transfer Mode (ATM),* and more modern technologies like *Multi Protocol Label Switching (MPLS),* but I'll talk about the legacy phone-company network and some of its terminology as well. You'll also learn everything you'll need to know about different speed links including T1s and E1s, SONET fiber links, and the plain old telephone service (POTS) lines that connect us to the Public Switched Telephone Network (PSTN), to arm you with the knowledge you need to meet the CompTIA Network+ objectives.

For up-to-the-minute updates for this chapter, please see www.lammle.com or www.sybex.com/go/comptianetwork+studyguide.

What's a WAN?

As local area networks (LANs) grew and developed, it became necessary to be able to connect their resources together over long distances—not just locally. At first, we achieved this goal via the phone company network known as the Public Switched Telephone Network (PSTN). And so, the first successful network that could establish voice communications over disparate locations was born.

Because few of us remember back to a time when there was no such thing as phone service, PSTN was an obvious solution because it was already a fully operational circuit-switching network, where every phone call established a unique circuit from one endpoint (phone) to another through a path of switches. So, instead of reinventing the wheel to design LANs, early network planners used packet switching as their communications-delivery method. And clearly, the task of wiring these packet-switched networks to enable communication over vast locales wasn't exactly something that could be done quickly, so early wide area networks (WANs) also used the existing phone company network. But this solution wasn't all that great because it was costly and imposed some ugly limitations on networks trying to transfer their data to each other.

So there's the history for you. Today's WANs are communications networks that cover broad geographic areas that still frequently use phone companies (service providers) along with their circuit-switched networks to connect LANs together. Competition can be great, and with the Internet entering the playing field and giving us an alternative way to connect LANs, we benefit tremendously from the resulting reduction for the cost of our connectivity. These new connection options, along with their related protocols and technologies can greatly reduce the cost of a WAN's infrastructure, and lowered transport costs are a huge relief for network administrators and designers.

Anyway, remember that WAN protocols and technologies all occupy the lower three layers of the OSI model—the Physical layer, Data Link layer, and sometimes the Network layer. The various types of connections, technologies, topologies, and devices used with WANs as well as creating WAN connections using different transmission media like air (wireless), space (satellite), and both copper and glass fiber for wired connections will all be covered in this chapter. But before we go there, you need to know some basic WAN terms.

Even though I could include wireless networks in this chapter as last-mile WAN solutions, we've already covered those solutions back in Chapter 12, "Wireless Technologies."

Defining WAN Terms

Before you run out and order a WAN service type from a provider, it would be a really good idea to understand the following terms that service providers typically use:

Customer premises equipment (CPE)   *Customer premises equipment (CPE)* is equipment that's owned by the service provider but located on the subscriber's (your) property.

CSU/DSU   *Channel service unit/data service unit (CSU/DSU)* is a Layer 1 device that connects your serial ports on your router to the provider's network and connects directly to the *demarcation point* (demark) or location. These devices can be external, as shown a little later in Figure 16.1, or internal cards on the router. The CSU/DSU provides clocking of the line to the CPE (your router, in this case) and provides other important options, like voltage regulation.

Demarcation point   The demarc is the precise spot where the service provider's (local exchange carrier) responsibility ends and the CPE begins. It's generally a device in a tele-communications closet owned and installed by the telecommunications company (telco). It's your responsibility to cable—a task called *extended demark*—from this box to the CPE, which is usually a connection to a CSU/DSU or ISDN interface.

Local loop   A cable consisting of a pair of copper wires called the *local loop* connects the demarc to the closest switching office known as a *central office (CO)*.

Central office (CO)   A phone company building that connects the customer's network to the provider's switching network. Good to know is that a CO is sometimes referred to as a *point of presence (POP)*.

Toll network   The *toll network* is a trunk line inside a WAN provider's network. This network is a collection of switches and facilities owned by the ISP.

With all this being said, let's take a look at Figure 16.1, which uses all these items to describe a typical WAN connection.

FIGURE 16.1   A typical wide area network

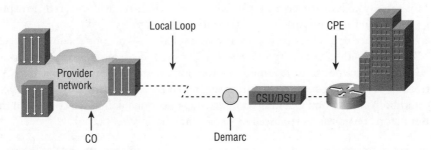

You would find the typical WAN as shown in Figure 16.1 when you order a T1 or Frame Relay circuit. Definitely familiarize yourself with these terms, because they're crucial to understanding WAN technologies.

The Public Switched Telephone Network (PSTN)

The portion of the PSTN that runs from your house to the rest of the world is known as *plain old telephone service (POTS),* and it's a popular method for connecting remote users to a local network because of its simplicity, low cost, and easy installation. But connecting to PSTN via ISDN, DSL, a cable modem, or even your cellular service is becoming all the rage today.

Two key concepts to keep in mind about PSTN are public and switched. *Public* basically means that, for a fee, anyone can lease the use of the network without having to deal with running any cabling, and *switched* explains how the phone system works. Even though one or more wires are actually connected to your home and/or office, all of them aren't always online, being used. But it's still available to you in its offline state so you can get online and join the network pretty much whenever you want. Think of it like a standing reservation, which your phone number is used as an I.D. to access. Because you initiate the connection by dialing a certain phone number, it's easy to imagine how technically impractical it would be—even impossible—for this method to work if every phone number stayed connected all the time. If they did, the resulting backbone cabling requirements and problems would essentially be insurmountable.

Take, for instance, the U.S. and worldwide telephone systems. The actual numbering sequence varies in other countries, but the concept is identical. The phone company runs the local loop from the demarc to the CO. All the pairs from all the local loop cables within a small regional area come together at a central point a lot like a patch panel in a unshielded twisted-pair (UTP)-based LAN does.

This centralized point has a piece of equipment attached called a *switch*, which opens a communications session when it's initiated by a user who's dialed the phone number of the receiver and keeps it open until the "conversation" ends, when the switch closes it. On one side of the switch is the neighborhood wiring, and on the other side are lines that either connect to another switch or to a local set of wiring.

Let me make this really clear. When you want to make a call, you pick up the phone, which completes a circuit that in most cases gives you a dial tone. The tone is the switch's way of saying, "I'm ready." When you don't get that dial tone, it means either that there's a break in the equipment chain or that the switch is too busy processing other requests. In many areas of the world, you hear a fast on-and-off tone after giving a command string (phone number) to the local switch. This means that other switches the local switch is attempting to communicate with are too busy at that time.

Recently, this tone thing has been replaced with a voice recording saying something like, "We're sorry. All circuits are busy. Please try your call later." Sometimes you even get offered the shady-sounding, "For only 99 cents, you can interrupt this call" added to the message. This happens frequently on holidays or during natural disasters, because the local area's phone company uses only the minimum number of wires called *trunk lines* required to handle the norms of usage capacity plus a few auxiliary lines for peak usage. They keep equipment to a minimum because wiring and switches are really expensive; it's essentially a trade-off between providing 100-percent uptime and keeping the costs of leasing the connection from the phone company reasonably affordable.

WAN Connection Types

With all that in mind, it's time to go over the various types of WAN connections you'll find on the market today. Figure 16.2 shows the different WAN connection types that can be used to connect your LANs together.

FIGURE 16.2 WAN connection types

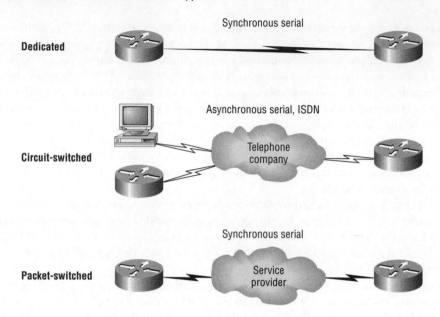

Okay—let me explain the different WAN connection types you see pictured here:

Leased lines These are usually referred to as a *point-to-point* or dedicated connection. A dedicated *leased line* is a pre-established WAN communications path that goes from the CPE through the DCE switch and then over to the CPE of the remote site. The CPE enables DTE networks to communicate at any time with no cumbersome setup procedures to muddle through before transmitting data. When you've got plenty of cash, this is the way to go because it uses synchronous serial lines up to 45Mbps. High-Level Data Link Control (HDLC) and Point to Point Protocol (PPP) encapsulations are frequently used on leased lines, and I'll go over them with you in detail in a bit.

Circuit switching When you hear the term *circuit switching*, think phone call. The big advantage is cost—you only pay for the time you actually use. No data can transfer before an end-to-end connection is established. Circuit switching uses dial-up modems or ISDN and is used for low-bandwidth data transfers. Okay—I know what you're thinking: "Modems? Did he say modems? Aren't those only in museums by now?" After all, with all the wireless technologies available, who uses modems these days? Well, some people do have ISDN: It's still viable, and there are many places on Earth where you still need a modem to get yourself dialed in. Plus, circuit switching can be used in some of the newer WAN technologies as well.

Packet switching This is a WAN switching method that allows you to share bandwidth with other companies to save money. *Packet switching* can be thought of as a network that's designed to look like a leased line yet charges you more like circuit switching does. But less isn't always more—there's definitely a downside, and if you need to transfer data constantly, just forget about this option. Instead, get yourself a leased line. Packet switching will only work for you if your data transfers are the bursty type—that is, not continuous. Frame Relay and the super-old X.25 are packet-switching technologies with speeds that can range from 56Kbps up to T3 (45Mbps).

LANs use packet switching with the source and destination addresses in the packet header to let the network move the packet closer and closer to the destination in the same way the Post Office takes your letter and keeps it moving closer and closer to its destination. This method avoids the necessity of establishing an actual contiguous electrical circuit from one end to the other, which is the method phone companies use to facilitate a phone call in their circuit-switched network.

Most WAN connections work on the phone company's circuit-switched network where the point-to-point nature of most connections eliminates the need for addressing because there's only one possible destination between endpoints. But you still need a proper addressing scheme within your LAN to ensure that data packets reach their correct destinations.

Bandwidth or Speed

The need for speed involves the necessity to move whatever volume of data-, voice-, and video-loaded packets across vast distances to communicate. As companies' volume requirements have grown, so has the appetite for ever bigger, faster connections. Speed or bandwidth is measured in bits per second or multiples of bits per second, such as kilobits (thousands of bits) per second, and so on.

The winner of the "slowest type of WAN connection" prize is (surprise) the much-maligned dial-on-demand dial-up connection. Modern dial-up modems typically have a maximum theoretical transfer speed of 56Kbps, although in most cases 40–50 Kbps is the norm. Factors such as phone-line noise as well as the quality of the modem itself play a large part in determining connection speeds. Modems are required to *modulate/demodulate* the signal, which means translating the analog signal our ears hear into a digital stream for transfer across a digital network. Some connections may be as slow as 20Kbps in extremely "noisy" environments like hotel rooms where phone lines are shared with an abundant number of extensions.

Megabyte (MB) and gigabyte (GB) usually refer to the amount of storage capacity available, whereas bandwidth and speed refer to units that measure how much data (bits) can be sent per second. In the networking world, speed is essentially the measurement of how fast the data flows (Hz) and also refers to how fast data flows within memory systems. Sometimes these two terms are used interchangeably.

T-Series Connections

The basic, first level in bandwidth or speed for leased lines that provide synchronous connections between sites is known as the T1 line. It serves up 24 Digital Signal 0 (DS0), 64Kbps channels in our country, Japan, and South Korea. A slightly bigger/faster version with 30 DS0 channels is available in Europe; it's called the E1 or E carrier line.

The name T1 came from the carrier letter assigned by AT&T to the technology. They are also known as T carrier lines. Essentially, the *T* is a part number that was assigned by AT&T. T1s offer Digital Signal 1 (DS1) bit patterns to transmit packets; DS1 has to do with the service to be sent over a T1—originally, 24 digitized voice channels. The terms T1 and DS1 have become synonymous and include a bunch of different services from voice to data to clear-channel pipes. The line speed is always consistent at 1.544Mbps (millions of bits per second), but the payload can vary greatly.

T-series connections are digital connections that you can lease from the telephone company. They can use copper pairs like regular phone lines, or they can be brought in as part of a backbone (also called a trunk line). At this point, T-series connections use time-division multiplexing (TDM) to divide the bandwidth into channels of equal bit rate.

T-series connection types are denoted by the letter *T* plus a number. Each connection type differs in its speed and in the signal used to multiplex the channels. Table 16.1 lists some of the T-series connections and their maximum data rates. The most commonly used T-series lines are T1 and T3.

TABLE 16.1   T-Series Connections

Connection	Maximum Speed
T1	1.544Mbps
T1C	3.152Mbps
T2	6.312Mbps
T3	44.736Mbps
T4	274.176Mbps

The T1 Connection

Okay—as I said, a T1 is a 1.544Mbps digital connection that's typically carried over two pairs of copper wires. This 1.544Mbps connection uses DS1 and aggregates 24 discrete, 64Kbps channels that use DS0. Each channel can carry either voice or data. In the POTS world, T1 lines are used to convert and bundle analog phone conversations over great distances due to the better quality of a digital signal and using much less wiring than would be needed if each pair carried only one call. This splitting into independent channels also allows a company to combine voice and data over one T1 connection or to use the T1 as if it were an unchannelized 1.544Mbps pipe. You can also order a fractional T1 (FT1) circuit that's delivered on a T1 but doesn't allow the use of all 24 channels.

The European version of the T1 is the E1, which operates at 2.048Mbps and uses 30 64Kbps channels (thirty DS0's). It was designed later, based on T1s—they just made theirs a little bigger. You'll also find the J1, which is the Japanese version of the T1 and which operates at 1.544 Mbps, just like the T1.

 Real World Scenario

What Is a Good Speed for a Business?

Many of you who happen to be in charge of setting up your company's Internet connection may think that a T1 is the best speed for your business; but unfortunately, T1 connections to the Internet can be really pricey. If you're in the business of selling Internet connections like an ISP is, you can justify spending the big bucks on large bandwidth pipes. Another example of when it would make sense for you to opt for a T1 is if you have loads of users on your network—at least 50 or more.

But even if you've got bunches of users on your network, it could be worth it to check out alternative solutions for your business that offer similar speeds at lower costs, like DSL or a cable modem. You can always use a virtual private network (VPN) if you need the security. And there are inexpensive wireless connection options out there as well that provide good bandwidth. It's always a good idea to do your research before buying.

The T3 Connection

A T3 line works similarly to a T1 connection but carries a whopping 44.736Mbps. This is equivalent to 28 T1 circuits (or a total of 672 DS0 channels), and it uses a signal known as Digital Signal 3 (DS3) that's definitely not the same as the DS1 signal and is generally delivered over fiber-optic cable. Many local ISPs have T3 connections to their next-tier ISPs. Also, very large multinational companies use T3 connections to send voice and data between their major regional offices.

As with the T1, the T3 has a European counterpart (the E3), which operates at 34.368Mbps. And the Japanese Digital Hierarchy specifies the J3 circuit, which operates at 32.064Mbps.

Transmission Media

Another aspect of WAN technologies that can have a big effect on the speed, bandwidth, and the volume of data that can be transferred is the type of transmission media. Wireless transmissions use air as a transmission media. This not only creates a bit of challenge concerning security but also presents us with signal degradation—the further the signal has to travel from the original source, the weaker it gets. A solution to this last hang-up comes through using microwave repeaters that retransmit signals through the air and bolster them. This approach is a lot more efficient because it can preserve signal strength over much greater distances.

The most far-reaching technology uses the air and even empty space to send electromagnetic signals to satellites from which they are then re-sent to distant geographic locations.

Wired Connections

Back on Earth, wired connections use either copper wire or glass fiber to carry bits as voltages or light pulses, respectively. That attenuation issue I just talked about under wireless technology, where the signal gradually weakens over distances, also relates to copper wire transmissions and limits the length of wire you can use. Fiber gives us a lot more bandwidth and is a lot less susceptible to noise, but it costs more to buy and install. In the U.S, the standard for synchronous data transmission on optical fiber is called *Synchronous Optical Network (SONET)*, and the international equivalent of SONET is Synchronous Digital Hierarchy (SDH). SONET defines a base data rate, or *throughput,* of 51.84Mbps, and multiples of this rate are known as optical carrier (OC) levels like OC-3, OC-12, and so on. Table 16.2 depicts common OC levels and their associated data rates

TABLE 16.2   Common Optical Carrier Levels (OC-*x*)

Level	Data Rate
OC-1	51.84Mbps
OC-3	155.52Mbps
OC-12	622.08Mbps
OC-48	2.488Gbps
OC-192	9.953Gbps

Regardless of the media used to carry WAN traffic, the growing volume of voice and video traversing data networks has lead to new traffic problems. Regular data traffic can arrive out-of-order and be reassembled back into its original order on the receiving end, but voice and video data require real-time delivery in order to be understandable. Clearly, this makes regular data a lot less vulnerable to congestion or busy traffic conditions that delay voice and video communications and seriously mess them up. The explosion in the popularity and amount of multimedia being sent over data networks is a big reason why the never-ending quest for greater bandwidth and speed to avoid traffic jams on WAN links is so vital today.

Wireless Technologies

Okay—let's get back to that distance issue. You know that different technologies offer different distance ranges and that optical fiber carries signals much further than copper cabling can. You also know that fiber comes with a much higher price tag to match its higher capacity and that it's much harder to install.

But we haven't covered *Bluetooth*, which is a type of wireless technology that's only used for short-distance wireless transmissions. Bluetooth is actually a wireless protocol that creates *personal area networks* (PANs). It utilizes a short-range communications technology enabling data transmission between fixed and/or mobile devices. It's not exactly a news bulletin that most of us have mobile phones, and on some of them we can even get our email. Some states, with more surely to follow soon, have passed laws making it illegal not to use a wireless headset while driving and talking. Those headsets use Bluetooth technology, as do wireless keyboards and mice, for example.

Getting all of our wireless toys to play nicely with each other and synch up can be a challenge, and meeting that need is exactly what the people who created Bluetooth intended to do—develop a single digital wireless protocol, capable of connecting multiple devices and overcoming problems arising from trying to synchronize them. Bluetooth achieves this using a radio technology called *frequency hopping spread spectrum*, which chops up the data being sent and transmits chunks of it through the air on up to 75 different frequencies.

Microwave radio relay is a technology for transmitting digital and sometimes even analog signals between two locations on a line-of-sight radio path through the atmosphere. During microwave radio relay, radio waves are transmitted between the two locations with directional antennas that form a fixed radio connection between them. A really long connected series of links can form line-of-sight transcontinental communication systems. (If this sounds familiar, it should—you read an entire chapter on wireless—remember Chapter 12?) Anyway, although having a dedicated microwave connection is still common because it allows you to purchase your own frequency range from the FCC to ensure you don't get any interference, a much less costlier installation is the wireless 802.11 specification (also discussed in Chapter 12), which provides us with long-distance solutions and a healthy amount of bandwidth, too.

A *communications satellite (comsat)* is an artificial satellite stationed in space for telecommunications purposes. Modern communications satellites use a variety of orbits. Here's a list of them:

- Geostationary orbits
- Molniya orbits, named after a series of communications satellites from Russia (*Molniya* means lightning in Russian)
- Low-polar and non-polar Earth orbits from which the satellite can first boost communications signals and then send them back to earth

There are other elliptical orbits, too, but I'm not going to go into them in this book because you're not reading this to help you get your FCC license. Instead, you want to pass the CompTia Network+ exam; and to do that, you do need to understand point-to-multipoint services and how communications satellites provide a microwave radio-relay technology as shown in Figure 16.3.

FIGURE 16.3 An example of a satellite point-to-multipoint

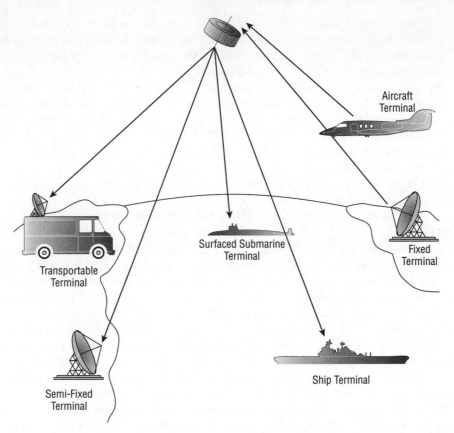

This technology is also used for mobile applications like GPS communications to ships, vehicles, planes, and hand-held terminals, as well as for fun stuff like watching football on satellite HDTV and radio broadcasting. These all require capabilities that are impractical or impossible to use with other technologies like cable.

Broadband Services

Now, before I get into telling you all about the WAN protocols required to meet the CompTIA objectives, I've got to talk about cable modems and DSL as solutions for connecting to WANs. I think it will really help you understand the practical differences between DSL and cable-modem networking, and they happen to be CompTIA objectives as well.

Dedicated broadband services include transmissions over media in a broad range of frequencies. The various forms of *digital subscriber line (DSL)* services are broadband in the sense that digital information is sent over a high-bandwidth channel above the baseband voice channel on a single pair of wires. Ethernet digital signals sent over a cable modem from your local cable television service provider are a competitor for DSL service.

Although it's true that DSL and cable Internet services do indeed have a lot in common, they still have some basic, essential differences that are really important for you to understand:

Speed   Most would tell you that cable is faster than DSL Internet, but cable doesn't always win the race in the real world.

Security   DSL and cable are based on different network-security models, and until recently, cable has been the reputed loser in this contest. But now it's pretty much a toss-up, and both offer adequate security that meets the needs of most users. And when I say adequate, I mean that there are still some very real security issues relating to both alternatives, no matter what your ISP says.

Popularity   Cable Internet is definitely "best in show" in the U.S. but DSL is beginning to catch up.

Customer satisfaction   Here, the reverse is true—in the U.S., DSL is top dog. Still, do you really know anyone who's satisfied with their ISP?

Figure 16.4 shows how a connection can terminate from modems to either a PC directly or to a router. Typically, your router would run Dynamic Host Configuration Protocol (DHCP) on that interface as well as Point to Point Protocol over Ethernet (PPPoE), which we discussed back in Chapter 13, "Authentication and Access Control."

FIGURE 16.4   Broadband access using cable or DSL

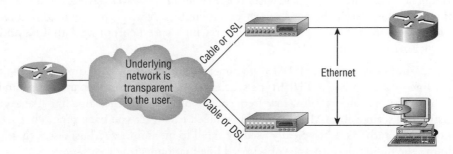

Both DSL and cable high-speed Internet services are available to millions of residential and business consumers worldwide, but in some areas, only one (sometimes neither) service is available. Surprisingly, some of the differences between DSL and cable modem have nothing to do with the actual technologies—it comes down to the individual ISP. All other things being equal, issues like cost, reliability, and quality of customer support for both installation and maintenance vary significantly from one provider to the next.

DSL Technology and *x*DSL

DSL is not a complete end-to-end solution. It is really a Physical layer transmission technology like dial, cable, or wireless. DSL connections are deployed in the *last-mile* of a local telephone network or local loop. The term *last-mile* has been used quite a bit in the last few years with broadband-type connections. It basically means the same thing as local loop and defines the physical connection from the customer to the first aggregation device of the provider network.

A DSL connection is set up between a pair of modems on either end of a copper wire that is between the CPE and the digital subscriber line access multiplexer (DSLAM). A DSLAM is the device located at the providers' CO that concentrates connections from multiple DSL subscribers.

xDSL is really a family of technologies that have become popular for data transmission over phone lines because *x*DSL uses regular PSTN phone wires to transmit digital signals and is extremely inexpensive compared with other digital communications methods. The *x* in xDSL represents the various letters that refer to different DSL flavors. *x*DSLs use high-frequency signals whereas regular phone calls use low-frequency signals over the same lines.

Communicating via *x*DSL requires an interface to a PC. All *x*DSL configurations require a DSL modem called an *endpoint* and a network interface card (NIC) in your computer. The NIC can be connected directly to the DSL modem using a straight-through Ethernet UTP patch cord with standard RJ-45 connectors on each end. But if there are other connecting devices between the computer and the cable modem, you'll need either a special switchable port or an Ethernet crossover cable for things to work well.

A nice feature of *x*DSL implementations is that they cost tens of dollars instead of the hundreds (possibly thousands) that you would have to pony up for a dedicated, digital point-to-point link like a T1. These cost-effective implementations include the following:

High bit-rate digital subscriber line (HDSL)   HDSL was the first DSL technology to use a higher-frequency spectrum of copper twisted-pair cables. HDSL was developed in the USA as a better technology for high-speed, synchronous circuits. It was typically used to interconnect local-exchange carrier systems and to carry high-speed corporate data links and voice channels using T1 lines.

Symmetric digital subscriber line (SDSL)   Symmetric (same rate in both directions) digital subscriber line (SDSL) provides T1/E1 type speeds symmetrically for both uploading and downloading data but doesn't allow low-frequency phone calls on the same line like asymmetric digital subscriber line (ADSL) does. How much it will set you back ranges between the cost of ADSL and T1s. It's typically used by small to medium-sized businesses that don't require the higher performance of a leased line for connecting to a server.

Very high data-rate digital subscriber line (VDSL)   VDSL or very high bitrate DSL (VHDSL) provides faster data transmission over single, flat, untwisted or twisted pairs of copper wires. This capacity for blazingly fast speeds mean that VDSL is capable of supporting high-bandwidth applications like HDTV, telephone services like the popular Voice over IP (VoIP), as well as general Internet access over a single connection. VDSL is deployed over existing wiring used for POTS and lower-speed DSL connections. Second-generation VDSL2 systems utilize bandwidths of up to 30MHz to provide data rates exceeding 100Mbps simultaneously in both the upstream and downstream directions. The maximum available bit rate is achieved at a range of about 300 meters with the signal performance degrading as the loop attenuation increases.

Asymmetric digital subscriber line (ADSL)   Asymmetric (meaning different upload and download speeds) DSL has become the most popular *x*DSL because it focuses on providing reasonably fast upstream transmission speeds (768Kbps) and very fast downstream transmission speeds (up to 9Mbps, although usually slower). This makes downloading graphics, audio, video, and data files from any remote computer a snap. The majority of web traffic is downstream. The best part is that ADSL works on a single phone line without losing voice call capability. This is accomplished with something called a *spl*itter that enables the use of multiple frequencies on your POTS line.

Cable Modem

Cable is a great cost-effective connection for a small office or home office (SOHO)—yes, there is an acronym for everything. Even in larger organizations, cable, or even DSL, can be great to have around as a backup link.

Here are a few cable network terms:

Headend   This is where all cable signals are received, processed, and formatted. The signals are then transmitted over the distribution network from the headend.

Distribution network   These are relatively small service areas that usually range in size from 100 to 2,000 customers. They're typically composed of a mixed, fiber-coaxial, or hybrid fiber coaxial (HFC) architecture, with optical fiber substituting for the distribution network's trunk portion. The fiber forms both the connection from the headend and an optical node that changes light to radio frequency (RF) signals that are then distributed through a coaxial cable throughout the specific service area - i.e. your home or office.

Data over cable service interface specification (DOCSIS)   This specification provides the interface requirements for a data over cable system, including that of high-speed data transfer to an existing Cable TV (CATV) system. All cable modems and similar devices have to measure up to this standard.

Figure 16.5 shows where you would be likely to find the various types of networks and how the terms I just listed would be used in a network diagram.

FIGURE 16.5   Cable network

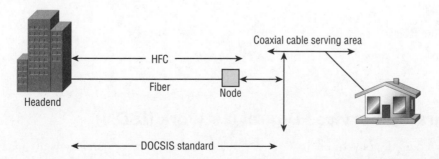

The problem with this is that ISPs often use a fiber-optic network that extends from the cable operator's master headend—sometimes even to regional headends—out to a neighborhood's hubsite, which finally arrives at a fiber-optic node that services anywhere from 25 to 2,000 or more homes. I'm really not picking on cable, but here's another issue: If you have cable, open your PC's command prompt, type **ipconfig**, and check out your subnet mask. It's probably a /20 or /21 class B address—yikes! You already know that translates to either 4,094 or 2,046 hosts per cable network connection. Definitely not good.

 When we say *cable*, we really mean using coax (coaxial) cable for transmission. Community antenna television (CATV) is now used as a means to offer cost-effective broadcasting to subscribers. Cable is able to provide voice and data, plus analog and digital video, without requiring you to cough up your whole paycheck.

Your average cable connection gives you a maximum download speed of 2Mbps. And remember—you have to share that bandwidth with all the other subscribers. As if that weren't enough, there are other things like overloaded web servers and plain old network congestion that factor into the mix as well. But your email-checking neighbors really aren't making that much of a difference. So who or what is? Well, if you're an online gamer, you will likely notice a bit more lag during peak periods, which could be a matter of virtual life and death. And if somebody in your neighborhood is uploading a large amount of data, like, say, an entire collection of pirated *Star Wars* movies, it could definitely max out the entire connection and bring everyone's browser to crawl-speed.

Cable-modem access may or may not be faster or easier to install than DSL, and your mileage will vary, depending on where you live plus a variety of other factors. But it's usually more available and a tad less pricey, making it a winner by a nose. But no worries; if cable access isn't available in your neighborhood, DSL is okay—anything is better than dial-up.

WAN Protocols

The technologies I'm going to focus on in this section are as follows:

- ISDN
- Frame Relay
- ATM
- MPLS

Integrated Services Digital Network (ISDN)

ISDN is a digital, point-to-point WAN technology capable of maximum transmission speeds of about 2Mbps (Primary Rate Interface [PRI]), although speeds of 128Kbps (Basic Rate Interface [BRI]) are more common in a SOHO environment.

Because it's capable of much higher data rates at a relatively low cost, ISDN is becoming a viable remote-user connection method—especially for those who work out of their homes. ISDN uses the same UTP wiring as POTS, yet it can transmit data at much higher speeds. But that's where the similarity ends. What makes ISDN different from a regular POTS line is how it uses the copper wiring. Instead of carrying an analog (voice) signal, it carries digital signals. This is the reason behind several key differences.

First, a computer connects to the 128Kbps ISDN line via an ISDN *Terminal Adapter (TA)* that's often incorrectly referred to as an ISDN modem. An ISDN TA is not a modem because it doesn't convert a digital signal from the computer to an analog signal on the subscriber line—ISDN signals are digital on the subscriber line. A TA is technically an ISDN-compatible device that has one or more non-ISDN ports for devices like computer serial interfaces and RJ-11 analog phones, giving these non-ISDN devices access to the ISDN network.

Second, an ISDN line has two types of channels. The data is carried on special *Bearer channels,* or *B channels,* each of which can carry 64Kbps of data. A BRI ISDN line has two B channels, and a PRI has twenty-three 64Kbps channels. One channel can be used for a voice call while the other can be used for data transmissions, and this is made possible by time-division multiplexing (TDM) on one pair of copper wires.

The other type of channel in ISDN is also multiplexed onto only one copper pair. It's used for call setup and link management and is known as the *signaling channel, D channel,* or *Delta channel.* This channel has only 16Kbps of bandwidth in BRI and 64Kbps in PRI.

To maximize throughput, the two B channels are often combined into one data connection for a total bandwidth of 128Kbps. This is known as *Bandwidth on Demand Interoperability Group* (BONDING) or *inverse multiplexing.*

This still leaves the D channel free for signaling purposes. In rare cases, you may see user data, such as credit-card verification, on the D channel. This was introduced as an additional feature of ISDN, but it hasn't caught on.

Some of the main advantages of ISDN are as follows:

- It has a fast connection.
- It offers higher bandwidth than POTS. BONDING yields 128Kbps bandwidth.
- There is no conversion from digital to analog.

  ISDN disadvantages include these:

- It's more expensive than POTS.
- Specialized equipment is required at the phone company and at the remote computer.
- Not all ISDN equipment can connect to every other type of equipment.
- Why use ISDN if you can get DSL or cable?

Remember that ISDN is a type of dial-up connection that must be initiated.

ISDN Terminal Adapters

Okay—so you now know that ISDN is another form of high-speed Internet access that delivers digital services (on 64Kbps channels) over conditioned telephone copper pairs. As I mentioned earlier, the device you must hook up to your computer to access ISDN services is properly known as an ISDN Terminal Adapter, which doesn't change from digital to analog like a modem does. It just changes between digital transmission formats.

The box itself is about the size of a modem and happens to look pretty similar to one. And also like DSL modems, it has a phone jack and an Ethernet jack. You connect a phone cord from the phone jack to the wall jack where your ISDN services are being delivered, and then you connect an Ethernet cable from your PC to the ISDN TA's Ethernet jack. Older, less-capable TAs used an Electronic Industries Association / Telecommunications Industry Alliance (EIA/TIA) 232 serial port for PC connectivity. These similarities are why people confuse ISDN TAs with standard modems.

Frame Relay Technology

Frame Relay is a WAN technology in which variable-length packets are transmitted by switching. *Packet switching* involves breaking messages into chunks at the sending device. Each packet can be sent over any number of routes on its way to its destination. The packets are then reassembled in the correct order at the receiver. Because they are packet-switched and the exact path is unknown, a cloud is used when creating a diagram to illustrate how data travels throughout this service.

From everything you've learned so far, just telling you that Frame Relay is a packet-switched technology should make you immediately realize a couple of things about it:

- Frame Relay doesn't work like a point-to-point leased line (although it can be made to look and act like one).

- Frame Relay is usually less expensive than leased lines are, but there are some sacrifices to make to get that savings.

So, why would you even consider using Frame Relay? Take a look at Figure 16.6 to get an idea of what a network looked like before Frame Relay.

Now check out Figure 16.7. You can see that there's now only one connection between the Corporate router and the Frame Relay switch. That saves some major cash.

FIGURE 16.6 Before Frame Relay

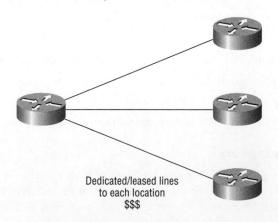

Dedicated/leased lines
to each location
$$$

FIGURE 16.7   After Frame Relay

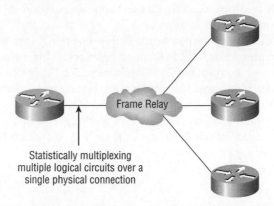

Statistically multiplexing
multiple logical circuits over a
single physical connection

Let's say you need to add seven remote sites to the corporate office, and you have only one free serial port on your router. Frame Relay to the rescue! Of course, I should probably mention that you now also have one single point of failure, which is not so good. But Frame Relay is used to save money, not to make a network more resilient.

Coming up, I'm going to cover the Frame Relay technology information you need to know about when studying for the CompTIA Network+ exam.

Committed Information Rate (CIR)

Frame Relay provides a packet-switched network to many different customers at the same time. This is a really good thing because it spreads out the cost of the switches among many customers. But remember, Frame Relay is based on the assumption that all customers won't need to transmit data constantly—or even all at the same time.

Frame Relay works by providing a portion of dedicated bandwidth to each user, and it also allows the user to exceed their guaranteed bandwidth if resources on the telco network happen to be available. So basically, Frame Relay providers allow customers to buy a lower amount of bandwidth than they really use. There are two separate bandwidth specifications with Frame Relay:

Access rate   The maximum speed at which the Frame Relay interface can transmit.

CIR   The maximum bandwidth of data guaranteed to be delivered. In reality, it's the average amount that the service provider will allow you to transmit, based on what you purchased.

If these two values are the same, the Frame Relay connection is pretty much just like a leased line. But they can also be set to different values. Here's an example: Let's say that you buy an access rate of T1 (1.544Mbps) and a CIR of 256Kbps. By doing this, you're guaranteed that the first 256Kbps of traffic you send will be delivered. Anything beyond that is called a *burst*—a transmission that exceeds your guaranteed 256Kbps rate and can total any amount up to the T1 access rate (if that amount is in your contract). If your combined committed burst (the basis for your CIR) and excess burst sizes, known as the maximum burst rate (MBR) exceed the access rate when combined, you can pretty much say goodbye to your additional traffic. It will most likely be dropped, although this happening depends on the subscription level of a particular service provider.

In a perfect world, this always works beautifully—but remember that little word *guarantee*—as in guaranteed rate, of 256Kbps to be exact? This means any burst of data you send that exceeds your guaranteed 256Kbps rate will be delivered on something called a "best effort" delivery basis. Or maybe not—if your telco's equipment doesn't have the capacity to deliver it at the time you transmitted, then your frames will be discarded, and the DTE will be notified. Timing is everything—you can scream data out at six times your guaranteed rate of 256Kbps (T1) *only if* your telco has the capacity available on its equipment at that moment.

Virtual Circuits

Frame Relay operates using *virtual circuits* as opposed to the actual circuits that leased lines use. These virtual circuits are what link together the thousands of devices connected to the provider's "cloud." Frame Relay provides a virtual circuit between your two DTE devices, making them appear to be connected via a circuit when in reality they're dumping their frames into a large, shared infrastructure. You never see the complexity of what's actually happening inside the cloud because you only have a virtual circuit.

And on top of all that, there are two types of virtual circuits—permanent and switched. Permanent virtual circuits (PVCs) are by far the most common type in use today. What *permanent* means here is that the telco creates the mappings inside their gear and as long as you pay the bill, they'll remain in place.

Switched virtual circuits (SVCs) are more like phone calls. The virtual circuit is established when data needs to be transmitted, and it's taken down when the data transfer is complete.

 I have never seen a Frame Relay service using SVCs offered by a telco in North America. It's used mainly in private Frame Relay networks.

Data Link Connection Identifiers (DLCIs)

Frame Relay PVCs are identified to DTE end devices by *Data Link Connection Identifiers (DLCIs)*. A Frame Relay service provider typically assigns DLCI values, which are used on Frame Relay interfaces to distinguish between different virtual circuits. Because many virtual circuits can be terminated on one multipoint Frame Relay interface, many DLCIs are often affiliated with it.

Let me explain. Suppose you have a central HQ with three branch offices. If you were to connect each branch office to HQ using a T1, you would need three serial interfaces on your router at HQ, one for each T1. Simple, right? Well, suppose you use Frame Relay PVCs instead. You could have a T1 at each branch connected to a service provider and only a *single* T1 at HQ. There would be three PVCs on the single T1 at HQ, one going to each branch. And even though you'd have only a single interface and a single CSU/DSU, the three PVCs would function as three separate circuits. Remember what I said about saving money? How much for two additional T1 interfaces and a pair of CSU/DSUs? Answer: A lot! So, why not go ahead and ask for a percentage of the savings in your bonus?

Asynchronous Transfer Mode (ATM)

*Asynchronous Transfer Mode (*ATM*)*, not to be confused with automated teller machines, first emerged in the early 1990s. ATM was designed to be a high-speed communications protocol that does not depend on any specific LAN topology. It uses a high-speed cell-switching technology that can handle data as well as real-time voice and video. The ATM protocol breaks up transmitted data into 53-byte cells. A *cell* is analogous to a packet or frame, except that an ATM cell is always fixed in length and is relatively small and fast, whereas a frame's length can vary.

ATM is designed to switch these small cells through an ATM network very quickly. It does this by setting up a virtual connection between the source and destination nodes; the cells may go through multiple switching points before ultimately arriving at their final destination. The cells may also arrive out of order, so the receiving system may have to reassemble and correctly order the arriving cells. ATM, like Frame Relay, is a connection-oriented service in contrast to most Data Link protocols, which are best-efforts delivery services and do not require virtual circuits to be established before transmitting user data.

Data rates are scalable and start as low as 1.5Mbps, with speeds of 25Mbps, 51Mbps, 100Mbps, 155Mbps, and higher. The common speeds of ATM networks today are 51.84Mbps and 155.52Mbps; both of them can be used over either copper or fiber-optic cabling. An ATM with a speed of 622.08Mbps is also becoming common but is currently used exclusively over fiber-optic cable. ATM supports very high speeds because it's designed to be routed by hardware rather than software, which makes faster processing speeds possible.

Fiber-based service-provider ATM networks are running today at data rates of 10Gbps, and they're becoming more and more common. These fast speeds make real-time payloads like voice and video travel with data on an ATM network and arrive without too much delay, or *latency*. The small size of the payload, compared to the size of each cell's header, makes ATM less efficient than other WAN technologies. In other words, ATM networks are fast, but they get bad gas mileage.

So, what should you use in a large-scale WAN if ATM is not that efficient? MPLS. Let me explain...

Multi Protocol Label Switching (MPLS)

MPLS belongs to a new family of high-speed packet-switching technologies that add to the OSI model's hierarchy by adding a new layer header between Layer 2 (the Data Link layer) and Layer 3 (the Network layer). MPLS is therefore referred to as residing on Layer 2.5.

MPLS was designed to be compatible with IP, which is not the case with ATM. This gives MPLS a huge advantage because it can act as a unified data carrying technology for VPN traffic from both circuit-switched clients and packet-switched clients. VPN traffic acts as if it were private by authenticating the users on each end and then encrypting the data so it can't be read if captured. It can carry many kinds of traffic including Ethernet frames, IP packets, SONET frames, and ATM cells. Unlike ATM's short cell length, MPLS is able to work with packets that vary in length, but with today's faster media, the length makes less difference anyway. Figure 16.8 shows how packets can be encapsulated and sent through an MPLS network.

FIGURE 16.8   MPLS switching

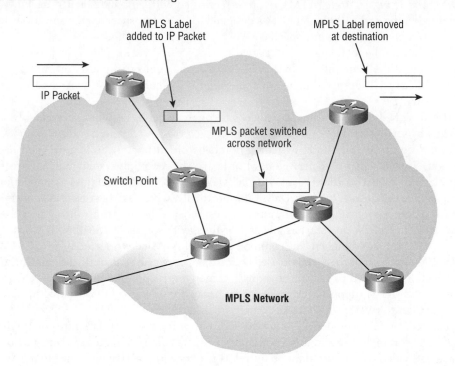

As your VPN data enters the carrier network, a label is attached to each packet. This label uniquely identifies your packet in a shared infrastructure and keeps it private. When the packet reaches its destination, the label is removed, returning the data packet to its original state. This process is seamless and unnoticeable to end users. You can think of MPLS as a special-delivery courier service for your network.

MPLS is replacing ATM on most WAN pathways due to its ability to implement quality of service (QoS) schemes like Resource Reservation Protocol (RSVP) that reserve bandwidth across a WAN network. Another factor is its quick hardware-routed speeds, which better support the real-time traffic like voice and video that we're increasingly seeing on today's converged networks. The only other strong competitor for MPLS is a protocol called Layer 2 Tunneling Protocol, version 3 (L2TPv3), which can also accommodate Layer 2 and 3 VPN connections.

Summary

In this chapter, you learned about the important issues involved in providing WAN connectivity between geographically separated network locations. You learned about the different kinds of WAN connections including point-to-point connections, circuit-switched service provider networks, and packet-switched service provider networks.

You also learned about the impact different transmission media and different distance parameters make with WAN connections. In addition, you learned about different choices for leased-line connections along with broadband technologies such as xDSL and cable modems.

You studied the different WAN protocols and technologies used in connecting today's high-speed WANs including ISDN, Frame Relay, ATM, and MPLS.

Exam Essentials

Be able to differentiate the kinds of WAN technologies.   You must be able to tell the speeds and capacities of the different remote-access and WAN technologies, as well as the media over which they are implemented.

Identify the basic characteristics of various Internet access technologies.   These include DSL, broadband cable, and POTS. It is important to know the differentiating features of these access technologies. Know their advantages and disadvantages so you can identify the best use of each.

Be knowledgeable about the differences between circuit-switched and packet-switched technologies, and know which protocols use either.   Frame Relay is a packet-switched technology, and ISDN is a circuit-switched digital solution. ATM is considered to be a cell-switched technology because it incorporates a 53-byte cell. Both MPLS and ATM are considered connection-oriented technologies because the connection is set up first.

Be clear about the differences involving speed and distance between different media and between different WAN protocols.   Wireless and fiber implementations are both growing, and their standards are facilitating faster speeds and coverage of greater distances.

Be able to differentiate between the different WAN protocols and technologies, their relative costs and speeds, and the types of implementations for which each would serve as a best solution.   ISDN is rarely used nowadays in its BRI configuration except for small home or office solutions. Frame Relay is relatively inexpensive, but service providers have overbooked their Frame Relay clouds, resulting in poor performance. ATM is fast but inefficient, and MPLS is fast and more efficient but complicated to administer.

Written Lab

In this section, write the answers to the following WAN-related questions:

1. What is the greatest advantage of PSTN (POTS)?

2. Which technology uses the term HFC?

3. You have one serial port on your router but need to connect many remote sites. What WAN protocol could you consider as an option?

4. What is the maximum speed for T1?

5. What does the acronym DSL stand for?

6. Which WAN technologies are considered packet-switching networks?

7. Which WAN technologies are considered circuit-switching networks?

8. Which WAN technology is considered a cell-switching network?

9. What are the different flavors of xDSL?

10. Which WAN protocol can carry traffic from both circuit-switching and packet-switching clients?

(The answers to the Written Lab can be found following the answers to the Review Questions for this chapter.)

Review Questions

1. Which of the following is not a WAN protocol or technology?

    A. ATM

    B. ISDN

    C. MPLS

    D. RIP

2. What OSI model layers do WAN protocols operate in?

    A. Layer 6, Layer 4, Layer 2

    B. Transport, Data Link, Network

    C. Physical, Data Link, Network

    D. Application, Data Link, Network

3. If you have a device in a telecommunications closet owned and installed by the telecommunications company (telco), and it's your responsibility to cable from this box to the CPE, which term should you use to refer to the device?

    A. Customer premises equipment

    B. Demarcation point

    C. Toll network

    D. Central office

4. You have an E 1. How many DS0's are used in this point-to-point connection?

    A. 24

    B. 25

    C. 30

    D. 32

5. Where does the local exchange carrier responsibility end and your responsibility begin on a WAN link?

    A. POP

    B. Central Office

    C. Demarc

    D. Smart Jack

6. You have a small-office/home-office environment. What WAN technology would most likely be used?

    A. T1

    B. T3

    C. Frame Relay

    D. Cable Modem

7. Which type of communication has a line speed of 1.544 Mbps (millions of bits per second)?

   A. T3

   B. T1C

   C. T1

   D. T4

8. Wireless transmissions use what as a transmission medium?

   A. POTS

   B. Copper wire

   C. Glass fiber

   D. Air

9. Which is not a common optical carrier level (OC-x)?

   A. OC-1

   B. OC-4

   C. OC-12

   D. OC-192

10. Which wireless protocol utilizes a short-range communications technology facilitating data transmission from fixed and/or mobile devices, creating wireless personal area networks (PANs)?

   A. Bluetooth

   B. Microwave radio relay

   C. Comsat

   D. Point-to-multipoint

11. What does the x in xDSL represent?

   A. Wire type

   B. Transmission speed

   C. DSL type

   D. Download speed

12. Which is not a type of xDSL?

   A. ADSL

   B. HDSL

   C. FDSL

   D. SDSL

13. What is the acronym DOCSIS stand for?

   A. Data over cable service interface spectrum

   B. Data over cable systems Internet specification

   C. Data over cable service Internet specification

   D. Data over cable service interface specification

14. What is the bandwidth for OC-12?

    A. 1.544Mbps

    B. 45Mbps

    C. 622Mbps

    D. 1000Mbps

15. Which WAN protocol utilizes cell-switching technology?

    A. Frame Relay

    B. ISDN

    C. ATM

    D. RIP

16. Which WAN protocol utilizes packet-switched technology?

    A. Frame Relay

    B. ISDN

    C. ATM

    D. RIP

17. What is the CIR in Frame Relay?

    A. Virtual circuit that is established when data needs to be transmitted

    B. Maximum speed at which the Frame Relay interface can transmit

    C. Rate at which the Frame Relay switch agrees to transfer data

    D. Rate at which the Frame Relay switch agrees to receive data

18. What does the acronym ATM stand for?

    A. Automated Teller Machine

    B. Asynchronous Transfer Mode

    C. Asynchronous Transfer Method

    D. Autonomous Transfer Mode

19. Which WAN has a transfer rate of 44.7Mbps?

    A. T1

    B. T3

    C. E1

    D. E3

20. What WAN protocol is described as residing in Layer 2.5 of the OSI model?

    A. Frame Relay

    B. ISDN

    C. MPLS

    D. RIP

Answers to Review Questions

1. D. Routing Information Protocol (RIP) is not a WAN protocol but a routing protocol used in internetworks.

2. C. These different protocols and technologies all occupy the lower three layers of the OSI model: the Physical layer, the Data Link layer, and sometimes the Network layer. Most WAN protocols work only at the Physical layer and Data Link layer, with MPLS being a 2.5 layer protocol.

3. B. The demarcation point is the precise spot where the service provider's responsibility ends and the CPE begins.

4. C. The European version of the T1 is the E1, which operates at 2.048Mbps and uses 30 64Kbps channels (thirty DS0's).

5. C. The demarc is the precise spot where the service provider's (local exchange carrier) responsibility ends and the CPE begins. It's generally a device in a telecommunications closet owned and installed by the telecommunications company (telco).

6. D. Cable is a great cost-effective connection for a small office or home office (SOHO)7. Which type of communication has a line speed of 1.544 Mbps (millions of bits per second)?

7. C. A T1 has a line speed of 1.544Mbps. This 1.544Mbps connection uses Digital Signal 1 (DS1) and aggregates 24 discrete, 64Kbps channels that use Digital Signal 0 (DS0). Other T-series connections have greater maximum connection speeds.

8. D. Wireless transmissions use the air as a transmission medium. The transmission medium can influence speed or bandwidth and thereby the volume of information that can be transferred over time.

9. B. OC-1, OC-3, OC-12, OC-48, and OC-192 are the normal service offerings. OC-1 has the lowest data rate at 51.84Mbps, up to the highest OC-192 at 9.953Gbps.

10. A. Bluetooth uses a radio technology called frequency hopping spread spectrum. It chops up the data being sent and transmits chunks of it through the air on up to 75 different frequencies.

11. C. The x in xDSL represents the different letters that refer to the DSL flavors. xDSLs use high-frequency signals, whereas regular phone calls use low-frequency signals over the same lines.

12. C. ADSL, HDSL, SDSL, VDSL or VHDSL, and VDSL2 are all common xDSL types. Synchronous Optical Network (SONET) is the standard for synchronous data transmission on optical fiber.

13. D. DOCSIS stands for data over cable service interface specification. All cable modems and like devices have to measure up to this standard.

14. C. Optical carrier 12 has speeds up to 622Mbps.

15. C. ATM uses a high-speed cell-switching technology that can handle data as well as real-time voice and video. The ATM protocol breaks up transmitted data into 53-byte cells.

16. A. Frame Relay is the frame WAN technology in which variable-length packets are transmitted by switching.

17. C. The Committed Information Rate (CIR) is the rate, in bits per second, at which the Frame Relay switch agrees to transfer data.

18. B. We're thinking in terms of a WAN, so B is obviously the correct choice. Asynchronous Transfer Mode was designed to be a high-speed communications protocol that does not depend on any specific LAN topology.

19. B. A T3 line works similarly to a T1 connection but carries a whopping 44.736Mbps. This is equivalent to 28 T1 circuits (or a total of 672 DS0 channels), and it uses a signal known as Digital Signal 3 (DS3).

20. C. MPLS belongs to a new high-speed family of packet-switching technologies that add to the OSI model's hierarchy by adding a new layer header between Layer 2 (the Data Link layer) and Layer 3 (the Network layer).

Answers to Written Lab

1. It is readily available.

2. Cable. In a modern network, hybrid fiber coaxial (HFC) is a telecommunications industry term for a network that incorporates both optical fiber and coaxial cable to create a broadband network.

3. Frame Relay. Although Frame Relay is not available in many markets today, it is a possible solution for the problem presented.

4. 1.544Mbps

5. Digital Subscriber Line

6. Frame-Relay and X.25

7. Modems (PSTN/POTS) and ISDN

8. ATM

9. HDSL, SDSL, VDSL, ADSL

10. MPLS

Chapter

17

Command-Line Tools

THE FOLLOWING COMPTIA NETWORK+ EXAM OBJECTIVES ARE COVERED IN THIS CHAPTER:

✓ **5.1 Given a scenario, select the appropriate command line interface tool and interpret the output to verify functionality**

- ▪ Traceroute
- ▪ Ipconfig
- ▪ Ifconfig
- ▪ Ping
- ▪ Arp ping
- ▪ Arp
- ▪ Nslookup
- ▪ Hostname
- ▪ Dig
- ▪ Mtr
- ▪ Route
- ▪ Nbstat
- ▪ Netstat

Most of us are running Transmission Control Protocol/Internet Protocol (TCP/IP) Version 4 on our networks these days so we absolutely need a way to test IP connectivity. But we also need be able to test and verify IPv6 networks. The reason for this is that even though Microsoft makes the majority of client platforms, a lot of these commands are really platform independent, and most of them can now use both IPv4 and IPv6. Even so, keep in mind that the Network+ exam focuses on the basic concepts of the function and use of the TCP/IP utilities that come with Windows.

You can use several utilities to verify TCP/IP function on Windows workstations, and most of them are listed in the chapter objectives. But there are a few others that I'm going to discuss with you because they're really important for anyone working in the networking field to know about. Here's a list of them:

- Traceroute (tracert in other environments)
- ipconfig/winipcfg (ifconfig in Unix)
- ping
- arp
- nslookup (dig in Unix)
- Mtr
- route
- nbtstat
- netstat
- ftp
- Telnet

And by the way… it's very important that you don't just blow through the output that I've supplied for each command. Instead, pay serious attention to it, because to meet the Network+ objectives, you'll be required to correctly identify each command's output.

So, let's cut right to the chase and take a look at some of these commands and their output. Oh, and do try and have fun with it!

For up-to-the-minute updates for this chapter, please see www.lammle.com or www.sybex.com/go/comptianetwork+studyguide.

Using *Traceroute*

For starters, let's pose these questions: "Where do all those packets really go when we send them over the Internet? And, how do all the packets actually get to their destinations?" Well, we can use the TCP/IP traceroute (tracert with Windows) command-line utility to help us answer both questions because its output will show us every router interface a TCP/IP packet passes through on the way to its destination.

Traceroute (trace for short), displays the path a packet takes to get to a remote device in all its glory by using something we call time to live (TTL), time-outs, and Internet Control Message Protocol (ICMP) error messages. And it's also a handy tool for troubleshooting an internetwork because we can use it to figure out which router along a path through that internetwork happens to be causing a network failure when a certain destination machine or network is, or suddenly becomes, unreachable.

To use tracert, at a Windows command prompt, type **tracert**, a space, and the Domain Name Service (DNS) name or IP address of the host machine you want to find the route to. The tracert utility will respond with a list of all the DNS names and IP addresses of the routers that the packet is passing through on its way. Plus, tracert uses TTL to indicate the time it takes for each attempt.

Following is the tracert output from my workstation in Boulder, Colorado to my Lammle.com server in Dallas, Texas:

```
C:\Users\tlammle>tracert www.lammle.com

Tracing route to lammle.com [206.123.114.186]
over a maximum of 30 hops:

  1     1 ms    <1 ms    <1 ms  dslmodem.domain.actdsltmp [192.168.0.1]
  2    53 ms    52 ms    52 ms  hlrn-dsl-gw36-228.hlrn.qwest.net
                                [207.225.112.228]
  3    52 ms    53 ms    52 ms  hlrn-agw1.inet.qwest.net [71.217.189.25]
  4    75 ms    75 ms    74 ms  dal-core-01.inet.qwest.net [67.14.2.53]
  5    76 ms    76 ms    76 ms  dap-brdr-01.inet.qwest.net [205.171.225.49]
  6    76 ms    76 ms    76 ms  205.171.1.110
  7    75 ms    76 ms   106 ms  xe-0-0-0.er2.dfw2.us.above.net [64.125.26.206]
  8    76 ms    76 ms    76 ms  209.249.122.74.available.above.net
                                [209.249.122.74]
  9    76 ms    76 ms    76 ms  65.99.248.250
 10    76 ms    76 ms    76 ms  pageuppro.pageuppro.com [206.123.114.186]
Trace complete.
```

Okay, were you able to see that the packet bounces through several routers before arriving at its destination? Good! This utility is useful if you are having problems reaching a web server on the Internet and you want to know if a wide area network (WAN) link is down, or if the server just isn't responding. What this means to you is that basically, wherever the trace stops is a great place to start troubleshooting. No worries here, though—the previous output shows that every router is up and responding. Lastly, notice in the output the "ms." This is the latency of each hop, meaning the delay. tracert or traceroute is a great troubleshooting tool to find out where your network bottlenecks are.

If you use traceroute or tracert and receive an asterisk, this indicates that the attempt to reach that router took longer than the default time-out value. This is very good to know because it can mean that either the router is extremely busy or that a particular link is slow. Another reason for getting an asterisk could be that the administrator has disabled the ICMP protocol on the router that the packet is trying to hop through.

Why would someone want to do that? For security reasons, that's why. It happens to be a typical strategic move done on the router(s) that interface to the ISP to conceal their actual location so bad guys can't hack into them and therefore, into your internetwork. It's a good idea, and I highly recommend doing it.

 If you are running traceroute and see repeating addresses and TTL timeouts, you probably have a routing loop.

Using *ipconfig* and *ifconfig*

The utilities known as ipconfig (in Windows), and ifconfig (in Unix/Linux/Mac) will display the current configuration of TCP/IP on a given workstation—including the current IP address, DNS configuration, Windows Internet Naming Service (WINS) configuration, and default gateway. In the following sections, we will discuss how to use both.

Using the *ipconfig* Utility

With the new Macs, Vista, and Windows Server 2008, you can see the IPv6 configuration because IPv6 is enabled by default. The output of the ipconfig command provides the basic routed protocol information on your machine. From a DOS prompt, type **ipconfig**, and you'll see something like this:

```
C:\Users\tlammle>ipconfig
Windows IP Configuration
Ethernet adapter Local Area Connection:
    Connection-specific DNS Suffix  . : domain.actdsltmp
    Link-local IPv6 Address . . . . . : fe80::2836:c43e:274b:f08c%11
    IPv4 Address. . . . . . . . . . . : 192.168.0.6
```

```
    Subnet Mask . . . . . . . . . . : 255.255.255.0
    Default Gateway . . . . . . . . : 192.168.0.1

Wireless LAN adapter Wireless Network Connection:
    Connection-specific DNS Suffix  . : qwest.net
    Link-local IPv6 Address . . . . . : fe80::20e7:7fb8:8a00:832b%10
    IPv4 Address. . . . . . . . . . : 10.0.1.198
    Subnet Mask . . . . . . . . . . : 255.255.255.0
    Default Gateway . . . . . . . . : fe80::21b:63ff:fef3:3694%10
                                      10.0.1.1

Tunnel adapter Local Area Connection* 6:
    Media State . . . . . . . . . . : Media disconnected
    Connection-specific DNS Suffix  . :

Tunnel adapter Local Area Connection* 7:
    Media State . . . . . . . . . . : Media disconnected
    Connection-specific DNS Suffix  . :
[output cut for brevity]
```

Wow, there sure are a lot of options in this output compared to earlier versions of Windows! First, what's up with all these interfaces showing? I only have two—one Ethernet and one wireless. You can see that my Ethernet adapter shows up first, and it has an IP address, a mask, and a default gateway, plus an IPv6 address and a DNS suffix. The next configured interface is the wireless local area network (LAN) adapter, which has an IP address, a mask, a default gateway, an IPv6 address, and the IPv6 default gateway, as well. This IPv6 default gateway address is simply my router advertising that it runs IPv6 and "I am the way out of the local LAN!"

The next adapters are disconnected because they are logical interfaces, and I'm not using them—my machine actually shows eight, but I cut the output because they provided no new information. They're automatically inserted because IPv6 is installed and running on my machine, and these adapters allow me to run IPv6 over an IPv4 only network.

But just in case the ipconfig doesn't provide enough information for you, try the ipconfig /all command—talk about details. Here's the beginning of that output:

```
C:\Users\tlammle>ipconfig /all
Windows IP Configuration
    Host Name . . . . . . . . . . . : globalnet-todd
    Primary Dns Suffix  . . . . . . : globalnet.local
    Node Type . . . . . . . . . . . : Hybrid
    IP Routing Enabled. . . . . . . : No
    WINS Proxy Enabled. . . . . . . : No
```

```
      DNS Suffix Search List. . . . . . : globalnet.local
                                          domain.actdsltmp
                                          qwest.net

Ethernet adapter Local Area Connection:
   Connection-specific DNS Suffix  . : domain.actdsltmp
   Description . . . . . . . . . . . : Intel(R) 82566MM Gigabit Network Connection
   Physical Address. . . . . . . . . : 00-1E-37-D0-E9-35
   DHCP Enabled. . . . . . . . . . . : Yes
   Autoconfiguration Enabled . . . . : Yes
   Link-local IPv6 Address . . . . . : fe80::2836:c43e:274b:f08c%11(Preferred)
   IPv4 Address. . . . . . . . . . . : 192.168.0.6(Preferred)
   Subnet Mask . . . . . . . . . . . : 255.255.255.0
   Lease Obtained. . . . . . . . . . : Monday, October 20, 2008 9:08:36 AM
   Lease Expires . . . . . . . . . . : Tuesday, October 21, 2008 9:08:39 AM
   Default Gateway . . . . . . . . . : 192.168.0.1
   DHCP Server . . . . . . . . . . . : 192.168.0.1
   DNS Servers . . . . . . . . . . . : 192.168.0.1
                                       205.171.3.65
   NetBIOS over Tcpip. . . . . . . . : Enabled

Wireless LAN adapter Wireless Network Connection:
   Connection-specific DNS Suffix  . : qwest.net
   Description . . . . . . . . . . . : Intel(R) Wireless WiFi Link 4965AGN
   Physical Address. . . . . . . . . : 00-1F-3B-3F-4A-D9
   DHCP Enabled. . . . . . . . . . . : Yes
   Autoconfiguration Enabled . . . . : Yes
   Link-local IPv6 Address . . . . . : fe80::20e7:7fb8:8a00:832b%10(Preferred)
   IPv4 Address. . . . . . . . . . . : 10.0.1.198(Preferred)
   Subnet Mask . . . . . . . . . . . : 255.255.255.0
   Lease Obtained. . . . . . . . . . : Monday, October 20, 2008 10:43:53 AM
   Lease Expires . . . . . . . . . . : Monday, October 20, 2008 2:43:53 PM
   Default Gateway . . . . . . . . . : fe80::21b:63ff:fef3:3694%10
                                       10.0.1.1
   DHCP Server . . . . . . . . . . . : 10.0.1.1
   DNS Servers . . . . . . . . . . . : 10.0.1.1
   NetBIOS over Tcpip. . . . . . . . : Enabled

Tunnel adapter Local Area Connection* 6:
   Media State . . . . . . . . . . . : Media disconnected
```

```
   Connection-specific DNS Suffix  . :
   Description . . . . . . . . . . : isatap.globalnet.local
   Physical Address. . . . . . . . : 00-00-00-00-00-00-00-E0
   DHCP Enabled. . . . . . . . . . : No
   Autoconfiguration Enabled . . . . : Yes

Tunnel adapter Local Area Connection* 7:
   Media State . . . . . . . . . . : Media disconnected
   Connection-specific DNS Suffix  . :
   Description . . . . . . . . . . : isatap.{9572A79F-3A58-4E9B-9BD0-
                                     8F6FF2F058FC}
   Physical Address. . . . . . . . : 00-00-00-00-00-00-00-E0
   DHCP Enabled. . . . . . . . . . : No
   Autoconfiguration Enabled . . . . : Yes
[output cut]
```

As you can see, it's more of the same—a whole lot more. The most important thing I want you to notice is that I've received the hardware information about each interface, including the Media Access Control (MAC) address. Also significant is that I can see the Dynamic Host Configuration Protocol (DHCP) lease times and DNS addresses now.

But why stop here? There are two more valuable options you need to use with the ipconfig command. They are /release and /renew.

When you change networks, you need to get the IP address of that subnet and/or virtual LAN (VLAN). Vista works most of the time without doing anything, but sometimes I do have to renew the IP configuration when changing networks. But that's easy—just type **ipconfig /renew** from a command prompt, and if you're connected to DHCP server that's available, you'll then magically receive an IP address.

Now, if it still doesn't work, you'll need to release and renew your TCP/IP settings. To release your current DHCP TCP/IP information, you must elevate your command prompt, or you'll get this warning:

```
C:\Users\tlammle>ipconfig /release
The requested operation requires elevation.
C:\Users\tlammle>
```

Should this happen to you, go to Start ➢ All Programs ➢ Accessories ➢ Command Prompt, right-click, and choose Run As Administrator. (Of course, you'll have to enter your name and password to do this if you are using Vista. But we love Vista, right? Okay, maybe not always.) Anyway, Figure 17.1 shows how I did this.

Once your Command Prompt has been duly elevated, you can use the ipconfig /release command and then the ipconfig /renew command to get new TCP/IP information for your host.

FIGURE 17.1   Elevating your command prompt

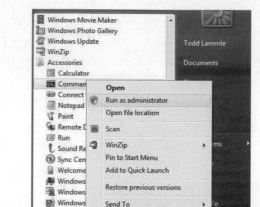

Using the *ifconfig* Utility

There is a utility in Linux/Unix/Mac that will give you information similar to what ipconfig shows. It's called ifconfig (short for "interface configuration"). Although ipconfig and ifconfig show similar information, there are major differences between these two utilities. The ipconfig utility is mainly used to view the TCP/IP configuration for a computer. You can use ifconfig to do the same thing, but ifconfig can also be used to configure a protocol or a particular network interface.

The general syntax of the ifconfig command is as follows:

```
ifconfig interface [address [parameters]]
```

The *interface* parameter equals the Unix name of the interface, such as eth0. If the optional address parameter is specified, the ifconfig command sets the IP address for the interface to the address you've specified. When the ifconfig command is used by itself with no parameters, all configured interfaces will be reported on. But if only the interface name is specified, you'll get output that looks like this:

```
# ifconfig eth0
eth0  Link encap 10Mbps Ethernet  HWaddr 00:00:C0:90:B3:42
inetaddr 172.16.0.2 Bcast 172.16.0.255 Mask 255.255.255.0 UP BROADCAST RUNNING
MTU 1500  Metric 0
```

```
    RX packets 3136 errors 217 dropped 7 overrun 26
    TX packets 1752 errors 25 dropped 0 overrun 0
```

Looking at this, we can see that the eth0 interface is a 10Mbps Ethernet interface. The interface's MAC and IP address information is displayed in this output as well. And, although not shown in the output, the ifconfig tool can show you the DNS information configured on the host.

Using the *ping* Utility

Ping is the most basic TCP/IP utility, and it's included with most TCP/IP stacks for most platforms. Windows, again, is no exception. In most cases, ping is a command-line utility, although there are many GUI implementations available. You use the ping utility for two primary purposes:

- To find out if a host is responding
- To find out if you can reach a host

Here's the syntax:

```
Ping hostname or IP address
```

If you ping any station that has an IP address, the ICMP that's part of that particular host's TCP/IP stack will respond to the request. This ICMP test and response looks something like this:

```
ping 204.153.163.2

Pinging 204.153.163.2 with 32 bytes of data:

Reply from 204.153.163.2: bytes=32 time<10ms TTL=128
Reply from 204.153.163.2: bytes=32 time=1ms TTL=128
Reply from 204.153.163.2: bytes=32 time<10ms TTL=128
Reply from 204.153.163.2: bytes=32 time<10ms TTL=128
```

Because I've received a reply from the destination station (204.153.163.2, in this case), I know that I can reach the host and that it's responding to basic IP requests. Don't forget that you can use name resolution and ping to a name such as ping www.sybex.com, and as long as that name can be resolved, you're golden.

Most versions of ping work the same way, but there are some switches you can use to specify certain information like the number of packets to send, how big a packet to send, and so on. And if you're running the Windows command-line version of ping, just use the /? or -? switch to display a list of the available options like this:

```
C:\Users\tlammle>ping /?
```

```
Usage: ping [-t] [-a] [-n count] [-l size] [-f] [-i TTL] [-v TOS]
            [-r count] [-s count] [[-j host-list] | [-k host-list]]
            [-w timeout] [-R] [-S srcaddr] [-4] [-6] target_name
```

The command will also output a table showing what each of the options does, presented here in Table 17.1.

TABLE 17.1 Options for *ping Switches*

Option	Description
-t	Pings the specified host until stopped. To see statistics and continue, press Ctrl+Break; to stop, press Ctrl+C.
-a	Resolves addresses to hostnames.
-n *count*	Specifies the number of echo requests to send.
-l *size*	Sends the buffer size.
-f	Sets the Don't Fragment flag in the packet (IPv4-only).
-i *TTL*	Specifies the time to live.
-v *TOS*	Specifies the type of service (IPv4-only).
-r *count*	Records the route for count hops (IPv4-only).
-s *count*	Specifies the timestamp for count hops (IPv4-only).
-j *host-list*	Uses a loose source route along the host-list (IPv4-only).
-k *host-list*	Uses a strict source route along host-list (IPv4-only).
-w *timeout*	Specifies the timeout in milliseconds to wait for each reply.
-R	Uses the routing header to test the reverse route also (IPv6-only).
-S *srcaddr*	Specifies the source address to use.
-4	Forces using IPv4.
-6	Forces using IPv6.

You can ping your local TCP/IP interface by typing **ping 127.0.0.1** or **ping localhost**. Understand that both addresses represent the local interface.

As you can see, there's a plethora of options you can use with the ping command from a Windows DOS prompt. But I really want you to focus on a few from the previous output. (I'm only going to go over a few of them, but you can get on your host machine and play with all the options.)

The -a switch is very cool because if you have name resolution (such as a DNS server), you can see the name of the destination host even if you only know its IP address. The -n switch sets the number of echo requests to send, where four is the default, and the -w switch allows you to adjust the time-out in milliseconds. The default ping timeout is 1 second (1000ms).

The -6 is also nice if you want to ping an IPv6 host. By the way, unless you really love typing 128-bit addresses, this is a wonderful example of how important name resolution is. And then there's -t, which keeps the ping running. Here's an example of a ping to an IPv6 address:

```
C:\Users\tlammle>ping -6 fe80::1063:16af:3f57:fff9

Pinging fe80::1063:16af:3f57:fff9 from fe80::1063:16af:3f57:fff9%25 with 32
bytes of data:
Reply from fe80::1063:16af:3f57:fff9: time<1ms
Reply from fe80::1063:16af:3f57:fff9: time<1ms
Reply from fe80::1063:16af:3f57:fff9: time<1ms
Reply from fe80::1063:16af:3f57:fff9: time<1ms

Ping statistics for fe80::1063:16af:3f57:fff9:
Packets: Sent = 4, Received = 4, Lost = 0 (0% loss),
Approximate round trip times in milli-seconds:
Minimum = 0ms, Maximum = 0ms, Average = 0ms
C:\Users\tlammle>
```

And if I want to have a continuous ping, I just use that -t option like this:

```
C:\Users\tlammle>ping -t 192.168.0.1

Pinging 192.168.0.1 with 32 bytes of data:
Reply from 192.168.0.1: bytes=32 time=7ms TTL=255
Reply from 192.168.0.1: bytes=32 time=1ms TTL=255
Reply from 192.168.0.1: bytes=32 time=1ms TTL=255
Reply from 192.168.0.1: bytes=32 time=1ms TTL=255
Reply from 192.168.0.1: bytes=32 time=1ms TTL=255
Reply from 192.168.0.1: bytes=32 time=1ms TTL=255
```

```
Ping statistics for 192.168.0.1:
Packets: Sent = 6, Received = 6, Lost = 0 (0% loss),
Approximate round trip times in milli-seconds:
Minimum = 1ms, Maximum = 7ms, Average = 2ms
Control-C
^C
C:\Users\tlammle>
```

This ping will just keep going and going like the Energizer Bunny until you press Ctrl+C. And by the way, it's an awesome tool for troubleshooting links.

Using the Address Resolution Protocol (ARP)

The *Address Resolution Protocol (ARP)* is part of the TCP/IP protocol stack. It's used to translate TCP/IP addresses to MAC addresses using broadcasts. When a machine running TCP/IP wants to know which machine on an Ethernet network is using a certain IP address, it will send an ARP broadcast that says, in effect, "Hey... exactly who is IP address xxx.xxx.xxx.xxx?" The machine that owns the specific address will respond with its own MAC address, supplying the answer. The machine that made the inquiry will respond by adding the newly gained information to its own ARP table.

In addition to the normal usage, the ARP designation refers to a utility in Windows that you can use to manipulate and view the local workstation's ARP table.

The Windows ARP Table

The *ARP table* in Windows includes a list of TCP/IP addresses and their associated physical (MAC) addresses. This table is cached in memory so that Windows doesn't have to perform ARP lookups for frequently accessed TCP/IP addresses like those of servers and default gateways. Each entry contains an IP address and a MAC address, plus a value for TTL that determines how long each entry will remain in the ARP table.

Remember that the ARP table contains two kinds of entries:

- Dynamic
- Static

Dynamic ARP table entries are created whenever the Windows TCP/IP stack performs an ARP lookup but the MAC address isn't found in the ARP table. When the MAC address of the requested IP address is finally found, or *resolved,* that information is then added into the ARP table as a dynamic entry. Whenever a request to send a packet to the host is sent to the Data Link layer, the ARP cache is checked first before an ARP broadcast is sent out. Remember, the ARP request is broadcast on the local segment—it does not go through a router.

The ARP table is cleared of dynamic entries whose TTL has expired to ensure that the entries are current.

Static ARP table entries serve the same function as dynamic entries but are made manually using the arp utility.

Using the *arp* Utility

Okay—you now know that ARP is a protocol included the TCP/IP suite. You also understand that ARP is used by IP to determine the MAC address of a device that exists on the same subnet as the requesting device. When a TCP/IP device needs to forward a packet to a device on the local subnet, it first looks in its own table, called an *ARP cache*, for an association between the known IP address of the destination device on the local subnet and that same device's MAC address. The cache is called that because the contents are periodically weeded out.

If no association that includes the destination IP address can be found, the device will then send out an ARP broadcast that includes its own MAC and IP information as well as the IP address of the target device and a blank MAC address field. Filling in that blank is the object of the whole operation—it's the unknown value that the source device is requesting to be returned to it in the form of an ARP reply. Windows includes a utility called arp that allows us to check out the operating system's ARP cache. To view this, from a Windows DOS prompt, use the arp command like this:

```
C:\Uses\tlammle>arp

Displays and modifies the IP to Physical address translation tables used by
address resolution protocol (ARP).

ARP -s inet_addr eth_addr [if_addr]
ARP -d inet_addr [if_addr]
ARP -a [inet_addr] [-N if_addr] [-v]
```

Table 17.1 describes the various options that you can use with the arp command.

TABLE 17.2   arp Option Descriptions

Option	Description
-a	Displays current ARP entries by interrogating the current protocol data. If inet_addr is specified, the IP and physical addresses for only the specified computer are displayed. If more than one network interface uses ARP, entries for each ARP table are displayed.

TABLE 17.2   arp Option Descriptions *(continued)*

Option	Description
-a	Displays current ARP entries by interrogating the current protocol data. If inet_addr is specified, the IP and physical addresses for only the specified computer are displayed. If more than one network interface uses ARP, entries for each ARP table are displayed.
-g	Same as -a.
-v	Displays current ARP entries in verbose mode. All invalid entries and entries on the loop-back interface will be shown.
inet_addr	Specifies an Internet address.
-N	Displays the ARP entries for the network interface specified by if_addr.
-d	Deletes the host specified by inet_addr. inet_addr may be wildcarded with * to delete all hosts.
-s	Adds the host, and associates the Internet address inet_addr with the physical address eth_addr. The physical address is given as six hexadecimal bytes separated by hyphens. The entry is permanent.
eth_addr	Specifies a physical address.
if_addr	If present, specifies the Internet address of the interface whose address translation table should be modified. If not present, the first applicable interface will be used.

Sheesh. Looking at that output really makes me wish we were all just running IPv6, because as you already should know, IPv6 doesn't need ARP as well as many other annoying features and protocols required when running IPv4.

Of note, the Windows arp utility is primarily useful for resolving duplicate IP addresses. For example, let's say your workstation receives its IP address from a DHCP server, but it accidentally receives the same address as some other workstation gets. And so, when you try to ping it, you get no response. Your workstation is basically confused—it's trying to determine the MAC address, and it can't because two machines are reporting that they have the same IP address. To solve this little snag, you can use the arp utility to view your local ARP table and see which TCP/IP address is resolved to which MAC address.

To display the entire current ARP table, use the arp command with the −a switch, like so:

```
C:\Users\tlammle>arp -a
```

```
Interface: 192.168.0.6 --- 0xb
```

```
Internet Address        Physical Address        Type
192.168.0.1             00-15-05-06-31-b0       dynamic
192.168.0.255           ff-ff-ff-ff-ff-ff       static
224.0.0.22              01-00-5e-00-00-16       static
224.0.0.252             01-00-5e-00-00-fc       static
239.255.255.250         01-00-5e-7f-ff-fa       static
255.255.255.255         ff-ff-ff-ff-ff-ff       static

Interface: 10.100.10.54 --- 0x10
Internet Address        Physical Address        Type
10.100.10.1             00-15-05-06-31-b0       dynamic
10.100.10.255           ff-ff-ff-ff-ff-ff       static
224.0.0.22              01-00-5e-00-00-16       static
224.0.0.252             01-00-5e-00-00-fc       static
239.255.255.250         01-00-5e-7f-ff-fa       static
```

By the way, the –g switch will produce the same result.

Now, from this output, you can tell which MAC address is assigned to which IP address. Then, for static assignments, you can tell which workstation has a specific IP address and if it's indeed supposed to have that address by examining your network documentation—you do have that record, right?

For DHCP-assigned addresses, you can begin to uncover problems stemming from multiple DHCP scopes or servers doling out identical addresses and other common configuration issues. And remember that under normal circumstances, you shouldn't see IP addresses in the ARP table for a given interface that aren't members of the same IP subnet as the interface.

If the machine has more than one network card (as may happen in Windows servers and on laptops with both Ethernet and wireless cards), each interface will be listed separately.

It's good to know that in addition to displaying the ARP table, you can use the arp utility to manipulate the table itself. To add static entries to the ARP table, you use the arp command with the –s switch. These static entries will stay in the ARP table until the machine is rebooted. A static entry essentially hard-wires a specific IP address to a specific MAC address so that when a packet needs to be sent to that IP address, it will automatically be sent to that MAC address. Here's the syntax:

```
arp –s [IP Address] [MAC Address]
```

Simply replace the *[IP Address]* and *[MAC Address]* sections with the appropriate entries, like so:

```
arp -s 204.153.163.5 00-a0-c0-ab-c3-11
```

Now, take a look at your new ARP table by using the arp -a command. You should see something like this:

```
Internet Address        Physical Address        Type
204.153.163.5           00-a0-c0-ab-c3-11       static
```

Finally, if you want to delete entries from the ARP table, you can either wait until the dynamic entries time out or use the -d switch with the IP address of the static entry you'd like to delete, like this:

```
arp -d 204.153.163.5
```

Doing so effectively deletes the entry from the ARP table in memory.

> The arp utility doesn't confirm successful additions or deletions (use arp -a or arp -g for that), but it will give you an error message if you use incorrect syntax.

Using the *nslookup* Utility

Whenever you're configuring a server or a workstation to connect to the Internet, you've got to start by configuring DNS if you want name resolution to happen (that is, if you want to be able to type **www.sybex.com** instead of an IP address). When configuring DNS, it's a very good thing to be able to test what IP address DNS is returning to ensure that it's working properly. The nslookup utility allows you to query a name server and quickly find out which name resolves to which IP address.

> The Unix dig (short for *domain information groper*) utility does the exact same thing as nslookup. It's primarily a command-line utility that allows you to perform a single DNS lookup for a specific entity, but it can also be employed in batch mode for a series of lookups. Detailed information on this command is beyond the scope of this study guide, but you can find more information on the Web by searching for "unix dig."

The nslookup utility comes with Windows NT and later, as well as most versions of Unix and Linux, but not with Windows 95/98. You can run it from a Windows command prompt. At the command prompt, you can start the `nslookup` utility by typing **`nslookup`** and pressing Enter. When you're inside this utility, the command prompt will change from something similar to `C:\>` sign to a shorter > sign. It will also display the name and IP address of the default DNS server you will be querying (you can change it, if necessary). Now, you can start using `nslookup`. The following output gives you a sample of the display after the `nslookup` command has been entered at the `C:\>` prompt.

```
C:\Users\tlammle>nslookup
Default Server:  gnt-corpdc1.globalnet.local
Address:  10.100.36.12

>
```

The primary job of `nslookup` is to tell you the many different features of a particular domain name, the names of the servers that serve it, and how they're configured. To get that, just type in a domain name at the > prompt, and the `nslookup` utility will then return this information:

```
> lammle.com
Server:  dslmodem.domain.actdsltmp
Address:  192.168.0.1

Non-authoritative answer:
Name:     lammle.com
Address:  206.123.114.186
```

What this tells you is that the server that returned the information is not responsible (authoritative) for the zone information of the domain for which you requested an address, and that the name server for the domain `lammle.com` is located at the IP address 206.123.114.186.

You can also ask `nslookup` for other information by setting a different option within `nslookup`. Just type **set** *option* at the > prompt and replace *option* with the actual option you want to use, for example, >set type=mx to determine the IP address of your email server. If you can't decide which one you want, use the question mark (?) at the greater than sign (>) to see all available options.

If you type in nslookup and receive this reply:

```
NS request timed out.
    timeout was 2 seconds.
***Can't find server name for address 206.123.114.186: Timed out
Default Server:  UnKnown
Address:  fec0:0:0:ffff::1
```

Then you know your DNS servers are not answering. You need to get over to the DNS server stat!

Resolving Names with the Hosts Table

The Hosts table is really a lot like DNS, except its entries are static for each and every host and server. Within the Hosts table, you'll find a collection of host names that devices reference for name-resolution purposes. And even though it works in both IP and IPv6 environments, it's unlikely you will use it these days, because the Hosts table is a way-ancient relic left over from old Unix machines.

But just because it's museum quality doesn't mean you won't run into it now and then, which is the main reason I'm talking to you about it. You can find the Hosts table in C:\Windows\System32\drivers\etc. Just double-click the file, and then choose to open the file in Notepad or other text editor. Here's the default information—it's really nothing more than an explanation of how to use it and the local hosts for both IP and IPv6:

```
# Copyright (c) 1993-2006 Microsoft Corp.
#
# This is a sample HOSTS file used by Microsoft TCP/IP for Windows.
#
# This file contains the mappings of IP addresses to host names. Each
# entry should be kept on an individual line. The IP address should
# be placed in the first column followed by the corresponding host name.
# The IP address and the host name should be separated by at least one
# space.
#
# Additionally, comments (such as these) may be inserted on individual
# lines or following the machine name denoted by a '#' symbol.
#
# For example:
#
#      102.54.94.97     rhino.acme.com          # source server
#       38.25.63.10     x.acme.com              # x client host

127.0.0.1       localhost
::1             localhost
```

Any information entered to the right of a pound sign (#) in a Hosts file is ignored, so you can use this space for comments.

Because it's a plain ASCII text file, you add the IP address under the local hosts and then the name to which you want to resolve the IP address. It's a pretty simple configuration, and again, one I don't recommend using because you have to type in the names of every host on every machine in your network. DNS is definitely the name resolution of choice for networks today.

Do not get the Hosts table confused with the hostname command. The hostname command doesn't do much but display the name of your host, as shown:

```
C:\Users\tlammle>hostname /?
```

Prints the name of the current host.

```
hostname
```

```
C:\Users\tlammle>hostname
globalnet-todd
```

Using the *Mtr* Command

Mtr or My traceroute is a computer program that combines the functions of the traceroute and ping utilities in a single network diagnostic tool. It also adds round-trip time and packet loss to the output—very cool.

Mtr probes routers on the route path by limiting the number of hops individual packets are allowed to traverse and listening to news of their termination. It will regularly repeat this process (usually once per second) and keep track of the response times of the hops along the path.

Mtr is great if you have Linux or Unix, but by default, it's not installed on Windows devices. Third-party applications of Mtr are available to install on Windows, but Microsoft did respond with its own version of Mtr—it's called pathping and provides the same functions as Mtr. Here's a look at the output and the options:

```
C:\Users\tlammle>pathping
```

```
Usage: pathping [-g host-list] [-h maximum_hops] [-i address] [-n]
                [-p period] [-q num_queries] [-w timeout]
                [-4] [-6] target_name
```

Table 17.3 lists the options of the Windows pathping command.

TABLE 17.3   *pathping* Options and Descriptions

Option	Description
-g *host-list*	Uses a loose source route along the *host-list*.
-h *maximum_hops*	Specifies the maximum number of hops to search for the target.

TABLE 17.3   *pathping* Options and Descriptions *(continued)*

Option	Description
-i *address*	Uses the specified source address.
-n	Does not resolve addresses to hostnames.
-p *period*	Waits *period* milliseconds between pings.
-q *num_queries*	Specifies the number of queries per hop.
-w *timeout*	Waits *timeout* milliseconds for each reply.
-4	Forces using IPv4.
-6	Forces using IPv6.

The Mtr utility is basically the same as traceroute and ping, but it does give you some additional output that can help you troubleshoot your network.

Using the *Route* Command

I went over static routing in Chapter 9, "Introduction to IP Routing," so you know that Windows devices like routers perform routing. Most of the time, it's a good idea to leave Windows alone, but it's still good to know how to add and delete routes on your Windows machines.

Probably the biggest reason for manipulating the routing table on a Windows server is to create a firewall. For instance, let's say we're running an application layer firewall on a Windows server located between the demilitarized zone (DMZ) and the internal network. This scenario would mean the routing that's happening on the server or hosts located in the DMZ wouldn't be able to reach the internal network's hosts and vice versa.

To circumvent this problem, we would need to employ both static and default routing, because Windows Vista and Server 2008 don't support routing protocols—running routing protocols on hosts and servers wouldn't be a good solution for today's networks, and Microsoft knows that.

To view the routing table on a Windows device, use the route print command, as shown in Figure 17.2.

FIGURE 17.2   route print output

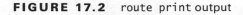

```
Command Prompt

Microsoft Windows [Version 6.0.6001]
Copyright (c) 2006 Microsoft Corporation. All rights reserved.

C:\Users\tlammle>route print
===========================================================================
Interface List
 20 ...00 05 9a 3c 78 00 ...... Cisco Systems UPN Adapter
 11 ...00 1e 37 d0 e9 35 ...... Intel(R) 82566MM Gigabit Network Connection
 10 ...00 1f 3b 3f 4a d9 ...... Intel(R) Wireless WiFi Link 4965AGN
  1 ........................... Software Loopback Interface 1
 14 ...00 00 00 00 00 00 00 e0  isatap.globalnet.local
 12 ...00 00 00 00 00 00 00 e0  isatap.{9572A79F-3A58-4E9B-9BD0-8F6FF2F058FC}
 17 ...00 00 00 00 00 00 00 e0  6TO4 Adapter
 37 ...00 00 00 00 00 00 00 e0  Microsoft ISATAP Adapter #5
 19 ...02 00 54 55 4e 01 ...... Teredo Tunneling Pseudo-Interface
 18 ...00 00 00 00 00 00 00 e0  isatap.globalnet.local
 28 ...00 00 00 00 00 00 00 e0  isatap.globalnet.local
 26 ...00 00 00 00 00 00 00 e0  isatap.globalnet.local
 29 ...00 00 00 00 00 00 00 e0  isatap.{9572A79F-3A58-4E9B-9BD0-8F6FF2F058FC}
 27 ...00 00 00 00 00 00 00 e0  isatap.domain.actdsltmp
===========================================================================

IPv4 Route Table
===========================================================================
Active Routes:
Network Destination        Netmask          Gateway       Interface  Metric
          0.0.0.0          0.0.0.0      192.168.0.1     192.168.0.6      20
       10.100.1.0    255.255.255.0     10.100.10.1   10.100.10.55     100
      10.100.10.0    255.255.255.0        On-link    10.100.10.55     276
     10.100.10.55  255.255.255.255        On-link    10.100.10.55     276
    10.100.10.255  255.255.255.255        On-link    10.100.10.55     276
      10.100.36.0  255.255.255.255     10.100.10.1   10.100.10.55     100
    64.190.251.30  255.255.255.255     192.168.0.1     192.168.0.6     100
        127.0.0.0        255.0.0.0        On-link       127.0.0.1     306
        127.0.0.1  255.255.255.255        On-link       127.0.0.1     306
  127.255.255.255  255.255.255.255        On-link       127.0.0.1     306
      192.168.0.0    255.255.255.0        On-link     192.168.0.6     276
      192.168.0.1  255.255.255.255        On-link     192.168.0.6     100
      192.168.0.6  255.255.255.255        On-link     192.168.0.6     276
    192.168.0.255  255.255.255.255        On-link     192.168.0.6     276
        224.0.0.0        240.0.0.0        On-link       127.0.0.1     306
        224.0.0.0        240.0.0.0        On-link     192.168.0.6     276
        224.0.0.0        240.0.0.0        On-link    10.100.10.55     276
  255.255.255.255  255.255.255.255        On-link       127.0.0.1     306
  255.255.255.255  255.255.255.255        On-link     192.168.0.6     276
  255.255.255.255  255.255.255.255        On-link    10.100.10.55     276
===========================================================================
Persistent Routes:
  None
```

In this output, you can see that each of the routes was added automatically when the system booted up. (This is all based on the configuration of your IP stack.) To see all the options available with the route command, type the route command and then press Enter. To add a route to your routing table, use the following syntax:

route [-f] [-p] [*Command* [*Destination*] [**mask** *Netmask*] [*Gateway*] [**metric** *Metric*]] [**if** *Interface*]]

Using the *route* Command Options

Let's start with the switches you can use:

-f   Using this command with any of the options like add, change, or delete will clear the routing table of all entries that aren't host routes (routes with the subnet mask 255.255.255.255), the loopback network route(s) (routes with a destination of 127.0.0.0 and the subnet mask 255.0.0.0), and any multicast routes (those with a destination of 224.0.0.0 and the subnet mask 240.0.0.0).

-p   If you use this with the add command, the individual route will be added to the registry and then used to initialize the IP routing table whenever TCP/IP is started. Important to remember is that by default, the routes you've statically added won't remain in the

routing table the next time TCP/IP boots. And if you use -p with the print command, you'll get shown a list of the persistent routes that are stored in the registry location of HKEY_LOCAL_MACHINE\SYSTEM\CurrentControlSet\Services\Tcpip\Parameters\ PersistentRoutes.

Now, let's take a look at how and when you would use the route command. Table 17.4 shows the command options available and what they do when using the route command with them.

TABLE 17.4   route Command Options

Command	Purpose
add	Adds a route
change	Modifies an existing route
delete	Deletes a route(s)
print	Prints a route(s)

Here's a description of some other tasks you can accomplish via the rest of the command's options:

destination   This will give you the network destination of a given route. If the host bits of the network address are set to 0, it will be depicted with the destination's IP network address, an IP address for a specific host route, or the default route of 0.0.0.0.

mask **netmask**   This will provide you with the *netmask*—often referred to as the *subnet mask*—that's associated with the destination network. The default destination subnet mask is 0.0.0.0, and typically you'll see 255.255.255.255 representing a host route. It's really important to remember that the destination address can't be more specific than its corresponding subnet mask. What I'm saying is that there absolutely can't be a bit set to 1 in the destination address if the equivalent bit in the subnet mask is a 0.

gateway   The gateway also depends on the network address and subnet mask, but it's even more specific and delimits what's called the *next-hop IP address*. For routes located on a local subnet, the gateway address maps directly to a particular interface. If the destination is on a remote network, the gateway IP address will direct packets to the neighboring router.

metric **metric**   *Metric* refers to the cost of a given route from the sending to the receiving device, and it's a value between 1 and 9999. Devices use this value to choose the best, or most efficient, routes among those in its routing table—the route with the lowest value wins. This decision can also include factors like the number of hops; the speed, reliability, and available bandwidth of the path being considered; plus the various administrative aspects associated with it.

if interface   This tool depends on information from the gateway address and determines the interface index for the specific interface that needs to receive the data. You can get a list of interfaces along with their relevant interface indexes by typing the **route print** command.

/?   Using this will allow you to view help at the command prompt.

Some Examples of the *route* Command

Even though the finer points of the route command demand that you use caution when deploying some of them, I'll still list the basics of the route command because it can be really useful. I highly recommend that you spend some time practicing them on a non-production server, though—especially at first.

- To display the entire IP routing table, type **route print**.

- To add a default route with the default gateway address 192.168.10.1, type **route add 0.0.0.0 mask 0.0.0.0 192.168.10.1**.

- To add a route to the destination 10.1.1.0 with the subnet mask 255.255.255.0 and the next-hop address 10.2.2.2, type **route add 10.1.1..0 mask 255.255.255.0 10.2.2.2**.

- If you want to, let's say, add a persistent route to the destination 10.100.0.0 with the subnet mask 255.255.0.0 and the next-hop address 10.2.0.1, type **route -p add 10.100.0.0 mask 255.255.0.0 10.2.0.1**.If you want to delete the route to the destination 10.100.0.0 with the subnet mask 255.255.0.0, enter **route delete 10.100.0.0 mask 255.255.0.0**.

- And finally, if you want to change the next-hop address of a route with the destination 10.100.0.0 and the subnet mask 255.255.0.0 from 10.2.0.1 to 10.7.0.5, type **route change 10.100.0.0 mask 255.255.0.0 10.7.0.5**.

Okay, let's move on to some other important Windows utilities.

Using the *nbtstat* Utility

Microsoft Windows uses an interface called Network Basic Input/Output System (NetBIOS), which relates names with workstations and is an upper-layer interface that requires a transport protocol—usually, TCP/IP. But IPv6 can be used as well. Deploying the nbtstat utility will achieve these three important things:

- Track NetBIOS over TCP/IP statistics
- Show the details of incoming and outgoing NetBIOS over TCP/IP connections
- Resolve NetBIOS names

Understand that because NetBIOS name resolution is primarily a Windows network utility, the nbtstat command is available only in Windows-based operating systems.

To display a basic description of nbtstat and its associated options, type **nbtstat** at the command line. Then, use these options to get a display of information about NetBIOS over TCP/IP hosts. Here are some of the tools, or *switches*, you can use:

–a	–A
–c	–n
–r	–R
–S	–s

All nbtstat switches are case sensitive. Generally speaking, lowercase switches deal with NetBIOS names of hosts, and the uppercase ones deal with the TCP/IP addresses of hosts.

The –*a* Switch

Making use of the–a switch will get you a remote machine's NetBIOS name table consisting of a list of every NetBIOS name the machine you've deployed the switch from knows of. The –a switch produced the output from server S1 shown in Figure 17.3.

So, using this switch arranges the NetBIOS name-table information in table form with output in four columns. The Name column displays the NetBIOS name entry for the remote host machine.

FIGURE 17.3   Sample output of the nbtstat –a command

```
C:\>nbtstat -a s1


    NetBIOS Remote Machine Name Table

   Name              Type       Status
  ─────────────────────────────────────
  S1             <20>  UNIQUE   Registered
  S1             <00>  UNIQUE   Registered
  ACME           <00>  GROUP    Registered
  ACME           <1C>  GROUP    Registered
  ACME           <1B>  UNIQUE   Registered
  S1             <03>  UNIQUE   Registered
  ACME           <1E>  GROUP    Registered
  ACME           <1D>  UNIQUE   Registered
  .__MSBROWSE__.<01>  GROUP    Registered
  INet~Services  <1C>  GROUP    Registered
  IS~S1......... <00>  UNIQUE   Registered

  MAC Address = 00-A0-C9-D4-BC-DC
```

The next column gives you a unique two-digit hexadecimal identifier for the NetBIOS name. This identifier represents the last byte of the NetBIOS name depicted in the Name column, and it's important because the same name could actually be used several times for the same machine. Plus, it identifies the specific service on the particular host that the name is referencing. Tables 17.5 and 17.6 list the hexadecimal identifiers for unique and group host names.

TABLE 17.5   Last-Byte Identifiers for Unique Names

Hex ID	Description
00	General name for the computer.
03	Messenger service ID used to send messages between a WINS server and a workstation. This is the ID registered with a WINS server.
06	Remote Access Server (RAS) server service ID.
20	File-serving service ID.
21	RAS client.
53	DNS.
123	Network Time Protocol (NTP).
1B	Domain master browser ID. A NetBIOS name with this ID indicates the domain master browser.
1F	Network Dynamic Data Exchange (NetDDE) service ID.
BE	Network monitor agent ID.
BF	Network monitor utility ID.

TABLE 17.6   Last-Byte Identifiers for Group Names

Hex ID	Description
01	Master browser for a domain to other master browsers.
20	Internet group name ID. This ID is registered with the WINS server to indicate which computers are used for administrative purposes.

TABLE 17.6   Last-Byte Identifiers for Group Names *(continued)*

Hex ID	Description
1C	Domain group name ID.
1D	Master browser name.
1E	Normal group name.

The Type column refers to (surprise) the type of NetBIOS name being referenced. Unique NetBIOS names refer to individual hosts, and Group names refer to the names of logical groupings of workstations—either domains or workgroups.

The Status column gives you information about the status of host's NetBIOS even if it hasn't been registered with the rest of the network.

The –*A* Switch

The –A switch works just like the –a switch and will give you the same output, but the syntax of the command is different. Obviously, you use an uppercase *A* instead of a lowercase one, and you also have to include the host's IP address instead of its NetBIOS name. To use it, type **nbtstat** followed by –A and finally the IP address of the specific host whose NetBIOS table you want to check out:

```
nbtstat –A 199.153.163.2
```

The –*c* Switch

Use the –c switch to display the local NetBIOS name cache on the workstation it's running on. Figure 17.4 shows sample output of the nbtstat –c command.

FIGURE 17.4   Sample output of the nbtstat –c command

```
Node IpAddress: [204.153.163.4] Scope Id: []

          NetBIOS Remote Cache Name Table

     Name          Type      Host Address    Life [sec]
   ---------------------------------------------------------
   S1          <00>  UNIQUE      204.153.163.2       420
```

Each entry in this display shows the NetBIOS name, the hex ID for the service that was accessed, the type of NetBIOS name (unique or group), the IP address that the name resolves to, and its life. The Life value shows how many seconds each entry will live in the cache. When this time expires, the entry will be deleted.

Sometimes, deploying nbtstat to display the cache will get you the response "No names in the cache," because all entries in the cache have expired. This is what happens if you don't regularly access machines or services with NetBIOS names.

The *–n* Switch

The –n switch will give you the local NetBIOS name table on a Windows device. Figure 17.5 shows output that's similar to the output of the –a switch, except for one important thing: What you're seeing is the NetBIOS name table for the machine you're running the command on instead of that of another host. Check it out.

FIGURE 17.5   Sample output of the nbtstat –n command

```
C:\NBTSTAT -n

Node IpAddress: [204.153.163.4] Scope Id: []

            NetBIOS Local Name Table

    Name              Type         Status
---------------------------------------------
DEFAULT       <00>  UNIQUE     Registered
WORKGROUP     <00>  GROUP      Registered
DEFAULT       <03>  UNIQUE     Registered
DEFAULT       <20>  UNIQUE     Registered
WORKGROUP     <1E>  GROUP      Registered
WORKGROUP     <1D>  UNIQUE     Registered
.._MSBROWSE__.<01>  GROUP      Registered
ADMINISTRATOR <03>  UNIQUE     Registered
```

The *–r* Switch

This switch is probably the one you'll use most often when you want to get hold of Net-BIOS over TCP/IP (NBT) statistics, because it tells you exactly how many NetBIOS names have been resolved to TCP/IP addresses. Figure 17.6 shows sample output of the nbtstat –r command.

FIGURE 17.6   Sample output of the nbtstat –r command

```
C:\>nbtstat -r


NetBIOS Names Resolution and Registration Statistics
---------------------------------------------------------

Resolved By Broadcast       = 2
Resolved By Name Server     = 0

Registered By Broadcast     = 12
Registered By Name Server = 0

    NetBIOS Names Resolved By Broadcast
---------------------------------------------------------
    ACME          <1B>
    ACME          <00>
```

What you can see here is that the statistics are divided into two categories. First, there are the NetBIOS Names Resolution and Registration Statistics. This is how many names have been resolved or registered either by broadcasts on the local segment or via lookup from a WINS name server.

Next you have the NetBIOS unique and group names and their associated hex IDs that were resolved or registered. In Figure 17.6, you can see that there's a distinct lack of information regarding names resolved by a name server. What this means is that the output is telling you that there's no WINS server operating—instead, all NetBIOS names were resolved by broadcast only.

> The −r switch comes in handy when you want to determine how a workstation is resolving NetBIOS names and whether WINS is configured correctly. If WINS isn't configured correctly or it's simply not being used, the numbers in the Resolved By Name Server and Registered By Name Server categories will always be zero.

The *−R* Switch

Unlike the −a and −A switches, −r and −R use the same letter but do *not* have anything in common.

Here's an example. Let's say you have a bad name in the NetBIOS name cache but the right name is in the LMHOSTS file instead. (The LMHOSTS file contains NetBIOS names of stations and their associated IP addresses.) Because the cache is consulted before the LMHOSTS file is, that bad address will remain in the cache until it expires.

This command is used when you want to purge the NetBIOS name table cache and reload the LMHOSTS file into memory. You do that using the nbtstat command with the −R switch, like so:

nbtstat −R

You can practice this nbtstat -R command on your host to purge the NBT remote cache table.

The *−S* Switch

Using the -S switch will display the NetBIOS sessions table that lists all NetBIOS sessions, incoming and outgoing, to and from the host from which you issued the command. The −S switch displays both workstation and server sessions but lists remote addresses by IP address only.

Figure 17.7 shows sample output of the nbtstat −S command.

FIGURE 17.7   Sample output of the nbtstat -S command

```
C:\NBTSTAT -S

            NetBIOS Connection Table
Local Name          State     In/Out  Remote Host           Input    Output
-----------------------------------------------------------------------------
S1          <00>    Connected   Out    204.153.163.4         256B     432B
S1          <03>    Listening
```

Here you can see the NetBIOS name being displayed along with its hex ID and the status of each session. An entry in the In/Out column determines whether the connection has been initiated from the computer on which you're running nbtstat (outbound) or whether another computer has initiated the connection (inbound). The numbers in the Input and Output columns indicate in bytes the amount of data transferred between the stations.

The –s Switch

As with the –A and –a switches, the lowercase –s switch is similar to its uppercase sibling. The nbtstat -s command produces the same output as nbtstat -S except that it will also attempt to resolve remote-host IP addresses into host names. Figure 17.8 shows sample output from the nbtstat -s command.

FIGURE 17.8   Sample output of the nbtstat -s command

```
C:\NBTSTAT -s

              NetBIOS Connection Table

Local Name          State     In/Out  Remote Host           Input    Output
-----------------------------------------------------------------------------
S1          <00>    Connected   Out    DEFAULT        <20>   256B     432B
S1          <03>    Listening
```

Note the similarities between Figure 17.8 and Figure 17.7.

As with any netstat command, the nbtstat command can place a number for an interval at the end to direct it to deploy once every so many seconds until you press Ctrl+C.

Using the *netstat* Utility

Using netstat is a great way to check out the inbound and outbound TCP/IP connections on your machine. You can also use it to view packet statistics like how many packets have been sent and received, the number of errors, and so on.

When used without any options, netstat produces output similar to the following, which shows all the outbound TCP/IP connections. This utility is a great tool to use to determine the status of outbound web connections. Take a look:

```
C:\Users\tlammle>netstat

Active Connections

  Proto  Local Address           Foreign Address          State
  TCP    10.100.10.54:49545      gnt-exchange:epmap       TIME_WAIT
  TCP    10.100.10.54:49548      gnt-exchange:epmap       TIME_WAIT
  TCP    10.100.10.54:49551      gnt-exchange:1151        ESTABLISHED
  TCP    10.100.10.54:49557      gnt-exchange:1026        ESTABLISHED
  TCP    10.100.10.54:49590      gnt-exchange:epmap       TIME_WAIT
  TCP    127.0.0.1:49174         globalnet-todd:62514     ESTABLISHED
  TCP    127.0.0.1:62514         globalnet-todd:49174     ESTABLISHED
  TCP    192.168.0.6:2492        blugro2relay:2492        ESTABLISHED
  TCP    192.168.0.6:2492        blugro3relay:2492        ESTABLISHED
  TCP    192.168.0.6:49170       64.12.25.26:5190         ESTABLISHED
  TCP    192.168.0.6:49171       oam-d05c:5190            ESTABLISHED
  TCP    192.168.0.6:49473       205.128.92.124:http      CLOSE_WAIT
  TCP    192.168.0.6:49625       64-190-251-21:ftp        ESTABLISHED
  TCP    192.168.0.6:49628       210-11:http              ESTABLISHED
  TCP    192.168.0.6:49629       varp1:http               ESTABLISHED
  TCP    192.168.0.6:49630       varp1:http               ESTABLISHED
  TCP    192.168.0.6:49631       varp1:http               ESTABLISHED
  TCP    192.168.0.6:49632       varp1:http               ESTABLISHED
  TCP    192.168.0.6:49635       199.93.62.125:http       ESTABLISHED
  TCP    192.168.0.6:49636       m1:http                  ESTABLISHED
  TCP    192.168.0.6:49638       spe:http                 ESTABLISHED
```

The Proto column lists the protocol being used. You can see that I'm connected to my Exchange server and an FTP server and that I have some HTTP sessions open; by the way, all of them use TCP at the Transport layer.

The Local Address column lists the source address and the source port (source socket). The Foreign Address lists the address of the destination machine (the host name if it's been resolved) plus the fact that the destination port is a TCP port. If the destination port is known, it will show up as the well-known port. In the previous output, you see http instead of port 80, and ftp instead of port 21.

The State column indicates the status of each connection. This column only shows statistics for TCP connections, because User Datagram Protocol (UDP) establishes no virtual circuit to the remote device. Usually, this column indicates ESTABLISHED when a TCP connection between your computer and the destination computer has been established. All sessions eventually time out and then close, and you can see that I have all of these listed in my `netstat` output.

> If the address of either your computer or the destination computer can be found in the HOSTS file on your computer, the destination computer's name, rather than the IP address, will show up in either the Local Address or Foreign Address column.

The output of the `netstat` utility depends on the switch. By using the netstat /? command we can see the options available to us.

C:\Users\tlammle>**netstat /?**

All of the `netstat` switch options are listed in Table 17.7.

TABLE 17.7   netstat Options and Descriptions

Option	Description
-a	Displays all connections and listening ports.
-b	Displays the executable involved in creating each connection or listening port. In some cases, well-known executables host multiple independent components, and in these cases the sequence of components involved in creating the connection or listening port is displayed. In this case, the executable name is in [ ] at the bottom; on top is the component it called, and so forth, until TCP/IP was reached. Note that this option can be time-consuming and will fail unless you have sufficient permissions.
-e	Displays Ethernet statistics. This may be combined with the -s option.
-f	Displays fully qualified domain names (FQDNs) for foreign addresses.
-n	Displays addresses and port numbers in numerical form.
-o	Displays the owning process ID associated with each connection.
-p proto	Shows connections for the protocol specified by proto; proto may be any of TCP, UDP, TCPv6, or UDPv6. If used with the -s option to display per-protocol statistics, proto may be any of IP, IPv6, ICMP, ICMPv6, TCP, TCPv6, UDP, or UDPv6.
-r	Displays the routing table.

TABLE 17.7   netstat Options and Descriptions *(continued)*

Option	Description
-s	Displays per-protocol statistics. By default, statistics are shown for IP, IPv6, ICMP, ICMPv6, TCP, TCPv6, UDP, and UDPv6; the -p option may be used to specify a subset of the default.
-t	Displays the current connection offload state. Redisplays selected statistics, pausing interval seconds between each display. Press Ctrl+C to stop redisplaying statistics. If omitted, netstat will print the current configuration information once.

Simply type **netstat** followed by a space and then the particular switch you want to use. Some switches have options, but no matter what, the syntax is basically the same.

Note that with Unix-type switches, the hyphen absolutely must be included. This is common in Microsoft operating systems for TCP/IP utilities that originate from Unix systems. I'm not going to exhaustively go over each and every switch, but make sure you practice all of these on your own Windows machine.

The –*a* Switch

When you use the –a switch, the netstat utility displays all TCP/IP connections and all UDP connections. Figure 17.9 shows sample output produced by the netstat –a command

FIGURE 17.9   Sample output of the netstat –a command

```
C:\ NETSTAT -a

Active Connections

Proto     Local Address       Foreign Address       State
TCP       default:1026        204.153.163.2:80      ESTABLISHED
TCP       default:1027        204.153.163.2:80      ESTABLISHED
TCP       default:1028        204.153.163.2:80      ESTABLISHED
TCP       default:1029        204.153.163.2:80      ESTABLISHED
UDP       default:nbname      *:*
UDP       default:nbdatagram  *:*
```

The last two entries in Figure 17.9 show that the protocol is UDP and gives the source-port nicknames nbname and nbdatagram. These are the well-known port numbers of 137 and 138, respectively. These port numbers are commonly seen on networks that broadcast the NetBIOS name of a workstation on the TCP/IP network. You can tell that this is a broadcast because the destination address is listed as *:* (meaning "any address, any port").

The State column has no entry because UDP is not a connection-oriented protocol and, therefore, has no connection state.

The most common use for the –a switch is to check the status of a TCP/IP connection that appears to be hung. You can determine if the connection is simply busy or is actually hung and no longer responding.

The –*e* Switch

The -e switch displays a summary of all the packets that have been sent over the Network Interface Card (NIC) as of that instant. The Received and Sent columns show packets coming in as well as being sent:

```
C:\Users\tlammle>netstat -e
Interface Statistics

                            Received              Sent

Bytes                        7426841           7226953
Unicast packets                25784             35006
Non-unicast packets             1115             12548
Discards                           0                 0
Errors                             0                71
Unknown protocols                  0
```

You can use the –e switch to display the following categories of statistics:

Bytes   The number of bytes transmitted or received because the computer was turned on. This statistic is useful for finding out if data is actually being transmitted and received, or if the network interface isn't doing anything at all.

Unicast Packets   The number of packets sent from or received at this computer. To register in one of these columns, the packet must be addressed directly from one computer to another, and the computer's address must be in either the source or destination address section of the packet.

Non-Unicast Packets   The number of packets that weren't directly sent from one workstation to another. For example, a broadcast packet is a non-unicast packet. The number of non-unicast packets should be smaller than the number of unicast packets. If the number of non-unicast packets is as high or higher than that of unicast packets, too many broadcast packets are being sent over your network. Definitely find the source of these packets and make any necessary adjustments to optimize performance.

Discards   The number of packets that were discarded by the NIC during either transmission or reception because they weren't assembled correctly.

Errors The number of errors that occurred during transmission or reception. (These numbers may indicate problems with the network card.)

Unknown Protocols The number of received packets that the Windows networking stack couldn't interpret. This statistic only shows up in the Received column because if the computer sent them, they wouldn't be unknown, right?

Unfortunately, statistics don't mean much unless they can be colored with time information. For example, if the Errors column shows 71 errors, is that a problem? It might be if the computer has been on for only a few minutes. But 71 errors could be par for the course if the computer has been operating for several days. Unfortunately, the `netstat` utility doesn't have a way of indicating how much time has elapsed for these statistics.

The –r Switch

You use the -r switch to display the current route table for a workstation so that you can see exactly how TCP/IP information is being routed. This will give you the same output as the `route print` command that we covered earlier in this chapter.

The –s Switch

Using the -s switch displays a variety of TCP, UDP, IP, and ICMP protocol statistics. But be warned—the output you'll get is really long, which may or may not be okay for you. For this book, it's way too long for me to insert. With that in mind, we can add another modifier called the -p switch.

The –p Switch

Like the -n switch, the -p switch is a modifier that's usually used with the -s switch to specify which protocol statistics to list in the output (IP, TCP, UDP, or ICMP). For example, if you want to view only ICMP statistics, you use the -p switch like so:

```
netstat -s -p ICMP
```

The `netstat` utility then displays the ICMP statistics instead of the entire gamut of TCP/IP statistics that the -s switch will typically flood you with. For a different example, let's use the -s and -p switches to retrieve some IPv6 information:

```
C:\Users\tlammle>netstat -s -p IPV6

IPv6 Statistics

  Packets Received              = 1400
  Received Header Errors        = 0
  Received Address Errors       = 6
```

```
Datagrams Forwarded                    = 0
Unknown Protocols Received             = 0
Received Packets Discarded             = 451
Received Packets Delivered             = 10441
Output Requests                        = 24349
Routing Discards                       = 0
Discarded Output Packets               = 3575
Output Packet No Route                 = 41
Reassembly Required                    = 0
Reassembly Successful                  = 0
Reassembly Failures                    = 0
Datagrams Successfully Fragmented      = 0
Datagrams Failing Fragmentation        = 0
Fragments Created                      = 0


C:\Users\tlammle>
```

Nice! Gets right to the point. Now, let's see the TCP connections my host has:

```
C:\Users\tlammle>netstat -s -p tcp

TCP Statistics for IPv4

    Active Opens                       = 7832
    Passive Opens                      = 833
    Failed Connection Attempts         = 1807
    Reset Connections                  = 2428
    Current Connections                = 11
    Segments Received                  = 1391678
    Segments Sent                      = 1340994
    Segments Retransmitted             = 6246

Active Connections

    Proto  Local Address          Foreign Address          State
    TCP    10.100.10.54:54737     gnt-exchange:1151        ESTABLISHED
    TCP    10.100.10.54:54955     gnt-exchange:1026        ESTABLISHED
    TCP    10.100.10.54:55218     gnt-exchange:epmap       TIME_WAIT
    TCP    127.0.0.1:2492         globalnet-todd:54840     ESTABLISHED
    TCP    127.0.0.1:54516        globalnet-todd:62514     ESTABLISHED
    TCP    127.0.0.1:54840        globalnet-todd:2492      ESTABLISHED
    TCP    127.0.0.1:62514        globalnet-todd:54516     ESTABLISHED
```

```
TCP     192.168.0.6:2492        blugro2relay:2492       ESTABLISHED
TCP     192.168.0.6:2492        blugro3relay:2492       ESTABLISHED
TCP     192.168.0.6:54527       64.12.25.26:5190        ESTABLISHED
TCP     192.168.0.6:54531       oam-d05c:5190           ESTABLISHED
TCP     192.168.0.6:55163       207.123.44.123:http     CLOSE_WAIT
```

`C:\Users\tlammle>`

This kind of efficiency is exactly why it's good you to use the -p modifier with the
-s switch.

> Because the Network+ exam doesn't cover them, we won't go into detail
> about what all these statistics mean for most of these commands. You can
> probably figure out most of them—for instance, Packets Received. For more
> details, go to Microsoft's support website at www.support.microsoft.com.

The –n Switch

The -n switch is a modifier for the other switches. When used with them, it reverses the natural tendency of netstat to use names instead of network addresses. In other words, when you
use the –n switch, the output always displays network addresses instead of their associated
network names. Following is output from the netstat command used with the netstat -n
command. It's showing the same information but with IP addresses instead of names:

`C:\Users\tlammle>`**netstat**

```
Active Connections

  Proto  Local Address           Foreign Address         State
  TCP    10.100.10.54:54737      gnt-exchange:1151       ESTABLISHED
  TCP    10.100.10.54:54955      gnt-exchange:1026       ESTABLISHED
  TCP    127.0.0.1:2492          globalnet-todd:54840    ESTABLISHED
  TCP    127.0.0.1:54516         globalnet-todd:62514    ESTABLISHED
  TCP    127.0.0.1:54840         globalnet-todd:2492     ESTABLISHED
  TCP    127.0.0.1:62514         globalnet-todd:54516    ESTABLISHED
  TCP    192.168.0.6:2492        blugro2relay:2492       ESTABLISHED
  TCP    192.168.0.6:2492        blugro3relay:2492       ESTABLISHED
  TCP    192.168.0.6:54527       64.12.25.26:5190        ESTABLISHED
  TCP    192.168.0.6:54531       oam-d05c:5190           ESTABLISHED
  TCP    192.168.0.6:55163       207.123.44.123:http     CLOSE_WAIT
```

```
C:\Users\tlammle>netstat -n

Active Connections

    Proto  Local Address         Foreign Address         State
    TCP    10.100.10.54:54737    10.100.36.13:1151       ESTABLISHED
    TCP    10.100.10.54:54955    10.100.36.13:1026       ESTABLISHED
    TCP    127.0.0.1:2492        127.0.0.1:54840         ESTABLISHED
    TCP    127.0.0.1:54516       127.0.0.1:62514         ESTABLISHED
    TCP    127.0.0.1:54840       127.0.0.1:2492          ESTABLISHED
    TCP    127.0.0.1:62514       127.0.0.1:54516         ESTABLISHED
    TCP    192.168.0.6:2492      65.55.239.100:2492      ESTABLISHED
    TCP    192.168.0.6:2492      65.55.248.110:2492      ESTABLISHED
    TCP    192.168.0.6:54527     64.12.25.26:5190        ESTABLISHED
    TCP    192.168.0.6:54531     205.188.248.163:5190    ESTABLISHED
    TCP    192.168.0.6:55163     207.123.44.123:80       CLOSE_WAIT

C:\Users\tlammle>
```

 Real World Scenario

Uses for *netstat*

You might be saying to yourself, "OK. Fine... I can use lots of cool switches with netstat, but really, what for?" I'm always finding uses for netstat. For instance, once I found a particularly nasty worm on my PC using netstat. I just happened to run netstat for giggles one day and noticed a very large number of outbound connections to various places on the Internet. My PC was sending out SYN packets to a large number of hosts (an indication that my computer was involved—unknowingly—in a large-scale denial of service attack). Upon further examination, I noticed that this activity would start shortly after bootup.

I tried running netstat after bootup and noticed that the first outbound connection was to TCP port 6667 to some Internet Relay Chat (IRC) server I'd never heard of—I didn't even have an IRC client on my machine at the time. The worm was particularly nasty to try to get rid of while active, so I turned off port 6667 on my firewall. That prevented the initial connection to the IRC server and, as I found out later, nicely prevented the worm from getting its instructions from the IRC server. I was then able to simply remove it. I would've never found out that this worm was working without netstat. Even my antivirus program missed it.

Using the File Transfer Protocol (FTP)

Okay, you already know that *File Transfer Protocol (FTP)* is a subset of TCP/IP, and that FTP is used for the transfer of files. In recent years, FTP has become a truly cross-platform protocol for transferring files. Because Internet (and thus TCP/IP) use has skyrocketed, almost every client and server platform has implemented FTP. Windows is no exception. Its TCP/IP stack comes with a command-line ftp utility.

To start the ftp utility, enter **ftp** at a command prompt. The result is an ftp command prompt:

```
C:\Users\tlammle>ftp
ftp>
```

From this prompt, you can open a connection to an FTP server and upload and download files as well as change the way FTP operates. To display a list of all the commands you can use at the ftp command prompt, type **help** or **?** and press Enter. To get help on a specific command, type **help**, a space, and then the name of the command. Here is some output from the help command:

```
ftp>help
Commands may be abbreviated.  Commands are:

!               delete          literal         prompt          send
?               debug           ls              put             status
append          dir             mdelete         pwd             trace
ascii           disconnect      mdir            quit            type
bell            get             mget            quote           user
binary          glob            mkdir           recv            verbose
bye             hash            mls             remotehelp
cd              help            mput            rename
close           lcd             open            rmdir
ftp>
```

In the following sections, I'll give you an introduction to uploading and downloading files, because every network technician and administrator positively needs to know how to do this. As they come up, I'll go over the specific commands necessary to perform those two operations, as well as any commands that relate to those processes. But first, let's look at how to begin the process.

Third-party applications are available that provide a GUI interface for FTP, which is easier than using a command line.

Starting FTP and Logging In to an FTP Server

Of the two FTP file operations (download and upload), the ability to download files is definitely the more crucial for you to have down as a network technician or sys admin. The reason it's so important for you to master is that network and client operating system drivers and patches are located on FTP servers all over the Internet.

The first steps in starting an FTP download session are to determine the address of the FTP site and start the ftp utility. The FTP site typically has the same name as the website except that the first three characters are ftp instead of www. For example, Microsoft's website is www.microsoft.com. Its FTP site, on the other hand, is ftp.microsoft.com. We'll use my personal FTP site as an example for the rest of this section because it works, so I can actually log in to it.

First, start the ftp utility as demonstrated earlier, and then follow these steps:

1. At the ftp command prompt, type **open**, a space, and the name of the FTP server, like this:

```
C:\Users\tlammle>ftp
ftp>open ftp.lammle.com
Connected to ftp.lammle.com.
220---------- Welcome to Pure-FTPd [TLS] ----------
220-You are user number 1 of 50 allowed.
220-Local time is now 11:45. Server port: 21.
220-IPv6 connections are also welcome on this server.
220 You will be disconnected after 15 minutes of inactivity.
User (ftp.lammle.com:(none)):enter
230 Anonymous user logged in
ftp>
```

As shown here, if the FTP server is available and running, you'll receive a response welcoming you to the server and asking you for a username. Right now, I just have Anonymous as the username (enabled by default on FTP server), which means that anyone can log in to it. (By the way, don't bother trying this on my server because I disabled it for obvious reasons as soon as I finished writing this section.)

You can also start an FTP session by typing **ftp**, a space, and the address of the FTP server (for example, **ftp ftp.globalnettraining.com**). This allows you to start the ftp utility and open a connection in one step. Here's an example:

```
C:\Users\tlammle>ftp ftp.globalnettraining.com
Connected to ftp.globalnettraining.com.
220 Microsoft FTP Service
User (ftp.globalnettraining.com:(none)):todd
331 Password required for todd.
```

```
Password:not shown when typed
230 User todd logged in.
ftp>quit
```

2. Enter a valid username, and press Enter.

3. Enter your password, and press Enter.(The password won't show up when you type it.)

> Most Internet web servers that allow just about anyone to download files also allow the username anonymous, as I demonstrated. In addition to anonymous, you can use the username ftp to gain access to a public FTP server. They are both anonymous usernames. Remember that FTP (and Unix) usernames are case sensitive.

Okay—all good, but if you want to access a private FTP server, as I'll demonstrate in a minute, you'll need to use the username and password given to you by the site's administrator. Oh, and sometimes you can use your email address as a password when accessing a public FTP server with a username like anonymous.

> You don't have to enter your entire email address to log in with the anonymous username. Most FTP server software doesn't actually verify the actual email address, only that it is, in fact, an email address. To do this, it checks for an @ sign and two words separated by a period. You just need to enter a very short email address to bypass the password (like u@me.com). This is especially helpful if you have a long email address, and it's a really good idea if you don't want to get a ton of junk email.

If you enter the wrong username and/or password, the server will tell you so by displaying the following and leaving you at the ftp command prompt:

```
530 Login Incorrect
Login failed.
```

This means you've got to try again and must start the login process over. If successful, the FTP server will welcome you and drop you back at the ftp command prompt. You're now ready to start uploading or downloading files.

Downloading Files

After you log in to the FTP server, you'll navigate to the directory that contains the files you want. Thankfully, the FTP command-line interface is similar to the DOS command-line interface. This is no surprise because DOS is based on Unix, and FTP is a Unix utility. Table 17.8 lists and describes the common navigation commands for FTP. (Remember that these are also case sensitive.)

After you navigate to the directory and find the file you want to download, it's time to set the parameters for the type of file. Files come in two types:

- ASCII, which contains text
- Binary, which is all other files

If you set ftp to the wrong type, the file you download will contain gibberish. So if you're in doubt, set ftp to download files as binary files. Check out Table 17.8.

TABLE 17.8   Common FTP Navigation Commands

Command	Description
Ls	Short for *list*. Displays a directory listing. Very similar to the DIR command in MS-DOS.
Cd	Short for *change directory*. Works almost identically to the MS-DOS CD command. Use it to change to a different directory and navigate the server's directory structure.
Pwd	Short for *print working directory*. Displays the current directory on the server. Useful if you forget where you are when changing to several locations on the server.
Lcd	Short for *local change directory*. Displays and changes the current directory on the local machine. Useful when you are downloading a file and aren't in the directory where you want to put the file.

To set the file type to ASCII, type **ascii** at the ftp command prompt. ftp will respond by telling you that the file type has been set to A (ASCII):

```
ftp>ascii
Type set to A
```

To set the file type to binary, type **binary** at the ftp command prompt. ftp will respond by telling you that the file type has been set to I (binary):

```
ftp>binary
Type set to I
```

To download the file, just use the get command like this:

```
ftp>get lammlepress.exe
200 PORT command successful.
150 Opening BINARY mode data connection for 'scrsav.exe'
(567018 bytes).
```

The file will start downloading to your hard drive. Unfortunately, with its default settings, the ftp utility doesn't give you any indication of the progress of the transfer. When the file has downloaded, the ftp utility will display the following message and return you to the ftp command prompt:

```
226 Transfer complete.
567018 bytes received in 116.27 seconds (4.88 Kbytes/sec)
```

You can download multiple files by using the mget command. Simply type **mget**, a space, and then something known as a *wildcard* that specifies the files you want to get. For example, to download all the text files in a directory, type **mget *.txt**.

Uploading Files

To upload a file to an FTP server, you've got to have rights on that specific server. These rights are assigned on a directory-by-directory basis. To upload a file, log in and then follow these steps:

1. At the ftp command prompt, type **lcd** to navigate to the directory on the local machine where the file resides.

2. Type **cd** to navigate to the destination directory.

3. Set the file type to ASCII or binary.

4. Use the put command to upload the file.

The syntax of the put command looks like this:

```
ftp>put local file destination file
```

Let's say you want to upload a file called 1.txt on the local server but you want it to be called my.txt on the destination server. To accomplish that, use the following command:

```
ftp>put 1.txt my.txt
```

And you'll get the following response:

```
200 PORT command successful.
150 Opening BINARY mode data connection for collwin.zip
226 Transfer complete.
743622 bytes sent in 0.55 seconds (1352.04 Kbytes/sec)
```

You can upload multiple files using the mput command. Simply type **mput**, a space, and then a wildcard that specifies the files. For example, to upload all the text files in a directory, type **mput *.txt**.

When you're finished with the ftp utility, just type **quit** to return to the command prompt.

Using the Telephone Network *(Telnet)* Utility

Part of the TCP/IP protocol suite, *telnet* is a virtual terminal protocol utility that allows you to make connections to remote devices, gather information, and run programs. Telnet was originally developed to open terminal sessions from remote Unix workstations to Unix servers. Although it's still used for that purpose, we now use it as a troubleshooting tool as well. Figure 17.10 shows the basic Telnet interface as it's being used to start a terminal session on a remote Unix host.

FIGURE 17.10   The Telnet utility

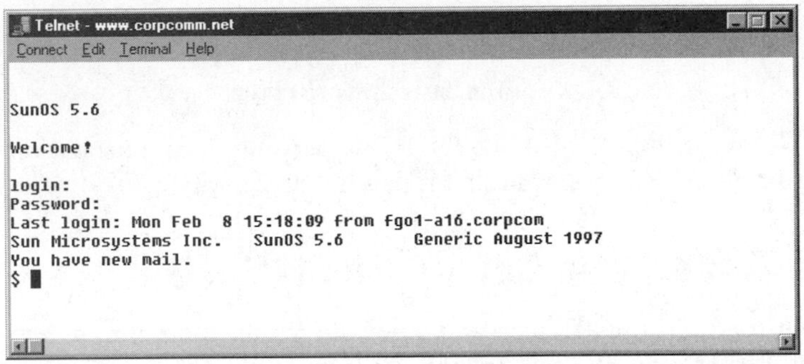

In today's Windows environments, Telnet is a basic command-line tool for testing TCP connections. You can Telnet to any TCP port to see if it's responding—something that's especially useful when checking Simple Mail Transfer Protocol (SMTP) and HTTP (web) ports.

As you learned back in Chapter 6, "Introduction to Internet Protocol (IP)," each upper-layer service in a TCP stack has a number for its address. And by default, each network service that uses a particular address will respond to a TCP request on that specific port.

How to Enable Telnet in Vista

Because most people have Vista operating systems running on their PCs these days, it's good to know that, by default, Vista installs without Telnet available. But there's a way around that one—if you really must have a Telnet client enabled in Vista, here's how to do it:

1. Open Control Panel.

2. Select Programs And Features.

3. In the left column, select Turn Windows Features On Or Off (get ready for the annoying User Account Control [UAC] prompt, and then enter your name and password).

4. Select the Telnet check box (and any other obscure services you may want enabled), and wait while Vista thinks for a while and then reboots.

Nice—now you can go to Start and then type **telnet** in the Start search box to get a Telnet window to open for you. You can also open a DOS prompt and just type **telnet** from there. Here are the options that Windows provides with telnet:

```
Microsoft Telnet> ?
Commands may be abbreviated. Supported commands are:

c    - close             close current connection
d    - display           display operating parameters
o    - open hostname [port]   connect to hostname (default port 23).
q    - quit              exit telnet
set  - set               set options (type 'set ?' for a list)
sen  - send              send strings to server
st   - status            print status information
u    - unset             unset options (type 'unset ?' for a list)
?/h  - help              print help information
```

Now that we've finished talking about Telnet, my personal recommendation is that you never use it again. What? Yes, you read that right, and here's why...

Don't Use Telnet, Use Secure Shell (SSH)

What? I just told you how to use Telnet, and now I am telling you not to use it. That's right, don't use Telnet! Telnet is totally insecure because it sends all data in crystal-clear text—including your name and password. And I'm pretty sure you know that's a really bad thing these days. If Microsoft doesn't even enable it on their latest OSs, than you know it really must be insecure.

So if you shouldn't use Telnet, what should you use instead? Secure Shell (SSH) is your answer. It provides the same options as Telnet, plus a lot more; but most important, it doesn't send any data in clear text. The thing is, your servers, routers, and other devices need to be enabled with SSH, and it's not configured by default on most devices.

Some configuration is usually necessary if you want things to work as they really should, and yes, sometimes it's a little painful to get everything running smoothly, but it's all worth it in the long run. Personally, I disable Telnet on all my routers and use SSH exclusively. No lie—I never use Telnet any more if I can help it. Even so, you should still understand Telnet and get in some practice with it in case you do ever need it.

> In my Sybex *Cisco CCNA Study Guide* I get into the skinny on how to configure SSH on all Cisco devices and use a SSH client; but because SSH is above the Network+ objectives, I'm not going to do that here. Still, keep this all in mind when building your networks.

Summary

In this chapter, you learned about many of the utilities for using and troubleshooting TCP/IP. These utilities include tracert, ping, arp, netstat, nbtstat, ipconfig, ifconfig, and nslookup.

You also learned how these utilities are used, including their various options and switches and how they all affect the use of these utilities. Finally, you learned about how these utilities work within the TCP/IP suite.

Exam Essentials

Know how to describe and use the troubleshooting information and statistics that arp, nbtstat, and netstat provide for you.   The arp utility shows whether an IP address is being resolved to your MAC address (or someone else's, in case of conflicts). The netstat utility produces TCP/IP statistics, and nbtstat produces NetBIOS over TCP/IP statistics.

Know how to diagnose a network by using TCP/IP's troubleshooting commands.   ping echoes back if a machine is alive and active on a network. tracert shows the path that the ping packets take from source to target. And telnet enables a user to participate in a remote text-based session.

Know what the tracert utility does.   The tracert utility finds the route from your computer to any computer on a network.

Know what the ping utility does.   ping determines whether a particular IP host is responding.

Know what the ftp utility does.   The ftp utility allows you to reliably download and upload files from and to an FTP server across the Internet.

Know what the ipconfig and ifconfig utilities do.   ipconfig displays TCP/IP configuration information for Windows NT and later operating systems. The ifconfig utility performs a similar function in Unix environments, in addition to performing certain interface-configuration tasks.

Know what the nslookup and dig utilities do.   Nslookup and dig allow you to look up DNS resolution information.

Written Lab

Write the answers to the following questions about command-line tools:

1. What command can you type from a command prompt to see the hops a packet takes to get to a destination host?

2. Which command will tell you if a host is alive somewhere on the network?

3. You need your IP address, subnet mask, default gateway, and DNS information. What command will you type in from a Windows command prompt?

4. You need to log in as a dumb terminal to a server or Unix host and run programs. What application will you use?

5. You need to add a route to your Windows servers routing table. What command will you use?

6. You want to log in to a server and transfer files. What application will you use?

7. You need to check your name-resolution information on your host. What command will you type in from the command prompt?

8. You want to use `netstat`, but you only want to see the IP address not the names of the hosts. Which modifier will you use?

9. You want the IP configuration on a Unix host. What command will you type in at the command prompt?

10. Which Windows command will show you the routing table of your host or server?

(The answers to the Written Lab can be found following the answers to the Review Questions for this chapter.)

Review Questions

1. Which TCP/IP utility is most often used to test whether an IP host is up and functional?

   A. ftp

   B. telnet

   C. ping

   D. netstat

2. Which TCP/IP utility will produce the following result?

   ```
   Interface: 199.102.30.152
   Internet Address    Physical Address      Type
   199.102.30.152      A0-ee-00-5b-0e-ac     dynamic
   ```

   A. arp

   B. netstat

   C. tracert

   D. nbtstat

3. Which Windows utility can you use to display NetBIOS over TCP/IP statistics, the current NetBIOS configuration and open connections?

   A. nbtstat

   B. netstat

   C. arp

   D. ipconfig

4. Which TCP/IP utility might produce the following output?

   ```
   Pinging 204.153.163.2 with 32 bytes of data:
   Reply from 204.153.163.2: bytes=32 time=1ms TTL=128
   Reply from 204.153.163.2: bytes=32 time=1ms TTL=128
   Reply from 204.153.163.2: bytes=32 time=1ms TTL=128
   Reply from 204.153.163.2: bytes=32 time<10ms TTL=128
   ```

   A. tracert

   B. ping

   C. WINS

   D. ipconfig

5. Which utility can you use to find the MAC and TCP/IP addresses of your Windows workstation?

   A. ping

   B. ipconfig

   C. ipconfig /all

   D. tracert

   E. telnet

6. Which ping commands will verify that your local TCP/IP interface is working? (Choose all that apply.)

   A. ping 204.153.163.2

   B. ping 127.0.0.1

   C. ping localif

   D. ping localhost

   E. ping iphost

7. Which switch for the Windows nbtstat utility will display all NetBIOS name-resolution statistics?

   A. -r

   B. /r

   C. -R

   D. /R

8. You need to find a NIC's specific MAC address and IP address. Which command line tool can you use to find this information without physical going to the computer?

   A. ping

   B. nbtstat

   C. arp

   D. netstat

   E. ftp

9. Which nbtstat utility switch will purge and reload the remote NetBIOS name table cache?

   A. -r

   B. -R

   C. /r

   D. /R

10. You are using the traceroute command and notice that after several hops, the addresses start repeating and the TTL-exceeded messages are returned. Which could be the problem in the network?

    A. Arp resolution

    B. A switching loop

    C. A routing loop

    D. A DNS problem

11. Which utility produces output similar to the following?

    ```
    1   110 ms   96 ms   107 ms fgo1.corpcomm.net [209.74.93.10]
    2   96 ms   126 ms   95 ms someone.corpcomm.net [209.74.93.1]
    3   113 ms   119 ms   112 ms Serial5-1-1.GW2.MSP1.alter.net      [157.130.100.185]
    4   133 ms   123 ms   126 ms 152.ATM3-0.XR2.CHI6.ALTER.NET      [146.188.209.126]
    5   176 ms   133 ms   129 ms 290.ATM2-0.TR2.CHI4.ALTER.NET      [146.188.209.10]
    6   196 ms   184 ms   218 ms 106.ATM7-0.TR2.SCL1.ALTER.NET      [146.188.136.162]
    7   182 ms   187 ms   187 ms 298.ATM7-0.XR2.SJC1.ALTER.NET      [146.188.146.61]
    8   204 ms   176 ms   186 ms 192.ATM3-0-0.SAN-JOSE9- GW.ALTER.NET
        [146.188.144.133]
    9   202 ms   198 ms   212 ms atm3-0-622M.cr1.sjc.globalcenter.net [206.57.16.17]
    10  209 ms   202 ms   195 ms pos3-1-155M.br4.SJC.globalcenter.net [206.132.150.98]
    11  190 ms    *       191 ms pos0-0-0-155M.hr3.SNV.globalcenter.net [206.251.5.93]
    12  195 ms   188 ms   188 ms pos4-1-0-   155M.hr2.SNV.globalcenter.net
        [206.132.150.206]
    13  198 ms   202 ms   197 ms www10.yahoo.com [204.71.200.75]
    ```

    A. arp

    B. tracert

    C. nbtstat

    D. netstat

12. You are the network administrator. A user calls you, complaining that the performance of the intranet web server is sluggish. When you try to ping the server, it takes several seconds for the server to respond. You suspect that the problem is related to a router that is seriously overloaded. Which workstation utility could you use to find out which router is causing this problem?

    A. netstat

    B. nbtstat

    C. tracert

    D. ping

    E. arp

13. Which `ipconfig` switch will display the most complete listing of IP configuration information for a station?

   A. /all

   B. /renew

   C. /release

   D. /?

14. Which utility will display a list of all the routers that a packet passes through on the way to an IP destination?

   A. netstat

   B. nbtstat

   C. tracert

   D. ping

   E. arp

15. Which Windows TCP/IP utility could you use to find out whether a server is responding on TCP port 21?

   A. tcp

   B. port

   C. ping

   D. netstat

   E. telnet

16. Which `arp` command can you use to display the currently cached ARP entries?

   A. arp

   B. arp –all

   C. arp /a

   D. ipconfig /arp

   E. arp /ipconfig

17. Which command line tool would best be used to verify DNS functionality?

   A. netstat

   B. nbtstat

   C. dig

   D. icmp

   E. arp

18. Which `arp` utility switches perform the same function? (Choose all that apply.)

    A. −g

    B. −A

    C. −d

    D. −a

19. Which command would you use at a workstation prompt to see the DNS servers that are configured to use? (choose 3)

    A. arp

    B. nslookup

    C. netstat

    D. nbtstat

    E. ipconfig

    F. ifconfig

20. Which `nbtstat` switch displays a list of all the NetBIOS sessions currently active on the local workstation?

    A. −a

    B. −r

    C. −s

    D. −I

Answers to Review Questions

1. C. The program Packet Internet Groper (ping) is used to find out if a host has the IP stack initialized.

2. A. The ARP utility is used to display the contents of the ARP cache, which tracks the resolution of IP addresses to physical (MAC) addresses and will produce the displayed output.

3. A. The *nbt* in nbtstat stands for "NetBIOS over TCP/IP." The purpose of nbtstat is to display the NetBIOS over TCP/IP statistics for a computer running both protocols.

4. B. The purpose of the ping utility is to test the communications channel between two IP hosts as well as how long it takes the packets to get from one host to another.

5. C. The ipconfig /all utility will display current configuration of TCP/IP on a given workstation—including the current IP address, DNS configuration, WINS configuration, and default gateway.

6. B, D. The address 127.0.0.1 is the special IP address designated for the local TCP/IP interface. The host name localhost is the host name given to the local interface. Therefore, pinging either the IP address or the host name for the local interface will tell you whether the local interface is working.

7. A. The command nbtstat -r displays all the name resolutions performed by the local client as well as their associated IP addresses. The -R switch will reload the cache.

8. C. The arp utility will show you the resolved MAC to IP address of all hosts on your network segment. Remember, this will only work for local hosts, not remote hosts.

9. B. To purge and reload the remote NetBIOS name cache, you must use nbtstat -R. Remember that the *R* must be uppercase and that it will not work correctly without the hyphen before it.

10. C. If you start seeing repeated addresses, and TTL timeouts, you have a network loop, meaning layer 3.

11. B. The tracert utility will give you that output. The tracert command (or trace for short) traces the route from the source IP host to the destination host.

12. C. The tracert utility will tell you which router is having the performance problem and how long it takes to move between each host. tracert can be used to locate problem areas in a network.

13. A. The ipconfig /all switch will display the most complete listing of TCP/IP configuration information also displaying the MAC address, DHCP lease times, and the DNS addresses.

14. C. The tracert utility returns all router names and addresses through which a packet passes on its way to a destination host.

15. E. The `telnet` utility can be used to test if a particular IP host is responding on a particular TCP port.

16. C. The `arp /a` command will display the current contents of the ARP cache on the local workstation.

17. C. Dig is an old unix command that will show you DNS server information.

18. A, D. The `arp` utility's −a and −g switches perform the same function. They both show the current ARP cache.

19. B, E, F. Nslookup, ipconfig, and ifconfig will show you the DNS servers that a computer is configured to use.

20. C. `nbtstat −s` will display pre-protocol statistics for IP, IPv6, ICMP, ICMPv6, TCP, TCPv6, UDP, and UDPv6.

Answers to Written Lab

1. `traceroute` or `tracert`

2. `ping`

3. `ipconfig /all`

4. Telnet

5. `route`

6. FTP

7. `nslookup`

8. `-n`

9. `ifconfig`

10. `route print`

Chapter

18

Software and Hardware Tools

THE FOLLOWING COMPTIA NETWORK+ EXAM OBJECTIVES ARE COVERED IN THIS CHAPTER:

✓ **5.2 Explain the purpose of network scanners**

- ▪ Packet sniffers
- ▪ Intrusion detection software
- ▪ Intrusion prevention software
- ▪ Port scanners

✓ **5.3 Given a scenario, utilize the appropriate hardware tools**

- ▪ Cable testers
- ▪ Protocol analyzer
- ▪ Certifiers
- ▪ TDR
- ▪ OTDR
- ▪ Multimeter
- ▪ Toner probe
- ▪ Butt set
- ▪ Punch-down tool
- ▪ Cable stripper
- ▪ Snips
- ▪ Voltage event recorder
- ▪ Temperature monitor

Specialized tasks require specialized tools, and installing network components is no exception. We use some of these tools, like network scanners, on an every-day basis, but most of the hardware tools I'll be covering in this chapter are used mainly in the telecommunications industry.

Still, in order to meet the CompTIA Network+ objectives, and also because you're likely to run across them in today's networking environments, it's very important that you're familiar with them.

NOTE For up-to-the-minute updates for this chapter, please see www.lammle.com or www.sybex.com/go/comptianetwork+studyguide.

Understanding Network Scanners

Network scanner has become a broad term often referring to a family of tools used to analyze our networks, but the CompTIA Network+ objectives are much less vague. So with regard to those critical objectives, know that *network scanners* refer to these three tools:

- Packet sniffers
- Intrusion Detection System / Intrusion Prevention System (IDS/IPS) software
- Port scanners

Packet Sniffers

Unlike port scanners, *packet sniffers* actually look inside every packet on a network segment. Packet sniffers come in many flavors, and some of them, like Microsoft's Network Monitor (NetMon), are even free today. Even though NetMon comes in more complex versions that are, well, not exactly free, the version that comes bundled with Windows Server does allow you to analyze network communications traffic. The full version will give you statistics on network utilization and packet traffic data as well as capture individual frames for analysis. These abilities really mean that NetMon is both a packet sniffer and *network analyzer*, and it's common for these to be combined and referred to as one and the same. The catch is that the free version from Microsoft—the one that's included with the company's server software—is a scaled down version that only looks at and monitors packets to and from the specific server that the software is running on!

All good, but personally, I use WireShark instead. It's also free, and you can easily download it from www.wireshark.org. A nice feature of WireShark is that it runs from Windows, OS X, Linux, and Unix platforms. It easily captures data on all my interfaces, including my wireless and virtual private network (VPN) connections and looks at all traffic on the network segment. There are tons of packet sniffers available, and to get your hands on most of them, you'll have to pony up some cash. Sometimes they're worth it, though, because these higher-end products can even provide solutions to problems you find on your network—nice.

Anyway, free or not, the basic purpose of packet sniffers (or network analyzers) is to collect and analyze each individual packet that is captured on a specific network segment to determine if problems like bottlenecks, retransmissions, and security breaches are happening. Packet sniffers are a must have for every network administrator to troubleshoot and find problems or security holes in your network. For example, you may discover that users are using an application on the network with usernames and passwords being sent unencrypted over the network.

You can also use packet sniffers to see if there is too much traffic on a segment, or even if a broadcast storm has been created by a bad Network Interface Card (NIC). And remember—I do mean on a network segment—you can't use them to catch packets passing through routers. Yes, they can help you find a hacker stalking around in there, but you'd really have to be looking closely and constantly to discover this. For that level of monitoring, you'd be better off using a tool known as IDS/IPS. It can really help you track and even defeat hackers. We'll talk about IDS/IPS in the next section. The more expensive network sniffers can help find anomalies in your network, like a hack, and even alert you of these problems. Figure 18.1 shows output from a packet sniffer

FIGURE 18.1   Output from a packet sniffer

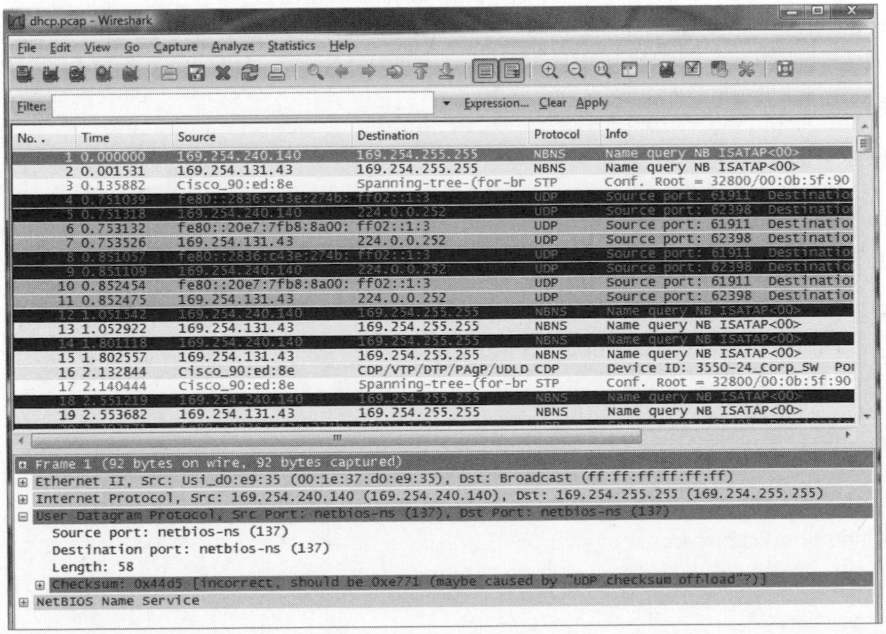

Okay, you can definitely see that a packet sniffer can provide you with huge amounts of information. This means you really need something to narrow things down and help you to more readily find the needle in the haystack that you're looking for, right?

In this case, help comes in the form of some handy built-in filters that can be used to gather information from just one specific host or server; without them, you'd have to go through possibly thousands of packets to find the problem. For the packet I've highlighted, you can see that there's a probable User Datagram Protocol (UDP) checksum error. And by the way, because UDP is connectionless, this is a pretty common error.

 You should download and start working with a network sniffer right away. As I mentioned, you can download WireShark at www.wireshark.org for free, so what are you waiting for? Go for it!

Now comes the fun stuff—let's take a look at ways we can find and stop hackers dead in their tracks.

Intrusion Detection and Prevention Software (IDS/IPS)

IDS detects unwanted attempts to manipulate network systems and/or environments; and IPS is a computer-security device that monitors network and/or system activities for any strange or malicious behavior. It can react in real time to prevent and even block nasty activities. IDS identifies, detects, and reports attempts of unauthorized access to the network as well as any suspicious activity, and IDS is the best software type for identifying an attack. However, if you want to stop the attack in its track you need to add an IPS device. So, unlike IDS, which can identify an attack and report it, IPS can stop the attack by shutting down ports or dropping certain types of packets.

A bunch of different IDS/IPS software is available on the market, and a lot of it is free. Again, predictably, the best ones aren't, and they can be a bit pricey. These high-powered versions run on Linux or other proprietary hardware. But there are still many IDS/IPS software applications available for Windows.

Snort is one of the most popular IDS/IPS software products around. It runs on both Linux and Windows, and it's a free, open source platform, which happens to be a big reason for its popularity. But that's not the only reason—just because it is free doesn't mean it doesn't offer up some pretty cool features. On the other hand, if you're dealing with a large, corporate environment, you need some serious weaponry, and Cisco offers an Adaptive Security Appliance (ASA) as an enterprise solution that's powerful, but definitely far from free. It's worth it, though.

Figure 18.2 shows a picture of the stack of Cisco ASA boxes I use in my security classes.

Personally, I think the Cisco box is the best IDS/IPS box on the market today. Still, Snort isn't bad; so if cost is an issue, rest assured you can use it, as well as several other tools, and be much better equipped than you would be without them working on your network to help you keep it secure.

FIGURE 18.2   A stack of Cisco ASAs

Figure 18.3 shows where you'd find a typical IDS/IPS in a network

FIGURE 18.3   IDS/IPS placement in an internetwork

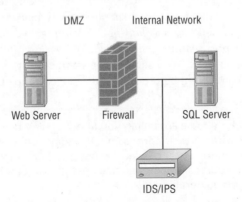

Okay… to be honest, this is a relatively simplistic view of IDS/IPS working within a network because of the device's complexity and the many different physical configurations possible. The important thing I want you to pay attention to is the fact that you would typically find

the IDS/IPS software positioned between your internal router and the firewall to the outside network (Internet). If you're using Snort, just add the software to a Linux box, and connect this box between the firewall and the router. This area would typically be your demilitarized zone (DMZ). The Basic Analysis and Security Engine (BASE) displays and reports intrusions and attacks logged in the Snort database in a web browser for convenient analysis.

Port Scanners

A *port scanner* is a software tool designed to search a host for open ports. Those of us administering our networks use port scanners to ensure their security, but bad guys use them to find a network's vulnerabilities and compromise them. To *portscan* means the act of scanning for Transport Control Protocol (TCP) and UDP open ports on a single target host to either legitimately connect to and use its services for business and/or personal reasons, or to find and connect to those ports and subsequently attack the host and steal or manipulate it for nefarious reasons.

In contrast, *port sweeping* means scanning multiple hosts on a network for a specific listening TCP or UDP port, like SQL. (SQL injection attacks are super-common today.) This just happens to be a favorite approach used by hackers when trying to invade your network. They port-sweep in a broad manner, and then, if they find something—in this case, SQL—they can port-scan the particular host they've discovered with the desired service available to exploit and get what they're after. This is why it's a really good idea to turn off any unused services on your servers and routers, and to run only the minimum services required on every host machine in your network. Do yourself a big favor and make sure this is in your security policy.

Remember that three-way handshake I discussed earlier? Well, it just so happens that an SYN scan is the most popular form of TCP scanning. Rather than use the operating system's network functions, the port scanner actually generates raw IP packets itself and monitors for responses. This scan type is also known as *half-open scanning*, because it never really opens a full TCP connection. The port scanner generates a SYN packet; and if the targeted port is open, it will respond with a SYN-ACK packet. The scanner host responds with an RST (reset) packet, closing the connection before the handshake is completed.

WARNING   Never use the tools I'm telling you about on any businesses or government agencies without their permission. It's against the law in a big way, and they do monitor and prosecute! Know that I am not exaggerating here, so please do yourself a favor and use the following tools only to test your own network for vulnerabilities.

Although a free program named Network Mapper (Nmap) can be used as a port scanner, you can use it to do so much more. I give it two thumbs up and recommend that you download Nmap (http://nmap.org/) and play with this cool program.

Nmap, like Snort, is open source. But Nmap runs on all platforms and can provide port-scanning ability, check all the open services running on each host, find firewalls, and even help tremendously with network management.

Figure 18.4 shows Nmap running on a Windows Vista platform, performing a Domain Name Service (DNS) resolution and then a port scan to the host being monitored (Zenmap is the name of the GUI interface it uses). Pretty chill, right?

FIGURE 18.4   Nmap in action

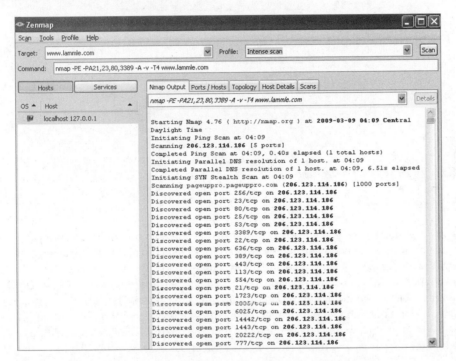

Nmap is very flexible and again, I really encourage you to check it out. One of the other nice features of Nmap is its documentation capacity. It comes with a complete set of instructions and equips you with documentation to help you troubleshoot and map your network.

Even though Nmap is pretty simple, there are even simpler tools out there—a whole lot of them. Angry IP is a program I also use that provides both IP-scanning and port-scanning abilities. It's definitely not as complex as Nmap, but because it's extremely easy to use, you might want to try out this free, open source program as well. Figure 18.5 illustrates port scanning with Angry IP.

You can see right away this is a much simpler program, but simple doesn't mean it isn't powerful. Angry IP slowed the PC I was scanning way down when I performed a full port scan on the host using this program. Check it out at http://www.angryziber .com/w/Home.

FIGURE 18.5   Angry IP Port Scanning

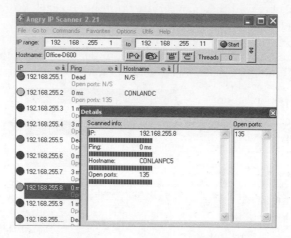

 Real World Scenario

Hacked and Blamed!

I've already mentioned that you shouldn't portscan on hosts that are not yours, but you need to be careful that someone else does not use your hosts or servers to portscan someone else's servers as well. A year or so ago, I had a server at an ISP, and some crackers had hacked into my server and were using it to portscan the Department of Defense (DoD) servers. I received a letter from the DoD informing me of this issue. They were very professional and even mentioned that it probably wasn't me that was doing the portscanning, but they said that if it happened again, they would prosecute me. They told me that I was responsible for my server and that if I did not stop the attackers, I would be liable.

Besides being terribly embarrassed, I was a little freaked out too! After looking at the server logs, I realized that the crackers were from France and that they had been in my server for three months. Instead of just locking down the ports and getting rid of the hackers, I formatted the server. Why? Because crackers/hackers are notorious for creating many backdoors once they are in a system, in case they get caught, so just locking them out would not have solved the problem. If this happens to you, a format is typically what you need to do. I also upgraded from Server 2000 to 2003, which helped with some of the security issues.

After you've downloaded all the software tools I just went over with you and practiced honing your skills with them (*only* on your own network, right?), you'll be ready to move on and explore the hardware tools that you need to be familiar with in order to meet the CompTIA Network+ objectives.

Identifying Hardware Tools

A great example of when the hardware tools and testers I'm about to cover would come in really handy is if you're dealing with failed fiber links between structures. As a system administrator running a network with a server, routers, and switches, it's entirely possible you'll never find yourself in a situation that calls for these tools. But if you're in network design or a field that requires installing cabling, then these hardware tools are going to be really valuable to you. Unlike the software tools we just talked about, none of these goodies are free, but they do come in a variety of flavors that run the gamut from real bargain to "You're joking—how much?" Some of them can indeed free you of thousands of dollars!

Cable testers are the most widely used hardware tool in today's LANs, so let's start this section with them.

Cable Testers

The best way to deal with a faulty cable installation is to avoid the problem in the first place by purchasing high-quality components and installing them carefully. Still, this isn't a perfect world—no matter how careful you are, problems are bound to arise anyway. The tools that I'm going to cover can be used to test cables at the time of their installation and afterward, if and when you need to troubleshoot cabling problems. Cable-testing tools can range from simple, inexpensive mechanical devices to elaborate electronic testers that automatically supply you with a litany of test results in an easy-to-read pass/fail format. Figure 18.6 shows an example of an inexpensive cable tester for twisted-pair wiring testing.

This little box can verify the connection through the cable and tell you if the cable is a straight-through or crossover. This is as cheap as they come.

Let's focus on the types of tools available for both copper and fiber-optic cable testing. This is not to say that you need all of the tools listed here. In fact, I'll try to steer you away from certain types of tools. Sometimes you'll get lucky and have the luxury of choosing between high-tech and low-tech devices available that perform roughly the same function. You can choose which ones you prefer according to the requirements of your network, your operational budget—even your temperament and time constraints. Some of the tools are extremely complicated and require extensive training to use effectively, whereas others can be used by pretty much anybody equipped with a functioning brain.

Other important considerations to keep in mind when selecting the types of tools you need are based on the descriptions of cable tests given earlier in this chapter, the test results required by the standards you're using to certify your network, and the capabilities of the people who will be doing the actual work. And don't forget the potentially painful cost of some of them.

FIGURE 18.6 An inexpensive cable tester

Wire-Map Testers

A *wire-map tester* is a device that transmits signals through each wire in a copper twisted-pair cable to determine if it's connected to the correct pin at the other end. Wire mapping is the most basic test for twisted-pair cables because the eight separate wire connections involved in each cable run are a common source of installation errors. Wire-map testers detect transposed wires, opens (broken or unconnected wires), and shorts (wires or pins improperly connected to each other). All of these problems can render a cable run completely inoperable.

Wire-map testing is nearly always included in multifunction cable testers, but sometimes it's just not worth spending serious cash on a comprehensive device. Dedicated wire-map testers that run about two to three hundred bucks are relatively inexpensive options that enable you to test your installation for the most common faults that occur during installations and afterward. If, say, you're installing voice-grade cable, a simple wire-mapping test is probably all that's needed.

A wire-map tester essentially consists of a remote unit that you attach to the far end of a connection and a battery-operated, handheld main unit that displays the results. Typically, the tester displays various codes that indicate the specific type of fault that it finds. You can also purchase a tester with multiple remote units that are numbered so that one person can test several connections without constantly traveling back and forth from one end of the connections to the other to move the remote unit.

> **WARNING** The one wiring fault that is not detectable by a dedicated wire-map tester is something known as *split pairs*. This fault flies under the radar because even though the pinouts are incorrect, the cable is still wired straight through. To detect split pairs, you must use a device that tests the cable for the near-end crosstalk that split pairs cause.

Continuity Testers

A *continuity tester* is an even simpler and less expensive device than a wire-map tester that's designed to check a copper cable connection for basic installation problems like opens, shorts, and crossed pairs. It will only set you back a few dollars, but such a device usually can't detect the more complicated twisted-pair wiring faults. It's still a nice option for basic cable testing, especially for coaxial cables that have only two conductors and so don't easily confuse whoever is installing them.

Like a wire-map tester, a continuity tester consists of two separate units that you connect to each end of the cable you want to test. Most of the time, the two units can snap together for storage and easy testing of patch cables.

Protocol Analyzer

A *protocol analyzer* is often confused with a packet sniffer because some products really are both. Remember—a packet sniffer looks at all traffic on a network segment. On the other hand, a protocol analyzer (surprise!) analyzes protocols. These tools come in both software and hardware versions, but compared to the products I listed earlier in this chapter, a network analyzer is likely to give you more information and help than a sniffer will. This is because a bona fide protocol analyzer can actually help you troubleshoot problems, whereas most sniffers just provide information for you to have a ball deciphering.

You can use a network protocol analyzer to accomplish the following:

- Help troubleshoot hard-to-solve problems
- Help you detect and identify malicious software (malware)
- Help gather information, such as baseline traffic patterns and network-utilization metrics
- Help you identify unused protocols so that you can remove them from the network
- Provide a traffic generator for penetration testing
- Possibly even work with an IDS

And last and perhaps most important for you, they can really help you learn about networking in general. This means if you want just want to find out why a network device is functioning in a certain way, you can use a protocol analyzer to sniff (there's that word again) the traffic and expose the data and protocols that pass along the wire.

 I've found a whole bunch of network analyzers you can use for free at http://www.snapfiles.com/freeware/network/fwpacketsniffer.html. But understand that there's no way I can verify the validity of this link after the publishing of this book. Again, the terms *sniffer* and *analyzer* are used to define the same product found at this link. Both Microsoft's NetMon and WireShark are called sniffers and analyzers, and they both are—at least to some degree.

Certifiers

Certification testers—or *certifiers*—are used to determine whether your network meets specific International Organization for Standardization (ISO) or TIA standards (Cat 5e, Cat 6, or Cat 7). They are the only option for you in this case. Also, if your network is wired with both copper and fiber, you really must use a certification tester.

Basically, a certifier is a combination cable tester and network analyzer, only better because it comes with more options. This is wonderful because it makes your job easier and makes you seem smarter to everyone around you—you're only as good as your tools, right? A good certifier will test the performance and response times of network resources like web, file, email, and even DNS and Dynamic Host Configuration Protocol (DHCP) servers. And, at the same time, it will certify your full Category 6 cable installation. After it finishes all this, you can provide your boss with a detailed network test report complete with dazzling, colorful graphics to make it simple to explain and understand—voila! You're instantly the genius of the day.

To get these smarts, all you need is a lot of money. These products are not for the small office, home office (SOHO) market, because they cost literally thousands of dollars, starting at about $5,000.

Time-Domain Reflectometer (TDR)

A *time-domain reflectometer (TDR)* is a tool that finds and describes faults in metallic cables like twisted wire pairs and coaxial cables. The equivalent device for optical fiber is an optical time-domain reflectometer (OTDR), which I'll talk about in a minute.

A TDR works in the same basic way that radar does. It transmits a short rise time pulse along the conductor, and if it turns out to be of a uniform impedance and properly terminated, the entire transmitted pulse is absorbed in the far-end termination; no signal is reflected back to the TDR. Any impedance interruptions will cause some of the incident signal to be sent back toward the source, letting you know all is not well.

So basically, any increases in the impedance create a reflection that reinforces the original pulse and decreases the impedance, thereby creating a reflection that opposes the original pulse. The resulting reflected pulse that's measured at the output/input to the TDR is displayed or plotted in measures of time. And because the speed of signal propagation is pretty consistent for a given type of transmission medium, the reading can also tell you about the cable length.

Because of this sensitivity to any variation in impedance, you can use a TDR to verify these things:

- Speed and condition of the cable
- Measure how long it takes to send a signal down a cable and how long it take to come back.
- Cable impedance characteristics
- Splice and connector locations and their associated loss amounts
- Estimated cable lengths

Now, let's take a look at a device that tests fiber-optic cables.

Optical Time-Domain Reflectometer (OTDR)

An *optical time-domain reflectometer (OTDR)* is an optoelectronic instrument used to give you the skinny on optical fibers. It works by putting out a series of optical pulses into the specific fiber you want to test. From the same end of the fiber, it extracts the light that's scattered and reflected back from anyplace over the length of the fiber that the amount of refraction changes. This is a lot like the way an electronic TDR measures reflections caused by impedance changes in a cable that you're testing. The strength of the return pulses is incorporated into a measure of time, which also conveniently gives you the fiber's length.

We use OTDRs to give us information about the following:

- The fiber's estimated length
- Its overall attenuation, including splice and mated-connector losses
- The location faults, such as breaks

Figure 18.7 shows the output from an OTDR testing a fiber connection.

The spike shows where a splice in the fiber is located, which has resulted in the signal being degraded. This is a very typical output. As the signal attenuates, you see a gradual but quick drop in decibels (db). Any connector will actually show a reflection, which, as mentioned, shows up as a spike in the OTDR output. The connector then creates more attenuation and loss of more db. The more splices, the less distance you can run with fiber.

FIGURE 18.7   Sample OTDR output

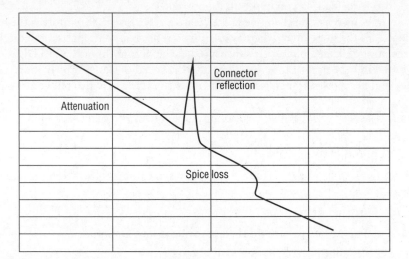

Multimeter

A *multimeter* or a multitester (also called a volt/ohm meter [VOM]) is a multitasking electronic measuring instrument. Your average multimeter typically includes features like the ability to measure voltage, current, and resistance. Multimeters come in analog and digital versions, and they range from basic hand-held devices useful for simple fault-finding and field-service work to more complex bench instruments that will give you measurements with a very high degree of accuracy.

They can be used to troubleshoot electrical problems in a wide array of electrical devices like batteries, motor controls, appliances, power supplies, and wiring systems. Figure 18.8 shows the multimeter that I use to help troubleshoot my networks.

Multimeters come in lots of flavors with different ranges of features and prices. Cheap ones cost less than ten bucks, but the top-of-the-line models can set you back up to five thousand.

Toner Probe

A *toner probe*, also called a tone generator, is a simple copper cable tester that is simple to use and can be used to trace a wire in a wall. It is a two-piece unit that's basically a tone generator and probe, sometimes called a "fox and hound" wire tracer. This type of device consists of one part that you connect to a cable with a standard jack—or to an individual wire with alligator clips that transmit a signal over the cable or wire—and another part that's a pen-like probe that emits an audible tone when it touches the other end of the cable, the wire, or even its insulating sheath.

FIGURE 18.8   A multimeter

Most often, you will use a toner probe to locate a specific connection in a punch-down block, because (annoyingly) some installers run all the cables for a network to the central punch-down block without labeling them. They (or you, if you're unlucky enough) then have to use a tone generator to identify which block is connected to which wall plate and label the punch-down block accordingly. This tool can identify a particular cable at any point between the two ends; and because the probe can detect the cable containing the tone signal through its sheath, it can help you to locate one specific cable out of a massive cable-spaghetti bundle in a ceiling conduit or other type of raceway.

Just connect the tone generator to one end, and touch the probe to each cable in the bundle until you hear the tone. Figure 18.9 shows a picture of my toner and the probe I use to find the tone on the other end of the cable.

Also, by testing the continuity of individual wires using alligator clips, you can use a tone generator and probe to find opens, shorts, and miswires. Open wire won't produce a tone at the other end, a short will produce a tone on two or more wires at the other end, and an improperly connected wire will produce a tone on the wrong pin at the other end.

FIGURE 18.9   A toner probe

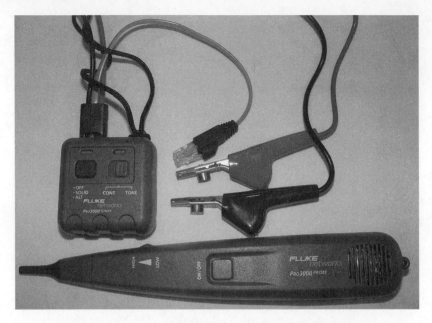

Sound like fun to you? Well, not so much—it takes a really long time, and it's super tedious. Worse, the whole process is almost as prone to errors as the cable installation itself. You have to either continually travel from one end of the cable to the other to move the tone generator unit or use a partner to test each connection, keeping in close contact using radios or some other means of communication to avoid confusion. So, considering the time and effort involved, investing in a wire-map tester is just a much more practical solution unless you're numbingly bored or really easily amused.

Butt Set

A *butt set* is essentially a portable telephone that allows you to test analog wet or dry lines and is used to monitor those lines. The most common type, shown in Figure 18.10, can both monitor and transmit.

You see these all the time with telco guys up on the telephone poles. They use their butt sets to connect to telephone lines, test them, and even make phone calls.

Another handy tool that will take the place of a butt-set is a *hound*. This non-canine device is nothing more than an inductively coupled amplifier with a small speaker in a hand-held tool. It's used to monitor the audio on a given line to verify you have the right pair before connecting it and typically is used with a toner probe. It will also monitor for noise.

Punch-Down Tool

Most networks today are built using twisted-pair cable of some sort. This cable is usually terminated in wiring closets using a tool known as a *punch-down tool*. It's called that because that's exactly what the tool does—punch down the wire into some kind of insulation displacement connector (IDC).

FIGURE 18.10   A butt set

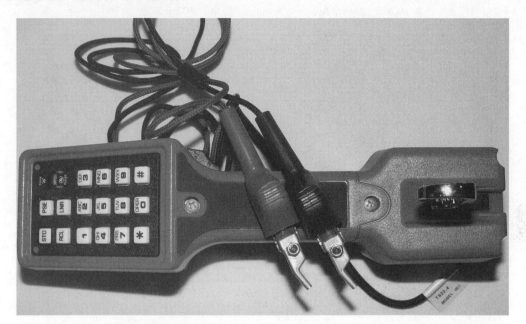

There are different types of punch-down tools. The most common is a punch down with replaceable blades for the different types of connectors (either 66 or 110). Figure 18.11 shows an example of this type of punch-down tool.

IDCs make contact by cutting through, or displacing, the insulation around a single conductor inside a twisted-pair cable.

FIGURE 18.11   An example of a punch-down tool

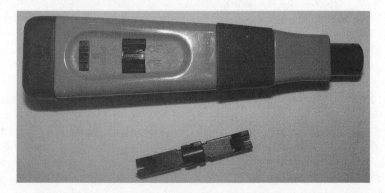

As shown in Figure 18.12, the punch-down tool pushes a conductor between the sides of a V inside an IDC, in this example a 10 block, allowing the small metal blade inside the connector to make contact with the inner conductor deep inside the wire.

FIGURE 18.12   Using a punch-down tool on a small 110 block

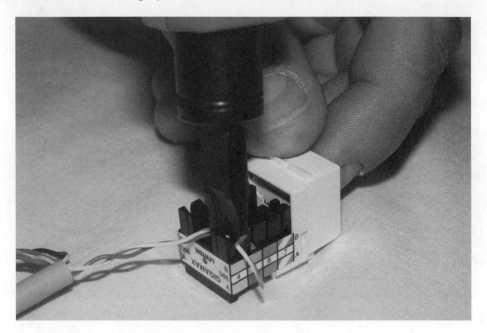

Now let's take a look at how to put a cable end together.

Cable Stripper/Snips

A *wire crimper*, often simply called crimper, is a handy tool found in most network technicians' tool bags. Crimpers are primarily used for attaching ends onto different types of network cables via a process known as—that's right—*crimping*. Crimping involves using your hands to apply a certain amount of force to press some kind of metal teeth into the inner conductors of a cable. Before you can crimp a connector onto the end, you've got to strip the cable with a type of *cable stripper* (or snips) and then properly put the wires into the connector.

Figure 18.13 shows what a cable stripper and snip looks like (this particular tool also includes a crimper).

Often, network technicians will make patch cables with a crimper. They'll take a small piece of Category 5e unshielded twisted-pair (UTP), strip the cable, and crimp two Registered Jack (RJ)-45 ends onto it to create the cable. Snips will create the type of cable needed to connect a host to a wall jack connection, for example. There are strippers and crimpers for the other types of cable as well—even specialized crimpers for fiber-optic ends.

FIGURE 18.13   A combination cable stripper, crimper, and snippers

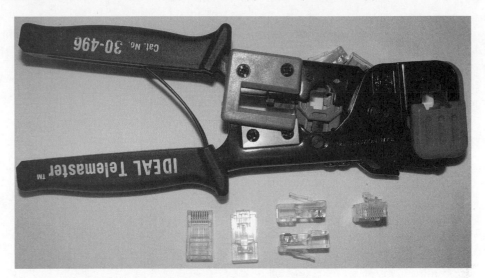

Voltage Event Recorder

Alternating current (AC) is basically the food that PCs and other network devices require in specific amounts to function properly. In the U.S., it's normally 110 volts and changes polarity 60 times a second (60 Hertz). These values are referred to as *line voltage*. Any deviation from these values can create some major problems for your PC or other electronics—like death.

This is why we have *surge protectors*. These little saviors use a special electronic circuit that monitors the incoming voltage level and trips a circuit breaker when the voltage level reaches critical mass. This kind of event is known as the *overvoltage threshold*. Even though having surge protector is definitely better than nothing, they too can fall victim to overvoltage events—I'm reminded of a friend whose home was struck by lightning during a thunderstorm and who found his surge protectors literally melted into the carpet! But they're still cool because even though they're really only somewhat protective, they are multiple-outlet strips that give us a lot more places to plug in our stuff.

By contrast, a quality *voltage event recorder* can troubleshoot and even provide preventative maintenance on your entire electrical system, whether it's a home or a huge factory. Although they do big things, they're typically small devices that just plug into a wall and record, over time, the power quality of a given circuit. The typical applications that you would use a voltage event recorder for include:

Recording voltage   The voltage event recorder monitors and records the supply voltage and checks whether the socket outlet is providing voltage within specifications.

Measuring distortion   The device measures frequency and harmonics, and it checks whether your uninterruptible power supply (UPS) system is functioning correctly.

Measuring flicker   It checks the switching loads on lighting systems.

Capturing voltage transients   And it can help you find intermittent, momentary events that may be affecting your equipment; the full waveform is captured with date, timestamp, and duration.

But you still have to do more to ensure the vitality of your electronic devices because they're very sensitive to temperature as well. This means you also need a way to monitor the temperature of the place(s) where your equipment is stored.

Temperature Monitor

A *temperature monitor* can save you and your precious devices from a total meltdown. By their very nature, networks often include lots of machines placed close together in one or several location(s)—like server rooms. Clearly, these devices, all humming along at once, generate quite a bit of heat, and heat is an arch enemy of all of them.

Just like us, electronics need to "breathe," and they're also pretty sensitive to becoming overheated, which is why you'll often need a jacket in a chilly server room. It's also why we need to set up and use temperature-monitoring devices. Twenty years ago or so, these didn't send alerts or give off any kind of alarms; they were just little plastic boxes that had pieces of round graph paper to graph temperature. This paper was good for a month, and for that duration, the paper would just spin around in a circle being drawn on by a pen attached to the temperature coil. As the temperature moved up or down, the pen moved in or out, leaving a circle line around the paper. All of this allowed you to manually monitor the temperature modulation in the server room over time. Although intended to "alert" you when and if there were climate changes, it usually did so after the fact and, therefore, too late.

Today, these temperature systems can provide multiple sensors feeding data to a single control point—nice. Now we can much more accurately track the temperature in our server rooms dynamically in real time. The central control point is usually equipped with HTTP software that can send alerts and provide alarms via a browser should your server room experience a warming event.

Temperature monitors also come in a variety of flavors. They vary in size and cost and come in hardware and/or software varieties. The kind you need varies and is based on the size of the room and the number of devices in it. You can even get one that will just monitor your PC's internal heat.

What type of indication or other problems will indicate you have a temperature problem in your server room? When you install new servers in a rack and you have network instability and other issues across all the servers in the rack but the power resources and bandwidth have been tested. This would be a good time to check your temperature monitor and verify that the servers are staying cool enough.

Summary

You need network tools, and you need to know how to use them. And as I said, you can get your hands on many of them for free; so download them and use them as soon as possible to get the experience you'll need to pass the CompTIA Network+ exam.

This chapter covered network scanners, including packet sniffers, IDS and IPS software, and port scanners. I also covered hardware tools, which are rarely free. The good news is that you don't need many of them yourself, but the company that owns all the equipment definitely does. Even though I've used all of the tools I talked about in this chapter, I don't own most of them personally—only the ones that are free or relatively inexpensive.

In the hardware tools section, I covered cable testers, analyzers, certifiers, TDR/OTDRs, and other critical tools that help you test the cables and devices in your network, monitor them, and keep them up and running smoothly.

Exam Essentials

Understand what network scanners are and how to use each one.   Network scanners are described as packet sniffers, IDS/IPS software, and port scanners. These devices can help you both troubleshoot and fix your network, as well as find and stop hackers in their tracks.

Remember what the basic purpose of a packet sniffer is.   The basic purpose of packet sniffers or network analyzers is to collect and analyze each individual packet that is captured on a specific network segment to determine if problems are happening.

Remember the main purpose of IDS/IPS software.   The IDS detects unwanted attempts to manipulate network systems and/or environment, and the IPS is a computer security device that monitors network and/or system activities for malicious behavior.

Understand what an OTDR is used for.   An optical time-domain reflectometer (OTDR) is an optoelectronic instrument used to test fiber-optic cabling. You can learn the cable's estimated length, attenuation (loss in db), and the location of faults.

Written Lab

Answer the following questions about software and hardware tools:

1. True/False: An IDS box can find and fix a problem as the attack occurs.

2. True/False: A TDR is used to test fiber connections.

3. True/False: An IDS box will report an attack but not fix an attack.

4. True/False: An OTDR is used to test fiber connections.

5. True/False: A network analyzer will see every packet on every segment of your network at the same time.

6. If you want to stop hackers before they get into your network, what type of network scanner will you use?

7. True/False: It is okay to scan the DoD network servers with a port scanner.

8. You need to monitor the temperature of your server room. What device should you use?

9. You want to monitor your UPS systems and make sure they are functioning correctly. What device should you use?

10. What type of device is used to put an RJ-45 end on a Cat 5e cable?

(The answers to the Written Lab can be found following the answers to the Review Questions for this chapter.)

Review Questions

1. Which is a tool of network scanners?
   A. Packet sniffers
   B. IDS/IPS software
   C. Port scanners
   D. All of the above

2. What is the purpose of packet sniffers?
   A. Discarding frames
   B. Sending transmissions from one port to another port
   C. Looking inside every packet on a network segment
   D. Monitoring the network for malicious behavior

3. You need to trace cables in multiple pair wiring. What tool will you use?
   A. Toner probe
   B. IDS
   C. cable tester
   D. butt set

4. What tool would you use to both find a break in a fiber optic connection and test the fiber connectivity on the network?
   A. Multimeter
   B. OTDR
   C. Butt set
   D. Toner probe

5. You need to create a cable that will connect your host to a wall jack connection. Which of the following will you use?
   A. IDS/IPS
   B. Snips
   C. Cable strippers
   D. Multimeter

6. Where is the IDS/IPS software typically placed within a network?
   A. Between the internal router and firewall connected to the ISP
   B. Between the printer and router connected to the ISP
   C. Between the computer and switch configured with VLANs
   D. Between the firewall and router connected to the email server

7. What is the purpose of a port scanner?

    A. Scan UDP for closed ports

    B. Sweep TCP for closed ports

    C. Search the network host for open ports

    D. None of the above

8. What is the purpose of wire-map testers?

    A. Check copper cable for crossed pairs only

    B. Analyzes protocols in software

    C. Help find unused protocols and remove them from the network

    D. Detect transposed wires, opens, and shorts in twisted-pair cables

9. Which of the following can check the speed and condition of the signal on a cable as well as measure the time it takes to send a signal down the wire and back?

    A. Multimeter

    B. TDR

    C. Tone generator

    D. event recorder

10. Which device should be used if you need to determine whether your network meets ISO or TIA standards?

    A. Angry IP

    B. Certifiers

    C. Nmap

    D. Routing table

11. Which software tool is used to view network traffic at the frame level?

    A. TDR

    B. Multimeter

    C. Port scanner

    D. Packet sniffer

12. Which function does a TDR not do?

    A. Estimate cable lengths

    B. Splice and connector locations and their associated loss amounts

    C. Display unused services

    D. Determine cable-impedance characteristics

    E. Sends a signal down a cable and measures how long it takes to come back

13. Which device would be used to measure voltage?

    A. Multimeter

    B. OTDR

    C. Butt set

    D. Toner probe

14. Which device would most likely be used to locate a specific connection in an unlabeled punch-down block?

    A. VOM

    B. Certifier

    C. TDR

    D. Toner probe

15. Which tool would be used to connect wire between two punch-down block blades?

    A. Punch-down tool

    B. Crimper

    C. Snips

    D. Strippers

16. Which tool is used to attach an RJ-45 connector to a CAT5 cable?

    A. Punch-down tool

    B. Crimper

    C. Snips

    D. Strippers

17. Which of the following would a technician use a punch down tool on?

    A. RJ-45 connector

    B. CSU/DSU

    C. 110 block

    D. Fiber ST connector

18. Which device monitors incoming voltage levels and overvoltage thresholds?

    A. Repeater

    B. Toner probe

    C. VOM

    D. Surge protector

19. Which application would a voltage event record be used for?

   A. Voltage recording

   B. Distortion measurement

   C. Flicker measurement

   D. Capturing voltage transients

   E. All of the above

20. You install new switches in your server room and they are having network instability and other issues across all servers in the rack. Which device would be used to alert you of a system overheating?

   A. Voltage event recorder

   B. Temperature monitor

   C. Surge protector

   D. Probe

Answers to Review Questions

1. D. Yup, all of the above. The CompTIA Network+ objectives cover all three in regard to tools used to analyze today's networks.

2. C. The basic purpose of packet sniffers or network analyzers is to collect and analyze each individual packet that is captured on a specific network segment to determine whether problems are happening. You can also use them to see if there is too much traffic on a segment.

3. A. A toner probe sends a signal down a pair of wires so that they can be traced. Typically a butt set is used to find this signal, but toner probe is the best answer to this question.

4. B. An optical time-domain reflectometer (OTDR) is an optoelectronic instrument used to give you the skinny on optical fibers. It works by putting out a series of optical pulses into the specific fiber you want to test and can tell you if a break in the fiber has occurred and where.

5. B. To create a patch cable (568A) to connect your host to a jack in the wall, you need to use a snips.

6. A. Remember that firewalls are the first line of defense for an Internet-connected network. If a network was directly connected to the Internet without a firewall, an attacker could theoretically gain direct access to the computers and servers on that network with little effort. The IDS/IPS software is usually positioned between your internal router and the firewall to the outside network (Internet).

7. C. Hope you answered C! A port scanner is just a piece of software designed to search a network for open hosts. Administrators of networks use port scanners to ensure security and bad guys use them to compromise it.

8. D. Wire-map testing is the most basic test for twisted-pair cables. It detects transposed wires, opens (broken or unconnected wires), and shorts (wires or pins improperly connected to each other).

9. B. A time-domain reflectometer (TDR) is a tool that finds and describes faults in metallic cables like twisted wire pairs and coaxial cables. The equivalent device for optical fiber is an optical time-domain reflectometer (OTDR). A TDR can also check the speed and condition of the signal on the cable.

10. B. A certifier is a combination cable tester and network analyzer, only better. It can test the performance and response times of network resources and certify your full Category 6 cable installation at the same time.

11. D. Unlike port scanners, packet sniffers actually look inside every packet on a network segment at the frame level.

12. C. Due to sensitivity to any variation and impedance A, B, D, and E are all reasons you'd use a TDR.

13. A. A multimeter or a volt/ohm meter (VOM) is used to measure voltage, current, and resistance.

14. D. Otherwise known as a "fox and hound" wire tracer, a toner probe would be useful in this situation. A toner probe will emit an audible tone when it touches the other end of the cable.

15. A. I hope you said A! A punch-down tool would be used if you needed to connect wire to a punch-down block. Most networks today have wiring closets, and to terminate the cables, you're certain to need a punch-down tool.

16. B. A wire crimper or crimper is used for attaching ends onto different types of network cables.

17. C. A punch down tool is used to punch down an RJ-45 cable to an insulation displacement connector, typically a 110 block.

18. D. An everyday surge protector monitors the incoming voltage level and trips a circuit breaker when the overvoltage reaches a certain level.

19. E. Using a voltage event recorder can help you troubleshoot and even provide preventative maintenance on your electrical systems.

20. B. Electronic devices are prone to overheating, which is why you should use a temperature monitor.

Answers to Written Lab

1. False

2. False

3. True

4. True

5. False. A typical network analyzer can see only one segment at a time.

6. An Intrusion Prevention System (IPS)

7. False. Unless you don't mind prison.

8. A temperature monitor

9. A voltage event recorder

10. A cable stripper/crimper

Chapter

19

Network Troubleshooting

**THE FOLLOWING COMPTIA NETWORK+
EXAM OBJECTIVES ARE COVERED IN THIS
CHAPTER:**

✓ **4.6 Given a scenario, implement the following network
troubleshooting methodology**

- Information gathering—identify symptoms and problems
- Identify the affected areas of the network
- Determine if anything has changed
- Establish the most probable cause
- Determine if escalation is necessary
- Create an action plan and solution identifying
  potential effects
- Implement and test the solution
- Identify the results and effects of the solution
- Document the solution and the entire process

✓ **4.7 Given a scenario, troubleshoot common connectivity
issues and select an appropriate solution**

- Physical issues:
  - Cross talk
  - Nearing cross talk
  - Attenuation
  - Collisions
  - Shorts
  - Open impedance mismatch (echo)
  - Interference

- Logical issues:
  - Port speed
  - Port duplex mismatch
  - Incorrect VLAN
  - Incorrect IP address
  - Wrong gateway
  - Wrong DNS
  - Wrong subnet mask
- Issues that should be identified but escalated:
  - Switching loop
  - Routing loop
  - Route problems
  - Proxy arp
  - Broadcast storms
- Wireless Issues:
  - Interference (bleed, environmental factors)
  - Incorrect encryption
  - Incorrect channel
  - Incorrect frequency
  - ESSID mismatch
  - Standard mismatch (802.11 a/b/g/n)
  - Distance
  - Bounce
  - Incorrect antenna placement

There is no way around it. Troubleshooting computers and networks is a combination of art and science, and the only way to get really good at it is by doing it—a lot! So it's practice, practice, practice with the basic yet vitally important skills you'll attain in this chapter. Of course, I'm going to cover all the troubleshooting topics you'll need to sail through the Network+ exam, but I'm also going to add some juicy bits of knowledge that will really help you to tackle the task of troubleshooting successfully in the real world.

First, you'll learn to check quickly for problems in the "super-simple stuff" category, and then we'll move into a hearty discussion about a common troubleshooting model that you can use like a checklist to go through and solve a surprising number of network problems. We'll finish the chapter with a good briefing about some common troubleshooting resources, tools, tips, and tricks to keep up your sleeve and equip you even further.

I won't be covering any new networking information in this chapter because you've gotten all the foundational background material you need for troubleshooting in the previous chapters. But no worries. I'll go through each of the issues described in this chapter's objectives, one at a time, in detail, so that even if you've still got a bit of that previous material to nail down yet, you'll be good to get going and fix some networks anyway.

To find up-to-the-minute updates for this chapter, please see www.lammle.com or www.sybex.com/go/comptianetwork+.

Narrowing Down the Problem

When initially faced with a network problem in its entirety, it's easy to get totally overwhelmed. That's why it's a great strategy to start by narrowing things down to the source of the problem. To help you achieve that goal, it's always wise to ask the right questions. You can begin doing just that with this list—ask yourself:

- Did you check the super simple stuff (SSS)?
- Is hardware or software causing the problem?
- Is it a workstation or server problem?
- Which segments of the network are affected?

Are There Any Cabling Issues? Did You Check the Super Simple Stuff?

Okay, yes—it sounds like a snake's hiss (appropriate for a problem, right?), but exactly what's on the SSS list that you should be checking first, and why? Well, as the saying goes, "All things being equal, the simplest explanation is probably the correct one"; so you probably won't be stunned and amazed when I tell you that I've had people call me in and act like the sky is falling when all they needed to do was check to make sure their workstation was plugged in or powered on. (I didn't say "super simple stuff" for nothing!) Your SSS list really does include things that are this obvious—sometimes so obvious, no one thinks to check for them. Even though anyone experienced in networking has their own favorite "DUH" events to tell about, almost everyone can agree on a few things that should definitely be on the SSS list:

- Check to ensure login procedures and rights.
- Look for link lights and collision lights.
- Check all power switches, cords, and adapters.
- Look for user errors.

The Correct Login Procedure and Rights

You know by now that if you've set up everything correctly, your network's users absolutely have to follow the proper login procedure to the letter (or number, or symbol) in order to successfully gain access to the network resources they're after. If they don't do that, they will be denied access; and considering that there are truly tons of opportunities to blow it, it's a miracle, or at least very special, that anyone manages to login to the network correctly at all.

Think about it. First, a user must enter their username and password flawlessly. Sounds easy, but as they say, "in a perfect world…" In this one, people mess up, don't realize it, and freak out at you about the "broken network" or the imaginary IT demon that changed their password on them while they went to lunch; and now, they can't log in. (The latter could be true—you may have done exactly that. If you did, just gently remind them about that memo you sent about the upcoming password-change date and time that they must have spaced about due to the tremendous demands on them.)

Anyway, it's true. By far, the most common problem is bad typing—people accidentally enter the wrong username or password, and they do that a lot. With some operating systems, a slight brush of the Caps Lock key is all it takes: The user's username and password are case-sensitive, and suddenly, they're trying to login with what's now all in uppercase instead—oops.

Plus, if you happen to be running one of the shiny new operating systems around today, you can also restrict the times and conditions under which users can log in, right? So, if your user spent an unusual amount of time in the bathroom upon returning from lunch, or if they got distracted and tried to log in from their BFF's workstation instead of their own, the network's operating system would've rejected their login request even though they still can type impressively well after two martinis.

And remember—you can also restrict how many times a user can log in to the network simultaneously. If you've set that up, and your user tries to establish more connections than you've allowed, access will again be denied. Just know that most of the time, if a user is denied access to the network and/or its resources, they're probably going to interpret that as a network problem even though the network operating system is doing what it should.

Real World Scenario

Can the Problem Be Reproduced?

The first question to ask anyone who reports a network or computer problem is, "Can you show me what 'not working' looks like?" This is because if you can reproduce the problem, you can identify when it happens, which may give you all the information you need to determine the source of the problem and maybe even solve it in a snap. The hardest problems to solve are the random variety that occur intermittently and can't be easily reproduced.

Let's pause for a minute to outline the steps to take during any user-oriented network problem-solving process:

1. Make sure the username and password is being entered correctly.

2. Check that Caps Lock key.

3. Try to login yourself from another workstation, assuming that doing this doesn't violate the security policy. If it works, go back to the user-oriented login problems, and go through them again.

4. If none of this solves the problem, check the network documentation to find out whether any of the aforementioned kinds of restrictions are in place; if so, find out whether the user has violated any of them.

Remember, if intruder detection is enabled on your network, a user will get locked out of their account after a specific number of unsuccessful login attempts. If this happens, either they'll have to wait until a predetermined time period has elapsed before their account will unlock and give them another chance, or you'll have to go in and manually unlock it for them.

The Link and Collision Lights

The link light is that little light-emitting diode (LED) found on both the Network Interface Card (NIC) and the hub. It's typically green and labeled *link* or some abbreviation of that. If you're running 10Base-T, a link light indicates that the NIC and hub are making a logical (Data Link layer) connection. If the link lights are lit up on both the workstation's NIC and the hub port to which the workstation is connected, it's usually safe to assume that the workstation and hub are communicating just fine.

The link lights on some NICs don't activate until the driver is loaded. So, if the link light isn't on when the system is first turned on, you'll just have to wait until the operating system loads the NIC driver. But don't wait forever!

The *collision light* is also a small LED, but it's typically amber in color, and it can usually be found on both Ethernet NICs and hubs. When lit, it indicates that an Ethernet collision has occurred. If you've got a busy Ethernet network on which collisions are somewhat common, understand that this light is likely to blink occasionally; but if it stays on continuously, it could mean that there are way too many collisions happening for legitimate network traffic to get through. Don't assume this is really what's happening without first checking that the NIC, or other network device, is working properly, because one or both could simply be malfunctioning.

Don't confuse the collision light with the network-activity or network-traffic light (which is usually green), because that light just indicates that a device is transmitting. This particular light *should* be blinking on and off continually as the device transmits and receives data on the network.

The Power Switch

Clearly, to function properly, all computer and network components must be turned on and powered up first. Obvious, yes, but if I had a buck for each time I've heard, "My computer is on, but my monitor is all dark," I'd be rolling in money by now.

When this kind of thing happens, just keep your cool and politely ask, "Is the monitor turned on?" After a little pause, the person calling for help will usually say, "Ohhh... ummmm... thanks," and then hang up ASAP. The reason I said to be nice is that, embarrassing as it is, this, or something like it, will probably happen to you too eventually.

Most systems include a power indicator (a Power or PWR light). The power switch typically has a 1 or an On indicator; but the system or device could still be powerless if all the relevant power cables aren't actually plugged in—including the power strip.

Remember that every cable has two ends, and both must be plugged in to something. If you're thinking something like, "Sheesh—a 4-year-old knows that," you're probably right; but again, I can't count the times this has turned out to be the root cause of a "major system failure."

The best way to go about troubleshooting power problems is to start with the most obvious device and work your way back to the power-service panel. There could be a number of power issues between the device and the service panel, including a bad power cable, bad outlet, bad electrical wire, tripped circuit breaker, or blown fuse, and any of these things could be the actual cause of the problem that appears to be device-death instead.

Operator Error

Or, the problem may be that you've got a user who simply doesn't know how to be one. Maybe you're dealing with someone who doesn't have the tiniest clue about the equipment they're using or about how to perform a certain task correctly—in other words, the problem may be due to something known as *operator error (OE)*. Here's a short list of the most common types of OEs and their associated acronyms:

- Equipment exceeds operator capability (EEOC)

- Problem exists between chair and keyboard (PEBCAK)

- ID Ten T error (an ID10T)

A word of caution here, though—assuming that all your problems are user related can quickly make an ID10T error out of you.

Although it can be really tempting to take the easy way out and blow things off, remember that the network's well-being and security are ultimately your responsibility. So, before you jump to the operator-error conclusion, ask the user in question to reproduce the problem in your presence, and pay close attention to what they do. Understand that doing this can require a great deal of patience, but it's worth your time and effort if you can prevent someone who doesn't know what they're doing from causing serious harm to pricey devices or leaving a gaping hole in your security. You might even save the Help Desk crew's sanity from the relentless calls of a user with the bad habit of flipping off the power switch without following proper shutdown procedures. You just wouldn't know they always do that if you didn't see it for yourself, right?

And what about finding out that that pesky user was, in fact, trained really badly by someone, and that they aren't the only one? This is exactly the kind of thing that can turn the best security policy to dust and leave your network and its resources as vulnerable to attack as that goat in *Jurassic Park*.

The moral here is, always check out the problem thoroughly. If the problem and its solution aren't immediately clear to you, try the procedure yourself, or ask someone else at another workstation to do so. Don't just leave the barn door wide open to assumptions, blaming others (or, worst of all, chance), because that's exactly what the bad guys out there are hoping you'll do.

 This is only a partial list of super-simple stuff. No worries. Rest assured, you'll come up with your own expanded version over time.

Is Hardware or Software Causing the Problem?

A hardware problem often rears its ugly head when some device in your computer skips a beat and/or dies. This one's pretty easy to discern because when you try to do something requiring that particular piece of hardware, you can't do it and instead get an error telling you that you can't do it. Even if your hard-disk fails, you'll probably get warning signs before it actually kicks, like a Disk I/O error or something similar.

Other problems drop out of the sky and hit you like something from the wrong end of a seagull. No warning at all—just splat! Components that were humming along fine a second ago can and do suddenly fail, usually at the worst possible time, leaving you with a mess of lost data, files, everything—you get the idea.

Solutions to hardware problems usually involve one of three things:

- Changing hardware settings
- Updating device drivers
- Replacing dead hardware

If your hardware has truly failed, it's time to get out your tools and start replacing components. If this isn't one of your skills, you can either send the device out for repair or replace it. Your mantra here is "backup, backup, backup," because in either case, a system could be down for a while—anywhere from an hour to several days—so it's always good to keep backup hardware around. And I know everyone and your momma has told you this, but here it is one more time: Back up all data, files, hard drive, everything, and do so on a regular basis.

Software problems are muddier waters. Sometimes you'll get General Protection Fault messages, which indicate a Windows or Windows program (or other platform) error of some type, and other times the program you're working in will suddenly stop responding and hang. At their worst, they'll cause your machine to randomly lock up on you. When this type of thing happens, I'd recommend visiting the manufacturer's support website to get software updates and patches or searching for the answer in a knowledge base.

Sometimes you get lucky and the ailing software will tell the truth by giving you a precise message about the source of the problem. Messages saying the software is missing a file or a file has become corrupt are great because you can usually get your problem fixed fast by providing that missing file or by reinstalling the software. Neither solution takes very long, but the downside is that whatever you were doing before the program hosed will probably be at least partially lost; so again, back up your stuff, and save your data often.

 Please re-read Chapter 17, "Operating Systems and Command-Line Tools," and Chapter 18, "Software and Hardware Tools," and use the software and hardware tools discussed in those two chapters to help you troubleshoot network problems.

Okay—it's time for you to learn how to troubleshoot your workstations and servers.

Is It a Workstation or a Server Problem?

The first thing you've got to determine when troubleshooting these kinds of problems is whether it's only one person or a whole group that's been affected. If the answer is only one person, think workstation—more than that, and it's probably part of the network (a segment) that's giving you grief.

So what do you do about it? Well, if it's the single-user situation, your first line of defense is to try to log in from another workstation within the same group of users. If you can do that, the problem is definitely the user's workstation, so look for things like cabling faults, a bad NIC, power issues, and OS's.

But if a whole department can't access a specific server, take a good, hard look at that particular server, and start by checking all user connections to it. If everyone is logged in correctly, the problem may have something to do with individual rights or permissions; but if no one can log in to that server, including you, the server probably has a communication problem with the rest of the network. And if the server has totally crashed, you'll either see messages regarding this nasty fact on the server's monitor, or you'll find its screen completely blank—screaming indications that the server is no longer running. All good, but it's important to keep in mind that these symptoms vary among network operating systems.

Which Segments of the Network Are Affected?

Figuring this one out can be a little tough. If multiple segments are affected, you may be dealing with a network-address conflict. If you're running Transmission Control Protocol/ Internet Protocol (TCP/IP), remember that IP addresses must be unique across an entire network. So, if two of your segments have the same IP subnet address, you'll end up with duplicate IP errors—an ugly situation that can be a real bear to troubleshoot and can make it tough to find the source of the problem.

If all of your network's users are experiencing the problem, it could be a server everyone accesses. Thank the powers that be if you nail it down to that, because if not, other network devices like your main router or hub may be down, making network transmissions impossible and usually meaning a lot more work on your part to fix.

Adding wide area network (WAN) connections to the mix can complicate matters exponentially, and you don't want to go there if you can avoid it; so start by finding out if stations on both sides of a WAN link can communicate. If so, get the champagne—your problem isn't related to the WAN—woo hoo! But if those stations can't communicate, it's not your lucky day: You've got to check everything between the sending station and the receiving one, including the WAN hardware, to find the culprit. The good news is that most of the time, WAN devices have built-in diagnostics that tell you whether a WAN link is working okay, which really helps you determine if the failure has something to do with the WAN link itself or with the hardware involved instead.

Is It Bad Cabling?

Back to hooking up correctly. After you've figured out whether your plight is related to one workstation, a network segment, or the whole tamale (network), you must then examine the relevant cabling. Are the cables properly connected to the correct port? More than once, I've seen a digital subscriber line (DSL) modem connection to the wall cabled all wrong—it's an easy mistake to make and an easy one to fix.

And you know that nothing lasts forever, so check those patch cables running between a workstation and a wall jack. Just because they don't come with expiration dates written on them doesn't mean they don't expire. They do go bad—especially if they get moved, trampled, or tripped over a lot. (I did tell you that it's a bad idea to run cabling across the office floor, didn't I?) Connection problems are the tell here—if you check the NIC and there is no link-light blinking, you may have a bad patch cable to blame.

It gets murkier if your cable in the walls or ceiling is toast or hasn't been installed correctly. Maybe you've got a user or two telling you the place is haunted because they only have problems with their workstations after dark when the lights go on. Haunted? No... Some genius probably ran a network cable over a fluorescent light, which is something that just happens to produce lots of electromagnetic interference (EMI), which can really mess up communications in that cable.

Next on your list is to check the medium dependent interface/medium dependent interface-crossover (MDI/MDI-X) port setting on small, workgroup hubs and switches. This is a potential source of trouble that's often overlooked, but it's important because this port is the one that's used to uplink to a switch on the network's backbone.

First, understand that the port setting has to be set to either MDI or MDI-X depending on the type of cable used for your hub-to-hub or switch-to-switch connection. For instance, the crossover cables I talked about way back in Chapter 3, "Networking Topologies, Connectors, and Wiring Standards," require that the port be set to MDI, and a standard network patch cable requires that the port be set to MDI-X. You can usually adjust the setting via a regular switch or a dual inline package (DIP) switch; but to be sure, if you're still using hubs, check out the hub's documentation. (You did keep that, right?)

Other Important Cable Issues You Need to Know About

They may be basic, but they're still vital—understanding the physical issues that can happen on a network when a user is connected via cable (usually Ethernet) is critical information to have in your troubleshooting repertoire.

Because most of today's networks still consist of large amounts of copper cable, they suffer from the same physical issues that have plagued networking since the very beginning. Newer technologies and protocols have helped to a degree, but they haven't made these issues a thing of the past yet. Some physical issues that still affect networks are listed and defined next:

Crosstalk   Again, harkening back to Chapter 3, remember that crosstalk is what happens when there's signal bleed between two adjacent wires that are carrying a current. Network designers minimize crosstalk inside network cables by twisting the wire pairs together, putting them at a 90-degree angle to each other. The tighter the wires are twisted, the less the crosstalk you have, and newer cables like Cat 6 cable really make a difference. But like I said, not completely—crosstalk still exists and affects communications, especially in high-speed networks.

Nearing or near-end crosstalk   This is a specific type of crosstalk measurement that has to do with the EMI bled from a wire to adjoining wires where the current originates. This particular point has the strongest potential to create crosstalk because the crosstalk signal itself degrades as it moves down the wire; so if you have an issue with it, it's probably to show up in the first part of wire where it's connected to a switch or a NIC.

Attenuation As a signal moves through any medium, the medium itself will degrade the signal—a phenomenon known as *attenuation* that's common in all kinds of networks. True, signals traversing fiber-optic cable don't attenuate as fast as those on copper cable, but they still do eventually. You know that all copper twisted-pair cables have a maximum segment distance of 100 meters before they'll need to be amplified or *repeated* by a hub or a switch, but single-mode fiber-optic cables can sometimes carry signals for miles before they begin to attenuate (degrade). If you need to go big, use fiber, not copper.

Collisions A network *collision* happens when two devices try to communicate on the same physical segment at the same time. Collisions like this were a big problem in early Ethernet networks, and a tool known as *Carrier Sense Multiple Access with Collision Detection* (CSMA/CD) was used to detect and respond to them. Nowadays, we use switches in place of hubs because they can separate the network into multiple collision domains, learn the Media Access Control (MAC) addresses of the devices attached to them, create a type of permanent virtual circuit between all network devices, and prevent collisions.

Shorts Basically, a *short circuit*, or *short*, happens when the current flows through a different path within a circuit than it's supposed to; in networks, they're usually caused by some type of physical fault in the cable. You can find shorts with circuit-testing equipment, but because sooner is better when it comes to getting a network back up and running, replacing the ailing cable until it can be fixed (if it can be) is your best option.

Open impedance mismatch (echo) Open impedance on cable-testing equipment tells you that the cable or wires aren't completing the circuit you're testing. If it happens on only one wire, it's probably a bad connection; but if it happens at the same place on all the wires in the same cable, the cable has probably been cut somehow. Some testing equipment will give you the location of the cut even if it's inside a wall.

Interference EMI and *radio frequency interference* (RFI) occur when signals interfere with the normal operation of electronic circuits. Computers happen to be really sensitive to sources of this, such as T.V. and radio transmitters, which create a specific radio frequency as part of their transmission process. Two other common culprits are two-way radios and cellular phones.

Your only way around this is to use shielded network cables like shielded twisted-pair (STP) and coaxial cable (rare today), or to run EMI/RFI-immune but pricey fiber-optic cable throughout your entire network.

Unbounded Media Issues (Wireless)

Okay, now let's say your problem-ridden user is telling you they only use a wireless connection. Well, you can definitely take crosstalk and shorts off the list of suspects; but don't get excited, because with wireless, you've got a whole new bunch of possible Physical-layer problems to sort through.

Wireless networks are really convenient for the user but not so much for administrators. They can require a lot more configuration, and understand that with wireless networks, you don't just get to substitute one set of challenges for another—you pretty much add all those fresh new issues on top of the wired challenges you already have on your plate.

Some of those new wireless challenges include

Interference   Because wireless networks rely on radio waves to transmit signals, they're more subject to interference, even from other wireless devices like Bluetooth keyboards, mice, or cell phones that are all close in frequency ranges. Any of these—even microwaves!—can cause signal bleed that can slow down or prevent wireless communications. Factors like the distance between a client and a wireless access point (WAP) and the stuff between the two can also affect signal strength and even intensify the interference from other signals. So, careful placement of that WAP is a must.

Incorrect encryption   You know that wireless networks can use encryption to secure their communications and that different encryption flavors are used for wireless networks, like Wired Equivalent Protocol (WEP) and Wi-Fi Protected Access 2 (WPA2) with Advanced Encryption Standard (AES). To ensure the tightest security, configure your wireless networks with the highest encryption protocol that both the WAP and the clients can support. Oh, and make sure the AP and its clients are configured with same type of encryption. This is why it's a good idea to disable security before troubleshooting client problems, because if the client can connect once you've done that, you know you're dealing with a security configuration error.

Incorrect channel   Wireless networks use many different frequencies within the 2.4GHz or 5Ghz band, and I'll bet you didn't know that these frequencies are sometimes combined to provide greater bandwidth for the user. You actually do know about this—has anyone heard of something called a *channel*? Well, that's exactly what a channel is, and it's also the reason some radio stations come in better than others—they have more bandwidth because their channel has more combined frequencies. You also know what happens when the AP and the client aren't quite matching up. Have you ever hit the scan on your car's radio and only kind of gotten a station's static-ridden broadcast? That's because the AP (radio station) and the client (your car's radio) aren't quite on the same channel. Most of the time, wireless networks use channel 1, 6, or 11, and because clients auto-configure themselves to any channel the AP is broadcasting on, it's not usually a configuration issue unless someone has forced a client onto an incorrect channel.

Incorrect frequency   Okay—so setting the channel sets the frequency or frequencies that wireless devices will use. But some devices, such as an AP running 802.11g and a, allow you to tweak those settings and choose a specific frequency. As with any relationship, it works best if things are mutual. So if you do this on one device, you've got to configure the same setting on all the devices you want to communicate, or they won't—they'll argue, and you don't want that. Incorrect-channel and frequency-setting problems on a client are rare, but if you have multiple APs and they're in close proximity, you need to make sure they're on different channels/frequencies to avoid potential interference problems.

ESSID mismatch   When a wireless device comes up, it scans for Service Set Identifiers (SSIDs) in its immediate area. These can be Basic Service Set Identifiers (BSSIDs) that identify an individual client, or Extended Service Set Identifiers (ESSIDs) that identify a certain AP. In your own wireless LAN, you clearly want the devices to find the ESSID that you're broadcasting, which isn't usually a problem: Your broadcast is closer than the neighbor's, so it should be stronger—unless you're in an office building or apartment complex that has lots of different APs assigned to lots of different ESSIDs because they belong to lots of different tenants in the building. This can definitely give you some grief, because it's possible that your neighbor's ESSID broadcast is stronger than yours, depending on where the clients are in the building. So if a user reports that they're connected to an AP but still can't access the resources they need or authenticate to the network, you should verify that they are, in fact, connected to your ESSID and not your neighbor's. You can generally just look at the information tool tip on the wireless software icon to find this out.

Standard mismatch As you found out in Chapter 12, "Wireless Technologies," wireless networks have many standards that have evolved over time, like 802.11a, 802.11b, 802.11g, and 802.11n. Standards continue to develop that make wireless networks even faster and more powerful. The catch is that some of these standards are backward compatible, and others aren't. For instance, most devices you buy today can be set to 802.11a/b/g, which means they can be used to communicate with other devices of all three standards. But some devices can't be configured to be backward compatible to 802.11a, because it used Orthogonal Frequency Division Multiplexing (OFDM) rather than Direct Sequence Spread Spectrum (DSSS). So, make sure the standards on the AP match the standards on the client, or that they're at least backward compatible. It's either that or tell all your users to buy a new cards for their machines.

Distance Location, location, location. You've got only two worries with this one: Your clients are either not far away enough or they're too far from the AP. If your AP doesn't seem to have enough power to provide a connectivity point for your clients, you can move it closer to them, increase the distance that the AP can transmit by changing the type of antenna it uses, or use multiple APs connected to the same switch or set of switches to solve the problem. If the signal is too strong, and it reaches out into the parking area or further out to other buildings and businesses, place the AP as close as possible to the center of the area it's providing service for. And don't forget to verify that you've the latest security features in place to keep bad guys from authenticating to and using your network.

Bounce For a wireless network spanning large geographical distances, you can install repeaters and reflectors to bounce a signal and boost it to cover about a mile. This can be a good thing, but if you don't tightly control signal bounce, you could end up with a much bigger network than you wanted. To determine exactly how far and wide the signal will bounce, make sure you conduct a thorough wireless site survey.

Incorrect antenna placement Most of the time, the best place to put an AP and/or its antenna is as close to the center of your wireless network as possible. But you can position some antennas a distance from the AP and connect to it with a cable—a method used for a lot of the outdoor installations around today. If you want to use multiple APs, you've also got to be a little more sophisticated about deciding where to put them all; you can use third-party tools like the packet sniffers WireShark and AirMagnet on a laptop to survey the site and establish how far your APs are actually transmitting. You can also hire a consultant to do this for you—there are many companies that specialize in assisting organizations with their wireless networks and the placement of antennas and APs. This is important because poor placement can lead to interference and poor performance, or even no performance at all.

Okay, now that you know all about the possible physical network horrors that can befall you on a typical network, it's a good time for you to memorize the troubleshooting steps that you've got to know to ace the CompTIA Network+ exam.

Troubleshooting Steps

In the Network+ troubleshooting model, there are nine steps you've got to have dialed in:

1. Information gathering—identify symptoms and problems.
2. Identify the affected areas of the network.
3. Determine if anything has changed.
4. Establish the most probable cause.
5. Determine if escalation is necessary.
6. Create an action plan and solution, identifying potential effects.
7. Implement and test the solution.
8. Identify the results and effects of the solution.
9. Document the solution and the entire process.

To get things off to a running start, let's assume that the user has called you yet again, but now they're almost in tears because they can't connect to the server on the intranet and they also can't get to the Internet. (By the way, this happens a lot, so pay attention—it's only a matter of time before it happens to you!)

 Absolutely, positively make sure you memorize this nine-step trouble-shooting process in the right order when studying for the Network+ exam!

Step 1: Information Gathering—Identify Symptoms and Problems

Before you can solve the problem, you've got to figure out what it is, right? Again, asking the right questions can get you far along this path and really help clarify the situation. A good way to start is by asking the user the following:

- Exactly which part of the Internet can't you access? A particular website? A certain address? A type of website? None of it at all?

- Can you use your web browser?

- If the hitch has to do with an internal server to the company, ask, "Can you ping the server?" and talk the user through doing that.

- Ask the user to try to telnet or FTP to an internal server to verify local network connectivity; if they don't know how, talk them through it.

Okay—here's another really common trouble ticket that just happens to build on the last scenario... Now let's say you've got a user who's called you at the Help Desk. By asking the previous questions, you found out that this user can't access the corporate intranet or get out to any sites on the Internet. You also established that the user can use their web browser to access the corporate FTP site, but only by IP address, not the FTP server name. This information tells you two important things: that you can rule out the host and the web browser (application) as the source of the problem, and that the physical network is working.

Great—now that you've nailed down the problem, you need to find out if it's an isolated case that's specific to your user's host, or if this is happening on other areas of the network as well. This leads us to...

Step 2: Identify the Affected Areas of the Network

I probably don't need to tell you that computers and networks can be really fickle—they can hum along fine for months, suddenly crash, and then continue to work fine again without ever seizing in that way again. That's why it's so important to be able to reproduce the problem and identify the affected area to narrow things down so you can cut to the chase and fix the issue fast. This really helps—when something isn't working, try it again, and write down exactly what is and is not happening.

Most users' knee-jerk reaction is to straight-up call the Help Desk the minute they have a problem. This is not only annoying but also inefficient, because you're going to ask them exactly what they were doing when the problem occurred, and most users have no idea what they were doing at the computer because they were focused on doing their jobs instead. This is why if you train users to reproduce the problem and jot down some notes about it *before* calling you, they'll be much better prepared to give you the information you need to start troubleshooting it and help them.

So with that, here we go. The problem you've identified results in coughing out an error message to your user when they try to access the corporate intranet. It looks like this:

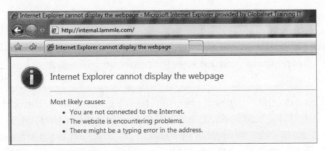

And when this user tries to ping the server using the server's hierarchical web name, it fails too:

You're going to respond by checking to see whether the server is up by pinging the server by its IP address:

```
Command Prompt

Microsoft Windows [Version 6.0.6001]
Copyright (c) 2006 Microsoft Corporation.  All rights reserved.

C:\Users\tlammle>ping 206.123.114.186

Pinging 206.123.114.186 with 32 bytes of data:
Reply from 206.123.114.186: bytes=32 time=75ms TTL=56
Reply from 206.123.114.186: bytes=32 time=75ms TTL=56
Reply from 206.123.114.186: bytes=32 time=74ms TTL=56
Reply from 206.123.114.186: bytes=32 time=75ms TTL=56

Ping statistics for 206.123.114.186:
    Packets: Sent = 4, Received = 4, Lost = 0 (0% loss),
Approximate round trip times in milli-seconds:
    Minimum = 74ms, Maximum = 75ms, Average = 74ms

C:\Users\tlammle>
```

Nice—that worked, so the server is up, but you could still have a server problem. Just because you can ping a host, it doesn't mean that host is 100% up and running, but in this case, it's a good start.

And you're in luck because you've been able to re-create this problem from this user's host machine. By doing that, you now know that the URL name is not being resolved from Internet Explorer, and you can't ping it by the name either. But you can ping the server IP address from your limping host, and when you try this same connection to the `internal.lammle.com` server from another host nearby, it works fine, meaning the server is working fine. So, you've succeeded in isolating the problem to this specific host—yes!

 It is a huge advantage if you can watch the user try to reproduce the problem themselves, because then you know for sure whether the user is performing the operation correctly. It's a really bad idea to assume the user is typing in what they say they are.

Step 3: Determine if Anything Has Changed

Moving right along, if you can reproduce the problem, your next step is to verify what has changed and how. Drawing on your knowledge of networking, you ask yourself and your user questions like these:

Were you ever able to do this? If not, then maybe it just isn't something the hardware or software is designed to do. You should then tell the user exactly that, as well as advise them that they may need additional hardware or software to pull off what they're trying do.

If so, when did you become unable to do it? If, once upon a time, the computer was able to do the job and then suddenly could not, whatever conditions surrounded and were involved in this turn of events become extremely important. You have a really good shot at unearthing the root of the problem if you know what happened right before things changed. Just know that there's a high level of probability that the cause of the problem is directly related to the conditions surrounding the change when it occurred.

Has anything changed since the last time you could do this? This question can lead you right to the problem's cause. Seriously—the thing that changed right before the problem began happening is almost always what caused it. It's so important that if you ask it, and your user tells you, "Nothing changed… it just happened," you should rephrase the question and say something like, "Did anyone add anything to your computer?" or "Are you doing anything differently from the way you usually do it?"

Were any error messages displayed? These are basically arrows that point directly at the problem's origin, because error messages are designed by programmers for the purpose of pointing them to exactly what it is that isn't working properly in computer systems. Sometimes error messages are crystal clear, like "Disk Full"; or they can be cryptically annoying little puzzles in themselves. If you pulled the short straw and got the latter variety, it's probably best to hit the software or hardware vendor's support site, where you can usually score a translation from the "programmerese" the error message is written in, into plain English so you can get back to solving your riddle.

Are other people experiencing this problem? You've got to ask this one because the answer will definitely help you target the cause of the problem. First, try to duplicate the problem from your own workstation, because if you can't, it's likely that the issue is related to only one user or group of users—possibly their workstations. (A solid hint that this is the case is if you're being inundated with calls from a bunch of people from the same workgroup.)

Is the problem always the same? It's good to know that when problems crop up, they're almost always the same each time they occur. But their symptoms can change slightly as the conditions surrounding them change. A related question would be, "If you do x, does the problem get better or worse?" For example, ask a user, "If you use a different file, does the problem get better or worse?" If the symptoms lighten up, it's an indication that the problem is related to the original file that's being used.

 Understand that these are just a few of the questions you can use to get to the source of a problem.

Okay—so let's get back to our sample scenario. So far, you've determined that the problem is unique to one user, which tells you that the problem is specific to this one host. Confirming that is the fact that you haven't received any other calls from other users on the network.

And when watching the user attempt to reproduce the problem, you note that they're typing the address correctly. Plus, you've got an error message that leads you to believe that the problem has something to with Domain Name Service (DNS) lookups on his host. Time to go deeper…

Step 4: Establish the Most Probable Cause

After you observe the problem and isolate the cause, next on the list is to establish its most probable cause. (If you're stressing about now, don't, because though you may feel overwhelmed by all this, it truly does get a lot easier with time and experience.)

You must come up with at least one possible cause, even though it may not be completely on the money. And you don't always have to come up with it yourself. Someone else in the group may have the answer. Also, don't forget to check online sources and vendor documentation.

Again, back to our scenario, in which you've determined the cause is probably an improperly configured DNS lookup on the workstation. The next thing to do is to verify the configuration and probably reconfigure DNS on the workstation; we'll get to this solution in the next section.

Understand that there are legions of problems that can occur on a network—and I'm sorry to tell you this, but they're typically not as simple as the example we've been using. They can be, but I just don't want you to expect them to be. Always consider the physical aspects of a network, but look beyond them into the realm of logical factors like the DNS lookup issue we've been using.

The probable causes that you've got to thoroughly understand to meet the Network+ objectives are as follows:

- Port speed
- Port duplex mismatch
- Incorrect virtual local area network (VLAN)
- Incorrect IP address
- Wrong gateway
- Wrong DNS
- Wrong subnet mask

Let's talk about these logical issues, which can cause an abundance of network problems. Most of these happen because a device has been improperly configured:

Port speed   Because networks have been evolving for many years, there are various levels of speed and sophistication mixed into them—often within the same network. Most of the newest NICs can be used at 10Mbps, 100Mbps, and 1000Mbps. Most switches can support at least 10Mbps and 100Mbps, and an increasing number of switches can also support 1,000Mbps. Plus, many switches can also autosense the speed of the NIC that's connected and use different speeds on various ports. As long as the switches are allowed to autosense the port speed, it's rare to have a problem develop that results in a complete lack of communication. But if you decide to set the port speed manually, make positively sure to set the same speed on both sides of a link.

Port duplex mismatch   There are generally three duplex settings on each port of a network switch: full, half, and auto. In order for two devices to connect effectively, the duplex setting has to match on both sides of the connection. If one side of a connection is set to full and the other is set to half, they're mismatched. More elusively, if both sides are set to auto, but the devices are different, you can also end up with a mismatch because the device on one side defaults to full and the other one defaults to half.

Duplex mismatches can cause lots of network errors and even the lack of a network connection. This is partially because setting the interfaces to full duplex disables the CSMA/CD protocol. This is definitely not a problem in a network that has no hubs (and therefore no shared segments in which there could be collisions), but it can make things really ugly in a network where hubs are still being used. This means choosing your settings is based on the type of devices you have populating your network. If you have all switches and no hubs, feel free to set all interfaces to full duplex; but if you've got hubs in the mix, you have shared networks, so you're forced to keep the settings at half duplex. With all new switches produced today, leaving the speed and duplex setting to auto (the default on both switches and hosts) is the recommended way to go.

Incorrect VLAN Switches can have multiple VLANs each, and they can be connected to other switches using trunk links. As you now know, VLANs are often used to represent departments or the occupations of a group of users. This makes the configurations of security policies and network access lists much easier to manage and control. On the other hand, if a port is accidentally assigned to the wrong VLAN in a switch, it's as if that client was magically transported to another place in the network. If that happens, the security policies that should apply to the client won't anymore, and other policies will be applied to the client that never should have been. The correct VLAN port assignment of a client is as important as air; when I'm troubleshooting a single-host problem, this is the first place I look.

It's pretty easy to tell if you have a port configured with a wrong VLAN assignment. If this is the case, it won't be long before you'll get a call from some user screaming something at you that makes the building shake, like, "I can get to the Internet but I can't get to the Sales server, and I'm about to lose a huge sale. DO SOMETHING!" When you check the switch, you will invariably see that this user's port has a membership in another VLAN like Marketing, which has no access to the Sales server.

Incorrect IP address The most common addressing protocol in use today is IPv4, which provides a unique IP address for each host on a network. Client computers usually get their addresses from Dynamic Host Configuration Protocol (DHCP) servers. But sometimes, especially in smaller networks, IP addresses for servers and router interfaces are statically assigned by the network's administrator. An incorrect address on a client will keep that client from being able to communicate and may even cause a conflict with another client on the network; and a bad address on a server or router interface can be disastrous and affect a multitude of users. This is exactly why you need to be super careful to set up DHCP servers correctly and also when configuring the static IP addresses assigned to servers and router interfaces.

Wrong gateway A *gateway*, sometimes called a *default gateway* or an *IP default gateway*, is a router interface's address that's configured to forward traffic with a destination IP address that's not in the same subnet as the device itself. Let me clarify that one for you: If a device compares where a packet wants to go with the network it's currently on, and finds that the packet needs to go to another network, the router and the device will send that packet to the gateway to be forwarded to the other network. Because every device needs a valid gateway to obtain communication outside of its own network, it's going to require some careful planning when considering the gateway configuration of devices in your network.

If you're configuring a static IP address and default gateway, you need to verify the router's address. Not doing so is a really common "wrong gateway" problem that I see all the time.

Wrong DNS   DNS servers are used by networks and their clients to resolve a computer's hostname to its IP addresses and to enable clients to find the server they need to provide the resources they require, like a domain controller during the login and authentication process. Most of the time, DNS addresses are automatically configured by a DHCP server, but sometimes these addresses are statically configured instead. Because lots of applications rely on hostname resolution, a botched DNS configuration usually causes a computer's network applications to fail just like the user's applications in our example scenario.

If you can ping a host using its IP address but not its name, you probably have some type of name-resolution issue. It's probably lurking somewhere within a DNS configuration.

Wrong subnet mask   When network devices look at an IP address configuration, they see a combination of the IP address and the subnet mask. The device uses the subnet mask to establish which part of the address represents the network address and which part represents the host address. So clearly, a subnet mask that is configured wrong has the same nasty effect as a wrong IP address configuration does on communications. Again, a subnet mask is generally configured by the DHCP server; if you're going to enter it manually, make sure the subnet mask is tight or you'll end up tangling with the fallout caused by the entire address's misconfiguration.

Okay—with all that in mind, let's move on with our troubleshooting steps.

Step 5: Determine if Escalation Is Necessary

Although it's true that CompTIA doesn't expect you to fix every single network problem that could possibly happen in the universe, they actually do expect you to get pretty close to determining exactly what the problem is; and if you can't fix it, you'll be expected to know how to escalate it and to whom. You are only as good as your resources—be they your own skill set, a book like this one, other more reference-oriented technical books, the Internet, or even a guru at a call center.

I know it seems like I talked to death physical and logical issues that cause problems in a network, but trust me, with what I've taught you, you're just getting started. There's a galaxy of networking evils that we have not even touched on because they're far beyond the objectives for Network+ certification and, therefore, the scope of this book. But out there in the real world, you'll get calls about them anyway, and because you're not yet equipped to handle them yourself, you need to escalate these nasties to a senior network engineer who has the additional experience and knowledge required to resolve the problems.

Some of the calamities that you should escalate are as follows:

- Switching loops
- Routing loops
- Routing problems
- Proxy Address Resolution Protocol (ARP)
- Broadcast storms

After you escalated the problem, you are done with the 9-step trouble-shooting model and you now need to meet with the emergency response team to determine the next step.

And just as with other problems, you have to be able to identify these events, because if you can't do that, how else will you know that you need to escalate them?

Switching loops   Today's networks often connect switches with redundant links to provide for fault tolerance and load balancing. Protocols such as Spanning Tree Protocol (STP) prevent switching loops and simultaneously maintain fault tolerance. If STP fails, it takes some expertise to reconfigure and repair the network, so you just need to be concerned with being able to identify the problem so you can escalate it. Remember, when you hear users complaining that the network works fine for a while, then unexpectedly goes down for about a minute, and then goes back to being fine, it's definitely an STP convergence issue that's pretty tough to find and fix. Escalate this problem ASAP!

Routing loops   Routing protocols are often used on networks to control traffic efficiently while preventing routing loops that happen when a routing protocol hasn't been configured properly or network changes didn't get the attention they deserved. Routing loops can also happen if you or the network admin blew the static configuration and created conflicting routes through the network. This evil event affects the traffic flow for all users, and because it's pretty complicated to fix, again, it's up, up, and away with this one. You can expect routing loops to occur if your network is running old routing protocols like Routing Information Protocol (RIP) and RIPv2. Just upgrading your routing protocol to Enhanced Interior Gateway Routing Protocol (EIGRP), Open Shortest Path First (OSPF), or *Intermediate* System-to-*Intermediate* System (IS-IS) will usually take care of the problem once and for all. Anyway, escalate this problem to the router group—which hopefully is soon to be you.

Routing problems   Routing packets through the many subnets of a large enterprise while still maintaining security can be a tremendous challenge. A router's configuration can include all kinds of stuff like access lists, Network Address Translation (NAT), Port Address Translation (PAT), and even authentication protocols like Remote Authentication Dial In User Service (RADIUS) and Terminal Access Controller Access-Control System (TACACS). Particularly diabolical, errant configuration changes can trigger a domino effect that can derail traffic down the wrong path or even to come to a grinding halt and stop traversing the network completely. To identify routing problem, check to see if someone has simply set a wrong default route on a router. This can easily create routing loops—I see it all the time. These configurations can be highly complex and specific to a particular device, so they need to be escalated to the top dogs—get the problem to the best sys admin in the router group.

Proxy ARP   Address Resolution Protocol (ARP) is a service that resolves IP addresses to MAC addresses. Proxy ARP is just wrong to use in today's networks, but hosts and routers still have it on by default. The idea of Proxy ARP was to solve the problem of a host being able to have only one configured default gateway. To allow redundancy, Proxy ARP running on a router will respond to a ARP broadcast from a host that's sending a packet to a remote network—but the host doesn't have a default gateway set. So, the router responds by being the proxy for the remote host, which in turn makes the local host think the remote host is really local; as a result, the local host sends the packets to the router, which then forwards the packets to the remote host. Most of the time, in today's networks, this does not work well, if at all. Disable Proxy ARP on your routers, and make sure you have default gateways set on all your hosts. If you need router redundancy, there are much better solutions available than Proxy ARP! This is another job for the routing group.

Broadcast storms   When a switch receives a broadcast, it will normally flood the broadcast out all the ports except for the one the broadcast came in on. If STP fails between switches or is disabled by an administrator, it's possible that the traffic could continue to be flooded repeatedly throughout the switch topology. When this happens, the network can get so busy that normal traffic can't traverse the network—an event referred to as a *broadcast storm*. As you can imagine, this is a particularly gruesome thing to have to troubleshoot and fix because you need to find the one bad link that is causing the mess while the network is probably still up and running—but doing so at a heavily congested crawl. Escalate ASAP to experts!

Step 6: Create an Action Plan and Solution, Identifying Potential Effects

Finally—you can now get back to that poor user you left on hold a few steps ago and solve their problem. To do that, you need to check the DNS configuration on your host. But first, let me point out something about the neglected user's network. All hosts are using DHCP, so it's really weird that a single user is having a DNS resolution issue.

Let's look into the matter by first checking the IP configuration of the hosts that just happen to includes DNS information. You use the `ipconfig /all` command to shows the IP configuration. The `/all` switch will give you the DNS information you need:

```
Administrator: Command Prompt
Ethernet adapter Local Area Connection:

   Connection-specific DNS Suffix  . : domain.actdsltmp
   Description . . . . . . . . . . . : Intel(R) 82566MM Gigabit Network Connecti
on
   Physical Address. . . . . . . . . : 00-1E-37-D0-E9-35
   DHCP Enabled. . . . . . . . . . . : Yes
   Autoconfiguration Enabled . . . . : Yes
   Link-local IPv6 Address . . . . . : fe80::2836:c43e:274b:f08c%11(Preferred)
   IPv4 Address. . . . . . . . . . . : 192.168.0.6(Preferred)
   Subnet Mask . . . . . . . . . . . : 255.255.255.0
   Lease Obtained. . . . . . . . . . : Friday, November 14, 2008 7:21:34 AM
   Lease Expires . . . . . . . . . . : Sunday, November 16, 2008 2:39:01 PM
   Default Gateway . . . . . . . . . : 192.168.0.1
   DHCP Server . . . . . . . . . . . : 192.168.0.1
   DNS Servers . . . . . . . . . . . : 1.1.1.1
                                       2.2.2.2
   NetBIOS over Tcpip. . . . . . . . : Enabled
```

Check out the DNS entries: 1.1.1.1 and 2.2.2.2. Is this right? What are they supposed to be? You can find this out by checking the addresses on a working host, but let's check the settings on your troubled host's adapter first. Click Start, then Control Panel, then Network And Sharing Center, and then Manage Network Connections on the left side of the screen, which will take you to this screen:

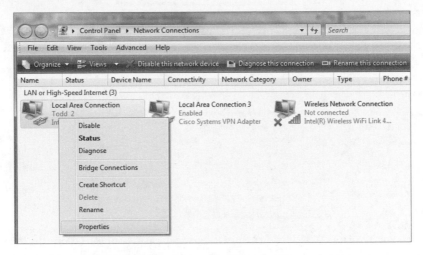

Now, click the interface in question, and click Properties. You receive this screen:

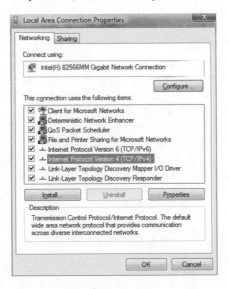

From here, you highlight Internet Protocol Version 4, and click Properties (or just double-click). From this screen, do you see what may be causing the problem?

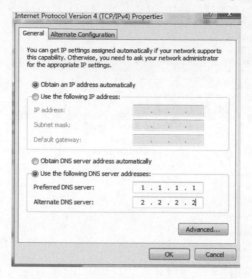

As I said, you're using DHCP right? But DNS is statically configured on this host. Interesting enough, when you set a static DNS entry on an interface, it will override the DHCP provided DNS entry. So, to fix the problem and get your user back in the game, just click Obtain DNS Server Address Automatically, and then click OK. Voila!

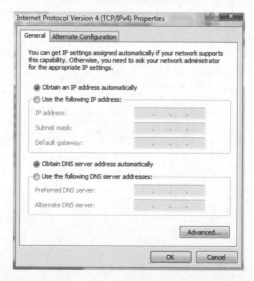

It's pretty much common sense that you should only change settings like this when you fully understand the effect your changes will have, or when you're asked to by someone who does. The incorrect configuration of these settings will disable the normal operation of your workstation; and, well, it seems that someone (the user, maybe?) did something they shouldn't have, or you wouldn't have had the pleasure of solving this problem.

> You have to be super careful when changing settings, and always check out a troubled host's network settings. Don't just assume that because they're using DHCP, someone has screwed up the static configuration.

Step 7: Implement and Test the Solution

Now that you've made your changes, you've got to follow through and test your solution to see if you really solved the problem. In this case, you ask the user to try to access the intranet server (because that's what they called about). Basically, you just ask the user to try doing whatever it was they couldn't do when they called you in the first place. If it works—sweet—problem solved. If not, try the operation yourself.

Let's take a look at the output of `ipconfig /all` and see if you received new DNS server addresses:

```
Command Prompt

Windows IP Configuration

    Host Name . . . . . . . . . . . . : globalnet-todd
    Primary Dns Suffix  . . . . . . . : globalnet.local
    Node Type . . . . . . . . . . . . : Hybrid
    IP Routing Enabled. . . . . . . . : No
    WINS Proxy Enabled. . . . . . . . : No
    DNS Suffix Search List. . . . . . : globalnet.local

Ethernet adapter Local Area Connection 3:

    Connection-specific DNS Suffix  . : globalnet.local
    Description . . . . . . . . . . . : Cisco Systems VPN Adapter
    Physical Address. . . . . . . . . : 00-05-9A-3C-78-00
    DHCP Enabled. . . . . . . . . . . : No
    Autoconfiguration Enabled . . . . : Yes
    Link-local IPv6 Address . . . . . : fe80::6cd5:2e37:bd94:1004%21(Preferred)
    IPv4 Address. . . . . . . . . . . : 10.100.10.58(Preferred)
    Subnet Mask . . . . . . . . . . . : 255.255.255.0
    Default Gateway . . . . . . . . . :
    DNS Servers . . . . . . . . . . . : 10.100.36.12
                                        10.100.36.13
    Primary WINS Server . . . . . . . : 10.100.36.13
    NetBIOS over Tcpip. . . . . . . . : Enabled
```

All good; you did. And you can test the host by trying to HTTP to the intranet server and even pinging by host name. Congratulations on solving your first trouble ticket!

If things hadn't worked out so well, you would go back to Step 4, select a new possible cause, and redo Steps 5 and 6. If this happens, keep track of what worked and what didn't so you don't make the same mistakes twice.

Step 8: Identify the Results and Effects of the Solution

A trap that any network technician can fall into is solving one problem and thinking it's all fixed without stopping to consider the possible consequences of their solution. The cure can be worse than the disease, and it's possible that your solution falls into this category. So before you fully implement the solution to a problem, make sure you totally understand the ramifications of doing so—clearly, if it causes more problems than it fixes, you should toss it and find a different solution that does no harm.

WARNING   Many people update a router's operating system or firmware just because a new version of code is released from the manufacturer. Do not do this on your production routers—just say no! Always test any new code before upgrading your production routers: Like a bad solution, sometimes the new code provides new features but creates more problems, and the cons outweigh the pros.

Step 9: Document the Solution and the Entire Process

I can't stress enough how vital network documentation is. Always document problems and solutions so that you have the information at hand when a similar problem arises in the future. With documented solutions to documented problems, you can assemble your own database of information that you can use to troubleshoot other problems. Be sure to include information like the following:

- A description of the conditions surrounding the problem
- The OS version, the software version, the type of computer, and the type of NIC
- Whether you were able to reproduce the problem
- The solutions you tried
- The ultimate solution

 Real World Scenario

Network Documentation

I don't know how many times I've gone into a place and asked where their documentation was, only to be met with a blank stare. I was recently at a small business that was experiencing network problems. The first question I asked was, "Do you have any kind of network documentation?" I got the blank stare. So, we proceeded to search through lots of receipts and other paperwork—anything we could find to help us understand the network layout and figure out exactly what was on the network. It turned out they had recently bought a WAP, and it was having trouble connecting—something that would've taken me five minutes to fix instead of searching through a mess for a couple hours!

Documentation doesn't have to look like a sleek owner's manual or anything—it can consist of a simple three-ring binder with an up-to-date network map; any receipts for network equipment; a pocket for owner's manuals; and a stack of loose-leaf paper to record services, changes, network-addressing assignments, access lists, and so on. Just this little bit of documentation can save lots of time money and prevent grief, especially in the critical first few months of a new network install.

Troubleshooting Tips

Now that you've got the basics of network troubleshooting down pat, I'm going to go over a few really handy troubleshooting tips for you to arm yourself with even further in the quest to conquer the world's networking evils.

Don't Overlook the Small Stuff

The super simple stuff (SSS) with which we opened this chapter should never be over-looked—ever! For a quick review of that section, just remember that problems are often caused by little things like a bad power switch; a power switch in the wrong position; a card or port that's not working, indicated by a link light that's not lit; or simply operator error (OE). Even the most experienced system administrator has forgotten to turn on the power, left a cable unplugged, or mistyped a username and password—not me, of course, but others…

And make sure that users get solid training for the systems they use. An ounce of prevention is worth a pound of cure, and you'll experience dramatically fewer ID10T errors this way.

Prioritize Your Problems

Being a network administrator or technician of even a fairly small network can keep you hopping, and it's pretty rare that you'll get calls for help one at a time and never be interrupted by more coming in. Closer to reality is receiving yet another call when you already have three people waiting for service. So, you've got to prioritize.

You start this process by again asking some basic questions to determine how severe the problem being reported is. Clearly, if the new call is about something little, and you already have a huge issue to deal with, you should put the new call on hold or get their info and get back to them later. This is because if you establish a good set of priorities, you'll make much better use of your time. Here's an example of the rank you probably want to give to networking problems, from highest priority to lowest:

- Total network failure (affects everyone)
- Partial network failure (affects small groups of users)
- Small network failure (affects a small, single group of users)
- Total workstation failure (single user can't work at all)
- Partial workstation failure (single user can't do most tasks)
- Minor issue (single user has problems that crop up now and then)

Mitigating circumstances can, of course, change the order of this list. For example, if the president of the company can't retrieve email, you'd take the express elevator to their office as soon as you got the call, right? And even a minor issue can move up the ladder if it's persistent enough.

Don't fall prey to thinking that simple problems are easier to deal with, because even though you may be able to bring up a crashed server in minutes, a user who doesn't know how to make columns line up in Microsoft Word could take a chunk out of your day. You'd want to put the latter problem toward the bottom of the list because of the time involved—it's a lot more efficient to solve problems for a big group of people than to fix this one user's problem immediately.

Some network administrators list all network-service requests on a chalkboard or a whiteboard. They then prioritize them based on the previously discussed criteria. Some larger companies have written support-call tracking software whose only function is to track and prioritize all network and computer problems. Use whatever method makes you comfortable, but prioritize your calls.

Check the Software Configuration

Often, network problems can be traced to software configuration, like our DNS configuration scenario; so when you're checking for software problems, don't forget to check types of configurations:

- DNS configuration
- WINS configuration
- HOSTS file
- The Registry

Software-configuration settings love to hide in places like these and can be notoriously hard to find (especially in the Registry).

Also, look for lines that have been commented out either intentionally or accidentally in text-configuration files—another place for clues. A command such as REM or REMARK, or asterisk or semicolon characters, indicates comment lines in a file.

The HOSTS file uses a pound sign (#) to indicate a comment line.

Don't Overlook Physical Conditions

You want to make sure that from a network-design standpoint, the physical environment for a server is optimized for placement, temperature, and humidity. When troubleshooting an obscure network problem, don't forget to check the physical conditions under which the network device is operating. Check for problems like these:

- Excessive heat
- Excessive humidity (condensation)

- Low humidity (leads to electrostatic discharge [ESD] problems)
- EMI/RFI problems
- ESD problems
- Power problems
- Unplugged cables

Don't Overlook Cable Problems

Cables, generally speaking, work fine once they are installed properly. If the patch cable isn't the problem, use a cable tester (not a tone generator and locator) to find the source of the problem.

Wires that are moved can be prone to breaking or shorting; and a short can happen when the wire conductor comes in contact with another conductive surface, changing the path of the electrical signal. The signal will go someplace else instead of to the intended recipient. You can use cable testers to test for many types of problems:

- Broken cables
- Incorrect connections
- Interference levels
- Total cable length (for length restrictions)
- Cable shorts
- Connector problems

 As a matter of fact, cable testers are so sophisticated that they can even indicate the exact location of a cable break, accurate to within six inches or better.

Check for Viruses

People overlook scanning for viruses because they assume that the network's virus-checking software has already picked them off. But to be effective, the software must be kept up-to-date, and updates are made available pretty much daily. You've got to run the virus-definition update utility to keep the virus-definition file current.

If you are having strange, unusual, irreproducible problems with a workstation, try scanning it with an up-to-date virus-scan utility. You'd be surprised how many times people have spent hours and hours troubleshooting a strange problem only to run a virus-scan utility, find and clean out one or more viruses, and have the problem disappear like magic.

Summary

In this chapter, you learned about all things troubleshooting, and you now know how to sleuth out and solve a lot of network problems. You learned to first check all the SSS and about how to approach problem resolution by eliminating what the problem is *not*. You learned the process of how to narrow the problem down to its basics and define it.

Next, you learned a systematic approach to troubleshooting using a nine-step trouble-shooting model to troubleshoot most of the problems you'll run into in networking. And you also learned about some resources you can use to help you during the troubleshooting process. You also learned how important documentation is to the health of your network.

Finally, I gave you a bunch of cool tips to further equip you, about prioritizing issues, checking for configuration issues, environmental factors—even hunting down viruses. As you venture out into the real world, keep these tips in mind; along with your own personal experience, they'll really help make you into an expert troubleshooter.

Exam Essentials

Know the nine troubleshooting steps, in order.   The steps, in order, are as follows:

1. Information gathering—identify symptoms and problems.

2. Identify the affected areas of the network.

3. Determine if anything has changed.

4. Establish the most probable cause.

5. Determine if escalation is necessary.

6. Create an action plan and solution, identifying potential effects.

7. Implement and test the solution.

8. Identify the results and effects of the solution.

9. Document the solution and the entire process.

Be able to identify a link light.   A link light is the small, usually green, LED on the back of a network card. This LED is typically found next to the media connector on a NIC and is usually labeled Link.

Understand how proper network-use procedures can affect the proper operation of a network.   If a user is not following a network-use procedure properly (for example, not logging in correctly), that user may report a problem where none exists. A good network troubleshooter should know how to differentiate between a network hardware/software problem and a "lack of user training" problem.

Know how to narrow down a problem to one specific area or cause.   Most problems can be traced to one specific area or cause. You must be able to determine if a problem is specific to one user or a bunch of users, specific to one computer or a bunch of computers, and related to hardware or software. The answers to these questions will give you a very specific problem focus.

Know how to detect cabling-related problems.   Generally speaking, most cabling-related problems can be traced by plugging the suspect workstation into a known, working network port. If the problem disappears (or at the very least changes significantly), the problem is related to the cabling for that workstation.

Written Lab

In this section, write the answers to the following questions:

1. What is Step 3 of the 9-step troubleshooting model?

2. What is Step 9 of the 9-step troubleshooting model?

3. How is crosstalk minimized in twisted-pair cabling?

4. If you plug a host into a switch port and the user cannot get to the server or other services they need to access, what could the problem be?

5. If you don't have the Spanning Tree Protocol (STP) running on your switches, what problem could possibly occur?

6. When a signal moves through any medium, the medium itself will degrade the signal. What is this called?

7. What is Step 4 of the 9-step troubleshooting model?

8. What is Step 5 of the 9-step troubleshooting model?

9. What are some of the problems that, if determined, should be escalated?

10. What cable issues should you know and understand for network troubleshooting?

(The answers to the Written Lab can be found following the answers to the Review Questions for this chapter.)

Review Questions

1. Which of the following are not steps in the Network+ troubleshooting model? (Choose all that apply.)

    A. Reboot the servers.

    B. Gather information.

    C. Determine if anything has changed.

    D. Determine if escalation is necessary.

    E. Document the solution and the entire process.

    F. Reboot all the routers.

2. You have a user who cannot connect to the network. What is the first thing you could check to determine the source of the problem?

    A. Workstation configuration

    B. Connectivity

    C. Patch cable

    D. Server configuration

3. A user cannot access the local intranet. Which action will not help you determine how to narrow the problem down to the intranet?

    A. Accessing the intranet from your workstation

    B. Accessing the intranet from the user's workstation as yourself

    C. Replacing the patch cable on the workstation

    D. Asking another user to access the intranet from the problem user's workstation

4. Several users can't log in to the server. Which action would help you to narrow the problem down to the workstations, network, or server?

    A. Run `tracert` from a workstation.

    B. Check the server console for user connections.

    C. Run `netstat` on all workstations.

    D. Check the network diagnostics.

5. A user can't log in to the network. She can't even connect to the Internet over the LAN. Other users in the same area aren't experiencing any problems. You attempt to log in as this user from your workstation with her username and password and don't experience any problems. However, you cannot log in with either her username or yours from her workstation. What is a likely cause of the problem?

    A. Insufficient rights to access the server

    B. A bad patch cable

    C. Server down

    D. Wrong username and password

6. A user is experiencing problems logging in to a Unix server. He can connect to the Internet over the LAN. Other users in the same area aren't experiencing any problems. You attempt logging in as this user from your workstation with his username and password and don't experience any problems. However, you cannot log in with either his username or yours from his workstation. What is a likely cause of the problem?

   A. The Caps Lock key is pressed.

   B. The network hub is malfunctioning.

   C. You have a downed server.

   D. You have a jabbering NIC.

7. You receive a call from a user who is having issues connecting to a new VPN. Which is the first step you should take?

   A. Find out what has changed

   B. Reboot the workstation

   C. Document the solution

   D. Identify the symptoms and potential causes

8. A workstation presents an error message to a user. The message states that a duplicate IP address has been detected on the network. After establishing what has changed in the network, what should be the next step using the standard troubleshooting model?

   A. Test the result.

   B. Select the most probable cause.

   C. Create an action plan.

   D. Identify the results and effects of the solution.

9. You have gathered information on a network issue and determined the affected areas of the network. What is your next step in resolving this issue?

   A. You should implement what the best solution for the issue is

   B. You should test the best solution for the issue

   C. You should check to see if there have been any recent changes to this affected part of the network.

   D. You should consider any negative impact to the network that might be caused by a solution

10. A user calls you, reporting a problem logging in to the corporate intranet. You can access the website without problems using the user's username and password. At your request, the user has tried logging in from other workstations but has been unsuccessful. What is the most likely cause of the problem?

    A. The user is logging in incorrectly.

    B. The network is down.

    C. The intranet server is locked up.

    D. The server is not routing packets correctly to that user's workstation.

11. You have just implemented a solution and you want to celebrate your success. But what should you do next before you start your celebration?

    A. Gather more information about the issue

    B. Document the issue and the solution that was implemented

    C. Test the solution and identify other effects it may have

    D. Escalate the issue

12. You can ping the local router and web server that a local user is trying to reach, but you cannot reach the web page that resides on that server. From Step 4 of the troubleshooting model, what is a possible problem that would lead to this situation?

    A. Your network cable is unplugged.

    B. There is a problem with your browser.

    C. Your NIC has failed.

    D. The web server is unplugged.

13. When troubleshooting an obscure network problem, what physical conditions should be reviewed to make sure the network device is operating correctly? (Choose all that apply.)

    A. Excessive heat

    B. Low/excessive humidity

    C. ESD problems

    D. All of the above

14. Which of the following is not a basic physical issue that can occur on a network when a user is connected via cable?

    A. Crosstalk

    B. Shorts

    C. Open impedance mismatch

    D. DNS configurations

15. You are troubleshooting a LAN switch and have identified the symptoms. What is the next step you should take?

    A. Escalate the issue

    B. Create an action plan

    C. Implement the solution

    D. Determine the scope of the problem

16. A user calls you, complaining that he can't access the corporate intranet web server. You try the same address, and you receive a Host Not Found error. Several minutes later, another user reports the same problem. You can still send email and transfer files to another server. What is the most likely cause of the problem?

    A. The hub is unplugged.

    B. The server is not routing protocols to your workstation.

    C. The user's workstation is not connected to the network.

    D. The web server is down.

17. You have implemented and tested a solution and identified any other effects the solution may have, what is your next step?

    A. Create an action plan

    B. Close the case and head home for the day

    C. Reboot the Windows server

    D. Document the solution

18. Users are reporting that they can access the internet but not the internal company website. Which of the following is the most likely problem?

    A. The DNS entry for the server is non-authoritative

    B. The intranet server is down

    C. The DNS address handed out by DHCP is incorrect

    D. The default gateway is incorrect

19. Several users have complained about the server's poor performance as of late. You know that the memory installed in the server is sufficient. What could you check to determine the source of the problem?

    A. Server's NIC link light

    B. Protocol analyzer

    C. Performance-monitoring tools

    D. Server's System Log file

20. You lose power to your computer room and the switches in your network do not come back up when everything is brought online. After you have identified the affected areas, established the cause and escalated this problem, what do you do next?

    A. Start to implement a solution to get those users back online asap

    B. Create an action plan and solution

    C. Meet with the emergency response team to determine the next step.

    D. Copy all the working routers configurations to the non-working switches

Answers to Review Questions

1. A, F. Rebooting servers and routers are not part of the troubleshooting model.

2. B. You need to check basic connectivity. The link light indicates that the network card is making a basic-level connection to the rest of the network. It is a very easy item to check, and if the link light is not lit, it is usually a very simple fix (like plugging in an unplugged cable).

3. C. Replacing the patch cable is a much more difficult troubleshooting step than testing intranet access from different workstations. Because workstations are usually grouped together, it would be easier to have many people first try to access at once than to crawl around behind a desk or cubicle to replace a patch cable.

4. B. Although all of these are good tests for network connectivity, checking the server console for user connections will tell you whether other users are able to log into the server. If they can, the problem is most likely related to one of those users' workstations. If they can't, the problem is either the server or network connection. This helps narrow down the problem.

5. B. Because of all the tests given and their results, you can narrow the problem down to the network connectivity of that workstation. And because no other users in her area are having the same problem, it can't be the hub or server. You can log in as the user from your workstation, so you know it isn't a rights issue or username/password issue. The only possible answer listed is a bad patch cable.

6. A. Because other users in the same area aren't having a problem, it can't be a downed server, network hub, or jabbering NIC. And because both you and the user can't log in, more than likely it's a problem specific to that workstation. The only one that would affect your ability to log in from that station is the Caps Lock key being pressed. That will cause the password to be in all uppercase (which most server operating systems treat as a different password), and thus it will probably be rejected.

7. D. Since this is a new connection, you need to start by troubleshooting and identify the symptoms and potential causes.

8. B. According to the Network+ troubleshooting model, the next step would be Step 4, establishing the most probably cause.

9. C. After determining the affected area, you need to find out if any changes has taken place.

10. A. Because the user can't log in correctly from any machine, more than likely he is using the wrong procedure for logging in. Because no one else is having that problem (including yourself), the problem must be related to that user.

11. C. After you have implemented a solution, you need to test if the solution works and identify other effects it may have.

12. B. Because you cannot reach the web page that resides on the server, the problem is most likely related to a problem to your browser.

13. D. From a design standpoint, the physical environment for a server should be optimized for items such as placement, temperature, and humidity. When troubleshooting, don't forget to check the physical conditions under which the network device is operating. Check for problems such as those mentioned here as well as EMI/RFI problems, power problems, and unplugged cables.

14. D. Because most of today's networks still consist of large amounts of copper cable, networks can suffer from the physical issues that have plagued all networks since the very beginning of networking (and the answers here are not a complete list). Newer technologies and protocols have lessened these issues but have not resolved them completely.

15. A. Once you have determined that the switch is either the problem, or the configuration of the switch is the problem, you need to escalate the issue.

16. D. Because other people are experiencing the problem, most likely the problem is either network or server related. Because you can transfer files to and from another server, it can't be the network. Thus, the problem is related to the web server.

17. D. After investigating the problem thoroughly and successfully testing and resolving an issue, you need to document the solution.

18. B. Since users can get to the internet, this means the DNS server is working, and they have the correct default gateway. The intranet server is probably down.

19. C. Performance-monitoring tools can give you an idea how busy the server and the rest of the network are. These tools use graphs to indicate how much traffic is going through that server.

20. C. Once you escalate the problem, you are done with the 9-step model. Meet with the escalation team to determine the next step.

Answers to Written Lab

1. Determine if anything has changed in the network.

2. Document the solution and the entire process.

3. Network designers minimize crosstalk inside network cables by twisting the wire pairs together, putting them at a 90 degree angle to each other.

4. The port has the wrong VLAN assignment.

5. Switching loops. If someone plugs two cables between switches, and STP is not running, a switching loop will occur.

6. Attenuation

7. Establish the most probable cause.

8. Determine if escalation is necessary.

9. Switching loops, routing loops, routing problems, Proxy ARP, broadcast storms

10. Crosstalk, attenuation, collisions, shorts, open impedance mismatch, interference

Chapter

20

Management, Monitoring, and Optimization

THE FOLLOWING COMPTIA NETWORK+ EXAM OBJECTIVES ARE COVERED IN THIS CHAPTER:

✓ **4.2 Identify types of configuration management documentation**

- Wiring schematics

- Physical and logical network diagrams

- Baselines

- Policies, procedures, and configurations

- Regulations

✓ **4.3 Given a scenario, evaluate the network based on configuration management documentation**

- Compare wiring schematics, physical and logical network diagrams, baselines, policies and procedures, and configurations to network devices and infrastructure

- Update wiring schematics, physical and logical network diagrams, configurations, and job logs as needed

✓ **4.4 Conduct network monitoring to identify performance and connectivity issues using the following:**

- Network monitoring utilities (e.g., packet sniffers, connectivity software, load testing, throughput testers)

- System logs, history logs, event logs

✓ **4.5 Explain different methods and rationales for network performance optimization**

- Methods:
  - QoS
  - Traffic shaping
  - Load balancing
  - High availability
  - Caching engines
  - Fault tolerance
- Reasons:
  - Latency sensitivity
  - High bandwidth applications
    - VoIP
    - Video applications
- Uptime

If you didn't just skip to the end of this book, you've trekked through enough material to know that without a doubt, the task of designing, implementing, and maintaining a state-of-the-art network doesn't happen magically. Ending up with a great network requires some really solid planning before you buy even one device for it. And planning includes thoroughly analyzing your design for potential flaws and optimizing configurations everywhere you can to maximize the network's future throughput and performance. If you blow it in this phase, trust me—you'll pay dearly later in bottom-line costs and countless hours consumed troubleshooting and putting out the fires of faulty design.

Start planning by creating an outline that precisely delimits all goals and business requirements for the network, and refer back to it often to ensure you don't deliver a network that falls short of your client's present needs or fails to offer the scalability to grow with those needs. Drawing out your design and jotting down all the relevant information really helps in spotting weaknesses and faults. If you have a team, make sure everyone on it gets to examine the design and evaluate it, and keep that network plan up throughout the installation phase. Hang on to it after implementation has been completed as well, because having it is like having the keys to the kingdom—it will enable you to efficiently troubleshoot any issues that could arise after everything is in place, up, and running.

High-quality documentation should include a baseline for network performance, because you and your client need to know what "normal" looks like in order to detect problems before they develop into disasters. Don't forget to verify that the network conforms to all internal and external regulations and that you've developed and itemized solid management procedures and security policies for future network administrators to refer to and follow.

I'll begin this chapter by going over the fundamentals of things like plans, diagrams, baselines, rules, and regulations, and then move on to covering critical hardware and software utilities you should have in your problem resolution arsenal, like packet sniffers, throughput testers, connectivity packages, and even different types of event logs on your servers. And because even the best designs usually need a little boost after they've been up and running for a while, I'll wrap things up by telling you about some cool ways you can tweak things to really jack up a network's performance, optimize its data throughput and, well, keep it all humming along as efficiently and smoothly as possible.

For up-to-the-minute updates for this chapter, please see www.lammle.com or www.sybex.com/go/comptianetwork+studyguide.

Managing Network Documentation

Okay, I'll admit it—creating network documentation is one of my least favorite tasks in network administration. It just isn't as exciting to me as learning about the coolest new technology or tackling and solving a challenging problem. Part of it may be that I figure I know my networks well enough—after all, I installed and configured them, so if something comes up, it should be easy to figure it out and fix it, right? And most of the time I can do that; but as networks get bigger and more complex, it gets harder and harder to remember it all. Plus, it's integral for my clients to have seriously solid documentation in hand to refer to after I've left the scene and turned their network over to them. So while I'll admit that creating documentation isn't something I get excited about, I know from experience that having it around is critical when problems come up—for myself and for my client's technicians and administrators, who may not have been part of the installation process and simply aren't familiar with the system.

So, no whining! Begrudgingly or not, we're going to create some sweet documentation. Because you probably don't want to redo it, it's a really good idea to keep it safe in at least three forms:

- An electronic copy that you can easily modify after configuration changes

- A hard copy in a binder of some sort, stored in an easily accessible location

- A copy on an external drive to keep in a really safe place (even offsite) in case something happens to the other two or the building or part of it burns to the ground

Why the hard copy, you ask? Well, what if the computer storing the electronic copy crashes and burns just when a major crisis develops? Good thing you have the paper on hand! Plus, sometimes you'll be troubleshooting on the run—maybe literally, as in running down the hall to the disaster's origin. Having that binder containing key configuration information on board could save you a lot of time and trouble; plus, it's also handy for making notes to yourself as you troubleshoot. And depending on the size of the intranet and the amount of people staffing the IT department, you may even need to have several hard copies. Just always make sure they're only checked out by staff who are cleared to have them, and that they're all returned to a secure location at the end of each shift. You definitely don't want that information in the wrong hands.

Now that I have (I hope) got you totally convinced that you need to have documentation, let's take a look into the different documentation types so you can learn how to assemble it. Network documentation basically falls into three categories:

- Schematics and diagrams

- Baselines

- Policies, procedures, and regulations

Schematics and Diagrams

No, reading network documentation can't exactly compete with racing your friends on jet skis, but it's really not that bad. It's better than eating canned spinach, and sometimes it's actually interesting to check out schematics and diagrams—especially when they describe innovative, elegant designs, or when you're hunting down clues needed to solve an intricate problem with an elusive solution. If something isn't working between point A and point B, I can't tell you how many times a solid diagram of the network that precisely describes exactly what exists between point A and point B has totally saved the day. Other times these tools come in handy is when you need to extend your network and you want a clear picture of how the expanded version will look and work. Will the new addition cause one part of the network to become bogged down while another remains underutilized? You get the idea.

Diagrams can be simple sketches created while brainstorming or troubleshooting on the fly; or they can be highly detailed, refined illustrations created with some of the flashy software packages available today, like Microsoft Visio, SmartDraw, and a host of computer-aided design (CAD) programs. Some of the more complex varieties, especially CAD programs, are super pricey. But whatever the tool that's used to draw pictures about our networks, they basically fall into these three groups:

- Wiring diagrams/schematics
- Physical network diagrams
- Logical network diagrams

Wiring Schematics

Wireless is definitely the wave of the future, but for now even the most extensive wireless networks have a wired backbone they rely on to connect them to the rest of humanity.

That skeleton is made up of cabled and other physical media like coax, fiber, and twisted pair. Surprisingly, it is the latter—specifically, unshielded twisted pair (UTP)—that screams to be pictured in a diagram. You'll see why in a minute. To help you follow me, let's review what we learned in Chapter 3, "Networking Topologies, Connectors, and Wiring Standards." Let's start by checking out Figure 20.1 (a diagram!) that pictures the fact that UTP cables use a Registered Jack (RJ)-45 connector.

FIGURE 20.1   RJ-45 connector

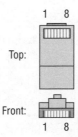

Okay—what we see here is that pin 1 is on the left and pin 8 is on the right, so clearly, within your UTP cable, you need to make sure the right wires get to the right pins. No worries if you got your cables premade from the store, but if you make them yourself because it saves money and allows you to customize cable lengths (wise), this is really important. Table 20.1 matches the colors for the wire associated with each pin, based on the Electronic Industries Association / Telecommunications Industry Alliance EIA/TIA 568B wiring standard.

TABLE 20.1   Standard EIA/TIA 568B wiring

Pin	Color
1	White/Orange
2	Orange
3	White/Green
4	Blue
5	White/Blue
6	Green
7	White/Brown
8	Brown

Standard drop cables or *patch cables* have the pins in the same order on both connectors. If you're connecting a computer to another computer directly, you should already know that you need a *crossover cable* that has one connector with flipped wires—specifically, pins 1 and 3, and pins 2 and 6 get switched to ensure that the send port from one computer's Network Interface Card (NIC) gets attached to the receive port on the other computer's NIC. Crossover cables were also used to connect older routers, switches, and hubs through their uplink ports; Figure 20.2 shows you what this would look like.

 The crossover cable shown in Figure 20.2 is for connections up to 100Base-TX. If you are using 1000Base-T4, all four pairs of wires get crossed at the opposite end, meaning pins 4 and 7 and pins 5 and 8 get crossed as well.

 The Automatic MDI/MDI+ Configuration standard (an optional feature of the 1000Base-T standard) makes the need for crossover cables between gigabit-capable interfaces a thing of the past.

FIGURE 20.2   Two ends of a crossover cable

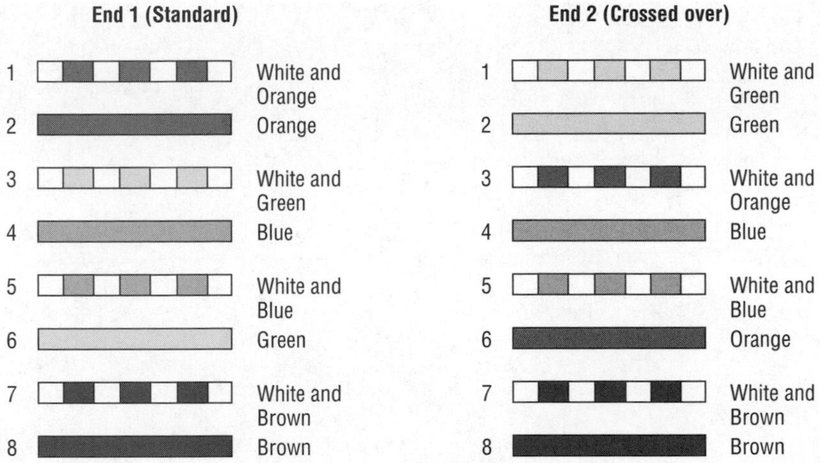

End 1 (Standard)		End 2 (Crossed over)	
1	White and Orange	1	White and Green
2	Orange	2	Green
3	White and Green	3	White and Orange
4	Blue	4	Blue
5	White and Blue	5	White and Blue
6	Green	6	Orange
7	White and Brown	7	White and Brown
8	Brown	8	Brown

This is where having a diagram is as good as gold. Let's say you're troubleshooting a network and discover connectivity problems between two hosts. Because you've got the map, you know the cable running between them just happens to be a brand new custom-made one, so you go there immediately knowing that cable probably wasn't made well and is causing the snag.

Another reason it's so important to diagram all things wiring is that all wires have to plug in somewhere, and it's really good to know where that is. Whether it's into a hub, a switch, a router, a workstation, or the wall, you positively need to know the who, what, where, when, and how of the way the wiring is attached.

After adding a new cable segment on your network you need to update the wiring schematics.

For medium to large networks, devices like hubs, switches, and routers are rack-mounted and would look something like the switches in Figure 20.3.

Knowing someone or something's name is important because it helps us differentiate between people and things—especially when communicating with each other. If you want to be specific, you can't just say, "You know that router in the rack?" This is why coming up with a good naming system for all the devices living in your racks will be invaluable for ensuring that your, err, wires don't get crossed (sorry!). Figure 20.3 displays switches with labels taped on them to designate them Sales and Marketing (names not displayed in the picture), which indicates they're located in Sales and Marketing, respectively. Last, you can see on some of the cables that they are marked XO for crossover.

FIGURE 20.3   Rack-mounted switches

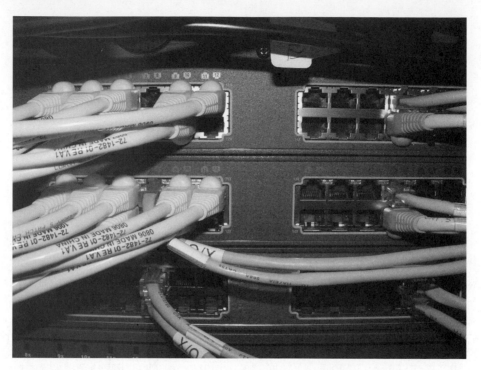

 Real World Scenario

Avoiding Confusion

Naming your network devices is no big deal, but for some reason, coming up with systems for naming devices and numbering connections can really stress people out.

Let me ease the pain. Let's say your network has two racks of switches, creatively named Block A and Block B. (Sounds like a prison, I know, but it's just to keep things simple for this example. In the real world, you can come up with whatever naming system works for you.)

Anyway, I'm going to use the letters FETH for FastEthernet; and because each rack has six switches, I'm going to number them (surprise!) 1–6. Because we read from left to right, it's intuitive to number the ports on each switch that way, too.

Having a solid naming system makes thing so much more efficient—even if it's a bit of a hassle to create. For instance, if you were the system administrator in this example, and suddenly all computers connected to FETHB-3 couldn't access any network resources, you would have a pretty good idea of where to look first, right?

Okay, I know it probably seems like we're edging over into obsessive-compulsive disorder territory, but stay with me here; in addition to labeling, well, everything so far, you should really label both ends of your cables, too. If something happens (earthquake, tsunami, temper tantrum, even repairs), and more than one cable gets unplugged at the same time, it can get messy scrambling to reconnect them from memory—fast.

Physical Network Diagrams

A *physical network diagram* contains all the physical devices and connectivity paths on your network and should accurately picture how your network physically fits together in detail. Again, I know it seems like overkill, but ideally, your network diagram should list and map everything you would need to rebuild your network from scratch if you had to. This is actually what this type of diagram is designed for. However, another example of physical network diagram is the firmware revision on all the switches and access points in your network. Besides having your physical network detailed, you need to understand the connections, types of hardware, and their firmware revisions. This document is very helpful in troubleshooting.

If you can't diagram everything, at least make sure all network devices are listed. As I said, physical network diagrams can run from simple, hand-drawn models to insanely complex monsters created by software packages like SmartDraw, Visio, and AutoCAD. Figure 20.4 shows a simple diagram that most of us could draw by hand.

For the artistically impaired, or if you just want a flashier version, Figure 20.5 exhibits a more complex physical diagram. This is an actual sample of what SmartDraw can do for you, and you can get it at www.smartdraw.com. In addition, Microsoft Visio provides many or possibly more of these same functions

FIGURE 20.4   Simple network physical diagram

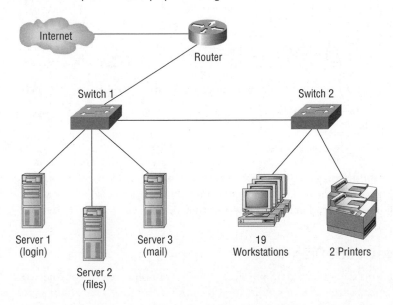

FIGURE 20.5   Network diagram with firewalls from SmartDraw

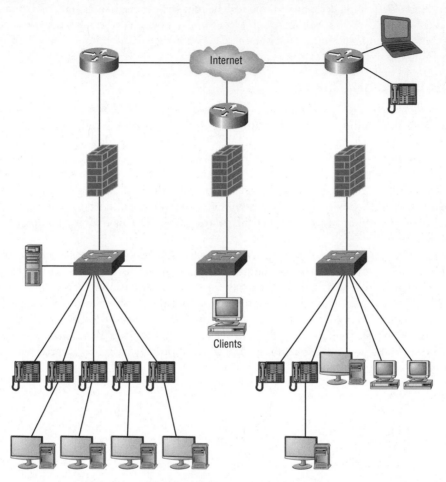

Clients

My last example, also courtesy of SmartDraw, includes diagrams of hardware racks, as revealed in Figure 20.6.

Don't throw anything at me, but I need to bring up one last thing: Never forget to mirror any changes you make to your actual network in the network's diagram. Think of it like an updated snapshot. If you give the authorities your college buddy's baby picture after he goes missing, will that really help people recognize him? Not without the help of some high-tech, age-progression software, that's for sure—and they don't make that for networks, so it's better to just keep things up to date.

Logical Network Diagrams

Physical diagrams depict how data physically flows from one area of your network to the next, but a *logical network diagram* includes things like protocols, configurations, addressing schemes, access lists, firewalls, types of applications, and so on, that apply logically to your network. Figure 20.7 shows what a logical network diagram could look like.

FIGURE 20.6   Hardware-rack diagram from SmartDraw

Rack Diagram

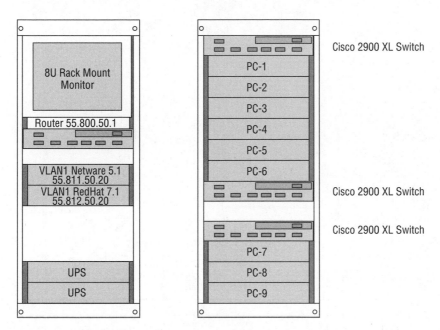

And just as you mirror any physical changes you make to the network, like adding devices or even just a cable, on your physical diagram, you map logical changes like creating a new subnet, virtual local area network (VLAN) or security zone on your logical network diagram as well. It is important that you keep this oh-so-important document up to date.

Baselines

In networking, *baseline* can refer to the standard level of performance of a certain device or to the normal operating capacity for your whole network. For instance, a specific server's baseline describes norms for factors like how busy its processors are, how much of the memory it uses, and how much data usually goes through the NIC at a given time.

A network baseline delimits the amount of available bandwidth available and when. For networks and networked devices, baselines include information about four key components:

- Processor
- Memory

- Hard-disk (or other storage) subsystem
- Network adapter or subsystem

FIGURE 20.7 Logical network diagram

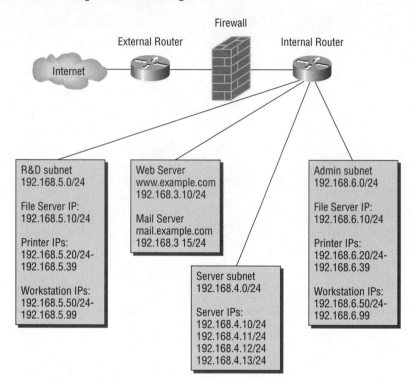

After everything is up and running, it's a good idea to establish performance baselines on all vital devices and your network in general. To do this, measure things like network usage at three different strategic times to get an accurate assessment. For instance, peak usage usually happens around eight a.m. Monday through Friday, or whenever most people log in to the network in the morning. After hours or on weekends is often when usage is the lowest. Knowing these values can help you troubleshoot *bottlenecks* or determine why certain system resources are more limited than they should be. Knowing what your baseline is can even tell you if someone's complaints about the network running like a slug are really valid—nice!

It's good to know that you can use network-monitoring software to establish baselines. Even some server operating systems come with software to help with network monitoring, which can help find baselines as well.

In my experience, it's wise to re-baseline network performance at least once a year. And always pinpoint new performance baselines after any major upgrade to your network's infrastructure.

Policies, Procedures, and Regulations

It's up to us, individually and corporately, to nail down exactly what solid guidelines for *policies* and *procedures* for network installation and operation should include. Some organizations are bound by regulations that also affect how they conduct their business, and that kind of thing clearly needs to be involved in their choices. But let me take a minute to make sure you understand the difference between policies and procedures.

Policies govern how the network is configured and operated as well as how people are expected to behave on it. They're in place to direct things like how users access resources, and which employees and groups get various types of network access and/or privileges. Basically, policies give people guidelines as to what they are expected to do. Procedures are precise descriptions of the appropriate steps to follow in a given situation, such as when an employee is terminated, or what to do in the event of a natural disaster. They often dictate precisely how to execute policies.

Of note, one of the most important aspects of any policies or procedures is that they're given high-level management support, because neither will be very effective if there aren't any consequences for not following the rules.

I talked extensively about security policies in Chapter 14, "Network Threats and Mitigation," so if you're drawing a blank, you can go back there for details. Here's a summary list of factors that most policies cover:

- Clean-desk policies

- Network access (who, what, and how)

- Acceptable-use policy

- Disposal of network equipment

- Use of recording equipment

- How passwords are managed (length and complexity required, and how often they need to be changed)

- Types of security hardware in place

- How often to do backups and other fault-tolerant measures

- What to do with user accounts after an employee leaves the company

Procedures are the actions to be taken in specific situations:

- Disciplinary action to be taken if a policy is broken

- What to do during an audit

- How issues are reported to management

- What to do when someone has locked themselves out of their account

- How to properly install or remove software on servers

- What to do if files on the servers suddenly appear to be "missing" or altered

- How to respond when a network computer has a virus

- Actions to take if it appears that a hacker has broken into the network

- Actions to take if there is a physical emergency like a fire or flood

Okay—so you get the idea, right? For every policy on your network, there should be a credible related procedure that clearly dictates the steps to take in order to fulfill it. And you know that policies and procedures are as unique as the wide array of companies and organizations that create and employ them. But all this doesn't mean you can't borrow good ideas and plans from others and tweak them a bit to meet your requirements.

 An example of a network access policy is using a biometric lock on the door to the server room.

In contrast, *regulations* are rules imposed on your organization by an outside agency, like a certifying board or a government entity, and they're usually totally rigid and non-mutable. The list of possible regulations that your company could be subjected to is so exhaustively long there's no way I can include it in this book. Different regulations exist for different types of organizations depending on if they're corporate, non-profit, scientific, educational, legal, governmental, and so on, and they also vary by where that organization is located.

For instance, U.S. governmental regulations vary by county and state, federal regulations are piled on top of those, and many other countries have multiple regulatory bodies as well. The Sarbanes-Oxley Act of 2002 (Sar-Ox) is an example of a regulation system imposed on all publicly traded companies in the United States. Its main goal was to ensure corporate responsibility and sound accounting practices, and although that may not sound like it would have much of an effect on your IT department, it does, because a lot of the provisions in this act target the retention and protection of data. Believe me, something as innocent sounding as deleting old emails could get you in trouble—if any of them could've remotely had a material impact on the company's financial disclosures, deleting them could actually be breaking the law. All good to know—be aware, and be careful.

I'm not going to give you a laundry list of regulations for you to memorize here, but I will tell you that IT regulations center around something known as the CIA triad:

Confidentiality   Only authorized users have access to the data.

Integrity   The data is accurate and complete.

Availability   Authorized users have access to the data when access is needed.

Also, one of the most commonly applied regulations is the ISO/IEC 27002 standard for information security, previously known as ISO 17799, and renamed in 2007. It was developed by the International Organization for Standardization (ISO) and the International Electrotechnical Commission (IEC), and it is based on British Standard (BS) 7799-1:1999.

The official title of ISO/IEC 27002 is *Information technology - Security techniques - Code of practice for information security management.* Although it's beyond our scope to get into the details of this standard, know that it covers 12 main areas:

- Risk assessment
- Security policy
- Organization of information security

- Asset management
- Human-resources security
- Physical and environmental security
- Communications and operations management
- Access control
- Information systems acquisition, development, and maintenance
- Information security incident management
- Business-continuity management
- Compliance

So what do you take with you from this? Your mission is clear. Know the regulations your company is expected to comply with, and make sure your IT policies and procedures are totally in line with any regulations so it's easy for you to comply with them. No sense getting hauled off to jail because you didn't archive an email, right?

Monitoring the Network and Optimizing Its Performance

We've talked about how important creating a good plan for your network design is to its ultimate success, but I still have to tell you that no matter how much time and energy you put into your plan, it's not going to be perfect. To be real, you'll still probably go through a challenge, or five. Not to discourage you—working thoroughly through the planning stage definitely pays off big-time; it's just not possible to foresee everything. Plus, things can always get better, right? There will always be ways to improve and optimize your network's performance.

And those two things are exactly what we're going to focus on next. First, I'll show you some cool ways to monitor your network and nail its problem areas through using a variety of logs on your servers. After that, we'll get into the skinny on how to optimize your system's performance.

Network Monitoring and Logging

There are a lot of ways to find out what's really going on within your network. Most administrators opt to directly keep tabs on network performance by looking at important factors like data rates and available bandwidth, using the many tools on the market designed to help with that. Another good strategy for assessing a network's health and well-being is via the more indirect route of monitoring the logs that your server operating systems keep. These can help you spot problems on your physical network as well as services or applications that aren't running properly and that could eventually bring the network or its resources down and make your users really unhappy.

Network Monitoring

Some key network-monitoring tools and diagnostic utilities around today are software additions that run on an existing server operating system like Windows Server 2008 or Unix. Others are standalone hardware devices that you plug into your network, but both are basically the packet sniffers we talked about back in Chapter 14. Although it's true that hackers can and do use sniffers to capture network traffic and gather data for an attack, we make good use of them, too. And strange but true, being a bit of a hacker yourself can make you a much better sys admin—knowing your enemies and their methods can help you find the same holes they would use for evil and use those technique to plug security holes and even optimize your network's performance.

Packet sniffers allow you to examine network traffic down to details of individual packets. You can put the packet's header under the microscope: It contains vital information about the protocol being used to encapsulate it, plus the source and destination IP addresses. This is super-valuable information—if I'm seeing the speed of traffic on a specific segment grind to a crawl, one of first the things I'll look for is only one IP address that's spewing tons of data. If so, it could mean that I've got a failing network adapter, because a common symptom of a dying NIC is to become extremely "chatty" by sending out broadcast packets and clogging things to the point that legitimate traffic can't get through. Like getting a deluge of junk mail and being forced to read every last bit of it, a broadcast packet is technically addressed to everyone, meaning that all the other NICs on the segment have to stop and read their junk—not so good.

 Good news—routers are, by default, configured to prevent broadcasts from going from one segment to another. Most switches sold today are also able to prevent broadcasts from spreading to multiple network segments, but not by default.

When you hear people refer to things like *load testing*, *connectivity testing*, and *throughput testing*, they're really talking about network monitoring. You'll also hear network monitors referred to as *protocol analyzers*. Microsoft has a graphical utility called Network Monitor that can be used to capture network traffic. The current version is 3.2, and it's supported by Windows XP, Vista, Server 2003, and Server 2008. You can download it from Microsoft's website, but for it to work, your network adapter must be able to work in promiscuous mode (yes, you read that right!). Several third parties specialize in producing network monitors; for example, Fluke Networks, which makes some cool tools like the OptiView Network Analyzer.

Server Logs

Windows Server 2003 and 2008 (and most other Windows operating systems) come with a tool called Event Viewer that provides you with several logs containing vital information about events happening on your computer. Other server operating systems have similar logs, and many connectivity devices like routers and switches also have graphical logs that gather statistics on what's happening to them. Figure 20.8 shows an Event Viewer System Log display from a Windows Server 2003 machine

FIGURE 20.8   Windows Event Viewer System Log

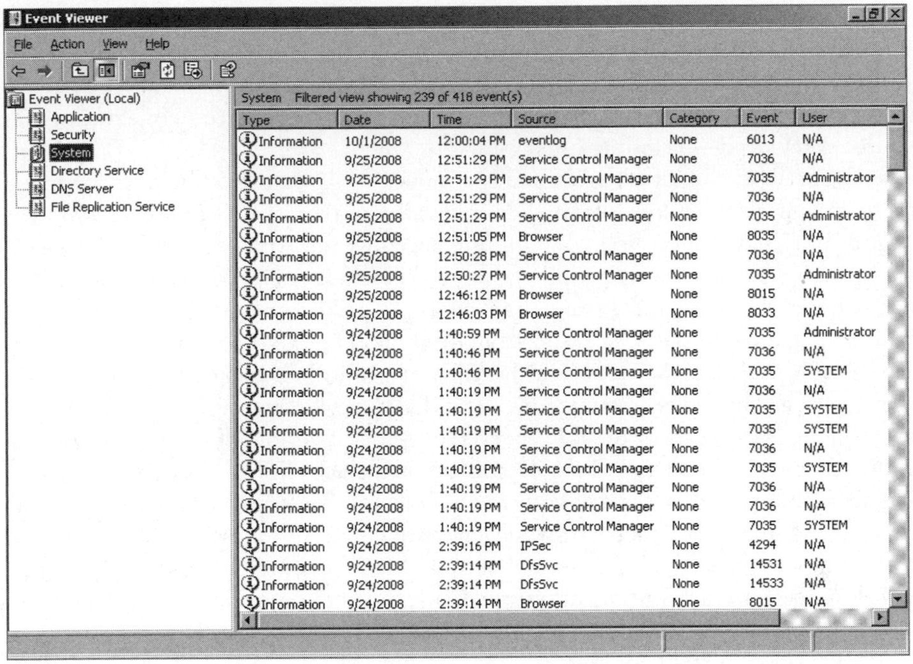

On Windows servers, a minimum of three separate logs hold different types of information:

Application   Contains events triggered by applications or programs determined by their programmers. Examples include LiveUpdate, the Microsoft Office suite, and SQL and Exchange servers.

Security   Contains security events like valid or invalid logon attempts and potential security problems. By default, it's not enabled, so you've got to set it up manually.

System   Contains events generated by Windows system components, including drivers and services that started or failed to start.

The basic "Big Three" can give us lots of juicy information about who's logging on, who's accessing the computer, and which services are running properly (or not). If you want to find out whether your Dynamic Host Configuration Protocol (DHCP) server started up its DHCP service properly, just check out its system log. Because the computer depicted in Figure 20.8 is configured as a domain controller, its Event Viewer serves up three more logs: Directory Service, DNS Server, and File Replication Service, for a total of six.

Windows 2000 Server and Windows Server 2003 came with System Monitor—another graphical tool used to create network baselines, provide performance logs, and identify bottlenecks. And Windows Server 2008 includes a new monitoring and optimization tool called System Center Operations Manager 2007, also known as OpsMgr.

Reasons to Optimize Your Network's Performance

So why do we have networks, anyway? I don't mean this in a historical sense, I mean pragmatically. The reason they've become such precious resources is that as our world has become smaller and more connected, we need a way to keep in touch like never before. Networks make accessing resources easy for people who can't be in the same location as the resources they need—including other people.

In essence, networks of all types are really complex tools we use to facilitate communication from afar and to allow lots of us to access the resources we need to keep up with the demands imposed on us in today's lightning paced world. And use them we do—a lot. And when you have many, many people trying to access one resource like a valuable file server or a shared database, our systems can get as bogged down and clogged as a freeway at rush hour. Just as road rage can result from driving on one of those not-so-expressways, frustrated people can direct some serious hostility at you if the same thing happens when they're trying to get somewhere using a network that's crawling along at snail speed.

This is why optimizing performance is in everyone's best interest—it keeps you and you network's users happily humming along. Optimization includes things like splitting up network segments, stopping unnecessary services on servers, offloading one server's work onto another, and upgrading outmoded hardware devices to newer, faster models. I'll get to exactly how to make that happen coming up soon; but in this next section, I'm going to talk about the theories behind performance optimization and even more about the reasons why you want to make sure performance is at its best.

In a perfect world, there would be unlimited bandwidth; but in reality, you're more likely to find Bigfoot than that. So, it's helpful to have some great strategies up your sleeve.

If you look at what computers are used for today, there's a huge difference between the files we transfer now versus those transferred even three to five years ago. Now, we do things like watch movies online without them stalling, and we can send humongous email attachments. Video teleconferences are more common than Starbucks locations—well, almost. The point is that the files we transfer today are really huge compared to what we sent back and forth just a few years ago. And although bandwidth has increased to allow us to do what we do, there are still limitations that cause network performance to suffer miserably. Let's start with a few reasons why you need to carefully manage whatever amount of precious bandwidth you've got.

Latency Sensitivity

Most of us have clicked to open an application or clicked a web link only to have the computer just sit there staring back at us, helplessly hanging. That sort of lag comes when the resources needed to open the program or take us to the next page are not fully available. That kind of lag on a network is called *latency*—the time between when data is requested and the moment it actually gets delivered. The more latency, the longer the delay, and the longer you have to stare blankly back at your computer screen, hoping something happens soon.

Latency affects some programs more than others. If you are sending an email, it may be annoying to have to wait a few seconds for the email server to respond, but that type of delay isn't likely to cause physical harm to you or a loved one. Applications that are adversely affected by latency are said to have high *latency sensitivity*. A common example of this is online gaming. Although it may not mean actual life or death, playing certain online games with significant delays can mean the untimely demise of your character—and you won't even know it. Worse, it can affect the entire experience for those playing with you, which can get you booted from some game servers. On a much more serious level, applications like remote surgery also have high latency sensitivity.

High-Bandwidth Applications

Many of the applications we now use over the network would have been totally unserviceable in the past because of the high amount of bandwidth they consume. And even though technology is constantly improving to give us more bandwidth, developers are in hot pursuit, developing new applications that gobble up that bandwidth as soon as it becomes—even in advance of it becoming—available. A couple of good examples of high-bandwidth applications are VoIP and video streaming:

VoIP *Voice over Internet Protocol (VoIP)* describes several technologies that work to deliver voice communications over the Internet or other data networks. In many cases, VoIP includes not only voice but video transmissions as well. VoIP allows us to send voice, video, and data all over the same connection to another location. Its most common application is video teleconferencing.

Many companies are investing in VoIP systems to reduce travel costs. Ponying up for pricey plane tickets, lodging, and rental cars adds up fast, so investing in a good VoIP system that allows the company to have virtual conferences with people in another state or country pays for itself in no time.

But sadly, VoIP installations can be stressed heavily by things like really low bandwidth, latency issues, packet loss, jitter, security flaws, and reliability concerns. And in some cases, routing VoIP through firewalls and routers using address translation can prove pretty problematic as well.

Video applications Watching real-time video on the Internet today is great if you have a decent high-speed connection. You can watch the news, sports, movies, and pretty much anything else that you watch on television. Although viewing digital media online is so common that anyone born after the year 2000 won't be able to remember a time when you needed to watch videos on anything other than a computer, again, this requires lots of bandwidth, and excessive use can cause traffic problems even on robust networks.

Uptime

Uptime is the amount of time the system is up and accessible to your end users, so the more uptime you have the better. And depending on how critical the nature of your business is, you may need to provide four-nine or five-nine uptime on your network—that's a lot. Why is this a lot? Because you write out four-nines as: 99.99%, or better, write out five-nines as: 99.999%! Now that is some serious uptime!

How to Optimize Performance

You now know that enough bandwidth is to networking as enough water is to life, and you're one of the lucky few if your network actually has an excess of it. Cursed is the downtrodden administrator who can't seem to find enough, and more fall into this category than the former. At times, your very sanity may hinge upon ensuring that your users have enough available bandwidth to get their jobs done on your network; and even if you've got a 1Gbps connection, it doesn't mean all your users have that much bandwidth at their fingertips. What it really means is that they get a piece of it, and they share the rest with other users and network processes. Because it's your job to make sure as much of that 1Gbps is there to use when needed as possible, I'm going to discuss some really cool ways to make that happen for you.

Quality of Service (QoS)

Quality of service (QoS) refers to the way the resources are controlled so that the quality of services is maintained. It's basically the ability to provide different priority of one or more types of traffic over other levels, to different applications, data flows, or users so that they can be guaranteed a certain performance level.

QoS methods focus on one of five problems that can affect data as it traverses network cable. Those problems include the following:

Delay   Data can run into congested lines or take a less than ideal route to the destination, and it's delays like these can make some applications, such as VoIP, fail. This is the best reason to implement QoS when real-tine applications are in use in the network—to prioritize delay sensitive traffic.

Dropped packets   Some routers will drop packets if they receive a packet while their buffers are full. If the receiving application is waiting for the packets but doesn't get them, it will usually request that the packets be retransmitted—another common cause of a service(s) delay.

Error   Packets can be corrupted in transit and arrive at the destination in an unacceptable format, again requiring retransmission and resulting in delays.

Jitter   Not every packet takes the same route to the destination, so some will be more delayed than others if they travel through a slower or busier network connection. The variation in packet delay is called *jitter*, and this can have a nastily negative impact on programs that communicate in real-time.

Out-of-order delivery   Out-of-order delivery is also a result of packets taking different paths through the network to their destinations. The application at the receiving end needs to put them back together in the right order for the message to be completed, so if there are significant delays or the packets are reassembled out of order, users will probably notice degradation of an application's quality.

QoS can ensure that applications with a required bit rate receive the necessary bandwidth to work properly. Clearly, on networks with excess bandwidth, this is not a factor; but the more limited your bandwidth is, the more important a concept like this becomes.

Applications that generally require some level of QoS include online gaming, VoIP, streaming multimedia, and safety-critical applications like remote surgery. There are eight levels of QoS priorities. The lowest level, 0, is called "best effort" but doesn't really mean that—it actually means something more like "your data will get there when it gets there." The highest level, 7, is used for things like remote surgery when data needs to get there in real-time or else! Table 20.2 displays the eight QoS levels.

TABLE 20.2   Eight Levels of QoS

Level	Description
0	Best effort
1	Background
2	Standard (spare)
3	Excellent load (business-critical applications)
4	Controlled load (streaming media)
5	Voice and video (interactive voice and video, less than 100ms latency and jitter)
6	Layer 3 Network Control Reserved Traffic (less than 10ms latency and jitter)
7	Layer 2 Network Control Reserved Traffic (lowest latency and jitter)

QoS levels are established per call, per session, or in advance of the session by an agreement known as a Service Level Agreement (SLA).

Traffic Shaping

Traffic shaping, or packet shaping, is another form of bandwidth optimization. It works by delaying packets that meet a certain criteria to guarantee usable bandwidth for other applications. Traffic shaping is basically traffic triage—you're really just delaying attention to some traffic so other traffic gets A-listed through. Traffic shaping uses *bandwidth throttling* to ensure that certain data streams don't send too much data in a specified period of time, as well as *rate limiting* to control the rate at which traffic is sent.

Most often, traffic shaping is applied to devices at the edge of the network to control the traffic entering the network, but it can also be deployed on devices within an internal network. The devices that control it have what's called a *traffic contract* that determines which packets are allowed on the network and when. You can think of this kind of like the stoplights on busy freeway on-ramps, where only so much traffic is allowed onto the road at one time, based on predefined rules. Even so, some traffic (such as like carpools and emergency vehicles) is allowed on the road immediately. Delayed packets are stored in the managing device's first-in, first-out (FIFO) buffer until they're allowed to proceed per the conditions in the contract. If you're the first car at the light, this could happen immediately. If not, you get to go after waiting briefly until the traffic in front of you is released.

Load Balancing

Load balancing refers to a technique used to spread work out to multiple computers, network links, or other devices.

Using load balancing, you can provide an active/passive server cluster in which only one server is active and handling requests. For example, your favorite Internet site might actually consist of 1 of 20 servers that all appear to be the same exact site, because that site's owner wants to ensure its users always experience quick access. You can accomplish this on a network by installing multiple, redundant links to ensure that network traffic is spread across several paths and to maximize the bandwidth on each link.

Think of this as like having two or more different freeways that will both get you to your destination equally well—if one is really busy, just take the other one.

High Availability

High availability is a system-design protocol that guarantees a certain amount of operational uptime during a given period of time. The design attempts to minimize unplanned downtime—the time users are unable to access resources. Organizations that serve critical functions obviously need this; after all, you really don't want to blaze your way to a hospital E.R. only to find that they can't treat you because their network is down!

There's a difference between planned downtime and unplanned downtime. Planned downtime is good—it's occasionally scheduled for system maintenance and routine upgrades. Unplanned downtime is bad: It's a lack of access due to system failure, which is exactly the issue high-availability resolves.

One of the highest standards in uptime is the ability to provide five-nine availability, which I spoke of earlier. This actually means the network is accessible 99.999% of the time—way impressive! Think about this. In 1 non-leap year, there are 31,536,000 seconds. If you are available 99.999% of the time, it means you can be down only .001% of the time, or a total of 315.36 seconds, or 5 minutes and 15.36 seconds per year—wow!

There's a difference between uptime and availability. Your servers may be up but not accessible if a cable gets cut or something, and that outage would definitely count against your availability time.

Caching Engines

A *cache* is a collection of data that duplicates key pieces of original data. Computers use caches all the time to temporarily store information for faster access, and processors have both internal and external caches available to them, which speeds up their response times.

A *caching engine* is basically a database on a server that stores information people need to access fast. The most popular implementation of this is with web servers and proxy servers, but caching engines are also used on internal networks to speed up access to things like database services.

Fault Tolerance

Fault tolerance means that even if one component fails, you won't lose access to the resource it provides. To implement fault tolerance, you need to employ multiple devices or connections that all provide a way to access the same resource(s).

A familiar form of fault tolerance is configuring an additional hard drive to be a mirror image of another so that if either one fails, there's still a copy of the data available to you. In networking, fault tolerance means that you have multiple paths from one point to another. What's really cool is that fault-tolerant connections can be configured to be available either on a standby basis only or all the time if you intend to use them used as part of a load-balancing system.

Summary

In this chapter, I talked a lot about the documentation aspects of network administration. I started off discussing physical diagrams and schematics and moved on to the logical form as well as configuration-management documentation. You learned about the importance of these diagrams as well as the simple to complex forms they can take and the tools used to create them—from pencil and paper to high-tech AutoCAD schematics. You also found out a great deal about creating performance baselines. After that, I delved deep into a discussion of network policies and procedures, and how regulations can affect how you manage your network.

Next, you learned about network monitoring and optimization and how monitoring your network can help you find issues before they develop into major problems. You found out about the fact that server operating systems and intelligent network devices have built-in graphical monitoring tools to help you troubleshoot your network. Also covered was how to check logs on servers or network devices to find out what's been happening on them, such as who has logged in or how much traffic has passed through them.

Finally, we got into performance optimization and the many theories and strategies you can apply to optimize performance on your network. All of them deal with controlling the traffic in some way and include methods like QoS, traffic shaping, load balancing, high availability, and the use of caching servers. You now know how important it is to ensure that you have plenty of bandwidth available for any applications that vitally need it, like critical service operations, VoIP, and real-time multimedia streaming.

Exam Essentials

Understand the difference between a physical network diagram and a logical network diagram. A physical diagram shows all of the physical connections and devices, and in many cases the cables or connections between the devices. It's a very detail-oriented view of the hardware on your network. A logical network diagram takes a higher-level view, such as your subnets and which protocols those subnets use to communicate with each other.

Understand the difference between policies, procedures, and regulations. A policy is created to give users guidance as to what is acceptable behavior on the network. Policies also help resolve problems before they begin by specifying who has access to what resources and how configurations should be managed. Procedures are steps to be taken when an event occurs on the network, such as what to do when a user is fired or how to respond to a natural disaster. Regulations are imposed on your organization; you are required to follow them, and if you don't, you may be subject to punitive actions.

Know how your servers and network devices can help you monitor your network. Most servers and network devices have monitoring tools built in that are capable of tracking data and events on your network. These include graphical tools as well as log files.

Understand several theories of performance optimization. There are several ways to manage traffic on your network to speed up access and in some cases guarantee available bandwidth to applications. These include QoS, traffic shaping, load balancing, high availability, and using caching servers.

Know some examples of bandwidth-intensive applications. Two examples of high-bandwidth applications are Voice over IP (VoIP) and real-time video streaming.

Written Lab

In this section, write the answers to the following management questions:

1. In which type of network diagram do you typically list the IP addresses of your servers and router ports?

2. Which network-performance optimization technique uses a contract to determine which data can get on to the network?

3. The lowest level of QoS is called _____.

4. The variation in packet delay on a network is called_____.

5. Spreading network traffic across multiple connections is called_____.

6. A standard of normal network performance is called_____.

7. If you need to connect two PCs directly together using their network adapters, what type of cable do you need?

8. Which network-performance optimization technique uses bandwidth throttling?

9. What are requirements imposed on the way you manage your network called?

10. The steps you should take when, for example, a network user is fired, are called_____.

(The answers to the Written Lab can be found following the answers to the Review Questions for this chapter.)

Review Questions

1. UTP cables use which type of connector?

   A. RJ-11

   B. RJ-25

   C. RJ-45

   D. BCN

2. Which type of cable will have the pins in the same order on both connectors?

   A. Crossover cable

   B. Patch cable

   C. Console cable

   D. Telephone cable

3. Which pins are switched in a crossover cable?

   A. 1 and 2, and 3 and 4

   B. 1 and 3, and 2 and 6

   C. 2 and 4, and 5 and 7

   D. 1 and 4, and 5 and 8

4. UTP cable has specific colors for the wire associated with each pin. Based on the TIA/EIA 568B wiring standard, what is the correct color order, starting with pin 1?

   A. White/Orange, Orange, Blue, White/Green, White/Blue, Green, White/Brown, Brown

   B. Orange, White/Orange, White/Green, Blue, White/Blue, White/Brown, Brown, Green

   C. White/Orange, Orange, White/Green, Blue, White/Blue, Green, White/Brown, Brown

   D. White/Green, Green, White/Orange, Blue, White/Blue, Orange, White/Brown, Brown

5. When measuring the performance of a network components or system, which of the following are key components to baseline? (Choose all that apply.)

   A. Hard disk

   B. Memory

   C. Processor

   D. Network adapter

   E. All of the above

6. Which of the following govern how the network is configured and operated as well as how people are expected to behave on the network?

   A. Baselines

   B. Laws

   C. Policies

   D. Procedures

7. You have upgraded the firmware on your switches and access points. What documentation do you need to update?

   A. Baselines and configuration documentation

   B. Physical network diagram

   C. Logical network diagram

   D. Wiring schematics

8. A user reports slowness on a network. The network administrator can begin to monitor the system by using what to look into the problem?

   A. Baseline

   B. Load balancing

   C. Packet sniffing

   D. Regulations

9. Load testing, connectivity testing, and throughput testing are all examples of what?

   A. Load balancing

   B. Network monitoring

   C. Packet sniffer

   D. Traffic shaping

10. Which type of server log will give information about specific programs?

    A. Application

    B. Security

    C. System

    D. None of the above

11. Which type of server log will give you information about drivers and services?

    A. Application

    B. Security

    C. System

    D. None of the above

12. What can provide different priority levels to different applications, data flows, or users to help guarantee performance levels?

    A. 1Gbps connection

    B. Bandwidth

    C. Uptime

    D. Quality of service

13. Which of the following is not a level of QoS?

    A. Best effort

    B. Excellent load

    C. Controlled load

    D. Completed load

14. You have added a new cable segment to your network. You need to make sure you document this for troubleshooting purposes. What should you update?

    A. The disaster recovery plan

    B. The wiring schematics

    C. The router connections document

    D. The baseline document

15. What is the basic purpose of QoS (choose 2)?

    A. Block access to certain web sites

    B. Make your entire network run faster

    C. Provide priority of one of more type of traffic over others

    D. Block access to web resources for just certain users or groups

    E. Prioritize delay sensitive traffic

16. Which network-performance optimization technique can delay packets that meet certain criteria to guarantee usable bandwidth for other applications?

    A. Traffic shaping

    B. Jitter

    C. Logical

    D. Load balancing

17. A network administrator needs to spread network traffic across multiple connections in which only one server is active and handling requests at a time. Which strategy could be used to help optimize traffic?

    A. Load balancing

    B. Traffic shaping

    C. Obtaining a 1Gbps connection

    D. Following the regulations

18. Which of the following are reasons to optimize network performance? (Choose all that apply.)

    A. Maximizing uptime

    B. Minimizing latency

    C. Using VoIP

    D. Using video applications

    E. B and D

    F. All of the above

19. What term describes technologies that can deliver voice communications over the Internet?

    A. Jitter

    B. Uptime

    C. Voice over Internet Protocol

    D. None of the above

20. To optimize performance on your network, which of the following control traffic in some way? (Choose all that apply.)

    A. QoS

    B. Traffic shaping

    C. Load balancing

    D. Caching services

    E. All of the above

Answers to Review Questions

1. C. UTP cables use an RJ-45 connector. RJ-11 and RJ-25 are often used for terminating telephone lines.

2. B. Standard cables, known as drop cables or patch cables, will have the pins in the same order on both connectors

3. B. On a crossover cable, one connector has flipped the wires. Specifically, pins 1 and 3 get switched, and pins 2 and 6 get switched.

4. C. If you are going to make your own UTP cables (drop/patch cables) to customize length, you need to make sure that the right wires get to the right pins.

5. E. A baseline is the standard level of performance of a network component or a system of components. For networks and networked devices, these are four key components to baseline.

6. C. Policies govern how the network is configured and operated as well as how people are expected to behave on the network, such as how users are able to access resources and which types of employees get network access.

7. A. A physical network diagram contains all the physical devices and connectivity paths on your network and should accurately picture how your network physically fits together in detail. This document will also have the firmware revision on all the switches and access points in your network.

8. C. A good choice here would be to use a packet sniffer. Packet sniffers allow you to examine network traffic down to details of individual packets. The key piece that network administrators are usually looking for is the packet header, or the beginning of each packet. The packet header will contain the protocol being used as well as the source and destination IP addresses.

9. B. Network monitoring can have several names, including load testing, connectivity testing, and throughput testing. You will also hear network monitors referred to as protocol analyzers.

10. A. The application log contains events triggered by applications or programs. These events are determined by the programmers. Examples of software that provide application logs include LiveUpdate, the Microsoft Office suite, and SQL and Exchange servers.

11. C. The system log contains events generated by Windows system components. Example events include drivers and services that started or failed to start.

12. D. QoS is the ability to provide different priority levels to different applications, data flows, or users so that they can be guaranteed a certain performance level.

13. D. There are eight levels of QoS, and "completed load" is not one of them.

14. B. If you add a new cable segment to the network you need to update the wiring schematics document.

15. C, E. Quality of service (QoS) is basically the ability to provide different priority of one or more types of traffic over other levels, to different applications, data flows, or users so that they can be guaranteed a certain performance level.

16. A. Traffic shaping, also known as packet shaping, is a form of bandwidth optimization. It delays packets that meet a certain criteria to guarantee usable bandwidth for other applications. Essentially, with traffic shaping, you're delaying some traffic so other traffic can get through. Traffic shaping uses bandwidth throttling to ensure that certain data streams don't send too much data in a specified period of time.

17. A. Load balancing refers to a technique used to spread work out to multiple computers, network links, or other devices. You can load-balance work on servers by clustering servers so that multiple machines all provide the same service, but only one will respond at a time.

18. F. There are many bandwidth-intensive programs, like VoIP and video streaming. These are just a few of the reasons why it's necessary to try to optimize network performance.

19. C. Voice over Internet Protocol (VoIP) is a general term that describes several technologies that are able to deliver voice communications over the Internet or other data networks.

20. E. There are many theories and strategies you can apply to optimize performance on your network. All of them deal with controlling the traffic in some way. Strategies include QoS, traffic shaping, load balancing, high availability, and the use of caching servers. You want to ensure you have plenty of bandwidth available for those applications that need it, such as critical service operations, VoIP, and real-time multimedia streaming.

Answers to Written Lab

1. Logical

2. Traffic shaping

3. Best effort

4. Jitter

5. Load balancing

6. A baseline

7. Crossover

8. Traffic shaping

9. Regulations

10. Procedures

Appendix

A

Subnetting Class A

Class A subnetting is not performed any differently than Classes B and C, but there are 24 bits to play with instead of the 16 in a Class B address and the 8 in a Class C address.

Let's start by listing all the Class A masks:

255.0.0.0	(/8)		
255.128.0.0	(/9)	255.255.240.0	(/20)
255.192.0.0	(/10)	255.255.248.0	(/21)
255.224.0.0	(/11)	255.255.252.0	(/22)
255.240.0.0	(/12)	255.255.254.0	(/23)
255.248.0.0	(/13)	255.255.255.0	(/24)
255.252.0.0	(/14)	255.255.255.128	(/25)
255.254.0.0	(/15)	255.255.255.192	(/26)
255.255.0.0	(/16)	255.255.255.224	(/27)
255.255.128.0	(/17)	255.255.255.240	(/28)
255.255.192.0	(/18)	255.255.255.248	(/29)
255.255.224.0	(/19)	255.255.255.252	(/30)

That's it. You must leave at least 2 bits for defining hosts. And I hope you can see the pattern by now. Remember, we're going to do this the same way as a Class B or C subnet. It's just that, again, we simply have more host bits and we just use the same subnet numbers we used with Class B and C, but we start using these numbers in the second octet.

Subnetting Practice Examples: Class A Addresses

When you look at an IP address and a subnet mask, you must be able to distinguish the bits used for subnets from the bits used for determining hosts. This is imperative. If you're still struggling with this concept, please reread the section, "IP Addressing," in Chapter 2. It shows you how to determine the difference between the subnet and host bits and should help clear things up.

Practice Example #1A: 255.255.0.0 (/16)

Class A addresses use a default mask of 255.0.0.0, which leaves 22 bits for subnetting since you must leave 2 bits for host addressing. The 255.255.0.0 mask with a Class A address is using 8 subnet bits.

- *Subnets?* 2^8 = 256.
- *Hosts?* $2^{16} - 2$ = 65,534.
- *Valid subnets?* What is the interesting octet? 256 – 255 = 1. 0, 1, 2, 3, etc. (all in the second octet). The subnets would be 10.0.0.0, 10.1.0.0, 10.2.0.0, 10.3.0.0, etc., up to 10.255.0.0.
- *Broadcast address for each subnet?*
- *Valid hosts?*

The following table shows the first two and last two subnets, valid host range, and broadcast addresses for the private Class A 10.0.0.0 network:

Subnet	10.0.0.0	10.1.0.0	...	10.254.0.0	10.255.0.0
First host	10.0.0.1	10.1.0.1	...	10.254.0.1	10.255.0.1
Last host	10.0.255.254	10.1.255.254	...	10.254.255.254	10.255.255.254
Broadcast	10.0.255.255	10.1.255.255	...	10.254.255.255	10.255.255.255

Practice Example #2A: 255.255.240.0 (/20)

255.255.240.0 gives us 12 bits of subnetting and leaves us 12 bits for host addressing.

- *Subnets?* 2^{12} = 4096.
- *Hosts?* $2^{12} - 2$ = 4094.
- *Valid subnets?* What is your interesting octet? 256 – 240 = 16. The subnets in the second octet are a block size of 1 and the subnets in the third octet are 0, 16, 32, etc.
- *Broadcast address for each subnet?*
- *Valid hosts?*

The following table shows some examples of the host ranges—the first three and the last subnets:

Subnet	10.0.0.0	10.0.16.0	10.0.32.0	...	10.255.240.0
First host	10.0.0.1	10.0.16.1	10.0.32.1	...	10.255.240.1
Last host	10.0.15.254	10.0.31.254	10.0.47.254	...	10.255.255.254
Broadcast	10.0.15.255	10.0.31.255	10.0.47.255	...	10.255.255.255

Practice Example #3A: 255.255.255.192 (/26)

Let's do one more example using the second, third, and fourth octets for subnetting.

- *Subnets?* 2^{18} = 262,144.
- *Hosts?* $2^6 - 2 = 62$.
- *Valid subnets?* In the second and third octet, the block size is 1, and in the fourth octet, the block size is 64.
- *Broadcast address for each subnet?*
- *Valid hosts?*

The following table shows the first four subnets and their valid hosts and broadcast addresses in the Class A 255.255.255.192 mask:

Subnet	10.0.0.0	10.0.0.64	10.0.0.128	10.0.0.192
First host	10.0.0.1	10.0.0.65	10.0.0.129	10.0.0.193
Last host	10.0.0.62	10.0.0.126	10.0.0.190	10.0.0.254
Broadcast	10.0.0.63	10.0.0.127	10.0.0.191	10.0.0.255

The following table shows the last four subnets and their valid hosts and broadcast addresses:

Subnet	10.255.255.0	10.255.255.64	10.255.255.128	10.255.255.192
First host	10.255.255.1	10.255.255.65	10.255.255.129	10.255.255.193
Last host	10.255.255.62	10.255.255.126	10.255.255.190	10.255.255.254
Broadcast	10.255.255.63	10.255.255.127	10.255.255.191	10.255.255.255

Subnetting in Your Head: Class A Addresses

This sounds hard, but as with Class C and Class B, the numbers are the same; we just start in the second octet. What makes this easy? You only need to worry about the octet that has the largest block size (typically called the interesting octet; one that is something other than 0 or 255)—for example, 255.255.240.0 (/20) with a Class A network. The second octet has a block size of 1, so any number listed in that octet is a subnet. The third octet is a 240 mask, which means we have a block size of 16 in the third octet. If your host ID is 10.20.80.30, what is your subnet, broadcast address, and valid host range?

The subnet in the second octet is 20 with a block size of 1, but the third octet is in block sizes of 16, so we'll just count them out: 0, 16, 32, 48, 64, 80, 96...voila! (By the way, you can count by 16s by now, right?) This makes our subnet 10.20.80.0, with a broadcast of 10.20.95.255 because the next subnet is 10.20.96.0. The valid host range is 10.20.80.1 through 10.20.95.254. And yes, no lie! You really can do this in your head if you just get your block sizes nailed!

Okay, let's practice on one more, just for fun!
Host IP: 10.1.3.65/23

First, you can't answer this question if you don't know what a /23 is. It's 255.255.254.0. The interesting octet here is the third one: 256 – 254 = 2. Our subnets in the third octet are 0, 2, 4, 6, etc. The host in this question is in subnet 2.0, and the next subnet is 4.0, so that makes the broadcast address 3.255. And any address between 10.1.2.1 and 10.1.3.254 is considered a valid host.

Written Lab 1

Given a Class B network and the net bits identified (CIDR), complete the following table to identify the subnet mask and the number of host addresses possible for each mask.

Classful Address	Subnet Mask	Number of Hosts per Subnet ($2^x - 2$)
/16		
/17		
/18		
/19		
/20		
/21		
/22		
/23		
/24		
/25		
/26		
/27		
/28		
/29		
/30		

Written Lab 2

Decimal IP Address	Address Class	Number of Subnet and Host Bits	Number of Subnets (2^x)	Number of Hosts ($2^x - 2$)
10.25.66.154/23				
172.31.254.12/24				
192.168.20.123/28				
63.24.89.21/18				
128.1.1.254/20				
208.100.54.209/30				

Answers to Written Lab 1

Classful Address	Subnet Mask	Number of Hosts per Subnet ($2^H - 2$)
/16	255.255.0.0	65,534
/17	255.255.128.0	32,766
/18	255.255.192.0	16,382
/19	255.255.224.0	8,190
/20	255.255.240.0	4,094
/21	255.255.248.0	2,046
/22	255.255.252.0	1,022
/23	255.255.254.0	510
/24	255.255.255.0	254
/25	255.255.255.128	126
/26	255.255.255.192	62
/27	255.255.255.224	30
/28	255.255.255.240	14
/29	255.255.255.248	6
/30	255.255.255.252	2

Answers to Written Lab 2

Decimal IP Address	Address Class	Number of Subnet and Host Bits	Number of Subnets (2^x)	Number of Hosts ($2^x - 2$)
10.25.66.154/23	A	15/9	32768	510
172.31.254.12/24	B	8/8	256	254
192.168.20.123/28	C	4/4	16	14
63.24.89.21/18	A	10/14	1,024	16,382
128.1.1.254/20	B	4/12	16	4094
208.100.54.209/30	C	6/2	64	2

Appendix B

About the Companion CD

IN THIS APPENDIX:

- ✓ What you'll find on the CD
- ✓ System requirements
- ✓ Using the CD
- ✓ Troubleshooting

What You'll Find on the CD

The following sections are arranged by category and summarize the software and other goodies you'll find on the CD. If you need help with installing the items provided on the CD, refer to the installation instructions in the "Using the CD" section of this appendix.

Some programs on the CD might fall into one of these categories:

Shareware programs are fully functional, free, trial versions of copyrighted programs. If you like particular programs, register with their authors for a nominal fee and receive licenses, enhanced versions, and technical support.

Freeware programs are free, copyrighted games, applications, and utilities. You can copy them to as many computers as you like—for free—but they offer no technical support.

GNU software is governed by its own license, which is included inside the folder of the GNU software. There are no restrictions on distribution of GNU software. See the GNU license at the root of the CD for more details.

Trial, *demo*, or *evaluation* versions of software are usually limited either by time or by functionality (such as not letting you save a project after you create it).

Sybex Test Engine

For Windows

The CD contains the Sybex test engine, which includes all of the assessment test and chapter review questions in electronic format, as well as two bonus exams located only on the CD.

PDF of the Book

For Windows

We have included an electronic version of the text in `.pdf` format. You can view the electronic version of the book with Adobe Reader.

Adobe Reader

For Windows

We've also included a copy of Adobe Reader so you can view PDF files that accompany the book's content. For more information on Adobe Reader or to check for a newer version, visit Adobe's website at `www.adobe.com/products/reader/`.

Electronic Flashcards

For PC, Pocket PC, and Palm

These handy electronic flashcards are just what they sound like. One side contains a question or fill-in-the-blank question, and the other side shows the answer.

System Requirements

Make sure your computer meets the minimum system requirements shown in the following list. If your computer doesn't match up to most of these requirements, you may have problems using the software and files on the companion CD. For the latest and greatest information, please refer to the ReadMe file located at the root of the CD-ROM.

- A PC running Microsoft Windows 98, Windows 2000, Windows NT4 (with SP4 or later), Windows Me, Windows XP, or Windows Vista
- An Internet connection
- A CD-ROM drive

Using the CD

To install the items from the CD to your hard drive, follow these steps:

1. Insert the CD into your computer's CD-ROM drive. The license agreement appears.

Windows users: The interface won't launch if you have autorun disabled. In that case, click Start ➤ Run (for Windows Vista, Start ➤ All Programs ➤ Accessories ➤ Run). In the dialog box that appears, type **D:\Start.exe**. (Replace *D* with the proper letter if your CD drive uses a different letter. If you don't know the letter, see how your CD drive is listed under My Computer.) Click OK.

2. Read the license agreement, and then click the Accept button if you want to use the CD.

The CD interface appears. The interface allows you to access the content with just one or two clicks.

Troubleshooting

Wiley has attempted to provide programs that work on most computers with the minimum system requirements. Alas, your computer may differ, and some programs may not work properly for some reason.

The two likeliest problems are that you don't have enough memory (RAM) for the programs you want to use or you have other programs running that are affecting installation or running of a program. If you get an error message such as "Not enough memory" or "Setup cannot continue," try one or more of the following suggestions and then try using the software again:

Turn off any antivirus software running on your computer. Installation programs sometimes mimic virus activity and may make your computer incorrectly believe that it's being infected by a virus.

Close all running programs. The more programs you have running, the less memory is available to other programs. Installation programs typically update files and programs; so if you keep other programs running, installation may not work properly.

Have your local computer store add more RAM to your computer. This is, admittedly, a drastic and somewhat expensive step. However, adding more memory can really help the speed of your computer and allow more programs to run at the same time.

Customer Care

If you have trouble with the book's companion CD-ROM, please call the Wiley Product Technical Support phone number at (800) 762-2974. Outside the United States, call +1(317) 572-3994. You can also contact Wiley Product Technical Support at http://sybex.custhelp.com. John Wiley & Sons will provide technical support only for installation and other general quality-control items. For technical support on the applications themselves, consult the program's vendor or author.

To place additional orders or to request information about other Wiley products, please call (877) 762-2974.

Glossary

10Base-T An implementation of Ethernet that specifies a 10Mbps signaling rate, baseband signaling, and twisted-pair cabling.

100Base-T Based on the IEEE 802.3u standard, 100Base-T is the Fast Ethernet specification of 100Mbps baseband that uses UTP wiring. 100Base-T sends link pulses (containing more information than those used in 10Base-T) over the network when no traffic is present. *See also* 10Base-T, Fast Ethernet, IEEE 802.3 CSMA/CD Networking.

100Base-TX Based on the IEEE 802.3u standard, 100Base-TX is the 100Mbps baseband Fast Ethernet specification that uses two pairs of UTP or STP wiring. The first pair of wires receives data; the second pair sends data. To ensure correct signal timing, a 100Base-TX segment cannot be longer than 100 meters.

A

access control list (ACL) A list of rights that an object has to resources in the network. Also a type of firewall. In this case, the lists reside on a router and determine which machines can use the router and in what direction.

access link Switch port assigned to only one VLAN.

ACK *See* acknowledgment.

acknowledgment (ACK) A message confirming that the data packet was received. This occurs at the Transport layer of the OSI model.

ACL *See* access control list.

Active Directory The replacement for NT Directory Service (NTDS) that is included with Windows Servers. It acts similarly to Novell Directory Services (NDS) because it is a true X.500-based directory service.

active hub A hub that is powered and actively regenerates any signal that is received. *See also* hub.

ad hoc RF network A network created when two RF-capable devices are brought within transmission range of each other. A common example is handheld PDAs beaming data to each other.

adapter Technically, the peripheral hardware that installs into your computer or the software that defines how the computer talks to that hardware.

address Designation to allow PCs to be known by a name or number to other PCs. Addressing allows a PC to transmit data directly to another PC by using its address (IP or MAC).

address learning The process by which switches/bridges receive a frame and place the source address of the frame in the content addressable memory (CAM) table.

address mask   A bit combination descriptor identifying which portion of an address refers to the network or subnet and which part refers to the host. Sometimes simply called the mask. *See also* subnet mask.

address record   Part of a DNS table that maps an IP address to a domain name. Also known as an A (or host) record.

address resolution   The process used for resolving differences between computer addressing schemes. Address resolution typically defines a method for tracing Network layer (Layer 3) addresses to Data Link layer (Layer 2) addresses.

Address Resolution Protocol (ARP)   The Network-layer protocol that IP uses to ascertain the MAC address of a known IP address when IP determines that the destination is on the local subnet and communication with the destination must therefore occur at the Data Link layer.

administrative distance (AD)   A number that is used by routing protocols to determine the trustworthiness of a route. If two route updates are received on a router with different AD's, the router will only accept the one with the lower AD and discard the other route update.

ADSL   *See* asymmetrical digital subscriber line.

Advanced Encryption Standard (AES)   A block-cipher adapted form of encryption that was created by Vincent Rinjndael and standardized by the U.S. government. It is now used worldwide. Before we used AES, the Data Encryption Standard (DES) was widely used.

alias record   *See* CNAME record.

antivirus   A category of software that uses various methods to eliminate viruses in a computer. It typically also protects against future infection. *See also* virus.

Application layer   The seventh layer of the OSI model, which deals with how applications access the network and describes application functionality, such as file transfer, messaging, and so on.

application-specific integrated circuit (ASIC)   An integrated circuit (IC) customized for a particular use, rather than intended for general-purpose use: for example, a chip designed solely to run a LAN switch.

ARP table   A table used by the Address Resolution Protocol (ARP) that contains a list of known TCP/IP addresses and their associated MAC addresses. The table is cached in memory so that ARP lookups do not have to be performed for frequently accessed TCP/IP addresses but aged out so that associations do not become stagnant. *See also* Address Resolution Protocol (ARP), Media Access Control (MAC), Transmission Control Protocol/Internet Protocol (TCP/IP).

asymmetrical digital subscriber line (ADSL)   An implementation of DSL where the upload and download speeds are different. *See also* digital subscriber line (DSL).

Asynchronous Transfer Mode (ATM)   A connection-oriented network architecture based on broadband ISDN technology that uses constant-size 53-byte cells instead of packets. Because cells don't change size, they are switched much faster and more efficiently than packets across a network.

ATM   *See* Asynchronous Transfer Mode.

Attachment Unit Interface (AUI) port   Port on some NICs that lets you connect the NIC to different media types by using an external transceiver.

attenuation   Attenuation is the degradation of a signal and affects the propagation of waves and signals in electrical circuits, in optical fibers, as well as in air (radio waves).

auto-detect mechanism   A means by which network devices can auto-detect options such as speed and duplex, just to name two. A LAN switch is a good example of how a port can auto-detect 10 or 100Mbps or full- and half-duplex operation with the network card that is attached to the port via cable.

B

B channel   *See* bearer channel.

backbone   The part of most networks that connects multiple segments together to form a LAN. The backbone usually has a higher speed than the segments. *See also* local area network, segment (LAN).

bandwidth   In network communications, the amount of data that can be sent across a wire in a given time. Each communication that passes along the wire decreases the amount of available bandwidth.

bandwidth throttling   A method of ensuring that a bandwidth-intensive device, such as a server or your ISP, will limit (throttle) the quantity of data it transmits and/or accepts within a specified period of time. For servers, bandwidth throttling helps limit network congestion and server crashes. For ISPs, bandwidth throttling can be used to limit users' speeds across certain applications, or limit upload speeds.

baseband   A transmission technique in which the signal uses the entire bandwidth of a transmission medium.

baseline   A category of network documentation that indicates how the network normally runs. It includes such information as network statistics, server-utilization trends, and processor performance statistics.

bearer channel (B channel)   A channel in an ISDN line that carries data. Each bearer channel typically has a bandwidth of 64Kbps.

best-effort transmission   Transmission that occurs between devices without any form of connection establishment or acknowledgment of received data. Best-effort transmission is performed by protocols that are both connectionless and unreliable, such as UDP, IP, and Ethernet.

binding   *See* bonding.

bit   A binary digit that takes a value of either 0 or 1 and that is the basic unit of information storage and communication in digital computing and digital information theory. Four bits equal a nibble. Eight bits equal a byte.

bonding   A procedure where two ISDN B channels are joined together to provide greater bandwidth. BONDING stands for Bandwidth ON Demand Interoperability Group, but it's often seen written in lowercase as a more generalized term referring to inverse multiplexing. Bonding can also refer to binding multiple Ethernet segments together to gain greater bandwidth and throughput.

Boot sector virus   An especially nasty virus that hides in the boot sector and is loaded with the operating system. A boot sector (sometimes called a bootblock) is a sector of a hard disk that contains code for booting programs.

Border Gateway Protocol (BGP)   The core routing protocol of the Internet. It is a very advanced routing protocol and is not used within corporations; instead, it can be used to make multiple connections to the Internet and perform load balancing. It works by maintaining a table of IP networks or prefixes that designate network reachability among autonomous systems. It is described as a path or Distance Vector protocol.

bottleneck   A location in the network that creates congestion because it cannot handle the load. A router interface or server can be a bottleneck.

bounded media   Network media used at the Physical layer, where the signal travels over a cable of some kind.

bridge   A network device, operating at the Data Link layer, that logically separates a single network into segments but lets the two segments appear to be one network to higher-layer protocols.

broadband   A network-transmission method in which a single transmission medium is divided so that multiple signals can travel across the same medium simultaneously.

broadcast address   A special network address that refers to all users on the network. For example, the TCP/IP address 255.255.255.255 is the broadcast address. Any packets sent to that address will be sent to everyone on that LAN.

broadcast domain   The collection of all devices that will receive each other's broadcast frames. Each interface on a router terminates a broadcast domain. Routers will not forward broadcasts to other interfaces. They can be made to turn certain broadcasts into unicasts to specific devices, but they will not propagate broadcasts. VLANs created on LAN switches are broadcast domains. Any broadcast created by a device attached to a switch port assigned to a VLAN will be received only by those devices attached to switch ports assigned to the same VLAN.

broadcast storm   Broadcast storms are typically created by network loops or a bad NIC. Because of the loop or bad NIC, worthless broadcasts can be sent in the millions and this can create an extreme amount of broadcast and multicast traffic on a computer network and render the network unable to transport normal traffic.

buffer   A place in memory to store incoming packets. All computers have buffers.

burned-in address (BIA)   Usually, a MAC address that has been burned into an EEPROM on a networking device, becoming a permanent physical address for the device.

bus   A pathway in a PC that allows data and signals to be transmitted between the PC components. Types of buses include ISA and PCI.

bus topology   A topology where the cable and signals run in a straight line from one end of the network to the other.

butt set   A special type of telephone used by technicians for installing and testing local-loop telephone lines.

byte   A basic unit of measurement of information storage in a computer and is considered to be a unit of memory addressing. A byte most often consists of eight bits.

C

cable   A physical transmission medium that has a central conductor of wire or fiber surrounded by a plastic jacket.

cable map   General network documentation indicating each cable's source and destination as well as where each network cable runs.

cable modem   A device used to interconnect computing and networking equipment, via Ethernet, with a television cable company's data network through the same cable circuit used to deliver television programming. The standard for data communications over the cable television network is known as the data over cable service interface specification (DOCSIS).

cable tester   A special instrument that is used to test the integrity of LAN cables. *See also* time-domain reflectometer (TDR).

call setup   The overall length of time required to establish a circuit-switched call between users.

carrier   A signal at a frequency that is chosen to carry data. The addition of data to the frequency is called modulation, and the removal of data from the frequency is called demodulation. This is used on analog devices like modems.

Carrier Sense Multiple Access with Collision Avoidance (CSMA/CA)   A media access method that sends a Request to Send (RTS) packet and waits to receive a Clear to Send (CTS) packet before sending. Once the CTS is received, the sender sends the packet of information.

Carrier Sense Multiple Access with Collision Detection (CSMA/CD)   A media access method that first senses whether there is a signal on the wire, indicating that someone is transmitting currently. If no one else is transmitting, it attempts a transmission and listens for someone else trying to transmit at the same time. If this happens, both senders back off and don't transmit again until some specified period of time has passed. *See also* collision.

categories   Different grades of cables that determine how much protection is offered against interference from outside the cable. Category 1 allows voice data only. Category 2 allows data transmissions up to 4Mbps. Category 3 allows data transmissions up to 10Mbps. Category 4 allows data transmissions up to 16Mbps. Category 5 allows data transmissions up to 100Mbps. The only cables we use now are Cat 5+ and Category 6, which provides up to 1Gbps.

Central Office (CO)   The office in any metropolitan or rural area that contains the telephone switching equipment for that area. The CO connects all users in that area to each other as well as to the rest of the PSTN. *See also* Public Switched Telephone Network (PSTN).

centralized computing   Computing done at a central location using terminals that are attached to a central computer. The computer itself may control all the peripherals directly, or they may be attached via a terminal server.

certificate authority (CA)   An entity that issues digital certificates for use by other companies or institutions. A CA is a characteristic of many Public Key Infrastructure (PKI) schemes.

Challenge Handshake Authentication Protocol (CHAP)   A client/server authentication method that uses MD5 encryption and a random value to authenticate a client. The authentication server "challenges" the client to come up with the same value based on the random value and the secret shared between client and server.

channel service unit (CSU)   Generally used with a T1 Internet line, it is used to terminate the connection from the T1 provider. The CSU is usually part of a CSU/DSU unit. It also provides diagnostics and testing if necessary.

CHAP   *See* Challenge Handshake Authentication Protocol.

checksum   A hexadecimal value computed from transmitted data that is used in error-checking routines.

circuit switching   A switching method where a dedicated connection between the sender and receiver is maintained throughout the conversation. POTS and ISDN, for example, establish circuit-switched connections through dialed numbers. *See also* packet switching.

Class A network   Part of the Internet Protocol hierarchical addressing scheme. Class A networks have only 8 bits for defining networks and 24 bits for defining hosts and subnets on each network.

Class B network   Part of the Internet Protocol hierarchical addressing scheme. Class B networks have 16 bits for defining networks and 16 bits for defining hosts and subnets on each network.

Class C network   Part of the Internet Protocol hierarchical addressing scheme. Class C networks have 24 bits for defining networks and only 8 bits for defining hosts and subnets on each network.

classful   Relates to the default characteristics of and constraints placed on an IP address based on the class of address in question. For example, a Class C address, by default, has 24 network bits and 8 host bits, limiting it to no more than 254 hosts per network. Classful defaults are considered in the absence of detailed configuration information, such as a nondefault subnet mask.

classful routing   The use of routing protocols that do not send subnet mask information when a route update is sent out.

Classless Inter-Domain Routing (CIDR)   The new routing method used by InterNIC to assign IP addresses. CIDR can be described as a "slash x" network. The x represents the number of bits in the network that InterNIC controls.

classless routing   Routing that sends subnet-mask information in the routing updates. Classless routing allows Variable-Length Subnet Masking (VLSM) and supernetting. Routing protocols that support classless routing are RIP version 2, EIGRP, and OSPF.

client   The part of a client/server network where the computing is usually done. In a typical setting, a client will use the server for remote storage, backups, or security such as a firewall.

client/server network   A server-centric network in which all resources are stored on a file server and processing power is distributed among workstations and the file server.

clustering   A computing technology where many servers work together so that they appear to be one high-powered server. If one server fails, the others in the cluster take over the services provided by the failed server.

CNAME record   A DNS record type that specifies other names for existing hosts. This allows a DNS administrator to assign multiple DNS host names to a single DNS host. Also known as an *alias record*.

coaxial cable   Often referred to as coax. A type of cable used in network wiring. Typical coaxial cable types include RG-58 and RG-62. 10Base-2 Ethernet networks use coaxial cable. Coaxial cable is usually shielded, which means that it is more immune to interference then unshielded cables.

collision   The error condition that occurs when two stations on a CSMA/CD network transmit data (at the Data Link layer) at the same time. *See also* Carrier Sense Multiple Access with Collision Detection (CSMA/CD).

collision domain   The group of devices whose frames could potentially collide with one another. Each interface on a bridge, switch, or router terminates a collision domain. These devices become responsible for recovering from collisions that occur due to their forwarding of frames out other interfaces.

collision light   An LED on a NIC or hub that indicates when a collision has occurred.

concentrator   *See* hub.

connectionless   Communication between two hosts that have no previous session established for synchronizing sent data. If the service is also unreliable, the data is not acknowledged at the receiving end. This can allow for data loss.

connectionless services   *See* connectionless, connectionless transport protocol.

connectionless transport protocol   A transport protocol, such as UDP, that does not create a virtual connection between sending and receiving stations before transmitting user data between them. *See also* User Datagram Protocol. (UDP)

connection-oriented   Communication between two hosts that have a previous session established for synchronizing sent data. If the service is also reliable, the data is acknowledged by the receiving device. This allows for guaranteed delivery of data between PCs.

connection-oriented transport protocol   A transport protocol that establishes a virtual connection between sending and receiving stations before any user data is transmitted between them. TCP is a connection-oriented protocol. *See also* Transmission Control Protocol (TCP).

Control Panel   A special window inside Microsoft Windows operating systems (Windows 95 and above) that has icons for all of the configurable options for the system.

controller   Part of a PC that allows connectivity to peripheral devices. A disk controller allows the PC to be connected to a hard disk. A network controller allows a PC to be connected to a network. A keyboard controller is used to connect a keyboard to the PC.

convergence   The process required for all routers in an internetwork to update their routing tables and create a consistent view of the network, using the best possible paths. No user data is passed during an STP convergence time.

cost   A value given to a route between PCs or subnets to determine which route may be best. The word *hop* is sometimes used to refer to the number of routers between two PCs or subnets. *See also* hop.

country codes   The two-letter abbreviations for countries, used in the DNS hierarchy. *See also* Domain Name Service (DNS).

CRC   *See* cyclical redundancy check.

crossover cable   The troubleshooting tool used in Ethernet UTP installations to test communications between two stations, bypassing the hub. Crossover cables can also be used to interconnect two DTE devices, such as PCs and routers, or two DCE devices, such as hubs and switches. *See also* unshielded twisted-pair (UTP) cable, medium dependent interface (MDI), medium dependent interface-crossover (MDI-X).

crosstalk   A type of interference that occurs when two LAN cables run close to each other. If one cable is carrying a signal and the other isn't, the one carrying a signal will induce a "ghost" signal (crosstalk) in the other cable.

CSMA/CA   *See* Carrier Sense Multiple Access with Collision Avoidance.

CSMA/CD   *See* Carrier Sense Multiple Access with Collision Detection.

customer premises equipment (CPE)   Items such as telephones, modems, and terminals installed at customer locations and connected to the service provider network.

cyclical redundancy check (CRC)   An error-checking method in data communications that runs a formula against data before transmissions. The sending station then appends the resultant value (called a checksum) to the data and sends it. The receiving station uses the same formula on the data. If the receiving station doesn't get the same checksum result for the calculation, it considers the transmission invalid, rejects the frame, and asks for a retransmission.

D

D channel   *See* delta channel (D channel).

daemon   Pronounced "demon," a program that acts like a terminate-and-stay-resident (TSR) application by loading into memory and lurking there for any trigger that calls on its services.

data communication equipment (DCE)   Equipment that provides clocking to DTE equipment. DCE equipment starts at the CSU/DSU and is defined as a connection all the way to the providers network.

Data Encryption Standard (DES)   A deprecated cryptographic block cipher that falls to brute-force attacks due to its short 56-bit key. Triple DES (3DES), which was widely used before AES became a standard, is a block cipher formed from the DES cipher by using it three times.

data frame   A frame is the Protocol Data Unit encapsulation at the Data Link layer of the OSI reference model. A data frame encapsulates packets from the Network layer and prepares the data for transmission on a network medium.

Data Link Connection Identifiers (DLCIs)   Used to identify virtual circuits in a frame relay network.

Data Link layer   The second layer of the OSI model. It describes the logical topology of a network, which is the way that packets move throughout a network. It also describes the method of media access. *See also* Open Systems Interconnect (OSI).

data over cable service interface specification (DOCSIS)   *See* cable modem.

data packet   A unit of data sent over a network. A packet includes a header, addressing information, and the data itself. A packet is treated as a single unit as it is sent from device to device. Also known as a *datagram*.

data terminal equipment (DTE)   Any device located at the user end of a user-network interface serving as a destination, a source, or both. DTE includes devices such as multiplexers, routers, protocol translators, and computers. The connection to a data network is made through data communication equipment (DCE) such as a modem, using the clocking signals generated by that device. *See also* data communication equipment (DCE).

datagram   A logical collection of information transmitted as a Network-layer unit over a medium without a previously established virtual circuit. IP datagrams have become the primary information unit of the Internet. At various layers of the OSI reference model, the terms *cell*, *frame*, *message*, *packet*, and *segment* also define these logical information groupings.

de-encapsulation   The technique used by layered protocols in which a layer removes header information from the Protocol Data Unit (PDU) from the layer below. *See also* encapsulation.

default gateway   The router that all packets are sent to when the workstation doesn't know where the destination station is or when it can't find the destination station on the local segment.

delta channel (D channel)   A channel on an ISDN line used for link management. For Basic Rate Interface (BRI) circuits, the D channel is 16Kbps. For the Primary Rate Interface (PRI), the D channel is 64Kbps. *See also* Integrated Services Digital Network (ISDN).

demarcation point (demarc)   The point on any telephone installation where the telephone lines from the central office enter the customer's premises.

demilitarized zone (DMZ)   A physical or logical subnetwork that contains and exposes an organization's external services to a larger, untrusted network, usually the Internet. Named after the military usage of the term; also known as a demarcation zone or perimeter network.

denial of service (DoS) attack   Type of hack that prevents any users—even legitimate ones—from using the system.

destination port number   The address of the PC to which data is being sent from a sending PC. The port portion allows for the demultiplexing of data to be sent to a specific application.

DHCP   *See* Dynamic Host Configuration Protocol.

digital subscriber line (DSL)   A digital WAN technology that brings high-speed digital networking to homes and businesses over POTS. There are many types, including HDSL (high-speed DSL) and VDSL (very high data-rate DSL). *See also* plain old telephone service (POTS), asymmetrical digital subscriber line (ADSL).

Direct Sequence Spread Spectrum (DSSS)   A modulation technique used by the original IEEE 802.11 standard, as well as by the 802.11b standard, that creates a redundant bit pattern for each bit that is transmitted. This way, if one or more bits in the bit pattern are damaged in transmission, the original data may be recoverable from the redundant bits. *See also* Frequency Hopping Spread Spectrum (FHSS), Orthogonal Frequency Division Multiplexing (OFDM).

directional antenna (Yagi)   A point-to-point antenna that, when used as a wireless access point, is not suitable for general client access but rather for point-to-point bridging of access points. *See also* omnidirectional antenna (Omni).

directory   A network database that contains a listing of all network resources, such as users, printers, groups, and so on.

directory service   A network service that provides access to a central database of information, which contains detailed information about the resources available on a network.

Discretionary Access Control (DAC)   Defined by the Trusted Computer System Evaluation Criteria as a means of restricting access to objects based on the identity of subjects and/or groups to which they belong.

Distance Vector routing protocol   A route discovery method in which each router, using broadcasts, tells every other router what networks and routes it knows about and the distance to them.

distributed denial of service (DDos) attacks   *See* denial of service (DoS) attack.

distributed WAN   An approach used by companies to provide WAN optimization by accelerating a broad range of applications accessed by distributed enterprise users via eliminating redundant transmissions, staging data in local caches, compressing and prioritizing data, and streamlining chatty protocols.

DIX   Another name for a 15-pin AUI connector or a DB-15 connector.

DNS   *See* Domain Name Service.

DNS server   Any server that performs address resolution by translating DNS host names to IP addresses. *See also* Domain Name Service (DNS), Internet Protocol (IP).

DNS zone   An area in the DNS hierarchy that is managed as a single unit. *See also* Domain Name Service (DNS).

DOCSIS   *See* cable modem.

DoD Networking Model   A four-layer conceptual model describing how communications should take place between computer systems. The four layers are Process/Application, Host-to-Host, Internet, and Network Access.

domain   A group of networked Windows computers that share a single SAM database.

Domain Name Service (DNS)   The network service used in TCP/IP networks that translates host names to IP addresses. *See also* Transmission Control Protocol/Internet Protocol (TCP/IP).

dotted decimal   Notation used by TCP/IP to designate an IP address. The notation is made up of 32 bits (4 bytes), each byte separated by a decimal. The range of numbers for each octet is 0–255. The leftmost octet contains the high-order bits, and the rightmost octet contains the low-order bits.

DSL   *See* digital subscriber line.

DSSS   *See* Direct Sequence Spread Spectrum.

dumb terminal   A keyboard and monitor that send keystrokes to a central processing computer (typically a mainframe or minicomputer) that returns screen displays to the monitor. The unit has no processing power of its own, hence the moniker "dumb."

duplicate servers   Two servers that are identical for use in clustering.

dynamic ARP table entries   *See* dynamic entry.

dynamic entry   An entry made in the ARP table whenever an ARP request is made by the Windows TCP/IP stack and the MAC address is not found in the ARP table. The ARP request is broadcast on the local segment. When the MAC address of the requested IP address is found, that information is added to the ARP table. *See also* Internet Protocol (IP), Media Access Control (MAC), Transmission Control Protocol/Internet Protocol (TCP/IP).

Dynamic Host Configuration Protocol (DHCP)   A protocol used on a TCP/IP network to send configuration data, including TCP/IP address, default gateway, subnet mask, and DNS configuration, to clients. *See also* default gateway, Domain Name Service (DNS), subnet mask, Transmission Control Protocol/Internet Protocol (TCP/IP).

dynamic packet filtering   A type of firewall used to accept or reject packets based on the contents of the packets.

dynamic ports   *See* dynamic VLAN.

dynamic routing   The use of route-discovery protocols to talk to other routers and find out what networks they are attached to. Routers that use dynamic routing send out special packets to request updates of the other routers on the network as well as to send their own updates.

dynamic VLAN   An administrator will create an entry in a special server with the hardware addresses of all devices on the internetwork. The server will then report the associated VLAN to a switch that requests it, based on the new device's hardware address.

dynamically allocated port   A TCP/IP port used by an application when needed. The port is not constantly used.

E

EEPROM   *See* electrically erasable programmable read-only memory.

electrically erasable programmable read-only memory (EEPROM)   A special integrated circuit on expansion cards that allows data to be stored on the chip. If necessary, the data can be erased by a special configuration program. Typically used to store hardware configuration data for expansion cards.

electromagnetic interference (EMI)   The interference that can occur during transmissions over copper cable because of electromagnetic energy outside the cable. The result is degradation of the signal.

electronic mail (email) software   An application that allows people to send messages via their computers on the same network or over the Internet.

EMI   *See* electromagnetic interference.

encapsulation   The technique used by layered protocols in which a layer adds header information to the Protocol Data Unit (PDU) from the layer above. As an example, in Internet terminology, a packet contains a header from the Data Link layer, followed by a header from the Network layer (IP), followed by a header from the Transport layer (TCP), followed by the application protocol data.

encoding   The process of translating data into signals that can be transmitted on a transmission medium.

encryption key   The string of alphanumeric characters used to decrypt encrypted data.

endpoint   The two ends of a connection for transmitting data. One end is the receiver, and the other is the sender.

Enhanced Interior Gateway Routing Protocol (EIGRP)   An advanced routing protocol created by Cisco, combining the advantages of Link State and Distance Vector protocols. EIGRP has superior convergence attributes, including high operating efficiency. *See also* Interior Gateway Protocol (IGP), Open Shortest Path First (OSPF), and Routing Information Protocol (RIP) and Routing Information Protocol version 2 (RIPv2).

Ethernet   A shared-media network architecture. It operates at the Physical and Data Link layers of the OSI model. As a media-access method, it uses baseband signaling over either a bus or a star topology with CSMA/CD. The cabling used in Ethernet networks can be coax, twisted-pair, or fiber-optic. *See also* Carrier Sense Multiple Access with Collision Detection (CSMA/CD). Open Systems Interconnect (OSI).

Ethernet address   *See* MAC address.

expansion slot   A slot on the computer's bus into which expansion cards are plugged to expand the functionality of the computer (for example, using a NIC to add the computer to a network). *See also* Network Interface Card (NIC).

Extensible Authentication Protocol (EAP)   An extension to PPP that supports multiple authentication methods, including Kerberos, passwords, certificates, smart cards, and so on. IEEE 802.1x is the standard that dictates how EAP is used within Ethernet frames.

Exterior Gateway Protocol (EGP)   Protocols used to connect autonomous systems (AS's) together. An example is BGP.

extranet   An intranet interconnected and intercommunicating with networks that are under separate administrative control by way of an arrangement between the administrative entities. *See also* internetwork, intranet.

extranet VPN   A VPN in which the various sites are owned by different enterprises. If all the sites in a VPN are owned by the same enterprise, the VPN is a corporate intranet.

F

Fast Ethernet   The general category name given to 100Mbps Ethernet technologies.

FHSS   *See* Frequency-Hopping Spread Spectrum.

Fiber Channel   A type of server-to-storage system connection that uses fiber-optic connectors.

fiber-optic   A type of network cable that uses a central glass or plastic core surrounded by a plastic coating.

file server   A server specialized in holding and distributing files.

File Transfer Protocol (FTP)   A TCP/IP protocol and software that permit the transferring of files between computer systems. Because FTP has been implemented on numerous types of computer systems, files can be transferred between disparate computer systems (for example, a personal computer and a minicomputer). *See also* Transmission Control Protocol/Internet Protocol (TCP/IP).

file virus   *See* virus.

firewall   A combination of hardware and software that protects a network from attack by hackers who could gain access through public networks, including the Internet.

flat network   A network that is one large collision domain and one large broadcast domain.

flow control   A methodology used to ensure that receiving units are not overwhelmed with data from sending devices. Pacing, as it is called in IBM networks, means that when buffers at a receiving unit are full, a message is transmitted to the sending unit to temporarily halt transmissions until all the data in the receiving buffer has been processed and the buffer is again ready for action.

forward/filter decision   Process in which a frame is received on an interface, and the switch then looks at the destination hardware address and finds the exit interface in the MAC database. The frame is only forwarded out the specified destination port.

FQDN   *See* fully qualified domain name.

frame   A logical unit of information sent by the Data Link layer over a transmission medium. The term often refers to the header and trailer, employed for synchronization and error control, that surround the data contained in the unit.

frame filtering   Process in which a switch reads the destination hardware address of a frame and then looks for this address in the filter table built by the switch. It then sends the frame out only to the port where the hardware address is located; the other ports do not see the frame. Frame filtering is used on Layer 2 switches to provide more bandwidth.

frame relay   A WAN technology that transmits packets over a WAN using packet switching. *See also* packet switching.

frame tagging   Process by which switches within a VLAN that spans multiple connected switches (which Cisco calls a switch-fabric) keep track of frames as they are received on the switch ports, and also keep track of the VLAN they belong to as the frames traverse this switch-fabric. Switches can then direct frames to the appropriate port.

frequency division multiplexing (FDM)   A multiplexing technique whereby the different signals are sent across multiple frequencies.

Frequency-Hopping Spread Spectrum (FHSS)   A modulation technique specified by the original IEEE 802.11 standard but not supported by manufacturers. DSSS is the modulation technique of choice of 802.11 equipment makers. FHSS modulates the data signal with a carrier signal that hops through a random, yet predictable, sequence of frequencies. A hopping code determines the transmission frequencies. The receiver is set to the same code, allowing it to listen to the incoming signal at the right time and frequency to properly receive the signal. *See also* Direct Sequence Spread Spectrum (DSSS), Orthogonal Frequency Division Multiplexing (OFDM).

FTP   *See* File Transfer Protocol.

FTP proxy   A server that uploads files to and downloads files from a server on behalf of a workstation.

full backup   A backup that copies all data to the archive medium.

full duplex   The capacity to transmit information between a sending station and a receiving unit at the same time. *See also* half duplex.

fully qualified domain name (FQDN)   An address that uses both the host name (workstation name) and the domain name.

G

gateway   The hardware and software needed to connect two disparate network environments so that communications can occur.

H

half duplex   The capacity to transfer data in only one direction at a time between a sending unit and receiving unit. *See also* full duplex.

hardware address   A Data Link layer address assigned to every NIC at the MAC sublayer. The address is in the format *xx:xx:xx:xx:xx:xx*. Each *xx* is a two-digit hexadecimal number. *See also* Media Access Control (MAC), Network Interface Card (NIC).

hardware loopback   A small plug used in a NIC that connects the transmission pins directly to the receiving pins, allowing diagnostic software to test whether a NIC can successfully transmit and receive. *See also* Network Interface Card (NIC).

heartbeat   The data transmission between two servers in a cluster to detect when one fails. When the standby server detects no heartbeats from the main server, it comes online and takes control of the responsibilities of the main server. This allows for all services to remain online and accessible.

hierarchical addressing   Any addressing plan employing a logical chain of commands to determine location. IP addresses are made up of a hierarchy of network numbers, subnet numbers, and host numbers to direct packets to the appropriate destination.

high bit-rate digital subscriber line (HDSL)   The first DSL technology to use a higher-frequency spectrum of copper, twisted-pair cables.

honeypot   A trap set to detect, deflect, or in some manner counteract attempts at unauthorized use of information systems. This can be a wired or wireless trap to collect information about the attacker.

hop   One pass through a router. *See also* cost, router.

hop count   A means of limiting the number of routers a packet can cross on the way to its destination. As a packet travels over a network through multiple routers, each router will increment the hop-count field in the packet by one as it crosses the router.

host   Any network device with a TCP/IP network address. *See also* Transmission Control Protocol/Internet Protocol (TCP/IP).

host address   A logical address configured by an administrator or server on a device. It logically identifies this device on an internetwork.

Host-to-Host layer   A layer in the DoD model that corresponds to the Transport layer of the OSI model. *See also* DoD Networking Model, Open Systems Interconnect (OSI).

HTML   *See* Hypertext Markup Language.

HTTP   *See* Hypertext Transfer Protocol.

hub   A Physical layer device that serves as a central connection point for several network devices. A hub repeats the signals it receives on one port to all other ports. *See also* active hub.

hybrid routing protocol   A routing protocol that uses the attributes of both Distance Vector and Link State. Enhanced Interior Gateway Routing Protocol (Enhanced IGRP) is an example of a hybrid routing protocol.

Hypertext Markup Language (HTML)   A set of codes used to format text and graphics that will be displayed in a browser. The codes define how data will be displayed.

Hypertext Transfer Protocol (HTTP)   The protocol used for communication between a web server and a web browser.

Hypertext Transfer Protocol over SSL (HTTPS)   A URI scheme used to indicate a secure communication such as payment transactions and corporate information systems.

I

ICMP   *See* Internet Control Message Protocol.

IEEE   *See* Institute of Electrical and Electronics Engineers.

IEEE 802.*x* standards   Standards for LAN and MAN networking.

IEEE 802.1 LAN/MAN Management   Standard that specifies LAN/MAN network management and internetworking.

IEEE 802.2 Logical Link Control   Standard that specifies the operation of the Logical Link Control (LLC) sublayer of the Data Link layer of the OSI model. The LLC sublayer provides an interface between the MAC sublayer and the Network layer. *See also* Media Access Control (MAC), Open Systems Interconnect (OSI).

IEEE 802.3 CSMA/CD Networking   Standard that specifies a network that uses Ethernet technology and a CSMA/CD network access method. *See also* Carrier Sense Multiple Access with Collision Detection (CSMA/CD).

IEEE 802.5 Token Ring   Specifies a logical ring, physical star, and token-passing media access method based on IBM's Token Ring.

IEEE 802.10 LAN/MAN Security   A series of guidelines dealing with various aspects of network security.

IEEE 802.11 Wireless LAN   Standards for implementing wireless technologies such as infrared and spread-spectrum radio.

IETF   *See* Internet Engineering Task Force.

implicit deny   A default test statement found at the end of each access list.

Independent Computing Architecture (ICA)   A proprietary protocol for an application server system, designed by Citrix Systems. ICA lays down a specification for passing data between server and clients but is not bound to any one platform.

Institute of Electrical and Electronics Engineers (IEEE)   An international organization that sets standards for various electrical and electronics issues.

Integrated Services Digital Network (ISDN)   A telecommunications standard that is used to digitally send voice, data, and video signals over the same lines. *See also* delta channel.

Interior Gateway Protocol (IGP)   A routing protocol used within an autonomous system to update the routing table on all the routers. Examples of IGP's are RIP, EIGRP, OSPF and IS-IS.

internal bridge   A bridge created by placing two NICs in a computer.

internal modem   A modem that is a regular PC card and is inserted into the bus slot. These modems are inside the PC.

International Organization for Standardization (ISO)   The standards organization that developed the OSI model. This model provides a guideline for how communications occur between computers.

Internet   A global network made up of a large number of individual networks interconnected through the use of public telephone circuits and TCP/IP protocols. *See also* Transmission Control Protocol/Internet Protocol (TCP/IP).

Internet Architecture Board (IAB)   The committee that oversees management of the Internet. It is made up of two subcommittees: the Internet Engineering Task Force (IETF) and the Internet Research Task Force (IRTF). *See also* Internet Engineering Task Force (IETF), Internet Research Task Force (IRTF).

Internet Control Message Protocol (ICMP)   A message and management protocol for TCP/IP. The ping utility uses ICMP. *See also* Ping, Transmission Control Protocol/Internet Protocol (TCP/IP).

Internet Engineering Task Force (IETF)   An international organization that works under the Internet Architecture Board to establish standards and protocols relating to the Internet. *See also* Internet Architecture Board (IAB).

Internet layer   Layer in the Internet Protocol suite of protocols that provides network addressing and routing through an internetwork.

Internet Protocol (IP)   The protocol in the TCP/IP protocol suite responsible for network addressing and routing. *See also* Transmission Control Protocol/Internet Protocol (TCP/IP).

Internet Research Task Force (IRTF)   An international organization that works under the Internet Architecture Board to research new Internet technologies. *See also* Internet Architecture Board.

Internet service provider (ISP)   A company that provides direct access to the Internet for home and business computer users.

internetwork   Also known as an internet, for short, the interconnection and intercommunication between autonomous networks. *See also* intranet, extranet.

Inter-Switch Link (ISL) routing   A Cisco proprietary method of frame tagging in a switched internetwork. Frame tagging is a way to identify the VLAN membership of a frame as it traverses a switched internetwork.

intranet   Often an internetwork encompassing only networks under a single administrative domain; very often used to refer to a large corporation's internal internetwork. *See also* internetwork, extranet.

Intrusion Detection System (IDS)   Software and/or hardware designed to detect unwanted attempts at accessing, manipulating, and/or disabling computer systems, mainly through a network such as the Internet. This detects problems but does not solve them. *See* Intrusion Prevention System (IPS).

Intrusion Prevention System (IPS)   A network security device that monitors network and/or system activities for malicious or unwanted behavior and can react, in real-time, to block or prevent those activities. Unlike IDS, IPS can stop a network attack.

inverse multiplexing   The network technology that allows one signal to be split across multiple transmission lines at the transmission source and combined at the receiving end.

IP   *See* Internet Protocol.

IP address   An address that is used by the Internet Protocol and identifies a device's location on the network.

IP proxy   A server technology that protects your network. With an IP proxy, all communications look as if they originated from a proxy server because the IP address of the user making a request is hidden. IP proxies use a technology known as NAT. *See also* Network Address Translation (NAT).

IP spoofing   An attack in which a hacker tries to gain access to a network by pretending their machine has the same network address as the internal network.

ipconfig   A Windows NT utility used to display a machine's current configuration.

IPv4   Provides logical addressing and routing through an internetwork. Has an address field of 32 bits.

IPv6   Provides logical addressing and routing through an internetwork. Has an address field of 128 bits.

IS-IS   Interior gateway routing protocol that is typically only used within ISP's.

ISDN   *See* Integrated Services Digital Network.

ISDN terminal adapter   The device used to connect a local network (or single machine) to an ISDN network. It provides power to the line as well as translates data from the LAN or individual computer for transmission on the ISDN line. *See also* Integrated Services Digital Network (ISDN).

ISP   *See* Internet service provider.

J

Java   A programming language, developed by Sun Microsystems, that is used to write programs that will run on any platform that has a Java Virtual Machine installed.

Java Virtual Machine (JVM)   Software, developed by Sun Microsystems that creates a virtual Java computer on which Java programs can run. A programmer writes a program once without having to recompile or rewrite the program for all platforms.

jumper   A small connector (cap or plug) that connects pins. This creates a circuit that indicates a setting to a device.

JVM   *See* Java Virtual Machine.

K

Kerberos   An authentication and encryption method that can be used by Cisco routers to ensure that data cannot be "sniffed" off the network. Kerberos was developed at MIT and was designed to provide strong security using the Data Encryption Standard (DES) cryptographic algorithm.

kernel   The core component of any operating system, which handles the functions of memory management, hardware interaction, and program execution.

key   A folder in the Windows Registry that contains subkeys and values, or a value with an algorithm to encrypt and decrypt data.

L

LAN   *See* local area network.

LAN driver   The interface between the NetWare kernel and the NIC installed in the server. Also a general category of drivers used to enable communications between an operating system and a NIC. *See also* Network Interface Card (NIC).

laser printer   A printer that uses a laser to form an image on a photo-sensitive drum. The image is then developed with toner and transferred to paper. Finally, a heated drum fuses toner particles onto the paper.

latency sensitivity   Broadly, the time it takes a data packet to get from one location to another. In specific networking contexts, it can mean either (1) the time elapsed (delay) between the execution of a request for access to a network by a device and the time the mechanism actually is permitted transmission, or (2) the time elapsed between when a mechanism receives a frame and the time that frame is forwarded out of the destination port.

Layer 2 switch   A switching hub that operates at the Data Link layer and builds a table of the MAC addresses of all the connected stations. *See also* Media Access Control (MAC).

Layer 3 switch   Functioning at the Network layer, a switch that performs the multiport, virtual LAN, data-pipelining functions of a standard Layer 2 switch but can also perform basic routing functions between virtual LANs.

layered architecture   An industry-standard way of creating applications to work on a network, which allows the application developer to make changes in only one layer instead of the whole program.

layers   Term used in networking to define how the OSI model works to encapsulate data for transmission on the network.

LCP   *See* Link Control Protocol.

lease   In DHCP, the duration of time for which a client is allowed to use the parameters assigned to it by the server. *See also* Dynamic Host Configuration Protocol (DHCP).

leased line   A permanent connection between two points leased from the telephone companies.

Link Control Protocol (LCP)   The protocol used to establish, configure, and test the link between a client and PPP host. *See also* Point-to-Point Protocol (PPP).

link light   A small light-emitting diode (LED) that is found on both the NIC and the hub. It is usually green and labeled Link or something similar. A link light indicates that the NIC and the hub are making a Data Link layer connection. *See also* hub, Network Interface Card (NIC).

Link State route discovery   A route discovery method that transmits special packets (Link State Packets [LSPs]) that contain information about the networks to which the router is connected.

Link State routing   A type of routing that advertises a router's entire routing table only at startup and possibly at infrequently scheduled intervals. Aside from that, the router sends updates to other routers only when changes occur in the advertiser's routing table.

Link State routing protocol   A routing protocol whereby the router sends out incremental information only, such as updates to its own routing table.

Linux   A version of Unix, developed by Linus Torvalds. It runs on Intel-based PCs and is generally free. *See also* Unix.

load balancing   The act of balancing packet load over multiple links to the same remote network.

local area network (LAN)   A network that is restricted to a single building, a group of buildings, or even a single room. A LAN can have one or more servers. LANs are defined by the Data Link protocols they run. For example, Ethernet networks are LANs, but PPP networks are not. They are WAN links.

Local Connector (LC)   A type of optical fiber connector that terminates the end of an optical fiber and enables quicker connection and disconnection than splicing. The connectors mechanically couple and align the cores of fibers so that light can pass.

local groups   Groups created on individual servers. Rights can be assigned only to local resources.

local loop   The part of the PSTN that goes from the Central Office to the demarcation point at the customer's premises. *See also* Central Office (CO), demarcation point (demarc), Public Switched Telephone Network (PSTN).

log file   A file that keeps a running list of all errors and notices, the time and date they occurred, and any other pertinent information.

logical address   A Network layer address that defines how data is sent from one network to another. Examples of logical addresses are IP and IPv6.

logical bus topology   A type of topology in which the signal appears to travel the distance of the cable and is received by all stations on the backbone. Compare to a physical bus topology, in which this is actually the case. Logical bus topologies are most often implemented as physical star topologies. *See also* backbone.

Logical Link Control (LLC)   A sublayer of the Data Link layer that provides an interface between the MAC sublayer and the Network layer. *See also* Media Access Control (MAC), topology.

logical network addressing   The addressing scheme used by protocols at the Network layer.

logical network diagram   A network design that is placed on top of a physical network design. A logical network diagram or design is an example of an IP or IPv6 logical addressing scheme. Before you can create the logical network diagram, you must first have a physical network diagram.

logical parallel port   A port used by the CAPTURE command to redirect a workstation printer port to a network print queue. The logical port has no relation to the port to which the printer is actually attached or to the physical port. *See also* physical parallel port.

logical port address   A value that is used at the Transport layer to differentiate between the upper-layer services.

logical ring topology   A network topology in which all network signals travel from one station to another, being read and forwarded by each station.

logical topology   A way that information can flow. The same as a physical topology except that the flow of information, rather than the physical arrangement, specifies the type of topology.

loop avoidance   Term that typically refers to the spanning-tree protocol (STP) to stop loops in a switched network. Routing protocols, such as RIP and EIGRP have layer-3 loop avoidance schemes as well.

M

MAC   *See* Media Access Control.

MAC address   The address that is either assigned to a network card or burned into the NIC. This is how PCs keep track of one another and keep each other separate.

macro virus   *See* virus.

magnetic flux   This is represented by the Greek letter Φ (phi), and is a measure of the quantity of magnetism using the strength and the extent of a magnetic field.

mail exchange (MX) record   A DNS record type that specifies the DNS host name of the mail server for a particular domain name.

managed objects   Devices managed by SNMP.

Management Information Base (MIB)   Software on hosts used by SNMP to manage devices.

mechanical transfer registered jack (MT-RJ)   A jack used to connect pairs of optical fibers together. It uses a form factor and latch like the RJ-45 connectors, supports full duplex, costs less than ST or SC connectors, and is easier to terminate and install than ST or SC connectors.

media access   The process of vying for transmission time on the network media.

Media Access Control (MAC)   A sublayer of the Data Link layer that controls the way multiple devices use the same media channel. It controls which devices can transmit and when they can transmit.

media converter   A networking device that converts from one network media type to another—for example, from an AUI port to an RJ-45 connector for 10Base-T.

medium dependent interface (MDI)   The standard pin configuration for a wiring specification. The transmit and receive pairs of an MDI port are crossed with respect to those of an MDI-X port. MDI is generally considered to be the pin configuration used on the device acting as data terminal equipment (DTE). There is generally one port on Ethernet hubs or switches that can be switched between MDI and MDI-X. Hub or switch ports set for MDI allow the hub or switch to be connected to the standard MDI-X port of another hub or switch without the use of a crossover cable. *See also* medium dependent interface-crossover (MDI-X).

medium dependent interface-crossover (MDI-X)   A nonstandard pin configuration for a wiring specification, characterized by reversing the transmit and receive channels with respect to the MDI specification. MDI-X is generally considered to be the pin configuration used on the device acting as data circuit-terminating equipment (DCE). There is generally one port on Ethernet hubs or switches that can be switched between MDI and MDI-X. Hub or switch ports set for MDI allow the hub or switch to be connected to the standard MDI-X port of another hub or switch without the use of a crossover cable. If the switchable port is set for MDI-X, it can be used with a straight-through cable for connection to an end device, such as a PC or router. *See also* medium dependent interface (MDI).

member server   A computer that has Windows NT server installed but doesn't have a copy of the SAM database.

mesh topology   A network topology in which there is a connection from each station to every other station in the network.

Microsoft Challenge Handshake Authentication Protocol (MS-CHAP)   Microsoft's version of CHAP, designed for authentication communications between Windows clients and servers. *See also* Challenge Handshake Authentication Protocol (CHAP).

misuse-detection IDS (MD-IDS)   *See* Intrusion Detection System (IDS).

modem   A communication device that converts digital computer signals into analog tones for transmission over the PSTN and converts them back to digital on reception. The word *modem* is an acronym for *modulator/demodulator*.

MS-CHAP   *See* Microsoft Challenge Handshake Authentication Protocol (MS-CHAP).

Multi Protocol Label Switching (MPLS)   A data-carrying mechanism that belongs to the family of packet-switched networks, like frame relay and ATM, but is an upgrade from those protocols. MPLS operates at an OSI model layer 2.5.

multicast   Broadly, any communication between a single sender and multiple receivers. Unlike broadcast messages, which are sent to all addresses on a network, multicast messages are sent to a defined subset of the network addresses; this subset has a group multicast address, which is specified in the packet's destination address field. *See also* broadcast address, directed broadcast.

multicast group   A defined set of users or hosts that are allowed to read or view data sent via multicast. Multicast works by sending messages or data to IP multicast group addresses.

multipartite virus   *See* virus.

multiple input, multiple output (MIMO)   Protocol used by 802.11n to provide full-duplex wireless communication.

multiplexing   A technology that combines multiple signals into one signal for transmission over a slow medium. *See also* frequency division multiplexing (FDM), inverse multiplexing.

multipoint RF network   A radio frequency (RF) network consisting of multiple stations, each with transmitters and receivers. This type of network also requires an RF bridge as a central sending and receiving point.

N

name resolution   The process of translating (resolving) logical host names to network addresses.

NAT   *See* Network Address Translation.

National Computing Security Center (NCSC)   The agency that developed the Trusted Computer System Evaluation Criteria (TCSEC) and the Trusted Network Interpretation Environmental Guideline (TNIEG).

National Security Agency (NSA)   The U.S. government agency responsible for protecting U.S. communications and producing foreign intelligence information. It was established by presidential directive in 1952 as a separately organized agency within the Department of Defense (DoD).

nbtstat (NetBIOS over TCP/IP statistics)   The Windows TCP/IP utility that is used to display NetBIOS over TCP/IP statistics. See also Network Basic Input/Output System (NetBIOS), Transmission Control Protocol/Internet Protocol (TCP/IP).

NCSC   *See* National Computing Security Center.

NetBEUI   *See* NetBIOS Extended User Interface.

NetBIOS   *See* Network Basic Input/Output System.

NetBIOS Extended User Interface (NetBEUI)   A transport protocol that is based on the NetBIOS protocol and has datagram support and support for connectionless transmission. NetBEUI is native to Microsoft networks and is mainly for use by small businesses. It is a nonroutable protocol that cannot pass over a router but does pass over a bridge, because it operates at the Data Link layer. *See also* Network Basic Input/Output System (NetBIOS).

NetBIOS name   The unique name used to identify and address a computer using NetBEUI.

netstat   A utility used to determine which TCP/IP connections—inbound or outbound—the computer has. It also allows the user to view packet statistics, such as how many packets have been sent and received. See also Transmission Control Protocol/Internet Protocol (TCP/IP).

network   A group of devices connected by some means for the purpose of sharing information or resources.

Network Access layer   The bottom layer in the Internet Protocol suite that provides media access to packets.

network address   An address that is used with the logical network addresses to identify the network segment in an internetwork. Logical addresses are hierarchical in nature and have at least two parts: network and host. An example of a hierarchical address is 172.16.10.5, where 172.16 is the network and 10.5 is the host address.

Network Address Translation (NAT)   A TCP/IP service that many routers, firewalls, and IP proxies can provide. NAT translates addresses that are legal for an inside network but illegal for a corresponding outside network into addresses that are legal for the outside network. NAT also resolves the outside addresses back to the inside addresses as return traffic for the originating device comes back from the outside network. *See also* IP proxy.

network attached storage   Storage, such as hard drives, attached to a network for the purpose of storing data for clients on the network. Network attached storage is commonly used for backing up data.

Network Basic Input/Output System (NetBIOS)   A Session-layer protocol that opens communication sessions for applications that want to communicate on a network.

Network File System (NFS)   A protocol that enables users to access files on remote computers as if the files were local.

Network Interface Card (NIC)   A physical device that connects computers and other network equipment to the transmission medium.

Network layer   This third layer of the OSI model, which is responsible for logical addressing and translating logical names into physical addresses. This layer also controls the routing of data from source to destination as well as the building and dismantling of packets. *See also* Open Systems Interconnect (OSI).

Network Management System (NMS)   Software that works with SNMP to monitor and control network elements such as hosts, gateways, and terminal servers. These network elements use a management agent to perform the network-management functions requested by the network management stations.

network media   The physical cables that link computers in a network; also known as *physical media*.

network operating system (NOS)   The software that runs on a network server and offers file, print, application, and other services to clients.

network segmentation   The process of breaking up a large network into smaller networks. Routers, switches, and bridges are used to create network segmentation.

network software diagnostics   Software tools, either protocol analyzers or performance monitoring tools, used to troubleshoot network problems.

network-centric   A description of network operating systems that use directory services to maintain information about the entire network.

NFS   *See* Network File System.

nibble   A unit of information storage made up of four bits.

NIC   *See* Network Interface Card.

NIC diagnostics   Software utilities that verify that the NIC is functioning correctly and test every aspect of NIC operation. *See also* Network Interface Card (NIC).

NIC driver   *See* LAN driver.

node address   An address that identifies a specific device in an internetwork. It can be a hardware address, which is burned into the NIC, or a logical network address, which an administrator or server assigns to the node.

nonce   Protocol that is used with the Diffie-Hellman algorithm to exchange encrypted keys.

non-unicast packet   A packet that is not sent directly from one workstation to another.

NOS   *See* network operating system.

NSA   *See* National Security Agency.

N-series connector   A male/female screw-and-barrel connector used with Thinnet and Thicknet cabling.

nslookup   A utility that allows you to query a name server to see which IP address a name resolves to.

O

octet   Refers to 8 bits; one-fourth of an IP address.

OFDM   *See* Orthogonal Frequency Division Multiplexing.

offline   The general name for the condition when some piece of electronic or computer equipment is unavailable or inoperable.

Omni   *See* omnidirectional antenna (Omni).

omnidirectional antenna (Omni)   A point-to-multipoint antenna that provides equal power dispersion in almost all directions. Omni is the primary antenna type used with a wireless access point that is designed to offer service to clients in any direction simultaneously. Contrast with directional Yagi antennas. *See also* directional antenna (Yagi).

Open Shortest Path First (OSPF)   A Link State, hierarchical routing algorithm derived from an earlier version of the IS-IS protocol, whose features include multipath routing, load balancing, and least-cost routing. OSPF is the suggested successor to RIP in the Internet environment. *See also* Enhanced Interior Gateway Routing Protocol (EIGRP), Interior Gateway Protocol (IGP), and Internet Protocol (IP).

Open Systems Interconnect (OSI)   A model defined by the ISO to categorize the process of communication between computers in terms of seven layers. The seven layers are Application, Presentation, Session, Transport, Network, Data Link, and Physical. *See also* International Organization for Standardization (ISO).

OpenLinux   A version of the Linux network operating system developed by Caldera.

operator error (OE)   A problem with the user not knowing how to operate software or hardware. An OE problem can be a serious one.

organizationally unique identifier (OUI)   The first 24 bits of a 48-bit MAC address. Each OUI is assigned by the IEEE to a single manufacturer of devices that have MAC addresses assigned to them. As long as the manufacturer does not duplicate the last 24 bits of the MAC address, the assumption is that the entire MAC address will be unique worldwide. However, renegade manufacturers and manufacturing mistakes can result in duplicate MAC addresses. As long as the devices with duplicate addresses do not make it onto the same local network segment (the same IP subnet, for example), this conflict will never be an issue.

Orthogonal Frequency Division Multiplexing (OFDM)   A modulation technique used by 802.11a that is implemented with a system of 52 subcarriers. OFDM's spread-spectrum technique distributes the data over these 52 subcarriers, which are spaced apart at precise frequencies. This spacing helps prevent demodulators from seeing frequencies other than their own. *See also* Direct Sequence Spread Spectrum (DSSS), Frequency Hopping Spread Spectrum (FHSS).

OSI   *See* Open Systems Interconnect.

P

packet   The basic division of data sent over a network.

packet filtering   A firewall technology that accepts or rejects packets based on their content.

packet sniffer   Software run on a host that gathers packets and analyzes them. Can also be referred to as a packet analyzer as well.

packet switching   A method of switching that sends information as potentially smaller discrete packets, each one independently addressed for the intended recipient. Intermediate devices, such as switches and routers, can send these packets along one or more different paths to the same destination, making the autonomy of each packet imperative. A packet-switched connection is virtual, and the physical paths are shared, in contrast to the concept of the dedicated paths of circuit switching. *See also* frame relay, circuit switching.

passive detection   A type of intruder detection that logs all network events to a file for an administrator to view later.

passive hub   A hub that makes physical and electrical connections between all connected stations. Generally speaking, these hubs are not powered.

PAT   See Port Address Translation.

patch   Software that fixes a problem with an existing program or operating system.

patch cable   A central wiring point for multiple devices on a UTP network. *See also* unshielded twisted-pair (UTP) cable.

patch panel   A central wiring point for multiple devices on a UTP network. The patch panel itself contains no electronic circuits. Generally, patch panels are in server rooms or located near switches or hubs to provide an easy means of patching over wall jacks or hardware.

PDU   *See* Protocol Data Unit.

peer communication   The use of headers to allow corresponding protocol processes in two devices to communicate with one another as if there were a direct connection between the devices at the protocol's layer.

peer-to-peer network   Computers that are hooked together and have no centralized authority. Each computer is equal and can act as both a server and a workstation.

peripheral   Any device that can be attached to a computer to expand its capabilities.

permanent virtual circuit (PVC)   A technology used by frame relay that allows virtual data communications (circuits) to be set up between sender and receiver over a packet-switched network.

PGP   *See* Pretty Good Privacy.

phishing   The criminally fraudulent process of attempting to acquire sensitive information such as usernames, passwords, and credit-card details by masquerading as a trustworthy entity in an electronic communication.

physical address   *See* MAC address.

physical bus topology   A network that uses one network cable that runs from one end of the network to the other. Workstations connect at various points along this cable.

Physical layer   The first layer of the OSI model. This layer controls the functional interface. *See also* Open Systems Interconnect (OSI).

physical media   *See* network media.

physical mesh topology   A network configuration in which each device has multiple connections. These multiple connections provide redundant connections.

physical network diagram   A network drawing that details the physical network layout, including routers, switches, and sometimes servers. After the physical network is designed and a diagram is created, a logical network diagram can be designed as a second layer to the physical network diagram.

physical parallel port   A port that is on the back of a computer and allows a printer to be connected with a parallel cable.

physical port   An opening on a network device that allows a cable of some kind to be connected. Ports allow devices to be connected to each other with cables.

physical ring topology   A network topology that is set up in a circular fashion. Data travels around the ring in one direction, and each device on the ring acts as a repeater to keep the signal strong as it travels. Each device incorporates a receiver for the incoming signal and a transmitter to send the data on to the next device in the ring. The network is dependent on the ability of the signal to travel around the ring.

physical star topology   A network in which a cable runs from each network entity to a central device called a hub. The hub allows all devices to communicate as if they were directly connected. *See also* hub.

physical topology   The physical layout of a network, such as a bus, star, ring, or mesh.

ping   A TCP/IP utility used to test whether another host is reachable. An ICMP request is sent to the host, which responds with a reply if it is reachable. The request times out if the host is not reachable.

Ping of Death attack   Type of attack in which a large ICMP packet is sent to overflow the remote host's buffer. This usually causes the remote host to reboot or hang.

plain old telephone service (POTS)   The classic analog circuit commonly used to connect to the Public Switched Telephone Network (PSTN) to make voice calls for conversations and modem and facsimile sessions. *See* asymmetrical digital subscriber line (ADSL), digital subscriber line (DSL), Public Switched Telephone Network (PSTN).

plenum-rated coating   A coaxial cable coating that does not produce toxic gas when burned.

point of presence (POP)   The physical location where an interexchange carrier has placed equipment to interconnect with a local exchange carrier.

point-to-point   Network communication in which two devices have exclusive access to a network medium. For example, a printer connected to only one workstation would be using a point-to-point connection.

Point-to-Point Protocol (PPP)   The protocol used with dial-up connections to the Internet. Its functions include error control, security, dynamic IP addressing, and support for multiple protocols.

Point to Point Protocol over Ethernet (PPPoE)   A PPP protocol that can be used over Ethernet for authentication purposes.

Point-to-Point Tunneling Protocol (PPTP)   A protocol that allows the creation of virtual private networks (VPNs), which allow users to access a server on a corporate network over a secure, direct connection via the Internet. *See also* virtual private network (VPN).

POP3   *See* Post Office Protocol version 3.

port   A numerical value used in the headers of such protocols as TCP and UDP to signify the identity of the next-highest-layer protocol responsible for the control information that follows the header containing the port number. Using this value, the protocol is able to hand its payload to the appropriate protocol at the next layer higher, creating the appearance of simultaneously multiplexing the PDUs of multiple higher-layer protocols.

Port Address Translation (PAT)   A process that allows a single IP address to represent multiple resources by altering the source TCP or UDP port number.

port numbers   Used at the transport layer with TCP and UDP to keep track of host-to-host virtual circuits.

positive acknowledgment with retransmission   A connection-oriented session that provides acknowledgment and retransmission of the data if it is not acknowledged by the receiving host within a certain time frame.

positive forward acknowledgement   A term used to describe acknowledgement schemes, such as the one used by TCP, that only acknowledge properly received PDUs (no negative acknowledgements to indicate errors in reception) and do so by specifying the next PDU identifier (the sequence number in TCP) the recipient expects to receive, not previously received identifiers.

Post Office Protocol version 3 (POP3)   The protocol used to download email from an SMTP email server to a network client. *See also* Simple Mail Transfer Protocol (SMTP).

POTS   *See* plain old telephone service.

Power over Ethernet (PoE)   A protocol that allows power to be send over unused wires in an Ethernet cable to provide power to devices like access points and phones.

PPP   *See* Point-to-Point Protocol.

PPTP   *See* Point-to-Point Tunneling Protocol.

prefix routing   A method of defining how many bits are used in a subnet and how this information is sent in a routing update. For example, RIP version 1 does not send subnet mask information in the route updates. However, RIP version 2 does. This means that RIP v2 updates will send /24, /25, /26, and so on with a route update, which RIP v1 will not.

Presentation layer   The sixth layer of the OSI model; responsible for formatting data exchange such as graphic commands and conversion of character sets. Also responsible for data compression, data encryption, and data stream redirection. *See also* Open Systems Interconnect (OSI).

Pretty Good Privacy (PGP)   A shareware implementation of RSA encryption. *See also* RSA Data Security, Inc.

print server   A centralized device that controls and manages all network printers. The print server can be hardware, software, or a combination of both. Some print servers are actually built into the network printer NICs. *See also* Network Interface Card (NIC).

print services   The network services that manage and control printing on a network, allowing multiple and simultaneous access to printers.

private key   A technology in which both the sender and the receiver have the same key. A single key is used to encrypt and decrypt all messages. *See also* public key.

Process/Application layer   Upper layer in the Internet Protocol stack that is responsible for network services.

protocol   A predefined set of rules that dictates how computers or devices communicate and exchange data on the network.

protocol address   A generic term for Network-layer addresses, such as IP or IPX addresses, that alludes to the protocol dependency of the address.

protocol analyzer   A software and hardware troubleshooting tool that is used to decode protocol information to try to determine the source of a network problem and to establish baselines.

Protocol Data Unit (PDU)   A generic term used to describe the end product of a protocol. It can be thought of as the entire data structure handed down by a protocol to the protocol at the next lowest layer or the information placed on the network media by the Physical layer. A PDU will consist of the original user data and any upper-layer control information (headers and trailers) imposed by upper-layer protocols encapsulated by the control information of the protocol creating the PDU.

protocol suite   The set of rules a computer uses to communicate with other computers.

protocol switching   A process in which a packet, as it arrives on a router to be forwarded, is copied to the router's process buffer, and the router performs a lookup on the Layer 3 address. Using the route table, an exit interface is associated with the destination address. The processor forwards the packet with the added new information to the exit interface, while the router initializes the fast-switching cache. Subsequent packets bound for the same destination address follow the same path as the first packet.

proxy   A type of firewall that prevents direct communication between a client and a host by acting as an intermediary. *See also* firewall.

proxy cache server   An implementation of a web proxy. The server receives an HTTP request from a web browser and makes the request on behalf of the sending workstation. When the response comes, the proxy cache server caches a copy of the response locally. The next time someone makes a request for the same web page or Internet information, the proxy cache server can fulfill the request out of the cache instead of having to retrieve the resource from the Web.

proxy server   A type of server that makes a single Internet connection and services requests on behalf of many users.

PSTN   *See* Public Switched Telephone Network.

public   For use by everyone. Also a popular name for certain Unix and FTP folders.

public key   A technology that uses two keys to facilitate communication: a public key and a private key. The public key is used to encrypt a message to a receiver. *See also* private key.

Public Key Infrastructure (PKI)   A cryptography arrangement that binds public keys with respective user identities by means of a certificate authority (CA) server.

public network   The part of a network that is on the outside of a firewall and is exposed to the public. *See also* firewall.

Public Switched Telephone Network (PSTN)   The U.S. public telephone network. It is also called the plain old telephone service (POTS). *See also* Central Office (CO).

punch-down tool   A hand tool used to terminate twisted-pair wires on a wall jack or patch panel.

PVC   *See* permanent virtual circuit.

Q

QoS   *See* quality of service.

quad decimal   Four sets of octets separated by a decimal point; an IP address.

quality of service (QoS)   Data prioritization at the Network layer of the OSI model. It results in guaranteed throughput rates. *See also* Open Systems Interconnect (OSI).

R

radio frequency interference (RFI)   Interference on copper cabling systems caused by radio frequencies.

README file   A file that the manufacturer includes with software to give the installer information that came too late to make it into the software manuals. It's usually a last-minute addition that includes tips on installing the software, possible incompatibilities, and any known installation problems that might have been found right before the product was shipped.

reference model   *See* Open Systems Interconnect (OSI).

regeneration process   A process in which signals are read, amplified, and repeated on the network to reduce signal degradation, which results in longer overall possible length of the network.

Registered Jack (RJ) connector   A modular connection mechanism that allows for as many as eight copper wires (four pairs). RJ connectors are most commonly used for telephone (such as the RJ-11) and network adaptors (such as RJ-45).

reliable   The quality of a protocol that uses acknowledgments to allow the recipient to confirm error-free receipt of data from a source device. *See also* unreliable.

remote-access protocol   Any networking protocol that is used to gain access to a network over public communication links.

remote-access server   A computer that has one or more modems installed to enable remote connections to the network.

remote-access VPN   A type of VPN that allows remote users like telecommuters to securely access the corporate network wherever and whenever they need to.

Remote Authentication Dial-In User Service (RADIUS)   A protocol that is used to communicate between the remote-access device and an authentication server. Sometimes an authentication server running RADIUS is called a RADIUS server.

remote copy (rcp)   An old Unix command to perform a remote copy. It is not secure.

Remote Desktop Protocol (RDP)   A multichannel protocol that allows a user to connect to a computer running Microsoft Terminal Services. The server listens by default on TCP port 3389.

remote shell (rsh)   A command-line computer program that can execute shell commands on another computer across a network. The remote system on which rsh executes the command needs to be running the rshd daemon.

Rendezvous   An IP-based ZeroConf open-service discovery protocol that allows devices to be added to and removed from networks without configuration.

repeater   A Physical-layer device that amplifies the signals it receives on one port and resends or repeats them on another. A repeater is used to extend the maximum length of a network segment.

replication   The process of copying directory information to other servers to keep them all synchronized.

RFI   *See* radio frequency interference.

RG-58   The type designation for the coaxial cable used in Thin Ethernet (10Base-2). It has a 50-ohm impedance rating and uses BNC connectors.

RG-62   The type designation for the coaxial cable used in ARCnet networks. It has a 93-ohm impedance and uses BNC connectors.

ring topology   A network topology in which each computer in the network is connected to exactly two other computers. With ring topology, a single break in the ring brings down the entire network.

RIP, RIPv2   *See* Routing Information Protocol (RIP) and Routing Information Protocol version 2 (RIPv2)

RJ (Registered Jack) connector   *See* Registered Jack (RJ) connector.

roaming profiles   Profiles downloaded from a server at each login. When a user logs out at the end of the session, changes are made and remembered for the next time the user logs in.

rogue access point   An access point not authorized to be up and running the corporate office. A very large security issue, and expensive software can find these AP's and shut them down.

rollover   Used to connect an RS-232 from your PC to a console connection on a router or switch.

route   The path to get to the destination from a source.

route cost   The number of router hops between source and destination in an internetwork. *See also* hop, router.

routed protocol   A protocol (such as IP or IP6v) used to transmit user data through an internetwork. By contrast, routing protocols (such as RIP, IGRP, and OSPF) are used to update routing tables between routers.

router   A device that connects two networks and allows packets to be transmitted and received between them. A router determines the best path for data packets from source to destination. *See also* hop.

routing   A function of the Network layer that involves moving data throughout a network. Data passes through several network segments using routers that can select the path the data takes. *See also* router.

Routing Information Protocol (RIP) and Routing Information Protocol version 2 (RIPv2)
A Distance Vector routing protocol used by IP and IPv6. It uses hops or ticks to determine the cost for a particular route.

routing protocol   One of a collection of protocols designed to allow routers to dynamically learn routes from one another, reducing or eliminating the need for manual configuration of routes. Examples of routing protocols are RIP, IGRP and EIGRP, OSPF, IS-IS, BGP, NLSP, and ATM's Private Network-to-Network Interface (PNNI).

routing table   A table that contains information about the locations of other routers on the network and their distance from the current router.

RS-232   A connection on your PC that is typically 9-pins. This is being phased out by a USB connection.

RSA Data Security, Inc.   A commercial company that produces encryption software. RSA stands for Rivest, Shamir, and Adleman, the founders of the company.

S

Secure Copy Protocol (SCP)   A protocol to securely transfer files between files on a network.

Secure Hypertext Transfer Protocol (HTTPS or S-HTTP)   A protocol used for secure communications between a web server and a web browser. This is an alternative mechanism to the HTTPS URI scheme for encrypting web communications carried over HTTP. Written as either HTTPS or S-HTTP.

Secure Shell (SSH)   A network protocol that allows data to be exchanged using a secure channel between two networked devices.

security log   A log file used in Windows NT and 2000 Event Viewer to keep track of security events specified by the domain's Audit policy.

security policy   A rule set in place by a company to help ensure the security of a network. This may include how often a password must be changed or how many characters a password should be.

segment   A unit of data smaller than a packet. Also refers to a portion of a larger network (a network can consist of multiple network segments). *See also* backbone.

sequence number   A number used to determine the order in which parts of a packet are to be reassembled after the packet has been split into sections.

server   A computer that provides resources to the clients on the network.

server and client configuration   A network in which the resources are located on a server for use by the clients.

server-centric   A network design model that uses a central server to contain all data as well as control security.

service accounts   Accounts created on a server for users to perform special services. Examples are backup operators, account operators, and server operators.

Session layer   The fifth layer of the OSI model, which determines how two computers establish, use, and end a session. Security authentication and network-naming functions required for applications occur here. The Session layer establishes, maintains, and breaks dialogs between two stations. *See also* Open Systems Interconnect (OSI).

shared key   A password or other object shared by two devices communicating across a link, often used to create a one-way hash that is transmitted and compared by the recipient to a one-way hash it creates using the same shared key. The shared key is generally not sent across the link.

share-level security   Form of network security where, instead of assigning users rights to network resources, passwords are assigned to individual files or other network resources (such as printers). These passwords are then given to all users who need access to these resources. All resources are visible from anywhere in the network, and any user who knows the password for a particular network resource can make changes to it.

shell   A Unix interface based solely on command prompts. There is no graphical interface.

shielded   Term that describes cabling that has extra wrapping to protect it from stray electrical or radio signals. Shielded cabling is more expensive than unshielded.

shielded twisted-pair cable (STP)   A type of cabling that includes pairs of copper conductors, twisted around each other, inside a metal or foil shield. This type of medium can support faster speeds than unshielded wiring.

shortest-path-first protocols   *See* Open Shortest Path First (OSPF).

S-HTTP   *See* Secure Hypertext Transfer Protocol.

signal   A transmission from one PC to another. This could be a notification to start a session or end a session.

signal encoding   The process whereby a protocol at the Physical layer receives information from the upper layers and translates all the data into signals that can be transmitted on a transmission medium.

signaling method   The process of transmitting data across the medium. Two types of signaling are digital and analog.

Simple Mail Transfer Protocol (SMTP)   A program that looks for mail on SMTP servers and sends it along the network to its destination at another SMTP server.

Simple Network Management Protocol (SNMP)   The management protocol created for sending information about the health of the network to network-management consoles.

SMTP   *See* Simple Mail Transfer Protocol.

Smurf attack   An attack that generates a lot of computer network traffic to a victim host.

SNMP   *See* Simple Network Management Protocol.

social engineering   The art of manipulating people into performing actions or divulging confidential information.

socket   A combination of a port address and an IP address.

software address   *See* logical address.

source address   The address of the station that sent a packet, usually found in the source area of a packet header.

source port number   The address of the PC that is sending data to a receiving PC. The port portion allows for multiplexing of data to be sent from a specific application.

Spanning Tree Protocol (STP)   The bridge protocol (IEEE 802.1D) that enables a learning bridge to dynamically avoid loops in the network topology by creating a spanning tree using the spanning-tree algorithm. Spanning-tree frames called Bridge Protocol Data Units (BPDUs) are sent and received by all switches in the network at regular intervals. The switches participating in the spanning tree don't forward the frames; instead, they're processed to determine the spanning-tree topology itself.

SSH File Transfer Protocol (SFTP)   A network protocol that provides file transfer over any reliable data stream. It is typically used with SSHv2 (TCP port 22) to provide secure file transfer but is intended to be usable with other protocols as well.

star topology   A network topology in which all devices on the network have a direct connection to every other device on the network. These networks are rare except in very small settings due to the huge amount of cabling required to add a new device.

state table   A firewall security method that monitors the states of all connections through the firewall.

state transition   Digital signaling scheme that reads the "state" of the digital signal in the middle of the bit cell. If it is five volts, the cell is read as a one. If the state of the digital signal is zero volts, the bit cell is read as a zero.

static ARP table entry   Entry in the ARP table that is manually added by a user when a PC will be accessed often. This speeds up the process of communicating with the PC because the IP-to-MAC address does not have to be resolved.

static routing   A method of routing packets in which the router's routing is updated manually by the network administrator instead of automatically by a route-discovery protocol.

static VLAN   A VLAN that is manually configured port by port. This is the method typically used in production networks.

straight tip (ST)   A type of fiber-optic cable connector that uses a mechanism similar to the BNC connectors used by Thinnet. This is the most popular fiber-optic connector currently in use.

subnet mask   A group of selected bits that identify a subnetwork within a TCP/IP network. *See also* Transmission Control Protocol/Internet Protocol (TCP/IP).

subnetting   The process of dividing a single IP address range into multiple address ranges.

subnetwork   A network that is part of another network. Also referred to as a subnet. The connection is made through a gateway, bridge, or router.

subnetwork address   A part of the 32-bit IPv4 address that designates the address of the subnetwork. Also referred to as a subnet address.

subscriber connector (SC)   A type of fiber-optic connector. These connectors are square shaped and have release mechanisms to prevent the cable from accidentally being unplugged.

supernetting   The process of combining multiple IP address ranges into a single IP network.

switch   In networking, a device responsible for multiple functions such as filtering, flooding, and sending frames. It works using the destination address of individual frames. Switches operate at the Data Link layer of the OSI model.

switched   Term used to describe a network that has multiple routes to get from a source to a destination. This allows for higher speeds.

symmetric digital subscriber line (SDSL)   Type of DSL that provides different speeds upstream than downstream. It is the opposite of ADSL.

symmetrical keys   Keys that are used to both encrypt and decrypt data.

SYN flood   A denial of service attack in which the hacker sends a barrage of SYN packets. The receiving station tries to respond to each SYN request for a connection, thereby tying up all the resources. All incoming connections are rejected until all current connections can be established.

Synchronous Optical Network (SONET)   A standard in the U.S. that defines a base data rate of 51.84Mbps. Multiples of this rate are known as optical carrier (OC) levels, such as OC-3, OC-12, and so on.

T

TA   *See* Terminal Adapter (TA).

TCP   *See* Transmission Control Protocol.

TCP/IP   *See* Transmission Control Protocol/Internet Protocol.

TDMA   *See* Time Division Multiple Access.

TDR   *See* time-domain reflectometer.

telephony server   A computer that functions as a smart answering machine for the network. It can also perform call-center and call-routing functions.

Telnet   A protocol that functions at the Application layer of the OSI model, providing terminal-emulation capabilities. *See also* Open Systems Interconnect (OSI).

template   A set of guidelines that you can apply to every new user account created.

Terminal Access Controller Access-Control System Plus (TACACS+)   An enhanced version of TACACS, similar to RADIUS. *See also* Remote Authentication Dial-In User Service (RADIUS).

Terminal Adapter (TA)   In ISDN, the device (often erroneously referred to as an ISDN modem) that is used to interconnect ISDN-incompatible devices, such as PC serial ports or Ethernet interfaces and POTS phones, to an ISDN network for eventual connection to an ISDN circuit.

terminal emulator   A program that enables a PC to act as a terminal for a mainframe or a Unix system.

TFTP   *See* Trivial File Transfer Protocol.

Thick Ethernet (Thicknet)   A type of Ethernet that uses thick coaxial cable and supports a maximum transmissions distance of 500 meters. Also called 10Base-5.

Thin Ethernet (Thinnet)   A type of Ethernet that uses RG-58 cable and 10Base-2.

three-way handshake   Term used in a TCP session to define how a virtual circuit is set up. It is called this because it uses three data segments.

Time Division Multiple Access (TDMA)   A method to divide individual channels in broadband communications into separate time slots, allowing more data to be carried at the same time. It is also possible to use TDMA in baseband communications.

time to live (TTL)   A field in IP packets that indicates how many routers the packet can still cross (hops it can still make) before it is discarded. TTL is also used in ARP tables to indicate how long an entry should remain in the table.

time-domain reflectometer (TDR)   A tool that sends out a signal and measures how much time it takes to return. It is used to find short or open circuits. Also called a *cable tester*.

tone generator   A small electronic device that is used to test network cables for breaks and other problems by sending an electronic signal down one set of UTP wires. Used with a tone locator. *See also* tone locator, unshielded twisted-pair (UTP) cable.

tone locator   A device used to test network cables for breaks and other problems. It senses the signal sent by the tone generator and emits a tone when the signal is detected in a particular set of wires.

toner probe   A device that allows telephone and cable technicians to find and to test cables. The probe listens for the tone coming from a tone generator.

topology   The physical and/or logical layout of the transmission media specified in the Physical and Logical layers of the OSI model. *See also* Open Systems Interconnect (OSI).

traceroute   *See* tracert.

tracert   A Microsoft-based TCP/IP command-line utility that shows the user every router interface a TCP/IP packet passes through on its way to a destination. The command `traceroute` is used in such environments as the Cisco IOS CLI. See also Transmission Control Protocol/Internet Protocol (TCP/IP).

trailer   A section of a data packet that contains error-checking information.

transceiver   The part of any network interface that transmits and receives network signals.

transmission   The sending of packets from the PC to the network cable.

Transmission Control Protocol (TCP)   The protocol found at the Host-to-Host layer of the DoD model. This protocol breaks data packets into segments, numbers them, and sends them in random order. The receiving computer reassembles the data so that the information is readable for the user. In the process, the sender and the receiver confirm that all data has been received; if not, it is resent. This is a connection-oriented protocol. *See also* connection-oriented transport protocol.

Transmission Control Protocol/Internet Protocol (TCP/IP)   The protocol suite developed by the DoD as an internetworking protocol suite that could route information around network failures. Today it is the de facto standard for communications on the Internet.

transmission media   Physical cables and/or wireless technology across which computers are able to communicate.

transparent bridging   The bridging scheme used in Ethernet and IEEE 802.3 networks that passes frames along one hop at a time, using bridging information stored in tables that associate end-node MAC addresses with bridge ports. This type of bridging is considered transparent because the source node does not know it has been bridged, because the destination frames are addressed directly to the end node.

Transport layer   The fourth layer of the OSI model, which is responsible for checking that data packets created in the Session layer were received error free. If necessary, it also changes the length of messages for transport up or down the remaining layers. *See also* Open Systems Interconnect (OSI).

Triple Data Encryption Standard (3DES)   *See* Data Encryption Standard (DES).

Trivial File Transfer Protocol (TFTP)   A protocol similar to FTP that does not provide the security or error-checking features of FTP. *See also* File Transfer Protocol (FTP).

Trojan horse   A virus or other malicious process that hides within another, possibly trusted, program that the user executes without knowing the Trojan horse is embedded. Execution of the host program generally launches the Trojan horse.

trunk lines   The telephone lines that form the backbone of a telephone network for a company. These lines connect the telephone(s) to the telephone company and to the PSTN. *See also* Public Switched Telephone Network (PSTN).

trunk link   A link used between switches and from some servers to the switches. Trunk links carry traffic for many VLANs. Access links are used to connect host devices to a switch and carry only VLAN information for the VLAN of which the device is a member.

T-series connections   A series of digital connections leased from the telephone company. Each T-series connection is rated with a number based on speed. T1 and T3 are the most popular.

TTL   *See* time to live.

tunneling   A method of avoiding protocol restrictions by wrapping packets from one protocol in another protocol's frame and transmitting this encapsulated packet over a network that supports the wrapper protocol. *See also* encapsulation.

twisted-pair cable   A network transmission medium that contains one or more pairs of color-coded, insulated copper wires that are twisted around each other in a common jacket.

type   A DOS command that displays the contents of a file. Also short for data type.

U

UDP   *See* User Datagram Protocol.

Uniform Resource Locator (URL)   One way of identifying a document on the Internet, consisting of the protocol that is used to access the document and the domain name or IP address of the host that holds the document. For example, http://www.sybex.com.

uninterruptible power supply (UPS)   A natural-line conditioner that uses a battery and power inverter to run the computer equipment that plugs into it. The battery charger continuously charges the battery. The battery charger is the only thing that runs off line voltage. During a power problem, the battery charger stops operating and the equipment continues to run off the battery.

Universal Serial Bus (USB)   A versatile, chainable serial-bus technology that connects up to 127 devices at speeds of 1.5Mbps and 12Mbps (versions 1.0 and 1.1—1.5Mbps is the subchannel rate) as well as 480Mbps (version 2.0—Hi-Speed USB).

Unix   A 32-bit, multitasking operating system developed in the 1960s for use on mainframes and minicomputers.

unreliable   The quality of a protocol that does not use acknowledgments to allow a receiving device to inform the source that it received its transmitted data without error. *See also* reliable.

unshielded   Term that describes cabling that has little or no wrapping to protect it from stray electrical or radio signals. Unshielded cabling is less expensive than shielded.

unshielded twisted-pair (UTP) cable   Twisted-pair cable consisting of a number of twisted pairs of copper wire with a simple plastic casing. Because no shielding is used in this cable, it is very susceptible to EMI, RFI, and other types of interference. Specifications for the types of Ethernet cables are 568A, which defines a straight through cable, and 568B, which defines a cross-over cable. *See also* crossover cable, electromagnetic interference (EMI), radio frequency interference (RFI).

upgrade   To increase an aspect of a PC by, for example, adding more RAM, changing to a faster CPU, and so on.

UPS   *See* uninterruptible power supply.

URL   *See* Uniform Resource Locator.

user   The person who is using a computer or network.

User Datagram Protocol (UDP)   A protocol at the Host-to-Host layer of the DoD model that corresponds to the Transport layer of the OSI model. Packets are divided into segments, given numbers, sent randomly, and put back together at the receiving end. This is a connectionless protocol. *See also* connectionless transport protocol, Open Systems Interconnect (OSI).

user-level security   A type of network security in which user accounts can read, write, change, and take ownership of files. Rights are assigned to user accounts, and each user knows only their own username and password, which makes this the preferred method for securing files.

V

very high data-rate digital subscriber line (VDSL)   A DSL technology that provides faster data transmission over a single flat untwisted or twisted pair of copper wires. VDSL is capable of supporting high-bandwidth applications such as HDTV as well as telephone services (Voice over IP) and general Internet access over a single connection.

virtual circuit   A logical circuit devised to ensure reliable communication between two devices on a network. Defined by a virtual path identifier/virtual channel (really the only time *channel* is used) identifier (VPI/VCI) pair, a virtual circuit can be permanent (PVC) or switched (SVC). Virtual circuits are used in frame relay and X.25. Known as virtual channel in ATM. *See also* permanent virtual circuit (PVC).

virtual COM port   A serial port that is used as if it were a serial port, but the actual serial-port interface does not exist.

virtual LAN (VLAN)   A technology that allows users on different switch ports to participate in their own network separate from, but still connected to, the other stations on the same or a connected switch.

virtual private network (VPN)   A network that uses the public Internet as a backbone for a private interconnection (network) between locations.

virus   A program intended to damage a computer system. Sophisticated viruses are encrypted and hide in a computer and may not appear until the user performs a certain action or until a certain date. *See also* antivirus.

virus engine   The core program that runs the virus-scanning process.

VLAN   *See* virtual LAN (VLAN).

Voice over Internet Protocol (VoIP)   A general term for a family of transmission technologies for delivery of voice communications over the Internet or other packet-switched networks.

VPN   *See* virtual private network.

VPN concentrator   A device that can terminate multiple VPN connections. Typically found at a corporate office that remote offices connect to.

W

WAN   *See* wide area network.

web proxy   A type of proxy that is used to act on behalf of a web client or web server.

web server   A server that holds and delivers web pages and other web content using the HTTP protocol. *See also* Hypertext Transfer Protocol (HTTP).

wide area network (WAN)   A network that crosses local, regional, or international boundaries.

Windows Internet Naming Service (WINS)   A Windows NT service that dynamically associates the NetBIOS name of a host with a domain name. *See also* Network Basic Input/Output System (NetBIOS).

WinNuke   A Windows-based attack that affects only computers running Windows NT 3.51 or 4. It is caused by the way the Windows NT TCP/IP stack handles bad data in the TCP header. Instead of returning an error code or rejecting the bad data, it sends NT to the Blue Screen of Death (BSOD). Figuratively speaking, the attack nukes the computer.

wire crimper   Used for attaching ends onto different types of network cables by a process known as crimping. Crimping involves using pressure to press some kind of metal teeth into the inner conductors of a cable.

Wired Equivalent Protocol (WEP)   A security protocol for 802.11b wireless LANs that gets its name from the fact that it is designed to provide a security level roughly equivalent to a wired LAN. This is done by encrypting the data that is transmitted wirelessly.

wireless (I know—duh!)   An 802.11 specification that allows data transmission over unbounded media.

wireless access point (WAP)   A wireless bridge used in a multipoint RF network.

wireless bridge   A bridge that performs all the functions of a regular bridge but uses RF instead of cables to transmit signals.

workgroup   A specific group of users or network devices, organized by job function or proximity to shared resources.

workstation   A computer that is not a server but is on a network. Generally, it is used to do work, whereas a server is used to store data or perform a network function. In the simplest terms, a workstation is a computer that is not a server.

World Wide Web (WWW)   A collection of HTTP servers running on the Internet. They support the use of documents formatted with HTML. *See also* Hypertext Markup Language (HTML), Hypertext Transfer Protocol (HTTP).

worm   A program that is similar to a virus but that propagates over a network. *See also* virus.

WWW   *See* World Wide Web.

X

X Windows   A graphical user interface (GUI) developed for use with the various flavors of Unix.

_x_DSL   A family of technologies that provides digital data transmission over the wires of a local telephone network, called a digital subscriber line (DSL).

Y

Yagi   *See* directional antenna (Yagi).

Index

Note to Reader: Bolded page references indicate definitions and main discussions of a topic. *Italicized* page references indicate illustrations and tables.

F

L

N

X

Y

Z

The Best CompTIA Network+ Book/CD Package on the Market!

Get ready for your CompTIA Network+ certification with the most comprehensive and challenging sample tests anywhere!

The Sybex Test Engine features:

- All the review questions, as covered in each chapter of the book.
- Challenging questions representative of those you'll find on the real exam.
- Two full-length bonus exams available only on the CD.
- An Assessment Test to narrow your focus to certain objective groups.

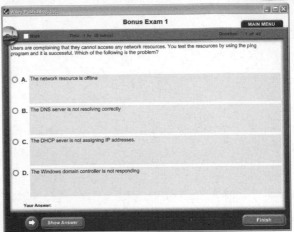

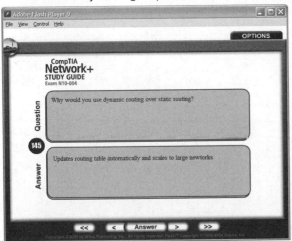

Use the Electronic Flashcards for PCs or Palm devices to jog your memory and prep last-minute for the exam!

- Reinforce your understanding of key concepts with these hardcore flashcard-style questions.
- Download the Flashcards to your Palm device and go on the road. Now you can study for the CompTIA Network+ exam (N10-004) anytime, anywhere.

Search through the complete book in PDF!

- Access the entire *CompTIA Network+ Study Guide* complete with figures and tables, in electronic format.
- Search the *CompTIA Network+ Study Guide* chapters to find information on any topic in seconds.

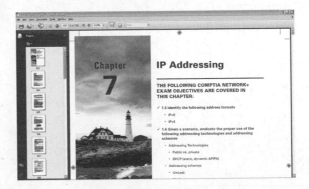

Study with the Best—
Pass the test!

You've made the right choice in selecting a CompTIA Authorized Partner to prepare for your CompTIA exam. CompTIA Authorized materials are reviewed and approved by industry experts, so you can feel confident on test day knowing that you prepared for your exam with the best materials available.

What can certification mean for you?

- A Standout Resume
- New Job Opportunities
- More Money
- Career Advancement
- Job Security

Get Certified

Make sure to take the next step and earn your CompTIA certification. Certified professionals report higher job satisfaction and even more pay! Visit: **www.comptiastore.com** to buy your exam voucher and schedule your test.

CompTIA.